Introducing Organizational Behaviour and Management

Introducing Organizational Behaviour and Management

David Knights and Hugh Willmott

SOUTH-WESTERN
CENGAGE Learning

Australia • Brazil • Japan • Korea • Mexico • Singapore • Spain • United Kingdom • United States

SOUTH-WESTERN
CENGAGE Learning™

**Introducing Organizational Behaviour
and Management**
David Knights and Hugh Willmott

Publishing Director: John Yates

Publisher: Thomas Rennie

Development Editor: James Clark

Content Project Editor: Sonia Patel

Manufacturing Manager: Helen Mason

Senior Production Controller: Maeve Healy

Marketing Manager: Anne-Marie Scoones

Typesetter: Newgen Imaging Systems

Cover design: Jackie Wrout, Land-Sky Ltd

Text design: Design Deluxe, Bath, UK

© 2007, Cengage Learning EMEA

For product information and technology assistance,
contact **emea.info@cengage.com**.

For permission to use material from this text or product,
and for permission queries,
email **clsuk.permissions@cengage.com**.

The Author has asserted the right under the Copyright, Designs and Patents Act 1988 to be identified as Author of this Work.

British Library Cataloguing-in-Publication Data
A catalogue record for this book is available from the British Library.

ISBN: 978-1-84480-0353

Cengage Learning EMEA
High Holborn House, 50-51 Bedford Row
London WC1R 4LR

Cengage Learning products are represented in Canada by Nelson Education Ltd.

For your lifelong learning solutions, visit
www.cengage.co.uk

Purchase e-books or e-chapters at:
http://estore.bized.co.uk

Printed by C&C Offset, China
3 4 5 6 7 8 9 10 – 11 10 09

Brief contents

Contents

List of cases

Preface

About this book

Existing organizational behaviour textbooks tend to suffer from the tendency to be *exhaustive*. They try to cover everything in unwarranted detail and in a way that students often find remote or removed from their own, everyday experiences. These books cram in lots of information but they do not help their readers to appreciate recurrent themes or to read more deeply into the subject. They also give the impression that the body of knowledge in the field of management and organization is unified. Yet, arguably, it is deeply divided across a range of issues and perspectives.

Packing in excessive and potentially mind-numbing detail and conveying an impression of unanimity is unfortunate, not least because it is precisely the divisions and associated debates that produce colour and interest. It is somewhat ironic that existing textbooks try to be comprehensive, yet they exclude much critical and controversial material. Their exhaustiveness makes them unnecessarily intimidating as well as unduly dull and deadening. We have sought, in our text, to be more selective in what we present, more accessible in how material is presented, and more attentive to differences of approach.

This text is written by scholars who are committed to thinking differently about the field or focus of their respective chapters. Writing on topics in which they have a specialist interest, they have a direct feel for key contributions and issues. Every one of the contributors to this text has worked closely with us in teaching and/or research. And it is this long-standing association that gives the chapters thematic continuity. Each chapter provides stand-alone treatment of its topic that is thematically linked to other chapters by the following framework:

- *Adopts a selective rather than exhaustive approach* to the established introductory organizational behaviour topics but remains with the principal topics that frame the more orthodox textbooks.
- *Covers both mainstream and critical literatures* – largely by exploring them in separate sections.
- *Links chapter content to everyday experience.* A basic assumption of the text is that students already know from their own day-to-day experience a good deal about work organizations (e.g. schools, retailers, service providers). A major value of this textbook resides in developing and illuminating this knowledge through drawing out students' reflections upon its significance and implications. Examples used are of direct relevance to their everyday experiences.
- *Introduces and applies a conceptual framework* based upon six core concepts – power, identity, knowledge, freedom, inequality, insecurity – to discuss the issues presented in each chapter.
- *Seeks to engage the reader* by breaking up the text through the use of case studies, boxed issues, key point summaries, review questions and other ways of preventing the analysis becoming dense and turgid.

The last point is particularly important, as we want you to retain key ideas and examples long after sitting examinations. It may be helpful to make a mental note of these points and perhaps to return to them occasionally as you are reading the text.

Approach and style

The aim of this text is to provide a fresh approach to addressing and rethinking core aspects of managing and organizing. This text encourages students to reflect upon their experience rather than merely acquire information. Instead of equating relevance with exhaustiveness, the relevance of our text is framed in terms of the experience of students who recurrently organize and manage their lives and participate in institutions. The book treats the subject matter not just as something to learn in order to pass exams and gain qualifications, but also as a key to understanding the contemporary world of work and organizations in relation to our everyday lives.

Structure and format

Our text is different as it presents two distinct and highly contrasting perspectives on organizational behaviour. An account of the key elements of the subject matter found in mainstream texts familiarizes the reader with what is conventionally studied in this field. However, although the orthodox approach presented could be treated as an end in itself, it is not treated as such here. Rather it is treated as a foil for introducing a critical or unorthodox perspective on organizational behaviour.

Each chapter introduces its focal topic and presents an overview of the key, diverse orthodox treatments of it. But each chapter also re-examines the issues by exploring what the mainstream literature says, and what it fails to say, about issues of **identity, (in)security, freedom, power, inequality** and **knowledge** – the six central concepts around which the more critical content of this book is organized.

In seeking to make the subject matter more relevant and accessible we treat organizational behaviour as first and foremost an activity that is not dissimilar to what we experience in everyday life. Our argument is that instead of excluding the human detail of organizations in favour of a focus on functions and tasks, as do many textbooks, we should reverse the emphasis. This is because we believe that students will find it easier to learn about organizations when they see that work relations and management activities are not so distant from their own everyday lives.

This textbook, therefore, moves away from a focus on the various stakeholders in organizations – managers and employees, shareholders and financiers, suppliers and customers, government personnel and interest or pressure groups – as rational and instrumental functionaries. These functions are not ignored but we show how managers and employees carry them out as gendered, sexually charged, ethnically located, emotionally embodied, and more or less passionate human beings.

Key features

The book is packed with pedagogical features, which have been carefully designed to help you in studying and learning when using this text:

Aims provide an outline of some of the key themes of the chapter and set the chapter in context.

Learning objectives provide you with an overview of the key concepts that underpin the chapter, highlight what you will learn and help you monitor your progress.

Case studies throughout the text illustrate the ideas explored in the chapter.

Thinkpoints throughout each chapter highlight important concepts and encourage you to think about the subject matter as you are reading it, helping you to discover as much as possible about the subject for yourself.

Discussion questions can be used as the basis of discussion and are included throughout the text, allowing you to check your understanding of the material covered.

Exercises help you further check your understanding of key concepts and ideas covered in the chapter.

Chapter summaries at the end of each chapter link to the learning objectives and recap the key issues of the chapter, helping you to check your understanding before reading on.

Conclusion summarizes the chapter and facilitates reflection upon the significance of the chapter's contents.

Further reading at the end of each chapter allows you to explore the subject further and acts as a starting point for projects and assignments.

Glossary at the end of the book includes thumbnail explanations of key terms in the book. For ease of reference the words included in the glossary are highlighted in bold red in the text.

Website an extensive website accompanies *Introducing Organizational Behaviour and Management* providing you with a comprehensive set of additional online resources.

We hope you will find reading this text enjoyable and stimulating as well as useful and informative.

David Knights and Hugh Willmott

Acknowledgements

We would like to thank the following people:

- Our students over several years at UMIST (now Manchester Business School), and for much shorter periods at Nottingham, Keele, Exeter and Cambridge Universities, whose comments and feedback have influenced the (selective) content and attempted (interactive) style of this text.

- Our colleagues, all of whom were involved with us in teaching and research at UMIST, and who have made this project possible by contributing chapters based upon their interests in the context of our requirements.

- Geraldine Lyons, our commissioning editor at Cengage Learning who provided unstinting advice, guidance, enthusiasm and support, and remained good-humoured throughout; and the many other staff at Cengage who have taken the completed manuscript to publication, including Paula Harris, James Clark and Sonia Pati.

- Secretarial and administrative staff who have assisted us in preparing and revising the manuscript, including Valeen Calder, Annie Dempsey, Andrea Derrick, Julie Hargreaves, Carmen Neagoe, Jane Pope and Katherine Webster.

- Sasha Willmott for commenting extensively on chapter drafts and Jamie Knights for a less extensive commentary about our tendency to use jargon. They are not to blame for our inability to respond to their comments as adequately as they might reasonably hope.

- And, above all, our long-suffering wives and families who encouraged us to prepare the text and have patiently endured our preoccupation with its completion.

Reviewers

- Dr Pawan Budhwar, Aston University
- Antonie van Nistelrooij, Vrije University, Amsterdam
- Terry McNulty, University of Liverpool
- Margaret McPhee, University of East Anglia
- Hadyn Bennett, Zayed University, UAE
- Valerie Caven, Nottingham Trent University
- Peter Copping, Consultant and Researcher in HR
- Patricia Findlay, The University of Edinburgh.

Contributors

David Knights is Research Professor in the Institute of Public Policy and Management at Keele University. He is a founding and continuing editor of the journal *Gender, Work and Organisation*. He is also the founder and continuing director of the Financial Services Research Forum that funds academic research and engages in critical debate on this sector with practitioners from corporations, government departments, regulators, consumer interests and voluntary bodies. He has published widely in the field of management and organization analysis. His most recent books are *Management Lives* (with H. Willmott) and *Organization and Innovation* (with D. McCabe). He is on the editorial board of over ten journals.

Joanna Brewis is Professor of Organization and Consumption at the School of Management, University of Leicester. She has previously worked at UMIST and the Universities of Portsmouth and Essex. While not engaged in intellectual pursuits such as buying shoes, reading chick-lit and watching *ER*, Jo writes on the intersections between the body, sexuality, identity and processes of organizing, and teaches research methodology.

Alessia Contu is a Lecturer in the Department of Management Learning and Leadership at the Lancaster University Management School. Her work revolves around critical views of management and organization and the attempts to develop studies of concrete formations of capitalist relations of work to understand the significance of antagonism and its possibilities for politics and social change. The areas she is particularly interested in and has written about include: learning practices in organizations and the ideology of learning; hegemony, ethics and democracy in organizations and organizing practices; the role of Lacanian psychoanalysis in understanding the political; and organization of work, politics of production and resistance.

Hugh Willmott is Research Professor, Cardiff Business School. He has previously held appointments at the Universities of Cambridge, Manchester and Aston, and visiting appointments at the Universities of Copenhagen, Lund and Cranfield. His books include *Making Quality Critical*, *The Re-engineering Revolution*, *Managing Knowledge*, *Management Lives*, *Studying Management Critically* and *Fragmenting Work*. He has published widely in social science and management journals and currently is a member of the editorial boards of the *Academy of Management Review*, *Organization Studies* and *Journal of Management Studies*.

Christopher Grey is Professor of Organizational Theory at the Judge Business School, University of Cambridge and Fellow of Wolfson College. Recent publications include *A Very Short, Fairly Interesting and Reasonably Cheap Book About Studying Organizations* (Sage, 2005) and the *Critical Management Studies Reader* (Oxford University Press, 2005), edited with Hugh Willmott.

Glenn Morgan is Professor of Organizational Behaviour at Warwick Business School, University of Warwick, and an Associate of the ESRC Centre for Globalization and Regionalization based at the University of Warwick. He is Editor of the journal *Organization*, the critical journal of organization, theory and society. His main interests concern how globalization processes, including multinationals and transnational regulatory bodies, develop and impact on actors, firms and institutions in different national contexts.

Dr Pamela Odih (PhD University of Manchester Institute of Science and Technology UK), is a Lecturer in Sociology at Goldsmiths University of London. Gendered time and its bearing on consumption and wider gender relations is her specialist area. Recent publications include Odih, P. (2003) 'Gender, work and organization in the time/space economy of just-in-time labour', *Time and Society* 12(2/3): 293–314. Forthcoming publications include Odih, P. (2007) *Advertising Consumer Subjectivity in Modern and Postmodern Time(s)*. (Sage) and Odih, P. (2007) *Work, Time and Identity in Cultural Context* (Open University Press).

Dr Damian O'Doherty is a Lecturer in Organization Analysis at the Manchester Business School in the University of Manchester. He is currently writing on the development of organization theory and its utility in organization analysis, and in particular whether this thing called 'organization theory' has a future. Dr. O'Doherty has published widely in areas of labour process analysis and the philosophy of organization. He is an executive board member of the Standing Conference in Organization Symbolism and sits on the editorial committees of a number of scholarly journals, including *Culture and Organization* and *Ephemera*.

John Roberts is a Reader in Organizational Analysis at the Judge Business School, University of Cambridge. His current research is focused on corporate governance and in particular the dynamics of accountability in and around boards of directors. He has published widely on this topic as well as on the associated issues of ethics and corporate social responsibility.

Andrew Sturdy is Professor of Organizational Behaviour at Warwick Business School, University of Warwick. He has a particular interest in the production and use of management ideas, especially the role of management consultants and their clients.

Theodore Vurdubakis is Professor of Organization and Technology. A graduate of Athens University he completed his PhD at the University of Manchester Institute of Science and Technology (UMIST) where he taught for 15 years. His research interests include the role of technologies in social organization and he is currently working on an Economic and Social Research Council (ESRC) project looking at knowledge management and enterprise resource planning systems (ERP).

Frank Worthington is a Senior Lecturer in Management at The University of Liverpool Management School. His main teaching and research interests include the study of behaviour in organizations and the theory and practice of management and employee relations from a labour process perspective.

Edward Wray-Bliss is a Senior Lecturer in Management, School of Management, University of Technology, Sydney. His research focuses upon a range of ethical and political issues in organizations and has included writings on sex discrimination, workforce drug testing, telephone call-centres, business ethics, management 'quick fixes', as well as the ethics of academic research. He has published on these issues in a number of academic journals and edited books.

Walk-through tour

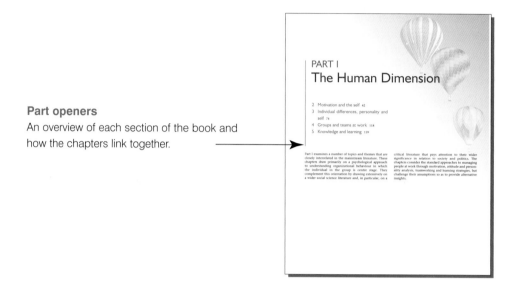

Part openers
An overview of each section of the book and how the chapters link together.

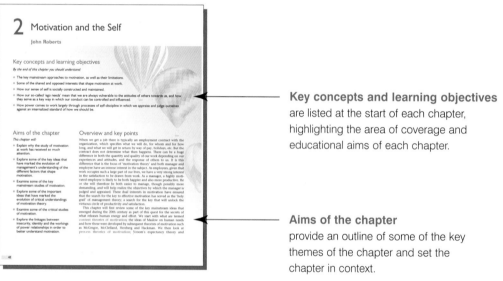

Key concepts and learning objectives
are listed at the start of each chapter, highlighting the area of coverage and educational aims of each chapter.

Aims of the chapter
provide an outline of some of the key themes of the chapter and set the chapter in context.

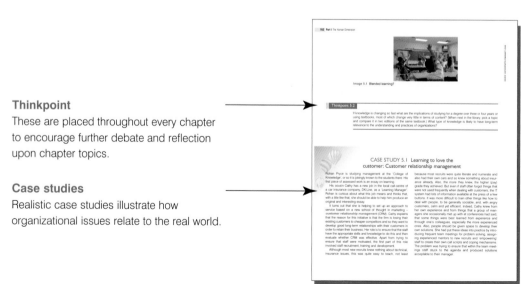

Thinkpoint
These are placed throughout every chapter to encourage further debate and reflection upon chapter topics.

Case studies
Realistic case studies illustrate how organizational issues relate to the real world.

Exercises and Recap questions
Interactive exercises and questions accompany each chapter, to test your understanding and explore concepts more thoroughly

Conclusions
Summarize and review the main concepts and key points covered in each chapter

Glossary
A comprehensive glossary explains key terms used throughout the textbook.

A COMPANION WEBSITE ACCOMPANIES

Introducing Organizational Behaviour and Management

David Knights and Hugh Willmott

Visit the companion website at **www.thomsonlearning.co.uk/knightswillmott** to find valuable teaching and learning materials including:

For lecturers

- Instructor's manual
- Suggested essay questions
- Powerpoint® slides
- Comparison with competing textbooks

For students

- Web links
- Chapter overviews
- Glossary

Introduction

David Knights and Hugh Willmott

Key concepts and learning objectives

Our intention for this book is to introduce management and organizational behaviour (OB) in a way that:

- Values your *own knowledge* and its contribution to understanding management and organizing.

- Encourages you to scrutinize and develop what you know about management and organization.

- Appreciates how the study of management and organization draws from a number of academic disciplines (e.g. sociology, politics, psychology and economics). It is, in this sense, multidisciplinary.

- Develops an awareness of how knowledge of management and organizations reflects and reproduces the particular framework or *perspective(s)* of the author (e.g. 'mainstream' or 'critical').

- Recognizes how different perspectives conjure up and provide contrasting and competing ways of making sense of management and organizations.

- Understands how knowledge of organization(s) is significantly dependent upon people's preoccupations and priorities and, in this sense, is *politically charged*.

- Challenges the way organizations are conventionally understood in mainstream texts as 'things' consisting of parts (e.g. people, functions, goals). This approach, we believe, is mechanical and removed from human experience.

- Appreciates how, fundamentally, 'management' and 'organization' are concepts. This encourages awareness of the diverse and multiple ways in which they are conceived. Each meaning associated with 'management' or 'organization' does not simply describe something 'out there' because it contributes to the very construction of what it claims to describe.

- Considers how the interrelated concepts of power, identity, knowledge, freedom, inequality and insecurity provide a framework for analysing aspects of organizational behaviour.

- Shows how key concepts in the study of management and organization are as relevant for making sense of everyday life as they are for studying behaviour in organizations.

Aims of this book

- This book seeks to connect the study of management and organization to readers' everyday experience.

- As this connection is made, the study of managing and organizing becomes more engaging and less remote.

- Ideas and insights explored in the following chapters should become more personally meaningful and therefore easier to recall.

Overview and key points

Much of our waking lives is spent in organizations: as students, for example, in schools or universities; as consumers in leisure organizations, such as shops and clubs; or as producers in work organizations, such as factories or offices (which, of course, include shops, schools and clubs). By relating our everyday *experience* to the study of management and organizations, we are likely to become more aware of how much we already know about them. Recognizing that we are already very familiar with organizations can increase our confidence when studying them. It can also encourage us to develop our understanding, question what we already know, and it may even result in us changing our habitual ways of thinking and acting. We illustrate this process in Figure 1.1.

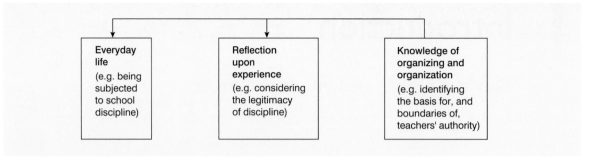

Figure 1.1 Experience, reflection and knowledge of management and organization

It would of course be possible to make further connections in this diagram – for example, by adding more boxes, by using double-headed arrows or by representing the elements as overlapping circles. How might additional elements and linkages offer other interesting ways of connecting our experiences, our reflections and our knowledge of organizations?

Before moving to the main part of the introduction, please have a look at the two boxes below.

Box 1.1: Learning as a challenging process

Learning best takes place when we relate meaningfully to what is being learned. If we take this view to heart, then it can make little sense for us to tell you *exactly* what you will have learned from each chapter of this book as each of the circumstances of each reader will differ. Instead, we encourage you to appreciate and explore your own understandings of the relevance of the various ideas and issues that we examine.

A very good and often enjoyable way to do this is by engaging in discussions with other students on your course. Consider how others are interpreting this text, and how these interpretations can challenge or advance your own understanding. For example, what assessments do you and they make of the arguments about learning and organizations presented in this chapter? What kinds of concepts and language are being used to articulate these views? What differences are emerging and how would you characterize these differences? Do others share your interpretation of these differences? Do these mixed reactions illustrate our point about the creativity, wilfulness and unpredictability of people?

Box 1.2: What you will find in this book

Each chapter of this book comprises an overview of key contributions to the mainstream study of its topic, followed by a reappraisal based upon a more critical approach to its analysis. What we mean by this is elaborated later in this chapter where we summarize our analytical framework based upon the concepts of insecurity, identity, inequality, power, freedom and knowledge. In each chapter we invite readers to go beyond the retrieval and storage of information from this book to reflect upon how the study of OB has relevance for everyday experience, and how this experience has relevance for OB.

Introduction

This book explores how people are organized and managed at work. Managing people is repeatedly identified by managers as the most demanding as well as the most important aspect of their jobs. Managing people is often troublesome. Why might this be?

Unlike other factors of production (e.g. raw materials and technology), human beings are wilful and comparatively unpredictable. Their creative power is crucial to production but it can also be deployed to frustrate, and not just facilitate, what they are paid to do. Organizational behaviour (OB) has emerged as a body of knowledge that identifies, explores and frequently suggests methods of controlling or 'empowering' the tricky 'people dimension' of managing and organizing.

As a field of study, 'organizational behaviour' comprises a wide variety of topics – such as motivation, leadership and organizational design – that relate to different aspects of behaviour in organizations. Examining these topics has involved incorporating perspectives and insights from a number of disciplines including psychology, economics, sociology and politics. (We elaborate this understanding later in this chapter in the 'What is Organizational behaviour?' section.)

Numerous disciplines that explore the complexity and diversity of collective human activity have contributed to the formation and development of OB. Something of this complexity is apparent in the sometimes conflicting purposes and objectives embraced by, or attributed to, 'management' and 'organizations'. These include: producing profits for shareholders, generating income for oneself and one's family, acquiring or building knowledge and skills, caring for others and so on. People rarely have just one purpose, and the various purposes do not always fit together neatly or achieve consistency one with another (see Box 1.3). To further complicate and confuse matters, people in organizations are affected by the changing circumstances in which they participate.

Providing a single definition of 'organization' is difficult and potentially unhelpful. At the same time we recognize that as we approach a new area of study, it can be helpful to have a working sense, or concept, of what we are studying. Provisionally, then, we will say that 'organization' is a concept used by both practitioners (e.g. managers) and analysts (e.g. academics) to make meaningful, and also to organize, the activities and interactions of people who are conceived to be doing organizational work, such as being engaged in creating, developing, and distributing products or services.

More specifically, in the current context, the concepts of 'organization(s)' and 'management' are deployed to indicate that people are able to accomplish together what they would find difficult or impossible to achieve when acting on their own or in smaller groups. They provide us with the possibility of thinking (or 'theorizing') about our experience, and especially, the practical, *collective* activity, such as the effort involved in making products or delivering services. (We explore the competing logics of organizing later in this chapter, in the 'Organizational behaviour as a contested terrain' section.)

Why study organizational behaviour?

Given the demanding nature of organizing and managing people, it is not surprising that OB is widely regarded as the foundation of management studies. Within the notion of 'behaviour', we include thinking and feeling as well as acting. OB aspires to have relevance for understanding the behaviour of people working at all hierarchical levels – from the workers employed part-time or on a casual basis on the shop floor or in the office to the most senior executive. Each is involved in processes of

Box 1.3: What about 'purpose'?

In order to explain their behaviour to others, individuals or groups often claim a purpose. But these claims may be rationalizations or simply socially acceptable accounts. Purposes, therefore, are not to be taken at face value or as the causes of behaviour. They are often invoked to make behaviour seem rational and coherent. Purposes are not self-evident. Sometimes we are only dimly aware of purposes after the event of their achievement. Only then are they identified 'on the hoof' (ad hoc) or after the next event (post hoc). (See Chapter 2.)

organizing and being organized, and managing and being managed. Whereas the management of lower hierarchy employees is transparent, it is also the case that boards of directors (or their equivalent), as well as less obviously personal assistants (PAs) or secretaries, often manage their senior executives.

We have emphasized how managing and organizing people to produce goods and provide services can be a demanding and perverse undertaking. As a student, you may well have experienced casual work, often undertaking jobs that are classified as 'unskilled' (and therefore poorly paid because there is no market shortage of people able to undertake them) but which require considerable concentration and effort, and can have damaging consequences if done badly. Equally, you may have found yourself in jobs where you have time on your hands and where your initiative and skills are underutilized or not used at all, except perhaps unofficially in looking for ways of minimizing your involvement in unpleasant tasks.

In principle, studying OB should enable you to better understand how and why people are organized; to identify and assess the likely consequences of making changes; and to introduce changes in ways that anticipate and minimize counter-productive effects (see Box 1.4). As we have emphasized and illustrated, we believe that this understanding is facilitated by considering organization as a concept rather than a description or an entity, and by applying the insights derived from our conceptual framework that link identity, insecurity, power, inequality, freedom and knowledge (see Appendix: The conceptual framework).

Connecting ideas and experience

Consider your experience as a participant in a higher educational organization. With due consideration to what we have already said about how purposes are invoked and ascribed, one or more of your purposes in studying this course, which may change over time, might be identified from the following list:

1. Intellectual curiosity.
2. To understand the basics of business.
3. To enhance your management capabilities.
4. To avoid an alternative choice of degree that you view as impractical/boring/intellectually demanding.
5. To obtain a degree with the minimum of effort.

You can readily add to this list.

What about the purposes of your teachers, the university authorities (whoever you deem them to be) or the government?

You might also reflect upon how our 'attributes' towards studying (and work more generally) are influenced by our interactions with others – parents and teachers as well as fellow students. Such considerations are often described in OB in terms of motivation, involvement or group dynamics. They are significant for OB in so far as they affect the quality and direction of collective action. In the context of

---

Box 1.4: The relevance of organizational behaviour

OB may be of most direct relevance for understanding general management but its importance extends to specialist areas, such as accounting, production and marketing where, inevitably, organizing and managing people remain central activities. Indeed, OB is a 'subject' taken by a growing number of students, either as a single degree or as a core element of degree programmes in engineering, modern languages and sports studies among others. Specialists within different areas of management and business are inevitably working with others on whose cooperation and 'good behaviour' they depend. Likewise, generalist managers are involved in coordinating their activities with specialist functions of accounting (e.g. through constructing and monitoring budgets) and production (e.g. through liaison with suppliers and customers regarding production requirements and schedules). Crucially, these are not simply impersonal activities requiring technical skills but, rather, involve organizing capabilities that are identified as leadership, communication and motivation. Equally, everyday experiences, including work experience, have relevance for appreciating, assessing and challenging the body of knowledge that comprises OB.

higher education, this would include the extent to which students actively seek and encourage participation in class discussions, how much willingness there is to question the 'received wisdom' found in textbooks, and generally whether education is experienced as a process of passive or active learning.

Learning and relevance Think of some information that you find easy to remember – for example, popular singers, CD tracks, sports stars, soap opera characters and story lines, etc.

- What makes it easy for you to recall this information?
- Why is it often difficult to retain other kinds of information, such as the contents of some of the courses that you are studying?

Discuss with fellow students your conclusions. How might learning be organized differently to make easier what you find difficult?

The mixed and shifting motivations of students (as listed above, p. 4) presents teachers and text-book writers with a dilemma. Do we seek to 'manage' your learning by providing you with easily digestible 'nuggets of knowledge' that you can memorize and regurgitate with the minimum of effort or thought? This could be seen as the most 'efficient' (i.e. low-effort) way to satisfy (4) and (5) in the list, but is it 'effective' in enabling you to understand something of the basics of management and business (2) as a lived, practical activity, let alone in enhancing your management and organizing capabilities (1)? Think about the design of modules and courses that you have taken in the past, or are currently attending. In their contents and delivery, do some approximate to the 'efficiency' model while others incorporate some concern with 'effectiveness'.

As with all forms of management, this text might encourage and enable you to 'play the game' of appearing to be interested in (1) or (2) while secretly you remain closer to (5) or (4) or vice versa. If you can relate OB to your experience of everyday life, you may find it 'less boring' (4) than some courses and/or at least a comparatively 'easy option' (5). We, of course, believe that our approach is more capable of feeding and nurturing your intellectual curiosity (1), your understanding of business (2) and ultimately your management capability (3). We may, on the other hand, be wide of the mark. You might prefer something more conventional that is perhaps 'boring' but also less demanding because it does not expect your engagement. Instead it requires only that you memorize and regurgitate its contents.

It is worth pausing briefly to note the similarities and continuities, as well as some significant differences, between organizing people at work and processes of teaching and learning. Challenges and frustrations in the lives of teachers and students are often paralleled in the experiences of managers and workers. For this reason, when studying OB it is frequently helpful to reflect upon our own educational experiences in order to bring to life, and grasp the relevance of, key topics and concepts. We now move on to identify some of the distinguishing features of OB.

What is organizational behaviour?

OB draws upon elements from a wide range of social scientific disciplines. For example:

- *Sociology* examines human behaviour in relation to various social, political, psychological and economic conditions that affect it, but in turn are produced or reproduced by it.
- *Psychology* concentrates on how individuals think and behave.
- *Politics* focuses on competitive struggles for political power and influence in society (see Chapter 8).
- *Economics* examines how wealth is produced and distributed.

Each discipline generates a distinctive way of conceiving of 'organization(s)' and interpreting behaviour in them. There is also a tendency for each discipline to be antagonistic, or even closed to its rivals. Despite this limitation, the different approaches provide a check and challenge to our particular prejudices about organizations. They serve to focus and organize our thinking, and that is why we call them 'disciplines' (see Box 1.5).

Box 1.5: Single discipline domination

Despite incorporating some elements of 'rival' disciplines, most OB studies and textbooks are often dominated by a single discipline. A large number of introductory OB texts are influenced most strongly by the discipline of psychology. This influence has meant that the key OB topics are often focused upon the individual and group processes. An example is Ian Brooks (1999), who defines OB as 'the study of human behaviour in organizations with a focus on individual and group processes and actions'.

This text includes a consideration of the psychology of individuals and group processes (see 'The distinctiveness of this text' section later in this chapter), as is evident in our emphasis upon freedom, insecurity and identity as three of six key analytical concepts (see Appendix: The conceptual framework). At the same time, we understand the attitudes, motivations and dynamics of individuals and groups in terms of their social, not just their psychological, formation and development. We extend our vision to include an appreciation of how seemingly 'psychological' factors and forces are shaped by and deeply embedded in social relations that stretch beyond both organizational members and the boundaries attributed to organizations. People at work are simultaneously family members with diverse social affiliations (of gender, class, ethnicity, etc.) that directly or indirectly colour their behaviour as individuals and their participation in groups.

When considering the work undertaken by managers or other organizational members, for example, we recognize the importance of their perceptions and motivations for understanding their behaviour. We also appreciate how perceptions and motivations are formed and coloured by wider, historical and cultural (i.e. sociological) experiences and relations both at work and beyond the workplace. Behaviour in organizations is not just about perceptions and motivations. It is also, and perhaps more importantly, about the economic and political conditions and consequences of work. It is therefore highly relevant to pay attention to the historical and cultural formation of managers' and employees' material and symbolic aspirations (e.g. pay, pensions and position, as well as other possibilities or opportunities for improving their situation such as promotion, share options and moving jobs). In this context, we need to appreciate how, for example, managers of private sector companies (PLCs) are *legally* accountable to shareholders as especially privileged stakeholders.

When placed in this wider context, awareness increases of how the disciplines of economics and politics are directly relevant for understanding work organizations. People who work in organizations come from diverse social backgrounds and have varied social responsibilities and affiliations outside, as well as within their workplaces. Quite widely divergent motivations and interests are forged and pursued in the process of developing and defending an individual and collective sense of security and identity. As a consequence, it cannot be presumed that, for example, employees or other stakeholders (e.g. customers, suppliers) fully support decisions (e.g. lay-offs, pay constraints, price rises, product range reductions) that are intended to advance the interests of shareholders.

SOURCE: © ISTOCKPHOTO.COM/LISE GAGNE

Image 1.1 College as a global village

Beyond mechanical prescription

We can illustrate the distinctiveness and value of our approach by considering the 'skill profile' attributed to effective managers (see Box 1.6), such as head teachers or departmental heads in schools. What is your reaction to the contents of this skill profile? Do you consider that knowledge of this profile would make managers that you have known more effective? If not, what else might be relevant? Give these questions a few moments of thought before continuing.

The 'skill profile' identified in Box 1.6 is based upon extensive research, with much of the data drawn from responses by managers' subordinates. Yet it contains few surprises or insights. In our experience, small groups of school students or undergraduates are able to produce very similar lists within a matter of minutes. If this is the case, it places in doubt the value of such lists, because they do little more than recycle and reinforce common-sense thinking (see Box 1.7).

Box 1.6: The effective manager's skill profile

- Clarifies goals and objectives for everyone involved.
- Encourages participation, upward communication and suggestions.
- Plans and organizes for an orderly work flow.

- Has technical and administrative expertise to answer organization-related questions.
- Facilitates work through teambuilding, training, coaching and support.
- Provides feedback honestly and constructively.

Source: From Kinicki and Kreitner, 2003, p. 8; emphases omitted.

Box 1.7: Isn't it all just commonsense?

When knowledge about something is considered to be 'commonsense', we tend to treat it as a self-evident or unquestionable 'truth'. How often have you been told, especially by parents or supervisors, to use your commonsense, or to be sensible? The term is used to convey the view that there is no room for debate or discussion about what is meant. Indeed, to challenge commonsense is to appear stupid or unreasonable. We use the term 'commonsense' to indicate what is believed to be obvious to any competent human being. 'Commonsense' is assumed to be clear-cut and straightforward, and so it is, but only as long as we do not challenge it. Terms that are not immediately recognizable as, or reducible to, commonsense – such as 'organization' or 'social structure', as contrasted to 'pecking order', for example – demand a little more thinking than commonsense expects.

An everyday example of commonsense is the notion that the sun rises and sets. Rising and setting is what the sun appears to do, yet if we accept contemporary scientific authority, then we should talk about the earth rotating: what commonsense tells us is misleading. Another, more directly relevant example of commonsense is the way that people describe economic self-interest as human nature. If we consider this claim more carefully, we find that it is problematic. This is because economic self-interest is also often denigrated as greediness – as in the 2002 scandals at Enron and WorldCom where false accounts were perpetrated to ensure high stock market ratings and big bonuses for the managers of those companies. In these examples, greed was condemned and executives have been urged to moderate their self-interest, suggesting that it can be controlled and therefore it is not essential to human nature. If something is human nature, it is the equivalent of the dog

barking when it senses that its territory is being invaded; and, as any dog owner knows, this is nigh impossible to prevent. In the example of economic self-interest, therefore, we can see that despite its claims to truth, commonsense is self-contradictory and rather impervious to reflection. It allows two mutually inconsistent or diametrically opposed views to be held at one and the same time.

We rarely think about organizations in a systematic way or seek to understand precisely why or how they failed to meet our expectations. There is a tendency to account for such failures by relying upon commonsense – for example, by diagnosing the failure as a 'lack of communication' or 'poor organization' as if, by labelling the problem in this way, we need pay it no further attention. Alternatively, we find a scapegoat like the incompetent boss. In principle, the study of OB can provide us with the conceptual and analytical resources for thinking beyond these sweeping and dismissive, commonsense 'explanations'. We might then better understand what renders communication 'lacking' or organization 'poor'. Or, to put this another way, we might begin to open the 'black box' of behaviour in organizations to discover what lurks inside.

Commonsense frequently relies upon assumptions that, on reflection, are shown to be simplistic. When the earth is conceived to be at the centre of the universe, it is 'obvious' that the sun rises and sets; when materialistic societies are conceived to be the most 'civilized', the greed that they inspire is readily identified as an essential feature of human nature. On reflection, economic self-interest is found not to be an essential quality of human nature. It is, rather, an effect of how in contemporary, materialistic societies, the individual and wealth are elevated as key values. In short, greed has become a widespread, normal pattern of

▶

behaviour – so widespread that economic self-interest is commonsensically regarded as inherent to human nature. But, saying this, there is no suggestion (either) that altruism (as the opposite of self-interest) is essential. Instead, we are drawn to the view that human nature is open and ambivalent. For this reason, to cite human nature as an explanation of a person's actions may be commonsensically plausible but, on reflection, it begs more questions than it answers. It invites us, for example, to ask why human nature is identified in particular ways that appeal to commonsense?

Having signalled its dangers and limitations, from time to time most of us, including scientists, rely upon commonsense thinking, or at least are prepared to suspend disbelief in it. We will, for example, rely frequently on a commonsense understanding of organization as an entity, even though we repeatedly question this commonsense 'truth'. Everyday conversations and communications would simply collapse if every word or statement that relied on commonsense were incessantly challenged or questioned.

What, then, is the alternative? In a nutshell, one possible alternative aims to provide insights into why, in practice, it is so difficult to develop and apply skills identified as effective. Take the example of goals and objectives. The list of effective skills implies that goals are already established and merely require elucidation. In practice, however, they are frequently ambiguous and conflicting as we noted earlier. Those involved may well perceive that the goals identified by the 'effective manager' are incompatible with their own preferences and priorities. In which case, 'participation' may well be more troublesome and even counter-productive in securing employee compliance. Even in situations where others can be persuaded to share goals or communicate and respond positively to honest feedback, competing priorities and limited resources frequently compromise or undermine effective managers' efforts to 'organize an orderly work flow' or 'facilitate work through teambuilding'. It is dangerous to assume that becoming an effective manager simply involves the acquisition of the desired skill profile. If this were so, a manager might be led to believe in the effectiveness of mindlessly applying those 'skills' to particular situations in the absence of interpreting appropriate usage on each and every occasion.

Box 1.8: Why are organizational behaviour texts so wide of the mark?

When considering the skill profile attributed to effective managers (see Box 1.6) we claimed that texts based upon such thinking are of limited value and relevance. This view immediately begs the question why, then, are they so popular and widely adopted? Our response is that their appeal resides in the highly positive image or 'spin' that they give to organizations and managers. This reassuring and even slightly glamorous image is attractive to future employers as well as to students as it portrays management as a respectable and responsible profession where the manager's role is 'simply' to enable others to achieve established, shared goals and objectives. Largely absent from the benign image of organizations and management presented in most OB texts is any recognition of how the practicalities of management are shaped – impeded as well as enabled – by insecurities and inequalities that are endemic to modern organizational life.

If this analysis is accepted, then what *is* of value to prospective managers? It is not, we believe, lists of effective skills or techniques. Rather, effective management involves drawing upon embodied insights into work relations as a means of developing a better understanding of how to manage without following simple prescriptions.

Our skill profile example is typical of an approach that introduces OB through the provision of abstract lists or idealistic prescriptions of management behaviour that students tend to find self-evident and/or remote from everyday experience. Because they are removed from an understanding of the ever-shifting complexities of human behaviour at work, they are likely to be of little assistance in practical situations of managing. Forms of management education and training based upon such prescriptive thinking tends to reinforce a passive learning experience in which students absorb and regurgitate information without ever reflecting upon its value to them, except as instrumental rational means of attaining a certification.

Without an awareness of the messy, politically charged practicalities of organizing and managing, any amount of worthy (and, we would add, often patronizing) prescription will be of little value and may even be damaging. It is foolhardy, and potentially disastrous, to apply a set of principles or 'best practices' without first making an assessment of the particular situation and developing an evaluation of their relevance.

We acknowledge that there can be value in identifying a set of skills that are seen to render managers effective. However, such profiles and checklists do not enable us to discern and diagnose why and in what circumstances these skills may be effective. In our view the point of studying OB is to scrutinize and move beyond apparently self-evident but ultimately simplistic and misleading ideas about working and managing in organizations. We elaborate our views in a later section of this chapter where we directly address the question 'Why study organizational behaviour?' For the moment, we focus upon organizations as the context for the study of human behaviour.

Thinking about organizations

So far, we have concentrated upon behaviour in organizations, but what about organizations themselves? When beginning to think about organizations, specific examples may spring to mind. We might think of a major retailer (e.g. Ikea), a manufacturer (e.g. Hewlett-Packard), a public sector organization, like the Health Service or a government department, a school, an office or a pub (see Box 1.9).

It is not difficult to reel off an extensive list of organizations, but what, if anything, do they have in common? Again, it is easy to identify some common features. Most organizations involve employment relations, a division of labour, hierarchy, and a degree of permanence or continuity. What other common features would you add to this list?

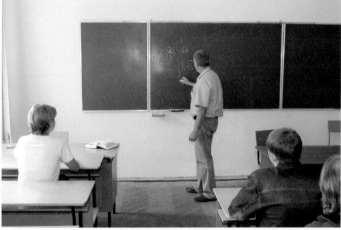

Image 1.2 Diverse work organizations: factory, school, office, public house

With the construction of this list, we appear to have identified a number of the distinctive characteristics of organizations. The difficulty is to find a single item on this list that is *exclusive* to organizations. Consider employment. We can think of examples of forms of employment that are not directly associated with organizations. Within the 'black economy' (e.g. where people work unofficially for cash in hand), many people are employed without being a member of an organization or indeed being recognized as employed for the purposes of tax and national insurance. Within organizations, a division of labour is present wherever members do not undertake identical tasks. But this is true of many other institutions, such as the family where certain jobs are frequently reserved by, or left to, particular members. For example, household tasks are often subjected to a gendered division of labour where women carry out most of the childcare responsibilities, cooking and cleaning, while men tend the garden or engage in DIY.

To take another example, a degree of permanence exists in families but we would not today readily identify families as organizations, even though, in small local enterprises, family members may run a business. In the pre-industrial era, work and family were not as separate as today, since domestic production was pre-eminent. The development of the internet and tele-computing communications has once again brought home and work closer together. Many people, like ourselves, do some or much of our work back in the family home partly because this allows us to concentrate, say, on writing this text without continuous interruptions from colleagues and students. However, through mobile communications, we usually make ourselves available to those who need to be in contact with us. Nonetheless, families are not readily conceived as organizations, perhaps largely because relations between their members are comparatively permanent, personal and intimate.

Thinkpoint 1.2

Working from home How many people do you know who work from home, at least part of the time, and what kinds of jobs do they do? What, if anything, differentiates the experience of doing these jobs from those carried out in offices, factories or other employer premises? Drawing upon your knowledge of people who work from home, what are some of the pros and cons of such work experience? How would you view 'housework' in the context of working from home?

There is further discussion of 'organization' in a later section in this chapter (see 'The distinctiveness of work organization: Instrumental rationality'). For the moment, it is worth repeating our earlier emphasis on organization as a concept that directs our attention and energies in particular ways, rather than assuming it to be a distinctive kind of social institution. It is also worth re-emphasizing that our purpose throughout this text is to connect its content with your experience of studying and working in a variety of settings or of consuming various products or services. In doing so, the intent is to make the contents of OB less remote and more personally relevant. In line with this approach, we now introduce an example from everyday life.

Box 1.9: What is a pub? A sociologist's answer

According to Clark (1983): . . .

the 'typically English pub' has its particular place in 'English' culture for its symbolic role as an 'icon of the everyday'. . . . Historically, in Britain, public houses have served as the social focus for geographical and occupational communities. The public house has taken different forms over time and has its origins in the 'inns', 'taverns' and 'alehouses' of the pre-industrial era. In that period, alehouses were more numerous than any other type of public meeting-place and were the focus for a huge range of social and economic activity. Ordinary people went there to buy and sell goods, to borrow money, to obtain lodging and work, to find sexual partners, to play folk games and gamble in addition to the usual eating, dancing, smoking and carousing.

However, it was not until the early 1800s that the purpose-built public house as we know it began to be built in large numbers and the 'alehouse' gave way to the 'public house'. By the beginning of the 19th century the term 'alehouse' had all but disappeared and by 1865, according to the *Oxford English Dictionary*, the word 'pub' had entered the language. (Watson, 2002, p. 18)

Organizational behaviour and everyday life: Going down the pub

We have already noted how difficult it is to draw a hard-and-fast distinction between organizations and other social institutions such as the family. The pub – or public house – provides a further example. For those who work in pubs, they are in many ways organizations that employ their specialist skills. In contrast, for regular customers, their 'local' is more like an extension of their family or community. In the following example of a pub – the Dog and Duck – we deliberately chose an example of an organization that is (a) familiar to most students and (b) ambivalent and shifting in its status as an organization.

In exploring the case of the Dog and Duck, we begin to introduce some of our key concepts (in italics) to demonstrate their relevance for analysing everyday life, including the pub as a work organization and a place of leisure where products (e.g. drinks and food) and services (such as live music and sports events) are consumed.

Our students tell us that the pubs that become student venues generally offer cheap deals on drinks and lower prices generally. In terms of material *inequality* (see the Appendix), many students are (albeit temporarily) low down on the social scale. The exceptions are students whose parents provide them with plenty of money, secure a large loan, or who get a well-remunerated job while at university. Even when not 'hard up', however, many students prefer drinking in student pubs rather than more expensive bars and clubs. Why is this? Take a moment to reflect upon what draws students to particular pubs. Do these work organizations have distinctive features?

Generally, student pubs are friendly toward young people and the management and staff are willing to put up with the boisterousness and noise where students gather in large numbers. They also provide attractions that students value, like pool tables and juke box music. But, beyond this, how does the student pub make you feel 'at home', relaxed and comfortable, and in what kinds of conditions

CASE STUDY 1.1 Jackie at the pub (1)

Jackie finished off her assessed work that was to be handed in the next day and felt she needed a drink. Her flatmates had gone out earlier that evening but she knew where they would be – at their local, the Dog and Duck. Her mates usually congregated in the pub around 7.00pm most weeknights because there were special deals on the drinks – two for the price of one. The landlady and landlord were happy for their pub to be full of students and did not hassle them when they got a bit rowdy. Also, in student jargon, the pub was good for 'pulling'. Jackie was now in her second semester of her first year and had already 'pulled' a couple of pretty fit lads she first met in the Dog and Duck. But the main reason for going to the D&D – or the 'B&Q' (the Bitch and Quackers) as it was known to her friends for reasons that Jackie would be embarrassed to explain – was that you could guarantee that your friends would be there.

However, on this occasion, Jackie arrived quite late because it had taken her longer than expected to finish her essay. Her mates had all disappeared. She had some idea that they would have gone off to one of the student discos in the town, but she was rather tired and so decided to have a quick drink on her own before heading back for a long-promised early night. At this time in the evening, most of the students had left and the bar was filling up with 'locals'. Like the students, the locals knew each other and therefore didn't ordinarily talk to the few remaining students unless they themselves were

'on the pull'. This was the first time that Jackie had found herself in the pub on her own and she felt a little embarrassed just standing at the bar with a drink. So she sat down in a corner of the pub, hoping she would be left alone. However, within a few minutes a group of young people, mainly lads, came towards her table. They seemed friendly enough and were talking in an animated way about the poor performance of the local football team. Jackie felt that she could fancy one of these lads. When he asked if anyone else was sitting at her table, the absence of other glasses made it difficult for her to refuse, and anyway her desire for a quiet drink had now been overtaken by her interest in the faceable lad.

Soon the conversation turned to the changing clientele in the pub and some of the group began running down the students, describing them as 'toffee-nosed' and 'cliquey'. It was clear to Jackie that they resented the 'takeover' of their local by the students, something that had happened earlier in the year when a new management at the pub made an effort to attract students. The pub had been quiet between about 6.30pm, when the early drinkers on their way home left and 8.30pm when the later regulars appeared after their evening meal. Jackie felt even more embarrassed that these locals were 'slagging off' students, as she thought, because she felt that they must know that she was a student, and were deliberately winding her up. She wasn't at all sure how, or even whether, to respond.

would you feel threatened? Does drinking with other students confirm or reinforce your *identity* (see the Appendix) as a student? Does that provide a key to understanding why we tend to gravitate to places where there are people like ourselves? When we find ourselves in a room largely full of strangers, we usually seek out a person we know. Why? Case Study 1.1 provides a story or scenario about going down the pub.

Like any other institution, the pub reflects a complex set of *power* relations (see the Appendix). As a customer, Jackie is dependent upon the staff of the pub to be served and, ultimately, for protection against verbal and physical abuse. But, as a customer, Jackie is important to the pub managers since they are determined to pursue the potentially highly profitable custom of students. Power relations operate to identify her not only as a student but also as a valued customer – and, quite possibly, as a customer who can encourage or dissuade her mates to use the pub. So even though Jackie and her friends occupy a comparatively low rung on the income scale, the existence of material *inequality* does not imply an absence of power as long as her custom, and that of her student friends, is valued. However, as our vignette or brief story shows, other customers, or even pub staff, may not share the positive value being ascribed by the pub managers to students as clientele.

Having read this account of Jackie's visit to the pub, what do you think you would have done in her position? Consider first what you perceive her position to be. What features of this position do you regard as significant? Once you have clarified your understanding of Jackie's situation, consider some possible responses Jackie could make:

- Pretend not to be listening to what they are saying?
- Confront the locals and attempt to defend the students?
- Pretend not to be a student and find a way of joining in on the stereotyping of them, if only as a way of attracting the attention of the Beckham-double? (After all, it is not too far-fetched to think that he may have targeted Jackie as a potential chat-up.)
- Ignore the attack but try to get into conversation with them?
- See the lads engaging in an alternative kind of 'chat-up' by trying to provoke some reaction instead of using a well-worn (institutionalized!) chat-up line – such as asking your name and what you did – so take the lads' (attention) in your stride?

Can you think of other ways that a student in Jackie's position might react?

We will return later to develop our analysis of this story. For the moment, we note only that what happened to Jackie indicates in a practical way how, even in places of leisure, experiences are

"Just for the minutes did anyone manage to catch
the chairman's parting words?"

Image 1.3

unpredictable because others – in this example, other customers – act in ways that are experienced as intrusive and objectionable, and which can be characterized as friendly, wilful or mischievous. Traditionally, the pub has been associated not only with symbolic violence, as experienced by Jackie, who felt personally affronted by the lads' 'slagging off' of students, but also physical violence when, fuelled by alcohol, frayed tempers spill over into punch-ups.

Outright physical violence involving an exchange of blows is exceptional but not unknown in other work organizations. Symbolic violence, however, is much more widespread. It can be based on physical characteristics (e.g. sexual or racial harassment) or take the form of verbal bullying. Many critics of the workplace argue that simply the demand to perform repetitive, physical work tasks that hardly engage the brain is a form of symbolic violence, in which case a majority of employees experience it at some point. We hope to show in this text how employees suffer a sense of frustration less from the routine nature of their tasks than from the absence of any power to influence how tasks are decided and organized. In our case, Jackie's levels of stress and *insecurity* (see the Appendix) – in the form of anxiety, embarrassment, irritation and frustration – were raised by her sense of powerlessness and lack of control. While she desperately wanted to challenge the lads' stereotypical views about students, she felt inhibited and intimidated. Whether or not it was their intent, they had succeeded in winding her up and she was finding it difficult to calm down and collect her thoughts. The study of organizations encounters conflict and contested points of view in more ways than in the direct expression of verbal or physical violence.

Symbolic violence – in the form of mild or vehement expressions of disagreement – might include, for example, differences of opinion among bar staff (and customers) about the desirability of students as clientele, and the verbal and non-verbal communication directed at this group. In this process, there is an elevation of the symbolic value or identity (see the Appendix) of one group through a negation of the other. In its most extreme versions, there is a complete polarization so that the other(s) or 'out-group' are demonized as unworthy of proper human respect. At football matches, this has resulted in the necessity for institutional forms of crowd control, such as physical segregation and other restrictions on the away supporters.

Such violence extends to disagreements among researchers, consultants, and indeed employees about the usefulness and meaning of concepts that are deployed to analyse behaviour and pursue practices in organizations. These disagreements – such as our criticizing conventional texts – may not result in the trading of blows but they can, and do, involve passionate exchanges of views and uneasy 'stand-offs'. Even when people recognize discussion and debate to be healthy and a source of new ideas, they may still feel threatened when their own ideas are challenged. Take a moment to reflect on some of the ideas or beliefs that you are attached to and would defend against a challenge. Often these are so deeply ingrained or taken for granted (e.g. your gender, class, nationality, race or religion) that it takes considerable reflective effort to bring them to mind.

Organizational behaviour as a contested terrain

In leading textbooks, OB tends to be presented as largely cut-and-dried and settled, thus lacking any controversy, conflict or contest, yet such appearances are deceptive. There are fundamental differences of view – cultural, political and ethical – about how organizations are organized, how they should be organized and how they can be studied. To some extent, these mirror and amplify differences of opinion and preference among people working in organizations (between factions of senior managers, for example) about how to organize and manage their operation. As a general rule, theories that articulate and confirm our preconceptions and prejudices tend to be most appealing, as they are the easiest to grasp and make us feel secure in our views and identities. So, in general, women are more likely than men to appreciate how relations of gender implicitly or explicitly affect the workplace, especially in areas of recruitment, selection and promotion. We invite you to discuss and reflect upon why this may be the case.

Here we are highlighting the continuities between practitioners' and researchers' ways of making sense of behaviour in organizations. At the same time, it is relevant to note that these practitioners and researchers are positioned in different relations of power – relations of power that provide access to distinctive ways of thinking and that assign different weights and values to such thinking. Some researchers favour and elaborate forms of analysis that highlight and explore how organizing is largely consensual and routine; others contend that organizing is precarious and conflict-ridden. Such analyses can serve to illuminate practitioners' everyday experiences, but practitioners themselves, especially managers, may find more favour and comfort with ideas that assume organizing to be consensual and conflict-free; or, at least, which assume consensus to be the normal and natural state of affairs.

Differences within and between practitioners and researchers can be confusing and frustrating, not least for students of OB. But these differences are also what make the field dynamic and engaging. Glossing over these differences can make OB easier to present and absorb, but this does students and practitioners few favours when highly complex organizational processes are examined in technically simplistic and politically naive ways. Challenging thinking that skirts around or skates over this complexity is necessary for developing an awareness of it. It is through such conflict and debate – in practice as well as theory – that intellectual reflection and organizational innovation is stimulated. At least, it is difficult to imagine how reflection and innovation would occur without them.

Exercise 1.1

Encountering organization Consider an organization where you have worked or have been a customer. List some differences of view, or grievances, among employees and/or customers that you encountered. How do these concerns connect to how activities were being organized and managed. Are there other issues that *you* would raise as an employee or as a customer? Reflect upon how your values and preoccupations lead you to raise these issues.

Competing logics of organizing

We have repeatedly stressed that organizations are politically charged, complex, social institutions (see Chapter 8). Their complexity does not arise directly from their scale or even from the diversity of their operations, but rather from conflicting priorities and preferences of their members who, in turn, are caught up in webs of others' demands upon them (e.g. families, customers, shareholders, etc.). An expression of these conflicting priorities is found in the existence of competing logics of organizing material and human resources to provide diverse goods and services. We have seen, for example, how Jackie found herself in a situation complicated by the competing priorities and

Image 1.4

preferences of the pub managers and the local customers. Whereas the new managers wanted to maximize the use of the premises at all times, this priority risked losing their established customer base of local regulars who resented 'their pub' being taken over by students.

A much broader example of competing logics of organizing concerns the issue of how 'public goods', such as health and education, should be provided. In recent years, questions have been asked with increasing frequency and urgency about the adequacy, and even the viability, of provision of such goods by public sector organizations. Public sector organizations have been repeatedly criticized for being too bureaucratic, unresponsive and insufficiently alert to (changing) customer preferences and expectations. Their critics point to an ingrained inflexibility (i.e. of managers, professional staff and workers) as the greatest obstacle to delivering value-for-money public goods (e.g. education).

During the 1980s and 1990s many people were persuaded that the answer to problems identified in the public sector – such as waste, rigidity and inefficiency – was to run it as a private business (see Box 1.10).

For elements of the public sector that were not privatized, the 'modernization' plan was to populate the public sector with 'professional managers' and to introduce more entrepreneurial ideas from the private sector. This process has included provisional targets and financial incentives for staff. It has encouraged competition and discipline associated with performance measurement and comparisons between different services. In the United Kingdom, the reforms included the introduction of performance measures in the form of league tables to schools and hospitals, for example, so that their 'customers' (i.e. parents and doctors) would make an informed choice between alternative service providers. In making a choice of school or university course, you (or your parents) may have been influenced by such tables.

Thinkpoint 1.3

League tables Consider the pros and cons of introducing league tables to measure the performance of schools or university departments. Imagine that you are advising a government in a country that has no equivalent to these tables. Consider the probable effects of their use upon the organization – e.g. scope and delivery – of educational provision. What arguments would you make to recommend or resist the introduction of league tables? How would you illustrate your position by reference to your own experience and knowledge as a recipient of educational services?

Box 1.10: Privatization and the 'new enterprise culture'

The case for the privatization of public services, either through substitution or contracting out to the private sector, is based on the claim that employees and especially managers in most organizations, including many in the private sector, have to be shaken out of their complacency and become more willing to take risks and be innovative in pursuit of efficiency, productivity and improved performance. In many countries, a number of publicly owned utilities (e.g. electricity, gas, transport and telecommunications) were 'sold off' to the private sector through a process of 'privatization'.

The supporters of this move argued that it would serve to modernize these services by making their provision more cost-effective, in addition to releasing capital that could fund tax cuts, reduce debt or boost the financing of services retained within the public sector (e.g. armed forces). Its critics pointed to the loss of control of key services, the damaging consequences of making them objects of profit, the erosion of conditions for public services workers and the redistribution of wealth from the poor to the rich by expanding the private sector. For organizations that remain in the public sector, what is needed, it is claimed, is a set of targets linked to incentives that can substitute for the profit motive and competition, which are seen to drive private sector managers to deliver high levels of performance. Public sector management, its critics complain, lacks incentives to make radical reforms. Enabling managers to exercise greater prerogative, unhampered by established traditions of collective bargaining and custom and practice regarding such things as manning levels and job design, is the key to raising the quality as well as the cost-effectiveness of public service delivery.

While there is a continuing controversy about the wisdom of privatization, or selling off the family silver as Lord Macmillan once described it, the idea that the private sector has much to offer the public sector remains. In the United Kingdom, confidence in the capacity of private ownership and associated forms of organizing and managing reflects a wider embracing of values that have been characterized as part and parcel of a new 'enterprise culture'. Balanced against this, highly visible failures of privatization (e.g. UK railways) have somewhat tempered public opinion and policy making in this area.

In the United Kingdom, the substitution of private for public forms of financing and organizing has been welcomed, or at least tacitly supported, by a majority of people. This is unsurprising because a reluctance to fund public services through taxation increases has left them (us) on the receiving end of under-investment in a public sector run down and demoralized by this neglect.[1] Almost everyone has a tale to tell of poor or worsening standards of public housing, healthcare and education. People suffering a bad experience with the public sector are already receptive to the suggestion that government should be run like a business, with professional managers being given the prerogative and discretion to manage resources.

'New managerialism' in the public sector

What this new managerialism means or at least claims, in less abstract terms, is that only by running public services like a business can citizens (as customers) receive the value-for-money and quality services to which they are entitled (see Box 1.11). The reform of public services is advocated in order to ensure that they are run for the benefit of those who use them, and not for 'the bureaucrats' who provide them. Paradoxically though, the result of such 'reforms' is an increase of managerial and monitoring staff whose salaries are paid by slashing the numbers, and eroding the terms and conditions, of the front-line employees who are being 'modernized'. Various private sector managerial techniques of budgets, targets, financial incentives, project management, performance league tables and accounting procedures are applied to the public sector.

After the scandals at Enron and WorldCom, the ideology that commends the running of public services like a business may be less convincing. 'New managerialism' does not acknowledge how too much faith in a managerial view can readily lead to corruption and greed. This then might undermine the very conditions necessary for a successful economy (such as confidence, trust and security).

'So, do you still think the government should be run like a business?..'

Image 1.5

SOURCE: CLAY BENNETT/ © 2002 THE CHRISTIAN SCIENCE MONITOR (WWW.CSMONITOR.COM).

Box 1.11: The organization and managerialization of everything

Managerialism refers to a view that assigns to managers the exclusive power to define the goals of the organization and their means of achievement. In extreme form, it proposes that everything can be managed efficiently through the application of 'correct' techniques. Elements of this can be seen in the delivery of programmed education provided in modularized chunks, using standardized overhead transparencies and student workbooks. Likened to the provision of (fast) food, this has been described as the 'McDonaldization' of education. To cater for a mass education market, textbooks are being produced to a standard formula and, like burgers, are probably not to be recommended as part of a healthy diet.

Thinkpoint 1.4

Would you privatize? How do you feel about efforts to 'privatize' or 'modernize' the public sector? In considering this question, you might examine reports of the Fire Brigades Union dispute that occurred during the autumn of 2002 into 2003. You might also reflect upon your experience as a consumer of public services – education, health, transport, local public facilities, etc. Here you could assess the effects of privatization and modernization upon the availability, scope and quality of such services.

The recurrent complaint of those who favour enterprise or market-based solutions to all forms of resource allocation is that the public services have been organized primarily for the benefit of producers (e.g. public sector employees) rather than their customers. This echoes the discovery of an earlier generation of OB researchers who found that bureaucracies suffered considerably from what they described as goal displacement (Merton *et al.*, 1952). Conforming to the internal rules of the organization (perhaps for reasons of career advancement) was shown to be more important than fulfilling the objectives (service to clients) that the rules were designed to facilitate.

However, this complaint about self-serving public sector bureaucrats also deflects attention from the importance placed upon shareholders, rather than customers, in the organizing logic that distinguishes private sector service provision. Private sector companies are obliged not only to operate profitably, but also to compete to raise the return on capital deployed. Of course, they may fail to do this, in which case they are starved of capital, experience a cash flow crisis, and eventually go to the wall unless they are bailed out by government. Or they succeed in staying afloat by engaging in sharp (e.g. anti-competitive) practices, which restrict consumer choice and raise prices. Alternatively, they engage in 'creative accounting' to inflate their earnings or conceal the extent of their liabilities and expenses. Private sector companies frequently claim that it is their priority to serve customers as a way of retaining or increasing market share, but neither will be pursued unless they contribute to profits. The users of privately supplied public services in the United Kingdom (e.g. children taught by agency teachers or travellers using the privatized rail system) have routinely discovered this to their cost, sometimes with their lives.

It has become increasingly clear that the private sector does not have all the answers (see Box 1.12). In the worst case, customers experience increased prices, lower levels of service and safety and massive inconvenience – as in the case of the railways in the United Kingdom. Contractual services are also often far from perfect. For example, hospitals have been encouraged to contract out their cleaning to private companies. Through a bidding process, the costs may end up being lower, but the quality of the cleaning is often poor and perhaps dangerous to the health of patients.[2] Incentives can work in perverse ways. Basically, a low-cost supplier will tend to 'cut corners' in order to maintain profit margins rather than raise standards. (A comparison of the private and public sectors is set out in Table 1.1.)

In an effort to counteract this endemic problem of purely market-based relations, increasing interest is being shown in private–public partnerships. In principle, the entrepreneurial features of private business are conceived to shake up and inspire improvements in public sector organizations without entirely abandoning an ethos of public service delivery. The assumption underlying this move was that market competition between private contractors would reduce the cost while maintaining or even improving quality. However, this calculation does not take significant account of the capacity/expertise of inexperienced staff in the public sector to secure a good deal.

Box 1.12: Denting confidence in private sector rationality

During the 1990s, the failure of many dot-com companies and e-commerce ventures indicated that private sector methods and strategies are not guaranteed to be superior to other (e.g. democratic, bureaucratic) ways of running an organization. In historical terms, the bursting of the dot-com bubble is not new;[3] and indeed, on a smaller scale, a high proportion of new businesses go bust every year. This is the nature of private enterprise and indeed the stock market has been likened to a giant global gambling casino (Strange, 1997). When the market crashed, those that spread their risks across a wide range of investments fared much better than those who were sucked into the idea that the boom could go on forever. Perhaps we should be just as circumspect when it comes to delivering public services.

Table 1.1 Comparing private and public sectors

Sector	Private	Public
Focus	Produce what is profitable for investors	Provide what is demanded by voters
Governance	Accountability to shareholders	Accountability to electorate
Logic of organization	Innovation to produce better returns on capital invested	Standardization to provide continuity of service and security of employment
Shortcomings	Lack of concern with anything (e.g. the environment, ethics, other stakeholders) that does not contribute to profits	Under-investment, bureaucratic rigidity and ineffective use of resources

Instead of surrendering, as it were, much of the public sector to private sector operators and their market-driven logics, there is increasingly an attempt to forge longer-term partnerships between the two sectors to secure the best of both worlds. Supporters of this middle way suggest that entrepreneurial flair can be transferred without damaging the ethos of public service delivery. In place of the lowest bidder, 'best value' is taken as the baseline for evaluating competing private sector bids for public service contracts. Best value can incorporate a concern with the ethos of the contractor, including their track record on collaborating in long-term partnerships, to find mutually acceptable ways of securing cost-effective improvements in service delivery.

Whether or not faith in public–private partnerships is justified or sustained, there is no doubt that a defining feature of capitalist business is risk. Critics of the 'enterprise culture' have asked the question: 'If you are ill do you want to be treated by an entrepreneur or a doctor following professional and regulated standards of good practice?' This question became all the more poignant or significant when in 2002 senior executives at major international companies (e.g. Enron, WorldCom) were exposed for fraudulently massaging their balance sheets to secure better stock market share prices. As major shareholders, many of these executives were the direct beneficiaries of the increased valuations and in many cases offloaded their shares prior to the company's collapse (see Box 1.13).

Contexts of organizational behaviour

Apart from the tragedy for employees losing their jobs, the Enron and WorldCom scandals had the effect of scaring already jittery investors who had experienced the pain of the dot-com bubble into a mass exodus from the stock market that brought share prices tumbling down and reminded people of the Great Crash on Wall Street in 1929. Because the whole world experienced several

Box 1.13: 'Enronomics'

The collapse of Enron followed by WorldCom begged a number of questions: How many more companies might be fraudulent? It led investors to ask: 'Can we trust executives – even, and perhaps especially, those with MBAs – with our money?' Almost overnight, senior executives and their so-called independent audit firms suffered worldwide disrepute. From being popular American heroes, corporate executives were reduced to pariahs – viewed with increasing suspicion and scorn when previously they had been lavished with bonuses and praise.

years of deep recession and mass unemployment after the 1929 crash, any parallel is viewed with great fear.

Of course, not every company is an Enron or a WorldCom, and not every dot-com company was badly managed or went bankrupt. But their 'excesses' are a reminder that the values and priorities of private business are financial profit. Companies stay in business only so long as investors (e.g. shareholders and banks) have confidence in the executives to deliver an acceptable rate of growth on their capital. When confidence is dented, investment is withdrawn as capital is transferred towards less risky ventures. Depleted of capital, financially weak companies based upon optimistic or 'unrealistic' business models then struggle to survive when an economic downturn favours companies with sufficient reserves to slash prices and/or weather the storm.

Combined with misgivings about the performance of privatized public utilities and private contracting, the 1990s dot-com bubble burst and the subsequent loss of confidence in audited accounts can only help to moderate the enthusiasm of governments for exclusively private sector solutions to public sector reform. In the wake of major scandals and collapses, the idea that 'government should be run like a business' is destined to lose some of its common-sense appeal. Perhaps, after all, solutions for organizational problems are not so simple, and maybe despite the problems of rigidity characteristic of bureaucratic organizations, there is some merit in the checks and balances built into 'old' public sector management (Du Gay, 2000).

At the time of writing (early 2003) world markets were struggling to avoid or climb out of recession, which, despite governments' best endeavours, tend to occur in cycles. Part of this problem was a global crisis of over-production (i.e. too many goods/services chasing too few consumers) but depressed stock markets resulting from global uncertainty about an Iraqi war plus the accounting scandals discussed above exacerbated the sense of crisis. Despite relatively high rates of employment, exceptionally low income tax and interest rates that would normally fuel consumer spending, the talk of economic gloom was fuelling the crisis. Contexts such as this cannot be ignored when studying organizations because they provide good or legitimate reasons (or excuses) for decisions that, for example, lead to downsizing, mergers and acquisitions, or liquidating a company.

Instead of focusing narrowly upon the behaviour of individuals and groups in organizations, we have sought to locate 'organizing' within a wider context – such as the private or public sectors of goods and services production (see Box 1.14). It is important to remember that organizing takes place within wider historical, cultural and institutional contexts. Organizational behaviour is embedded in this context, which it reproduces or transforms. How would you characterize the contemporary context? Modern? Capitalist? Industrial? Post-industrial? These and other terms may spring to mind, but there is also a case for describing contemporary society as simply organized. Many contemporary activities and arrangements are characterized as the properties of organizations – bodies that cater for virtually every aspect of our lives.

Organizations have become central to, and now dominate, processes of producing and consuming goods and services of all kinds. To earn a wage or salary, a majority of people find employment within organizations – the self-employed being an exception (although many of them are contracted to work for organizations on a casual or temporary basis). While we usually work in one organization, we spend most of our earnings in other organizations, notably in the retail outlets where we buy food, clothing, cars, mortgages and so on. Organizations provide us with most of our material, and a considerable number of our less material (i.e. leisure and other service) wants. In their absence, many people would struggle to obtain an equivalent income, and there would be an acute shortage of goods and services. Organizations have become crucial to our material lives and perhaps survival.

Box 1.14: The 'unnaturalness' of organizations

The provision of goods and services through the creation of organizations is clearly not a 'natural' (i.e. a part of the human condition like food, water and oxygen) or necessary way of sustaining our lives. We need only think of how (even today, and more so in the past) a majority of people in the world produce and consume their everyday goods by depending much more on family and community than they do upon the activities and arrangements that we describe as organizations.

Back to the pub: The personal and the organizational

When thinking of organizations, there remains a tendency to think first of manufacturing industry or perhaps an established public sector organization, such as a school or hospital. We could easily have situated Jackie's experience of organization in a school, office or factory instead of a pub. The pub is however an interesting space as it combines processes of production, in the form of service delivery and sometimes brewing, with processes of consumption that are partly commodified (e.g. through purchasing and branding of goods) but largely self-organized (e.g. through socializing, conversing, etc.).

In contemporary, post-industrial societies, leisure has become a distinctive sphere of (recreational) life by virtue of other time that is sold to an employer or taken up with routine chores and 'maintenance' activities. Historically the 'public house' has been a recreational space and of central significance in 'disposing' of leisure time. Increasingly, however, advanced industrial societies are becoming de-industrialized as manufacturing is more profitably undertaken in industrializing economies where access to labour and raw materials is cheaper, more plentiful and less regulated. As the proportion of income available to be disposed on non-essentials (e.g. accommodation, food, clothing) has grown, the leisure sector has enjoyed sustained growth by commodifying the means of entertainment. That is to say, forms of leisure are increasingly 'packaged' for sale in the market-place rather than self-organized within families or communities.

Let us therefore go back to our narrative about Jackie in the Dog and Duck, a pub owned by the brewery, which has not (yet) sought to give it a 'theme' or 'facelift'. Remember she was sitting in a corner of the pub, having to listen to a gang of locals openly engaged in what she experienced as a character assassination of students.

We invite you to reflect further upon Jackie's visit to the pub (see Case study 1.2), concentrating this time upon the landlord and landlady's approach to managing this organization. To assist in this process, we encourage you to consider, preferably with other students on your course, the following questions:

1. Jackie is taking a course on organization studies. How do you think her experience of working in the pub might help with her studies and, how might her studies help her in the work?

CASE STUDY 1.2 Jackie at the pub (2)

Instead of choosing the various options suggested after presenting our vignette earlier, Jackie decided to leave the table and return to standing at the bar. After a short time she entered into conversation with the landlady and landlord who, for a few minutes, were sitting on the customer side of the bar. The conversation meandered through a number of topics, until Jackie felt sufficiently relaxed to bring up the experience of being criticized by the locals.

The landlady sympathized with Jackie, recognizing that there was a good deal of animosity between the locals and the students, especially since they had made considerable efforts to attract students into the pub. Ordinarily there was little trouble as the students were inclined to move on to other bars or discos nearer the centre of town before the locals came in. The landlord went on to explain his policy in seeking to attract the students when he became the tenant of the pub 12 months ago. He pointed out that they were hoping to make their tenancy a great success, as this was the way to obtain a much bigger pub from the brewery. Eventually they were hoping to buy their own pub in a nice coastal village in Cornwall where the tourist trade during the summer would provide financial security and allow them more time to pursue their hobbies – of astronomy and art work – during the quieter winter months. As they were talking, some customers were becoming impatient at not getting immediate service, and the landlord went back behind the bar for a while. The landlady then confided in Jackie that the growth in business in the pub had presented a staff problem for them.

As she left the pub Jackie felt a lot more at ease. The friendliness of the landlord and landlady had reassured her that students were really welcome and she knew that, in future, she could always talk to them when waiting for her friends to arrive. In fact she had found herself saying that if ever they were short of staff, she would be happy to help out. On her next visit to the pub, Jackie was asked by the landlord if she could do a few hours the following night when one of the staff had to visit her mother in hospital.

2. How does the case illustrate the concepts of identity, insecurity, power and inequality, and illuminate the practicalities of management and organization? *(See the Appendix for further discussion of these concepts.)*

3. Are there any other questions relating to this case study that you feel are important? If so, discuss these and feedback your results to our website.

It might be assumed that organizations have relevance, value or significance only as instruments for producing and providing goods and services. Yet organizations are also of central importance in producing and providing *a* sense of identity for both employees and customers. It is through our participation in organizations (e.g. as producers or consumers) that we develop, confirm or manage our sense of identity – for example, as employable (in work organizations), as prosperous (in retail outlets), as sick or cured (in hospitals), as well-educated or ignorant (in schools), and as enjoying ourselves (in pubs and clubs). But, as we have seen in our case study of the Dog and Duck, pubs can also be contexts where our identities are threatened in ways that fuel our insecurities. We saw how Jackie experienced this when the local lads voiced their assault on students – an assault that was provoked by insecurities aroused because of the pub's concern to attract students into their local.

Formation, development and change in our identities occur through social interactions – with ourselves as well as others – as we reflect upon our experiences and resolve, perhaps, to change our ways. This is, of course, not easy as is evidenced but the number of new year resolutions that are broken as our habitual patterns of action override our good intentions before the end of January.

Inescapably, what happens in organizations has personal as well as **instrumental** significance. Our experiences in organizations reinforce (or threaten) our sense of who we are and what is meaningful and valuable to us (and about us). In this process, relations of power operate to enable or obstruct how interactions and identities are accomplished. For example, Jackie's identity as a student is not just created by herself but also by the locals and the landlord and landlady. This identity degrades her value in the eyes of the locals but enhances it from the perspective of the landlady. She regards Jackie as a potential employee who can assist in developing a student clientele.

From Jackie's standpoint, her limited income as a student made the opportunity to do some part-time bar work more attractive than for someone in a healthier financial situation. But it was not simply material inequality that rendered Jackie more alert to this job opportunity. She also regarded it as a chance to enhance her status in the eyes of her parents who had been exerting pressures upon her to find part-time work. It is hardly surprising then, that Jackie felt much better after having had a more pleasant interaction with the landlord and landlady, being eventually offered a part-time job behind the bar. A few months later, after demonstrating a flair for interacting with customers, she was asked by the landlord if she would be able to manage the pub for a weekend. We take up the story on her first night in this enhanced role (see Case study 1.3).

CASE STUDY 1.3 Jackie at the pub (3)

Jackie was in some trepidation about managing the pub and, in particular, the reactions of the two other bar staff. They were both slightly older and also locals. John was pretty relaxed and she didn't expect much of a problem, not least because he displayed a 'soft spot' for her and this gave her a sense of control. Christine, however, was a different kettle of fish. When Christine had found herself working behind the bar with a student, she had felt threatened. As the elder and more experienced bartender of the three, Christine was upset that she had not been asked to manage the pub. This was particularly galling because she had ambitions to become a landlady.

Things were going all right on this Saturday evening until it got very busy. One of the customers was clearly expressing impatience at not getting served. Both Jackie and John were serving customers but Christine was engaged in a lengthy chat with a friend who was sitting at the bar. Jackie asked Christine if she could serve the waiting customer and she appeared to accept the request but then continued to chat with her friend. A bit of a row then occurred as Jackie tried to get Christine to come into the back where they could discuss the problem. Christine simply blew her top, condemning Jackie for embarrassing her in front of the customers. Christine walked out, saying she was not going to be bossed about by a trumped-up student who knew nothing about bar work.

The pub was very busy and it was going to be extremely difficult to manage with just two bar staff. At the first opportunity

Jackie tried to ring the landlord but couldn't get an answer. So she rang one of her flatmates – Carol – to see if she would come and help out. Fortunately Carol agreed to come at once and, despite needing a lot of help, the evening went reasonably smoothly. Eventually the landlord rang back and Jackie was able to explain the situation. He was sympathetic but was also a bit worried about how to replace Christine who, he feared, was gone for good. Maybe Carol, he suggested, would fill in for Christine, although Christine was working more hours than might be expected from a full-time student. Carol seemed quite keen. She had seen how Jackie had flourished since taking the job, plus the money was not to be sneezed at.

Jackie had experienced a big boost to her self-esteem by being asked to manage the pub. In contrast, not being chosen to manage the pub was a terrible blow to Christine. Not least, this was because she was more experienced in pub work, older, and of even more importance, she had ambitions to run a pub of her own. This helps us to understand Christine's reactions when Jackie sought to manage her defiance. Christine's defiance threatened Jackie's sense of identity, and especially her stand-in role as manager of the pub. She felt that her position as temporary manager had been undermined in the eyes of the clientele, and that her standing with the landlord and landlady would be damaged. Jackie was also concerned about how the landlord would react to the possible loss of Christine as a valued employee. While she had been embarrassed by Christine's walkout, Jackie's dignity and self-esteem remained intact by virtue of her not exploding in the same way as Christine. However, she felt some mild resentment towards the landlord who, she believed, must have had some inkling of how Christine might react. She felt that she had been placed in a difficult situation, and it crossed her mind that the landlord and landlady had perhaps seized, or even created, an opportunity to force Christine out so as to replace her with someone who they could trust to act as a reliable manager in their absence.

Once again, we encourage you to reflect upon staff relations at the Dog and Duck as illustrative of different aspects of behaviour in organizations. Here are some questions:

1. If Jackie is right that the landlord had contrived a situation that would provoke Christine into walking out, what implications does this have for 'the effective manager's skill profile' presented and discussed earlier.

2. How are the concepts of insecurity, identity, knowledge, power, freedom and inequality (see the Appendix) relevant for exploring and analysing the dynamics of the relationship and interactions between Jackie, Christine and the landlord?

3. Can you draw some parallels between the actions of the landlord, Jackie and Christine and your own experiences of work or leisure relationships?

4. Can you think of media reports of disputes at work, past or present, whose content might be illuminated through a similar analysis to the one we have sketched to interpret aspects of organization and management at the Dog and Duck?

Jackie's experience illustrates how organizations are not only important to our material existence, but they also have *symbolic* significance. For organizations involve not just our objectives and interests, but also our feelings, sentiments and identities. Organizations are among the core institutions – including the family and school – that foster and shape our aspirations and our attachment to particular social identities.

Organization and institutionalization

When we highlight the personal and social significance of organizations, we are also acknowledging their status and importance as institutions within which people – employees and customers – become institutionalized. You have probably heard the phrase 'the British pub is an institution' and never thought to reflect upon what it means. The phrase signals, we suggest, the distinctiveness of the social interactions as emblematic of British society. More sceptically, it could be argued that the pub is invoked to support a romantic ideal of how many people prefer to think of Britain.

Of course, there are many institutions that are not readily or plausibly identified as organizational. For example, a series of activities may become institutionalized around preparing for mealtimes, such as breakfast. The kind of breakfast that is prepared and the particular interactions, or grunts, exchanged with others during the process of preparing and consuming breakfast, assumes a pattern that becomes 'normal' and taken-for-granted. It is only when this pattern is disturbed, intentionally or otherwise (e.g. a valued ingredient runs out or a guest requests a very different kind of breakfast), that an awareness of the routine is aroused. The routine is an element of 'an institution' in the sense that it is the outcome of an orderly set of social relations that ensures, most of the time, that, in the case of the breakfast routine, the desired ingredients have been bought and that the usual grunts are exchanged (see Box 1.15).

It's just routine Consider some other routines (e.g. going to lectures) and how their presence and significance only comes to light when they are disrupted, or when we reflect critically upon them by imagining the possibilities of their disruption.

An example of 'breaking with routine' is the inability to 'make' the 9.00am lecture because of a hangover or lack of sleep the night before (assuming, of course, that such a routine was ever established). Student life can result in late nights and leisure becoming the routine, and this might only be disrupted when realizing that the lifestyle could result in failing the degree.

The significance of routines

Actions and relations are institutionalized in the sense that there is regularity and routine – for example, in how pupils relate to teachers, how doctors treat patients and how ticket inspectors check passengers. This process does not occur automatically. Rather, actions become institutionalized as people become attached to routines for material reasons (i.e. income flows from the routines of a job) or social acceptance (i.e. 'fitting in' with the routines of our mates). In both cases, our identity is confirmed, thereby making us feel secure – unless, of course, we are striving to establish a sense of identity in opposition to established conventions and lifestyles (in which case, we are involved in a process of institutionalizing alternative values and forms of behaviour).

As we noted earlier, over the past decade or more, pubs as work organizations have been expanding their services in an attempt to appeal to new customers. Providing play areas for children can attract young families, those seeking to eat out inexpensively can be catered for by pub food, and some pubs might (like the Dog and Duck) seek to specialize by encouraging a potentially profitable segment (e.g. students). In each case, the traditional clientele may feel (as we saw at the Dog and Duck) 'pushed out' or denied their institutionalized expectations when going down the pub.

More generally, employees as well as customers in many organizations have been obliged to make sense of, and deal with, disruptions to established practices and routines as companies have sought to use their (human and material) facilities in more productive, profitable and cost-effective ways. Think, for example, of the use of call-centres to replace face-to-face services, the shift to self-service

Box 1.15: Institutions and institutionalization

When sets of actions and relations are seen as fairly predictable, they are termed 'institutions'. Institutions involve common ways of doing things. Members of institutions (e.g. students within a university system) may not always agree with the rules (e.g. examination regulations) but usually comply (e.g. because of the concern to gain a degree). Processes of institutionalization are simply the outcome of our routinely behaving in accordance with what the institution (e.g. the family, school or work organization) deems appropriate. So, for example, in schools and work organizations, the process of institutionalization includes the acquisition of habits, aspirations and discipline (e.g. time-keeping and deference to authority) that enable classes to run on time, students to attend and a degree of order to be maintained.

Image 1.6 Everyday routines – having a meal, cleaning the fridge

(e.g. bank ATMs, supermarket consumption) or the exploitation of brands to generate customer loyalty and a high pricing strategy. Do these changes have implications for how people use products and services (e.g. how customers use pubs) and become 'institutionalized' through their interactions within them?

Thinkpoint 1.6

Branding and consumption When companies brand products (e.g. themed pubs), what assumptions are they making about the organization of consumption (and the production of such goods and services)?

Whenever we participate in an institution, we take with us implicit as well as explicit knowledge of the routines and conventions that we expect to find in such contexts. As a regular customer in a supermarket, for example, we learn how the store is arranged in terms of how the goods are grouped and where they can be found on the shelves. Again, this knowledge may be so taken-for-granted that it surfaces only when there is a 'reorganization'. Such changes are usually justified by a managerial calculation that they will produce more traffic down the aisles and thereby increase revenues. It disrupts our shopping pattern, and perhaps makes us more aware that we had such a pattern, but it is effective from the viewpoint of the supermarket's managers and shareholders if it has the effect of us purchasing other goods that had previously been invisible to us.

What such disruptions risk, of course, is a negative reaction from customers who, in the absence of any marked loyalty, may respond by changing their routines as they decide to shop elsewhere. A parallel analysis could be applied to the locals, as customers, at the Dog and Duck (see earlier) who were reacting negatively to what they were finding on the equivalent of 'the shelves' in the supermarket – that is, the influx of a student clientele. Can you think of other examples where a change in what is available to consumers upsets their routine?

The centrality of people

As we all know, our everyday relationships with parents, friends or lovers can be difficult. The more we try to organize them the more difficult they often become. Work organizations exhibit these same difficulties, except we do not usually or necessarily share the same intensity of commitment and loyalty to relationships at work. In general, it is easier to leave the organizations in which we work than to walk out of personal relationships, unless of course they coincide!

Organizing in everyday life Think about a tension or conflict you have had personally with someone close and reflect on the degree to which it can illuminate an aspect of organizing, being organized or relating to some organized activity (e.g. a place of education, work, consumption or leisure). If convenient, this could be done in pairs whereby one of you probes the other and vice versa so as to try and avoid the tendency that we all have of rationalizing (i.e. reinterpreting unpleasant experiences in a more favourable light in terms of our own part in them). Consider, for example, how a sense of 'fairness' is negotiated or imposed, or reflect upon how trust is established or undermined.

When faced with pressures to increase productivity or improve levels of service, managers may attempt to coerce staff into working harder (e.g. by bullying or imposing penalties). Earlier, when considering the actions of the landlord at the Dog and Duck, we raised the possibility that he engineered the situation that resulted in a staff member (Christine) walking out. When detected or even suspected by staff, such methods reinforce the impersonality of the relationship, and make it more difficult to engineer more personal or involved forms of motivation and leadership. This tells us something significant about work organizations. Participation in them is usually based on an impersonal contract of employment in which a wage is paid for the application of skill and effort. In itself, this impersonal contract carries with it no moral obligation to work diligently or to be loyal to the employer.

People in organizations may be more or less willing to accept being organized. Ultimately, willing cooperation or grudging compliance depends upon their sense of the legitimacy (fairness) of the demands made upon them, and of course the capacity of managers to influence the conditions that make compliance the normal employee response. We saw earlier how compliance is not to be taken for granted when Christine was unwilling to be managed by a younger barmaid in the pub in which they both worked. People can be creative, responsible, dedicated and loyal, but, equally, they can act in ways that, from a managerial perspective, are destructive, subversive, irresponsible and disloyal.

Views of organization: Entity, process and concept

Identifying organization

On the face of it, what 'organization' means is obvious or self-evident. Ask anyone to name six organizations, and they would have few problems providing a list. What would you name? Let's make the question a little more testing by asking you to identify six *educational* organizations. Which six would you choose from the list in Table 1.2?

Table 1.2 Types of educational organization

❖ School	❖ Workplace	❖ University	❖ Community centre
❖ Family	❖ Hockey club	❖ Night class	❖ Beach party
❖ Friendship group	❖ Garden centre	❖ Chat room	❖ Toddler group
❖ Bookshop	❖ Library	❖ Cinema	❖ Media

Once you have chosen the six that, in your view, are 'educational organizations', think back to what led you to pick them. If you now had to justify your selection, what would you say? What is it about your six selections that differentiate them as 'educational *organizations*'?

Perhaps the most obvious candidates are 'school' and 'university'. These, commonsensically, are bodies that provide educational goods or services. When we think of 'education' we tend to privilege *formal* methods of teaching – as found in classrooms. That is what education commonsensically means, even if there are alternatives which challenge that understanding, like 'the school of hard knocks' which celebrates learning through the 'university of life' – doing and making mistakes.

Parents, for example, are also involved in educating their children – by teaching them how to speak and to interact with others. Parents may also try to compensate for perceived shortcomings in their children's formal education by supplementing it with their own instruction or employing tutors. Governments may even build this view of 'responsible parenting' into educational policy by, for example, prosecuting (even gaoling) parents of truanting children for not instilling the values of education in their offspring. So, do we count the family as an educational *organization*?

In the workplace, various kinds of education abound, both in training and through learning from others as mates and mentors. The same could be said for many other forms of human association. In the process of meeting up with friends, going to discos, clubs, pubs and parties, playing sports and even watching TV, visiting retail stores, chat rooms, etc., we become educated about various aspects of the world in which we live. Many of these activities are 'organized' and/or take place in organizational contexts. Indeed, they can and do provide alternative forms of education, even to the point of placing in question the authority and value of formal education. From a critical perspective, formal education can be seen as a narrow indoctrination into certain 'respectable' patterns of belief and behaviours that restrict rather than expand intellectual and moral horizons. Critics of formal education might well wish to place some scare quotes around much of the 'education' provided by schools and universities. Purposely, we also placed on the bottom row of our list a number of non-educational organizations/institutions that, nonetheless, may facilitate education. The last two – cinema and media – indicate that almost anything can be educational; it depends on how we relate to them.

When education is seen as a process, almost everything we do has educational significance and implications; it all depends on how we *relate* to what we do. Learning can be seen as synonymous with our everyday practices of talking, interacting and relating with one another and the world around us. Take the case of organizations. Why assume that we know little or nothing about organizations or organizing just because we have never attended an OB course or read a textbook and, therefore, jump to the conclusion that we are ignorant of the subject? In doing so, we effectively disempower ourselves as we cede authority to 'experts' who are deemed to possess a monopoly of knowledge in this field – a view that allows our experience of organizations and organizing to be ignored or marginalized. Instead, we might usefully recognize how frequently and continuously we have participated in organizations and organizing processes, and how much we have 'picked up' or learned in this process. Unfortunately, many textbooks fail to recognize and facilitate the exploration of this knowledge as part of studying OB.

Box 1.16: Education in business schools

Associated with the idea that organizations are distinguished by the presence of formal, impersonal relationships and procedures is a conception of business and management education that emphasizes and reinforces this understanding. The ultimate expression of this thinking is the treatment of people as mere factors of production or commodities.

Since the Enron and WorldCom scandals, there has been considerable soul-searching about the education of executives. The content of MBAs (Masters of Business Administration), in particular, has been criticized for the lack of attention to the ethics of managing. Finance-centred courses in particular have encouraged and legitimized the ruthless pursuit of shareholder value fuelled by the rising value of stock options used to compensate executives. Commonsensically, the term 'education' is reserved for what happens in schools, colleges and universities, and increasingly tends to focus upon abstracted forms of knowledge comprising sets of information and techniques. Even case studies, which offer a potential means of exploring issues of politics and ethics in decision making, tend to concentrate on the analysis of information and the identification and application of appropriate techniques. This commonsense notion of education revolves around treating education as a 'thing', which is confined to specific settings, rather than a process that occurs within all spheres of everyday life.

In the next three sub-sections, we consider some different ways in which 'organization' can be defined, identified and analysed.

An entity view

Box 1.17: Mainstream definitions of 'organization'

- 'Organization refers to social arrangements such as factories, bureaucracies, armies, research and development teams, and so on, created to achieve technical, productive ends'. (David Buchanan and Andrei Huczyinski, *Organizational Behaviour: An Introductory Text*, third edition, London: Prentice Hall, 1997, p. 552.)

- 'An organization is a consciously coordinated social unit, composed of two or more people, that functions on a relatively continuous basis to achieve a common goal or set of goals. It's characterized by formal roles that define and shape the behaviour of its members'. (Stephen P. Robbins, *Essentials of Organizational Behaviour*, seventh edition, Upper Saddle River, New Jersey: Prentice Hall, 2003, p. 2.)

When considering the definitions set out in Box 1.17, you may well respond by thinking: 'Yes, that makes sense. It is a bit technical but it is along the lines I was expecting'. We acknowledge the contribution of such thinking, at least to the extent that it highlights how, in work organizations, there is a great deal of emphasis on the means to achieve what are presumed to be shared objectives. In families or in friendship groups, in contrast, doing things more efficiently or effectively is generally of lesser importance than preserving the quality of our relationships, as an end in itself. In this respect, at least, there is logic when studying organizations in emphasizing the impersonal and objective criteria of appointment and promotion, as often based primarily upon qualifications and/or measurable length of service.[4] In the process, however, other ways of understanding organizations are screened out.

Mainstream definitions reflect and reinforce the common-sense understanding of 'organizations' as *entities* consisting of a distinguishing set of characteristics. Organizations are portrayed as unified entities comprising 'formal' rules and structures. Roles, or positions, are hierarchical – meaning that those who occupy senior positions always 'define and shape' the behaviour of subordinates (see Box 1.18).

Box 1.18: Roles, security and power

The notion of role is not unlike that used in the theatre but the script is unwritten and therefore, in principle, more open to interpretation, improvisation and inspiration than is the case for the actor. A role, however, consists of a set of expectations and obligations. To the extent that people identify with these roles as a source of security and/or sense of power, they operate to constrain the individual almost as much as scripts constrain actors on stage.

Definitions should not be dismissed as simply the ritualistic elements of a textbook. Definitions are significant insofar as they distil and frame a particular way of thinking that is exemplified through a text. How 'organization' is defined frequently provides an important clue to how the boundaries of the field are being drawn and how its contents are being examined.

Like the common-sense idea of education as something that occurs within specific organizations, the definitions provided in Box 1.17 are not so much wide of the mark as limiting and potentially misleading. They focus attention principally upon aspects of organizing that coincide with the concerns of those occupying the senior ranks of organizations. It is a view of organizations developed by their designers, and it is one that portrays organizations as malleable, instrumental tools for achieving their established objectives. Minimal attention is given to the conflicting priorities of other members of the organization or the dangers in managing organizations as if such conflicts were of little consequence.

Definitions found in mainstream textbooks may appear to be uncontroversial and politically neutral, but this is far from the case. Their adequacy and credibility can be challenged on account of the exclusion of issues of power, domination and exploitation. Silence on these issues casts doubt upon the practical relevance as well as the scholarly standing of their contents. It is important to recognize how their contents operate not only to describe but also to define and discipline how organization is thought about and how we act within them (including ourselves as lecturers and students).

The effect of these texts, when we accept them as common-sense truths, is to equate the meaning of organization with their contents. They invite us to accept their knowledge of organizations without presenting alternatives and without actively encouraging us to reflect critically upon their analyses and prescriptions. To assume that organizations are created and/or maintained simply 'to achieve technical, productive ends' is simplistic since it excludes consideration of many (mixed) 'motives' and 'preoccupations' that inspire and shape their design and development. Similarly, presuming that the goals of senior managers are identical to those of other members of the organization is politically unrealistic. To believe (commonsensically) in the entity view is the equivalent of thinking of the sun rising, rather than the earth rotating.

A process view

To say that organization is a process rather than an entity is not to deny that there are activities occurring that are identifiable as 'organized', and that are located, as it were, in organizations. By conceiving of organization as a process, however, the study of (organizing) processes is not confined to what are commonsensically identified as large, formal organizations or their structures, roles and so forth. The focus of analysis is not upon organizations as entities, but upon processes of organizing wherever organized activities occur – in families, beach parties, toddler groups, etc.

Box 1.19: A process view of 'organization'

'The concept of "the organization" is extremely difficult to define and, additionally, depends upon what use is to be made of the definition . . . For this reason, *our focus is not on organization as a thing but on organization as process*: the activity of organizing and being organized. All particular organizations are examples of this process . . . The process of organization in this context is the configuration of people and things in ways that are not given in nature . . . when we talk about organizations we mean any organization, whether big or small, multinational or local, formal and informal, for profit and not for profit, involuntary or voluntary'. (Norman Jackson and Pippa Carter, *Rethinking Organizational Behaviour*, London: Prentice Hall, 2000, p. 7, emphasis added.)

The process view draws our attention to the ways in which organizing, in diverse settings, is accomplished through social interactions in which we seek to manage ourselves as well as others. It understands behaviour in all human associations as a process of skilful negotiation in accomplishing whatever is done. This view invites us to scrutinize how various activities happen or are disrupted in the everyday life of an organization, whether this is in settings commonsensically identified as 'organization(s)' or outside of such settings. Importantly, it recognizes the continuity of organizing processes across institutions, and does not confine them to, or reserve them for, 'organizations'. Organizations – such as the multinational enterprise or the local voluntary group – are understood to be products or expressions of such 'organizing processes' that should not to be reduced simply to formal role-playing or goal-orientated behaviour.

A process view of organization might perhaps be seen as more theoretical. Yet it is arguably more focused on the practices that comprise organization than on the entity approach. For an entity definition tends towards a concern with prescriptions and models, such as the allocation of tasks, the grouping of activities, systems of measurement and reward, and so on, rather than the activities and interactions that comprise organizing as a dynamic process.

A concept view

As Jackson and Carter (2000) point out, the difficulty of single, universal definitions is that they cannot take account of how a definition will change in relation to how it is used in a particular context. We see no problem, in principle, in engaging alternative definitions of organization for different purposes. Yet it would be devious not to declare our own preference for a third, 'concept' view of organizing and organization. In doing so, we acknowledge that 'the concept of "the organization" is extremely difficult to define' (Jackson and Carter, 2000, p. 7). Its meaning is multiple and contested. Does this imply that differences over the meaning of organization can be settled? In our view, they cannot. Instead each definition, or way of conceiving of organization, is partial and political. It is partial not in the sense that it reveals just one aspect of organization, but, rather, because each definition necessarily excludes other ways of thinking about organization as it supports and champions a *particular* view. It is political because it invites and encourages people to 'see' *and organize* the world in particular ways. As a consequence, the world – including the world of organizing and organizations – takes a form associated with specific ways of thinking and associated actions. When a particular complex of thought and action assumes prominence and dominance, it becomes the 'common-sense' view (until it is disrupted and supplemented by an alternative).

What makes the 'concept view' distinctive? The concept view understands that 'organization' is first and foremost a word that assumes a variety of meanings and exerts a number of effects. The concept view recognizes that 'organization' can be conceived as an entity; and it can also be conceived as a process. But it is neither an entity nor a process. Organization is rather a concept to which a variety of meanings are attributed – including the view that it is a concept. We have already observed how, for those who favour a process view of organizations, it is the *activity of organizing*, wherever this takes place. Definitions of both entity and process make reference to organizations as identifiable social units or as examples of organizing activities. The concept view draws attention to how all definitions are politically charged as they construe activity in particular ways and anticipate or expect certain behaviours in the future. In this sense, ideas of organization do not just describe but also *prescribe* (i.e. outline what should happen) and act to *discipline* the behaviour of their members. That is what makes them partial and political.

Thinkpoint 1.7

It's kind of hard to define . . . Given our concern to make studying organizations more interesting and connected to everyday life, you might justifiably object that our attention to definitions is contradictory. Surely, you might say, definitions are abstract and boring and that is why, in everyday life, we prefer to point to the object that we are talking about rather than define it. Our response is that definitions remain important for communication and disciplining thought. Clarifying how terms are being defined can minimize the danger of talking at cross-purposes. Even so, we prefer to regard definitions as 'views'. The term 'definition' tends to imply that words can capture the basic features or essence of what they aspire to describe, whereas 'view' better conveys our understanding that words operate to make us see, make sense of and perform the world around us in particular ways.

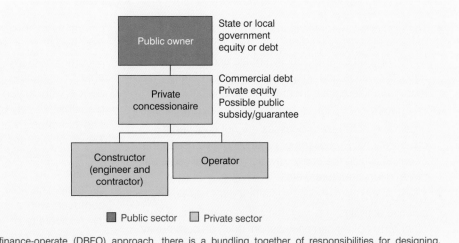

SOURCE: ADAPTED FROM WWW.FHWA.DOT.GOV/PPP/DBFO.HTM

With the design-build-finance-operate (DBFO) approach, there is a bundling together of responsibilities for designing, building, financing and operating, which are transferred to private sector partners. A common feature of such schemes is their part or total financing by debt leveraging revenue streams. For example, direct user fees (tolls) on roads constructed by the DBFO approach can provide a revenue source. In such cases, future revenues are leveraged to issue bonds or other debt that provide funds for initial capital and project development costs (e.g. building roads, hospitals, etc.).

Figure 1.2 Public–private partnership: design, build, finance, operate (DBFO)

The principal merit of identifying organization as a concept is that it disrupts the tendency to assume that language (e.g. organization) reflects or captures some element(s) of the world that are external to it – such as the features of the 'entities' and 'processes' the views discussed earlier claim to describe. To put this another way, the concept view reminds us of our involvement, as subjects or agents, in helping to produce, sustain and change the social world of organizations that otherwise appears to exist independently of us.

Box 1.20: The origin of the term 'organization'

The word can be traced to the Latin word organum, meaning a musical instrument and the disciplined playing of pre-arranged notes. Organization then continues to have this association with order and discipline (hence the ease with which the entity view prevails) but the discipline is implicit rather than explicit as in a musical score. Moreover, perhaps (to retain the musical analogy) an organization is more akin to music such as jazz, rock or heavy metal where there are greater degrees of interpretation and improvisation. Over time, it has come to assume a related but rather different meaning in which there remains continuity with order and discipline, and where the disciplined setting and playing of notes has parallels with activities that are identified as what is meant by organization. As we have seen, however, this emphasis on discipline and order is implicit rather than explicit in mainstream definitions of organization, and the political nature of the definition is thereby concealed. This does not mean that alternative definitions (e.g. the process view – see Box 1.19) are free of politics. Refusing to follow the convention of defining organizations as formal structures designed to achieve shared goals is a political statement, but one that disrupts rather than conserves commonsense ways of thinking and acting.

The concept view indicates that there is no one universal way to define or study organizations. When we accept or adopt a particular view, we are engaging in a political, reality-defining act. In that moment of decision, we act in a way that construes any object (e.g. organization) in the world as 'this' rather than 'that'. From this it follows that different definitions of 'organization' should not be evaluated according to their claimed correspondence to what they aspire to describe.

We conceive of organization as a potent concept, while commonsense tends to treat it as an entity. Organizations are identified and discussed as if they exist 'out there' in a way that implies that they are virtually identical with the buildings or that social space they occupy. Most textbooks on organizational behaviour perpetuate this common-sense understanding as they favour an entity definition of organizations. We have sought to question this approach.

Box 1.21: Overview – 'Organization' as entity, process and concept

- *The entity view*. Organizations are particular kinds of unified entities. Such features as their design for achieving particular productive goals and the formal roles that define and shape the behaviour of their members differentiate them from one another.

- *The process view*. Organizations comprise processes of organizing but these processes are not confined to organizations. Processes of organizing give rise to the activities, which the entity view aspires to delineate as tasks, roles, structures, etc.

- *The concept view*. Organization is a term used to characterize activities in a way that differentiates them from other forms of human association, such as community or family. It also indicates how we are active agents in organizing whatever it is that the entity or process view defines as organization.

When we examine different definitions of organizations or texts that amplify these definitions, it is tempting, yet ultimately mistaken, to ask the question: 'How realistic is this view?' The difficulty with this question is that it assumes that we have direct access to reality and are able to evaluate definitions in terms of their correspondence with it. On reflection, this seems unlikely. More plausibly, we rely upon a set of interpretations, prejudices and hunches to assess the credibility of different views. These views are relevant in enabling us to elaborate, refine or even abandon our interpretations and thereby (re)direct our actions. Learning from competing views is certainly possible, but it should not be conflated or confused with assessing their correspondence with reality. A diversity of views can open up alternative lines of action and/or provide ways of challenging dominant thinking, but their summation does not produce a more comprehensive grasp or map of the terrain. Attention is more appropriately directed to scrutinizing the values, preferences and *effects* embedded in different conceptions of organization and organizing.

Distinctiveness of work organization: instrumental rationality

'Bureaucratic work shapes people's consciousness in decisive ways. Among other things, it regularizes people's experience of time and indeed routinizes their lives by engaging them on a daily basis in rational, socially approved, purposive action' (*Jackall, 1998, p.p. 5–6*).

'Community and family are conserving institutions. In general, their members act to maintain stability and to prevent, or at least to slow down, change. But the modern organization is a destabilizer. It must be organized for innovation, and innovation, as the great Austro-American economist Joseph Schumpeter said, is "creative destruction" ' (*Drucker, 1992, p. 96*).

Earlier, when considering the entity view of organizations, we noted how organizations are conventionally and commonsensically associated with the use of an instrumentally rational means to achieve explicit purposes or goals. Such instrumental rationality is reflected in the definitions of organization provided by the entity view, where 'organization' is seen largely in terms of the technical or functional means to achieve 'a common set of goals'.

In discussing instrumental rationality, we have repeatedly drawn upon the entity view of organization – for example, when we talk about organizations (as entities) pursuing objectives or refer to managers in organizations engineering employee loyalty. This is not surprising because we understand the entity view to be closely associated with, or even a product of, instrumental rationality. Organization is conceived as an entity as it is identified as an instrument for attaining objectives as defined by senior managers. In other words, we regard the entity view as a product of the instrumental rationality that it also aspires to advance. Equally, both are seen to reflect commonsense because, as soon as we use the word organization, we tend to associate it with the concrete entity (i.e. the building) in which it is located and the very entity is assumed only to exist to serve some instrumental purpose.

Box 1.22: Instrumental rationality

An instrumentally rational organization or person is concerned primarily, if not exclusively, with the most effective means to achieve specific ends or objectives. The *value* of those objectives is taken for granted and therefore is not open to debate or challenge. One might suggest, for example, that private companies are preoccupied with the best means to increase profits; or that public corporations are concerned with the most efficient means of providing a public service such as health or education. Each is geared to increasing labour productivity and reducing the costs of production.

We have also suggested that organizing is fundamental to human existence but that this activity occurs within different kinds of institutions (e.g. the family or peer groups) and is not confined to organizations. We have differentiated (work) organizations from other institutions by the degree of dependence upon instrumental rationality. While instrumental rationality may be present to some degree in many institutions, it is most dominant and legitimate within (work) organizations. This is why we describe them as organizations, rather than families or communities. We can say, then, that the concept of organization, and the associated notion of organizational behaviour brings with it a particular, instrumentally rational view of *how to organize* – what is expected from us when becoming a member of an organization.

Box 1.23: Legitimacy

Legitimacy is a term used to convey an unquestionable or legal right to something. Once it is legitimate to exercise power over someone, it is difficult to challenge that right, although this does not rule out resistance. Indeed it is only by challenging or resisting the legitimacy of established power relations that social change occurs. People had to resist the legitimate power of slave-owners to abolish slavery, the absolute sovereignty of the monarchy and aristocrats to achieve democracy, and the imperial powers of Western nations to achieve independence for ex-colonies and protectorates.

Given the pervasiveness of organizations in modern societies and the centrality of instrumental rationality in schools and workplaces, it would be surprising if their influence did not extend to family life and friendship groups who may come to resemble organizations when planning, resourcing and implementing an event or set of tasks. Peer groups often try to organize an event, trip, or perhaps just a party; and then what they do can begin to look like the activities associated with organizations.

Consider the party. Someone proposes a party and usually individuals or groups agree to take on particular tasks such as arranging an appropriate venue, ordering or preparing the food and drink, getting the music sorted, etc. This way of 'making it happen' is routinely conceived or calculated to be the least time-consuming and individually onerous. So, a leisure group can, for limited periods, look not dissimilar to a work organization. You might raise the objection that the peer group does not get paid, or seek to make a profit. These are relevant distinctions but ones that define an *economic* work organization as opposed to an organization per se. What makes holding a party similar to a work organization is reliance upon instrumental rationality that supports the logic of a division and coordination of the labour involved in making it happen.

Box 1.24: Mixing rationalities

The predominance of a means–ends (instrumental) rationality is, we have suggested, what distinguishes the entity view of organization from other human associations such as families, friends or communities where we expect love, loyalty and commitment to prevail. In principle, organizations are those institutions to which a greater influence of calculative, means–ends rationality is attributed. There are, however, continuities and overlaps.

Instrumental reasoning enters other social institutions and arrangements when, for example, someone marries for money, uses friends to advance their career, or engages in community work to enhance their status and reputation. Conversely, managers often try to secure loyalty, cooperation and commitment from employees by emphasizing family and community values of solidarity. But, of course, their motivation is an instrumental one: they calculate, perhaps correctly, that developing a more attentive and friendly attitude towards their staff will improve morale and employee retention. In 2003, the UK government passed family friendly legislation that gave employees with children under six the right to flexible working hours. A popular device for securing both cooperation and commitment is teamworking drawn from team sports. Here an identification and solidarity with the 'in-group' in opposition to the 'out-group' is used as a competitive device for raising productivity. However, where cooperation and collaboration between different groups or teams is important, this competitive ethos may be counter-productive.

Conversely, a family can be seen as an economic work organization when, for instance, some of its members run a small business, such as the corner shop or a small farm. In such cases, there is generally a blending (or uneasy union) of instrumentally rational principles, such as a division of labour with respect to particular tasks (and associated responsibilities), and other, familial values that demand a degree of flexibility and commitment – qualities in a workforce that are more difficult to engender and mobilize in the absence of family and community ties. The significance and impact of instrumental rationality is well illustrated when, for example, a hobby or leisure activity, like playing football, is turned into a job that provides a source of income (see Box 1.25). What previously was pursued casually and in an ad hoc manner then becomes a target of more careful calculation, as time becomes money.

Manchester United is not just a work organization because, unlike many football clubs throughout the world, it has been highly profitable and has an international image and thus is a global brand – something that has been a major attraction to corporate predators wishing to take it over. It is also a work organization because it is identified as such by others (e.g. staff, investors, etc.) who emphasize its likeness (in terms of hierarchical and formalized organizing practices, for example) to other institutions that are characterized as work or business organizations. This identity is further reinforced by players insofar as they regard their activity as work (albeit comparatively pleasurable) in which they participate in the development and promotion of a business and expect a substantial income in exchange for their efforts, skill and time. It is difficult not to be aware of the superficiality of family-like solidarity and loyalty within football when key members of the team (e.g. David Beckham) are 'sold off' to help balance the books. Business values almost always take precedence when push comes to shove – something, that invariably disaffects hard-core fans who are more interested in retaining star players than in making profits for shareholders who have only a financial interest in 'their' club. A similar analysis could be made of the British royal family, which its members privately but revealingly describe as 'The Firm'.

Box 1.25: Family, community, organization and Manchester United

Concepts such as 'family' or 'community', rather than 'organization', may be emphasized when characterizing a football team. Managers often seek to engender a 'happy family' atmosphere among their teams, despite its obvious superficiality when key players can be 'sold off' to make room for the latest superstar or to 'balance the books'. A family friendly image has also become a major marketing tool of the big clubs, with family stands, etc.

Consider the appalling tragedy at Hillsborough football ground in Sheffield. Due to a combination of barriers, overcrowding on the terraces and police incompetence large numbers of spectators died or were seriously injured because of a sudden surge of fans crushing those in front of them. The outcome of this tragedy was government insistence on seating-only stadiums, an unintended consequence of which was to make football more of a family spectator pastime as the standing-only terraces were swept away.

Fans of Manchester United have appealed to family and community notions when seeking to question or resist multinationals taking over the club. In 2000 the community of fans demonstrated their power when Rupert Murdoch and his media empire tried to takeover the club partly to strengthen its TV rights monopoly over the most attractive football matches. The official fan club mobilized the community of Manchester United fans to persuade the directors not to pursue the offer, and this probably had some effect. Eventually the Competition Policy Committee outlawed the bid on monopolistic grounds, but it is likely that the community protest had some effect on the outcome. It had much less effect, though not for want of trying, when Malcolm Glazier bought the club through enormous borrowing in 2005 and saddled what was previously the most profitable soccer club in the world with huge debts. Amidst considerable anger from the fans and even the wider public, Manchester United became a private company owned solely by Malcolm Glazier, whose interest would seem to be the purely financial one of exploiting the brand to maximum effect. It is expected that he will sell the club on once this further exploitation of the brand is realized.

Game-playing and resistance

In practice, there can be considerable resistance to instrumental rationality in organizations. As we have repeatedly noted, other rationalities are present that are resistant to being supplanted or colonized by instrumental rationality. People enter organizations with their own values, their own objectives and their own sense of what is reasonable. In doing so, they may think, or be persuaded, that it is appropriate to forget or suspend their values and priorities once they set foot in the office or factory. But they may also resent and resist demands to be compliant. Or they may become more instrumentally rational – not by directly pursuing corporate objectives but by calculating how to set, protect and fulfil their own agendas, while managing an impression of dedication, loyalty and commitment. Career systems allow some coincidence of personal and corporate agendas as commitment can be demonstrated and rewarded with promotion and/or pay. But because of the complexities of organizations, where outcomes cannot easily be attributed directly to the efforts or skills of a single individual, there can be a lot of game-playing in which individuals claim responsibility for 'successful' outcomes and endeavour to shift the blame for 'unsuccessful' ones.

Box 1.26: Game-playing in higher education

Students and staff engage in various forms of game-playing. Lectures, tutorials/seminars, and self-study or library work are regarded as the instrumentally rational way of enabling large numbers of students to gain degree-level education. This education is meant to involve a creative component that takes students beyond the comparatively programmed and packaged experience of A levels. In practice, many management students (at least) discover that much degree level work is less demanding and less creative than some of their A level courses.

There is often ambivalence about this. On the one hand, it is frustrating and disappointing, with a sense of being cheated or 'conned'. On the other hand, it is a relief and leaves more time for leisure pursuits. What tends to emerge is a conspiracy of silence – a kind of grand game-playing – in which neither students nor staff are inclined to acknowledge this particular 'elephant in the room'. Staff say that some creative input into essays is required but then often penalize students when it appears. To do otherwise, would require considerable time in assessing the merit of eccentric

▶

approaches that deviate from the model answers often required to standardize the assessment process.

Cutbacks in resources and associated pressures to secure research grant income and generate publications make it unlikely that staff will sacrifice their careers or their leisure time by giving assignments that are demanding to assess. Students realize that regurgitating lectures and textbooks is a less risky way of achieving a good (but perhaps not outstanding) mark. Both students and staff act in an instrumentally rational way to reproduce a system that is ostensibly organized to provide degree level education but which routinely falters in its delivery. At the same time, performance systems for teaching as well as research are introduced, which staff become adept at 'gaming' in order to provide the required evidence of educational quality. In this, students are encouraged to collude by accepting the logic of the calculation that the value of their degree depends in some measure upon the reputation of the department that is being assessed.

Less-privileged (i.e. lower-ranking) staff in organizations generally have fewer opportunities to play games that substantially improve their material (income) or symbolic (social status) wealth. Nonetheless, they may pretend to be committed while remaining psychologically distant from what they are doing. This occurs frequently when they are engaged in mundane routine tasks such as performing data entry, routine office work, or working on the mass assembly line in car production and other manufacturing work. Staff may daydream or spend much of their time chatting except when the supervisor appears, at which time they put their heads down and give the impression of being engaged on the task. Occasionally resistance to the instrumentally rational pursuit of production goals will be more disruptive or subversive. Workers may purposely slow down the machine or sabotage the conveyor belt by causing it to break down. In this way, they demonstrate the dependence of managers and shareholders upon their productive efforts. This dependence is even more dramatically demonstrated when there is a strike or 'work to rule' in labour relations. For then there are no products and services from which profits can be extracted.

Theory and practice

An underlying assumption of educational provision, including the delivery of OB modules, is that exposure to academic or 'scientific' knowledge about behaviour in organizations will make workers, and especially managers, more efficient and effective. More specifically, it is anticipated that the expertise, or at least the qualifications (e.g. an MBA), will add legitimacy to the exercise of authority. Either way, there is an expectation that knowledge of human behaviour will result in improved practices.

This view is seductive but also problematic. Its limitations are manifest in the manager who is highly qualified – let us imagine someone who possesses a first degree in business studies followed by an MBA – yet is notoriously bad at organizing and managing people. Such a manager has sat through numerous courses, including OB modules, to gain such qualifications, and has also passed examinations that apparently demonstrate an expert knowledge of the field. So, why doesn't this expertise translate itself into effective ways of managing and organizing people?

We doubt that there is a simple or universal answer to this question. To assume that there is would be to fall into the trap of believing that a medical model is appropriate for 'treating' problems attributed to organizations: all that is required is to diagnose what is wrong, prescribe the medicine and await the recovery. The assumption that organizations can be likened to the human body has attracted many students, and particularly management consultants, who propose a whole range of prescriptions for diverse symptoms of 'organizational ill health'. We have yet to find the organizational equivalent of the aspirin, let alone antibiotics; and we argue that we never will because organizations are not the same as bodies. To put this another way, the theory – including its conception of the relationship between practice and theory – is poorly aligned with the practice.

Nor are organizations like machines. Yet the metaphor has been another influential way of thinking about organizations, with the assumption that knowledge of engineering will yield effective solutions to perceived problems. Indeed, some of the most influential classical, and a number of more recent theorists of organization (e.g. Fayol, Taylor, Crosby and Deming) were engineers by training. Students of organizations have sought to treat them as machines in order to bridge the gap between theory and practice in one 'quick fix'. Our own view is that thinking drawn from the social sciences rather than biology or engineering is more relevant. Ideas of contextual embeddedness, for example, can help us to explore possible reasons for the gap between theory and practice.

On the basis of what we have explored so far, we can sketch a number of reasons for the theory–practice gap, and we invite you to add others:

- Theory presented in textbooks, or underpinning influential practice provides an over-rosy ('idealized' to use a bit of social scientific jargon) view of complex behaviour, leading to simplistic interventions. Textbook knowledge fails to appreciate particular, contextually embedded aspects of the situation and thereby offers seemingly universal but locally inappropriate solutions to problems.

- Students view knowledge of organizations and management instrumentally as a means of gaining qualifications. There is little thought for, or grasp of, its potential relevance for the messy practice of managing and organizing. Knowledge is often viewed inappropriately as a reliable instrument of power and thereby applied mechanically or naively to practice.

- Politics and power operate to frustrate consultants and managers' efforts to reorganize activities by applying theories, even of the most sophisticated variety. Attempts to impose control provoke resistance that is unanticipated because it is assumed that those being managed will share managers' sense of priorities.

- The practice of managing and organizing involves, above all else, interaction with people – colleagues and superiors as well as subordinates. There is little in management textbooks or indeed in education and training that directly addresses this critical issue.

What other possible factors behind the theory–practice divide can you think of?

We have cautioned against using commonsense as a guide to the study of organization (see earlier examples). Yet we have also recognized how it is drawn upon in developing theory and in management practice. Jackie was hardly consulting a textbook when running the pub for the weekend. She just drew on her everyday experience of organizing, and as we have said, this is extensive for us all. If you think about it, every day of our lives consists of a great deal of organizing. Some, of course, we have learned consciously at school or elsewhere. Knowing this, the managers of the pub could assume that Jackie would be able to add up the takings at the end of the day and communicate with the other bar staff. Yet, as we saw, in the case of Christine, not all such tasks are simple. What Jackie did not appreciate or anticipate was how Christine would interpret and react to the landlord's decision, and how this would result in an embarrassing and threatening display of defiance. What Jackie lacked was a theory of organizational behaviour that would have sensitized her to this possibility and thereby enabled her to think through how she might deal with such an eventuality. Yet even had she studied OB, there is no guarantee that in the heat of the moment she would have been able coolly to apply its insights rather than just react spontaneously as she did.

Distinctiveness of this text

In general, the curriculum and teaching of OB has given priority to ideas that are conservative and broadly pro-managerial. OB has been superficially pro-managerial in the sense of presuming that managers *alone* have a monopoly of knowledge of, and an almost divine right to determine, how work should be organized. As a consequence, the orthodox treatment of OB has taken the form of a technology of control, with each of its topics (e.g. motivation, leadership) being presented as an element of a control toolkit. Ideas and perspectives that do not fit neatly into this toolkit are either ignored or accommodated as just one more dimension to consider. Efficiency, performance and/or profit are seen to inform everything that occurs in organizations, whereas social and moral responsibility are either seen as outside the sphere of OB or simply tagged on as an afterthought. Even where ethical issues are included, and this has become more relevant in recent time because of various corporate scandals, the focus is on compliance with regulations to avoid bad publicity or financial sanctions against the organization. In short, the concern with business ethics (see Chapter 14) is simply another instrumental means to the end of preserving the status quo.

Our text attempts to be different primarily by presenting and contrasting alternative conceptions – orthodox or mainstream and critical – of OB. In each of the following chapters, an account of the subject matter found in mainstream texts familiarizes the reader with what is conventionally studied in this field. The orthdox approach is not presented here as an end in itself, however. Instead – as we have shown in relation to the 'entity' concept of organization – orthodox thinking is treated as a foil for introducing critical or unorthodox thinking on OB. To do this, we rely upon an approach with which all the contributors have been closely associated for several years.

Box 1.27: Orthodox and critical wings of organizational behaviour

What do we mean by 'orthodoxy'? The term orthodox is used to describe what most people *currently* recognize as a legitimate way of doing or thinking about things – it is conventional and conservative, or a continuation of the way things have always or traditionally been done. The orthodox view regards managing as a technical activity and organization as a neutral instrument for achieving shared goals.

What do we mean by 'critical'? The term 'critical' is used to signal an interest in interrogating and challenging received wisdom – both theory and practice – by drawing upon social

science perspectives that are routinely ignored or excluded from OB. Critical refers to approaches that challenge the orthodoxy in some way. The critical view regards organization as a political instrument for achieving contested goals.

Of course, if widely accepted, a critical approach may become the orthodoxy. Examples that spring to mind include the challenge to religion made by science, the challenge to monarchy posed by republicanism, the discrediting of imperialism generated by anti-colonialists, and the challenge to anti-apartheid in South Africa represented by the (after the fact) heroic figure of Nelson Mandela.

Each chapter of this book addresses a core topic of OB. In each chapter both mainstream and critical contributions to knowledge of this topic are presented and explored through one or more of the six central concepts – identity, (in)security, freedom, power, inequality and knowledge – around which the more critical content of this book is organized (see the Appendix for a definition of these concepts).

Throughout the book, we endeavour to make the subject matter more relevant and accessible by viewing organizational behaviour first and foremost as practices of organizing and meaning-making, involving thinking, feeling and acting, that are not so dissimilar to everyday life. An important implication of this approach is that it acknowledges, rather than denies, the politically and emotionally messy human detail of organizations. This approach, as we explained earlier, makes it easier to learn about organizations as work relations and management activities are understood to be less remote from everyday life.

More specifically, we seek to appreciate and emphasize the continuities between the experiences of students and employees. Both are engaged in, and shaped by, a world in which organizations are as central as they are familiar. We also endeavour to capitalize upon the closeness of this understanding with the view that we all learn best when we can identify and participate in the 'object' of our learning. This may sometimes demand a leap of imagination and a refusal to compartmentalize our everyday lives (e.g. going to clubs, pubs, bars or parties) from what we are studying. Of course we are not suggesting that the social world of the student is equivalent, let alone identical, to that of a manager or administrator. As we have emphasized earlier, we do not deny the distinctiveness of organizations in which the working lives of employees are routinely conditioned by the demands and trappings of instrumental rationality. But, at the same time, we reject the reduction of the messy complexities of organizing to the abstracted and idealized ways of representing this complexity in the mainstream, orthodox OB literature.

In turn, this approach leads us to recognize and stress that (i) instrumental rationality is neither politically and morally neutral nor free of specific values for it cultivates a particular, impersonal and disembodied way of living; and (ii) it is introduced and applied by economically and politically interested managers and employees who are also gendered, sexually charged, ethnically located, emotionally involved, and more or less passionate human beings. These interests, emotions and identities after all comprise some of the most fundamental of our experiences, whether at work or not (Knights and Willmott, 1999). Put at its simplest, we challenge the very idea that the organization is separate from life outside it and vice versa. To explore this connection, contributors to this text have been guided by a framework of six interrelated concepts.

Six key concepts

The central concepts that provide the framework for all the chapters are outlined here, together with the principal and secondary disciplines that are ordinarily associated with them (see Table 1.3).

Table 1.3 Key concepts and disciplines

Concepts	Principal discipline	Secondary discipline
Insecurity	Psychology	Economics
Identity	Social psychology	Sociology
Inequality	Economics	Sociology
Power	Sociology and politics	
Knowledge	All disciplines	
Freedom	Philosophy, politics and economics	

We deployed these six concepts earlier in this chapter but now seek to define them a little more closely in relation to Jackie's experiences in the pub. If you return to the vignette, you will recall that when first standing at the bar Jackie had felt uncomfortable and perhaps a little *insecure*, as all the students had already left the pub to go to the disco. Our assumption is that uncertainties and associated insecurities are a widespread feature of working in organizations. They may range from a general feeling of uneasiness to more fundamental questioning of its purpose, accompanied by unvoiced doubts such as 'is this all there is?'

Box 1.28: Insecurity

Insecurity arises when people are unable to interpret a situation in a way that confirms their own sense of themselves – for example, as a 'bright student' or as a 'caring person'. Social situations are especially difficult in this respect since we can never be fully sure of, let alone control, how others view us. Yet, it is through our sense of how others view us that we develop and evaluate self-identity. 'Knowing' someone reduces the stress or tension of this uncertainty in social encounters. However, this uncertainty cannot be entirely eliminated as people are continually changing as a result of new circumstances, experiences and relationships.

When the local lads who sat at her table started criticizing students, Jackie felt her *identity* was under attack. Perceiving her identity as a student, she did not like the lads undermining it. People routinely attribute an identity to us, in past as a way of dealing with their own uncertainties and insecurities. We also, often subconsciously, take on identities and only realize the extent of our identifications when they are challenged. Much of the time we are unconsciously striving to reproduce an habitual sense of identity (or identities – student, brother/sister, son/daughter, man/woman, etc.) that we have largely taken for granted.

As we all know, attacks on our identity can be almost as bad as being physically assaulted. As an example, in 2002 the Republic of Ireland and Manchester United soccer captain, Roy Keane, became a household name less for his footballing brilliance than for his violence (both physical and verbal) in what can only be seen as an attempt to assert and/or defend his identity against the Irish manager of the 2002 World Cup squad. Zidane's head butt in the 2006 World Cup final provides a further example.

Box 1.29: Identity

Identity refers to how people are identified or classified – as a man, brother, student, fighter, etc. Our sense of self-worth or significance is related to our social identity. But an identity is not only an image presented by oneself or attributed to us by others. It is also associated with expectations and obligations about how to behave. When how we behave is consistent with what others expect there will tend to be coherence between our sense of self-identity and the social identity ascribed to us.

Returning to Jackie, when she was on her own in the pub, she felt *power*-less to intervene to defend her own identity. She had a sense of being subjected to the *power* of the locals and thereby unable to do much about their ridiculing students. More generally, her very sense of identity as a student was an effect of the power that produced this identification. We frequently think of power as a possession – the lads had it, Jackie lacked it – but it is perhaps more illuminating to conceive of power as shaping who we are and what we do. Thinking of power in this way enables us to consider the extent to which both the lads and Jackie were objects and agents of power (e.g. the power that defined Jackie as a student) – the power that placed them in a particular way in relation to each other.

Box 1.30: Power

Power has traditionally been associated with the coercive and repressive means through which respectively a class of capitalists exploits proletarian labour (Marx), political elites control the masses (Pareto) or management cadres dominate subordinate employees (Burnham). Such concepts of power see it as a wholly negative control of one group or person over another. More recently, an alternative has rejected this negative or purely coercive conception of power. Instead, allowing that there are no social relations that are 'free' of power, it is seen not just as constraining in its effects but also productive and positive (Foucault, 1980, 1982). An individual or group can exercise power positively by transforming individuals into subjects who find meaning, purpose and identity in the practices that it demands or expects. The effect of power then can be to make those over whom it is exercised more creative, productive and powerful, which, of course, does not imply that they always and everywhere accept or defer to the ostensibly powerful. Sometimes subjects will exercise their own power to resist what is demanded or expected of them.

Why did Jackie feel powerless to resist the negative stereotypes or stigmas of students that the local lads were constructing? Largely it was because of being outnumbered and this *inequality* making her feel insecure in a way not dissimilar to when she had stood alone at the bar. This situation of inequality would have been reversed had she come to the pub earlier when the students outnumbered the locals. However, were we to examine the future prospects of the students compared to those locals who had not attended university, we would probably conclude that many of them suffered more from inequality – in terms of housing, employment opportunities, life expectancy, pension provision, etc. – than the students.

Box 1.31: Inequality

Inequality describes differences in wealth and status, such as the inequalities of income and privilege between managers and employees and between men and women, or those suffered by ethnic minorities. These inequalities may be seen as institutionalised insofar as they are embedded in, and reproduced by, working relations (e.g. hierarchy and job segregation by gender or ethnicity) and employment practices (e.g. recruitment and promotion). They are also reproduced by other social formations such as markets, where inequalities of wealth are reinforced because money, makes money, or the family, where inheritance guarantees intergenerational inequality.

Indeed, it is this *knowledge* of how inequality works that might explain the perhaps semi-conscious purge for the locals to verbally abuse the students. Arguably, the locals were feeling swamped by students who had begun to 'take over' a pub that they regarded as 'theirs'. This antagonism was, in all likelihood, prompted and fuelled by an implicit awareness and resentment of how students can trade on their knowledge to secure privileged jobs and a superior social status in life.

Box 1.32: Knowledge

Knowledge is sometimes referred to as power ('power is knowledge'), and this is probably because invariably, when exercising power, knowledge is drawn upon. Knowledge – both everyday knowledge and more specialist knowledge – leads us to interpret and produce the world in particular historically and culturally specific ways. Just think of how disempowered we feel when, as we move out of our sphere of knowledge, we do not *know* the language or *know* the culture. It is not coincidence that a majority of football managers are ex-footballers as they can draw upon their knowledge of playing as well as of more recently acquired management skills.

Knowledge and power are so intimately related that Foucault (1980) insisted on speaking about power/knowledge relations. However, it is not just that knowledge is a resource for the exercise of power. Knowledge is also often an effect of, or produced by, the exercise of power. So, for example, the very exercise of power over a football team will generate knowledge of how to exercise that power, and this is why nothing is seen to entirely substitute for experience. Acquiring knowledge through education is something that you are doing as students, and you may be doing it largely not for its own sake but as a means to getting a 'good' job.

Perhaps the reason why the local lads were antagonistic to the students was because they also resent the *freedom* that students appear to enjoy. Students do not have to get up at a certain time every day for work, enjoy long holidays, experience few controls, etc. The locals overhear them recounting exciting experiences overseas in the summer vacation and they always seem to be partying.

Box 1.33: Freedom

Freedom has often been defined as autonomy or an absence of constraints on the individual. However, while we all may seek fewer constraints on our choices and behaviour, a moment's reflection would suggest that an absence of all constraints would be chaotic or anarchic. We have to use our freedom (and power) responsibly so that it at least does not directly violate other people's freedom. We can see here that our very concept of freedom is based on a (humanistic) constraint of being respectful to the 'other'. With the development of the environmental movement, this respect is extended from the world of human beings to that of nature. Human freedom or autonomy then, as Foucault (1982) reminds us, is both liberating and disciplining.

We use this conceptual framework to interpret the key elements of, and present an alternative to the orthodox or mainstream treatment of OB topics. In addition to providing some insights into behaviour in organizations, these six concepts can also readily be related to your own experiences, thereby making the study of OB more meaningful and memorable.

Box 1.34: Mainstream, orthodox texts

Mainstream texts tend to present a (exhaustive) body of knowledge that aspiring managers are invited to absorb in a way that is abstracted from their everyday experience. In the absence of any overall and explicit sense-making framework, it is difficult to grasp the relevance of the knowledge and to incorporate it into what is done in organizations. In contrast, by exploring a web of concepts, students are able to draw and build upon their own experience of organizations. Then, the relevance and value of the orthodox body of knowledge can be scrutinized and selectively drawn upon.

We are not of course suggesting that the combination of these concepts is all that matters. Clearly you could think of lots of other concepts (e.g. emotion, rationality) that would help us to understand behaviour in organizations, including Jackie's experiences and actions. However, when speaking about Jackie's emotions or rationality, it would be difficult to ignore one or more of the six concepts. Her emotions revolve around insecurity and identity, and her rationality is dependent on (because it is exercised through) her freedom, knowledge and power. Jackie also deploys both rationality and emotion in securing knowledge and maintaining her position within a system of social inequality through succeeding in education, and through her social skills and capacity to present a favourable impression to the landlord and landlady, thereby gaining a job as a barmaid.

Each concept in our framework is intuitively relevant for understanding people in organizations. For example, we are all routinely ascribed an *identity* – as students, employees, customers, suppliers, etc. – that will have some influence upon how we present (and manage) ourselves. We may invest in more than one identity, and sometimes these may conflict. At this point, you may usefully return to the case study of the pub to list the different identities that relate to Jackie and consider whether there are conflicts between them. Take the issue of gender and sexual preference. These are important identity issues for most people. Misconceptions and misunderstandings in these areas can cause considerable offence, embarrassment and pain when they are not a source of amusement and pleasure. When others (e.g. customers) identified Jackie as a barmaid, she was seen differently. The sexist stereotype of this role might help to explain the numerous sexual advances that she experienced, some of which she found flattering or amusing, but most of which she experienced as awkward or demeaning. Again, you might wish to reflect upon the possible explanations of such mixed reactions.

As employees, we may comply with certain expectations but we may also seek to challenge and change them. In dealing with others, including those who hope to persuade or coerce us to perform organizational tasks, we mobilize everyday *knowledge* of others as well as of ourselves. In doing so, we exercise both *power* and *freedom*. In this process, we encounter relations of *inequality* as we discover that others have more money/income or status than ourselves. This, combined with the difficulties of fulfilling or wanting to challenge other people's expectations, can make us feel insecure – as was Jackie when, as a student, she felt personally subjected to a character assassination of students by the locals. This was so despite the oblique nature of their assault.

This way of thinking about behaviour in organizations rarely surfaces in mainstream, orthodox OB texts. Why not? It is because, on the whole, orthodox texts are preoccupied with conveying an exhaustive and comprehensive list of theories and topics so that their authors cannot be criticized as failing to cover all the literature.

They are less concerned with showing how behaviour in organizations can be illuminated and made meaningful to students by approaching its topics through a linked set of concepts or a conceptual framework. Such a framework provides a basic analytical *aide-mémoire* that has wide applicability for interpreting, and participating in the dynamics of OB. Of course, we hope that you find it helpful when studying OB. But we hope even more that you will continue to find it useful when you have completed your studies and are facing the challenges of working with people in organizations.

References

Brooks, I. (1999) *Organizational Behaviour: Individuals, Groups and the Organization*, London: FT Pitman.

Buchanan, D. and Huczyinski, A. (1997) *Organizational Behaviour: An Introductory Text*, third edition, London: Prentice Hall.

Clark, P. (1983) *The English Alehouse: A Social History 1200–1850*, London: Longman.

Drucker, P. (1992) 'The New Society of Organizations', *Harvard Business Review*, 70(5): 95–104.

Du Gay, P. (2000) *In Praise of Bureaucracy*, London: Sage.

Foucault, M. (1980) *Power/Knowledge*, edited by Colin Gordon London: Tavistock.

Foucault, M. (1982) 'The Subject and Power', in H. Dreyfus and P. Rabinow (eds) *Michel Foucault: Beyond Structuralism and Hermeneutics*, Brighton: Harvester Press.

Huczynski, A. and Buchanan, D. (2001) *Organizational Behaviour: An Introductory Text*, fourth edition, London: Financial Times/Prentice Hall.

Jackall, R. (1998) *Moral Mazes: The World Corporate Managers*, New York: Oxford University Press.

Jackson, N. and Carter, P. (2000) *Rethinking Organizational Behaviour*, London: Financial Times/Prentice Hall.

Kinicki, A. and Kreitner, R. (2003) *Organizational Behaviour: Key Concepts, Skills and Best Practices*, New York: McGraw-Hill.

Knights, D. and Willmott, H. C. (1999) *Management Lives: Power and Identity in Work Organisations*, London: Sage.

Merton, R. K., Gray, A. P., Hockey, B. and Selvin, H. C. (1952) *Reader In Bureaucracy*, New York: Free Press.

Robbins, S. (2003) *Essentials of Organizational Behaviour*, seventh edition, Upper Saddle River, New Jersey: Prentice Hall.

Strange, S. (1997) *Casino Capitalism*, Manchester: Manchester University Press.

Watson, D. (2002) 'Home From Home: The Pub and Everyday Life', in T. Bennett and D. Watson (eds) *Understanding Everyday Life*, Oxford: Blackwell.

Notes

1 In addition, those who bought shares in privatized industries at knock-down prices made substantial capital gains, provided that they sold their investments before the privatization bubble was burst by scandal and subsequent regulations.

2 We have direct experience of contract cleaners rarely doing more than emptying the waste bins in universities, but in hospitals cleanliness is more than a mere aesthetic.

3 When the high valuation given to internet and new technology stocks was dramatically cut.

4 These are the kinds of criteria used to justify the shortlisting of candidates. Thereafter, other less readily auditable and quantifiable criteria come into play, such as assessments of their character and ability to lead, or the knock-on effects of appointing particular or disappointing individuals.

PART I
The Human Dimension

Part I examines a number of topics and themes that are closely interrelated in the mainstream literature. These chapters draw primarily on a psychological approach to understanding organizational behaviour in which the individual in the group is centre stage. They complement this orientation by drawing extensively on a wider social science literature and, in particular, on a critical literature that pays attention to their wider significance in relation to society and politics. The chapters consider the standard approaches to managing people at work through motivation, attitude and personality analysis, teamworking and learning strategies, but challenge their assumptions so as to provide alternative insights.

2 Motivation and the Self

John Roberts

Key concepts and learning objectives

By the end of this chapter you should understand:

- The key mainstream approaches to motivation, as well as their limitations.

- Some of the shared and opposed interests that shape motivation at work.

- How our sense of self is socially constructed and maintained.

- How our so-called 'ego needs' mean that we are always vulnerable to the attitudes of others towards us, and how they serve as a key way in which our conduct can be controlled and influenced.

- How power comes to work largely through processes of self-discipline in which we appraise and judge ourselves against an internalized standard of how we should be.

Aims of the chapter

This chapter will:

- Explain why the study of motivation at work has received so much attention.

- Explore some of the key ideas that have marked the evolution of management's understanding of the different factors that shape motivation.

- Examine some of the key mainstream studies of motivation.

- Explore some of the important ideas that have marked the evolution of critical understandings of motivation theory.

- Examine some of the critical studies of motivation.

- Explore the linkages between insecurity, identity and the workings of power relationships in order to better understand motivation.

Overview and key points

When we get a job there is typically an employment contract with the organization, which specifies what we will do, for whom and for how long, and what we will get in return by way of pay, holidays, etc. But the contract does not determine what then happens. There can be a huge difference in both the quantity and quality of our work depending on our experiences and attitudes, and the response of others to us. It is this difference that is the focus of 'motivation theory' and both manager and employee have an intense interest in the subject. As employees, given that work occupies such a large part of our lives, we have a very strong interest in the satisfaction to be drawn from work. As a manager, a highly moti-vated employee is likely to be both happier and also more productive. He or she will therefore be both easier to manage, though possibly more demanding, and will help realize the objectives by which the manager is judged and appraised. These dual interests in motivation have ensured that the search for the key to effective motivation has served as the 'holy grail' of management theory; a search for the key that will unlock the virtuous circle of productivity *and* satisfaction.

This chapter will first review some of the key mainstream ideas that emerged during the 20th century as part of this quest for the secrets of what releases human energy and effort. We start with what are termed **content theories of motivation**; the ideas of Maslow on human needs and how these were developed by subsequent theorists of motivation such as McGregor, McClelland, Herzberg and Hackman. We then look at **process theories of motivation**; Vroom's expectancy theory and

Image 2.1 Beyond the carrot and the stick

contemporary theories of motivation and the emphasis they place on an employee's autonomy and self-motivation, supported by management empowerment.

In the second half of the chapter we will take a more critical look at what is involved in motivation. We look first at Marx's analysis of 'alienation' at work and his suggestion that in capitalism there is a fundamental conflict of interests between owners and their agents and employees. Secondly, we take a critical look at the current interest in promoting individual autonomy at work and suggest that motivation techniques now involve not just the use of economic insecurity but also the deliberate manipulation of a person's sense of self and self-worth.

Mainstream approaches to motivation and the self

Introduction

Late in the 19th century Frederick Taylor developed one of the earliest conceptions of management and the management role – his 'principles of scientific management'. Here we merely want to touch on some of these principles as they reflect a set of assumptions about motivation against which many of the writers on whom we will later focus can be seen to be reacting and responding.

Taylor was the first person to have attempted to provide a rationale for the emergent role of the manager in increasingly large American enterprises. The foreman or chargehand was no longer merely the stand-in for the absent owner, free to exercise power in a personalized and arbitrary fashion. Instead, Taylor drew upon the wider authority and methodology of science to offer a version of what the manager should do. The division of labour between worker and manager was seen in terms of a separation of the planning function from that of execution. It was the manager's job to make a 'scientific' study of tasks and on this basis to develop the most efficient form of work that could then be taught to new employees. The division of labour could then be greatly extended, allowing relatively unskilled labour to be trained in the most efficient means for carrying out a particular part of a task. It was also part of the management task to then control this labour through close monitoring and through the use of piece rates to ensure that the economic rewards of work were tied to actual productivity. It is this attempt to relate reward to the efficiency of effort and output that has led many to insist that Taylor placed a primary motivational value upon money.

For Taylor there was no necessary conflict between the interests of workers and those of management. Instead, if managers were to exercise their responsibilities in the ways in which he described, then what was possible was a rational division of labour that made optimal use of the purely manual skills of labour through the mental skills associated with the study and optimization of work, planning and monitoring by managers. The laziness or 'systematic soldiering' that Taylor observed in employees could in this way be resolved in the service of both the organization and the employee. Both would gain economically from the application of this new managerial rationality.

The separation of mental and manual capabilities, the focus on the efficiency gains of an intense division of labour, coupled with management training and monitoring, offer us an early image of the beliefs and practices that shaped human motivation. One of the targets and exemplars for Taylor for these new management techniques was a pig-iron shoveller called Schmidt – a man who was seemingly deficient in all respects bar brute physical strength. Once his labour had been scientifically studied and analysed his capacity for shovelling increased enormously and seemed to offer clear evidence of the potential gains for all, including Schmidt, of this new scientific version of the manager's role in relation to labour.

In the 1920s and 1930s a set of American studies at the Western Electric Company, often referred to as the Hawthorne Experiments, began to unravel the assumptions of Taylor's early work. The experiments began with a scientific study of the impact of different levels of illumination on worker output. Much to the surprise of all those involved, output increased whatever adjustments were made to the level of lighting; a result that gradually led to the recognition of the importance of individuals' social needs. The economic atom that Schmidt symbolized is seen now as a person who craves the attention of the manager, and who, as a social being, is found to be highly responsive to the pressures brought to bear by his or her work group. While the Hawthorne studies are typically held to have founded the human relations movement, it was left to later theorists to draw out and develop the more complex view of human motivation that the studies began to uncover. In what follows we will briefly review some of the seminal studies and theories that then shaped something of a revolution in how managers were supposed to understand, and ideally practise motivation.

Central problems and major issues in mainstream approaches

The major issues that mainstream motivation theory has sought to address are:

- What motivates a person? Should we look for the answer 'inside' the person in their 'needs' for money, status or power? Should we look outside at the work they do and how they are managed?
- Is there a universal truth to be discovered, or is motivation highly contingent and dependent on the specific character of a person and situation?
- How does motivation change over time? Is what motivates the same as what demotivates?
- Can my manager know more about what motivates me than I do, or does my motivation depend on the sense I make of my experiences?
- Can a manager motivate someone else or is motivation always something I do to myself?
- What allows or gets in the way of such self-motivation?

Key ideas and contributions

Motivation: It is about fulfilling human needs (Abraham Maslow) Although Maslow was writing over 60 years ago, his ideas about a '**hierarchy of needs**' have retained a peculiar currency. At the bottom of the hierarchy are what he called 'physiological' needs; the needs for food, sleep, drink, etc. Maslow suggests that while such needs are unsatisfied then we are completely preoccupied by them and all our capacities are put to the service of meeting them. Other needs or concerns are in this way marginalized and become unimportant. But Maslow, writing in a US context, suggests that the dominance of such physiological needs is very rare; appetite should not be confused with hunger in this sense – men live by bread alone only when there is no bread.

So what happens when such physiological needs are routinely met. It is here that Maslow introduces his notion of a hierarchy of needs. He suggests that as one level of need is met 'at once other (and "higher") needs emerge' and come to dominate. In this sense the meeting of a need is

CASE STUDY 2.1 A problem (of motivation) at PYT plc (1)

Peter Drake has just been appointed as the Sales Manager of the Manchester office of PYT plc. He has been with PYT since leaving school nine years ago. At school he had done all right, and his teachers had told him that if he worked hard at his A levels he could get to college. Peter, however, was keen to get out and start earning some money as soon as possible, but he was clear that, unlike his dad who was a school caretaker, manual work was not for him; he wanted a job in an office. The job at PYT seemed ideal. He started as a telephone sales representative, and four years later became a section leader.

PYT had a contract with the national telephone company to publish a telephone directory of business services. Every business in the country had a free entry in the directory but PYT made its money from selling additional advertising space to individual businesses. Looking back, Peter thought that part of his success was simply a matter of good luck and timing. When he first joined PYT it had only been going for a year and he quickly discovered that there were rich pickings to be had. The product was new to the UK and the potential market for additional advertising was huge. The company did not put him straight on the phones but instead took him away for a two-week training course at a hotel in the south of England. Here he was taught all the benefits of the product and introduced to the skills of selling.

His mum and dad had always told Peter that he would go far because he had the 'gift of the gab' and telephone sales offered him the chance to make good use of this. For every bit of additional space he sold he was paid a commission that meant that, in a good month, he could add something like 50 per cent to his basic salary. Within a year he had bought himself a car and had moved into a shared flat in town. Compared to his friends who had gone to college, he had loads of money and the chance of getting on if he did well.

Peter had just got back from his first sales managers' meeting – a meeting of all the Office, Regional and National Account managers, held in Birmingham with the Sales Director. The picture of the state of the company that Peter had gathered from this meeting was not very encouraging. Given the strength of PYT's sales training, new sales had always been good, but two problems had begun to emerge. The latest figures indicated that a growing number of their customers were not renewing their adverts from one year to the next. In the past this had not mattered much – there were plenty of new 'punters' to be caught – but the Sales Director had pointed out that, if current trends continued, in three years time they would be losing more business than they were selling. Their licence for publishing the directory was also due for renewal in two years time. Matters were possibly being made worse by the fact that staff turnover in the offices was approaching 100 per cent. Not only was this a big cost to PYT, given its initial training costs, but it also meant that there was no incentive for staff to be realistic in what they sold to customers. Staff would oversell one year and then leave rather than go back to the same customer a year later. At the meeting the Sales Director had announced a number of changes and initiatives that were to be introduced across the company to address the situation. There were to be immediate changes to the incentive system; in future staff would only be paid commission for any net gain in sales (new sales less drop-out from the previous year). Managers were also encouraged to change the profile of the people they recruited; it was thought that older, more mature people would probably stay longer. Finally there was the suggestion that part of the problem was poor management and Peter heard that he was to attend a one-week management development course next month.

Question

Drawing on the above and your own experiences, what factors do you think might affect the motivation of a group of sales staff?

important in allowing other, more social needs to emerge. At the same time, however, a need that is satisfied no longer motivates.

The second set of needs that Maslow identified in his hierarchy he termed 'safety' needs. Such a need for safety, Maslow suggests, is evidenced in our taste for routine and predictability. When safety is disturbed, panic or terror set in. Maslow suggests that, in developed societies, one must look to the neurotic or the 'economic or social' underdog to see where these needs dominate. According to Maslow (1989, p. 26) 'Their reaction is often to unknown, psychological dangers in a world that is perceived to be hostile, overwhelming, and threatening. Such a person behaves as if a great catastrophe were almost always impending'.

As with physiological needs, once met safety needs no longer dominate attention and leave room for yet higher needs to emerge. The next hierarchal set of needs to emerge is framed by Maslow in terms of needs for 'love, affection and belongingness'. While some of these needs may well be met through relationships outside work, in the context of work Maslow was thinking of a person's need to find their place within a group; a need to make contact and establish friendships with colleagues.

The fourth set of needs that emerge, once 'love' needs are met, Maslow termed 'esteem' needs. He describes these in the following terms: 'all people in our society (with a few pathological exceptions) have a need or desire for a stable, firmly based, (usually) high evaluation of themselves, for self-respect, for self-esteem, and for the esteem of others' (Maslow, 1989, p. 27). This, he suggests, should be based on real capacity, achievement and respect for others. He further divides these needs in terms of, first, 'the desire for strength, for achievement, for adequacy, for confidence in the face of the world, and for independence and freedom', and secondly, as the desire for 'reputation or prestige, recognition, attention, importance or appreciation'. If such needs are met, he suggests that they lead to feelings of 'self confidence, worth, strength, capability and adequacy, of being useful and necessary in the world'. If they are thwarted they lead to feelings of 'inferiority, of weakness and of helplessness'.

But even with the meeting of such 'esteem' needs, Maslow suggests that a 'new discontent and restlessness will soon develop', which arises from needs for what, at the top of the hierarchy, he terms the need for 'self-actualization'. He uses this term to refer to the desire for self-fulfilment; the desire to make actual all that is potential within the self.

Importantly, Maslow sees the thwarting of these basic needs as a source of sickness. For him a 'healthy man is primarily motivated by his needs to develop and actualize his fullest potentialities and capacities'. Such a notion of health is very demanding. In so far as the pursuit of such self-actualizing needs characterizes only a few people in organizations, then the sad conclusion is that there is much sickness in our organizations.

Exercise 2.1

Consider the following questions:

1 From your own experience and what you know of the experiences of your parents, siblings or friends, what merits are there to Maslow's idea of a hierarchy of needs?

2 Think of occasions when each of the different needs – physiological, safety, love, esteem and self-actualization – have been dominant in your mind. What feelings arise with the satisfaction of each need? What feelings dominate when these needs are frustrated?

3 Can you see in different others the dominance of different needs?

4 In terms of each set of needs, think about what might need to be done by colleagues, managers and those who design organizations to make the meeting of such needs possible.

5 Where in the hierarchy would you place money as a motivator?

6 What is your potential?

7 How 'sick' is our society in terms of the satisfactions it offers people in their work?

In what follows we will explore how Maslow's ideas have been taken up and developed in at least two different directions. The first looks at how behaviour at work, or the lack of motivation, may be the *unintended consequence* of how manager's think about employees – they simply do not understand their needs. The second takes these needs more seriously and then looks at the design of work to understand what motivates.

Motivation: It is managers' assumptions that matter (Douglas McGregor) We turn to Douglas McGregor's work immediately after looking at Maslow because there is a clear and explicit link between Maslow's view of 'sickness' as the failure to be able to meet one's basic needs and McGregor's attempts to think this through in terms of the effects that *manager's own assumptions* have on how they then go about seeking to motivate others. While Maslow focused on defining a hierarchy of largely unconscious needs that shape conduct, McGregor is more interested in how managers' *beliefs* about what drives others (and themselves perhaps) feed through into their practice of motivation.

The story McGregor tells contrasts a conventional conception of management's task – theory X – with a new, theoretically informed theory Y. **Theory X** propositions are as follows (McGregor, 1989, p. 315):

1. 'Management is responsible for organizing the elements of productive enterprise – money, materials, equipment, people – in the interest of economic ends.

2. With respect to people, this is a process of directing their efforts, motivating them, controlling their actions, modifying their behaviour to fit the needs of the organization.

3. Without this active intervention by management, people would be passive – even resistant – to organizational needs. They must therefore be persuaded, rewarded, punished, controlled – their activities must be directed.'

McGregor suggests that other, less conscious assumptions inform this conventional theory including the belief that the average person is lazy, lacks ambition, prefers to be led and dislikes responsibility. These assumptions, he suggests, shape organizations in the way that they come to be embedded in structures, policies and practices.

It is not that these assumptions are wrong, but rather that they are *assumptions*, and, once embedded in management structures, policies and practices, they begin to have effects on how people behave. McGregor's innovation was to suggest that while behaviour supporting the assumptions of theory X could easily be discovered in organizations, it was the result not of human's inherent nature, but rather an unintended consequence of management philosophy, policies and practice. The problem of motivation lies not in the worker but in the mind and assumptions and resulting conduct of the manager.

It is at this point that McGregor draws on Maslow's work to offer a critique of current management practice. He suggests that arbitrary management action, uncertainty over continued employment, favouritism or discrimination, all serve to keep safety needs strong in the employment relationship. Similarly, he suggests that management can fear group resistance to the pursuit of its objectives and therefore leave what he calls employees' 'social' needs unsatisfied. In relation to the needs for self-esteem, status and respect, McGregor suggests that, at least at lower levels in the hierarchy, these needs

Image 2.2

are completely ignored, and thereby thwarted. This is even more so for the needs for self-actualization: 'People, deprived of opportunities to satisfy at work the needs which are now important to them, behave exactly as we might predict – with indolence, passivity, resistance to change, lack of responsibility, unreasonable demands for economic benefits. It would seem that we are caught in a web of our own weaving' (McGregor, 1989, p. 320).

McGregor then offers an alternative '**theory Y**' based on what he argues is a more adequate set of assumptions about human nature and motivation (McGregor, 1989, p. 321).

1. Management is responsible for organizing the elements of productive enterprise – money, materials, equipment, people – in the interest of economic ends.

2. People are *not* by nature passive or resistant to organizational needs – they have become so as a result of their experience in organizations.

3. The motivation, the potential for development, the capacity for assuming responsibility, the readiness to direct behaviour towards organizational goals are all present in people. Management does not put them there. It is the responsibility of management to make it possible for people to recognize and develop these human characteristics for themselves.

4. The essential task of managers is to arrange organizational conditions and methods of operation so that people can achieve their own goals best by directing their effort toward organizational objectives.

Change, McGregor suggests, will inevitably be slow, but in job enrichment and new forms of decentralization, delegation, participation and consultation he sees hope of the gradual implementation of theory Y. Management by objectives is to replace management by control. External control will be replaced by '*self-control and self-direction*'.

Thinkpoint 2.1

Think about the good and bad teachers, lecturers or managers that you have encountered. How do you think your own behaviour was influenced by the assumptions they seemed to have about your ability and motives?

What motivates managers? (McClelland and Burnham) A striking feature of studies of motivation is that they are typically addressed to those who would motivate others. As an exception to this, in the 1970s David McClelland and David Burnham published an article in *Harvard Business Review* called 'Power is the great motivator' that focused directly on manager's motivation. Drawing on studies of managers in the United States they contrasted three possible sets of motives – the need for achievement, the need for power, and the need to be liked. They argued that the 'need for achievement' had typically been assumed to be the measure of business success, for example, with successful entrepreneurs. Their innovation was to question whether such a need for achievement was related to good management, particularly in large complex organizations. They argued that, in practice, a high need for achievement may encourage an individual to focus on personal improvement, and encourage them to do things themselves. The need to achieve might typically also be associated with a need for concrete short-term feedback. Against this they argued that, in large complex organizations, the key requirement is to manage others to perform, and this will often mean a lack of immediate and personal feedback for the manager. Here they suggested that the 'need for power' might be more important and appropriate than the 'need for achievement'.

They decided that perhaps the best index of a manager's effectiveness would be the climate he or she creates around themselves and that this would be reflected in the morale of subordinates. It was this that they then measured. Their version of a good manager was as follows (McClelland, 2003, p. 109):

a good manager is one who, among other things, helps subordinates feel strong and responsible, rewards them properly for good performance, and sees that things are organized so that subordinates feel they know what they should be doing. Above all, managers should foster among subordinates a strong sense of team-spirit, of pride in working as part of a team.

Through their surveys they found that some 70 per cent of managers had a higher than average need for power, suggesting that the need for power is important in managers. They also found a strong correlation between the strength of a manager's need for power and good team morale. But the results also contained a surprise, for the main driver of high morale turned out to be not whether a manager's need for power was higher than their need to achieve, but whether it was higher than their need to be liked. This latter group they termed 'affiliative managers', whose strongest need was to be liked. This, they argued, would result in a kind of weakness that would make exceptions out of sentiment or the desire to be thought well of by a particular subordinate. The result would be a team-wide perception of unfairness that led to low morale. This thought about the impact of perceived fairness on motivation has been further developed in Adams '**equity theory**', and more recently by Greenberg's work on '**procedural justice**'.

Maslow's early ideas about a hierarchy of needs and the way in which these were then taken up by McGregor define at least two key axes along which motivation can be understood – the nature of human needs and, as importantly, a manager's assumptions about the needs of those they manage. McClelland and Burnham's studies were an interesting addition, for in Maslow's terms, they suggest that a manager's love and status needs may well get in the way of effectiveness. Manager's should need power but in a mature and non-egocentric way if they are to manage well.

Exercise 2.2

Consider the following question: In your experience of teachers, lecturers and managers can you think of instances where it seemed as if their own needs to be liked, or for power or for achievement, helped or hindered their work?

In the next section we will explore another, slightly different approach to motivation; one that gives primary importance to the work itself as a source of motivation. We will begin by looking at the very influential ideas of Frederick Herzberg.

Motivation: What satisfies is different from what causes dissatisfaction (Frederick Herzberg) Herzberg made the useful observation that it is often the manager rather than the employee who is motivated. Managers want to get people to do things – in this sense they are motivated – but the means they use, he suggests, often serve only to produce movement rather than motivation in employees. His own views on motivation emerged as result of his asking this question to a wide variety of people in different jobs: 'what job events had occurred in their work that had led to extreme satisfaction or extreme dissatisfaction on their part?' Answers typically suggested that the factors that cause dissatisfaction are almost entirely different from those that cause satisfaction. His conclusion was that job satisfaction and dissatisfaction involve different feelings and are not polar opposites. As he puts it (Herzberg, 2003, p.p. 55–56): 'The opposite of job satisfaction is not job dissatisfaction but, rather, *no* job satisfaction: and similarly, the opposite of job dissatisfaction is not job satisfaction, but *no* job dissatisfaction.'

Herzberg argued that two different needs of human beings are involved here. One set of needs can be thought about as stemming from human's animal nature – the built-in drive to avoid pain from the environment, plus all the learned drives that become conditioned to the basic biological needs. The other set of needs relates to what he argued was a unique human characteristic – 'the ability to achieve and, through achievement, to experience psychological growth'.

Image 2.3

The growth or 'motivator factors', he argued, were intrinsic to the job. They are achievement, recognition, the work itself, responsibility and growth or advancement. The dissatisfaction–avoidance or what he termed 'hygiene factors' are extrinsic to the job and include company policy and administration, supervision, interpersonal relationships, working conditions, salary, status and security. 'Motivators are the primary cause of satisfaction, and hygiene factors the primary cause of unhappiness on the job' (Herzberg, 2003, p. 57).

On the basis of his studies Herzberg was scornful of many of the personnel practices that were the outgrowth of the Hawthorne experiments and the human relations movement. Things like sensitivity training, employee participation and counselling. The primary implication of his work was that the focus of motivational effort should be on work itself and the way it could be 'enriched' to bring about the more effective utilization of personnel.

Rather than pursue Herzberg's ideas on job enrichment we will look at some slightly later work of Hackman, who, in collaboration with Oldham, tried to discover what creates what they called 'intrinsic' motivation, and what job characteristics are associated with such motivation.

Motivation: It is the design of jobs that can make a difference (Hackman) A lot of the problems of motivation fall away when someone is well matched to the job they are doing. In such circumstances working hard and performing well happens simply because it is rewarding and satisfying. Hackman and Oldham (1980) talk about this happy congruence of person and job as 'internal motivation', and suggest that this depends upon three key conditions:

1. The work should be experienced as 'meaningful' – as something that matters to the person.
2. Work must involve the experience of 'responsibility' for the results.
3. A person must have 'knowledge of the results' of their work. Without this kind of feedback a person will have no basis upon which to feel good or bad about what they are doing.

Problems of motivation arise when one or more of these 'critical psychological states' is missing. While the three psychological states are internal to the person, Hackman and Oldham suggest that they are related to five key job characteristics.

In order to experience work as *meaningful*, three job characteristics are necessary:

1. '*Skill variety*'. A job needs to involve a variety of different activities drawing upon a variety of skills.
2. '*Task identity*'. A job needs to involve completion of a whole or complete piece of work with a visible outcome.
3. '*Task significance*'. A job and its output needs to make a difference to others either inside or beyond the organization.

In order to encourage feelings of *responsibility* for what one does, a job needs to involve substantial freedom, autonomy and discretion in how it is carried out. Only with this will there be a sense that outcomes are the result of one's own efforts and therefore something for which one has personal responsibility.

Box 2.1: Comment

The ideas of Maslow, McGregor, McClelland, Herzberg and Hackman that we have looked at so far, when taken together sketch the three main dimensions around which motivation has and continues to be thought about; (a) the person and their needs, (b) the manager's needs and beliefs and (c) the characteristics of the job itself. Together they bring us a long way from Taylor's view of scientific management. The employee is not merely a body but a human with 'social' needs. Taylor's scientific view turns out to a set of assumptions he was making about others and these assumptions were part of the motivational problem. They assumed the need for close control and monitoring without seeing how this thwarted human needs. The fragmentation of jobs that he then promoted in the name of efficiency in effect robbed work of any 'intrinsic' motivation.

Finally, in order to have *knowledge of the results* of what one does a person needs feedback. Such feedback they suggest needs to come directly from the work, rather than indirectly through one's boss.

In contrast to Maslow's focus on needs, Hackman and Oldham conclude that: 'motivation at work may actually have more to do with how tasks are designed and managed than with the personal dispositions of the people who do them'.

The theories that we have looked at so far are often referred to as 'content' theories; they offer a concrete view of what motivates – needs, behaviour, and different aspects of work and the organization of work. Such theories are then contrasted with what are called 'process' theories that explore motivation as the outcome of experience and the sense made of experience. We will begin with the ideas of Vroom, who in the 1970s developed what he called an expectancy theory of motivation.

Motivation: It is a person's expectations that count (Victor Vroom) One of the problems of Maslow's theory of needs is that motivation seems to be the product of needs that are largely given as part of 'human nature' and that for the most part are largely unconscious. This is a convenient myth for managers for it denies that what people do – the level of effort that they put into their work – is in part the *product of their experiences at work* and the sense that they have made of these. The employee is not just a need-driven entity but rather a self-conscious person making sense of their experiences and adjusting their effort in the light of earlier experience. It is here that Victor Vroom, writing in the early 1970s, made an important contribution to conventional theories of motivation with what became known as 'expectancy theory'.

In line with earlier behaviourist theories, Vroom assumes that humans are motivated to maximize pleasure and minimize pain, but humans are capable of choice, and such choices will depend upon their perceptions and the beliefs and attitudes that are formed from these. 'Valence', 'instrumentality' and 'expectancy' were the terms that Vroom selected to identify three sets of belief involved in deciding to commit effort to a course of action.

Valence refers to largely emotional orientations people have in relation to particular outcomes. These can be both positive (I want these) and negative (I'm keen to avoid these.) It is also possible to be indifferent to some outcomes. What was significant about Vroom's formulation was to suggest that in relation to work it is people's *expectations* rather than actual outcomes that matter. For example, the effort you make at any moment will be driven by what you expect to get out of your course, rather than its actual outcomes. So valence is about the expected levels of satisfaction and/or dissatisfaction that employees expect to flow from their efforts.

The second term – instrumentality – explores the factors that shape the expectations or valence for an employee. Something is instrumental if it is believed to lead to something else. So you may expect that reading this text will allow you to write a good essay and get a good degree, which in turn may mean that you can get the job you really want. However, the relation between effort and outcome is not certain, or rather we will have different expectations, born of experience, of the certainty or otherwise with which outcomes will follow from effort. For example, your past experience may lead you to believe that there is a strong positive relationship between your essay writing efforts and the feedback and results that you get. This will create a positive valence. On the other hand, your experience may have been negative or frustrating and leave you feeling that it was not worth the effort, or that those who make no effort are also rewarded by high marks. How have your own efforts on your course been changed by the sense you have made of your experiences so far?

The third belief involved in Vroom's model he termed expectancy, and he writes of this as the 'action–outcome' association in a person's mind. Several things might shape your expectations about the outcome of your essay writing. Do you think that you have the ability to do the course? Will your lecturers give you the help you need? Will the library have the right books?

It is the combination of beliefs about valence, instrumentalities and expectancies that results in a certain level and pattern of motivation. Motivation and the performance that flows from this is the product of *choice*; choice shaped by expectations born of past experiences.

One implication of Vroom's ideas is that, like it or not, managers and the jobs they design, and the decisions and systems that they put in place, are shaping employees' expectations and choices as to whether it is worth the effort, or at least how much effort to make for what. The second implication is that the employee is not a 'need' driven entity but rather a self-conscious person capable of autonomous choice. Behaviour is shaped not just by needs but by 'cognitions'; by an active process of sense making.

Motivation: A new competitive imperative In the late 1970s and early 1980s a new urgency was given to the topic of employee motivation by the emergence of Japan as a major competitor in the world economy. Many of the subsequent studies of the Japanese employment system, often by Western academics or consultants, were used to hold up a less than flattering mirror to the West's own

CASE STUDY 2.2 A problem (of motivation) at PYT plc (2)

Peter's management training course was a real eye-opener to him. He had never thought much about human needs or management styles. What he knew about managing came from what he'd learnt working for his old boss, Mr Thomas. But the course had made him think about this experience a bit differently. For some reason Peter had always got on well with Mr Thomas; he encouraged Peter even when things were not going so well and it was Mr Thomas who had encouraged Peter to put in for his first promotion. But with the rest of the staff Mr Thomas was often very strict; and some of his colleagues used to call Peter the 'teacher's pet' as a result. Mr Thomas regularly listened in to sales calls and told people where they were going wrong. You had to ask permission if you wanted to leave your desk, and apart from at breaks, talking to colleagues was discouraged. At the end of each day he would check on who had sold what to whom and, if people had failed to meet their targets, it was not unusual for him to shout at them in front of the whole office.

Thinking about this on the course, Peter began to wonder whether this was good management. He had been particularly impressed by the ideas about 'theory X' and 'theory Y', and that being a manager should really be about creating opportunities for people to grow. His own time at PYT had allowed him to grow a lot and become a supervisor and now office manager. It was clear enough that profits were important but he liked the idea that he was also able to help people develop and grow. That way there was no 'us' and 'them'.

Question

Drawing on all the ideas presented above, what suggestions could you give Peter for improving staff motivation at PYT? What might he need to do to implement theory Y in relation to both staff and managers? What other factors would he need to consider to improve motivation?

Box 2.2: 'From Control to Commitment in the Workplace'

Richard Walton's 1985 *Harvard Business Review* article announced a 'significant change' that was under way throughout US industry in approaches to organization and the management of work. Comparing two plants, Walton argued that the differences could be traced to two 'radically different strategies' for managing the workforce; a strategy based on 'imposing control' and a strategy based on 'eliciting commitment'. The traditional 'control' strategy involved a rigid division of labour and individual accountability that assumed low levels of staff skill and motivation. Managers in control mode were organized in a hierarchy of specialist roles with clear status demarcation. Labour was treated as no more than a variable cost, and assumed to have an inevitably adversarial relationship to controlling managers. Walton argued that at the heart of this traditional model was the 'wish to establish order, exercise control and achieve efficiency in the application of the workforce'(Walton, 1985, p. 78). However this wish, Walton argued, was now threatened both by changing worker expectations and the inability of this strategy to meet the 'standards of excellence' set by world-class competitors. Market success, he suggested, required a superior level of performance that

needed 'the deep commitment, not merely the obedience – if you could obtain it – of workers', and it is in the context of this need that the new strategies of eliciting commitment began to emerge. Unions and managers began talking of common interests and the need for mutual trust, layers of hierarchy were stripped out and overt status differentials reduced. Responsibility for integration and quality were being pushed back down to the shop floor. Jobs were being redesigned to be broader and more flexible and included responsibility for continuous improvement. Accountability was shifted from the 'individual' to the 'team' with an acknowledgement of the 'heightened importance of group achievement, the expanded scope of individual contribution, and the growing concern for such questions of "equity" as gain sharing, stock ownership and profit sharing'. To help elicit commitment from the workforce companies were giving employees some assurance of security with retraining, and consultation. Unlike the old control strategy with its exclusive focus on the rights of shareholders, management now acknowledged the 'legitimate claims' of a company's multiple stakeholders – owners, employees, customers and the public.

management and motivational practices. The contrast was perhaps sharpest at the level of production workers in Japan. Here a system of company unions and associated security for core employees apparently allowed for much greater flexibility and responsibility among employees and was enabling the Japanese to achieve both high-quality and low-cost production. That other systems could be both more profitable and encourage greater employee motivation was alarming.

The result in the West has been two decades in which human resource strategies have come to be seen as central to business recovery, and old motivational certainties have been augmented by a growing emphasis upon the team, on creating commitment and on encouraging high performance. The high-performance team it is argued is now a competitive necessity. While Walton announces an American corporate revolution, in practice there is a great deal of continuity between current human resource management and the earlier theories of motivation that we have already looked at. In this way current motivation theory both builds upon the past as well as adding new points of emphasis and focus. Some aspects of these – the focus on groups and teams, and on organizational culture – will be covered in other chapters. Here we will look at the emphasis that is now placed on autonomy and self-management and the ways that the manager can support these.

In one sense, Walton's recognition of the counter-productive consequences of control marks the triumph of motivation theory over management. What starts with a concern to find ways that managers can control employees' motivation ends with the grudging recognition that people manage themselves, and that, at best, managers can seek to create the conditions under which employees will commit their energies to the organization. But in another way, recognizing and coming to understand the reality of 'self-management' has also opened up new avenues for management influence.

Self-motivation: It is the ideals we have for the self that motivate (Harry Levinson) One clear statement of the reality of self-motivation came from a psychoanalyst and management writer, Harry Levinson, who in a *Harvard Business Review* article in the 1970s – 'Management by Whose Objectives' – suggests that we need to begin with an understanding of a person's own objectives since managers' objectives will have no incentive effect if they are unrelated to a person's own dreams and wishes. These he talks about as an 'ego-ideal' (Levinson, 2003, p. 111):

> If a person's most powerful driving force is comprised of needs, wishes, and personal aspirations, combined with the compelling wish to look good in her own eyes for meeting those deeply held personal goals, then management by objectives should begin with her objectives. . . . Each of us has a built-in road map, a picture of his or her future best self. Psychologists speak of this as an ego-ideal, which is comprised of a person's values, the expectations parents and others have held out for competences and skills, and favourite ways of behaving. An ego-ideal is essentially the way an individual thinks he or she ought to be.

Some of the focus on leadership, on corporate vision and values, and on culture management (see Chapters 7 and 9) can be understood as attempts to shape such ideals.

Self-motivation is shaped by a person's sense of 'self-efficacy' (Albert Bandura) Another aspect of the self that has become the object of attention is a person's belief about how effective they are. As part of his 'social cognitive theory', Albert Bandura suggests that a person's sense of their own efficacy is one of the most important and pervasive influences on how they act. Some people, he suggests, do not even try to do something because they simply doubt that they have what it takes to succeed. Conversely, others have a strong belief in their capacity to succeed even in the face of setbacks and obstacles.

Such beliefs about self-efficacy will have a pervasive effect on what a person aspires to do and how to approach almost any aspect of work in an organization, including a person's resilience to stress. Bandura suggests that we cannot influence our own motivation and actions very well if we do not keep track of our thought patterns and performance, what is happening around us and the effects we are having. Self-observation of behaviour is part of the solution, as are various forms of goal-setting and emotional 'self-regulation'. Although such beliefs will most probably have been shaped early in life, Bandura suggests a number of strategies that can be pursued to develop and strengthen a 'resilient' sense of self-efficacy. As regards perceptions of self-efficacy, he says (Bandura, 2000, p. 121):

> People of high efficacy focus on the opportunities worth pursuing, and view obstacles as surmountable. Through ingenuity and perseverance they figure out ways of exercising some control even in environments of limited opportunities and many constraints. Those beset with self-doubts dwell on impediments which they view as obstacles over which they can exert little control, and easily convince themselves of the futility of effort. They achieve limited success even in environments that provide many opportunities.

Exercise 2.3

Think about your own sense of 'self-efficacy'. Is it 'high' or 'low'? How might this be shaping what you do, along with what you try to do? With these ideas, how might you try to strengthen your sense of how effective you can be? How might others help in this?

As a resource for thinking about motivation, Bandura's ideas focus not on an assumed set of needs that we possess by virtue of being human, but rather on the very ways in which we have come to think about ourselves. In terms of the development of motivation theory, this involves a step change – a new focus of knowledge on thought processes within the person.

Self-motivation: It is the goals set for the self (Locke and Latham) This theory, which the authors claim has been tested on over 40 000 people in many countries, suggests that the most simple and direct explanation of why some individuals perform much better than others lies in the fact that they have different performance goals. The theory builds on four broad propositions:

1. Difficult goals lead to higher performance than easy goals, or no goals, or abstract injunctions like 'do your best'.
2. The higher the goal the higher the performance.
3. Praise, feedback or participation in decision making makes a difference to what people do only in so far as it increases commitment to a difficult goal.
4. In addition to affecting choice, effort and the persistence of effort, goal-setting can also increase the effort people make to discover ways of meeting a goal.

Latham and Locke argue that, in addition, a goal must be challenging and specific. Their idea is that as well as serving as *targets* to attain, goals are 'the standards by which one judges one's adequacy or success'. There is a competitive element here so that part of the pleasure of setting high goals is that they are higher than other people's goals. Moreover, high goals are accompanied by expectations that achievement will bring feelings of self-efficacy, as well as recognition by one's peers, along with the more tangible benefits of salary increases and promotion.

Latham argues that 'the management of oneself lies at the core of goal setting theory' and that 'without commitment goal-setting is meaningless'. In other words goal-setting is something that we should do in order to motivate ourselves. But managers can support this self-management. Feedback is important because measurement signals what is actually valued in an organization rather than what is claimed to be valued. Relatedly coaching aimed at improving performance through increasing a person's sense of self-efficacy can be most effective. Managers should set 'SMART' *goals* – that is, goals should be specific, measurable, attainable, relevant and have a clear time frame. The manager's own expectations of employees can also be important in shaping the goals they set themselves.

Self-motivation involves empowerment (Thomas and Velthouse) While empowerment is often presented as a management initiative, Thomas and Velthouse (1990) argue that empowerment should be understood in terms of four different cognitions related to a person's sense of meaning, competence, choice and impact. Meaning is about my assessment of the value of a task in relation to my own ideals and standards. Competence relates to my beliefs about my own capability (self-efficacy). Choice refers to my beliefs as to whether I can direct my own actions, and Impact to my sense of being able to 'make a difference'. Conger (2000) later suggests that understanding empowerment requires understanding the psychology of power and control. Power must be understood as 'an intrinsic need for self-determination along with a belief in self-efficacy'. But if employees have such a need for self-determination, management can effect this in a variety of ways.

- *Factors that undermine empowerment cognitions.* A rigid and impersonal hierarchy may limit a person's sense of being able to exercise initiative, or exercise real responsibility. Authoritarian styles of management can deny any sense of self-determination. Rewards may be allocated in a way that is perceived as unfair or unresponsive to competence or creativity. Similarly, as we have seen, jobs that have little meaning or challenge, or where there is overload or conflict, readily produce a sense of powerlessness.

- *Factors that encourage empowerment cognitions.* Organizational policies and cultures that emphasize self-determination, collaboration over competition, and high performance standards and open communication systems help create the conditions for empowerment. Leadership or supervision that sets high expectations while expressing confidence, allows autonomy, and sets inspirational or at least meaningful goals, also contributes to empowerment. Jobs with high variety, relevance, autonomy and control as well as good advancement prospects empower, as does rewarding innovative and creative performance.

Self-motivation: Selective recognition by managers helps (Luthans)   Along with a focus on how management can create the conditions for empowerment cognitions, the other focus in the 1990s has been on the effect of recognition on performance. Some of this takes us back to our initial focus on the impact of pay on performance. The 1980s and 1990s saw a renewed interest in pay as a way to influence performance, and both attract and retain employees. Along with traditional practices, many advocated new forms of profit sharing and share ownership schemes for employees at all levels as an inducement for better performance. Interest in such traditional forms of recognition were accompanied by a new awareness of the power of 'social recognition'. Luthans and Stajkovic (2000), for example, argue (at p. 167) that: 'If social recognition is provided on a contingent basis in managing employee behaviour it can be a powerful motivator of employee behaviour'. Such a use of 'contingent recognition' by management, they suggest, both shapes expectations of future reward as well as offering a signal of belonging. It also has a direct regulatory effect.

> Based on the recognition received and, thus, the perceived prediction of desired consequences to come, people will self-regulate their future behaviours by forethought. By using forethought, employees may plan courses of action for the near future, anticipate the likely consequences of their future actions, and set performance goals for themselves. Thus people first anticipate certain outcomes based on recognition received, and then through forethought, they initiate and guide their actions in an anticipatory fashion. *(Luthans and Stajkovic, 2000, p. 170)*

By using recognition selectively managers can influence how staff will manage themselves. Self-management it seems does not mark the end of managers' attempts to control staff after all. Rather, a clearer understanding of the self – the ideals, and standards by which we judge ourselves, our beliefs about our own competence, and the value, meaning and effects of what we do – offers both a new object for our own self-observation and self-management, and new opportunities for managers to influence the very ways in which we exercise our autonomy.

Image 2.4

Contribution and limitations of the mainstream theories of motivation

We began this review of mainstream theories of motivation with the work of Frederick Taylor, his development of a 'scientific' view of management, and, within this, his assumption that money in the form of piece rates would be enough to motivate Schmidt, the pig-iron shoveller. In the subsequent century of work on motivation our understanding has come a long way.

We saw how the humanist views of Maslow challenged the patronizing views of Taylor, insisting that managers recognize a much broader range of needs, beyond money, in their employees. McGregor took this a step further by suggesting, with his distinction between theory X and Y managers, that the laziness Taylor imagined to be a part of Schmidt, may have been no more than a reflection of Taylor's own negative assumptions and the way that these informed his treatment of Schmidt. Herzberg's and Hackman's work then challenged Taylor's views on the separation of mental from manual labour, and the efficiency of an intense division of labour, by insisting that it was the nature of jobs, rather than human needs that was the key to motivation. Schmidt was not stupid or lazy, but bored out of his head by the mindless, fragmented work that he was asked to do. To be meaningful and motivating jobs need to allow one to use a variety of skills, to deal with complete tasks rather than fragments, and allow one to feel that what one does is important to others and the success of the organization.

But these early attempts to uncover the universal truths, or 'content', of what motivates – individual needs, the task, the managers' assumptions and conduct – were themselves challenged by ideas that insisted that motivation is a dynamic 'process'. Schmidt had perhaps learnt through long experience to expect little beyond money from his work. He was not, as Taylor imagined, just a body to be trained, or even a bundle of needs, but a self-conscious person who acted on the basis of the sense he made of his experiences.

Now if the employee is a self-conscious, thinking being, just like the manager, then suddenly motivation theorists realized that motivation could never be what a manager *does* to an employee. People motivate themselves, and the most that managers can do is to create an enabling

CASE STUDY 2.3 A problem (of motivation) at PYT plc (3)

Val had worked as a sales representative at PYT for a couple of years when she was promoted to a vacant post on John's team of sales executives. She was a bit worried about this move; she wasn't sure she could handle the larger clients, and John had the reputation of being fiercely ambitious and felt much less approachable than her present boss Mel. Her fears were quickly confirmed. She was having some problems with her partner outside work and she began to slip behind on her sales targets for her first campaign. John said he would give her some training and spent one Friday morning listening in to her calls. But the training in practice involved John telling her all the things she was doing wrong. She tried to explain to him that it was just a bad patch she was going through. She even hinted at the troubles she was having outside work but John ignored this. By the end of the morning she was feeling awful about herself and finally burst into tears and rushed out of the office. She went to the doctor and was off sick for the next week. When Mel, her old team leader, heard about what had happened she was furious with John for what she saw as the

way he had undermined Val. He, however, insisted that she was simply 'no good' and 'not up to it' and would have to leave or take a demotion. When Val returned fearfully the next week, John took her into an office and told her that she had the choice either to leave the company or go back to her old job on Mel's team. Val was shattered. It was Mel who later came and found her in the toilets, took her out to lunch, and tried to persuade her to give it a go with her old job. 'Never mind what John said, I know that you're a great sales person and I want you on my team.' Val went back to work for Mel, but it was weeks before she began to regain her confidence.

Question

How do theories of self-motivation in relation to ideals, self-efficacy, targets, empowerment and selective recognition help understand Val's contrasting experiences of being managed at PYT? What does her experience suggest about the problems of these new forms of self-motivation?

environment for this. Under the pressure of growing international competition since the 1970s this has led to an explosion of interest, and study, of all the different dimensions of self-motivation. In part this depends on the ideals we have of what we should seek to become, the beliefs we have acquired about how effective we can be, and the goals we set for ourselves. The role of managers in relation to self-motivation involves them thinking about whether the environment they create is empowering for staff, and whether they create opportunities for achievement, as well as offer staff recognition.

So after this century-long journey of 'discovery' about motivation have we reached the promised land of healthy, productive and satisfied employees? What does your own experience tell you? Is this the sense you have of your own experiences of working, or those of your friends or parents?

Many of the studies we have described were sincerely motivated by a concern to address what the writers felt was the waste of human potential at work, but the interest their work aroused was perhaps less noble in its intentions. Who was investing in developing our understanding of motivation, and why? On the one hand, managers like to think well of themselves and how they treat their staff. But, on the other hand, they know that their own success will depend on their ability to get as much as they can from staff. So although thinking about motivation seems to have moved way beyond Taylor, in another way it still shares his *instrumental* interest in efficiency. Other people are still seen as a means to an end. Managers' interests lie in about making full use – exploiting – other people; their job and future career as a manager depends on this. We might also ask why it has taken a century for theory to discover that employees are people like us. Do we really need social scientific studies to discover what should be obvious from our own experience of families and friendship. And why is it still so easy in the course of our work to find discontent and unacceptable conduct?

The unspoken story in all these studies of motivation is about power. The desire to fully use others' power in the service of our careers and the organization, and all the resources – research and training – that are put into this. The power that allowed Taylor to treat Schmidt like a mindless machine, and kept Schmidt working despite this. The power that makes the use of motivation theory a sort of optional extra for managers; something that they can embrace but also ignore if they choose to do so.

Superficially, the recognition of the damaging impact of imposed control, and the apparent recognition of employee autonomy suggests that, in theory at least, motivating managers have given up using their power in this way – they merely empower and enable. But as we shall explore in what follows, the more recent attention to the autonomous self – its ideals, self-beliefs and aspirations – can be seen as an even more intense, intrusive and effective form of power in the service, not of the employee, but of corporate profit.

Box 2.3: James Wolfensohn – President of the World Bank

'I personally feel that the world is out of balance. The way the world is dealing with problems of poverty and peace seem to be disconnected. Military spending is now probably US$1000 billion and spending on subsidies or tariffs to protect the developed world farmers is about US$300 billion. Meanwhile the rich countries offer no more than US$50–60 billion in aid to developing countries while blocking most of their agricultural exports – one of the few ways these countries could pull themselves out of poverty.'

'The three things are linked. There are 5 billion people in the developing world, 3 billion earning under US$2 a day,

and 1.2 billion earning under US$1 a day. If you can't give them hope, which comes from getting a job or doing something productive, giving them their self respect, these people become the basis upon which terrorists or renegades or advocacy groups can flourish. Its an essentially unstable situation.'

'If you cannot deal with the question of hope or economic security there is no way that with military expenditure you can have peace . . . if you do nothing about poverty and development you're not going to have stability.'

Source: The *Australian*, 4 February 2004.

Critical perspectives on motivation and the self

Overview

While many of the studies that we have looked at in the first part of this chapter were very critical of current management practice, what they all share is a hope or a belief that the 'problem' of motivation can be solved through the development and application of knowledge; i.e. a better understanding of human needs, the redesign of work and more appropriate management behaviour. Critical views of motivation theory challenge the adequacy of these mainstream approaches on two very different but related bases. In the first – views shaped by Marx's analysis of the structures of capitalism – we return to the role that economic interests have in shaping conduct at work. While mainstream theory emphasizes the unitary nature of interests in organizations, for Marx, capitalism involves an essential *conflict of interests* between ownership (and its agents) and those who must sell their labour in order to live. Acknowledging this fundamental conflict of interests arguably offers a more historically accurate account of how management have been able either simply to ignore employee interests, or alternatively have (selectively) recognized them only in order to maximize profits. Either way, it points to management's instrumental interests in motivation; their interest is not in making work more satisfying for employees but in getting more out of them. It also suggests that much motivation theory can be seen as an 'ideology' that justifies hierarchy and inequality and presents the sectional interests of owners and their agents as if they were universal and shared. A real change in motivational practice would require a different structure of ownership and the power relations that this creates.

The second critical account of motivation draws upon ideas about the 'social construction' of the 'self', as well as the work of Michel Foucault and those who have been influenced by his analysis of what he calls the operation of 'disciplinary power'. As we have seen, over time mainstream motivation theory has come to emphasize the motivational importance of individual autonomy and self-management and used this to suggest that the exercise of management control has often been counter-productive and should be replaced by strategies of empowerment that promote employee commitment. Here power and individual autonomy are treated as opposites, as indeed they often are in classic Marxist accounts. But in this final section of the chapter we want to explore how power comes to shape the very ideals that we set for the exercise of individual autonomy. Our knowledge of the 'self' is socially produced, and as a result is never under my autonomous control. Motivation here is seen to be animated by the desire to fix and secure the very sense we have of ourselves as this is reflected in the attitudes of others' towards us. Many of the new motivational strategies involved in contemporary 'human resource management' can be seen to rely upon and play with these aspects of the ego.

Marxist analyses

'Men make history, but not under conditions of their own choosing.' *(Karl Marx)*

The profound creativity of human action Typically when we first join an organization it already exists – it has a history, buildings, rules that govern its operation, established procedures and systems. From this perspective it is as if our actions and thoughts and motives have nothing at all to do with the nature of the organization in which we work; the purposes of the organization and our purposes can be thought about in isolation from each other. Take university, for example. It is easy to see it simply as the context in which you can pursue your own individual goals of getting a degree, having a good time, etc. This sharp separation between subjective reality and the organization as an objective reality can encourage us to have a very limited view of work and the effects of what we do. It can lead us to ignore or deny the profoundly creative aspect of what we and others do.

For Marx, what distinguishes humans from other animals is that we do not have a biologically fixed or instinctually predetermined relationship either with ourselves or with the world. There is, therefore, neither a fixed human nature to which we might refer, or seek to discover, in order to understand human motivation; nor is there a fixed structure of external determinants of human responses. Instead, human nature is itself only shaped and reshaped through work and the consciousness that arises through such work. Work or labour then becomes a central explanatory concept – it is not to be understood as an aspect of a person's life alongside leisure, family, sport and so on, but rather as an historical process through which we humans create and recreate ourselves and our world. Moreover, work organizations cannot be understood in isolation from the social and political relationships in which they are embedded. Nor can the present social or organizational reality be treated as if it is somehow 'natural' and not itself the product of historical forces and itself subject to change and further development.

The process of production Let's take a closer look at what is involved in action / work / labour. Work can be thought of as a relationship between us and the world, or as our way of relating to the world. It involves a moment of conception in which we draw upon all our existing tacit knowledge and understanding to conceive of what we will do. For the most part we act habitually, doing what we have always done through drawing upon the skills and knowledge that we have accumulated in the course of our lives. Look at an infant or a child and it is immediately obvious how much and how long it takes each of us to acquire even the most basic of skills.

The second moment involved in work is one of externalization. we combine our accumulated knowledge, skills and thought with materials to hand and produce something – this can be an idea, work, picture or other kind of object.

Finally what has been created becomes part of the external world – objectification – and is available for both ourselves and others, and for future generations.

While all labour involves such processes of conception, externalization and objectification, there are two further potentials – reification and alienation – that are important for our understanding of human motivation (see Box 2.5).

When you go to the library to find books to write an essay what is your sense of your relationship to these? Are they oppressive, non-human 'truths' that you must wade through simply to get your essay written. Here work, and its means of production – books and articles – are felt to have no relationship to you and your own thoughts and experience. Instead these objects dominate and oppress you. Alternatively, are the books merely the objectification of other people's thoughts – thoughts that were shaped by their own history and interests and reflections – upon which you can then draw in shaping your own thoughts and opinions. Here, writing becomes a creative relationship between yourself and the objective world through which both you and the world are developed and changed.

The contradictions of capitalism and alienation The story that Marx tells of human history is a story about the relationship between an evolving 'means of production' – the accumulating knowledge, skills

---

Box 2.4: Tacit knowledge

Tacit knowledge is a set of skills and ways of understanding that is so familiar that we take it for granted as what we know of how things are, and can only with difficulty explain or describe it. A good example is riding a bicycle. Like so many of the skills upon which we depend, riding a bicycle is something that we learnt, possibly with some difficulty. It took time and effort to coordinate our legs working on the pedals with steering. We fell off a few times before we learnt the basic skill and then refined it. We also had to learn the rules of the road so that we stop and give way at the right places, and ride on the correct side of the road and are not a danger to ourselves and others. But today we just get on a bike and cycle and do not even have to think about what we are doing deliberately. Despite our obvious 'practical' skill, however, when we try to teach someone else to cycle we are hard pressed to find the words that explain it. It's obvious, taken for granted.

Box 2.5: Reification and alienation

Reification: to treat something as if it has an independent existence of its own, rather than as the product of human thought or work.

Alienation: a reversal of the relationship between the producer and their product such that what is humanly produced comes to dominate the producer.

and artefacts through which we manage our relationship to nature – and the forms of social relationships or 'relations of production' that come into existence around any particular set of productive relations. Although he offered a broad historical sketch of these relationship starting with tribal society, then the ancient societies of Greece and Rome, and then an agrarian based 'feudal' society, Marx's key concern was with the emergence and dynamic of productive and social relationships under capitalism.

For Marx there is a contradiction at the very heart of capitalism. On the one hand the move from feudal to capitalist society involved a massive positive development in the means of production and, in this process, the emergent merchant class played a progressive role. In part this was achieved, as Adam Smith described, through an intensification of the division of labour, such that traditional craft skills were broken down into specialized tasks that could be carried out by a number of workers. But the success of the market also stimulated technological innovation and the huge increase in productive capability that industrialization allowed. In principle, such positive developments in the means of production should have been associated with the progressive liberation of humans from need. For Marx, however, the experience of work under capitalism turned into the exact opposite. Marx analysed these paradoxical effects of capitalism in terms of four forms of 'alienation'; four ways in which under capitalism what is humanly produced comes to impoverish the human producer.

ALIENATION FROM THE PRODUCT Under feudalism, although the worker would have had to give a proportion of what was produced to his lord, he was in other respects his own proprietor who was free to produce according to his own immediate needs and those of his family. Under capitalism this relationship to the land as a means of production is broken and, instead, increasing numbers of workers become entirely dependent upon the sale of their own labour on the market. Their labour becomes just like any other commodity, and what they produce is no longer determined by what they or others need but by monetary exchange driven by the search for profit and the accumulation of capital. For Marx, the key 'class' division emerges between those who must sell their labour in order to live and those who, by virtue of owning the means of production, are able to expropriate not only the surplus produced through their own efforts but also the surplus produced by others. This conflict of interest at the very heart of capitalism is expressed in the different meaning of wages; for the employee they are their only means of living, for the owner they are a cost to be minimized. The more the worker produces the cheaper labour becomes.

ALIENATION FROM THE PROCESS OF PRODUCTION Work does not allow the worker 'to develop freely his mental and physical energies'. Work can no longer be experienced as an end in itself but rather is just a means to ends that are external to work. Marx took as evidence of this the fact that 'as soon as there is no physical or other compulsion, men flee from labour like the plague'.

ALIENATION FROM OTHERS For Marx the 'individual' of economic theory was a peculiar invention of capitalist society. The person is fundamentally social and it is impossible to conceive of the person as somehow apart and distinct from the society and culture out of which he or she emerges. Yet under capitalism relationships between people come to be dominated by the logic of the market. Colleagues become rivals for jobs and for wages, as means or obstacles to one's own success. Others are seen solely through the calculative lens of profit or advantage.

ALIENATION FROM THE SELF Finally, and in a sense as an accumulation of these effects, Marx talked of capitalism as involving the alienation of both the worker and owner from themselves, from their own social nature. While an individual is always the product of the society in which he or she is born,

Box 2.6: The 'isolated individual'

'The "isolated individual" is a fiction of utilitarian theory; no human being exists who has not been born into and thus shaped by an ongoing society. Each individual is thus the recipient of the accumulated culture of the generations which have preceded him, and in his own interaction with the natural and social world in which he lives, is a contributor to the further modification of that world as experienced by other.' 'Individual life and species life are not different things;' Marx asserts. 'Though man is a unique individual he is equally the whole, the ideal whole, the subjective existence of society as thought and experienced' (Giddens, 1971, p. 13).

under capitalism awareness of this relationship is reversed and the social is subordinated to the pursuit of individual goals. We begin to treat the self and others like a market commodity.

It is important to point out that the alienation that is being talked of here is not from some ideal natural man; there is no such thing. Alienation arises instead from the contradiction between the socialized nature of production and the privatized ownership of the means of production under capitalism, which itself sets up a tension between the productive possibilities of capitalism and the experiences of those who produce within it. The solution, however, also lies within capitalism, for Marx believed that by bringing people together in large numbers – in cities and factories – there would be the potential for these contradictions themselves to be overthrown. To date, at least capitalism has proved remarkably adaptable.

Core assumptions of the Marxist perspective

- Man is a social animal rather than a self-seeking 'individual'.
- Production for exchange rather than use is a feature of capitalism rather than a universal of economic activity.
- Under capitalism, production is motivated not by the meeting of human needs but by the pursuit of profit and the accumulation of capital.
- The self-seeking opportunism that is the grounding assumption about the nature of human beings in neo-classical economics is better understood as historically specific to capitalism.
- There are different interests for different groups in organizations that are shaped not by 'individual' needs but by class position – whether one is an owner, or must rather sell one's labour in order to live.

If the interests of labour and owners (and their agents, management) are fundamentally opposed, then this suggests two things as regards motivation. First, it suggests that the problem of motivation is built into capitalist organizations. This explains why motivation has become a 'holy grail' of

CASE STUDY 2.4 A problem (of motivation) at PYT plc (4)

Emily had worked at PYT for the past eight months. She'd worked in a shop before that, but had not liked the weekend working. At least here her weekends were her own. She had got married last year and her and her husband, Robin, spent most weekends doing up the house they'd bought.

She enjoyed the training course that PYT sent her on when she first arrived and she'd been amazed to discover that the techniques they had taught her really worked. The trick seemed to be to get people talking after you'd told them that you were just phoning to check their entry in the directory. The 'open' questions she'd been taught to use – Where exactly is your shop? Have you been there long? What sort of area is it? – really did seem to get people talking and then she'd change to closed questions – Would you like a quarter or half page? Shall I go ahead and book that for you? – to try and make the sale. She was surprised how many people went along with what she suggested.

Sometimes she felt a bit guilty with the small businesses – she wasn't sure they needed to spend that much – but then, as they'd taught her, advertising is important if you want to

grow your business. She liked working on Ruth's team and when she'd made her first sales Ruth had shouted it out and everybody clapped. The thing she still felt most uncomfortable about was some of the other people in the office. They were a bit posh and were always talking about the designer clothes they'd bought, the restaurants they'd been to and the expensive holidays they were going on. She and Robin barely had enough to live on, what with the new house. Emily had started taking a Selfridge's bag with her when she went shopping. She couldn't afford to shop there but at least they wouldn't know that she had to buy her clothes at cheaper stores. But Emily saw PYT as a place where she might be able to make something of herself. If she worked hard and was successful then perhaps she could get to be a manager in a year or so.

Question

Can you find examples of Marx's four versions of alienation in Emily's attitude to herself, her work and her co-workers?

management writers that has been pursued for over a century. Secondly, it suggests that the problem will never be solved within capitalism and so the managerial quest for performance and satisfaction will be endless, in part because it wants to solve the problem without addressing its root cause, which lies in the exploitation made possible by private ownership.

Rethinking motivation: Efficient and rational for whom?

MOTIVATION THEORY AS IDEOLOGY In whose interests are theories of motivation developed and whose interests do they serve? Marx argued that at any moment in history the dominant class would typically disseminate ideas that serve to legitimize its own position of dominance. He talked of this as 'ideology' – presenting the interests of a particular group as if they were universal interests. Take Maslow's ideas of a hierarchy of needs. How might the idea of a hierarchy of needs serve to justify and legitimize the current structures of hierarchy and power in an organization? Now it is clear that Maslow and McGregor were critical of the way organizations fail to meet human needs, but as their ideas have been popularized by management texts, these critical aspects of their ideas are typically edited out. Instead their ideas are read as if they offer a 'natural' justification for hierarchy. It is tempting to simply assume that those doing lower level, or menial work in an organization are somehow at a lower level of development, preoccupied with lower level needs, while those at the top have 'grown' and are (rightly) rewarded with the opportunity for 'self-actualization'.

MOTIVATION AND ECONOMIC INEQUALITY While knowledge of motivation might be said to have developed over the years, it is still up to management, rather than the employee, particularly at lower levels of an organization, as to whether these ideas are taken seriously. Motivation is in this sense an optional extra for management – they can always fall back on the force implicit in the employment contract to get people to do what is required. The fear of unemployment is all the motivation that most people need. The theories have not led management to address or change the structures of power in which they work. It is for managers to introduce empowerment – employee power on managers'

Image 2.5

CASE STUDY 2.5 A problem (of motivation) at PYT plc (5)

As Damian Rawls, the Sales Director, had feared, PYT was continuing to haemorrhage customers and Peter was becoming increasingly alarmed at the prospect of the office missing its half-year profit target. Damian was on the phone to him every week now to ask about how the office was doing and had just told Peter that he was going to visit the office next week to take a closer look at operations. Peter immediately called his section leaders, Mel, John and Ruth, into his office.

Perhaps Peter did not know how thin his office walls were, but staff heard him shouting at them: 'I don't care if the staff are under huge pressure, we've just got to meet these targets'.

Question

Are profits all that matter? If we need a job in order to live then why should managers give another thought to our motivation?

terms – rather than acknowledge a real dependence upon employees. All this means that a concern for motivation can be applied selectively and strategically. If you need a high level of commitment and loyalty, or if you fear the power of a union or a political shift of power towards the interests of labour, then perhaps we should invest in winning hearts and minds, or treat certain groups of employees very carefully. However, if unemployment is high and replacements easy to find, if the costs of motivation exceed the likely benefits, then there is no need to weigh employee needs against the interest in profit. The rhetoric changes but not the power structures.

THE POWER OF DIVIDING   One final criticism of conventional theories emerges from a consideration of Marx's views on alienation. For Marx the contradictions of capitalism were likely to be removed by its own internal dynamics. As an unintended consequence of capitalist production, the organization of work would bring large groups of employees together in factories and offices, and as citizens. Given the conflict of interest around production between wages and profits he believed that people would begin to see their true interests. While as an 'individual' I might be weak relative to my employer, as a member of a trade union or a political party I could be powerful. While conventional theories of motivation acknowledge the 'social' needs for belonging, affection and recognition, these do not extend to the collective needs for concerted resistance or political action. But they also point to the political significance of what has been termed 'individualized' attention. By focusing on the 'individual' employee, by emphasizing the hierarchical differences between individuals, by keeping them absorbed with their careers and promotion prospects, a whole set of forces are set up that avoid or preclude collective action.

Important empirical studies

LABOUR AND MONOPOLY CAPITAL (HARRY BRAVERMAN)   Braverman's reinterpretation of Taylor's scientific management in the 1970s draws its inspiration from Marx's analysis of the dynamics of capitalism. What Taylor suggested was the product of the application of scientific methods to the study and organization of work is seen by Braverman in terms of the logic of capitalism that sets the pursuit of profit on a collision course with the human importance of meaningful work. What Taylor offered as a rational separation of mental and manual work is seen by Braverman as a process of de-skilling, driven by concerns to reduce costs, intensify work effort and reduce the potential for worker resistance.

Braverman's starting point is the 19th century craftsman; the coherence, knowledge and skill embodied in craft work, and the relatively autonomous organization of craft labour within craft unions. The scientific application of seemingly neutral rationality to such work by proponents of scientific management can be seen to be driven by the logic of profit rather than a universally beneficial efficiency. The separation of mental and manual labour is from this point of view an act of theft in which management captures the skills and knowledge of skilled labour and on this basis is able to de-skill and fragment jobs, and in the process extract more output for less cost. Coherent jobs with their own intrinsic satisfactions are broken down into relatively meaningless fragments and these fragmented tasks can then be performed by unskilled labour that is both much cheaper and more easily replaced than the skilled craftsman.

Braverman's work was important because its focus on the labour process was an important antidote to the rather abstract and idealized images of employment coming from management writers. The early introduction of new computer-controlled technologies in the 1970s where skilled work was recorded on computer tape pointed to the continuing relevance of his critique of Taylor. Braverman's (1974) book inspired a host of critical studies of work but was itself criticized for its rather passive portrayal of the worker and the degradation of work under the relentlessly unfolding logic of capitalism. Workers are portrayed as the victims of strengthened management control.

MANUFACTURING CONSENT (BURAWOY)   One of the difficulties Marxist accounts of work face is to explain why, given the conflict of interest between profit and wages, there is so little resistance on the part of organized labour to its own exploitation. Explaining this seeming paradox was the task that Michael Burawoy set himself in his 1979 study, *Manufacturing Consent*. Where Braverman explains work intensification in terms of increased management control achieved through the separation of conception from execution, Burawoy suggests that work intensification has been achieved through a management strategy of worker 'self-organization'.

What his empirical study observed was workers' enthusiastic participation in worker-led games of 'making out'; attempts by a host of means to maximize bonus payments. Playing such games,

Burawoy suggests, creates a sense of personal autonomy and choice, it relieves the boredom and drudgery of work and gives people a sense of accomplishment. While such games are played in the spirit of an assertion of autonomy against management, by playing the game people inadvertently come to accept the rules of the game; a logic of capital in which labour is systematically disadvantaged. The pleasures and apparent freedoms of the game ensure greater productivity. Importantly, Burawoy's study observes how the bonus system games, and the defence of wage differentials between different groups of workers, have the effect of separating people off from one another and encouraging workers to see work in the same instrumental terms as they themselves are viewed by management. The game gives us a sense of being in control, of being able to use the company rather than just being used, but the result is that we work ourselves hard.

Power and the 'self'

Marxist analyses focus on how ownership gives some the power to exploit others through creating economic insecurity. The second set of ideas that we will explore suggest that modern motivation techniques play not just on economic insecurity but a person's insecurity about the value of the self. These ideas involve questioning the very notion of 'individual' autonomy and raise the possibility that power works not to constrain this autonomy from the outside but instead by shaping our very notion of what it is to be an individual. It is here that notions of economic power associated with the private ownership of property can be seen to be intimately linked with personal concerns with self-identity and security. To begin to introduce these ideas we will in what follows look a little more closely at how a person's sense of self is developed and maintained, and then see how this becomes a key lever for motivating both ourselves and others at work.

The formation of the 'self' In everyday language we often talk about the self as if it were a something that we have. We treat the self as if it were the psychological equivalent of our bodies; something that is relatively fixed, stable and independent from the world. Although the self is unique to us, here it is being thought about as if it were indeed a 'something' – an object. Here we will look at some ideas about how such a sense of a solid self emerges.

How far back can you remember? Usually people have no memories that they can easily bring to mind much before the ages of three or four. Even then the memories are fragmented – a particular scene or taste or event – always laced with the doubt that it might be something that others have talked about rather than an actual memory. So why is there this critical gap in our memory and what does this mean for our understanding of what it is to be or have a 'self? Does it mean that early experiences are simply unimportant? This seems unlikely and here we will pursue an alternative explanation; that we are not born with a developed sense of self but instead 'self-consciousness' is the product of early experiences and development.

One of the most influential early accounts of this process comes from an American pragmatist, George Herbert Mead. In his book, written in the 1930s, called *Mind, Self and Society*, he drew a distinction between three aspects of the self – the 'I', the 'me' and what he termed the 'generalized other'. Mead suggested that we are not born with a developed sense of self but merely the potential for such 'self' consciousness.

Finding my self in the mirror of others' responses Mead argued that I come to my first sense of self, not through defining my own experience for myself but, instead, through 'taking over' the attitudes of 'significant' others towards me. So I can think of myself surrounded by parents, grandparents and siblings and finding my first sense of self as if in the mirror of how these people responded to me. But language can be deceptive here for this is the very foundation of these differentiations of the self as 'I', 'me', 'my', 'others'. Mead argues that I become aware of the self first as a 'me', as an object to/for others, and indeed as a child acquires language s/he typically refers to the self initially in the third person – as 'me'. My sense of self as an active agent, as an author or subject, as 'I', only comes after I have begun to organize a sense of 'me' as the 'object' I am for others. Mead talked about the relation between the 'me' and the 'I' in terms of *the "I" of this moment becoming the "me" of the next*. As an 'I' the self has to be understood as a continuous, active but endless process of becoming. As lived the self is in a 'constant transition from a now thus to a new now thus'. But I can also reflect on this active process of being and experiencing, and in doing so come to define the self as this or that, 'me' or 'not me'. What is important to note is that I cannot ever quite capture the self in reflection; I can never reduce the self to the status of a known object. Instead the mind is constantly moving very rapidly between engagement with the world, and reflection on this engagement.

The self as a synthesis of images Mead's account of the formation of the self allows us to differentiate between the active, engaged and reflexive moments of selfhood. But in his description of my first sense of self being acquired through 'taking over' the attitudes of others towards me he also allows us to see the social nature of the self, and thereby come to understand some of the difficulties of achieving and maintaining a sense of autonomous 'self-identity'. My identity is a set of ideas as to what defines me uniquely as a human being, but Mead's analysis suggests that this definition of self is always socially constructed.

'Taking over' has a rather mechanical tone to it but, in practice, this involves my coming to understand who I am through making sense of others' responses to me. In reality this can mean that our initial sense of self is in many ways more about others around us than it is about the self. As a child it is too easy for us to ascribe the other's response as being to do with who we are rather than what is happening to them. For example, a mother who is depressed can leave a child feeling as if they do not quite exist and a parent who is angry can leave a child feeling that they are bad. Alternatively, the very different needs, aspirations and expectations of parents can simply make it difficult for the child to synthesize into a coherent unity all the different experiences they have with their 'significant others'. Ideally, of course, the parents will have the psychological maturity and space to respond accurately, and with love to the child's own initiative and this then founds a strong positive sense of the goodness of the self as a resource for future life. What should be emphasized here, however, is that our initial sense of self as 'me', is made up of my *synthesis* of others' responses to me – it is this synthesis that actually constitutes or creates my founding sense of 'me'. These processes go hand in hand with the acquisition of language as a ready-made set of differentiations between self and other, past and present, me and not me.

Learning what the self must be (to be loved) Even in the most loving of environments, part of what the parents will be concerned to do is to introduce the child to the 'norms' or standards of behaviour of the wider society in which the child must eventually take their place. While initially some physical constraints may be placed upon the child, with the entry of the child into language and the formation of an early sense of self, then it becomes increasingly possible for the behaviour of the child to be influenced *symbolically* by the parents. The response of 'significant others' to the child is in part shaped by their sense not only of who the child is but of what the child must be. Here praise ('what a good girl, well done') as well as criticism ('don't do that, that's very naughty') as well as straight bribery ('if you do that then you can . . .') are all used to try to direct the child's conduct towards desired ends. So the sense of self that we acquire from others contains not just a sense of who we are, but also a sense of what we must be in order to be liked, loved, recognized or belong. Such is our dependence that, again, our very existence seems to depend upon our being able to be what the other wishes us to be (or at least what we imagine we must be to win their recognition and love).

Acquiring a (guilty) conscience Psychologists talk of two related processes that together further differentiate the psychological structure of the early ego – the formation of an 'ego ideal' and a 'superego'. Part of what is involved in 'taking over' the attitudes of others is what Freud calls 'identification'; the internalization of some aspects of another as a part of the self. The ego ideal involves the internalization of some idealized aspect of the parent, which then serves as an internal standard against which the self is measured. It has a double aspect. On the one hand, it is an ideal of what we can be or should be like. It is akin to the borrowing of another's power – a sense of what one also might become. But any ideal is also necessarily a description of what we are not, and depending on the gap between the self and ideal self it can become an internalized

SOURCE: IMAGES.COM/CORBIS

Image 2.6 Acquiring a (guilty) conscience

voice that constantly berates and criticizes the self for being less than perfect – for our inadequacy, incompetence and insignificance. Freud referred to this 'critical agency' as a 'superego' that turns its frustration and anger not out towards others, but back upon the self for being bad, inadequate or not good enough.

What has happened then is that an external relationship with a very powerful other – a parental figure – has been internalized as a relationship between two aspects of the self; what we are and what we must be (to be loved). Such internalized ideals can be motivating. Think of those inspiring figures – teachers, parents, heroes – who have become models of what you would like to be like. But it is important to remember that ideals can never be fulfilled. The self is always in the process of becoming and will never become a perfect 'something' whose value is established unambiguously once and for all. But the *pursuit* of such perfection is another thing, and perhaps precisely because the self is 'open' there is a strong desire to know, fix and secure the self.

Securing the self at work   How then do these ideas about the formation of our early sense of self-consciousness help us to understand adult human motivation more fully, and in particular how power, self-identity and insecurity become linked? Although the force of our early experiences with others makes these founding experiences of the self highly consequential for how we think about ourselves for the rest of our lives, it would be wrong to imagine that once formed, our self actually becomes independent of others. If we have a good start in life then this gives us a certain basic security or confidence that allows us to more easily withstand negative experiences, but because the idea we have of the self or 'self-concept' is a 'synthetic' object, our sense of who or what we are (of 'me' in Mead's terms) is always vulnerable to the responses of others. We are all typically prone to treat the responses of others as if they were a mirror in which we see ourselves.

When we talk about 'self-identity' we are talking about the creation and maintenance of a certain synthesis of experiences; a sense of the continuity over time of our experience of being a self and of the coherence of our own and others 'objectifications' of the self. As a fundamental aspect of my knowledge of the world, my sense of self is obviously among my most precious possessions. But what if this knowledge is 'reified' – that is, treated not as an always partial and selective definition of me as 'this' or 'that', but rather as the 'whole' and 'objective' truth of who I am? This makes protecting my identity seem like a matter of life or death. I am therefore prone to be constantly comparing myself with others (am I better or worse than them) and alert to how they see me (do they like, admire, respect me, are they insulting me?). It is this vulnerability of the 'self' that is central to modern motivation techniques. In the mirror of the other's response I look both for confirmation/recognition and feel myself to be exposed to possible rejection or attack.

I once visited a factory in the north-west of England. It was a plastics factory and the operators each worked at the end of a large moulding machine, pressing and abstracting mouldings for car bumpers. The factory was staffed largely by Asian immigrants but managed by white English managers. I was shown round the factory by a white manager, and we had a conversation about the production process across an employee as if he was not there. Later I went to talk to this man who turned out to be a university educated schoolteacher who had come abroad and found factory work only because he could find no work as a teacher at home in Bangladesh. What do you think it was like for him to be ignored in the way that he was by the manager? How do you think this may have fitted with his earlier experiences at university? Over time what effect do you think being ignored, overlooked and disregarded would have on his sense of himself?

That each of us is self-conscious, with a sense of our uniqueness and capacity for autonomous action, means that we are both aware and typically resistant to others' attempts to control us overtly. At least in the management literature, if not in practice, part of the history of ideas about motivation that we have traced is a grudging but dawning recognition that the exercise of control is often likely to have negative motivational consequences. As we saw earlier, Walton argues that controlling managers are likely to produce not discipline but adversarial employment relation. I am another person not an object to be used merely for management's purposes, and if I feel myself being manipulated in that way I am likely to resist. Management's seeming recognition in recent years of individual autonomy looks promising, as if enlightened managers have given up control and are now wise enough to simply try to encourage individual commitment.

Here management power and employee autonomy seem to be at odds. But in what follows I want to argue the exact opposite; that power works precisely, and much more efficiently, through shaping the exercise of individual autonomy. It does this in part through coming to shape the very ideals in terms of which I come to judge my own and others' actions. And as Luthans observed, selective recognition by managers is a very powerful way to influence this self-management. To develop this alternative view of power we will briefly look at some of the ideas of Michel Foucault, in particular his analysis of what he called 'disciplinary power'.

The power of being made visible and knowing it   In his book *Discipline and Punish*, Foucault (1979) notes a shift in the late 18th century from what he calls a 'sovereign' view of power to what he terms 'disciplinary' power. We often locate power elsewhere with the 'powerful' – the boss, chief executive, prime minister, Queen – but Foucault argues that this idea merely conceals how, in fact, we practise power upon the self and upon each other. He offers a prison design by Jeremy Bentham, the 19th century utilitarian, as a model for this new form of the exercise of power. Cells in the prison were organized around a central tower, in which, behind blinds, a guard could watch over the prisoners. The key question to ask is what is the effect of the blinds?

On a railway station in central London a printed sign with a symbol of an eye tells me that I am being filmed by security cameras. As I drive back home later in the day, road signs tell me that there are speed cameras in operation. Again the question is why, if they want to catch me speeding or committing crimes, do they tell me in advance that I am being watched? Or closer to home perhaps, what is the effect of knowing that, at the end of the academic year, you are going to have to sit an exam?

It is because knowing that one is being watched, that what we do is visible, but not being able to know at any moment in time quite who is watching, changes our behaviour. Foucault suggests that in effect we can do away with the guards, at least for some of the time, since each of us prisoners will over time come to internalize the power relationship and will effectively watch over our own conduct, and those of others. As he puts it, we will 'simultaneously play both roles'. Foucault argues that a whole host of contemporary social technologies have similar effects. These technologies work through making us knowable and visible in certain ways, and through classifying, comparing, homogenizing, hierarchizing and excluding have the effect of both 'individualizing' and 'normalizing' people.

Let's explore what such processes might mean in the context of work and motivation. When Maslow and others began writing of basic human needs for belonging, for love and status, and recognition, they were exhorting managers to recognize employees as other human selves rather than just anonymous labour. Their intentions were no doubt humane, but given the 'synthetic' nature of the self and its vulnerability to others' responses, such *recognition* then becomes a powerful lever on conduct.

- At its simplest the adult relationship between boss and employee can have echoes of earlier power relationships; the boss can become the ideal around which I model myself, a person whom I want to please, for whom I want to be special.
- The hierarchy itself can also serve as a mirror of the value of the self. I can feel a failure when I compare myself to others higher up the hierarchy, and more successful compared to those 'lower' down. I can see promotion as an opportunity to 'make something of myself', and see my colleagues as competitors for such promotion.
- Through performance figures and accounting information the 'results' of my work are made visible to me and others. Praise and criticism, and the occasional dismissal or promotion, advertise what kind of employee I must be if I want to keep my job, if I want to be a success.
- In anticipation of desired recognition and feared blame I supervise my own conduct. Company standards over time become the lens through which I judge and supervise myself. I set myself targets and goals, I criticize my own performance and identify the strengths I need to build on and the weaknesses I need to work on.

SOURCE: © ISTOCKPHOTO.COM/CHRIS SCHMIDT

24 HOUR CCTV RECORDING IN OPERATION

Image 2.7 The power of being made visible

- I come to view my 'self' as a project – as my own bit of capital, to be developed, marketed, packaged and sold.
- As Foucault puts it, I become 'the principal of my own subjection'.

Key studies

Reframing human resource management (Barbara Townley) Barbara Townley has drawn extensively on Foucault's writing to offer a very different view of human resource management. Her work picks up on a recurrent theme in this chapter – the indeterminacy or incompleteness of the employment contract – and offers a very different view of the history we have traced. One way to read this history is as a gradual and progressive 'uncovering' or 'discovering' of the truth of motivation – a cumulative knowledge of individuals and their responses to different kinds of job and management. We can see this knowledge as an objective, even scientific, fact that any 'rational' manager should be keen to use. But Townley questions this view of knowing; what if it is not so much an uncovering of some essential truths about the 'self' but rather a way of producing the 'individual' at a particular point in history.

Following Foucault she argues that ways of knowing are also always a form of power relationship. The progressive study of motivation is both stimulated by the desire to render the person controllable, and the knowledge that is produced then has important power effects in the way that it becomes embodied in techniques and practices of organizing the workforce. Part of human resource management involves what she calls 'dividing practices'; work is separated from home, and jobs are ranked in terms of skills, responsibility, experience, seniority and function. Similarly, the individual comes to be categorized in increasingly elaborate ways, as we have seen, in terms of needs, expectations, skills, attitudes, goals and ideals. This knowledge then becomes embedded in ways of *examining* the person in processes of selection, training and development, appraisal, feedback and surveys. It also becomes embedded in ways of talking and getting employees to talk about the self in mentoring and coaching, appraisal and development. The accumulation of knowledge about motivation in this way can be seen, over time, as providing a way of distinguishing 'myself' from others, as well as shaping the norms through which I will judge and appraise myself and others. In the context of work at least it becomes the very means through which we think about the self.

'Someone to watch over me' (Wilkinson and Sewell) Graham Sewell and Barry Wilkinson (1992) drew on Foucault's ideas in a study of shop floor work at a UK engineering firm they called Kays. They suggested that the new physical layout of the shop floor and use of electronic data associated with the introduction of total quality management and just-in-time stock control had greatly increased the visibility of shop floor work and greatly decreased the opportunity for workers to exercise discretion. The quality of what was produced could be traced to particular individuals, and was then reinforced by the public display of quality and productivity information that advertised both desired standards and individual deviations from this. All this was backed up with an emphasis on teams who were given responsibility for achieving targets and continuous improvement. Following Foucault, they suggested that workers were much more effectively controlled under the new production systems. Increased visibility, the knowledge that every aspect of work was being monitored and the likelihood that any failure would bring public humiliation to an individual were enough to ensure that individual employees managed themselves in line with management expectations.

Happy families at Hephaestus (Catherine Casey) Casey's (1999) study of culture change in a transnational company she calls Hephaestus adds a psychological dimension to our understanding of quite how effective new forms of management control can be. Casey suggests that employees typically embraced the values of a happy family that management advertised; they believed the story that management told them. In this way the values of the organization came to act as an ideal that informed individual conduct and the way that they judged themselves and others.

Her argument is that modern management techniques work in part through encouraging such identification with ideals. Whereas in former times employee aggression would be channelled outwards towards management, now she suggests it is channelled back on the self for failing to live up to the ideal of a competent, caring and committed employee. The problem at Hephaestus was that the organization was not quite like the ideal it claimed to be. Repeatedly, members of the family were 'killed off', and the emphasis on being a good team member also involved team attacks on those who had let them down, and rivalry for the recognition of the team leader. The results for employees were considerable levels of individual stress caused by concerns about their own competence, and confused and ambivalent feelings about the official rhetoric of their being all part of one big happy family. For the most part, however, people went along with the official story, and challenged and criticized themselves and colleagues rather than management, for the hypocrisy of saying one thing and doing something different.

Contributions and limitations of critical approaches

The principal contribution of the approaches informed by Marx's analysis of the dynamics of capitalism is to draw attention yet again to the inequalities of power relations at work and how these inform management's selective interest in theories of motivation. While many of the mainstream writers were informed by concerns to improve the human condition, their ideas arguably gained currency because it was hoped that they could help managers to bridge the gap between employing labour and turning that into effective labour power. Capitalist organizations had managed quite well without theories of motivation, and, like John at PYT, managers can still rely on the fact that people need a job as a powerful force for motivation. Changing political, educational and economic conditions have altered the nature of work and employee expectations such that brute force and coercion are less possible, and their negative effects more obviously counter-productive, but employees' calculation of self-interest still goes a long way in ensuring that, as individuals, they will be compliant with what is asked of them. Particularly at lower levels of organizations it is still easy to find all the abuses of economic power; low wages, poor working conditions, and coercive and arbitrary management practices.

But if economic exploitation is a reality then, as we have seen, this creates a puzzle as to quite why those who are disadvantaged by a system are so willing to cooperate in their own exploitation. Some of this, as Burawoy argued, can be seen as the unintended side effects of their own attempts at 'making out', but it is here that ideas about the social construction of the self and in particular Foucault's ideas are particularly helpful. If theories of motivation in the end become the very means through which we come to understand, think and judge ourselves, and if motivation involves self-management, a preoccupation with making something of ourselves, a competitive orientation to others, and a tendency to view failure as a failure of the self rather than the product of economic forces over which we have no control, then the aggression that Marx hoped might be turned outwards against the institutions of private ownership is instead turned inwards against the self.

But these later views of power also disturb some of the reassurance that comes from a view of the world where the worker is cast as the victim of external forces and relatively powerless, at least as an individual, to make a difference. Foucault's analysis of the 'micro-physics of power' robs us of the

Image 2.8 Exploitation: a thing of the past?

illusion of being victims, or of the hope that if only we can rid ourselves of the 'bad' other – bosses, owners, lazy workers – then all will be well. We practise power upon ourselves and each other – manager and worker are in this sense both subjects – and it is much more difficult to even conceive of resistance if the effects of power are to be discovered in the very ways in which we think about ourselves.

This section began with a quote from James Wolfensohn, the President of the World Bank, talking about global poverty and inequality. What the motivational emphasis upon individual autonomy and self-discipline ensures, perhaps, is that we are simply too preoccupied with ourselves to notice or feel part of such global processes, let alone to figure out the role that our own conduct has in both reproducing the problem and creating the solution.

Chapter summary and conclusions

This chapter began with the ideas of Frederick Taylor and his principles of scientific management. Motivation here was about money and the potential for the interests of management in profit, and workers in higher wages, to be reconciled through a division of mental and manual labour. Such ideas stand in sharp contrast to the earliest ideas that we have explored in this chapter; those of Marx, and his suggestion that there is a fundamental contradiction at the heart of capitalism. We produce together, but then some people, by virtue of being owners, can exploit those who have only their labour to sell. The owners' interest in maximizing profits is always at odds with the employees' interests in maximizing their earnings. Economic power gives owners and managers a powerful lever to dictate the terms on which others work – in this sense economic insecurity is all the motivation that many need. But then there is a huge difference between dull conformity under pressure of coercion and enthusiastic participation. The challenge for management has been to find ways in which they can turn labour into committed employees. It is not enough for employees just to turn up; what is wanted is their commitment and energy and the effort that goes with this.

Marx's ideas, and the associated fears of industrial conflict and political change, haunt the subsequent study of motivation. For the mainstream theories that we considered there was and continues to be a problem of motivation, but for these writers the problem is assumed to be solvable within capitalism if only they can understand the individual more thoroughly. The early content theories that we considered were those of Maslow, McGregor, McClelland, Herzberg and Hackman. Each focuses on a different dimension as the explanation of motivation. For Maslow, motivation was to be achieved through a better understanding of human needs and the integration of this understanding into the organization of work. Maslow suggests a hierarchy of needs from physiological, through safety and belonging, to status and recognition, and finally self-actualization. McGregor, drawing

CASE STUDY 2.6 A problem (of motivation) at PYT plc (6)

PYT ceased to operate as a company when its contract to manage the directory was not renewed. One of the factors involved in the decision not to renew the contract was the discovery of certain financial irregularities by PYT auditors in the previous year. The new incentive structure for sales people – under which they were to be paid commission only on net new business – had a fatal flaw. Staff in one office realized that if a single record card was removed from the office of the support staff all records of net customer losses attributable to an individual sales person were lost, and their commission earnings were thereby greatly inflated. The scam was only discovered after eight months, by which time it had spread to a number of offices and cost nearly US$1 million. In this case, then, the highly incentivized pursuit of self-interest had an unanticipated yet disastrous effect on the common interest in the future of the business.

Question

Is there such a thing as a common interest in work organizations? How could we arrive at a shared definition of such a common interest?

upon Maslow, suggests that the behaviour associated with theory X is easily discovered in work organizations but is to be explained not in terms of some truth about workers – they are lazy, will refuse responsibility, etc. – but rather in terms of the assumptions management make about workers and the effects of these assumptions on workers. The problem of motivation is in the manager not the employee. McClelland develops this thought further with his exploration of managers' motivation – their needs for achievement, power and to be liked. His finding was that the need for power is the best predictor of good management in terms of the climate such managers create among staff – as long as they have their own ego needs under control.

But then Herzberg enters with a different story. The focus on management–employee relations misses the point. The key drivers of motivation are intrinsic to the job a person does; the work itself and the opportunities it offers for achievement, recognition and responsibility, all of which allow individuals to grow psychologically. These factors produce positive satisfaction, and should not be confused with the factors that cause dissatisfaction, which include supervision, salary and security. Removing sources of dissatisfaction will not produce satisfaction but rather an absence of dissatisfaction. Hackman and Lawler pursued this thought that it is the work itself that matters with their assertion that 'internal motivation' depends upon work being meaningful, involving the experience of responsibility, and where there is knowledge of the results. These motivations in turn imply the need for jobs to have skill variety, task identity and significance structured into them.

The second mainstream set of theories that we explored are often termed 'process theories'. In their earliest form – Vroom's expectancy theory – it was argued that motivation is the product of valence (what I want and do not want), instrumentality (my expectations of what leads to desired outcomes) and expectancy (my expectations about how what I want and how to achieve it are related). Importantly, the employee is rediscovered here as an intelligent person, making sense of their experiences and then acting on the basis of the expectations that these experiences have created.

These process views were further developed in the 1980s and 1990s under the weight of renewed competitive pressure to solve the problem of motivation through a recognition of individuals' capacities for self-motivation. Reluctantly, it seems that managers have finally learnt the lessons of earlier studies. Management cannot control staff – pull their strings like puppets or rely on coercion. This will at best only produce dull compliance if not outright opposition. People need to motivate themselves and the manager's task is to create the conditions that support this. We looked at Levinson's argument that it is a person's own ego-ideal – what they aspire to achieve – that motivates. Locke and Latham relatedly argued for the importance of stretching goals for motivation; ideally these are goals that we set for ourselves and to which we are committed. Bandura, as a social psychologist, takes us further into the mysteries of self-motivation with his ideas about the importance of our own 'self-efficacy'. Past experience will have shaped a set of beliefs we have about what we can do and its likely success, and these will shape what we attempt and how strongly we pursue the goals we set for ourselves. Managers can support such self-motivation by creating empowering conditions that allow people to feel that they can make a difference. Luthans also suggests that ideals, goals and people's views of themselves can be influenced by the selective use of recognition by managers.

Now taken at face value this history of motivation theory suggests a progressive movement towards enlightened management conduct. It begins with Taylor stripping out the mental content of work and insisting that thinking and planning was manager's work, along with close control and monitoring of mindless staff. Then gradually what he had taken away is rediscovered in employees – the range of different needs beyond money, the damaging results of certain management assumptions, the importance of whole and meaningful tasks. Then, with the process theories, the rediscovery of the thinking self-conscious employee, who is as capable of autonomous action as the manager, and who must therefore be encouraged to manage themselves, with management in a supporting and enabling role. The theory is seductive. We would all like to think of ourselves as in control – as able to make a difference. We have all been taught to work upon ourselves, to improve ourselves and make something of ourselves. What could possibly be wrong about that?

For Marx and those influenced by his thought the problem of motivation needs to be understood on a wider canvas. Getting people motivated will always be a problem under capitalism because, although we depend upon each other to produce wealth, private ownership of the means of production allows owners to exploit those who must sell their labour in order to live. Though profits are only made through labour, the interests of owners diverge since labour is a cost to be minimized if profits are to be maximized. Either managers can rely on job insecurity to ensure compliance, or if it is cost-effective, they can invest in winning hearts and minds. But still the contradictions persist.

While Marx looked at the power effects of ownership and focused on economic insecurity, more recent theories have explored how insecurity about the self, and management's power to create insecurity about the value of the self, is used to motivate. The seeming celebration of individual self-management in empowered organizations is here recast as a more subtle and effective form of domination. Power works not through constraining us from the outside but through shaping the way we think about ourselves, the goals we set ourselves and the judgements we make about ourselves. Managers and employees are no different from each other in this respect; both are shaped as subjects by the new forms of organizational control. But while we are encouraged to become and remain pre-occupied with ourselves then all sorts of collective and political opportunities for resistance and change are foreclosed. Inequality and injustice remain but we are now prone to blame ourselves and our colleagues for failure. We are so busy making something of ourselves, so eager to compete with our colleagues for promotion, so keen to have the security of belonging to a happy family, that we cannot even think that things could or should be otherwise.

Motivation theorists set out to discover the secrets of human nature so that more could be got out of it. Others with more humane interests wanted managers to see the employee in more than economic terms but still believed that the interests of managers and workers could be reconciled within capitalism. Others have identified not with the organization and its goals but with those who suffer from being managed. Mainstream theory here reappears as an ideology that masks the conflicts of interest at the heart of capitalism, and in the recent recognition of employee autonomy has simply found a new object for more subtle forms of domination.

Discussion questions

1 How has our understanding of how to motivate ourselves and others developed since Frederick Taylor first introduced his ideas about scientific management more than a century ago?

2 Which of the ideas covered in this chapter did you find particularly helpful in thinking about your own motivation?

3 What are the key differences and similarities between content and process theories of motivation?

4 Can managers motivate or is motivation always self-motivation?

5 In what ways is it impossible to understand motivation without also thinking about how power works on the self and in relationships?

6 Is Marx's concept of alienation still useful in understanding the modern experience of working?

7 Why is personal autonomy so important to motivation? In what ways is the image of the autonomous self always something of an illusion?

8 What are the key lessons that managers should draw from the study of management over the last century and a half?

Further reading

Richard Sennett, *The Corrosion of Character: The Personal Consequences of Work in the New Capitalism*, Norton and Company, London, 1998.

This is a follow-up study to an earlier classic that Richard Sennett and Jonathon Cobb wrote called *The Hidden Injuries of Class*. It is based on interviews with the now grown-up child of first generation immigrants in the United States, and offers a compassionate view of how they make sense of their own experiences of failure and dislocation arising from the globalization of capitalism.

Peter Fusaro and Ross Miller, *What Went Wrong at Enron*, Wiley and Sons, London, 2002.

This is a very readable account of the recent collapse of Enron. It offers a description of the fatal consequences of economic incentives for senior executives, and the way in which the

organizational culture – 'Rank and Yank' – helped to keep employees quiet as the company headed for collapse.

E. Locke (ed.), '*The Blackwell Handbook of Principles of Organizational Behaviour*, Blackwell, Oxford, 2000.

There are a number of good articles in this collection of current thinking about motivation. They are clear and easy to read but completely uncritical.

Tracy Kidder, *The Soul of a New Machine*, Allen Lane, 1982.

This is a great read and an exciting account of the development of a new computer. It is a story that illustrates both the frustrations of large organizations as well as the energies that can develop in a small group committed to a task they all believe in.

References

Bandura, A. (2000) 'Cultivate self-efficacy for personal and organizational effectiveness', in E. Locke (ed.) *The Blackwell Handbook of Principles of Organizational Behaviour*, Oxford: Blackwell.

Braverman, H. (1974) *Labor and Monopoly Capital*, New York: Monthly Review Press.

Burawoy, M. (1979) *Manufacturing Consent*, Chicago: Chicago University Press.

Casey, C. (1999) 'Come join our family: Discipline and integration in corporate organizational culture', *Human Relations*, 52(2):155–178.

Conger, J. (2000) 'Motivate performance through empowerment', in E. Locke (ed.) *The Blackwell Handbook of Principles of Organizational Behaviour*, Oxford: Blackwell.

Foucault, M. (1979) *Discipline and Punish: The Birth of the Prison*, London: Allen Lane.

Giddens, A. (1971) *Capitalism and Modern Social Theory: An Analysis of the Writings of Marx, Durkheim and Weber*, Cambridge: Cambridge University Press.

Hackman, J. R. and Oldham, G. R. (1980) *Work Redesign*, Reading MA: Addison-Wesley.

Herzberg, F. (2003) 'One more time: How do you motivate employees?', *Harvard Business Review on Motivating People*, Boston MA: Harvard Business School Press.

Latham, G. (2000) 'Motivate employee performance through goal-setting', in E. Locke (ed.) *The Blackwell Handbook of Principles of Organizational Behaviour*, Oxford: Blackwell.

Levinson, H. (2003) 'Management by whose objectives?', in *Harvard Business Review on Motivating People*, Boston MA: Harvard Business School Press.

Luthans, F. and Stajkovic, A. (2000) 'Provide recognition for performance improvement', in E. Locke (ed.) *The Blackwell Handbook of Principles of Organizational Behaviour*, Oxford: Blackwell.

McClelland, D. (2003) 'Power is the great motivator', in *Harvard Business Review on Motivating People*, Boston MA: Harvard Business School Press.

McGregor, D. (1989) 'The human side of enterprise', in H. Leavitt, L. Pondy and D. Boje (eds) *Readings in Managerial Psychology*, fourth edition, p.p. 314–324, New York: McGraw-Hill.

Maslow, A. (1989) 'A theory of human motivation', in H. Leavitt, L. Pondy and D. Boje (eds) *Readings in Managerial Psychology*, fourth edition, p.p. 20–35, Chicago: University of Chicago Press.

Mead, G.H. (1934) *Mind, Self and Society*, Chicago: University of Chicago Press.

Sewell, G. and Wilkinson, B. (1992) 'Someone to watch over me: Surveillance, discipline and just-in-time labour process', *Sociology* 26(12):271–289.

Thomas, K. and Velthouse, B. (1990) 'Cognitive elements of empowerment: An interpretative model of intrinsic task motivation', *Academy of Management Review* 15(4):666–681.

Townley, B. (1994) *Reframing Human Resource Management: Power, Ethics and the Subject at Work*, London: Sage.

Vroom, V. H. (1964) *Work and Motivation*, New York: Wiley.

Vroom, V. H. and Deci, E. (1992) *Management and Motivation*, Harmondsworth: Penguin.

Walton, R. (1985) 'From control to commitment in the workplace', *Harvard Business Review*, March–April:77–84.

3 Individual Differences, Personality and Self

Damian O'Doherty

Key concepts and learning objectives

By the end of this chapter you should understand:

- Personality type theories and how they differ from what are called trait theories of personality.

- The development of personality type theories from the ancient Greeks through Carl Jung to the more recent experimental and laboratory-based work of the Eysencks. We will also look at the influential Myers-Briggs type indicator of personality.

- The central ideas that inform what many people believe to be the biological basis of personality founded on research in neurophysiology and behavioural psychology. We will come to understand these ideas as essentialist in orientation – that is, they posit an *inherent* and *universal* core to explain who people are and what they do.

- The more idiographic approach associated with the writings of George Kelly, Carl Rogers and particularly Abraham Maslow.

- The ideas associated with the phenomenological analysis of personality. This begins to take us out of the conceptual confines of orthodox personality theory and opens up a more generous understanding of 'self'. George Herbert Mead (1863–1931) pioneered a phenomenological approach to personality, which allows us to see how a wider set of social forces shape the development and emergence of unique selves.

- The contribution of writers such Ronald Laing and Erich Fromm, who take the analysis even further to show how self is a dynamic and processual phenomena – one that develops and changes over time.

- A more existential interpretation of the individual in which it makes more critical sense to think about people through the concept of identity rather than personality.

Aims of the chapter

This chapter will:

- Explore concepts and ideas that have been used to build up theories about individual differences, personality and self.

- Examine the limits of orthodoxy in management and organization as we begin to understand 'personality' in the terms of subjectivity and identity.

Overview and key points

We tend to think of ourselves as a personality. Maybe we understand ourselves, for example, as an extravert or an introvert, or perhaps we are 'easy going', depressive or melancholic. We also attribute personality to our friends and colleagues. Personality is both complex and fascinating, but it is also elusive and difficult to define. Consider the amount of time we all spend trying to work out the personality of people around us – what makes them distinctive, or what makes them 'tick' – and the difficulties we have in understanding how and why different personalities clash or cohere within particular groups or social settings. A great deal of organizational behaviour (OB) can be explained through personality, and the astute manager is one who is both attentive to the different personalities of people at work, and subtle in their understanding of their dynamics and implications.

This chapter takes you on a journey from popular, mainstream ways of thinking about individual personality to more critical and theoretically innovative understandings of subjectivity and identity. The idea is to explore some of the most important concepts and ideas that have been used to build theories about individual differences, personality and self. We do not simply summarize the work of the major theories and ideas in convenient lists of revisable bullet points; instead we take you *into* the texts and thinking of some of the most important writers and thinkers to illustrate how and why they thought as they did and how they arrived at their conclusions. This will help us to start thinking for ourselves. In this way we will begin to see some of the implications of adopting the terminology of personality and of thinking of the management of work organization in terms of the supervision of personality. In order to make this move we must tackle some difficult issues surrounding the philosophy and methodology of the natural sciences. This will allow us to consider the relevance and application of these methods to management and OB. In other words, is management a science or an art? Once we have thought about these issues we will be in a better position to appreciate OB as a something that is perhaps better understood through the concepts of subjectivity and identity. Using these ideas helps us to open up and explore the world of organization in a different way. It makes it possible to conceive of organizations as complex and disorderly phenomena divided by conflict and irreconcilable differences in values and goals.

Work organizations are obviously concerned with a series of rational and economic issues relating to productivity and efficiency, but they are also characterized by a great deal of suffering, pain, and disappointment – much of which remains suppressed and unacknowledged. To begin thinking of the individual in terms of 'identity' instead of personality helps to unearth these 'deeper' issues that lurk just below the surface of everyday life in work and employment. Explosive and unpredictable, these forces in an organization can conspire to wreak havoc and disorganization. They demand thoughtful and mature management in order to shape and channel their dangerous energies into forms that are less disruptive to organization. This chapter will help to show that the way we choose to frame the problem of the individual will largely depend on our assumptions or understanding of the world and our role or possibilities within it. This is a political question or problem and it remains hidden in most introductions to OB.

Chapter structure

We begin the chapter by exploring the different definitions and interpretations of personality. This illustrates the confusion and often contradictory understandings that most people hold about personality. Academic theories about personality have tried to clear up this confusion and have adopted what are known as nomothetic or idiographic approaches. The thinking and methods of the natural sciences have been used predominantly to develop nomothetic theories of personality. Modern science inherits the ancient classification of personality, which identifies four basic temperaments. Later developments organized these four temperaments in terms of two fundamental dimensions of personality – namely changeability and emotion. The work of Carl Jung and his analytical psychology has also been tremendously influential for management research. Jung introduces ideas about a shadow world and the collective unconscious to explain how and why certain personalities develop, and it is largely because of Jung that we have become accustomed to thinking of people as either extravert or introvert. Katherine Briggs and Isabel Myers Briggs took up the work of Jung in the development of a practical tool for managers interested in personality: the Myers-Briggs Type Indicator test of personality. According to Myers-Briggs there are four basic underlying tendencies or preferences evident in the way we think and act and which define the *type* of personality we have.

Another major strand of modern research into personality looks at *traits* rather than personality types. There are a whole series of 'traits' that make up individuals – things like anxiety, guilt, tension, low self-esteem, impulsiveness, consistency and predictability. The foundations of this approach to thinking about personality are associated with the studies of Hans and Michael Eysenck, who laid the groundwork for how most people today think and study personality. The Eysencks used scientific laboratory tests to measure behavioural acts from which they inferred the existence of personality traits, traits which cohered or could be aggregated around two major categories (or forces) – extraversion and neuroticism. The relative influence of these two factors largely explains why people behave in different ways, and this is explained, in turn, by genetic inheritance.

The use of laboratories and the methods of natural science in the study of personality bring with it a whole series of assumptions and implications for management and OB. We introduce a critical interrogation of the scientific methodology to show that it is predisposed to seek explanations for personality in simple and reductive terms. Rather than challenge commonsense assumptions about traits such as 'anxiety', 'irrational behaviour', 'emotional' or 'hopeful', the Eysencks would take these as a given and go out and try to 'test' or measure them. In so doing they ignore the changing social and historical construction of these categories – what counts as 'moody', for example, is never fixed culturally or historically – and downplay the interrelation of social and individual/biological causation of personality and traits. The influence of the natural sciences is profound and largely explains the existence and faith that people have in things like psychometric testing as a way of recruiting and managing human resources in organization.

Idiographic approaches to personality emphasize its more living and protean nature. Personality can be seen to grow or shrink, people can withdraw into themselves or, as we say, *come out* of themselves; in brief, personality can develop and respond in relation to different social and contextual circumstances. In the second half of this chapter we explore these more humanistic and phenomenological dimensions of personality, looking in particular at the popular work of Abraham Maslow (introduced in Chapter 2). Where Maslow is somewhat idealistic and romantic, other writers in this tradition, such as Ronald Laing and Erich Fromm, take a deeper look at the existential dilemmas confronting individuals, and place personality within a broader study of 'identity'. This brings into focus the influence of society and the social construction of individuals in shaping and determining personal identity. Their thinking helps us to explain the emergence of more disturbing aspects of personality in contemporary society: narcissism and the authoritarian personality. Consideration of the existential dimensions of personality helps us to see how the vulnerability of individuals renders them susceptible to manipulation and forms of corporate colonization as detailed in studies by writers such as David Collinson and Catherine Casey. Towards the end of the chapter we begin to acquire concepts and tools that allow us to explore the political and contested nature of work organization, where powerful forces of disintegration and disorder can be seen to traverse and permeate through the individual.

Central problems in the field: Mainstream and critical

We can summarize the main problem in the field as one that hinges on the question of science and whether the methods of the natural sciences are appropriate in the study of personality. The mainstream tends to be more traditional and scientific in its approach to studying personality; the more critical studies of management and organization behaviour are less 'scientific', but perhaps more theoretically speculative and adventurous. However, both the mainstream and its critics have science and anti-scientific tendencies.

Subsidiary questions form around the problem of whether personality is the outcome of nature or nurture – that is, whether biological and genetic disposition determines and explains personality, or whether the 'environment' (historical and social conditions) better explains its emergence. Debates also rage about the extent to which personality is 'fixed' and enduring over time, or whether it is open and contingent over time, maturing, developing and shape-shifting. In other words, is personality a static 'entity' or one that is processual and open-ended? In recent years this question has been posed in terms of 'essentialism'.

The mainstream tends to be more 'behavioural' in its orientation, seeking clues to personality from the ways in which people behave or respond to stimuli, which is more often than not tested in artificial, laboratory conditions. The scientific approach is popular amongst many hard-pressed managers because it seems to offer relatively straightforward and simple, practical solutions to problems of OB. Where 'types' and the influence of 'traits' can be identified and catalogued, management can more quickly and efficiently recruit and select individuals, build teams and develop leadership in organizations. Or, at least, that is the promise. The critical approach favours a more sensate or 'inner' and experiential study of personality, studying its lived in-situ conditions of emergence where the complex, dynamic nature of its realization is manifest.

Mainstream and critical also divide over the degree of explanatory weight that one should attribute to personality, particularly the extent to which the most important features of OB can be understood through the study of personality. Critical thinkers tend to think more in terms of *identity*, which opens up other dimensions of being that allows one to explore the more political, existential, spiritual and emotional make-up of individuals. For critical thinkers the institution of science can be extremely dangerous, and might be better thought of as a disciplinary mode of conduct: disciplinary in the sense that it trains us to see and think in partial and limited ways, but also disciplinary in terms of its practical effects in the world. The individual can only be understood in a very limited way when it is thought about in terms of 'personality'. Critical thinkers want to go beyond the superficial, the mundane and the pragmatic, which continues to drive the thinking and activity of most managers in work organizations. They want to think in terms of wider and deeper questions, questions concerned with existential and political issues – the imminence of death, for example, or the quest for meaning and purpose. This is why the central problem for critical thinkers is the question about identity, not personality. The challenge posed by this more critical agenda is that unless we shift the terms of the debate into these more complex realms of being, and challenge the predominant inclination of managers to react with impatience to the perceived pressures and immediacy of organizational pressures, we will intensify unhealthy and pathological tendencies in work organization.

CASE STUDY 3.1 WaRP mAsters and Experienced Records

You might be sitting around with a group of friends at the Dog and Duck pub on a Friday evening when you hear *Funkadelica Dice*, a new record by the Manchester-based turntablists WaRP mAsters, who are mixing their latest blend of pastiche Latin breaks with modulated Detroit-style sound loops. Your conversation has momentarily stopped. Some people have started dancing. It's a truly awesome tune that some people heard for the first time at Glastonbury last year. But you might be wondering: how do they make records like that? Contracted to Experienced Records for an undisclosed fee, WaRP mAsters are two years into a five album deal and each record they have released to date has redefined cross-over trance-dance music. From underground cult to global phenomena, they are quite literally a new sensation and seem to have been on the front cover of every music magazine in the last six months. What a great industry to work in, you might be thinking.

You need a strong, vibrant personality for this job . . . Our success has been built upon people who are able to project themselves, to infuse and enthuse customers and colleagues alike. If you're not into meeting people, talking, networking, persuading, cajoling, able to go from speaking to some 19-year-old spaced-out fashion model (and that's the guys I'm talking about!) to a corporate exec at Sony Records . . . yes, and having a laugh, you know actually enjoying yourself, turning up in the evenings for socials, photoshoots, going the extra mile, then you can forget working for Experienced Records.

Image 3.1

SOURCE: © GETTY IMAGES/THOMAS HOEFFGEN

So says David Marsh, the human resources director at the UK-based head office for Experienced Records, a multinational recording, manufacturer and distributor of popular and classical music. It's April 2001 and their biggest recent success has been the signing of the Manchester underground cult band WaRP mAsters. In the next six weeks David is looking to recruit 12 university graduates into his UK sales and marketing teams. As part of their recruitment and selection exercise they run a psychometric test that it is claimed cuts through the presentation of self, those illusions and images projected by individuals, and even the deluded beliefs people often have about themselves. Only certain personalities have proven to be a success working in the music industry. The psychometric test used by Experienced Records is based on the latest scientific research and findings. It gets right to the heart of your personality so that David Marsh and his colleagues can base their selection decision on the type of person you actually are and not the kind of person you might like to think you are.

You may have heard, on the other hand, that it is all about who you know and not what you know that secures employment. Indeed it is well researched and reported (Jackall, 1988; Grey, 1994; Watson, 1994; Casey, 1995) that what is probably more important in career advancement is a political and organizational ability to curry favours and develop the right network of connections among the powerful, the cliques and cabals that actually 'run the show' in organizations. Here it is more about 'fitting in', being adaptable and chameleon-like, cultivating, developing and presenting the right attributes – that it is, in essence, all about image and manipulation. Especially in the music industry, personality might well be something that is expendable, something that is manufactured and packaged for commercial gain. Not only have 'personalities' been constructed and developed for the lead singers of many popular bands, but for those working 'behind the scenes' in management and organization who are likewise careful in the kind of image they present to the world, continually self-monitoring their behaviour and 'impression management' (Goffman, 1959) for personal and political goals. Consider the recent fate of the so-called 'Right Honourable Professor Cornelius Y. Tlee (himself)'! Many people will go further and claim that they will leave their personality at home when they go to work – that their 'true self' is something far different from the kind of image they project and use to advance their careers.

Personality, management and organization

'A control-freak!'. 'Spineless'. 'An egotistical maniac'. 'A fake!'. We all *have* a personality. Or, at least that is what we have come to believe. Some of us are loud and pushy, and others are quiet and reserved. There are those who are thoughtful, very rational and careful, while some are passionate and enthusiastic, perhaps not so cautious, but who express and generate a lot of energy around them. Flirtatious, gregarious, serious, fun-loving, 'dizzy' or morose: personality comes in many complex shades.

We also have a number of ways of classifying personality, from the relatively simple to the more complex. It is often said, for example, that someone has a 'nice' personality. On the other hand we might overhear a conversation in which it is remarked that David Marsh of Experienced Records is a good manager but that he oscillates unpredictably between what we will learn to call a 'type a' and a 'type b' personality. But which of these personalities is the one that is going to work most successfully in organizations today? You may well have your own personality but we need to remember that all of us have to work with a diverse range of other personalities in organizations, some of whom we are compatible with, and others who we find very difficult to work alongside. One thing that we do know about organization in the future is that nearly everyone will have to learn to manage other personalities as we learn to understand, shape and manage our own

The psychometric test

Many people will quickly associate personality and the workplace with the psychometric test. The psychometric test is one of the most controversial techniques currently being deployed by managers in organizations and excites fervent debate across a range of opinion. This is only the latest in a long line of personality assessments that extends from handwriting analysis and colour preference theory to story-telling ability and astrological readings. We will need to consider the theoretical basis upon which these tests have been devised if we are to establish the analytical building blocks that are needed to prise open some of the most pressing management problems in organizations today.

In order to recruit and develop employees in organizations, management frequently use psychometric tests, which puts them among some of the most popular of methods. Associated with the practices of management and forged out of what was referred to in the introductory chapter of this book as the 'entity view of organization', psychometric testing is also used to help management assess candidates for promotion. Indeed, the psychometric test is often our initial introduction to the world of work and our first experience of business organization.

In this chapter you will discover a number of different ways in which it might be claimed that personality can be 'extracted' from an individual and defined in a neat and succinct way. Following this assumption it would seem that despite our best efforts we cannot permanently hide or disguise our 'true' personality. According to many writers we inevitably project our personalities through a whole series of signs, some explicit and others more disguised, but nonetheless discernible. You may have seen a recent newspaper article, for example, in which it is reported that scientists have discovered that even the position and shape of your body during sleep reveals your type of personality! In another recent news item it was reported that scientists are claiming that they can identify the precise gene responsible for aggression. In years to come it seems we might even be able to eliminate undesirable personality attributes at the foetal stage of life.

In many areas of contemporary work organization, the significance of personality as a factor in determining success or failure is beginning to be realized by senior management. As Chapter 4 examines, working in teams has become an almost universal mode of organizing work today – but getting the right blend of personalities has proved to be a most confusing and complex task (Belbin, 1981; cf. Barker, 1999). In this chapter you are going to learn more about these kinds of issues as we seek to open up the debate concerning the nature of the relation between 'the individual' and 'the organization'. We spend quite a bit of time getting the basic foundations in place first. Most OB textbooks will simply offer a summary of the results of the major theories in personality; they will not take you through *how* these insights about personality have been arrived at. Mullins (1993, p.p. 97–128), for example, provides a comprehensive synopsis of most of the major theorists in personality study but the price of this coverage is an absence of any serious exploration of *how* and *why* different writers come to understand personality in so many diverse ways (cf. Huczynski and Buchanan, 2001; Thompson and McHugh, 2002). This approach encourages what we have been calling in this book a 'banking' concept of knowledge – an approach that does not really encourage the reader to explore the conceptual, interpretative and *political* dilemmas that underpin the development of theory and the understanding of personality.

We really need to consider the thinking and decisions that are made at this level if we want to understand the grounds upon which the debates and often heated disputes emerge to contest this highly sensitive subject matter. The most effective managers of future organizations may well be those who are able to tackle the problems associated with personality at work with this fine degree of discrimination and understanding. In order to begin to address this issue we will look in some depth at the thought that grounds two of the most popular and enduring theories of personality: the type indicator test, associated with the research team of mother and daughter Katherine Briggs and Isabel Myers; and trait theory, established and most exhaustively studied by the brothers Hans and Michael Eysenck. This allows us to start thinking in quite mature and sophisticated ways about the difficulties of management and helps us to see some of the fascinating spaces through which organization is chronically and perpetually being *dis*-organized. Exploring issues around personality can advance ways of thinking that disclose how patterns of disorganization are marked out across a complex series of lines of division, often in 'dimensions' of organization that many would prefer to ignore.

From personality to subjectivity and identity

In order to get beyond the clichés and stereotyping associated with a lot of the popular writing and discussion on 'personality' we will go on to examine the distinctions between what we call 'self' and 'personality'. Then we are going to recall and develop the less familiar concepts of 'subjectivity', 'insecurity' and 'identity' – concepts that will provide ways of delving a little deeper into the relationship and dynamics between the individual and organization. Insecurity and identity have already been introduced in Chapter 1 as two of the six key concepts (see the Appendix), and they are used in a number of ways in the different chapters of this book to develop what we have been calling the *process view* and the *concept view* of organization. In this chapter we extend and elaborate the ideas of subjectivity and identity as an alternative and potentially more insightful and productive way of thinking about individual differences in the workplace, particularly in terms of their significance for the actual practice of organization and management. However, to get to this mode of thinking we have to carefully question the status of science to consider whether the application of natural science methodology in the study of management and organization behaviour is useful or appropriate.

This chapter introduces and debates the contribution of personality theory to the understanding of individual differences in work organization. Within the mainstream thinking and practice of management, personality is seen as one of the most basic and fundamental features of organization. Quite simply we need to understand people at work *as personalities* if we wish to develop our skills as managers in ways that are competent and efficient. However, not only are there many ways of understanding personality but there is also a complex argument about the importance we should attach to 'personality'. The introduction and study of personality developed here enables us to situate the analytical focus on personality in the context of a more expansive theoretical approach, one that begins to think of people not so much as personalities but as 'subjects' who are more preoccupied with questions and uncertainties about identity. We will discover that this provides a way of understanding the contingent and precarious dynamics that preoccupy individuals at work, and so offers a more incisive and deeper understanding of the differences and tensions that are at play in organizations.

In sum, the first half of this chapter (through to the end of 'The science of personality' section) deals with the mainstream thinking in management and organization studies, before we introduce the more critical material that helps develop the process and concept views of organization. However, the material on Carl Jung begins to show how there is no hard and fast distinction between the critical and the mainstream. Rather, it is more a case of emphasis and interpretation; in other words, how we use or apply certain ideas, and for what purposes or ends (which reminds us that study and thinking about management and its practical day-to-day conduct in organizations is inevitably political and ethical). It is interesting then that Jung's work has mainly been used by mainstream writers to justify and contribute towards what is the predominant pragmatic approach to management study and practice in the United Kingdom. Here the ambition is definition, clarity and control of personality to facilitate the collective organization of people at work. However, as we show, a more careful reading of Jung reveals how his insights and thinking into personality provide little comfort for orthodox forms of management practice preoccupied with a restricted agenda of short-term economic calculation and control.

In brief, we will be working towards an understanding of individual differences at work that takes us beyond a rather impoverished and essentialist interpretation of the individual typical of those approaches, which take personality as its focus. This lays the foundations for students to begin to think about identity as a partly reflexive and open phenomenon, a condition of organization that marks out the space of what we call a contested terrain. This space admits and acknowledges the existence of a whole series of social and political forces that are routinely ignored by mainstream management. It also casts into relief the idea that organizations are political and hierarchical phenomena characterized by power struggles, conflict and inequality. We may then begin to understand what it means to talk about 'a corporate colonization of self' (Casey, 1995), and why some people see identity as a possible resource for resisting actions and initiatives adopted by certain groups in the study of organization (Collinson, 1992). Identity might offer a basis for resistance to management, but at the same time it can be dangerous and self-indulgent. Therefore, a preoccupation with identity at the expense of its wider social and political interrelations is ultimately self-defeating.

Introduction to personality

Definitions of personality

Box 3.1: Definition of personality

According to the *Webster's Encyclopedic Dictionary*, personality is the 'visible aspect of one's character'. In other words, this is what other people see or perceive. It is not necessarily then, what you might think of yourself, but how you come across to other people. The English word 'personality' is derived from the Latin *persona*, which means 'mask', as in the face-mask that was worn by actors on stage in the theatre. In the Latin, *persona* also has associations with 'role', as in one's *role* in life, in a play or a tale that is being told. The dictionary goes on to further clarify personality by saying that the person is an embodiment of a collection of qualities and that personality is the 'essential character of a person' or the 'organized pattern of behavioural characteristics of the individual'. It is often used to define the sum total of the physical, mental, emotional and social characteristics of an individual. Further enquiry into definition finds that the word personality is often used in a disparaging or hostile sense, as in the phrase, 'the conversation deteriorated into personalities'. We might also think here of a personality clash or the disparaging judgement often intended in the phrase 'a cult of personality'.

Our search for definition is getting confusing, complex and even a little contradictory. It seems to be at one and the same time, a mask or a disguise, something that is presented to others, or something that is presented to satisfy the demands of the situation or the environment, *and* the inner most authentic core of a person, which is what distinguishes people. As we go on to examine later in the chapter, personality occupies a strange, double space – both public and private, 'fluid' or malleable and objective or concrete. Once again we enter that wider problem identified in OB, but here played out in one of the building-blocks or sub-components of the academic discipline, where we are confused about whether we are dealing with an entity view of personality, a processual understanding, or a conceptual, approach.

Take a look around at your group of friends. Of all those people you know, who do you think is most likely to be a success working to sell and promote contemporary DJs and bands in the music industry? Some of your friends, for example, might be very popular. They are sociable, they seem to mix easily, and enjoy being with large groups of people. Others are likely to be quieter, reserved, or, as some people say, 'bookish'. Think carefully and try to make a list of all your friends or family and then next to their names list what you take to be a few of the most salient features of their personality. Indicate what you think might be their 'strengths' and 'weaknesses'. Are they impatient for example? Or, do they tend to talk too much and then not listen to others carefully enough? Then make a list of all the things you think the record company might be looking for in its ideal sales managers. It is important to be mindful of the fact that some elements of personality which *you* find disagreeable or unpleasant might in fact be deemed essential to the successful execution of a professional role with all its associated duties and responsibilities. Furthermore, remember that the record company will be thinking about the future. They are likely to want people who are flexible and adaptable, and not so stuck in their ways that they appear to have an over-rigid personality. We will be referring back to this list as the chapter develops so spend some time thinking carefully about the people you know. Bear in mind that people are often very different from the way they come across in social company. Therefore you might want to compile your list so you can distinguish how your friends might define their own personalities and how you or others might interpret their personality. Table 3.1 provides one or two examples.

Table 3.1 Examples of personality profiles

Name	Elements of personality as presented to others	Personality as you see it	Ideal job
Jackie Paper	Quiet, sensible, helpful, caring	Extravert, likes talking to people, quite 'deep', emotional	Bar Manager? The Caring Professions? Personnel Manager?
Christine Pharos	Loud, fun-loving, flirtatious, vivacious	Envious, insecure, quiet, suspicious	Band Manager? Marketing?

Nomothetic and idiographic approaches

One of the difficulties involved in drawing up a catalogue of personalities in this way is the problem you have no doubt encountered in this relatively simple and schematic exercise – namely, what is to count as relevant? What is relevant or significant in one person's character and what elements of personality would serve to distinguish and identify that person? Is there a difference? Many people doing this exercise for the first time find that they have no common reference against which to measure people. We arrive at a jumbled list of characteristics from which it is very difficult to really say what it is that defines somebody's personality. Typically we end up with that all too banal conclusion that everybody is different, that we are all unique and you cannot hope to generalize. In some ways this is probably true, but it does not help our recruitment manager, David Marsh at Experienced Records, who is trying to identify which of his applicants is likely to be the most successful in sales and marketing. This problem can be understood more formally as a reflection of different approaches or methodologies in the study of personality, namely a nomothetic approach as against an idiographic one (Eysenck and Eysenck, 1985, p. 3).

One way round this problem is to standardize the measurement of personality. That is, you extract two or three elements of personality that then form a template against which comparisons can be made. You might think, for example, that what is most important in somebody's personality is whether they are driven by emotion, or whether they are, instead, more logical and rational, using their intellect to guide their actions. Take a look at the table you have drawn and see if there are any commonalities that your friends and families share. Take the category emotion/intellect as a test case and try to assess your group against this scale. Do half your friends fall on the side of emotional and the other half you have categorized as rational? Can you quantify *how* emotional your friends are? Could you say that one of your friends is almost 100 per cent driven by their emotions, whereas another is only 80 per cent driven by emotion? What we need in order to be able to accurately measure people in this kind of way is some very accurate definitions of the category 'emotional'. We also need an outer limit, or an extremely emotional person, against whom we can then measure the rest of our population. Once we start constructing tools of measurement in this way, we are beginning to think of personality through a nomothetic methodology

Among some of the most important work that has been conducted in the nomothetic approach is the research and writings of Hans Jurgen Eysenck who studied personality from the 1940s through to the late 1980s. However, there is a long history of study and interest in this approach that takes us back to the pioneers of what is today's more formal research.

The four temperaments

Most people identify Hippocrates as 'the father of medicine' and it was he who first began to think about the classification and explanation of personality during the 3rd and 4th centuries BC. Interestingly, on graduation as physicians, students of medicine today still recite what is called the 'Hippocratic oath', a pledge of commitment to the ethics, duties and obligations of medical practice. Some people will tell you that Hippocrates, living on the island of Kos in ancient Greece, knew as much as there could possibly be known about personality, and that today we have not been able to progress much beyond what he knew over 2000 years ago.

Hippocrates tells us that from his observations and studies there are basically four temperaments – the melancholic, the choleric, the sanguine and the phlegmatic (Eysenck and Rachman, 1965). In more modern prose we might define the melancholic type as someone who seems to suffer from introspection and withdrawal, or heavy, downcast moods; somebody who is generally depressive in nature. The choleric person, by contrast, is quite cranky, fiery and irritable. We would experience

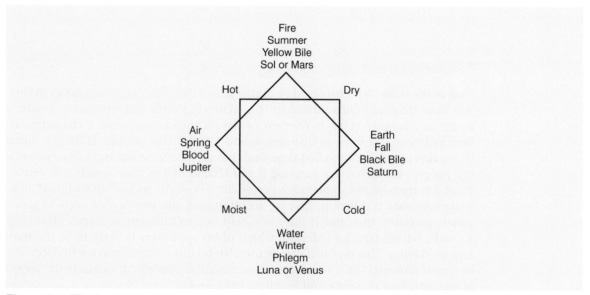

Figure 3.1 The humours or temperaments and reasons related to the qualities established in the Corpus Hippocrericum (5th century BC)

someone who is sanguine as cheerful, hopeful and basically optimistic; and the phlegmatic person would appear sluggish or apathetic, listless or laid back.

For Hippocrates, people are born and 'made up' out of four basic material substances: black bile, yellow bile, blood and phlegm. In Hippocratic observation these four body substances equate to the four basic 'universal' elements – earth, fire, air and water, respectively. The exact composition, the mixture or 'temperament' of one's inheritance, is largely determined by spiritual and material forces in action at the time of one's birth – including the 'pull' exerted by the arrangement of the planets (see Short, 2000). We are born under the sway of a certain physics of material energies so that we all tend to be composed of slightly different settlements and accommodations between competing forces. Born under the influence of the remote and slow-moving planet Saturn, for example, an individual is likely to be subject to an excess of black bile which leaves the individual predisposed to melancholia. For Hippocrates, these element were associated with particular calendrical seasons; so autumn or fall is the time of melancholia, and earth – as opposed to water, air or fire – its mediating and corresponding element. These ideas were taken up and developed by another Greek physician, Galen, who introduced a greater degree of order and classification to the exercise. He noted how people born with an excess of black bile tended to become melancholic, or, in our terms, depressive in character. Yellow bile equates to the choleric type; blood with a sanguine temperament; and phlegm with the phlegmatic person.

In 1798 the famous German philosopher Immanuel Kant published his *Anthropologie* in which he revises and translates the four basic Hippocratic types into a form that is more easily recognizable today. Kant downplayed the significance of 'mysterious' energies and forces mediated by the blood and bile and instead sought what we identify today as a more rational categorization of personality. He elaborates and develops descriptions of the four temperaments in ways that make distinctive what are typically modern characters. So, he describes people tending towards melancholia as those who:

> attribute great importance to everything that concerns them. They discover everywhere cause for great anxiety, and notice first of all the difficulties in a situation, in contradistinction to the sanguine person. They do not make promises easily, because they insist on keeping their word, and have to consider whether they will be able to do so. All this is so not because of moral considerations, but because interaction with others make them worried, suspicious and thoughtful; it is for this reason that happiness escapes them.

For Kant, you cannot have combinations of the basic temperaments, so somebody could not possibly be both sanguine and choleric. Wilhelm Max Wundt (1832–1920), a German physiologist and early psychologist, was the first to recognize that these categories should not be understood as sealed boxes but rather as continuums along common dimensions. In other words, where the influence of melancholia was fairly mild in one person they might begin to feel the effects of more choleric type factors. It is not simply a case of either-or, then, but of competing forces that find expression in a myriad of personality complexions. What explains the basic distribution of personality characteristics are the strength of feelings and the speed of change in a person's feelings. Somebody who is highly anxious would normally be considered a melancholic temperament where feelings are generally considered quite stable, but Wundt showed how anxiety could be observed in combination with people who are 'quickly roused'. He suggested that what explains the melancholic, the choleric, etc., and what underlies the four temperaments, are the fundamental dimensions of 'changeability' and 'emotion'. The Eysencks (1985, p. 45) developed a schematic diagram that helps us picture what Wundt was getting at, as shown in Figure 3.2.

Recap questions

1 Can you recall what the four basic bodily substances are? How do you think we might be able to identify the composition of bodily substances in each individual?

2 Return to your list of friends and families you made earlier. Can you redescribe these people in terms of the four temperaments? Does this make more sense to you; does it dig a little deeper into their personalities?

3 Now try to locate your group of friends on the continuums emotional–non-emotional and changeable–unchangeable. Do the descriptions offered in Figure 3.2 connect with your experience of these people?

4 Do you think personality can change? If so, what would this tell you about some of the theory we have been considering so far?

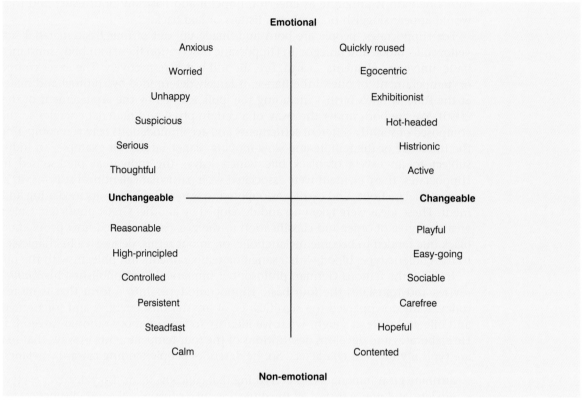

Figure 3.2 Diagrammatic representation of the classical theory of the four temperaments

Jung and personality theory

The work of Carl Jung (1875–1961) has become foundational for many working within personality theory. He identified a related but nonetheless different set of dimensions which he believed more accurately and more comprehensively explained distinctive personalities (Jung, 1923). After the break from his former teacher and colleague Sigmund Freud, Jung developed what was to become known as 'analytical psychology'. This approach proved extremely influential in what was to become the orthodox and mainstream teaching in management and OB. Management research conducted in the 1950s and 1960s, particularly that developed in the United States, bore the influence of Jung's potentially quite radical methodology and ideas. People like Henry Alexander Murray, David McClelland, Katherine Myers-Briggs, Abraham Maslow, and even Douglas McGregor, all display the trace of Jung's influence, however much they may have misused or abused his work.

Management research tends only to take those sections from Jung's voluminous writings that can be systematized and organized in ways that make it possible to produce highly proceduralized and rational laboratory-based, scientific research. Extracting only elements of his writing inevitably leads to distortions and on occasion encourages research that entirely misses the point of Jung's intention and ambition. Similarly, most of the popular OB textbooks tend to ignore or elide the puzzling, but potentially more rewarding aspects of Jung's work. This streamlining of his work is pursued in order to maintain the idea that there is an onwards and upwards development in thinking, by means of which we continually progress towards a state of more truth and accuracy. Those elements of Jung's work that do not permit simple formulaic prescription and application designed to serve and enhance a restricted and utilitarian agenda of organization are quietly forgotten (see Mullins, 1993, p.p. 107–109; Huczynski and Buchanan, 2001, p.p. 147–148; cf. Bowles, 1991; Case and Williamson, 2004). It is unlikely that Jung would have approved of what many have done with his work. This is particularly so where this has led to a belief in the possibility and legitimacy of cast-iron taxonomies of people.

The shadow world

Having said that, some simplification of his ideas is inevitable if we are to introduce the potential of his thinking. This will allow us to show at a later stage how his ideas have only been taken up and used to extend what we have been describing in this book as the 'entity view of organization'. For Jung, the individual is a participant in a 'collective unconscious'. As we can see from Figure 3.3 the collective unconscious and the personal unconcious form one part of a system called the 'inner world' out of which and through which the persona or personality is extruded to create a kind of surface between the inner and the outer world. At best we are only partly self-determining and autonomous agents and what we like to think of as 'the individual' is driven by a matrix of non-rational and unconscious forces. Indeed, for Jung it is possible that we are the mere playthings of agents and forces enacting a more universal drama staged in realms of existence that eclipse our more mundane reality. Something with which Harry Potter would no doubt concur! We are in effect, actors on two stages, split between two worlds. The rational everyday that we most immediately relate to, the here-and-now of the conscious world. But we are also simultaneously resident in another world that we can partly gain access to during certain modes of consciousness, such as our dreams. Despite its relative obscurity, this other 'shadow world' continues to exert its influence on us and determines some of the most profound things in our life, things such as destiny and fate (Jung, 1968).

According to Jung, some people are more in tune with the collective unconscious and find it easier to discover and navigate their way through it. You might recall that in our earlier discussion on the definition of personality we discovered that an important element in the term 'personality' is reserved for the idea of a role, as in our role in a play or a tale being told. We may be able to think, therefore, that in Jung's thinking, we have a role on another stage, or that – probably a more accurate reading of Jung – our role is yet to be found and shaped. Nonetheless, it is being spun out as a tale by forces and elements that are only partly available to the conscious, rational mind. We may well be then 'characters in search of an author' (Sievers, 1995), but an author for whom we are characters, little more than counters or gewgaws. For healthy, personal development, we must get in touch with and reclaim our share of the authoring function. It is essential that the two sides of one's personality are explored and cultivated; only out of the interaction of the two realms and the resolution of a series of dilemmas and contradictions thrown up out of this alternation is it possible for individuals to

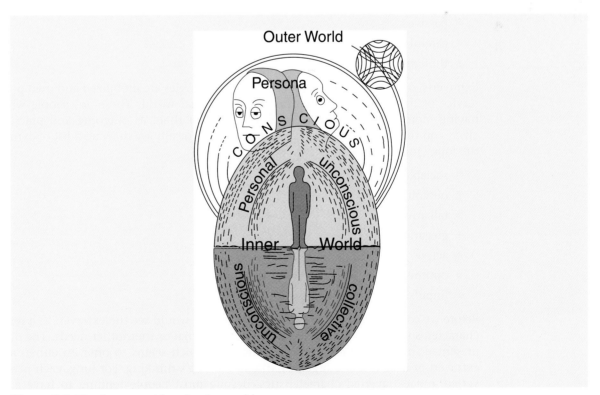

Figure 3.3 The inner world and outer world

progress in ways that allow them to fulfil their potential and destiny. Hence, for Jung it is the *contradictions* that are significant for understanding personality rather than those factors that tend to cohere on the surface to form personality 'type'. Personality type remains an abstraction and simplification, a unification that is simply an illusion or self-deception based on repression and control.

Thinkpoint 3.1

Corporate heroes People often fantasize about their role in organizations. Many corporate executives tell stories of organizational recovery in which they cast themselves in archetypal roles such as the hero, the saviour or the white knight (see Frye, 1957). Michael Edwardes' (1983) account of his time at the old British car manufacturers British Leyland is typical of this genre. Think of an organization where you have worked. This might even be your university. Are there people there who you might characterize or who see themselves in these roles? What role might you have played in this drama? Imagine a story that could be told of this organization in which the organization comes to assume a 'personality'. Is the organization friendly, perhaps, or is it maybe greedy?

Jung's theory of extraverts and introverts

In more basic terms it is the introverts who are more receptive to the force and influence of the collective unconscious. Introverts have a much more expansive and more developed inner world. For Jung, this inner world is not simply interior to the human subject, in the psyche or somewhere inside its bounded body, but is rather more like a vestibule that opens out into the more collective unconscious dimensions of existence. We tend to categorize introverts as those people who are characterized by the following traits:

- withdrawn
- unsociable
- prefers to be alone
- shy
- passive
- careful
- thoughtful.

Extraverts, on the other hand, are those whose energies are mobilized and used predominantly in the service of the rational pragmatism of the external world. These are people who we recognize as having more developed social skills. We think of them as outgoing and practical, those who are always on the go, getting practical things done. Typically we draw up a list of extraverts that includes the following characteristics:

- sociable
- outgoing
- talkative
- gregarious
- active
- optimistic
- impulsive.

Before we continue, it is worth recalling that Jung would see the extravert as a relatively unbalanced character, someone who is in flight from or in denial of their other needs. The dualism that is often presented in the textbooks, that classification which seems to offer an either-or – one is *either* an extravert or introvert – is largely anathema to Jung's thinking. For Jung, each person has both introverted and extraverted characteristics, despite most people tending to have a proclivity towards one or the other. In other words, they find it easier, or they are compelled to one end of the introvert/extravert continuum – that is, they may have a developed extraverted character, one that is mature or sometimes overdeveloped, but often at the expense of their more introverted traits, which are left somewhat in recession or abeyance. If these aspects of self are not attended to they can become quite problematic and unpredictable, in effect, forming a 'shadow personality' that dwells in a penumbra, eclipsed by the primary-dominant self. The fictional writings of the popular, contemporary Japanese writer Haruki Murakami explore the interplay of these two dimensions in the lives of his characters, notably in his book *Hard-Boiled Wonderland and the End of the World* (1993).

Exercise 3.2

Return to the list you made at the beginning of this chapter and see if you can identify people who you would describe as extravert or introvert. What is it that makes some of your friends extraverts and others introverts? Once you have redrafted your character list look again at the two columns in which you have tried to think about those elements of personality that are presented to others and those kinds of things that you feel are more representative of the real personality of your friends and family. Can you spot people who might have both extravert and introvert dimensions in their personality? Are there some who you might describe as 'unbalanced', or who are excessively extraverted or introverted?

Then, how would you describe yourself?

The Myers-Briggs type indicator test of personality

Isabel Myers-Briggs in collaboration with her mother Katherine C. Briggs developed what is widely considered to be a robust practical tool that enables psychologists to classify and identify people in ways they claim are consistent with the theory worked out by Jung in his 1923 publication, *Psychological Types*. According to the interpretation made by Myers-Briggs, the gist of the theory developed by Jung 'is that much apparently random variation in human behaviour is actually quite orderly and consistent' (Myers-Briggs, 1962, p. 1). Once the influence of certain key determining factors are isolated and understood the diversity of behaviour can be organized and classified in ways that form distinct personality types.

The research produced in preparation for the writing of the type indicator test originated out of a series of studies that first began back in 1942. The first period of research was focused on the writing of a number of preliminary questions, the responses to which were used to refine and develop the test. Myers-Briggs and her research collaborators tested these prototype questions on a group of 20 friends and relatives. Later, in the second stage of the research (1956–58), more than 200 new questions were tested out on 120 men and women, some of whom it transpires had prior knowledge and some familiarity with the emerging personality type indicator. Following this, the test questions were elaborated and clarified through a series of iterations and research projects conducted in North American Ivy League universities and then, later, among Pennsylvania and Massachusetts high school students.

People are the 'unique product of their particular heredity and environment', the author writes (Myers-Briggs, 1962, p. 51), yet there is a wide variation in the way people *accept* and *reject* different features of their environment. What we are receptive to and that which we respond to is unique to our personality and these responses tell us something about ourselves. For example, it is a truism that we all have different ways of looking. Yet it is also noted how some of us have a tendency to respond to colour or sound in the immediate empirical environment of our senses, whereas others are more disposed to reach out to the world through a more intuitive relationship, drawing on what some people call the sixth sense. People also differ in the way they reason. How we act and react to situations are also multiple and diverse. The satisfactions people seek and the goals or values that motivate them are likewise disparate and manifold.

This is not to say, however, that this diversity cannot be organized or classified. Myers-Briggs was looking to discover the underlying principles that would explain this constitutive make-up of people and hence personality. Despite this, the 1962 handbook is never clear whether people are endowed with a certain personality, in a sense fated by their birth and environment, or whether in fact people are compelled to make choices, the resulting decisions helping to form and shape personality. If this is the case, individuals remain, at least in part, autonomous, self-choosing agents, so that personality remains a more open and somewhat contingent product. This tension in the exposition reflects deeper, unresolved philosophical issues concerning the relationship between the individual and the environment. However, this ambiguity does not negate the value of the insights this research was able to generate, and indeed the tension between choice and determinism is suggestive of the struggle that individuals face in developing their own self-understanding.

The four preferences

Myers-Briggs writes that the basic differences that explain individuals 'concern the way people *prefer* to use their minds', and as she goes on to specify and clarify, 'specifically the way they use perception and judgement' (1962, p. 51; emphasis in original). She took from Jung the idea that there are four preferences that structure the individual personality, namely the degree to which people have a proclivity towards extraversion or introversion (EI), whether they prefer to use the senses or would rather rely on intuition (SN), the extent to which individuals are guided by thinking or feeling (TF) and, finally, their bias towards judgement or perception (JP) as a basic orientation in the world. We end up then with Table 3.2.

There are some quite subtle differences here in the way Myers-Briggs uses some of these terms, which stands in marked contrast to the way we have been using them up until now. What we do not get, for example, is the stereotypical list of features that normally accompany the category extravert and introvert. This probably reflects the legacy of Jung's work and the efforts of Myers-Briggs to respect his more rigorous understanding that extraverts and introverts are products of a more complex formation conducted at the level of the group through forces that are partly processed by means of unconscious dynamics. Both extraverts and introverts are valuable, she writes, and no judgement is intended as to which is a more useful or 'better' personality. Nonetheless, it is assumed that people are *either* extravert or introvert in essence, and the type indicator is designed to provide a way of identifying whether someone has a preference for extraversion or introversion. It is worth noting here that it is quite possible that somebody may be acting out as extravert, but in essence they are truly introvert. In other words they are going against their natural preference.

The SN index is designed to categorize people depending on their perceptual preferences. Do people tend to rely mainly on their five senses in their awareness of things – that is, what we might call the empirical faculties of sight, touch, hearing, smell and taste – to generate facts about the world around them? Or, do we rely to a greater extent on our more indirect form of perception, namely intuition, which is more in touch with unconscious dimensions of reality through which possibilities, ideas and associations are generated? Some people, for example, talk about a masculine 'hunch' in

Table 3.2 Index of personality preference: the Myers-Briggs personality index

Index	Preference as between	Affects individual's choice as to
EI	Extraversion or Introversion	Whether to direct perception and judgement upon environment or world of ideas
SN	Sensing or Intuition	Which of the two kinds of perception to rely on
TF	Thinking or Feeling	Which of these two kinds of judgement to rely on
JP	Judgement or Perception	Whether to use judging or perceptive attitude for dealing with environment

Source: Modified and reproduced by special permission of the Publisher, CPP, Inc., from Myers-Briggs Type Indicator Manual by Isabel Briggs Myers. Copyright 1962 by Isabel Briggs Myers, Inc. All rights reserved. Further reproduction is prohibited without the Publisher's consent. Myers-Briggs Type Indicator and MBTI are trademarks or registered trademarks of the Myers-Briggs Type Indicator Trust in the United States and other Countries.

their perception and awareness of events around them, and many will be familiar with the idea of 'feminine' intuition. We might think of this SN index as the way information about the world finds its way into the mind. Another basic difference arises in the way we use this information. There are individuals who predominantly use thinking, the logical and rational processes of the mind. Others tend to go with their feelings about situations and events.

Finally, the JP (judgement–perception) index is constructed to determine whether individuals tend to be driven by the desire to come to conclusions about the world, or instead whether they are more inclined towards the process of coming to an awareness of things around them. It is found that people who have a bias towards perception are not so preoccupied with forming conclusive judgements but, rather, remain open to the flux of possibility.

Individuals who take the Myers-Briggs test produce 'scores' that indicate the strength of E–I, S–N, T–F, J–P. In taking the test one scores points for each of these categories and the results are produced by calculating a simple sum from these figures. A typical test result might be E12, S26, T35, J20 indicating that this person is a combination of extravert, reliant on their senses and faculties of logical thought, and driven by judgement. The figure 12 is reached by the sum of all the extravert and introvert scores. In other words, there are more extravert responses than introvert; in fact, in this case, extravert responses exceed the introvert ones by 12. In total there are 16 different combinations: the popular ESTJ type is one kind of personality but there are also INFP types, ENTP personalities, ESFP and so on. In order to establish one's precise combination and strength of type factors one has to sit the test. The final version of the test takes the form of a questionnaire with 166 questions (Myers-Briggs, 1962), divided into three parts. There is no time limit but it is suggested that around 45 minutes is required on average. Parts 1 and 3 take the form of phrase questions in which you are asked to indicate a preferred response and Part 2 offers 51 word pair options where candidates are asked to express the one word that appeals to them the most. Let's take a look at some of these questions:

- **Part 1 Questions**

  41. In your crowd, are you
      - (A) one of the last to hear what is going on
      - (B) full of news about everybody

  48. Are such emotional 'ups and downs' as you may feel
      - (A) very marked
      - (B) rather moderate

  51. In your early childhood (at six or eight), did you
      - (A) feel your parents were very wise people who should be obeyed
      - (B) find their authority irksome and escape it when possible

- **Part 2 Word pair options**

  96. (A) affection   tenderness (B)
  103. (A) compassion   foresight (B)
  107. (A) make   create (B)

Myers-Briggs tells us that these questions and options have been devised and honed to *maximize* the chance of forcing option choices one way or another on the four type indicator scales. The assumption is clearly being made that people are either intuitive or sense orientated, which is evident in the very design of this test. Therefore, through trials and experiments those questions that proved most adept in separating people into this either-or categorization were the ones that were retained and used as models to refine and adjust the questionnaire.

In the original 1962 manual, Myers-Briggs offers a series of suggestions to indicate the benefits of the questionnaire: identifying likely career options for individuals; choosing the form of education through which different people would have the best chance of success – vocational as against academic, for example, or engineering as opposed to the arts; recruitment and selection decisions; and even more complex manpower planning decisions where different combinations and the balance between the different types are required in order to maximize productivity and efficiency. To illustrate some of these benefits Myers-Briggs (1962) provides in Appendix E of the manual a summary of a study conducted at a large bank: the case of the messenger girl.

The case of the messenger girl

Messenger girls were required to transport 'cylinders' and finished work between different departments of the bank. During the intervals between deliveries the girls were asked to monitor and maintain supplies of materials for the typists. The previous two incumbents in the post had both proved unsuitable and had not been particularly successful in their role. Type indicator tests were requested by the bank and then carried out on these two individuals. The first messenger girl was found to be an ESFJ, and as Myers-Briggs tells us one of the distinctive characteristics of the ESFJ type is over-talkativeness. In fact this particular employee had been periodically criticized for spending too much time talking with other employees. In effect she would turn every errand into a 'social occasion'. The second role holder was found to be as ISTJ, driven by her senses and just like the previous candidate, judgmental in disposition. By contrast she was introverted and thoughtful rather than extraverted and orientated by her feelings. Her problem had been judged to be one of inflexibility. Once engaged in a task she found it impossible to suspend current work that she was doing in order to run an errand.

On this evidence Myers-Briggs suggested the bank try an '– SFP type', the 'S for awareness of detail, F for desire to comply with expectation, and, above all, P for adaptability to the needs of the instant' (Myers-Briggs, 1962, E-3). The '–' indicates that the extravert/introvert index was not significant in this case. The appointment of a candidate with this type indicator proved to be highly successful.

Personality type and leadership style

More recent studies of leadership profiles and leadership success have extended this work of Myers-Briggs. Kuhnert and Russell (1990) and Church and Waclawski (1998), for example, have been able to identify the ENTP types as 'motivators'. While they may be 'high on themselves' and have an over-inflated sense of their impact on others, they are nonetheless perceived as transformational in their leadership style. What the studies define and identify as the 'innovators', on the other hand, tend to be orientated more towards the IN–P personality type. Recall that the '–' indicates that the TF (thinking–feeling) is not so relevant in forming this kind of approach to work; what is significant is the extravert–introvert dimension. The IN–P types have a more accurate awareness of how they come across to other people but they remain equally transformative by virtue of their capacity for innovation and creative problem solving. In essence their approach to transformation is different. Indeed they may facilitate transformation rather than seeking to drive it through by enthusiasm and force of personality. Introverted, in comparison to the motivators, and driven as much by 'feeling' as by 'rational thinking', the innovators are 'likely to be interested in theoretical and abstract thinking with a penchant for problem solving' (Church and Waclawski, 1998, p. 112), They are more concerned, the authors write, 'with the world of concepts than the world of social interaction'. We might conclude from this that the Myers-Briggs test proves useful in identifying leadership potential, but more than this, it helps us to see that there might be different routes to effective leadership. Each leadership style brings with it a different set of consequences, which tells us something about the kind of organization that is being created as a result of leadership.

Recap questions

1 What is the so-called shadow world and what is its significance for understanding personality and its management?

2 Define the four 'preferences' that Myers-Briggs identifies as the key components that help explain personality. How might this assist management?

Exercise 3.3

Think again of your group of friends sat round in the Dog and Duck pub. Can you guess how they might be classified under the Myers-Briggs type indicator (MBTI)? Are some of these people more judgemental than others, for example? What about yourself? Which 'type' of person do you think Dave Marsh from Experienced Records is looking for?

How legitimate do you think it is to identify people by way of the MBTI dimensions? You might be able to answer this question most effectively by considering whether you find it easy to make your choices from the example questions from the MBTI provided earlier in this section.

The science of personality

So far we have been looking at ways of identifying and classifying individual differences in terms of personality types and we have spent quite a bit of time exploring the influential Myers-Briggs personality type theory. While the Myers-Briggs type indicator is quite typical, there are in fact a whole series of alternative methods of identifying personality. In our suggested further reading, you will come across Raymond Cattell's 16 personality factor inventory (Cattell, 1965), the Minnesota multiphasic personality inventory (see Mischel, 1993, p.p. 181–185), and the California psychological inventory (Gough, 1957). The length of our exegesis on the Myers-Briggs type indicator, however, has been important in order to provide a little more depth than is typical of OB textbooks. Only in this way can we begin to show *how* Myers-Briggs arrived at her understanding of personality and provide the basis upon which you might begin to think *with* her personality type construct. Rather than simply expecting you to remember a list of bullet points we invite you to experience and think with the tools of this approach. Once you are able to do this you will then be in a position to explore some of the underlying methodological and theoretical commitments that are being made here, particularly with respect to the individual and individual differences. Without this careful exposition at this stage you will be unable to follow the analytical and conceptual moves that are made in the second half of the chapter.

An alternative to this personality-type form of taxonomy and its methods of allocation based on questionnaire responses is the observation and measurement of behavioural acts, or what is sometimes called 'action tendencies'. For many psychologists interested in personality the self-report questionnaire style approach, typical of type theories, lacks scientific rigour, accuracy or consistency. Ultimately, it is weak on explanatory power. Self-reporting is notoriously problematic and has a number of obvious methodological weaknesses: people do not always judge themselves accurately, nor can they always be trusted to do so; there is a tendency that people try to second-guess what the test is looking for; ideal images of self are often reported; and the inferences drawn from the test data by the psychologist can be very impressionistic, based more on a desire to fit people into pre-established categories than a commitment to understand the dynamics and consequences of personality.

Throughout their distinguished careers, Hans J. Eysenck and Michael W. Eysenck developed a whole series of scientific tests and sophisticated statistical modelling to identify and explain personality. The laboratory methods and their commitment to a rigorous model of scientific methodology based on the 'pure' natural sciences lends their work an air of certitude and authority. In their approach, personality is like any other scientific phenomenon. It can be explored and made observable through the application of laboratory techniques and explained by rational cause–effect type relations. The Eysencks' work is typical of the kind of scientific approach that leads to biological inheritance and geneticist explanations of personality. This is what we have called above an essentialist explanation, which is appealing for hard-pressed managers seeking quick-fix solutions to organizational problems but tends to be reductive and overly simplistic. Yet there is also a rather powerful and disturbing logic to the way in which this science unfolds and progresses. Over time it tends to constitute and *discipline* its object of study. The world responds and is made in its image. Pure observation, then, is a fallacy. Indeed, as science has discovered in its exploration of quantum mechanics, and in the study of chaotic systems and 'complexity', the very act of observation changes the existence and nature of that which is being observed (see Capra, 1991; Gleick, 1987). So, the language of science creeps into everyday managerial discourse and begins to act as a yardstick against which phenomena are measured and seen. The growing popularity of management techniques that assume the possibility of objectivity in identifying and measuring personality, and indeed that personality provides a reliable indicator of performance, is part of a trend in the management of organization that is seeking greater precision, prediction and reliability. The psychometric test 'normalizes' as its language and assumptions begin to be internalized and circulated by members of work organizations. For these reasons it is worth unpacking in some detail the Eysencks' work because of its influence on ways of understanding and studying personality and because it exemplifies in its most clear form the scientific approach to personality.

Trait theory

Unlike Myers-Briggs, the Eysencks begin from the assessment and observation of repeated actions that give evidence of the influence of inherent 'personality traits'. Traits are not directly observable, but

Image 3.2

SOURCE: © HULTON-DEUTSCH COLLECTION/CORBIS

can only be inferred. It is important to make these inferences because, in their absence, the regular and repeated activities of individual subjects could not be explained. Quoting Allport (1937, p. 129), the Eysencks note that traits are not active all the time, 'but they are persistent even when latent, and are distinguished by low thresholds of arousal' (Eysenck and Eysenck, 1985, p. 12). Traits are defined as the '*dispositional* factors that regularly and persistently determine our conduct in many different types of situations' (p. 17) and they are identified by way of observing statistically significant correlations between behavioural acts or action tendencies among test subjects. Personality type, for example, the 'extravert' or the 'introvert', is then a second order or superordinate average of correlated traits.

A personality type might be thought of as a higher order concept characterized by a greater degree of inclusiveness and it is, therefore, really nothing more than a series of inter-correlated traits. For most of their careers the Eysencks worked with the two major clusters of inter-correlated traits that formed around the types 'extraversion' (E) and 'neuroticism' (N). Extraversion we have already met, and once again it is here defined in opposition to introversion. Neuroticism is defined by things such as emotional volatility, inconsistency and unpredictable mood swings, and it is measured against stability and predictability. The traits or 'primary factors' that cohere around the neurotic type concept include anxiety, low self-esteem, feelings of guilt, tension, depression, displays of 'irrational' behaviour, being shy, moody or emotional.

Later in their careers the Eysencks introduced a third major type concept, namely 'psychoticism' (P), which they identified as an independent cluster of inter-correlated traits defined in opposition to 'impulse control'. Those who cannot control their 'impulses' tend towards the psychotic. Individuals are never identified as pure types – as extraverts or neurotics, for example. Rather, these are better thought of as 'mechanisms', the effects of which are 'normally distributed' (as in the bell curve used in statistical analysis) throughout the population. Extraversion, therefore, is 'felt' to varying degrees by *all* individuals. It tends to be exaggerated or over-developed in some people, but under-developed in others. The significance of these type concepts is that they allow us to define and make sense of regular, routine behavioural phenomena. We must remember that it is only behavioural phenomena that can be observed; extraversion for example, in itself, cannot be. Moreover, the importance of the three mechanisms – P, E, N – is that, statistically, these explain *most* of the variance in the behaviour of test subjects.

Factor analysis

In our everyday language we often think of people and describe their character as 'emotional'. Some might go so far as to claim that it is indeed a personality type rather than simply a trait. Why do the Eysencks then privilege only these three mechanisms and what is that defines a 'trait' as opposed to a personality 'type'? Furthermore, is this not a little reductive, reducing the subtle and variegated complexity of personality as it is typically experienced to two or three universal tendencies, which as they admit can never be observed in a pure state? The point is that the kind of research on personality conducted within that school of thought championed by the Eysencks is preoccupied with the question of statistical accuracy and prediction. So, while it is quite common to describe somebody's personality as 'shy', for the population as a whole – and as a statistical average – being shy tends to be associated or 'correlated' with a whole series of other traits that together form an aggregate personality type made up of all these traits. According to the Eysencks, being shy is not significant in terms of explaining behaviour and would form only one component that makes up introversion. The point is that neuroticism or extraversion are more powerful concepts than being shy and, as such, provide greater statistical accuracy in explaining behavioural variation. Another way of explaining this is to say that the set of people defined as neurotic personality types *contains* the population of individuals who are shy. In other words, a subpopulation of people who are shy will be moody and emotional, while others might have low self-esteem and suffer from guilt feelings. What they all share in common, however, and what explains a greater degree of their behaviour is that they all tend towards the neurotic dimension of personality. More formally, this technique of abstraction and measurement is called 'factor analysis' (Eysenck, 1950; Eysenck and Eysenck, 1985, p.p. 19–33).

The Eysencks' (1985) book *Personality and Individual Differences* provides a summation of their lifelong research in personality and it is from this text that we draw. In the second half of this publication the Eysencks describe the application and results of techniques derived from experimental laboratory-based science. These techniques are deployed in an effort to more rigorously isolate the determinants of personality and to more accurately identify its behavioural effects. In these tests the Eysencks attempt to examine and explain cognition and behaviour in terms of personality. Or, at least, they are attempting to *prove* that personality explains behaviour and cognition. From the statistical aggregation of their results researchers were able to identify patterns of stability and consistency in the repeated actions of test candidates in ways that seemed to demonstrate the influence of personality. So, in 'critical flicker fusion tests' it is found that extraverts are less able to discriminate and separate repetitive light flashes, which means that as the intensity of light increases – or the interval between the flashes decreases – the intermittent pulse resolves more quickly into what appears to be a continuous light stream. Similar results are found on acoustical tests. The Eysencks proposed two different theories or hypotheses to explain results like these – the inhibition theory (1957) and the arousal theory (1967).

Inhibition and arousal theory

According to the inhibition theory, extraverts are more prone to the build-up of 'reactive inhibition' during repetitive behavioural tasks. Testing certain forms of behaviour shows that extraverts are more quickly inhibited than introverts. Electroencephalogram (EEG) measurements show that electrical activity varies in different individuals: it would seem that some people have constitutively higher levels of activity than others. In terms of the later arousal theory, Eysenck (1967, p.p. 226–262) concluded that introverts have a greater degree of electrical activity or cortical arousal than extraverts. Crudely, we can say that individuals are compelled to seek stimulation if they are endowed with lower levels of arousal. Therefore, they need to stimulate cortical activity through interaction with others, or by finding external activities that will amplify their levels of arousal. Introverts are less prone to seeking external sources of satisfaction and arousal because there is inherently more activity going on in the viscera of their brain, in what is more accurately called the ascending reticular activating systems (ARAS; see Figure 3.4) (Eysenck and Eysenck, 1985, p. 197).

Drawing on a series of neurophysiological findings, the Eysencks note that the visceral brain is largely concerned with emotion. The more sensitive the visceral brain the more activity is stimulated in proportion to a given stimulus received at a peripheral sense organ. This stimulus then gets passed on through cortico-reticular loops to reticular formation, which is responsible for the organization of aggregate arousal levels. We can now explain why extraverts and introverts differ in their 'threshold limits' in response to critical flicker fusion tests. Threshold limits emerge out of a combination of the forces of arousal and inhibition, which are then regulated by the reticular formation system located in the human brain. The flickering of light registers less arousal in extraverts. Inhibitory reactions set in much quicker among extraverts, and, being less 'sensitive', their cortical arousal systems require a greater degree of stimulus. We might explain inhibitory reactions by recourse to that argument which suggests that extraverts, given their highly charged desire for external sources of stimulation, get bored more quickly; as they get bored extraverts become less receptive and their reactions slower to the intermittent pulse produced in the critical flicker test. The pulse becomes less defined and distinctive for the individual and begins to merge with the preceding and succeeding pulses of light. One can immediately see the appeal of these kinds of studies for work organizations that employ low skill workers for routinized and repetitive work tasks.

The Eysencks move from observed behavioural regularities and 'action tendencies' towards explanations at the level of personality, which is itself explained as a product of the neurophysiological system and the inherited physiological, neurological and biochemical make-up of the individual. On the basis of research and study into twins, comparing the behaviour and personality of those brought up together with those separated at birth, they argue that nearly two-thirds of the variance in personality as measured by the PEN dimensions can be accounted for by heredity. Personality, in other words, is genetically and biologically determined. Or at least that which is most significant

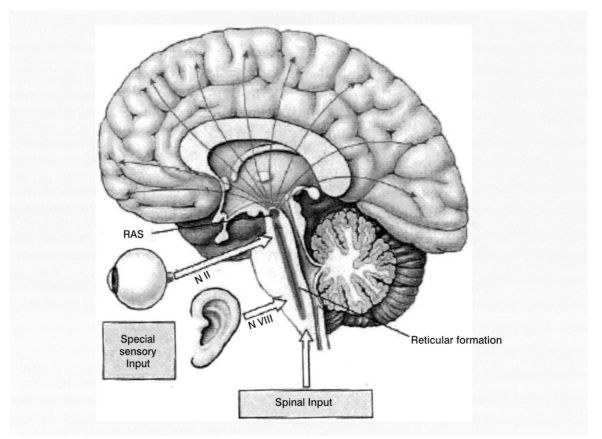

Figure 3.4 The reticular activating systems

in personality for the explanation of behaviour and cognitive abilities is largely hereditary. Their experiments and analysis will support interpretations that claim criminal behaviour is a consequence of personality, which as we have seen is itself the product of genetic inheritance.

Genetic re-engineering?

This kind of science pursues genetic explanation for social behaviour and seems driven by the quest to identify particular genes in order to explain criminality. Their approach reminds us of those studies, now discredited, that sought to explain sexuality and what was at one time called sexual 'deviance' (by which was meant essentially non-heterosexual tastes) by reference to genetic make up. If criminal behaviour and personality disorders could be explained at the level of genetics it is seductive and relatively simple to make what appears to be the next logical analytical move and conclude that genetic replacement will solve a whole series of social and organizational problems. Indeed, the Eysencks performed a great deal of research on physiological drug experimentation and extensive sections of their major publications report on behavioural modifications brought about by such interventions.

One can see from this why so much power has been invested into the development of techniques like psychometric testing. All kinds of developments are countenanced, from genetic screening through to the possibility of personality transplants (Huczynski and Buchanan, 2001, p. 167). Disruptive team members in work organizations would no longer be offered redundancy or expensive and time-consuming retraining but would simply have their genetic composition modified or re-engineered. Are we that far off given the widespread use of drug screening and psychometric testing in many work organizations? Following this logic one might easily be persuaded that mood and personality altering prescriptions for workers make good economic sense, especially for those engaged in highly dangerous team-dependent forms of work. It is probably in these areas that we will see the first application of 'corporate prescription' pharmaceuticals being used as part of a managerial strategy to improve productivity and efficiency. The military has always used body and mind altering substances, from bromide in tea during times of war, through to sleep depressant drugs for long-distance bomber pilots; but in the future we might see a more widespread use of battle-enhancing drugs. Given the kind of off-world outer space engineering routinely carried out by NASA these days, we might expect to find strong reasons for the development of certain organizational attributes like team cohesion by means of medication that alters or temporarily modifies individual personality.

The commercial and political incentives to identify specific bio-genetic codes in order to explain personality and behaviour are clearly vast. Recent developments in pharmaceutical products and the growth of bio-genetic engineering are themselves testimony to a deep-rooted societal belief in science, and evidence of a strong political will and commitment to science.

The 'personality' of science: Power and politics

At various points in this book we have sought to question the diverse assumptions and consequences inherent to particular forms of knowledge and research. So far in this chapter we have been studying theoretical and empirical research in personality that has developed out of the assumptions and practices associated with the natural sciences.

Our intention here is not to develop and extend a rigorous and lengthy critique of science. Texts that do this can be found in the 'Further reading' section below. However, we do need to make some preliminary observations at this stage if we are to prepare the ground and explain the move we make into more phenomenological and existential approaches to individuality and the self.

Biological and sociological explanations

One of the first things we notice is the restricted frame of reference for enquiry and analysis adopted in the work of researchers like the Eysencks. Their commitment to study the physiological and biological basis of personality ignores a whole series of other influences that undoubtedly shape personality. In addition to genetic factors there is surely a significant amount of social determination that explains personality. It seems common sense to argue that children brought up in parental homes where education and study have been valued and rewarded by parents who practise patience and tolerance will cultivate a personality undoubtedly different from a child who has been ignored, neglected or even abused. Likewise we might say that different types of work organization cultivate distinctive personalities among its employees; the causation, in other words, works the other way. Personality is the product of organization and socialization. This means that personality might well change over time as it is drawn out in various ways by differing forms and types of organization. The problem with this form of critique is that science values precision, accuracy and prediction, and what we have said here would seem a little imprecise and generalized. Science also tends to deal with macro-scale explanations, with aggregates and tendencies that hold for populations as a whole, rather than the isolated and exceptional or contingent case.

Most scientists, even the Eysencks, do not completely ignore social and environmental conditioning. However, what they argue is that on those dimensions that are being measured – psychoticism, extraversion and neuroticism – *most* of the causal influence can be identified and explained in genetic inheritance. Most of the measurable behavioural activities are likewise explained by these dimensions. So, environment is there, but its influence is relatively minor in areas of personality. Therefore it is not that significant. Moreover, if we push the logic of the Eysencks a little, we will find that environmental and social conditions are in fact understood to be an effect of personality – or, more strictly by the degree of relative balance within and across the dimensions of PEN. Anti-social behaviour and crime in the community is then a product or an outcome of certain types of personality (Eysenck, 1964; see also Gray, 1981). Extending this argument we would have to argue that it must also be certain types of personalities who find themselves unemployed, and so it is once again personality that is the cause of social deprivation. Of course, the argument threatens to become circular and self-reinforcing, unless, that is, theory can posit an underlying

Image 3.3

hereditary and genetic predisposition that finds expression in crime, unemployment and poverty. We are then left with the apparently simple solution, namely that to improve social conditions we need to more carefully select from the genetic pool. We can see here how close writers like the Eysencks come to eugenics. Indeed, throughout their research their work attracted a great deal of controversy and was, for many, fundamentally tainted by racist overtones.

One of the main problems with the search for genetic causation is that research sets off to seek explanatory factors for things like behavioural acts, personality or social problems, which are themselves not definitive or self-evident. The precise definitions of psychotic or neurotic are historically relative and remain subject to a great deal of dispute and debate. By this we mean that what might count as extraverted in the year 2006 will be different from how extraversion might be understood in 1006. Indeed it is probably unlikely that extraversion was even a meaningful category of analysis in pre-modern times. Just recently in the United Kingdom we have seen how the question of drug use and its legal regulation is constantly changing. What might have been described as a criminal act 20 years ago is now no longer identified as illegal. The 'criminal' is in fact a category socially constructed out of political and historical struggle. Consider the category of sexual deviance. Some 20 or 30 years ago homosexuality was outlawed and suppressed in many Western countries, but it has now become not only acceptable and rather 'conventional', but rightly celebrated as an expression of human diversity and freedom. If you look at any 'criminal' activity – even 'murder' and 'theft' – you will find that they are constantly being debated and negotiated. Not only historically, but also culturally and socially, even sub-culturally, such phenomena are understood and defined in a variety of ways. For one person an act might be murder, for another manslaughter, yet for someone else a crime of passion or the result of 'diminished responsibility' in which the causal agent is not deemed capable of exercising reason or recognizable forms of consciousness.

Thinkpoint 3.2

A 'criminal' personality?   Can you think of ways in which the very act of legislating, of inventing laws, is also an invention of criminality – or indeed represents an act carried out by criminals? In this respect it might be worth recalling the fact that the early founders of nation states acquired their land through the victory and conquests of war. Reflect on the foundation of the United States of America or Australia, and the treatment of their indigenous populations. Following this logic through, might we say that it is the rebels, the outlaws (Nelson Mandela?) – in one sense the criminal 'personalities' – who are absolutely essential for the birth of the modern nation state. How then might we distinguish 'the law' from 'outlaws', the criminals from the legislators? What are the implications of this for work organizations? Use the six key concepts as a way of approaching this question.

The methodology of science

One of the causes and consequences of the application of natural science methodology to the study of personality is the assumption that personality can be studied *as if* it could be measured and categorized in taxonomic form. Personality is approached in exactly the same way as the Mendeleyev table presents the 'periodic elements'. Moreover, its basic categories of analysis – society and the individual – operate like opposites, a dualism to orient and organize its study. This dualism opens up a problematic space *between* the two categories, which science then takes as its task the burden of explanation. As we have seen, for the Eysencks, social phenomena are explained as the product of personality. Extending this we could say that poor organizational performance and inefficiency is the product of weak selection techniques that are failing to identify and eliminate the 'carriers' of weak genetics. However, if the two poles of this dualism – society and individual – cannot be categorically defined or stabilized, these kinds of results and extrapolations are discredited.

We have seen that the 'criminal' personality is at best an historically relative phenomenon. At a more disaggregated level of analysis the constituent factors of personality – psychoticism, extraversion and neuroticism, for example – are themselves historically determined and contingent. If we continue our analysis into the deeper and even more fine-grained material substance of the human, into the 'physio-chemical' and genetic elements of the human, we find that these too are scientific concepts: words, labels and categories invented to 'map' the human organism. Analysis of this kind proceeds by way of carving up and labelling the human body. In order to be able to think and advance this procedure

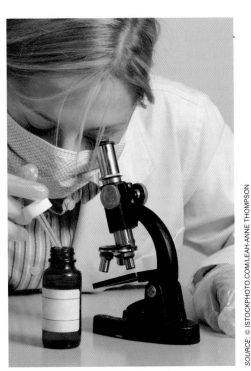

SOURCE: © ISTOCKPHOTO.COM/LEAH-ANNE THOMPSON

Image 3.4

it must be assumed *a priori* that the body is, and then treated as if it were, a skin-bound, isolatable phenomenon. As an entity it is further broken down into the minutiae of more singular 'atomic' entities that are understood to interact by way of discrete cause–effect relations, which then gives rise to more macro-scale observable outcomes (see Foucault, 1973). It is as if the human body contained its own programme whose logic unfolds independently of its external environment and then finds expression in personality. The problem is that the more we look into the detail the more we find that causes are themselves effects of other causes in what amounts to a complex spiral of relations. We soon realize that the macro (the 'social' or the 'environment' in mainstream personality research) seamlessly interfolds with the micro. The dualism between the macro and the micro, or the interior and exterior, does not hold. It is, then, at best a convenient fiction, a separation that renders impossible – *yet simultaneously generates the quest and belief in* – the isolation and definition of a first cause, a prime-mover, or in terms of personality, explanatory factors at the level of genetics and biology.

Science is forced to delimit its area of study so that it can artificially arrest this confusing interplay of forces and relations. It does this by carving out in controlled laboratory conditions phenomena that can be made demonstrable and explainable in terms of reductive cause–effect connections (see Latour, 1987).

Science harbours a self-generating and reproducing logic, and out of this dynamic it both feeds and keeps going. It is able to self-justify ever more research funding to endlessly pursue discrete, simple causality, in part because the influence of the excluded domain – that which falls outside the purview of their test experiments – inevitably feeds through to disrupt and distort the behaviour of those factors that *have been* labelled and isolated. In its pursuit of precision and accuracy, a degree of inconsistency and uncertainty in definition, in test variable behaviour, and relations between variables, is unavoidable where modern science is practised. Unforeseen consequences and side effects of science only further compel what is presented as an ever greater need for science. And the desire for a final root explanatory cause is so seductive and attractive, grounded as it is in our desperate modern quest to seek economy and simplicity. We break down phenomena into discrete parts that operate in delimited and defined areas of the human body so that we might identify the influence of a principal variable that provides a 'target' for simple remedial forms of intervention and resolution.

The logic of this practice can be seen in the way we instinctively react to ailments and disease. So, we accept the diagnosis that labels and defines our difficulties in terms of a depressive personality or example. Depression has now become common parlance and the term is bandied around so casually that people even begin to self-diagnose (Wurtzel, 1995). We then understand that depression is caused by low serotonin, a chemical triumphantly declared to have been isolated and observed under laboratory conditions. Therefore we take Prozac, which has been proved to alter 'serotonin' levels in the human brain. But why low serotonin? Moreover, are some people constitutively made up bio-chemically with low serotonin, or are serotonin levels themselves symptoms of something larger, more complex and intangible? Is there something more fundamental causing the low serotonin? Might serotonin be some kind of early-warning system for something that is going on more broadly in the human sensorium, itself part of a more 'holistic' set of forces and relations that traverse those fabricated divisions between the inside and the outside, the body and the environment, mind and matter, the social and the personal (see Bateson, 1972; and especially Pirsig, 1974 for an extended discussion)?

This brief introduction to the epistemology of natural science helps us to see that the very starting points that the Eysencks adopt for the study of personality are assumptions that lack any history or contextual sensitivity. They begin their research with an attempt to seek descriptive classification before they go on to examine ways of explaining personality and its behavioural consequences. But can you see how their assumptions are those typical of the modern Western world? What they decide is important to look for in the first instance – traits, which can be found located somewhere within a skin-bound entity called the individual – would not make sense to someone from the African or Far-Eastern world. It would not even occur to them that personality was a psychological phenomenon or in some way an outcome of the different mixtures of 'traits' associated with being 'cold', 'tough-minded', 'lively', 'venturesome', suffering from 'guilt feelings' or being 'irrational' (Eysenck and Eysenck, 1985, p.p. 14–15). What does it mean to be 'cold', for example? How to identify or understand what 'cold' might mean is highly dependent on historical and culturally specific meaning and attribution. Despite the claims made on behalf of rigour and objectivity, and their efforts to eliminate elements of subjectivism from scientific enquiry, it is important to remember that the Eysencks devised their own self-reporting questionnaire in order to establish and classify individual differences. The authors give the impression that they are starting their enquiries with zero bias so that the world can yield up its 'truths' and 'laws' – truths and laws, moreover, which are assumed to exist independently of scientific observation. However, they generate their questions out of an *a priori* list of traits that are assumed to make up the types 'extraversion', 'neuroticism' and 'psychoticism'.

The circularity of science

Traits deemed to make up the type 'neuroticism' are listed as 'emotional', 'moody', 'shy', 'irrational', 'tense', 'low self-esteem', 'guilt feelings', 'depressed' and 'anxious'. The questions they go on to construct are then designed to subsequently identify these characteristics. In brief, these questions *follow* the initial assumptions made about what it is they are looking for, which can be clearly seen in the following examples taken from their questionnaire: 'Are you often troubled by feelings of guilt', and 'Do you often feel that life is very dull?'. On the basis that there is a statistically significant correlation across responses to these questions, therefore generating a 'population' of 'yes' answers, this pattern of response can then be labelled with – or deemed to confirm – the category 'neuroticism'. It is always ambiguous whether the category comes before or after the experimental endeavours, suggestive of an element of bad faith or disingenuous methodology. The Eysencks try to measure the extent to which people self-report on feelings, behaviour, attitudes and values that will provide evidence of the existence of different traits. So, they ask a question 'Do you enjoy meeting people?' (Eysenck and Eysenck, 1985, p. 84), for example, as a way of identifying extraverts, and 'Does your mood often go up and down?', as a test question for neuroticism. What is important to think about first is what it is that motivates or prompts the researchers to even begin thinking about asking questions about mood swings or meeting people. There must be some expectation that extraverts enjoy meeting people, whereas introverts do not, and that neurotics suffer from mood swings whereas the emotionally stable do not. Questions are constructed and phrased in ways that betray the author's *pre-understanding*, or pre-scientific basic commitments to the meaning, classification and definition of personality. In sum, the procedure is *circular*.

Moreover, we would clearly want to ask whether the person devising the questions and the respondent share an understanding about things like 'self-esteem', 'mood swings', 'anxiety' or 'guilt'? Historically and geographically we know that there are many societies for whom the category 'guilt' would have no meaning, and even within our own there may be respondents who understand this question within the context of a moral or religious meaning and others who might attribute guilt simply to vague, temporary states of mild discomfort. We could extend this analysis to question what precisely is meant by 'troubled'. Is this something more than simply 'awareness' or daily reflection, for example? The point is that there is no overarching definition of guilt or 'troubled', and each respondent is likely to understand the term in a number of different ways. Positive responses to this question might then be picking up all manner of social attitudes rather than being indicative of some underlying individual trait or personality type. One cannot avoid the conclusion that what might be being recorded by the Eysencks is simply a categorization of prevailing social and historical norms, organized by attribution to 'personality', in which case we might be led to the interpretation that what is taking place here is little more than a rationalization of current social mores and attitudes.

As a form of rationalization or explanation, this is very restrictive and conservative. We have seen how these explanations can be used to justify pharmaceutical intervention and genetic modification as ways of tackling perceived 'personal', 'behavioural' or 'social' problems. These 'problems' are themselves historically relative, always contested and shifting, and better seen as the product of prevailing relations of power (between class, gender, race, etc.). Consider, for example, the category 'hysteria' and its indiscriminate application to women during Victorian times (see Foucault, 1979). It was not only male doctors who went about labelling women in this way, but because of the popularization and circulation of medical discourse in social relations at the time, fathers and husbands began using this term in their description and treatment of women. Just like the category 'depression' or a 'criminal personality', a 'neurotic' or an 'introvert', or what we will later discover is a 'proactive personality', these terms are *historical constructions* (that is, a definition of what it is to be normal rather than abnormal). As constructs they become 'normalized' through the circulation of discourse to provide ways of categorizing and then disciplining individuals. It would take a strong (or foolish?) individual to resist the common-sense language of the everyday and resist self-identification on its basis. Instead of tackling issues at this level in terms of history, power and social relations, however, the Eysencks simply provide grounds for changing or 're-engineering' the individual in order to make people conform and fit into predominant social values and categories.

Science begins from a set of assumptions that it can only return to by way of findings and conclusions. It can never escape its basic assumptions; or, in other words, the bias that it puts in to the research. In itself this might not be such a problem, or it might be an inescapable problem for any kind of research or intellectual activity. However, what we might want to do is to question the *value* of these starting points. With the Eysencks what we do find is an austere and obstinate commitment to statistical precision, prediction, accuracy and clarity in experimental and test procedures. This is their overriding preoccupation in all of their writings. Their texts are predominantly composed of explanations that describe the methods of statistical data generation, the identification of test variables and correlations, methods of evaluating the statistical significance of their findings, and a critique of other researchers in their field focused once again around the purity and exactitude of their statistical procedures and laboratory conditions. In fact, given that this is ostensibly a text on personality, there is very little discussion about people and personality; seldom do we encounter in their text what we might recognize as a real, flesh and blood person or personality.

Recap questions

1 What is meant by psychoticism, extraversion and neuroticism?

2 What are the typical features we associate with a scientific approach to personality?

3 Describe and illustrate the idea that there is a circularity or 'catch 22' logic to the practice of science.

4 What is the power of science?

Summary

In the detail of the primary texts we have discovered that there are some logical and methodological problems with this natural science approach to personality research and, moreover, a number of potentially dangerous and politically regressive consequences. On a more general level there are other considerations worth briefly mentioning:

- The behavioural predictions that are made are often of an abstract and simplistic kind that can only be produced and reproduced in strictly controlled laboratory conditions. The 'pursuit rotor test' (Eysenck and Eysenck, 1985, p.p. 268–9, 271), for example, which seeks to classify people by introversion and extraversion, involves using a metal stylus to follow a high-speed revolving metal disc. Subjects are artificially isolated from environmental or external sources of interference, which might be attended to or interacted with in a variety of ways by 'real' subjects involved in the complex, ongoing accomplishment of work tasks in organizations. These reactions might be as important to an understanding of personality as the abstract behavioural regularities produced in scientific laboratory conditions.

- It is questionable whether the Eysencks are really interested in personality at all. The root motivation of their research is the prediction of behavioural activity. For most of the time these behavioural acts are extremely routine and simplistic, or automatic, physiological and physiognomic responses to physical, chemical or electrical stimuli. While it is bound to throw up statistical regularities and correlations, to extrapolate back and explain the bimodal distribution or pattern of responses to the influence of two, or in their later research, three primary dimensions of personality is, nonetheless, reductive in the extreme. Moreover, it represents an attempt to conflate or juxtapose what might be better thought of as two partially autonomous realms of the human subject: the unreflexive, automatic workings of the physiognomic and physical, and the inconsistency and unpredictability of the psyche and the emotions – which might be equally important for the understanding of personality, at least if one is interested in a more nuanced interpretation of people and their personalities.

- Human subjects are understood to be what the British sociologist Anthony Giddens (1976), following Garfinkel (1967), calls 'cultural dopes'. In other words they are deemed to be mechanistic and machine-like in their interactions with the world of stimulus and need, lacking self-awareness and the capacity to mould and shape their response or, at a more complex level, their personality. Responses to stimuli, for example, are considered to be automatic and it is assumed that personality is persistent and stable over time. There appears to be little acknowledgement of learning, development or change. Indeed this possibility is excluded at the very outset of their research where the assumption is made that subjects inherit their personality by virtue of genetic and biological programming. It is almost as if people with, for example, neurotic personalities – accepting the validity of the term 'neuroticism' for the moment – are condemned to neuroticism, unless of course there is some genetic intervention or some biological re-engineering. Yet, from experience, we know that people do change. Freud treated many patients for neurosis and his writings report a considerable amount of success in his interventions and therapy. In addition it seems reasonable to assume that people become aware of their personality; they might realize, for example, that they are extremely impatient, but over time by attending to and developing other facets of their personality, aspects of their self that have not had a chance to mature, they are able to reduce or eliminate the play of impatience in their character make-up. Here, we are beginning to think of personality in a radically different way from the approach typical of the natural sciences.

Applications in organization and recent case studies

Despite these methodological and theoretical problems, problems that can only really be settled or resolved at the level of political and ethical debate, the promise of this kind of science for someone like David Marsh at Experienced Records is that things like job performance can be measured and determined by personality. Seibert, Kraimer and Crant (2001), for example, have recently built on work that has identified what is called a 'proactive personality', which is considered to be a predictor of career success (measured in terms of salary progression, promotion within two years and career satisfaction). Proactive personalities are those people who assume and exercise 'personal initiative' in work organizations, who affect environmental change, and who go beyond normal role expectations – that is they are driven to go the 'extra mile'. Barrick and Mount (1991) in testing the influence of what is called the 'Big Five' personality dimensions – extraversion, emotional stability, agreeableness, conscientiousness and culture (see Digman, 1989; 1990; Norman, 1963) – find that across a range of jobs the degree of conscientiousness is the most important factor in determining high job perform-ance. If personality can be thought of as a phenomenon that is essential and inherent to an individual, stable and enduring over time, something that can be accessed and quantitatively measured through methods such as the psychometric tests, and if the results of studies linking personality to job performance are robust and reliable, then we may have some confidence that personality type is a useful predictor of job success. However, there are a lot of 'ifs' here and we still might not be able to determine the direction of causality – i.e. whether personality is cause or effect of environment. Moreover, if someone has a personality that indicates high career potential, we may still not appoint because we may fear their ambition might mean they are footloose or impatient for promotion and salary increase such that we might easily lose them to competitor organizations. Once we make these acknowledgements we are beginning to recognize that appointment, progression and success in organizations might be driven by another agenda: one of power and politics.

Idiographic approaches to personality

The limitations associated with the hard sciences approach to personality and the hidden political assumptions and consequences latent within its practice have motivated some writers to adopt what are sometimes called **idiographic** methodologies. We have seen how the **nomothetic** orientation to the study of personality is motivated by the desire to uncover objective, law-like mechanisms that are deemed to explain personality and to locate individual personalities within relatively simple dimensions of classification and comparison. As we have seen most of this research emerges out of a concern with biology and behaviour. In the idiographic sensibility, the emphasis is more on the detailed, richer texture of personality that stresses change, evolution and development, where differences are emphasized and understood to be much more subtle, shifting and complex. For the Eysencks (1985) these approaches are unsatisfactory because they tend towards a 'nihilistic' state of affairs in which there seems to be no underlying categories or mechanisms to establish order, classification and understanding, and no attempt by idiographic writers to construct overarching norms and definitions. For the Eysencks, a consequence of this is the unacceptable submission by science to the idea that anything goes, in which we can no longer identify differences or similarities because of the lack of any common measure or standard. They claim we end up with a confusing disorder that says little more than everybody is different – but without any substantial scientific basis for being able to say this. However, this critique proves to be misguided and poorly focused. Freud, often considered to be one of the pioneers of a psychodynamic approach (see below), especially in his earlier writings, betrays as much concern with mechanism, laws, scientific methodology and classification as many writers considered to be guided by the nomothetic method.

Within the corpus of writings labelled 'idiographic', authors take greater licence to interpret and elaborate more speculatively on personality in ways that do not try to convince the reader with techniques of mathematical and statistical application and measurement. Instead their writing invites recognition and often an intuitive sense that their account is persuasive or correct. This is not to say that idiographic approaches lack rigour, consistency or veracity, only that the methods by which these standards are achieved are different. Idiographic writings are constructed with their own rigour and demonstrative precision as the writer builds up from simple principles that provide grounds for more sophisticated elaboration and reasonable speculation. Idiographic approaches are not so much concerned with experimental testing or behavioural prediction and precision. Indeed, the idea that personality can be distilled and categorized into observable and measurable 'behavioural variables' is anathema, a methodological preoccupation that is deemed to lose sight of personality in direct proportion to its ever more desperate effort to pin it down into the exactitude associated with classificatory grids and tables.

When one considers that emotional and spiritual dimensions of human life form important elements in personality, we might see why laboratory testing and experimentation remain crude and inappropriate. One may consider the capacity for love and empathy, for example, to be the most important dimensions of personality, but most of us would still find it difficult to believe that it was possible for science to define love and persuasively demonstrate or convince us that there was a 'normal distribution' of love against which the normal and deviant could be measured. Indeed, one of the most important aspects of idiographic writing is the relative demotion of personality per se and a recontextualization of personality within a broader and more expansive realm of self and being that draws in aspects of our being that we do not normally attend to. This is of particular significance when we seek to understand the theory and practice of management and more broadly the motivation and behaviour of individuals and collectives at work in organizations from within a more critical sensitivity. However, as a word of caution, there will be few who doubt that science will one day, if it has not done so already, claim to have found the genetic code for love or the sphere in the brain from which love derives.

Within the more idiographic (literally self-writing) approach there are a number of important theoretically distinctive schools of thought.

Psychodynamic approaches

Here the emphasis is on the development of personality over time, in which the individual is conceived as a processual phenomenon that over time is challenged to resolve a series of unconscious internal conflicts. The writings of Sigmund Freud (1900; 1933) pioneered this approach to personality and encouraged researchers to begin to see how behavioural oddities or personality problems were surface symptoms of more profound, underlying disorders in the psychic structure. He identified three interacting components in an individual psyche – the ego, id and superego. In Freudian analysis the ego is understood to be the mechanism that resolves primal desires, those desires that seek satisfaction through the discharge of the id, with the values and norms of society that demand their repression. The superego is the psychic mechanism that represents these social norms, and the ego is balanced in between these two competing pressures. It is from Freud's early work that we trace the

and even cosmological interaction. Personality eventually comes to be thought of as a relatively minor component or surface manifestation of this much deeper ontology or what it is to be human or a 'being'. It is in these terms that Maslow then raises the question of motivation. 'Most drives are not isolatable', he writes (1970, p. 20). Indeed, particular desires are not important, he goes on to argue. What is important is what these specific *moments* of desire 'stand for' in terms of the whole. Here Maslow acknowledges that this whole includes unconscious dimensions – of which we might only be dimly aware. In fact, in the detail of his exposition Maslow goes so far to say that one can never exhaustively list drives (1970, p. 25); drives are not discrete isolated entities but fluctuating and dynamic phenomena that can only ever be artificially stabilized and defined. The individual is at the vortex of overlapping and multiple motivations and these motivations are continually shifting and becoming, never ending, fluctuating and complex. In other words, the human being is never satisfied. One way to read and interpret Maslow would be to understand the human as a being that is condemned to frustration and incompletion. This becomes most explicit in his 1971 work *The Farther Reaches of Human Nature*. Personality is best seen then, perhaps as an *interruption*, an accommodation reached between man and the forces of nature that conspire to shed man of his all-too-human masks and costumes (recall that the word personality is formed out of the idea of *persona*, the face-mask worn by ancient Greek actors on stage).

Transcendence and self-actualization

Throughout his writings Maslow develops and employs a quite sophisticated understanding of the role of the human being in the world and, beyond that, to the position of the individual in the realms of a spiritual cosmos. He draws upon a diverse range of Western and Eastern philosophy, literature and esoteric mysticism to articulate his vision to readers. We might well wonder what could possibly be the managerial lessons of this understanding of personality. What we can say is that management and organization would look radically different from the way it does today and only the most far reaching of changes in the way we organize and manage work will provide the conditions within which personality is liberated from the shackles of control and inhibition. Practical examples of organizations that come closest to embodying this vision of human relations might be the Israeli kibbutz communities or local community self-development/spiritual groups. In the main these organizations tend not to be driven primarily by economics or the values of consumerism and materialism. Organizations such as these have struggled in recent years and have faced great difficulties in promoting alternatives to the expansion of consumerist values. On the other hand, there has been an upsurge of interest in alternative communities, ecology groups, collective forms of living, cooperative organizations, nomadic communities and groups of land reclamation activists that are suggestive of the possibility that there are more people dropping out of mainstream society in order to develop something more healthy and meaningful (Melucci, 1986; Crossley, 2002).

We might be suspicious of its up-beat, west coast American presentation, but the intention of Maslow's critique is radical and clear. Self-actualization might only be possible once we relinquish the control that the ego maintains over our experience and vision of the world. Maslow talks here in terms of 'peak-experiences' and self-actualized cults of people experimenting with sex therapy and 'encounter groups' as ways of overcoming our routine confinement in isolated and individualized forms of being. For 'peakers', sexual orgasm is a doorway into some mystical union with the cosmos (see Maslow, 1970, p.p. 181–195). This is wild stuff! And far from the sterilized rendition we are offered in management. It is only when we realize the scale and ambition of Maslow's work that we can really make sense of his exposition of a hierarchy of needs and its significance for understanding personality (see Chapter 2).

Box 3.2 Definition of transcendence

Literally this means to rise above or go beyond, to overpass or exceed all known limits. For some it means an achieved state of being that leaves behind all earthly and material worries or concerns, to be disconnected from all that is contingent and accidental in human experience. A transcendent personality would be then someone who is 'free'.

Critique of Maslow

There are certainly many problems and objections to Maslow's understanding of motivation and personality. From the perspective of this book his work appears idealistic and essentialist. That is, many of the assumptions that inform his views about self-actualization are those typical of an educated, male and middle class individual born and brought up in the United States of America. Self-actualized people are 'strongly ethical' with 'definite moral standards', we are told; they are democratic and will give their 'honest respect to a carpenter who is a good carpenter' (Maslow, 1970, p. 168). We can see from reading sections such as these how his writing becomes at times rather smug and self-satisfied. Self-actualized people seem to be remarkably similar to Maslow's own group of friends and acquaintances. In this respect his work is an autobiography but one that lacks the humility of critical reflexivity. He shows little awareness how partial and limited a view of the world this actually is and that democracy, ethics and morals, in its detailed specification and meaning, are all historically and culturally relative and far from the 'absolutes' he seems to assume. The dynamics that operate in his hierarchy of needs are also peculiarly abstract and insulated from any detailed treatment of social conditions and social forces. Individuals are assumed to be inherently driven by the quest for knowledge and self-actualization, as if this was something they were born with, rather than something that is produced historically through the discipline and regulation of social relations. There is no recognition of political economy, nor of the persistence of structured patterns of power and inequality in which it is only the relatively privileged who are able to think and aspire to this version of self-actualization. Moreover, many of the features of self-actualization might be better thought of as the historically relative products of modern capitalist society – ideals and images that are fostered and cultivated through education, mass media and commercial advertising.

We also lose sight of some of the precision around personality. We might have raised objections earlier to the categorical taxonomy of personality, but might personality 'type' offer quite a useful way of approaching the question of the individual and individual differences? At the very least it might provide a starting point for analysis. Maslow implies that everything, from the introvert to the extravert, the neurotic and psychotic, the narcissist to the obsessive compulsive, is subsumed into a universal dynamic where personality is explained away simply as a symptom of an interruption in the drive to self-actualize. There might be very good reasons why we might want to retain the category 'neurosis'. It helps understand and explain forms of human suffering as the product of forces operating at the level of the family, arising out of abuse or neglect, and interacting with wider forces of economic competition and political economy. An understanding at this intermediate level of abstraction is more likely to give rise to the desire for practical action and intervention within the family and community. The metaphysical speculations that Maslow indulges are far more likely to motivate private study and withdrawal; the questions he arrives at seem to demand forms of concentration and meditation that encourage solitude and withdrawal in ways that might paradoxically aggravate current social trends. The privatization of social relations, individualism, isolation and, ironically enough given his critique of science, the 'atomization' of individuals (see Houellebecq, 2000), might be made even worse if thoughtful and critically inclined people were to withdraw from the practical struggles of the everyday.

One reason for this neglect might be that Maslow is not really interested in personality; for Maslow what is more important is the question of the 'self' or the more generalized struggle of the human being. Perhaps one of reasons for this limitation is that Maslow arrives at these questions out of the study of personality, but he tries to inscribe his more universal interests and concerns back into the rather more limited discourse of personality and motivation. In the next section we briefly question the value of the categories of the 'individual' and 'personality' before looking at the more existential tradition of writers such as Ronald Laing and Erich Fromm. These writers are able to avoid some of these problems because personality gets relocated within the wider dynamics that operate across what is understood to be an existential and political context. We do not lose sight of the specificity of the

Recap questions

1 What is distinctive about the phenomenological approach to personality?

2 Outline Maslow's critique of science. What is a self-actualized personality?

3 How realistic are Maslow's ideas in the context of organization today and to what extent could they be applied to the management of personality?

here-and-now but we also retain the analytical power provided by an awareness of metaphysical and ontological depth. In part, these moves are made by shifting the focus of concern from personality to identity.

Self-actualization We might think of the ecstasy and spontaneity associated with self-actualization in terms of the kind of experience reported by mystical initiates or gold winning Olympic athletes, the artist realizing their vision or a collective musical experience. Consider the possibility of self-actualized experiences in the workplace. Is it possible that organizations can be developed in ways that might motivate individuals so that they can achieve self-actualization? What kind of workplaces might these be? Could it be that participants at clubs and raves are not simply consumers of an experience similar to this but are actually *workers* put to work by organizers and managers of these entertainment factories?

The end of the individual?

Today one feels responsible only for one's will and actions, and finds one's pride in oneself. All our teachers of law start from this sense of self and pleasure in the individual as if this had always been the fount of law. But during the longest period of the human past nothing was more terrible than to feel one stood by oneself. To be alone, to experience things by oneself, neither to obey nor rule, to be an individual – that was not a pleasure but a punishment; one was sentenced 'to individuality'.
(Nietzsche 1974, The Gay Science, *p. 117)*

The historical construction of 'the individual'

We still live in times where it is almost impossible to think that 'the individual' might not exist or that it may be a recent social 'invention', an arbitrary category in which we have all been disciplined and through which we are made to think. Society openly celebrates the individual: we believe ourselves to be individuals; we style our lives in *individual* ways; we have *individual* opinions; we believe at work the *individual* should be rewarded for their contribution; in sum, we sense that our self ends at our skin, which is a kind of container out of which we look on other skin-bound containers of individuality. There was a time, however, when we thought of ourselves not so much in terms of individuals but more as role holders in a wider collective, almost like an extended body-part of some collective being. Native Americans and the indigenous 'Australian' population, labelled 'the Aborigines' by English colonial settlers, lived in this way (see Chatwin, 1987; Devereux, 1996), and today there are many parts of the world in which this is still thought. It is possible to understand many Eastern and Islamic communities or societies, for example, in that way. Residues of this form of being in the world still survives today in the West, evident in the ideas of 'groupthink' and the behaviour of groups such as football crowds or rioting mobs where there seems to be a collective personality at work and where the rational, autonomous individual seems to dissolve or disappear (see Le Bon, 1960).

Group dynamics

We have also been looking at a number of theories and ideas in personality studies that might indicate that we are not simply individuals, but rather personality 'types'. In some versions of this theory the world might be made up of only 16 different types, or various combinations across three different personality dimensions. However, at the same time, many of us will think of personality as that which is the most distinctive feature of our individuality and share that experience of a generalized social pressure to have and express an exciting and fabulous, unique personality. This is what Dave Marsh at Experienced Records tells us he is looking for. Remember, however, how we earlier discovered that the word 'personality' also embodies the sense of 'mask', a fabrication or an illusion – something that is invented and acted out. It is possible that we only play out our personalities on the stage of social life but that we have become so good at our performance we have forgotten we are acting? We then need to ask who or what is doing the inventing and what are its benefits and disadvantages. In another tradition of thinking, developed out of the work of Melanie Klein and Wilfred Bion – the group dynamics approach (Bion, 1961; see also Kreeger, 1975; Lawrence, 1979) – it is possible to understand personality as a (partly unconscious) 'negotiation' between the individual and the group where personalities are selected and developed for the needs of the group. We can also think of this at a more societal level. This might sound a little fantastical but consider what would happen if six extremely extravert individuals formed a team to work for an extended period of time in a confined space. Six squabbling extraverts could not survive, and over time 'individuals' are likely to begin shaping and developing different personalities – or roles.

Exercise 3.4

In your seminar group organize a reading of Belbin's (1993) book *Team Roles at Work*. Share your ideas about what it is that makes a successful team. Then, reflect once more on your group of friends, perhaps those who have been sitting sharing a drink in the Dog and Duck. Are there any 'personality clashes'? How does your group resolve these if and when they break out in the open? In what ways could the group be 'disciplining' all of you to 'give room' to each other while maintaining bonds of friendship. What is missing from Belbin's analysis?

Identity and existential anxiety

One way of understanding the ambiguities around personality and individual differences is to recontextualize this problematic within an understanding of identity. Ronald Laing (1965), drawing on his study of the French philosopher Jean Paul Sartre (1958), argued that what was significant in the dynamics of individuality and personality was the broader 'existential' questions confronting each of us, namely questions around 'meaning' and 'purpose' in a world that seems to abandon each of us to transience and uncertainty within a vast universe that is beyond our comprehension – seemingly cold and remote, without ultimate direction or purpose. Each individual must inevitably face up to this insignificance but also to their own mortality, a finality that inevitably comes but we know not when (see also Brown, 1959). This combination of certainty and uncertainty means that we may not complete or fulfil our own objectives, our life may still remain unfinished, without 'closure'. We may then wonder if our life can be given any overall 'shape' or 'purpose', whether each of our everyday activities – the moments or 'parts' of our everyday, the routine and humdrum, through to the painful and distressing – can be provided with some overall contextual meaning. If the 'parts' do not add up to serve some greater value or ideal, some purpose or meaning, they can become disconnected and fragmented. We are then in danger of losing motivation for the everyday. It quite literally does not make any sense.

For the existentialists this provokes what is called 'anxiety' – a vague, disturbing unease with the world and ourselves, but a feeling that cannot really find a reason or object for that which is the cause. In response to this anxiety there is a tendency to withdraw into ourselves. Routines become reassuring, we seek the comfort of the familiar, the bosom of our family or friends where we can be ourselves, or at least where we can express that 'identity' with which we have become most comfortable. To not know who we are, or to face a future in which we might lose our sense of identity – the change from adolescence to adulthood for example – is to find ourselves in situations that are sometimes overwhelming. So overwhelming, in fact, that we retreat from those situations that are threatening; alternatively, we might regress or 'act out' a reassuring version of our self, but which might nonetheless be inappropriate, selfish or uncreative. The reassurance of the familiar identity prevents us from opening up new experiences and new circumstances. At the same time, faced with the enormity of possibilities in an universe where we seem insignificant, it is perhaps understandable that many think that all there is to rely on is ourselves and our sense of selfhood. In these circumstances our identity becomes a treasured 'resource'. Responding to these difficulties in a way that avoids depression, neurosis or more extreme forms of 'personality disorder' requires that the individuals assume personal responsibility for their situation and seek out their true 'authentic' self – which is not so much an inherited essence deep somewhere in our subjective interiority but more a question of decision, of creativity, or a leap into that which we will become. There is a certain assumption of fate in this analysis. As Nietzsche writes, we must learn to love this fate: *amor fati*. Only this can provide purpose and meaning. Everything else, from money, property, consumption, motivation at work, to passing pleasures, are simply 'surrogates' in comparison to this more existential leap, surrogates that are ultimately unsatisfying and only serve to amplify greater desire but frustration in chains of tension and release.

Ronald Laing: The schizophrenic self

Laing draws on this kind of existential thinking to chart a series of case studies that show the psychological dangers of remaining 'inauthentic' – that is, individuals who fail to stand up and choose, to discover and create their own identity, and instead act out that which has been 'given' to them or that has been 'demanded' of them by parents, family, community or religion. We might add that in today's world it is commercially developed role models – images in media and advertising, pop stars, movie actors, and maybe even characters in computer games – that usurp and colonize our anxiety for identity and self-meaning. Trying to maintain a public self, to be that person which is expected – to be 'happy', 'cheerful', 'good' or 'successful', for example – can lead to what Laing calls 'split personalities' through which we develop a person whom we display to society around us whilst knowing that this is only an act to disguise or cover up that person who we truly believe ourselves to be, the inner real self. Maybe the cover-up operation is maintained because of a sense that there might be nothing behind the costumes and masks, no real self that is struggling to get out. To sustain this act stokes up even greater levels of insecurity as we are forced to continually monitor and maintain our performance, to 'keep our guard up' and not let anyone see cracks in our performance. This causes us to spin around ever faster in self-reinforcing cycles of insecurity and identity, a 'snowballing' effect that motivates individuals to bolster the identity of their inauthentic selves but in ways that only serve to generate its equal and opposite reaction, the fear of its loss, or disconfirmation, or rejection. (Note the massive insecurity of those who continually seek 'respect' and the competitiveness that ensues as to who deserves more 'respect', who has not paid sufficient 'respect', etc.) For Laing this doubling or 'divided self' is inevitably doomed to become entrenched and pathological and helps explain the dynamics and condition of schizophrenia. Laing recognizes that the source of this problem does not reside in the individual; rather the schizophrenia is social. The family, and more broadly modern society, wired up with forces of competition and material greed, both *exaggerate* restlessness, desire and insecurity and offer images, ideals and models to (albeit temporarily) placate and relieve anxiety. Perhaps one of the most telling recent examples of this is the fashion industry and the images of beauty it organizes and disseminates of women, provoking an endless chase to acquire the latest 'look'.

Erich Fromm: The authoritarian and marketing personalities

Fromm (1942) works from a similar position to Laing, but what he emphasizes is that anxiety is provoked by the 'fear of freedom', a fear that he traces historically to show how modern secular society (note: his concerns are with the West) no longer provides enduring social structures within which man can find his role or place. Nor does modern society provide any unifying, religious answers to

Image 3.5

SOURCE: © ELLEN MIRET. TITLE TAKEN FROM A WORK BY HONDI DUNCAN BRASCO

those existential questions concerned with purpose and meaning. Without a universal foundation of belief and truth, modern (wo)man is rendered far more vulnerable to anxiety. But at the same time she faces a greater degree of choice and freedom in what to do and what to believe in following the demise of the medieval 'moral economy' (see Thompson, 1968). The emergence of capitalism seemed to sweep away all that which appeared solid, to unleash one of the most turbulent periods of social change and unrest. Faced with such uncertainty man has a tendency to look towards strong leaders to provide direction, guidance and reassurance. These leaders are themselves products of changing social and economic conditions and express on behalf of the group what are collective

SOURCE: © CORBIS

Image 3.6

anxieties. At the same time they seem to offer a role model of fortitude and identity in response to this distress and worry. Perhaps leaders are those who feel the threat of uncertainty and insecurity the most, or are those cynical enough to perceive these conditions as an opportunity to acquire status, power and leadership by amplifying those fears while offering simple and seductive solutions. Writers routinely point to Hitler and his ascendancy in 1930s Germany as an example of this kind of demagoguery and charismatic leadership, but we see it all around us today, whether we think of Thatcher in Britain during the 1980s, Ronald Reagan in the United States during the same period, Milosevic in Serbia during the 1990s, and even George Bush junior in more recent times.

Fromm argues that the modern political-economy stimulates the emergence of an 'authoritarian personality', and when we look around the world of work organization we can find many examples of such authoritarianism. During the 1980s, for example, there was a debate about the rise of the 'macho manager' (Mackay, 1986). In more recent developments such as total quality management, downsizing and business process re-engineering (Hammer and Champy, 1993; see Grint, 1994; Willmott, 1995), with its language of obliterating the organization, of 'shooting' those resistant to BPR (see Strassman, 1994), and taking a hammer to rules and procedures, we can see how prevalent and pervasive is the spread of authoritarian personalities (see also Jackall, 1988).

In his later writings, Fromm (1976) was drawn to consider the effects of the rise of mass consumption, advertising, marketing and entertainment, and found that in response a new type of personality was ascendant, what he called the 'marketing personality'. This type of personality is preoccupied with image and the 'right' presentation of self to others. People are becoming increasingly superficial, Fromm argues, driven by an insatiable desire to purchase the latest fads and fashions as social interaction, dominated by gossip and display, becomes ever more vacuous. It is almost as if we might be able to posit a relationship between collectivism and individualism. As people withdraw from communitarian and collective commitments, and the 'quality' of collective sociality declines, people take flight to seek more individualized forms of satisfaction, security and meaning. Communities where people once knew each other as neighbours and extended families and with whom they were able to share their preoccupations and concerns have declined, to be replaced by ever more fragmentation and isolation characterized by more insular and privatized forms of living. One symptom of this is the increased investment in privatized forms of home security as people seek to protect their own possessions and encourage criminals to seek out those properties less well protected by intruder alarms. Of course, this is a competition. Burglars become ever more sophisticated as they get used to newer forms of domestic security, and so one must always keep ahead of the Jones's. Meanwhile insurance costs increase at the same time that the fundamental basis upon which wider existential 'life insurance' and security can be nurtured and established is further eroded.

Exercise 3.5

In your seminar group discuss the problem of access to books and other library resources at your university. Consider some of the books on the 'Further reading' list at the end of the chapter. Who among the group thinks that the way to achieving the highest marks in coursework and exams is one in which we let individuals chase and accumulate material on their own without regard for others? If we *collectively* organized and shared the material in a way that raised the average mark but reduced the marks of those individuals who would have been top of the class, who would say there has been an improvement in educational standards? What do you think is of most benefit to society? Which of the two alternatives might raise the most anxiety? In your discussion can you identify certain personality 'types' from the different positions they take with respect to this debate?

Key contributions and major controversies in the field: Mainstream and critical

Our chapter has introduced the key contributions and major controversies in the field of individual differences, personality and the self. We have found that the mainstream approaches, building on the foundations and nomothetic orientation of writers such as the Eysencks and Myers-Briggs have developed increasingly refined and forensic techniques of observation, measurement and classification that 'explains' personality and its effects in work organization and wider society. Myers-Briggs has achieved some impressive results showing that the successful selection and deployment of staff to posts in organizations depends upon the correct identification of personality. Leadership style studies have shown that there is not one type of personality that can be considered 'successful' in terms of leadership; rather there are different types of leaders, with different types of personalities. According to Myers-Briggs we all have distinctive types of personalities based on the different ways we are predisposed to use our minds. Different personalities develop different leadership styles – some more motivational in style, while others are more innovative, but both styles can be successful modes of transformational leadership (Kuhnert and Russell, 1990; Church and Waclawski, 1998). It would all seem to depend on what we do with the type of personality we have, or how we can make it work for us, or what we do with our inherited dispositional traits. Belbin (1981) shows that successful teams need to seek a mix of different personality types. Recently, research examining the influence of the so-called Big Five personality dimensions finds that differences in job performance can be explained most by conscientiousness. The correct identification of this personality dimension would seem then to be an essential task of management in the recruitment, selection and promotion of its human resources so that it can retain and enhance its productivity and competitiveness.

However, it is here that we gain an insight into the limitations of this kind of research. For all their research and funding, all the years of study and publication, Barrick and Mount (1991) find that conscientiousness is the most important factor in explaining job performance. Moreover, this is a statistical finding discovered through extensive abstraction, measurement and calculation. But the finding is circular, and perhaps a little obvious. It amounts to saying that conscientious people work hard! Or, hard-working people are conscientious. It is equally plausible to argue that good job performance, with its attendant rewards, will encourage conscientiousness. In other words, the cause (conscientiousness) is in part an effect (high job performance). Also remember that conscientious people worked hard for Hitler's Third Reich. This suggests that we may need to think more critically about how we evaluate and study people at work and their organizational behaviour. The scientific abstraction of personality through the identification of discrete components that can be measured and statistically correlated with 'effects' such as job performance, transformational leadership or organizational success, is a technical orientation to the study of management and organization. It does not ask what are perhaps the more important questions. Why is high job performance a good thing, in itself? What kinds of work should be encouraged? Is personality the cause or consequence of wider social and historical conditions and influences? Can personality be thought of as a category or entity? Does it unfold and become manifest as the result of a predictable genetic or biological programme? What are the consequences of carving up the phenomena of the individual in terms of personality, rather than say identity.

These are the type of questions that mark out what is distinctive about the critical study of OB. Its main contribution has been to shift the terms of the debate away from a rather narrow and pragmatic preoccupation with personality towards a more expansive reflection on the question of identity. For the critical scholar the restrictive methodology of the natural sciences is the most controversial aspect of the research and study into personality and the individual at work. They question the extent to which 'personality' can be identified with any degree of accuracy, particularly statistical accuracy, and doubt that it remains predictable and consistent over time. One of the major achievements of writers such as Maslow, Laing and Fromm is to return the study of the individual to a richer and more expansive ontology of being, one that draws on 20th century developments in the philosophical understanding of our being – in particular by Martin Heidegger and John Paul Sartre. Critical studies have taken us out of some of the limitations associated with the preoccupation with personality. The study of identity invites a consideration of those deeper questions that seem to haunt our being, namely questions concerning the meaning or purpose of our being, the accident of our birth or the imminence but unpredictability of our death – questions that act as a source of motivation and preoccupation for members of work organizations.

But identity and its preoccupation, the constant search for its definition or expression and confirmation by others, can equally be dangerous and inhibiting. Critical scholars of identity have helped elucidate how there is a basic anxiety that arises from 'being in the world'. We constantly seek to flee this anxiety through the quest for an (egotistical) robust identity, which encourages efforts to acquire power and control over others, to crave identity confirmation through the allure of consumption, worldly goods and the marketing of 'idealized' identities. Contemporary organization is riddled with pathological forms of identity, schizophrenic tendencies, and authoritarian and narcissistic personalities. This helps us to see and understand organization as fractious and disorderly, and unstable and volatile – something that requires sensitive and sophisticated management.

However, in conclusion, perhaps the major controversy in the field is a deeper one, relating to a series of political differences in values and commitments that are fought out at the level of philosophical assumptions concerned with ontology and epistemology. Ontology refers to the way in which we understand and envision the relation between self and the world, or how we understand the type of world or cosmos in which we *believe we live*, or in which it makes sense for our lives and is therefore *relevant* to our preoccupations and concerns. The restricted scientific approach to personality works within but does not raise or question these bigger concerns. It seeks an economized representation of the world that renders things precise, knowable and definitive, and it is driven by the desire for control and order so that we can continue with(in) the immediacy of our secular and practical affairs. Critical studies of personality might risk being utopian or impractical but they invite a more imaginative relation with our world, one that raises deeper questions and possibilities for organization and our future, collective being in the world.

Summary

We began our study of personality with a fairly rough and ready schematic division that has become popular common sense, and we have been able to trace this understanding back to Hippocrates and the ancient Greeks. We then saw how Carl Jung deepened the exploration of personality. Drawing on astrology and alchemy he located personality within a much deeper, more complex cosmology that identified the influence of archetypes and the collective unconscious in the formation and distribution of personality types. Myers-Briggs attempted to standardize and proceduralize the work of Jung in ways that made it appear amenable to a more rigorous scientific method and application in mainstream management thinking and practice.

The Eysencks extended this scientific approach through the exercise of sophisticated statistical measurement and laboratory experiments. Preoccupied with the biological basis of personality and behavioural manifestations of different personalities, we noted how the Eysencks are motivated by classification, order and control. Our critique of the scientific method showed what an impoverished understanding of personality this was and helped us to clarify how these 'positivist' methods (see Chapter 1 and Burrell and Morgan, 1979) are not only consistent with the entity view of organization but through their interventions in social relations, actively contribute to forces that seek to render organization a machine-like entity. Although often denied, this remains inherently political.

The idiographic orientation to personality offers a richer and more generous comprehension of personality, showing how it is more 'open', shifting and changing over time in response to our deeper struggles and questions about freedom and meaning. Formed out of learning and social interaction, personality appears to be more of a processual phenomenon, and as part of wider organization this helps us to understand the process view of organization. The legacy of idealism, humanism and essentialism evident in the work of Maslow, but also in the work of psychologists such as Carl Rogers, Erik Erikson, and Heinz Kohut, which we have not had time to explore (but references can be found in the 'Further reading' section at the end of this chapter), restricts the scope of its analysis and conceals deeper *existential* struggles that make more sense when conceived in terms of identity. Shifting the analytical terrain to the question of identity also helps restore a concern with wider structures of power and inequality. This brings into focus the interactions between the individual and political economy. When we combine the existential with political–economic dynamics we can begin to understand how identity seems to offer a seductive retreat or defence against powerful forces of dissolution, disorder and insecurity. At the same time, identity can become unhealthy and pathological. Paradoxically, all of us could then be prey to the conservative appeal of the entity view of organization: anxious and inhibited, we might be unable to question or engage with the predominant relations of power and politics that restrict the development of the concept view of organization – development that relies upon imagination, risk, political 'voice' and (perhaps) *personality*.

CASE STUDY 3.2 Dave Marsh 'loses his rag'

'I've been working here for near on 15 years and I can say that new recruit we took on from McConcept University is a *disgrace*. I'll be hauling his ass up here first thing tomorrow morning . . . make no mistake, you know, like . . . When was it? . . . last year? Look, make no mistake, mate. You'll see. How long has he been with us? How long? What is it . . . what is it? . . . two years? I can't believe it . . . I tell ya, I mean . . . it's dumb and *disgusting*. Hicks from the sticks.'

Dave Marsh, the director of Human Resources at Experienced Records, is shouting down the phone to Richard Dream, Area Manager for the South-East UK market, responsible for the signing and development of new acts. His Australian accent is extremely broad when he gets angry in this way. He looks a little dishevelled; his hair is wild, his tie hanging loose from his shirt. Sales have not been going well. Banging his head against the window he kicks the radiator pipe as he stutters and salivates in his efforts to explain what is going on. Hitching up his sharp designer trousers suspended by distinctive red braces he lights up the stub of one his hand-rolled Cuban cigars, from a collection that under more propitious occasions he likes to flaunt and offer around to other executives. He's just had these cigars monographed with his initials to celebrate his recent promotion to the board. He now holds an executive position on the board of Experienced Records. Today, he is surrounded by newspaper cuttings and his office desk is spilling over with mountains of paperwork. The office walls are covered with framed black and white photographs of famous rock and roll artists of the past, smiling, with their arms around a younger looking Dave. You can pick out pictures of people like Mick Jagger, Eric Clapton, Paul McCartney and Chuck Berry. 'I'll throttle him, he sputters. 'And to think, I took the final decision on that psychometric test.'

One of Richard's team, Rowland Curtis, has been photographed in a London nightclub with new teen-act sensation, 18-year-old Cindy Tinkerdale, both apparently drunk and taking drugs. Cindy has recently become engaged to clean-cut boy-band favourite, Justin 'SurfBoy' Didsbury. One of the photographs reveals Cindy's underwear as she is trying to step into a London black cab. The photo spread is not at all flattering. In one, her eyes look intense and glazed; her make-up has run and smeared, and she looks as if she has been crying. Dave explains that he has been receiving 'serious flack' this morning from what he calls the 'ponces and queens' in media and public relations. 'I'll have him shot', Dave splutters. 'When we first took him on he was all extra-hours and hard work, in the background, working with the boys from image development, attending the right launches . . . Cindy was one of his creations! Now he's gone and potentially ruined her . . . I mean *maybe* we can angle a

drugs and rehabilitation story for her, get her on the chat shows, childhood neglect, too young in the business, learning the error of her ways, you know, that kind of thing. She's only had her first single out.' Dave hurls his play basketball at the net in the corner, narrowly missing and crashing into a stack of old copies of *Management Today*, which Dave has been collecting to acquire the latest trends and buzz words in management theory. 'If it wasn't for the test results I'd have tried to persuade Jeni a little more. She's a real cutie. You know, she was interested and she would have taken the job. She just needed a bit more encouragement. I remember that line she used after we told her that Rowland had got the job: "Oh well! I don't really see myself at the front end of the business, out in the limelight, meeting all those stars, that sort of thing. You know I'm probably better in the back-office admin" – and I could tell she hadn't put everything into the interviews and tests. I hate Rowland Curtis!'

Question

1 Using the ideas around Hippocrates' four temperaments, sketch out some of your initial thoughts about the various personalities in this case study at Experienced Records. Then compare this to what you can say of these characters by applying categories used in the Myers-Briggs test.

2 How do you think the Eysencks would understand these different characters? In what ways are they likely to explain these different personalities? Reading through the case study again, what might be being overlooked by the trait theory of personality?

3 Compare your impressions of Dave Marsh here with that impression you formed from Case study 3.1. What do you think might explain the apparent change? What kind of personality is he? Why did Dave 'lose his rag'?

4 What is the significance of personality in the organization and work that takes place in Experienced Records and the music industry more broadly? Is there anything here that Ronald Laing's work might help us to see or understand?

5 Think now more in terms of identity. What are the possible struggles that all these characters might share? Can you spot 'inconsistencies' in these characters? Consider the possibility that people might not be simply 'identities', but rather a multiplicity of different, half-formed identities, perhaps with one dominant at most times and in most situations.

6 Consider the influence of wider power relations and politics. How does power work in the music industry? What is holding Jeni back from career ambition, for example?

Further reading

General texts in personality theory

Mischel, W. (1993) *Introduction to Personality*, fifth edition, Orlando, FL: Harcourt Brace College Publishers.

Pervin, A. and John, O. P. (1996) *Personality: Theories and Research*, seventh edition, Chichester: Wiley.

Classic treatises

Eysenck, H. J. (1967) *The Biological Basis of Personality*, Springfield, IL: Charles C. Thomas.

Freud, S. (1933) *New Introductory Lectures on Psychoanalysis*, Harmondsworth: Penguin.

Fromm, E. (1942) *Fear of Freedom*, London: Routledge and Kegan Paul.

Maslow, A. H. (1954) *Motivation and Personality*, New York: Harper and Row.

Humanist studies: Idiographic approaches

Rogers, C. R. (1980) *A Way of Being*, Boston: Houghton Mifflin.

Erikson, E. (1968) *Identity: Youth and Crisis*, New York: Norton.

Kohut, H. (1977) *The Restoration of the Self*, New York: International Universities Press.

Critical studies of identity at work

Casey, C. (1995) *Work, Self and Society: After Industrialism*, London and New York: Routledge.

Collinson, D. (1992) *Managing the Shopfloor*, Berlin: De Gruyter.

Watson, T. (1994) *In Search of Management: Culture, Chaos and Control in Managerial Work*, London: Routledge.

Websites

http://www.humanmetrics.com/cgi-win/JTypes2.asp
Discover your personality by completing this online test based on the Myers-Briggs personality type indicator. Rather crude, but it is fun to do. Best taken with a large dose of salt!

http://www.colorquiz.com/
An even more simplistic modelling of personality based on the idea that colour preference can give clues to your personality. Again, quite amusing, albeit a little superficial; the principles upon which this is based remain rather unsound both theoretically and methodologically.

http://www.ship.edu/~cgboeree/perscontents.html
This website provides material on all the major theorists and writers we have been looking at in this chapter. You will find material here on Freud, Jung, Eysenck, Erikson and Fromm.

http://www.radpsynet.org/
A critical and radical organization committed to exposing and examining the politics and ideologies that inform most mainstream psychology. Papers, essays, critical reviews and an online discussion forum provide a space for people to question and interrogate many aspects of psychology. Includes important essays relevant to the study of personality.

References

Ackroyd, S. and Thompson, P. (1999) *Organizational Misbehaviour*, London: Sage.

Allport, G. (1937) *Personality*, London: Constable.

Barker, J. (1999) *The Discipline of Teamwork: Participation and Concertive Control*, London: Sage.

Barrick, M. R. and Mount, M. (1991) 'The Big Five personality dimensions and job performance: A meta-analysis', *Personnel Psychology* 44:1–26.

Bateson, G. (1972) *Steps to an Ecology of Mind*, New York: Ballantine.

Belbin, M. (1981) *Management Teams*, London: Heinemann.

Belbin, M. (1993) *Team Roles at Work*, London: Butterworth-Heinemann.

Best, S. and Kellner, D. (1991) *Postmodern Theory: Critical Interrogations*, London: Macmillan.

Bion, W. (1961) *Experiences in Groups*, London: Tavistock.

Bowles, M. (1991) 'The organizational shadow', *Organization Studies* 12:387–404.

Braverman, H. (1974) *Labour and Monopoly Capital*, New York: Monthly Review Press.

Brown, N. O. (1959) *Life Against Death*, Middleton, CT: Wesleyan University Press.

Burrell, G. and Morgan, G. (1979) *Sociological Paradigms and Organizational Analysis*, London: Heinemann.

Capra, F. (1991) *The Tao of Physics*, third edition, London: Flamingo.

Case, P. and Williamson, G. (2004) 'Alchemy, astrology and retro-organisation theory: An astro-genealogical critique of the Myers-Briggs type indicator', *Organization* 11(4): 473–495.

Casey, C. (1995) *Work, Self and Society: After Industrialism*, London and New York: Routledge.

Cattell, R. B. (1965) *The Scientific Analysis of Personality*, Baltimore: Penguin Books.

Chatwin, B. (1987) *The Songlines*, London: Jonathan Cape.

Church, A. H. and Waclawski, J. (1998) 'The relationship between individual and personality orientation and executive leadership behaviour', *Journal of Occupational and Organizational Psychology* 71:99–125.

Collinson, D. (1992) *Managing the Shopfloor*, Berlin: De Gruyter.

Crossley, N. (2002) *Making Sense of Social Movements*, Buckingham: Open University Press.

Devereux, P. (1996) *Re-Visioning the Earth*, New York: Simon and Schuster.

Digman, J. M. (1989) 'Five robust trait dimensions: development, stability, utility', *Journal of Personality* 57:195–214.

Digman, J. M. (1990) 'Personality structure: Emergence of the five-factor model', *Annual Review of Psychology* 41:417–440.

Edwardes, M. (1983) *Back from the Brink*, London: Pan.

Eysenck, H. J. (1950) 'Criterion analysis: An application of the hypethetico-deductive method to factor analysis', *Psychological Review* 37:38–53.

Eysenck, H. J. (1957) *The Dynamics of Anxiety and Hysteria*, London: Routledge and Kegan Paul.

Eysenck, H. J. (1964) 'The biological basis of criminal behaviour', *Nature* 203:952–953.

Eysenck, H. J. (1967) *The Biological Basis of Personality*. Springfield, IL: Charles C. Thomas.

Eysenck, H. J. and Eysenck, M. W. (1985) *Personality and Individual Differences: A Natural Sciences Approach*, New York and London: Plenum Press.

Eysenck, H. J. and Rachman, S. (1965) *The Causes and Cures of Neurosis*. San Diego, CA: R. R. Knapp.

Fincham, R. and Rhodes, P. (1999) *Principles of Organizational Behaviour*. Oxford: Oxford University Press.

Foucault, M. (1973) *The Birth of the Clinic*, London: Tavistock.

Foucault, M. (1979) *The History of Sexuality, Vol. 1*, Vintage: New York.

Foucault, M. (1989) *Madness and Civilization*, London: Tavistock.

Freud, S. (1900) *The Interpretation of Dreams*, Harmondsworth: Penguin.

Freud, S. (1933) *New Introductory Lectures on Psychoanalysis*, Harmondsworth: Penguin.

Fromm, E. (1942) *Fear of Freedom*, London: Routledge and Kegan Paul.

Fromm, E. (1976) *To Have or To Be?*, London: Abacus.

Frye, N. (1957) *Anatomy of Criticism: Four Essays*, Princeton, NJ: Princeton University Press.

Gabriel, J. (1999) *Organizations in Depth: The Psychoanalysis of Organizations*, London: Sage.

Garfinkel, H. (1967) *Studies in Ethnomethodology*, Englewood Cliffs, NJ: Prentice Hall.

Giddens, A. (1976) *New Rules of Sociological Method*, London: Hutchinson.

Gleick, J. (1987) *Chaos: Making a New Science*, London: Abacus.

Goffman, E. (1959) *The Presentation of Self in Everyday Life*, Harmondsworth: Penguin.

Gough, H. G. (1957) *Manual, California Psychological Inventory*, Palo Alto, CA: Consulting Psychologists Press.

Gray, J. A. (1981) 'A critique of Eysenck's theory of personality', in H. J. Eysenck, (ed.) *A Model for Personality*, Berlin: Springer.

Grey, C. (1994) 'Career as a project of self and labour process discipline', *Sociology* 28,2:479–497.

Grint, K. (1994) 'Reengineering History', *Organization* 1,1:179–202.

Hammer, M. and Champy, J. (1993) *Reengineering the Corporation: A Manifesto for Business Revolution*, London: Nicholas Brealey.

Herzberg, F. (1968) 'One more time: how do you motivate employees?', *Harvard Business Review* 46,1:53–62.

Hirschhorn, L. (1988) *The Workplace Within: Psychodynamics of Organization Life*, Cambridge: MIT Press.

Houellebecq, M. (2000) *Atomised*, London: Heinemann.

Huczynski, A. and Buchanan, D. (2001) *Organizational Behaviour: An Introductory Text*, fourth edition, London: Pitman.

Jackall, R. (1988) *Moral Mazes: The World of Corporate Managers*, New York: Oxford University Press.

Jermier, J., Knights, D. and Willmott, H. (eds.) (1994) *Resistance and Power in Organizations*, London: Routledge.

Jung, C. (1923) *Psychological Types*, London: Routledge and Kegan Paul.

Jung, C. (1968) *The Archetypes and the Collective Unconscious*, London: Routledge.

Kelly, G. (1955) *The Psychology of Personal Constructs*, New York: Norton.

Kets de Vries, M. and Miller, D. (1984) *The Neurotic Organization: Diagnosing and Changing Counterproductive Styles of Management*, San Francisco: Jossey-Bass.

Kreeger, L. (ed.) (1975) *The Large Group: Dynamics and Therapy*, London: Constable.

Kuhnert, K. W. and Russell, C. J. (1990) 'Using constructive developmental theory and biodata to bridge the gap between personnel selection and leadership', *Journal of Management* 16(3):595–607.

Laing, R. (1965) *The Divided Self*, Harmondsworth: Penguin.

Lasch, C. (1979) *The Culture of Narcissism*, New York: Norton.

Latour, B. (1987) *Science in Action*, Milton Keynes: Open University Press.

Lawrence, W. G. (1979) *Exploring Individual and Organizational Boundaries: A Tavistock Open Systems Approach*, New York: Wiley and Sons.

Le Bon, G. (1960) *The Crowd*, New York: Viking.

Lewin, K. (1935) *A Dynamic Theory of Personality*, New York: McGraw Hill.

McGregor, D. M. (1960) *The Human Side of Enterprise*, New York: McGraw-Hill.

Mackay, L. (1986) 'The macho manager: it's no myth', *Personnel Management* 18(1):25–28.

Marcuse, H. (1964) *One Dimensional Man*, Boston, MA: Beacon Press.

Maslow, A. H. (1954) *Motivation and Personality*, New York: Harper and Row.

Maslow, A. H. (1970) *Motivation and Personality*, second edition, New York: Harper and Row.

Maslow, A. H. (1971) *The Farther Reaches of Human Personality*, New York: Viking.

Melucci, A. (1986) *Nomads of the Present*, London: Radius.

Mischel, W. (1993) *Introduction to Personality*, fifth edition. Orlando, FL: Harcourt Brace College Publishers.

Mullins, L. (1993) *Management and Organizational Behaviour*, third edition, London: Pitman.

Murakami, H. (1993) *Hard-Boiled Wonderland and the End of the World*, New York: Vintage.

Myers-Briggs, I. (1962) *The Myers-Briggs Type Indicator*, Princeton, NJ: Educational Testing Service.

Nietzsche, F. (1974) *The Gay Science*, New York: Vintage.

Norman, W. T. (1963) 'Toward an adequate taxonomy of personality attributes: Replicated factor structure in peer nomination personality ratings', *Journal of Abnormal and Social Psychology* 66:574–583.

Pirsig, R. (1974) *Zen and the Art of Motorcycle Maintenance*, London: Bodley Head.

Rogers, C. (1970) *Carl Rogers on Encounter Groups*, New York: Harper and Row.

Sartre, J. P. (1958) *Being and Nothingness*, London: Routledge.

Schwartz, H. (1990) *Narcissistic Process and Corporate Decay: The Theory of the Organization Ideal*, New York: New York University Press.

Short, J. R. (2000) *Alternative Geographies*, London: Prentice Hall.

Seibert, S. C., Kraimer, M. L. and Crant, J. M. (2001) 'What do proactive people do? A longitudinal model linking proactive personality and career success', *Personnel Psychology* 54:845–874.

Sennett, R. (1977) *The Fall of Public Man*, New York: Alfred Knopf.

Sievers, B. (1994) *Work, Death and Life Itself*, Berlin: De Gruyter.

Sievers, B. (1995) 'Characters in search of a theatre: Organization as theatre for the drama of childhood and the drama at work', *Free Associations* 5,2:196–220.

Strassman, P. A. (1994) 'The hocus-pocus of reengineering', *Across the Board*, 34,6:35–38.

Thompson, E. P. (1968) *The Making of the English Working Classes*, Harmondsworth: Penguin.

Thompson, P. (1990) 'Crawling from the wreckage: The labour process and the politics of production', in D. Knights and H. Willmott (eds.) *Labour Process Theory*, London: Macmillan.

Thompson, P. and Bannon, E. (1985) *Working the System*, London: Pluto.

Thompson, P. and McHugh, D. (2002) *Work Organisations*, third edition, Basingstoke: Palgrave.

Townley, B. (1994) *Reframing Human Resource Management*, London: Sage.

Watson, T. (1994) *In Search of Management: Culture, Chaos and Control in Managerial Work*, London: Routledge.

Willmott, H. (1995) 'The odd couple? Re-engineering business processes, managing human relations', *New Technology, Work and Employment* 10,2:89–98.

Wurtzel, E. (1995) *Prozac Nation – Young and Depressed in America: A Memoir*, London: Quartet Books.

4 Groups and Teams at Work

Alessia Contu

Key concepts and learning objectives

By the end of this chapter you should understand:

- The traditional and mainstream views of teams at work and why they are important for work organization.

- The main contributions to the subject, and their differences, drawing upon various theoretical contributions and empirical studies.

- Critical perspectives on teamwork, the political issues they highlight in terms of inequalities, identity and resistance, and the opportunities they offer for understanding the difficulties and challenges of organizational life.

Aims of the chapter

This chapter will:

- Explore the meaning of teamwork.

- Explain how and why teamwork is used in organizations.

- Highlight the problems, open questions and limitations of mainstream models of teamwork.

- Indicate the contribution of critical approaches to teamwork.

- Explain and illustrate the implications of power, insecurity, identity and knowledge for understanding teamwork.

Overview and key points

The first part of this chapter introduces mainstream views of teams at work. Referring to a case study of a new media company, it elaborates the assumptions held and the importance attached to the idea that teamwork is good for organizational performance, and that teamwork favours flexibility, motivation and learning. The text makes connections to contemporary ideas about teamwork, as well as referring to past studies that have been significant for our understanding of the ways teams, and their members, behave.

In the second part of the chapter, problems of mainstream thinking are unravelled and addressed by drawing upon the work of radical and critical studies of teamwork to show that:

- The categories we create can become prescriptions and lose their relevance for understanding the challenges and difficulties of organized life.

- Organizational life is complex, ambiguous and embedded in relations of power.

- Teamwork is neither intrinsically good nor new.

- Radical and critical views can enhance democratic debate by questioning taken-for-granted assumptions about teamwork.

Mainstream views of teams at work

Introduction to mainstream thinking on groups and teams

Most people assume the benefits of working in teams and many recognize the importance of belonging to a group, of whatever kind, to get a job done. There are many types of groups, including self-managing teams, task forces, 'hot groups', 'Japanese teams' and so on.

Many management gurus, and also many academics, would without hesitation justify the role of teams in creating and sustaining successful organizations. It is these justifications that are presented and discussed in the first part of this chapter.

Thinkpoint 4.1

Have you ever worked as part of a team in a company or similar organization? What explanation or justification was offered by managers or team members for the organization of workers into teams?

First, however, we need to consider the message presented by advocates of teamwork. The message is clear: 'if the organization is to perform it must be organized as a team' (Drucker, 1992). Others foresee that 'teams will be the primary building blocks of company performance in the organization of the future' (Katzenbach and Smith, 1993, p. 173). Data published for the Department of Trade and Industry in the United Kingdom, which forms part of the Workplace Employment Relations Survey 1998 (WERS – Cully *et al.*, 1998) reports that 65 per cent of workplaces have the majority of their employees working in teams. Other international surveys (see Cohen *et al.*, 1996; Waterson *et al.*, 1999) indicate that managers have acted upon this message. According to one estimate in 2000, 80 per cent of all Fortune 2000 companies had over half of their employees working in teams (Flores and Gray, 2000, cited in Thrift, 2001, p. 420).

The reasons given to justify why teams are important, if not fundamental, for organizational success are diverse. Summarizing the arguments of both popular and academic mainstream literature, we can suggest that teamworking ranks highly on three dimensions that are central for today's organization: flexibility, motivation and learning (see Figure 4.2).

Key problem: What is a team?

Work organizations seem to have discovered the importance of teams. At the same time teams, or group or 'groupings' of various kinds, are everywhere. We support, or play, in sports teams, we have groups of friends, we love or even play in music bands. At university, teaching activities are often accomplished by collaborating – working with others as a unit, rather than individually.

There is a certain confusion associated with groups and teams, given that we often use these words interchangeably and on different occasions and circumstances. What is the difference between 'teams' and 'groups'? In sociology, for example, a group is a social unit that 'sits' between the individual and the collective/institution/organizational. Psychologists suggest that a group is a socio-psychological dimension where each individual satisfies the need of affiliation – i.e. of being part of something bigger than him or herself.

Thinkpoint 4.2

In thinking of the social units you belong to, what would you describe as a group? What as a team? What do you think is the difference between a group and a team?

Perhaps you have a *group* of friends with which you go to the pub regularly and whose company you enjoy very much. You probably would not call this group of friends a team. Yet, you would describe as a *team* the same group when it enters the Monday evening quiz and competes against other teams at the pub. We are calling a 'group' an ensemble of people who share certain interests and passions, or perhaps simply enjoy each other's company. Even if they do not themselves view each other as members of a group, they may well be identified as a group. The quiz team is still a group, because it is still an ensemble of people that arguably share an interest – i.e. participating in a quiz. But they now have a specific purpose, or goal – namely taking part in a quiz, perhaps with the objective of winning it. They have a task that is clear: combine their knowledge to answer the most questions correctly. They must collaborate with each other to answer the questions correctly. So, we seem to have identified key differences in the meaning of the word 'team' and that of 'group'.

Sometimes we are assigned to groups or teams by default as we enter certain institutions, such as university. We do not choose the people, or the time/space of engagement, or the type of engagement. We call these *formal* groups. As a student you might be assigned to a seminar group, or, for your course work, you might be required to complete a team-based project. Perhaps this last example is the one closer to what you might experience in your future working life. In the team-based project, the team is responsible for the delivery of an outcome (presentation, research report), just as at work a team can be responsible for the management and delivery of a project, such as a new product or service. The key point is that the idea of 'team' implies collaboration between 'players' or members to undertake a task.

Management writers consider it very important to be precise and explicit on the difference between work groups and teams. For Katzenbach and Smith (1993) the orientation to the task and clarity of performance goals are the fundamental characteristics for understanding the difference between work groups and teams, which they define in the terms set out in Box 4.1.

Disciplines that have influenced the teaching, training and the implementation and management of teams at work include sociology, psychology and psychoanalysis. Understanding how teams work and the behaviour of teams and their members might be important in your everyday student life as well as for your future career. This is a point that career advisers often emphasize in their presentations to students! Schools and universities are 'invited' by policy makers and governors to train students in teamworking skills (see Flores and Gray, 2000, p. 24), which is both cause and effect of the sheer number of companies employing teams at work in one form or another. So, when being assessed for a job as a trainee, the selectors might well try to discover whether you are a 'team player'. Does your behaviour enable others to contribute to defining and accomplishing a task, or do you either dominate or withdraw?

Image 4.1 Undergraduate outdoor teambuilding events can be used as ice-breakers, and as a way to sensitize students on the importance/relevance of teamwork

Box 4.1: Work groups and teams: Definitions by Katzenbach and Smith (1993)

Work group: a small number of people working in a collaborative style with individual input and accountability. An example can be your seminar group at university.

Team: a small number of interdependent people with complementary skills who are committed to a common purpose, performance goals and approach for which they hold themselves mutually accountable. The team has joint, specific 'collective work-products' such as experiments, reports, products, etc. An example can be your course work based on a team-based project.

The photograph here was taken during a teambuilding event for undergraduate students. Teambuilding is constituted by a series of games and exercises through which the participants learn to become a cohesive team. These games are based on the understanding of the nature of groups, their processes and behaviours, which goes under the name of 'group dynamics'.

It was Kurt Lewin and his colleagues, mainly at the MIT Centre for Group Dynamics, who suggested (building on a series of experiments, an example of which is included on page 131) that a group is a particular psycho-social dimension distinct from the individual one. In other words, a group is more than the sum of the individuals comprising it, an aspect that is signalled by the sense of cohesion of the team. Lewin describes this as the 'we-feeling' or 'belongingness' exhibited by the members, which is what the teambuilding event is designed to create – build a team out of what starts as a mere collection of three to eight individuals. Reynolds (1994, p. 45) proposes a list indicating the 'group processes' one should be aware of, and suggests some questions you can use to investigate and understand the processes of the groups you belong to:

- *Communication*. Who talks to whom, who supports whom? Who seems actively involved? Who does not?

- *Decision making*. How are decisions and choices made? Who is involved in this and in what way?

- *Power and influence*. What seems to be the basis and pattern of power and influence in the group? Does it change over time?

- *Conflict*. How are conflicts of ideas, opinions or interests worked out within the group? Are they resolved and if so how?

- *Ethos*. What does it seem to be like to belong in this group? Are there accepted norms of behaviours? What roles or rules developed?

However, not everything that happens in groups is easily subjected to scrutiny. Psychoanalytic approaches have shown that group processes are not always conscious – i.e. they are not always intentional and guided by a known and linear rationality. In particular, the work of Wilfred Bion has identified the existence of specific 'group phenomena', which are unconscious responses to the group situation characterized by a high emotional content, be that hate, love, fear or anxiety. For Bion (1961), every work group activity, hence also the ones you are involved in, can be obstructed, diverted, and on occasions assisted by these powerful emotional drives that cluster in what he calls the group's 'basic assumptions'. These are instantaneous, inevitable and instinctive ways in which individuals in a group combine and associate unconsciously in specific ways. There are three fundamental basic assumptions:

- *Dependency*. When the group is completely dependent on a leader who is invested with all the powers, just like a god, for providing answers to the anxieties of the group, hence providing security.

- *Expectancy or pairing*. When in the group there are two people (or sub-groups) that focus the attention of everyone. These are invested by the group with the hopes that something great will come – a Messiah – be it a person, idea or utopia, which will solve all the problems/issues/anxieties of the group. It is the hope itself that provides security.

- *Flight/Fight*. When the group transforms the insecurity into a threat from a person or an object that needs to be fought or escaped. It is the action itself that keeps the insecurity at bay.

Non-psychoanalytic approaches, mainly in social psychology, have been the main sources for management theory and managerial practice regarding or involving groups and teams (for example, in training and development). This is because social psychology tends to share the same set of assumptions of mainstream management theory – that is, to enhance control and predictability.

To illustrate some of the insights of social psychology for understanding team behaviour, let's return to the example of the team-based project. As is often the case in this situation, the project report is marked for the team as a whole. Each student is not assessed individually: the mark for each individual is the team mark. A complaint is often made that some people in the team do not 'pull their weight' and a few members end up doing most of the work. In this case the team might be affected by the 'free-riding tendency' (see Albanese and Van Fleet, 1985) – that is, the tendency of some individuals to reduce effort and contribution in a team situation. This phenomenon in social psychology is called 'social loafing' and is mainly said to occur in situations, where, for example:

- The number of participants is very high, making it difficult to assess individual's contributions.
- The interest in the task is low and rewards are unclear or irrelevant.
- There are no systems in place for checking and improving individual's contributions.

This diagnosis also suggests that the free-riding tendency can be effectively managed by limiting the size of the group and by introducing rewards and control systems.

Team-based work (such as the project for your course work) can be an anxiety-provoking and unfair experience. But it may also be exciting for the possibilities it offers – for example, of actually sharing the workload, of creating new interpersonal relationships and learning new things. This excitement, social psychology tells us, can also be frustrated or perhaps taken too far. Groupthink (Janis, 1972, 1982) is a phenomenon whereby the team tends to search for, and reach, an immediate agreement. The explosion of the NASA Shuttle *Challenger*, 73 seconds after it launched in January 1986, is considered one of the clearest examples of groupthink. Even if the engineers working for NASA raised concerns on the readiness and safety of the Shuttle's structure in the conditions expected at the launch, those concerns, and the information they were based on, were silenced. The NASA team gave the 'go' signal, initiating a tragedy that killed the seven astronauts of the *Challenger's* crew. Groupthink, it has been suggested, distorted the decision-making processes of the small groups of people involved in taking these delicate decisions. Reaching a premature consensus halted the collection and open evaluation of information and the analysis of alternatives. Learning stopped as any further development was effectively frozen by a consensus that was more based upon insecurity than upon an open and considered assessment of diverse sources of information and possible options. Groupthink, therefore, is also involved in a 'risk shift': an illusion of invulnerability and enthusiasm for a certain action or decision that polarizes the group towards higher risk. The risk that the group takes is higher than what people would risk individually.

When the group is affected by groupthink the issues at stake are poorly discussed and examined, leaving many possible solutions or routes unexplored. Dissenting voices are often stereotyped and marginalized, or 'invited' to reconsider their position, as happened in the case of the engineers working for NASA. This, ultimately, may invalidate team performance (see page 132 for the importance of dialogue) and participate in creating disasters that, like in the case of *Challenger*, could have been easily prevented.

Janis argues that many important historical fiascos in US foreign policy (for example, the involvement of the United States in the war in Vietnam) were at least partially due to groupthink. It has also been argued that the current US administration is affected by groupthink (see Levine, 2004). The decision to start the war against Iraq, and the actual management of the war itself, is said to present all the characteristics that Janis considered important for identifying groupthink:

- illusion of invulnerability
- belief in inherent morality of the group
- collective rationalization
- out of group stereotypes
- self-censorship
- illusion of unanimity
- direct pressure on dissenters
- self-appointed mindguards.

'Real' teams at work Teams are not in themselves a panacea (Dunphy and Bryant, 1996) and are not infallible (Plunkett and Fournier, 1991, p. 32). Yet, mainstream management theory suggests that when teams are introduced in the right way and nurtured as part of a wider organizational philosophy and strategy, they outperform individuals and collaborative groupings. In the management literature there is a wide utilization of the word 'team' and almost a blind acceptance of the value of teams for organizational success. Many authors have tried to identify the factors that intervene in heightening team performance (see Hackman, 1987; Campion, Medsker and Higgs,

1993; Cohen, Ledford and Spreitzer, 1996; Tannebaum, Beard and Salas, 1992; West, 2004). These authors have ventured to explain exactly what teamwork is, and in what sense teams are important for organizational success.

For Katzenbach and Smith (1993), for example, the connection between teams and organizational success is performance. Teams, or what they call 'real' teams, should be understood as discrete units of performance and not, or not only, as examples of positive organizational values such as sharing, collaborating or listening to others. Katzenbach and Smith (1993) propose that the importance and the impact of teams at work is dependent on how much they are *not* a simple new label attached by senior managers (or by your lecturers) to old ways of working; they are *not* to be equated with well-intentioned teambuilding events proposed by management consultants and they are *not* the same as recipes presented in the popular management books making the best sellers list. Teams, rather, are identified as a distinctive form of organizational technology – i.e. a particular way of organizing work that is designed to achieve specific ends. As Katzenbach and Smith (1993) put it, there is a 'wisdom' related to teams at work. To create 'real teams' (i.e. teams that reach high performance) managers need to learn a proper *discipline* which requires application, time and commitment.

Features of team discipline are:

- adequate level of complementary skills
- truly meaningful purpose
- specific goals and performance objectives
- clear working approach
- mutual accountability.

The discipline needed to create a high-performance team is demanding for all those involved. It cannot be improvised or faked, and it is intrinsically connected to a clear strategic commitment to create a high-performing organization. So senior executives, warn Katzenbach and Smith (1993), need to be realistic and clear on what high performance means for their organization. Then, they need to implement it correctly. There can be resistance to real teams, but effective discipline erodes this resistance and prepares for the advent of 'real', high-performing teams. We shall now consider an example of a team at work in a new media company.

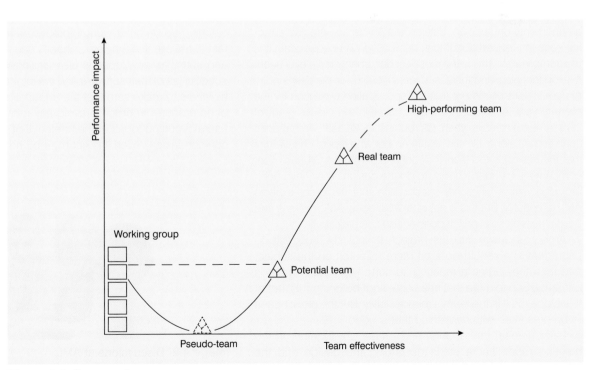

Figure 4.1 Team performance curve

Case study: AML, the digital media communication agency   AML is a digital marketing and communication agency. Among its services, the company designs and builds websites, and it develops marketing campaigns using multiple digital platforms – i.e. the internet, mobile phones, CDs, etc. The philosophy of work of AML is that better digital solutions can be obtained by working in

CASE STUDY 4.1 AML (1)

When I arrive at AML on Monday morning in mid-July, I join a meeting with Laura, a junior content designer, Teresa the account manager/producer who's also an expert in content design, and John a technical developer. They are discussing a document that Laura has produced over the weekend, which was supposed to express the ideas and solutions they came up with on the previous Friday. They had a series of e-mail exchanges over the weekend and they are now going through the amendments to the document that Laura has written. Laura reads the document aloud. The discussion is rather careful and specific. John asks Laura if it is possible to explain in detail the diagrams in the document, and also if she can explain better the folder view. John is a developer in his late twenties. He is helpful in proposing changes, such as a drop-down folder, that are well received by Laura and Teresa. But John is also rather distant and annoyed. He leaves the meeting twice excusing himself but without explanation, and so leaving his fellow workers stunned and puzzled. Then I understand why he is behaving in this way. He is irritated by the fact that Laura has not followed faithfully the brief they discussed on Friday, which was put together in a series of pieces of paper. John asks Laura: 'Have you got it? It is very important, have you taken it home?'

Having made the corrections, Laura is left to make the further amendments on her own. Later, when Amber, the creative director, sees the revised document, her reaction is unequivocal: 'It is too complicated. This is the messiest document I have ever seen. It is too technical and there is no consideration of the user's point of view.' Laura points out that the specification produced by the client is very technical. She tries to explain the client's point of view. Amber just says 'yeah, Ok, but this looks naff!' At that point John comes along. He sits next to Amber who repeats her verdict that the design is too technical. John explains that S4 (the client company) is telling them how to do the design. They have been provided with a functional specification that the client expects AML to beautify. But this is not what AML does. AML designs and builds 'perfect' solutions. It does not do cosmetic work.

Amber is drawn into the project. In fact she suggests to Laura that she should do a bit more research on the subject and then they agree a meeting 'to sort things out'. Amber is unhappy. She told me that she should not be doing this, not at this stage, as it is the team's responsibility. But the client needs to be presented with something that is good.

Later, Teresa, Laura, John and Amber are together in the meeting room. Laura starts describing the design and the problems. They are not starting from scratch because they have the S4 specification and Laura's document. In a way, the atmosphere is rather playful with jokes and laughter, but the joke also alludes to subtle tensions. John offers to prepare tea. When he comes back, Laura who knows he knows how she likes her tea, finds he has put in sugar and exclaims 'Revenge!'.

The meeting is now very different from the one in the morning. Amber just asks 'OK what are we trying to do? What do we need to achieve? Everything that is needed becomes a specific feature, even if there is a long discussion on what the feature might look like. So, for example, they agree that in the address book there will be cartoon characters that can be associated with the names in the address book. They all participate in coming up with suggestions and ideas, and at the end of the meeting the room is wallpapered with sheets of drawings, sentences and navigation diagrams. Laura, as content designer, has to put everything together in a document that presents exactly what was agreed in this meeting: the detailed content design of the project. Laura returns to her workstation to start doing that even though she thought she had already done that during the weekend. She is still smiling and, looking at me, she says 'You are not going to stay are you? It is already five o'clock.' Teresa and John are staying too because they are catching up on other work. Moreover, Teresa is the direct contact to the client. If they are unhappy she has to deal with them, and John, as developer, is also liaising with the client on the specificities of their software and the interface needed with it, so he wants to make sure that the explanation of the navigation is done properly. In order to avoid any mess he decides to help Laura in putting together the artefact that specifies the detailed content design, 'even if is not my job!' he adds.

Image 4.2 Discussions at AML

teams made up of multiple, complementary skills. So, by putting together content, graphic and technical experts, it is possible to design and produce solutions that are neither over-designed nor too technical, but a 'perfect' balance. Case study 4.1 provides an example of a real life working situation at AML, involving a series of meetings for creating what they call 'the detailed content design' of an e-mail system for a product at the interface between the internet and mobile phones. In this vignette they are discussing specifically the design of the mailing system address book.

Here are a few questions that can help you to think about the case and the various issues involved in understanding teams at work:

- How would you describe AML's work organization?

- Is this a 'real team'? Can you identify and summarize the features listed in Katzenbach and Smith (1993)?

- Where do you think there are problems? What do you think they are due to?

- Do you think the team could improve their performance? How? What should the managers do in order to help the team?

- In what ways are the three dimensions we have signalled earlier of flexibility, motivation and learning activated and affected?

- How do you explain the fact that the workers stay at work even if their working time is over?

Perhaps one of the reactions to the AML case is that they seem to be very disorganized! Yet, they do have an organization – the team – which has all the characteristics indicated by Katzenbach and Smith (1993). The common purpose is to design the outline of the mailing system, which is the joint work-product. The members of the team need to collaborate in order to achieve this objective – they could not design it individually. They all have different, complementary skills (content designer, developer and graphic designer), and each of them is fundamental and necessary for realizing the design. Yet, everything is rather loose and unclear. There are no templates that specify what a detailed content design should look like, for example. They spend a lot of time discussing what should be in a detailed content design, and also how it should be presented, which does not seem an efficient utilization of time. As soon as they show the document/artefact they have produced to the creative director, she says 'it's too naff'. This does not strike one as a useful, constructive comment, and it does not give any clear direction. Then, when Amber gets heavily involved in the second meeting, things seems to be different. She does not tell them what to do but she facilitates their thinking, helping them to achieve a successful balance between the user point of view, creativity, usability and the constraints dictated by the client's specifications. You might have noted that there are no clear rules about how each person should participate, or what they should do. Everything seems to be left to personal interpretation and willingness. Yet they also seem highly committed. They work a great deal, including weekends via e-mail exchanges, and well beyond 'normal' working hours. Accountability is also shared. They are accountable not only to Amber, the creative director, but also to each other. In the vignette we see how individuals' contributions, suggestions and ideas are not only expected but closely monitored and judged by the team members.

Many characteristics of AML are often associated with post-bureaucratic organizational forms. In the following section we shall consider how teams connect to these 'post-bureaucracies' and enter into the details of the key ideas around teams at work. As indicated earlier, teams in the mainstream are said to activate/enhance three main organizational dimensions: flexibility, motivation and learning. We shall look at these dimensions and suggest why teams are considered to be involved in enhancing and activating these dimensions.

Key ideas and contributions to thinking and important empirical studies

Many popular and academic authors include 'teams' as a central feature of their favoured prescriptions for improved organizational performance. Teams, for example, are identified as essential components of the implementation of the principles of total quality management (Oakland, 1996). They are the building blocks of 'excellent organizations' (Peters and Waterman, 1982), key elements of the 'learning organization' (Senge, 1990) and they are critical components of virtually all high-performance management systems that build profit by putting people first (Pfeffer, 1998).

and standardization, but these principles are inserted in a virtuous circle of continuous improvement, what we have said below is called *kaizen*. The system that makes this possible they call 'enabling' or 'learning bureaucracy':

> using learned analytical tools, their own experience and the expertise of leaders and engineers, workers create a consensual standard that they teach to the system by writing job descriptions. The system then teaches these standards back to the workers, who then by further analysis, standardisation, re-analysis, refinement and re-standardisation create an intensely structured system of continuous improvement. The salient characteristic of this bureaucracy is learning, not coercion.
> *(Adler, 1993, p. 104)*

CASE STUDY 4.2 NUMMI

NUMMI, a joint venture between Toyota and GM in Fremont, California, was formally established in 1984. It has approximately 350 teams in production made up of five to seven people and a leader. Small teams are supposed to encourage participative decision making and team bonding (Adler, 1993, p. 5). Each team is responsible for a different portion of the assembly line. Four teams form what is known as a group, with the first layer of management being the group leader. Each team has to coordinate its own work and the relations with other teams. Also, the cleanliness and tidiness of their workspace is the responsibility of the team. Team members are trained in all the tasks necessary to the team operation, and they can rotate when needed. Teams are responsible for quality checks and small repairs. Problems are solved when they occur. Any defective operation on the line is tackled immediately, rather than being pushed up to 'quality control' and being left to pile up for attention in a rectification section. In order to solve the problems when they appear, and even before they occur, workers must be able to do something that was unthinkable in the traditional production line, namely to stop the line.

Teams are also encouraged to utilize the 'Five Why's' – a questioning strategy designed to get to the bottom of the problem the team is facing. They are also asked to propose improvements to the system of production beyond immediate problem solving, through a system of suggestions or, for example, by joining quality circles. These are teams made up of workers as well as specialist engineers, looking at implementing suggestions and ideas with the goal of improving the system of production continuously.

Management's role in NUMMI, as in Toyota, is that of providing expertise to help production teams with problem solving. In order to compete with the performance gains – in quality as well as price – achieved by Toyota, other auto makers have followed their lead in introducing lean manufacturing methods. And the basic ideas of lean production have been applied in many other industries, with mixed results. The system organized around production teams has often proved to be extremely efficient, much more than traditional plants. The fact that teams are constantly attentive to the work and detect errors immediately reduces the rework needed at the end of the line. In other words, the essence of the teamwork in NUMMI is its flexibility because workers can do all the different tasks and are collectively responsible for improving their ability to work productively as a team. Each new idea, new successful implementation and new process is not only adopted by the team but is spread to the whole organization in a continuous race to improvement. This is known by the Japanese word *kaizen*.

By the end of 1986 NUMMI's productivity was the highest in GM and was twice that of the old plant. More then 90 per cent of the workers declared themselves to be satisfied with their employment in NUMMI and absenteeism fell from 20–25 per cent to 3–4 per cent. Both in Toyota and NUMMI there are formal agreements in place that seal a true reciprocal obligation between workers and employers (Womack *et al.*, 1990, p. 102). For example, there are agreements on a certain level of job security and policies, which avoid job cuts as a way out of financial crisis. The teams are part of a system in which the workers, the managers, the suppliers and the distributors are integrated and are said to share a common destiny, 'a community of fate' (Berders and Van Hootegem, 2000, p. 55). This is also obtained through the socialization of the employees into an organizational culture that values their work and their knowledge, putting them at the centre of the production process. Emblems of traditional differences in status such as different dress codes, different food facilities, parking spaces, etc. are erased in order to inspire a spirit of communality and equality. The main idea is that the whole organization shares the same values and same destiny, so everyone has to do their best to make the company succeed.

Teams for motivation: Participation, satisfaction and humane ways of working When teams are empowered to solve problems, to offer innovative solutions, all the workers become active participants in their work. They can shape the specificities of their working practices, and they can improve them, rather than being mere executors of managers' orders. In other words, employees' importance and value is recognized; and they are not considered as simple appendices of the machines or bureaucrats of impersonal organizations. The 'empowerment' of employees has become extremely significant in recent times. With the motto of 'people first', for example, Pfeffer (1998) proposes a seven point list for organizational success where enlightened 'people management' is at the centre of a profit-making organization that invests and treats its employees with respect, building up relations of trust and cooperation rather than relying upon expensive direct control systems. When people are empowered to work in teams they can manage themselves and develop real commitment and ownership of what they do. The autonomy and discretion that people enjoy in teams translates into intrinsic rewards and job satisfaction (Pfeffer, 1998, p. 74), which in turn has an impact on employee morale and productivity.

The assumptions underlying this view are part of an extended legacy that stretches back to the socio-technical tradition, the human relations movement, and the **quality of working life movement** (see Procter and Mueller, 2000; Buchanon, 2000; Huczynski, 1996). You can find some of these classical studies summarized at the end of this subsection. It is important to consider that this legacy emphasizes that:

- An organization is not only a technical system but also a **social system**; and both need to be managed.
- In social systems, groups are an important source of norms of conduct and informal rules.
- A democratic approach to a task, which favours participation and autonomy, enhances the quality and quantity of the output.

Scientific management considered material benefits primary for generating motivation in otherwise uninterested, idiosyncratic workers who require constant control and supervision to be kept on the task. In contrast, 'modern management thinking' maintains that social, psychological and moral factors also intervene in regulating workers' motivation and satisfaction. This is why many

---

Box 4.2: Learning and bureaucracy

For Adler there are three aspects involved in creating a 'learning and enabling bureaucracy':

1 The open, trustworthy and prompt relationship between management and workers' unions which 'on the basis of the recognition that job security is fundamental to an employee's well-being' agrees to a no-layoff policy and to a listening and prompt response on employees' demands.

2 Standardization of operation is a fundamental factor. This, in NUMMI, is extensive. NUMMI still uses the Tayloristic precepts of studying and defining procedures of time and motion. But these precepts, rather than being decided by some engineer detached from production and without any consultation with those on the shop floor, are actually devised by the workers themselves. In NUMMI, the workers 'hold the stopwatch'. The members of the team will observe and time each other, finding the most efficient and safest way to perform a certain operation. Then they break the work

down into small parts and try to improve each of these parts. The team then compares the results with other teams on the same station during other shifts and the best one becomes the standard procedure for that particular operation in the plant. The workers become themselves work engineers. In this respect they are 'empowered' because, rather than being told what to do, they find out for themselves what is the best way of doing something. They are managers of their own activity. They are not alienated appendices of a machine or mere executors of someone else's design. Rather they execute their own design.

3 The other aspect, which is connected with standardization, is that it offers a basis for continuous improvement. The improvements of one team, in a particular shift, for example, become the benchmark to be improved upon by the other teams. This introduces the challenge that continues the virtuous circle of the learning bureaucracy.

Teams for learning: Continuous improvement and innovation The issue of learning and knowledge creation and diffusion has increased in importance in recent decades, with many asserting that knowledge is the source of competitive advantage. A flourishing literature has developed that analyses, describes and often prescribes strategies, ideas and models for understanding, creating, facilitating and supporting organizations that learn, to improve or innovate by creating, transferring and managing successfully new and existing knowledge (Drucker, 1993; Senge, 1990; Nonaka and Takeuchi, 1995; Davenport and Pusak, 1998). The level and quality of creativity and problem solving required to innovate or improve on existing business solutions is very high. An individual working alone rarely produces the creative ideas or solutions required, for example, for complex or discontinuous innovation (Tushman and Nadler, 1998). If this seems blindingly obvious at an intuitive level, it should also be appreciated that theoretically the creation and transfer of knowledge – in the form of learning – has been increasingly recognized as a social phenomenon rather than an individual cognitive endeavour. This is why teams/groups, as a basic social unit, can be considered as media of knowledge creation and diffusion. Specifically, learning and knowledge creation occur:

- in the social context
- in interaction and participation in shared practices
- in processes of reflection and feedback
- in freedom to explore and implement new and daring concepts.

For all these reasons, many studies are concentrating on team learning and how this can be favoured and nurtured in organizations (Argote *et al.*, 2000; Wood and Bandura, 1989; Gibson and Vermeuler, 2003; Edmonson, 2002). As Peter Senge (1990, p. 236) puts it, 'there has never been a greater need for mastering team learning in organization than there is today'.

According to Senge, areas and issues that should be considered for facilitating team learning are:

- *Discussion and dialogue.* These are two different modes of communication, both important. Discussion enables members to dissect a topic or a problem from various points of view. Dialogue is a 'free flow of meaning' through which people can observe their own thinking, understand how it developed and enable it to cohere in a collective meaning.

- *Dealing with conflict and defensive routines.* Defensive routines are entrenched in often unacknowledged habits that we use to defend ourselves from the embarrassment and threat that comes with exposing our thinking. Reflection and mutual inquiry are skills employed for dealing with conflictual situations and defensive routines.

- *Practise team learning.* Create space and time (with specific sessions or learning laboratories) to practise discussion and dialogue and to develop skills for dealing with defensiveness.

Box 4.3: Peter Senge

Dr. Peter M. Senge is the founding chairperson of the Society for Organizational Learning (SOL) and a senior lecturer at the Massachusetts Institute of Technology. Dr. Senge is the author of *The Fifth Discipline: The Art and Practice of the Learning Organization*. He has lectured extensively throughout the world, translating the abstract ideas of systems theory into tools for better understanding of economic and organizational change. He has worked with leaders in business, education, healthcare and government. *The Journal of Business Strategy* (September/October 1999) named Dr. Senge as one of the 24 people who had had the greatest influence on business strategy over the last 100 years.

Image 4.4 Peter Senge, author of the *Fifth Discipline*

Source: http://www.solonline.org/aboutsol/who/Senge/

You can engage with your seminar group in a 'learning laboratory' to improve your skills at dialogue and negotiation. Centre your discussion on the question: 'How do we deal with conflicts?'

The ground rules that everyone has to respect are:

- *Suspension of assumptions*. Do not hold on to your position at any cost but try to understand your own and all the others' views.

- *Act as equals*. There might be differences between you – some people have better marks than others, or are considered more knowledgeable. Suspend these differences for the time you are in this 'learning laboratory'.

- *Spirit of inquiry*. Try to understand what are the deep assumptions beyond the positions you and others hold. Probe by asking what is the evidence or reason that justifies the positions people hold. Ask the question how have we come to accept these views.

You might have already recognized the possibility that if a team can be a medium of knowledge creation, learning as a social phenomenon does not occur exclusively within the restricted, officially prescribed formal boundaries of specific, formal or functional team membership. There are some authors (Lave and Wenger, 1991; Brown and Duguid, 1991) who have suggested we should also concentrate on what they call 'communities of practice' (COPs), which are made up of people who cluster around a specific practice (such as the design of digital solutions as in the case of AML) they are involved in, and for which they often share a keen interest. Participating in these communities, people develop new ways of doing or improving on existing practice, and the activities comprising the practice itself. In this process of participation they develop a certain identity (in the case of AML as web designers, for example) and become active and recognized members of that wider community. Learning occurs in the participation in the practice, as members engage and develop a specific language, share stories that help make sense of the practice and produce artefacts that are meaningful for all the members. We can be members of many COPs. In some we might be at the periphery whereas in others we might be at the centre, recognized as competent members, even experts of that practice.

To which COPs do you belong? Can you identify the key aspects, such as specific language, stories and artefacts, of each of the COPs you belong to?

If learning occurs at various levels and dimensions and it is not restricted to specific business units like formal teams, then we need to consider the implications for organizations. One of these implications is that multi-membership (see Figure 4.3) should be noted and managed (Wenger, 1998; Wenger and Snyder, 2000; Wenger, McDermott and Snyder, 2002), for example, by identifying the existing COPs, and by fostering and nurturing COPs and the members' freedom and ability to tap into the different levels and dimensions of learning and innovation.

Deploy the model of multi-membership and the concept of COPs to analyse the AML case study.

Table 4.1 Belbin's model for team management

Rules and descriptions – team role contributions	Allowable weaknesses
Plant	
Creative, unorthodox, imaginative; solves difficult problems	Ignores details; too preoccupied to communicate effectively
Resource investigator	
Extravert, enthusiastic, communicative; explores opportunities; develops contacts	Over-optimistic; loses interest once initial enthusiasm has passed
Coordinator	
Mature, confident, a good chairperson; clarifies goals, promotes decision making; delegates well	Can be seen as manipulative; delegates personal work
Shaper	
Challenging, dynamic, thrives on pressure; has the drive and courage to overcome obstacles	Can provoke others; hurts people's feelings
Monitor evaluator	
Sober, strategic and discerning; seeks all opinions; judges accurately	Lacks drive and ability to inspire others; overly critical
Teamworker	
Cooperative, mild, perceptive and diplomatic; listens, builds, averts friction, calms the nerves	Indecisive in crunch situations; can be easily influenced
Implementer	
Disciplined, reliable, conservative and efficient; turns ideas into practical actions	Somewhat inflexible; slow to respond to new possibilities
Completer	
Painstaking conscientious, anxious; searches out errors and omissions; delivers on time	Inclined to worry unduly; reluctant to delegate; can be a nit-picker
Specialist	
Single-minded, self-starting, dedicated; provides knowledge and skills in rare supply	Contributes on only a narrow front; dwells on technicalities; overlooks the big picture

Note: Strengths of contributors in any one of the roles is commonly associated with particular weaknesses. These are called allowable weaknesses. Executives are seldom strong in all nine team roles.

Source: Reprinted from team roles at work, Belbin (ed.), 1993, p. 23 with permission from Elsevier

Box 4.4: Research field

Researchers at Henley College studied teams involved in playing a business management game where each team played a 'company'. The game enabled the researchers to have an objective measure of team performance – i.e. the financial results of the 'companies' playing the management game. The researchers also measured and categorized the participants according to a set of broad human characteristics – mental ability, personality, character and orientation – via specific psychometric tests. They also closely observed teams during their activities. The researchers manipulated variables, one of which was the composition of the members of each team. The teams were then observed and scored on observation items. It is from an elaboration of these data that researchers identified nine roles that have proved to be significant, and that hindered performance when they were not taken up. Teams, for Belbin, are a matter of balance: 'What is needed is not well-balanced individuals but individuals who balance well with one another. In that way human frailty can be underpinned and strengths used to full advantage' (Belbin, 1993, p. 73).

The success of team roles could be explained by the fact that Belbin's model claims predictive capacity. This means that by applying the instruments provided to test and score people, it is possible to design the best team (in the given circumstances) to perform a specific task. Such a promise is very appealing and might explain the interest in Belbin's model shown by managers and students. Belbin's self-inventory is an easy test for students and managers alike. Managers can score themselves and their employees and apply what has come to be known as Belbin's method for designing teams. For £984 you could also participate in a two-day training course and become a Belbin accredited trainer or consultant (http://www.btinternet.com/~cert/accreditation.htm).

However, in organizational psychology the validity of Belbin's model and his team-role self-perception inventory has been questioned and retested, with mixed results. For example, Furnham, Steele and Pendleton (1993, p. 254) found that there is little psychometric support for the structure of Belbin inventories.

How do you make teams work?

ADDRESSING RESISTANCE Students and advocates of teams at work report that creating 'real teams' is difficult because there is often resistance to their implementation. Berneinsten (1992, p. 359), for example, reports that in the experiments at Volvo discussed earlier, 'to everyone's surprise some workers resisted changes because they preferred the traditional approach of doing a single task all day'. Weisbord (1992), in recounting his attempt to implement participative work design and teams in his company, points out that some ex-supervisors, as well as some workers, could not adapt to the self-managing teams: 'Sidney, our best shipper, a world class miracle of efficient distribution had about as much interest in participation as a gourmet chef would have in McDonald's. "I don't want more responsibility. Why can't I just pack orders?" ' (Weisbord, 1992, p. 98).

Do the quotes reported above signal a resistance to teamwork? This is anecdotal evidence, you might think, and you would be right. Mainstream researchers have rarely undertaken in-depth exploration of employees' experiences of teamwork. Some studies have attempted to identify the factors that intervene in producing resistance to working in teams. Kanter (1983), for example, considers that teams are not immune from organizational politics as people pursue personal agendas, internal competition, etc., resulting in a disruption of team cohesiveness and effective task accomplishment.

Some of the factors intervening in generating resistance that have been studied are: perceptions of fairness and trust; attitude towards change; and cultural values.

PERCEPTION OF FAIRNESS AND TRUST Some researchers have concluded that trust and fairness of treatment in the perception of employees is an important element in avoiding or engendering resistance to teamwork. According to Kirkman (2000), the aspects of work that have proven significant for employees' perception of fairness (Kirkman *et al.*, 1996; Jones and Lindley, 1998) are:

- pay
- distribution of workload
- criteria for decisions
- interpersonal treatment.

However, Kirkman (2000, p. 7) argues that one should not believe that fair management will *necessarily* reduce resistance. In the first place, there should be a desire of the worker to be self-managing or 'self-leading', as Manz (1990, p. 486) also stresses. There must be, these authors maintain, a certain philosophy held by the employees if they are to be willing and productive members of a team. It is a certain view and meaning of their work that makes working in teams personally meaningful and

Box 4.5: Definition of 'resistance'

Resistance in the mainstream literature is defined as any conduct that serves to maintain the status quo in the face of pressure to alter the status quo' (Zaltman and Duncan 1977, cited in Kirkman and Shapiro, 1997).

appealing for them. These non-fairness issues are related to dispositional factors, such as stable attitudes towards change and cultural values. These dispositional factors are clarified below.

TOLERANCE FOR CHANGE As Kirkman (2000) suggests, low tolerance towards change is negatively associated with the introduction of self-managing teams. People may well understand intellectually that change is required but they can have negative emotional responses that can be unconscious or conscious, such as a fear of not being able to develop the skills and behaviours required, or of not understanding the task. They can find it extremely difficult to cope with the novelty and ambiguity that self-managing teams might mean for them intellectually, physically and emotionally.

CULTURAL VALUES Hofstede (1980, 1983) has suggested that cultural values are based on durable, desirable conduct that is deemed proper, in particular, to certain societies (Kirkman and Shapiro, 1997, p. 11). So, values (e.g. shared problem solving rather than reliance upon a single authority figure) that facilitate self-managing teams may be resisted more in certain cultures than others. Yet, Kirkman notes that there can be variation in the values also within cultures. This model therefore, does not focus only on national differences (as was the case in Hofstede's research) but also on individual differences within a national culture (see also Kluckhohn and Strodtbeck, 1961; Maznevski and DiStefano, 1995). This implies the possibility of investigating any prospective or established worker, and identifying how he/she scores on the following categories:

- *Collectivism–Individualism*. This is evident in the attitude towards teamwork as a process that requires interdependency. It regards how much a person finds it desirable to share, collaborate and depend on others for results, thereby valuing the benefit of the group (collectivism) over self-interest (individualism). Individuals embedded in a collectivist culture are understood to be less likely to resist teamwork than those steeped in a individualist culture.

The following considerations have a bearing upon the attitude towards self-management:

- *Power distance*. This is the level (high or low) of acceptance of an unequal distribution of power. Individuals with high power distance expect and respect managers to lead them. Those with low power distance are more comfortable with a high degree of autonomy and responsibility and are more inclined to by-pass bosses, status and formality in order to get the job done. High power distance is expected to create resistance to self-management.
- *Orientation*. Doing versus being. This is the orientation towards work and non-work activities. Being-oriented people have a tendency to emphasize non-work activities, while doing-oriented people emphasize the accomplishment of goals at work. The being-oriented people are expected to have a higher resistance to self-managed teamwork because this may require a continuous process of goal-setting, higher commitment and effort at work.
- *Determinism versus free will*. This concerns the belief of who or what controls one's life. Determinists believe that outcomes and life's difficulties are controlled by forces outside oneself (God, fate, management, etc.). They are thought more likely to resist self-management.

Limiting and containing resistance, for example by selecting the individuals with the 'right' dispositions is what Kirkman's work is designed to achieve. Another of the main aspects related to team effectiveness is that of leadership. We discuss next how this relates to teams at work.

Addressing leadership Should teams, and especially the so-called self-managing teams, have a leader? What type of leadership should be utilized in organizations based on teamwork? It is true that self-managing and self-leading teams would not require, in principle, a leader or supervisor because this role is internal to the empowered team? Research (Wall *et al.*, 1992) has shown that self-managing teams reduce cost by removing traditional supervisory hierarchical levels. Employees are empowered to be autonomous and responsible in how they organize, coordinate and improve their work. Yet, this creates strong demands upon managers who are under pressure to maintain systems of direction and control. As Manz (1990) argues, following a study by Mulder (1971), employees lack the managerial knowledge and education, and therefore lack the 'expert power' attributed to managers. Therefore many management writers point at the fundamental role of leaders in companies where work is organized into teams. Not only, as we have said earlier, does management need to provide clear performance goals for the team (Hackman *et al.*, 1989; Katzenbach and Smith, 1993; Lipman, Blumen

Table 4.2 Traditional versus 'SuperLeadership'

Traditional leadership	SuperLeadership
• Direction	• Encourage self-goal-setting
• Instruction	• Encourage self-evaluation
• Command	• Encourage high self-expectancy
• Assigned jobs/tasks	• Facilitate self-problem solving
• Assigned goals	• Develop self-initiative and responsibility
• Hierarchical conflict resolution	• Encourage within-group conflict resolution
• Reprimand	• Provide training
	• Encourage opportunity thinking

and Leavitt, 1999; Shea and Guzzo, 1987), but the role and the behaviour of managers external to the team – the 'external' leaders (Manz and Sims, 1987; Hackman, 1992; Glaser, 1992) – is also fundamental for the success of the team.

Hackman (1992), for example, has argued that team leaders should focus on critical aspects of the team performance: clear direction, enabling structure, supportive organizational context, available coaching and adequate material resources that the leaders must constantly monitor and take action as required. Manz and Sims (1987) delineate, more in depth, what is for them the actual role and specific behaviour in order for such leaders to be effective and useful to the team. They suggest that the 'external leader' is one who is able to make the team lead itself. They call this 'SuperLeadership' (Manz and Sims, 1993; Manz, 1992). They consider it ineffective, and even dangerous, for the performance of the self-managing team to have traditional leadership (e.g. a foreman) using a top-down approach. In Table 4.2 you can see the set of behaviours associated with traditional leadership and you can compare it with that of the 'SuperLeader' (Manz and Sims, 1993, p. 209).

Exercise 4.3

Using Table 4.2, analyse and discuss leadership in the case of AML. Who is leading the team? What type of leadership can you identify? Illustrate your arguments with examples from the vignette.

In SuperLeadership, external managers and superiors are supposed to facilitate the team to lead itself. But how does a team specifically develop leadership? Glaser (1992) suggests that self-leadership is obtained through a process of progressive empowerment of the team – a shift of power and authority from the supervisors to the team itself. Self-leadership is the last stage of a four-stage process:

- *Stage 1*. The team is unempowered. Glaser calls this an underdeveloped group. The groups follows the direction of the facilitator, who deploys a top-down leadership style very similar to the traditional one of planning, directing and controlling.

- *Stage 2*. The team starts questioning aspects of its work through dialogue and requests feedback. The role of the leader starts being more that of a coach, offering counsel and advice in a continuous, open communication with the team.

- *Stage 3*. The team is, as Glaser defines it, 'somewhat empowered'. This is a team able to contribute possible strategies and to engage in some critical thinking regarding the planning, controlling and directing of its work.

- *Stage 4*. An effective, self-managing team is established. It is 'fully empowered' as the team itself takes responsibility for planning, direction and control. The team leader has the role of a SuperLeader, facilitating the members of the team to lead themselves, while control of the teamwork is, for the most part, in the hands of the team.

Summary of key mainstream contributions and empirical studies In the first part of this chapter we have provided some definitions and discussed the distinction between *team* and *group work* as they are defined in management theory. We have also considered some of the insights developed in psychology and psychoanalysis for understanding the experience of being in a group. We have seen that there are many group phenomena and that some of them are not necessarily positive for performance, such as the free-riding tendency and the groupthink.

In mainstream management theory teams are considered fundamental for today's organizations. It has been suggested that teams are important because they activate/enhance three organizational dimensions that are considered central for healthy and wealthy work organization: flexibility, motivation and learning. We have analysed and discussed many different empirical studies that are important for studying teams at work in the mainstream management literature. These included traditional industries such as the automobile industry. With the case of NUMMI we illustrated teams working in regimes of 'lean production', 'learning bureaucracy' and 'continuous improvement'; with Volvo, we discussed participative work design and self-managing teams. We also presented a case of a knowledge intensive company, AML, which develops, designs and builds 'perfect digital solutions'. This helped us in illustrating what are often referred to as post-bureaucratic organizational forms, with only two organizational hierarchical layers, and where interdependent members working in self-managing teams are fundamental for getting the job done.

The notions that sustain the positive view of teams at work for increasing morale, flexibility and ultimately productivity, we have argued, are not entirely a new phenomenon but belong to a long tradition of studies that gave origin to the 'human relations school' (Mayo, 1933, 1945), the socio-technical tradition of work design (Trist and Bamforth, 1951) and studies in social psychology devoted to understanding and facilitating social change and democratization through groups (Lewin, 1948). The empirical studies we have referred to are summarized in Table 4.3, where it is indicated how each of

Table 4.3 Summary of empirical studies

Authors	Key concepts	Key contributions
Mayo (1933, 1945)	• Social needs • Group norms and rules	• Informal groups have an impact on motivation and conduct in organizations. They need to be managed
Lewin (1948)	• Group cohesion: we-ness • Group dynamics • Group atmosphere	• A democratic participative atmosphere increases quality and quantity of output • Social relations can be changed and improved by intervening with/in group dynamics
Trist and Bamforth (1951)	• Autonomous responsibility • Socio-technical system	• Social systems can produce groups that show high levels of responsibility even when they have high autonomy • When introducing organizational change we need to intervene not only on the technical but also on the social system
Adler (1993) Adler and Borys (1996) Womack *et al.* (1990)	• Lean production • JIT • Learning bureaucracy	• Teams' responsibility for a practice increases flexibility, motivation and learning • Standardization, formalization and continuous improvement can be obtained also with team-based production
Berggren (1992) Bernstein (1992)	• Self-managing teams • Participative design and organization	• Democratic, participative design is feasible • Social and political factors intervene in favouring the success or failure of a new design

them has contributed to the debate on teams at work. Then we looked at aspects and issues that management theorists consider important for enhancing and perfecting team effectiveness and efficiency. Group development, roles design, resistance and leadership, it is suggested, are some of the areas that need to be attentively managed in order to obtain high-performing and successful teams.

Contribution and limitation of mainstream

Conceptual and methodological contributions and limitations One of the main contributions of the mainstream literature on teams at work is that it appears to offer a solution for everything: it explains how teams work, why they work and how you can make them work more effectively, and even how you can yourself become a successful team member. This can be useful in so far as it helps to reduce the anxiety of what to do when faced with a teamwork situation. Yet, if you have experienced it, team life is rarely as rosy as the mainstream literature seems to imply, and the prescriptions do not necessarily help in improving the situation. It is not always, or not 'just', a matter of 'wrong implementation' of teams at work. Too often, mainstream knowledge creates an overenthusiastic and simplistic view of organizational life that pictures teamwork as a **panacea** (Jenkins, 1996; Dunphy and Bryant, 1996; Sinclair, 1992). The categories and the prescriptions offered in the mainstream are often detached from the complexities and messiness of organizing people and resources. A list of bullet points that is mechanically applied without regard to the particularities of the situation can create more problems than it solves.

Much of the mainstream literature centres on the classification of what teams are and how it is possible to improve team effectiveness. The aim is to establish – by limited, often anecdotal and methodologically dubious studies – the basis for models that can establish conceptual differences (such as the distinction between 'real teams' and 'groupwork') and predict behaviours and results (for example, by limiting the number of individuals with cultural values that are not conducive to self-managing teams; or recruiting people to fill required roles). However, the possibility of finding comprehensive and universally predictive models is, as Benders and Van Hootegem (2000, p. 7) put it, a 'mission impossible'. Many have pointed out that when we leave the field of prescriptions (i.e. the magic bullet points) it is very difficult to make comparisons between different plants and experiences (Mueller, 1994; Benders and Van Hootegem, 1999, 2000; Van Amelsvoort and Benders, 1996; Buchanon, 2000). In the concrete experiences of work, the variances we can find are enormous and the issues at work numerous and awkward.

Thinkpoint 4.5

Can you employ any of the concepts of the mainstream to analyse and compare teams at work in NUMMI, Uddevalla and AML? What limitations do you find?

In the case of AML, many elements that are suggested in the mainstream, such as assessing employees for relevant roles and identifying resistances, and matching people to obtain role balance, are impossible given the resources available. Including the elements suggested in the literature in the recruitment and selection process could be a sensible thing to do, but it would be very costly – an aspect little considered in the mainstream literature where there is a silence on costs issues as well as the broader feasibility of introducing the prescriptions for 'proper' teamwork (Dunphy and Bryant, 1996; Sinclair, 1992). Their universal, one size fits all prescriptions do not take into consideration the specificity of the industry. In order to understand teams at work, we need to include a much wider set of issues based on a 'detailed examination of historical, technological and socio-political internal and external conditions of teamworking practice' (Knights and McCabe, 2000). Teamwork, in other words, should not be considered as a well-defined, fixed package but, rather, it is dependent upon, and influenced by a set of dynamic circumstances: 'issues of the extent and nature of delegated power, or whether socialisation of teams' members plays an important role, are contingent on a variety of national, corporate and local factors' (Thompson and Wallace, 1996, p. 105).

Specifically then, some of the suggestions given in the mainstream knowledge of teams at work, such as testing for roles and disposition to resistance, imply the existence of a labour market that contains a right balance in terms of roles, dispositions and skills from which the company can source

Critical writers contest the **idealized picture** of teamwork painted in the mainstream literature. This idealization can be seen in the somewhat benign nature of teamwork as creating a win-win work situation (Ezzamel and Willmott, 1998): employees are more satisfied and their work is 'smarter' because they have been treated like adult human beings with respect and they are given responsibility and autonomy. This makes it possible for the 'organization' to be more flexible, innovative and capable of sustaining and building its future.

The idealized, rosy picture is obtained by dismissing behaviours, ideas and issues that do not fit the creed sustained in the mainstream – what Sinclair (1992) calls the 'team ideology'. The mainstream promises a better organizational reality for managers and for workers alike. But, as we have seen, things often 'do not fit'. There are 'remains' – that is, elements that disrupt the nice, clear picture of teams at work.

Thinkpoint 4.6

How is the idealized picture sustained and maintained? Behaviours that 'do not fit' are quickly dismissed, if even noticed, in different ways in the mainstream. For example:

- *As irrational aberrations*, as in the case presented earlier of the Volvo operator who actually stated he preferred to be told what to do. The suggestion is that it is irrational to prefer the inhumane and alienating repetition of Taylorist organization to the empowering and democratic self-managing teams. What do you think?

- *As personal shortcomings or idiosyncrasies*, as in the example of the order filler (page 137) who was fantastic at his job but just could not understand how good and amazing the whole new system based on teamwork was.

- *As unfortunate individual/cultural predispositions*, as in the case of the Kirkman model (page 138) whereby if you are individualist and being-oriented and high in power disposition you are hopeless because the likelihood that you are going to be a bad team player is high!

- *As perceptions* of fairness, trust and justice, which makes these issues a subjective matter to be addressed and seemingly resolved by means of ethical codes of conduct and regulations.

Critical perspectives on teamworking question what, in the mainstream literature, are taken-for-granted 'truths' of teams at work, pointing out the contradictions of such teamwork theory and practice. First, we shall delve into contributions that aim to show another, arguably darker side to teamwork. This section is entitled 'The other side of the coin', which specifically highlights issues of inequality and autonomy/freedom. Concepts and ideas will be illustrated by reference to the NUMMI case presented earlier. As a significant part of the critical debate centres on the concept of control, a second section is dedicated to understanding teamworking by considering how issues of identity are of relevance for its critical analysis. Other empirical studies, including AML, will be used to illustrate these ideas.

The other side of the coin

Working smarter *and* harder One of the key considerations pointed out by critical writers is that teamworking is generally a top-down, management (or employer) driven process. As Procter and Mueller (2000) note, many of the original studies of teams at work, particularly those of the socio-technical tradition, were cases where employees had organized themselves in autonomous groups (see also Ezzamel, Willmott and Worthington, 2001), while today teamwork is introduced by management as part of a proper managerial strategy (Procter and Mueller, 2000, p. 8). This strategy has specific stated aims, one of the most important being to increase the efficiency of the workforce – as the slogan goes, 'by working smarter not harder'. Yet, many contend that often teamwork means working smarter *and* harder (Adler, 1993; Parker and Slaughter, 1988; Berggren, 1992; Garrahan and Stewart, 1992; McCabe and Black, 1996). In other words, teamworking can produce (and it often does) work intensification. Voices from the union movement have been extremely critical of practical applications of teamwork, specifically in regimes of 'lean production', so much so that it has been recast as 'mean production' (Parker and Slaughter, 1988; Grenier, 1989).

Production is 'mean' because of the negative effect upon the employees of minimizing stockpiles of parts and other forms of duplication in production. These are considered as waste in the lean, JIT design. Yet they function as 'buffers', which, Parker and Slaughter argue, make the system more bearable for the workers as they give them a breathing space that is lacking in the highly regimented lean design. Buffers also give managers a certain leeway, enabling them to keep things going, covering for problems or emergencies if they arise. CYA ('cover your ass'), by building in some elements of slack and redundancy, has often been considered a prudent operating procedure, as Parker and Slaughter (1988, p. 16) observe!

By aiming to eliminate waste of all kinds, lean production does not give any leeway and pressurizes all the 'components' of the system continuously, without any possibility of having a steady and tolerable pace. The pace of production is relentless and continuously stressed to higher and higher degrees, in many different ways, for example, by speeding up the line. Parker and Slaughter call this management-by-stress (MBS) as, when following the principles of *kaizen*, new standards are created that assign additional activities to the workers of a team that must also keep up with a faster assembly line. But higher stress is also felt every time there is an absentee from the team, or a new, novice worker is assigned to the team. Given that workers in the NUMMI teams are interchangeable, and a team is completely responsible for a certain area of work, then it is the team that is responsible for covering for slow workers, novices or absentees. Each worker has to continue with their normal tasks and all the team members are called to do a bit of the work of the novice or the absentee. In other words, the cost is on the team and the team leader and, as Parker and Slaughter (1988, p. 21) put it, 'no department's budget is hurt by absenteeism'.

Thinkpoint 4.7

What problems do you see with this system? Do you think this system ensures equality in the distribution of effort/cost? Do you think this system of work respects human dignity? What is human dignity for you?

Box 4.7: The meaning of 'human dignity' and inequality

Human dignity might appear an uncontested concept, but the example of what is understood by 'human dignity' in the context of the advocates of lean production is enlightening. Human dignity is central for the 'empowered' workforce yet, as Parker and Slaughter (1988) point out, the whole teamwork rhetoric employs a peculiar notion of humanity. They give the example of the answer given by Monden (1983), an advocate and popularizer of the practices of Toyota, to those who criticize the lack of buffers and slack. Monden suggests that allowing for slack 'does not give the opportunity for the worker to realise his [sic] worth. On the contrary, that end can be better served by providing the worker with a sense that his work is worthwhile and allowing him to work with his superior and his comrades to solve problems they encounter.' This example,

apart from showing the gendered organization of work, also succinctly points out how human dignity and human fulfilment is defined within a mainstream perspective, namely, to exercise one's abilities to solve problems with others. This view is *defined by management*, and somewhat 'given', ready made, to the workers who simply have to accept and actualize 'this dignity' in the terms and in practices that are established by management. A narrow view of human dignity established by a particular section of the population, namely management, is taken to stand for a universal and necessary view of human dignity. This instrumental view of human dignity at once poses a particular view as universal and also reproduces and legitimizes the structured system of inequalities in wealth and status that are normal features of capitalist societies.

Parker and Slaughter (1988) contend that this intensification of work is less humane than traditional forms of work organization. In the name of empowerment, this system cuts the possibility of breathing space and personal autonomy that 'buffers' of different kinds made possible. Teams have an unprecedented level of responsibility but also a limited possibility of exercising genuine autonomy, since the main objective of the system is to develop higher and higher degrees of efficiency (and productivity). It, therefore, requires strict adherence to its own rigid methods and procedures (Klein, 1989, p.p. 60–61).

These considerations are important and represent a departure from the mainstream for two reasons. They point to the other, ugly face of teamwork as an intensifying and stressful practice of work, which does not really square with mainstream images of teamwork as a more playful and fulfilling cooperation in achieving harmonized organizational ends. More fundamentally, it puts into question who benefits from the work smarter and harder logic. For Parker and Slaughter, the workers are not necessarily benefiting from this process of intensification of their labour, which instead serves the ends of 'those' exploiting the workers' capacity for labour, as they get more labour for less money and less managerial overheads, in a regime in which 'participation' is on management's terms.

Teamworking as control and consent over labour effort and cost With the shift to a critical view of teamworking, we pay attention to its role in the perpetuation of a particular socio-economic order – that of liberal capitalist societies. In liberal capitalism, the owners of the business organization (the 'shareholders') and its controllers and enactors (management) are, broadly speaking, concerned to maximize profit at the minimum cost. This is obtained by dividing and coordinating a set of productive activities where the surplus (income minus expenditures) generated in these activities (which, as we have seen earlier, are made natural and normal by the use of comparatively impersonal organizational ends) is privately appropriated (by the owners themselves).

Karl Marx, a political thinker, developed the understanding that, in capitalism, the planning, division and coordination of work are intended to ensure control of the workers in a process that is alienating and exploitative. By 'control' is meant the mechanism of exploitation. While wages are paid for the workers' *capacity* to engage in purposeful activities, the transformation that adds value to a given process of work happens only in the moment of its actual application. *Without control, this application is at a discretion of the workers*, and that is why management is employed to control workers in order to get the maximum application at a minimum cost. Control is needed to make sure that workers submit to the logic of capital accumulation, so as to eliminate what are considered 'unproductive' time and practices – what we called 'waste' in JIT. This understanding of work organization – which highlights the role of management in controlling workers in order to produce a surplus that can be distributed to shareholders – questions something that for us all is entirely normal. It is so normal, infact, that we take it for granted as our existence is routinely seen within the coordinates that this system produces and maintains. We expect and also wish to enter wage relations with an employer, with the inequalities and the subordination to, or over, others that this relation implies. We generally regard this as an unexceptional, even natural progression in life, signalling independence and the entrance into adulthood.

Thinkpoint 4.8

Do you think there are alternatives to this organization and division of labour and resources? How could those alternatives be realized? What problems do you foresee?

In other words, critical perspectives suggest that even if teamworking moves away from the fragmenting, individualizing logic of Taylorism, it maintains the same fundamental logic of workers' exploitation. But it is accomplished in a different way as the workers are given the means to influence, within narrow limits controlled by management, at least part of how the application of their labour should be accomplished. The logic (and the power relations that are sustained by it) is much the same, as the coordinates are that of maximum application of labour at minimum cost for the owners. This, in the case of NUMMI, was accomplished by work intensification so as to achieve

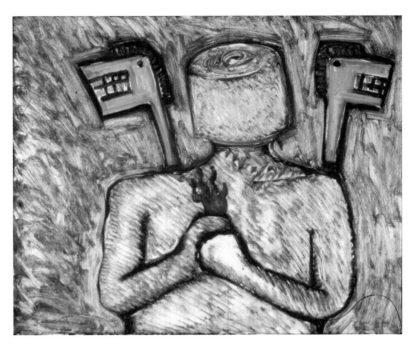

Image 4.5 Consent

maximum input per unit of work. But it can be accomplished in different ways. In AML, we saw how workers 'feel responsible' for finishing the detailed content design of the e-mail system address book. They stay at work late to get the job done. This means that they continue to work beyond 'normal working hours' – a concept that has become almost obsolete in many (e.g. knowledge-intensive) firms – and far beyond the working hours for which they are paid. This effort, then, is literally (money) and figuratively (time that could be spent doing other things in their life) at the workers' expense.

This example of AML illustrates what Friedman (1977) calls control by 'responsible autonomy', in which workers are encouraged and rewarded by management to exercise their discretion in ways that are responsible for attaining management's goals (e.g. greater productivity). Teamwork is a practice that can help facilitate this feeling of involvement in the work they do, and a sense of ownership of their practice that increases the responsibility they have for their work. Through teamworking, they actively **consent** to furthering their own exploitation and further their subordination. It is in this sense that teamwork is considered a subtle form of control, not least because it is clothed in a rhetoric of participation and employee involvement. It is intended to enhance work effort, thereby increasing productivity but saving on labour cost (see Pollert, 1996; McCabe and Black, 1996; Buchanan, 2000).

Thinkpoint 4.9

Why do people consent to this form of control? How is it that teamworking facilitates this consent?

Some writers, such as Parker and Slaughter (1988), have argued that the utilization of the team concept – what, as we have seen, Sinclair calls 'team ideology' – is a manipulation that 'cons' workers. It cons them into believing that the managerial strategies for intensification and consent are good for them, desirable and serve their interests as workers and as individual human beings. In other words, teamwork is regarded as a managerial strategy that realigns (most of the time successfully) 'individual motivation' with 'organizational need' (see Mueller, 1994); it reduces conflict and resistance at work; and it marginalizes or neutralizes the need for, and the role of, unions, as the employees' material and psychological needs are met through their (managed) identification with their team.

One of the problems with this view is that it implies that that the workers are ignorant and blinded in understanding their own real interest, while there are others, arguably radical theorists or union leaders, who are knowledgeable about what these interests are, and uncover them for the workers. This essentialist view of the human subject also assumes that there is such a thing as a 'real' interest, where real is understood as a fixed and determined knot in our lives that if undone would 'sort' our lives forever, or, at least, release us from our delusions (false consciousness) so showing us our true interest.

A murkier picture of teamwork

Many critical writers suggest the picture is much murkier than the one presented above, given that the contradictions of teamwork are evident and available to workers, managers and students, making teamwork a 'contested terrain' rather than an encompassing ideology that is readily and effectively applied by a cunning management to a naive workforce. Garrahan and Stewart (1992) contend that at Nissan workers willingly consent to their own subordination and further exploitation. The workers know very well what they are doing, but nevertheless they still do it. In other words, they are not simply 'conned' and manipulated by managerial strategy and its ideology (teamwork). Research on teamwork implementation presented by Pollert (1996) and McCabe and Black (1996) suggests that teamworking can create a set of ambiguities for the workers, which does not necessarily lead to consent (see Ezzamel *et al.*, 2001). Managers themselves experience conflicting demands that make the contradictions of teamwork more evident and give reason 'for the union to retain a foot hold' (Pollert cited in McCabe and Black, 1996, p. 114). In the politics of production, teamworking reflects local dynamics where its principles are partially implemented, imperfectly adopted and inconsistently applied. However, we should avoid slipping into a form of 'contingency analysis': 'when faced with the grand claims of would-be gurus, the danger is that we slip into a form of contingency analysis where a detailing of the context displaces theoretical reflection altogether' (Knights and McCabe, 2000, p. 6).

We need additional theoretical resources to question teamworking and problematize the issue of consent and the reproduction of relations of inequality, which, it has been suggested, this practice perpetuates. Many authors (see for example Ezzamel and Willmott, 1998; Ezzamel *et al.*, 2001; Knights and McCabe, 2003; McCabe and Knights, 2000; McKinlay and Taylor, 1996; Sewell and Wilkinson, 1992; Sewell, 1998) have attempted to address these questions, in particular by considering how workers' *subjectivity* – their sense of self – is central to resistance and consent. These views draw upon theoretical sources that we explore and illustrate next.

Self-discipline and surveillance Detailed ethnographies can enable us to make sense of how it is that workers' sense of identity comes to be shaped in conduct that secures willing consent and compliance to work smarter and harder, as teamwork becomes a means for control that increases their productivity and exploitation. The main point conveyed by these studies is that teamworking itself is a social practice through which workers discipline themselves, and each other, by continuous surveillance and by creating, as well as enforcing on themselves and on others, the identity of 'team-mate' (see Barker, 1993, 1999; Sewell and Wilkinson, 1992; Sewell, 1998). This knowledge exerts power as it is also a self-knowledge, by which workers can talk about themselves and 'rationalize' their conduct, by considering what it means to be a team player, and what it takes to be a good team member. How is self-identity specifically conceptualized? A key to answering how it is that people consent and willingly subject to the working harder and smarter logic is embedded in a certain understanding of subjectivity – i.e. what we say we are and how we identify ourselves, most of the time, as free, autonomous and rational beings.

In the mainstream literature, people are considered 'essential beings' – i.e. they 'carry' a sense of self that can be classified and measured in all sorts of scales and categories. In the case of teamwork, people might be categorized for their orientation, for their locus of control, for their personality trait or IQ. Critical writers, in particular those influenced by the work of Michel Foucault, challenge this essentialist and psychologized view of identity. They consider how our 'subjectivity' – i.e. our own sense of self – is constituted and reproduced everyday by actively participating in social practices and in acquiring and reproducing the knowledge that sustains and explains these practices. This means that our subjectivity is not so much described, as it is constituted, for example, by a knowledge that tells us that we have an IQ of 120, have a 'being-orientation', and are high in 'power distance'. Foucault calls this complex set of practices 'power/knowledge', as knowledge itself is productive of relations of power.

Our sense of self is then constantly maintained and reproduced by participation in social practices, by our social relations in the family and friends, by what we read, the products we buy and so on. But this is counter-intuitive, you might think, as you are and always will be your 'own person'. You might 'change' or 'mature', but deep down you are always 'your self'. In other words, there is a sense of continuity about your self-identity that you might feel very strongly about. For critical writers the coherency of our sense of self is like a narrative (see Ezzamel and Willmott, 1998) that we keep on telling us and others – what 'we really are' – but also 'what we really are not' and 'what we really would like to be'. This narrative is continuously negotiated and often comes under threat with feelings of anxiety and insecurities engendered by 'things' that do not fit either with what we thought of ourselves or what we thought of as our reality.

Thinkpoint 4.10

Reflect on your own narrative and thinking of your life as a university student and other experiences you might be undertaking (such as part-time jobs or voluntary work). What is your sense of self? What experiences have challenged the view you have of your self? What experiences have reinforced your sense of self?

An example in AML In the case of AML, John's sense of self is narrated as a knowleadgeable tehnical expert, a 'wizard' in producing elegant and creative technical solutions. To sustain this sense of self he had to collaborate with others. Yet teamworking in AML calls for an involvement with others in phases of design that, for him, is, as he put it in an interview, 'far too much'. He finds himself working as a content designer, while 'my job is technical, I am a technical expert'. In other words, this practice threatens his sense of self as technical expert. Perversely, however, he knows that the final product, will be viewed and assessed by others (his colleagues, his managers, the clients, and the members of the community of technical experts, the internet and mobile users) not simply as a technical solution but as a complete whole. So he engages yet more actively and forcefully in the practice of work to make sure that this 'really is' the elegant and usable solution, which is what sustains the narrative of himself as a 'wizard' and expert.

Further illustrations of the importance of identity in understanding teamworking as a technology that fashions compliant subjects can be derived from the ethnographic work of James Barker (1993, 1998). Barker's study of ISE, a US electronic company, is exemplary of the set of practices that the introduction of the self-managing teams can engender to create a pattern of discipline and surveillance, what he called 'concertive control'. Barker calls it concertive control (see also Tompkins and Cheney, 1985) because workers act in concert to develop the means of their own control (Barker, 1993, p. 4).

What is fascinating about Barker's study of ISE (see Case Study 4.5) is that the final result of the team activity has a strong resemblance to the traditional bureaucratic form of control – i.e. the card checking and ranking of performance. Nonetheless, the source of authority and the enforcement of this control is not the abstract impersonal rule of bureaucratic order but a diffuse set of mechanisms devised by the teams themselves and sustained by the team power/knowledge. Teamwork power/knowledge is composed also of the rules identified and recognized by team members as establishing and summarizing the proper conduct of a rightful teamwork ethic. Self-discipline and surveillance of the concertive control produced an even tighter iron cage than the traditional bureaucracy. Some have called this type of control 'chimerical control' exactly because it is not traditional top-down but is diffused and has hybrid and monstrous characteristics (Sewell, 1998, p. 12). The team members daily constructed, reproduced and maintained a power/knowledge of what they are, and what their work is, that makes them their own masters and their own slaves: 'ISE team workers are both under the eye of the norm and in the eye of the norm, but from where they are, in the eye, all seems natural and as it should be' (Barker, 1993, p. 435).

As we shift to a critical perspective, we consider teamworking as a social practice that institutes, maintains and creates certain power relations by means, as Knights and McCabe (2000) put it, of constituting particular kinds of subjectivities – in short, transforming individuals into teamworking subjects who assume a self-identity as team-mates or face problems or expulsion. For example, Barker points out that 'uncommitted workers' – that is uncommitted according to the team power/knowledge – do not last in the concertive system: 'If they wanted to resist their team control, they must be willing to risk their human dignity, being made to feel unworthy as "team-mates" ' (Barker, p. 436).

Resistance is futile(?) We seem to have painted a rather bleak picture of teamwork. On the one hand, we have suggested that considering teamwork as (traditional) ideology was empirically unsustainable, and theoretically flawed (see page 148). Then the concepts of concertive control, surveillance and discipline were proposed, which, however, from a different theoretical route, arrive at the same conclusion. The bars of the cage are even stronger as people are entrenched in what makes them what they

CASE STUDY 4.5 Teamwork and concerted control: Self-discipline and surveillance

Barker's ethnography of an electronic board assembly factory started at the beginning of the 1990s and lasted two years. The CEO had read the popular management writers (such as Drucker), praising the importance of teamwork and the recognition of employees' participation. He was fascinated and persuaded by this knowledge. He studied the system based on self-managing teams, and then implemented a new organizational design.

First he conducted a limited experiment or 'pilot', and then the whole production activity was organized into self-managing teams. Each individual was assigned to a team that became responsible for the manufacture or configuration of two or three electronic boards. The teams had to decide how to share the work, how to assign responsibilities, what were the ground rules of their work, etc. The company offered training in teambuilding and interpersonal skills and provided supporting advice. They were never told what to do but were guided, notably by the mission statement that was prepared for them by the ISE president. This expressed the values that the company expected from the team, and from each individual as a self-manager: personal initiative, responsibility in doing the work, commitment to the team, quality of individual and team contributions. Barker describes how team members at first experienced confusion and uncertainties because they did not know what to do. Yet, they soon realized it was 'really' up to them to decide how to do the work!

In an impressive number of meetings, teams started discussing closely what their work meant for them, what good quality was, what they expected from each other and so on. Barker notes how the team members started to talk about a sense of ownership and extreme commitment to the work they were doing, feeling that delivering the product on time was their responsibility. For example, there was an incident where some material arrived late, which then required the team to

stay late if they were to get the order out to the customer as scheduled. Lea Ann, one of the team members, called the team and put it to everyone that it would take two hours overtime to accomplish the task. Some people had various commitments, but they discussed the issue and eventually all agreed to stay. One of them, they agreed, could go at the normal time because she wanted to attend her children's play at school, but she promised that she would work late the next time it was required.

This is a compelling example of how a team translated into practice the values indicated by the company. The team acquired a set of values that became translated, particularly when new employees joined, in more and more visible signs of commitment. The teams created a series of mechanisms that facilitated and disciplined workers into forms of conduct that reproduced and reinforced their identity as proper, valuable and respected members of an effective and efficient team. Mutual surveillance was part of the conduct of team members. The rules of the team became progressively clearer and more explicit and were enforced in many different ways. For example, some teams had time set aside in their meetings to confront members whose behaviour did not conform to the team rules.

But there were also more subtle means of mutual surveillance – for example, in relation to lateness. Before teamworking, the supervisors might have turned a blind eye to lateness. But teams developed a zero tolerance for tardiness so that everyone's arrival was ranked everyday with a colour coded card system. If a worker collected too many red dots, this would call for a sanction. As one of the employees put it 'now the whole team around me is observing what I am doing'. The constant surveillance promoted self-discipline and compliance as it implied that to be a team member one has to follow the conduct expected, the standards of which are agreed and monitored by the team itself.

Image 4.6

are: their own self-identity as team members. Teamworking power/knowledge seems comparable to the technology of the Borg in *Star Trek*, the famous sci-fi series. The Borg pursues the quest for knowledge and for perfection by assimilating in the collective mind all the alien cultures encountered, so all the differences are maintained in a perfect whole. The collective changes all the time, but it always stays the same imperturbably, just like capitalism which has to change in order to avoid collapse. 'Resistance is futile!' states the Borg in front of the terrorized subject, to whom perfection and knowledge is given when the assimilation is completed. Are we all assimilated in a system that gives us a sense of self? Are the Borg right – resistance is futile?

Critical writers suggest that it is not futile. But, again, it is not a matter of finding or even proposing a single solution or recipe. The point is that making explicit the ambivalence and ambiguity of everyday working practices helps in making explicit the antagonism and negativity of social relations. This reminds us how much the sedimentation and taken-for-grantedness of these relations is the results of political acts. As such, these are not naturally given, can be changed and are constantly threatened at work.

As Garahan and Stewart (1992) note in their study of Nissan, not all employees totally identify with the 'team-mates' ethos and identity. There is resistance to practices that were intended to strengthen the Nissan culture and its values such as the sponsoring of sports events, family events and holidays for employees' children. Many employees would not, or could not, identify with such values, and many were cynical towards teamworking (see also Ezzamel *et al.*, 2001; Knights and McCabe, 2000, 2003). Some of the workers (but arguably also some of the managers) would consider themselves to have no alternative other than to 'shut up and put up' because losing employment was not considered a real option. Their sense of identity as providers for their own family or homeowners or consumers, etc. made it impossible for them to consider risking losing their jobs.

More broadly we should consider that for critical writers social practices (such as teamworking) never totalize or exhaust the field of possibilities altogether. In other words, it is impossible to ever determine the meaning, the results and the possibilities offered by a particular practice. This means and implies that teamworking as power/knowledge operates neither according to the aims of the managers nor workers but it establishes what the identities of both might be. Fundamentally the issue refers to the fact that binary logic – i.e. that teamwork either produces consent or produces resistance; or the logic that if it is a managerial tool then it produces only workers' exploitation – cannot be maintained. As the meaning of social practices (in this case of teamworking) is never determined once and for all, it is open to contestation and its closure is constantly under threat and open to rearticulation.

We can illustrate this openness and ambiguity of teamworking power/knowledge with reference to McKinlay and Taylor's (1996) study of Pyramid (see Case study 4.6).

In summary:

- As a social practice, teamwork is 'owned' neither by the managers nor by the workers. What is a 'manager' and what is a 'worker' is realized and reproduced in the teamworking practice, as well as by other practices, which create and maintain the meaning of self and the meaning of work in our lives.

- Teamworking as power/knowledge is not a monolith established once and for all at the service of management. But it is constantly open to rearticulation that can disrupt and subvert the status quo.

Recap questions

1 What is understood by teamwork in the critical tradition?

2 Why are teams said to be a managerial strategy for work intensification?

3 Can you illustrate these views?

4 In what ways does teamwork further inequalities and exploitation?

5 What are the problems with these views?

6 What is concertive control?

7 Why is teamwork considered a social form of what is called power/knowledge?

8 How does this critical understanding of teamwork reconceptualize identity?

9 How does this help us in conceptualizing consent and resistance?

10 What examples from your own experience can you use to illustrate the complex, contradictory, ambiguous and, in a sense, murkier picture of teamworking?

CASE STUDY 4.6 Resistance and teamworking

In Pyramid, a technological company, teamwork power/knowledge came to play a role that compromised the expected aims for which empowered teams were introduced. A clue to the role of teamworking in dislocating managerial expectations and design can be seen in the adoption of the system of peer review for the teams. This was introduced by the management as a way of obtaining knowledge about the shop floor, as well as a forum for the teams to reflect on themselves and their teambuilding processes. It was, in other words, a disciplinary mechanism.

This practice of peer review proved largely unpopular at first, and it was resisted by many employees, who, for example, started to use retaliatory scoring to get at each other. Eventually, however, the equalizing of scores became widespread, which, of course, made this technology useless. Interestingly, the equalizing was made possible by the mobilization of the team ethos itself. It was argued that if the team is reaching the target why should different people be scored more highly than others if the overall result was good? This makes explicit how teamworking as power/knowledge is open to constant rearticulation, which also establishes the interests it is serving and not the other way round. Rather than creating consent it created a sense of resistance to the scoring system

and the differences this was designed to establish among workers. In other words, it shows us how the system of inequalities, on which capitalist work relations are based, are actually subverted by taking teamworking 'too seriously' as the workers did in this case, over-identifying with the team ethos.

As a disciplinary mechanism, the peer review was supposed to classify, divide and rank the workers so that bonuses could be allocated to 'deserving' workers. The fact that this was done by the workers themselves should have tied them to their own self-evaluation. This also would provide the effect of a 'consensual' basis for bonus payments. But the workers disrupted these intended truth effects of the self-assessment exercise. They subverted the idea of consensual ranking and classification, as well as that of 'bonuses'. Managers faced with the impossibility of equality – because if bonuses were paid equally the profitability of the operation would be hurt – assigned the bonuses randomly. This response became a nodal point for the constitution of a clear antagonistic move, with teams going on a silent strike – what the employees called three weeks of 'go slow' – and a devastatingly high number of complaints filed against the managerial decision. This occurrence was symptomatic of the inequalities on which such workplaces are based.

Summary of key contributions, empirical studies and limitations in the critical approach

In the second part of this chapter we have analysed critically the concept and practice of teamwork. We referred to a number of empirical studies that have approached teamwork from a critical perspective. These studies are summarized in Table 4.4 and their main contribution to the debate in questioning teamwork is highlighted.

We have suggested that teamwork is often considered an ideology that, under the seductive slogan of 'working smarter not harder', in reality forces workers to work both smarter *and* harder. In other words, there is another, darker side to the rosy picture we have seen presented in the mainstream literature. By revisiting the NUMMI case and the AML case we have discussed how teamwork is a process that increases work intensification and furthers workers' exploitation, participating in eroding workers' rights and conditions. We have considered how one of the limitations of this view is that it assumes that workers are 'conned' by management into believing that teamwork is good for them. This critical structuralists view implies that workers are determined in their conduct and their belief by the managerial strategies and the manipulations they are able to engender, while both managers and critical social theorists are able to see what the workers' real interest is or should be. For example, critical structuralists think that workers' real interests should be that of resisting teamworking practices. However, some critical writers suggest that this privileged insight cannot be justified because, empirically, we observe that production, including teamworking, is a very contested terrain, and not a monolithic, whole encompassing ideology. Workers and managers are ambiguous in their understanding of teamwork and the way they participate in these practices. It is suggested that we can understand and address better the complexities and ambiguities of the experiences in production if, theoretically, we move away from essential notions of subjectivity. One's sense of self is not determined by managers' strategies but is produced, maintained and elaborated in the many practices, diffused mechanisms and technologies in which we participate in and in which we are constituted as subjects, like in the case of teamworking power/knowledge where people develop a knowledge about themselves and their conduct.

One of the limitations of this approach is that it appears to create a bleak picture of working practices because disciplinary mechanisms seem to produce entirely consenting subjects; excluding any sense of resistance. However, we have suggested that these mechanisms of power, of which teamworking is an example, cannot be considered to be owned by anyone in particular and cannot ever be defined in their meaning and consequences once and for all. In other words, even if teamworking can be intentionally introduced in order to exploit teamwork power/knowledge and increase self-control and discipline, that does not mean that it produces what top managers and shareholders desire. The practice of

Table 4.4 Summary of empirical studies

Authors	Key concepts	Key contributions
Parker and Slaughter (1988)	• Mean production • Management-by-stress	• Teamwork is a managerial strategy of work intensification
Barker (1993, 1999) See also Sewell (1998) Ezzamel and Willmott (1998) Sewell and Wilkinson (1992)	• Concertive control • Self-discipline • Surveillance • Consent	• Teamwork is itself a social practice that produces and maintains a self-identity • This enhances control and consent
MacKinlay and Taylor (1996) See also Knights and McCabe (2001, 2003) Ezzamel and Willmott (1998) Ezzamel et al., (2001)	• Openness of social practices • Resistance	• Teamwork as a social practice and its subject cannot be determined once and for all • Teamworking can also provoke resistance and antagonistic behaviour

teamwork can actually be disruptive of production for both managers and workers. This indicates that discipline and surveillance of teamworking power/knowledge can also be a subverting force. The case of Pyramid illustrated the fear of some of the mainstream management authors. In fact, workers over-identified with the teamworking ethos, thereby traversing the fantasy that teamwork sustains, namely the notion that contemporary workplaces are sites of social relation based on an equal and just exchange. This over-identification brought forth the inequalities on which the capitalist system of production is based and became a nodal point around which an antagonism against management was coagulated.

Final remarks

Teams and good performance are inseparable; you cannot have one without the other. But people use the word 'team' so loosely that it gets in the way of learning and applying the discipline that leads to good performance. For managers to make better decisions about whether, when or how to encourage and use teams, it is important to be more precise about what a team is and what it isn't. (*Katzenbach and Smith, 1993, p. 163*)

Some of my students and I love this quote because it condenses the taken-for-granted truth about teams and teamwork in mainstream management studies. But there is another truth that oozes from this quote on which I want to concentrate.

Some of my students find the quote appealing because they want to become managers. Arguably, they believe that if someone tells them precisely how they are supposed to manage properly, they will get it right and will be successful managers. This belief is directly attended by Katzenbach and Smith (1993), who propose to 'repair' the shortcomings of woolly thinking and bring in the due precision that will lead to good performance.

Who would not like that? If there were clear, sure recipes telling us what to do and how; if there was something of an indubitable descriptive precision; if there was a natural Truth, we would all know what to do at all times. How great that would be! No more uncertainties and doubts, nor that stomach-turning anxiety we occasionally or often feel but rarely mention. A template would describe and dictate our behaviour, working life and even family life and leisure. It would all be perfectly determined and we would be living in a world of . . . automatons. Yes, with a template for everything, everything would already be decided so we would be like sophisticated robots. We would not decide anything as the decision would be dictated by principles – of teamwork or total quality management, etc. Actually we would not even think of such a thing/concept as a decision. A decision requires an utter not-knowing. A real decision is a crazy step because it is something we take out of undecidability. It is after we have taken it that we find reasonable motives for taking 'this' decision rather than 'that' one. In other words, always it is the present that gives us a sense of the past and the future and not vice versa.

Mind you, the whole point of much of what we call knowledge is about telling us what to do, when and how. Much of management and organization theory is about explaining how things are organized in systems and how these systems help us to predict and control what we do. In organizations there are job descriptions, financial charts, business plans, procedures and contracts. All these indicate and even prescribe the role and behaviour of managers, workers, customers, clients and suppliers, and what these 'stakeholders' are supposed to do. You are reading this book because most likely you are a student in a university and your lecturer said you should read it, and because you are a conscientious student or because your family expect you to do your best at university, and perhaps, because you want to get a good mark and get a top, highly paid job.

So much is directed, ruled, regulated, decided. Yet there are things (ideas, behaviours, elements) that do not fit. As we have seen earlier, if employees really followed completely their job description or the implications of things such as teamworking, probably their units would arrive at a standstill. And, yes, your family may want you to be a conscientious student; but they also want you to be a rounded person, and have friends and keep fit and eat well and be a good citizen. So they probably would not want you to be over-conscientious! But when is the line reached? So many things are often contradictory and, anyway, you do not only do what your family wishes!

It is because things never fit perfectly, because there are some remains of what we are supposed to be and do that there are so many different views on life and interpretations and theories and cultures. Procedures, templates, desires, etc. can never tell us 'the truth' of what we are and what the world is about. We are not automatons. This is the sense of freedom, that is at once appealing, seductive, chastening and terrifying. There are alternatives to the way things are; they are not naturally given; they are not written in stone. They are 'sedimented' constructions, so much so that too often we forget that they are constituted. They are sedimented power relations, and power is not 'natural' – power is 'social'. That, in a nutshell, is the fundamental assumption upon which critical power/knowledge is constructed.

Alternatives are possible. Suspecting and undermining those who claim to have the truth, those who do not even consider that 'truth' is problematic, and showing and proposing alternatives that mobilize the values of equality and freedom, is part of what a radical and democratic project is about. And this is what this chapter, in showing mainstream and critical views, has tried to do in relation to the meaning and valence of teamwork. This is a way of making sense of the politics of one arena of management knowledge, and, as such, this knowledge itself, and your reading of it, is a political act.

Further reading

Barker, J. R. (1999) *The Discipline of Teamwork: Participation and Concertive Control*, London: Sage.

Danaher, G., Schirato, T. and Webb, J. (2000) *Understanding Foucault*, London: Sage.

Foulkes, S. H. and Anthony, E. J. (1957) *Group Psychotherapy: The Psychoanalytic Approach*, London: Penguin Books.

Marx, K. and Engels, F. (1888/1985) *The Communist Manifesto*, London: Penguin Books.

Procter, S. and Mueller, F. (eds) (2000) *Teamworking*, Basingstoke: Macmillan Business.

Wetherell, M. (ed.) (1996) *Identities, Groups and Social Issues*, London: Sage.

Websites

Social psychology and cultural studies sources:
http://www.socialpsychology.org/social.htm#group
http://www.cultsock.ndirect.co.uk/MUHome/cshtml/index.html

Radical and critical sources:
http://www.marxists.org/index.htm
http://www.wsws.org/

http://www.workersworld.net/
http://www.forumsocialmundial.org.br/
http://foucault.info/
http://www.thefoucauldian.co.uk/

Examples of teams and COPs consultants' sites:
Belbin: http://www.belbin.com/game-co-operate.html
Katzenbach: http://www.katzenbach.com/
COPs: http://www.solonline.org/
http://www.ewenger.com/

Portals and sites with resources, games and exercises on teambuilding and development:
http://www.grouprelations.com/
http://www.wilderdom.com/games/InitiativeGames.html
http://www.queendom.com/tests/career/team_roles_access.html
http://www.hrgopher.com/category/377.php
http://reviewing.co.uk/toolkit/teams-and-teamwork.htm

References

Adler, P. (1993) 'Time and motion regained', *Harvard Business Review* 71(1):97–108.

Adler, P. S. and Borys, B. (1996) 'Two types of bureaucracy: Enabling and coercive', *Administrative Science Quarterly* 41(1):61–89.

Albanese, R. and Van Fleet, D. D. (1985) 'Rational behaviour in groups: The free-riding tendency', *Academy of Management Review* 10(2):244–55.

Alvesson, M. (1993) 'Organizations as rhetoric: Knowledge-intensive firms and the struggle with ambiguity', *Journal of Management Studies* 30(6):997–1015.

Ancora, D. and Caldwell, D. (2000) 'Compose teams to assure successful boundary activity', *Blackwell Handbook of Principles of Organizational Behavior*, p.p. 199–210.

Ancora, D. G. and Caldwell, D. F. (2000) 'Bridging the boundary: External activity and performance in organizational teams', *Administrative Science Quarerly* 37(4):634–655.

Argote, L., Gruenfeld, D. and Naquin, C. *et al.* (2000) 'Group learning in organizations', in M. E. Gurner (ed.) *Groups at Work: Advances in Theory and Research*, New York: Erlbham.

Argote, L., Ingram, P., Levine, J. M. and Moreland, R. L. (2000) 'Knowledge transfer in organizations: learning from the experience of others', *Organizational Behavior and Human Decision Processes* 82(1):1–8.

Barker, J. (1993) 'Tightening the iron cage: Concertive control in self managing teams', *Administrative Science Quarterly* 38(3):408–437.

Barker, J. (1999) *The Discipline of Teamwork: Participation and Concertive Control*, London: Sage.

Belbin, M. (1993) *Team Roles at Work*, Oxford: Butterworth-Heinemann.

Belbin, M. (2004) *Management Teams: Why They Succeed or Fail?* Second edition, Oxford: Butterworth-Heinemann.

Benders, J. and Van Hootegem, G. (1999) 'Teams and their context: Moving the team discussion beyond existing dichotomies', *Journal of Management Studies* 36(5):609.

Benders, J. and Van Hootegem, G. (2000) 'How the Japanese got teams', in S. Procter and F. Mueller (eds.) *Teamworking*, Basingstoke: Macmillan Business.

Berggren, C. (1992) *The Volvo Experience: Alternatives to Lean Production in the Swedish Auto Industry*, Basingstoke: Macmillan Press.

Bernstein, P. (1992) 'The learning curve at Volvo', in R. Glaser (ed.) *Classic Readings in Self: Managing Teamwork*, Pennsylvania: Organization Design and Development, Inc.

Bion, W. R. (1961) *Experiences in Groups and Other Papers*, London: Tavistock Publications.

Brown, J. S. and Duguid, P. (1991) 'Organizational learning and communities-of-practice: Toward a unified view of working, learning and innovation', *Organization Science* 2(1):40–57.

Buchanan, D. (2000) 'An eager and enduring embrace: The ongoing rediscovery of teamworking as a management idea', in S. Procter and F. Mueller (eds.) *Teamworking*, London: Macmillan Business.

Campion, M. A., Medsker, G. J. and Higgs, A. C., *et al.* (1993) 'Relations between work group characteristics and effectiveness: Implications for designing effective workgroups', *Personnel Psychology* 46:823–850.

Cohen, S. and Ledford, G. (1994) 'The effectiveness of self-managing teams: A quasi experiment, *Human Relations* 47(1):13–43.

Cohen, S. G., Ledford, G. E. Jr. and Spreitzer, G. M. (1996) 'A predictive model of self managing work team effectiveness', *Human Relations* 49(5):643–675.

Cordery, J. L., Mueller, W. S. and Smith, L. M. (1991) 'Attitudinal and behavioural effects of an autonomous working group: A longitudinal field of study', *Academy of Management Journal* 34: 464–476.

Corger, J. and Kanungo, R. (1988) 'The empowerment process: Integrating theory and practice', *Academy of Management Review* 13: 471–482.

Davenport, T. H. and Pusak, L. (1998) *Working Knowledge: How Organizations Manage What They Know*, Cambridge, MA: Harvard Business School Press.

Drucker, P. (1993) 'Knowledge-worker productivity: The biggest challenge', *California Management Review* 41(2):812–856.

Drucker, P. F. (1992) 'The new society of organisations', *Harvard Business Review* Sept–Oct:95–104.

Dunphy, D. and Bryant, B. (1996) 'Teams: Panaceas or prescriptions for improving performance?', *Human Relations* 49(5):677–699.

Edmonson, A. C. (2002) 'The local and variegated nature of learning in organisations: A group-level perspective', *Organization Science* 13(2): 128–146.

Ezzamel, M. and Willmott, H. (1998) 'Accounting for team work: A critical study of group based system of organizational control', *Administrative Science Quarterly* 43(2):358–397.

Ezzamel, M., Willmott, H. and Worthington, F. (2001) 'Power, control and resistance in "the factory that time forgot" ', *Journal of Management Studies* 38(8):1953–1981.

Findlay, P., McKinlay, A., Marks, A. and Thompson, P. (2000) 'Flexible when suits them: The use and abuse of teamwork skills', in S. Procter and F. Mueller (eds.) *Teamworking*, London: Macmillan Business.

Flores, F. and Gray, J. (2000) *Entrepreneurship and the Wired Life: Work in the Wake of Careers*, London: Demos.

Friedman, A. (1977) *Industry and Labour: Class Struggle at Work and Monopoly Capitalism*, London: Macmillan.

Furnham, A., Steele, H. and Pendleton, D. (1993) 'A psychometric assessment of the Belbin Team-Role Self Perception Inventory', *Journal of Occupational and Organizational Psychology* 66:245–257.

Garrahan, P. and Stewart, P. (1992) *The Nissan Enigma: Flexibility at Work in a Local Economy*, London: Mansell.

Gersick, C. (1988) 'Time and transition in work teams: Toward a new model of group development', *Academy of Management Journal* 31(1):9–41.

Gersick, C. (1989) 'Marking time: Predictable transitions in task group', *Academy of Management Journal* 32(2):274–309.

Gibson, C. and Vermeuler, F. (2003) 'A healthy divide: Subgroups as a stimulus for team learning behavior', *Administrative Science Quarterly*, 00018392, June, Vol. 48, 2: 202–239.

Glaser, R. (1992) *Moving Your Team Towards Self Management*, King of Prussia, PA: Organization Design and Development Inc.

Grenier, G. (1989) *Inhuman Relations: Quality Circles and Anti-Unionism in American Industry*, Philadelphia: Temple University Press.

Hackman, J. R. (1987) 'The design of work teams', in J. Lorsch (ed.) *Handbook of Organizational Behavior*, Englewood Cliffs, NJ: Prentice Hall, p.p. 315–342.

Hackman, J. R. (1992) 'The psychology of self managing in organizations', in R. Glaser (ed.) *Classic Readings in Self: Managing Teamwork*, Pennsylvania: Organization Design and Development, Inc.

Hackman, J. R. and Morris, C. G. (1975) 'Group tasks, group interaction process and group performance effectiveness: A review and proposed integration', in L. L. Berkowitz (ed.) *Advances in Experimental Social Psychology*, 8: 47–100, New York: Academic.

Heller, F., Pusic, E., Strauss, G. and Wilpert, B. *et al.* (1998) *Organizational Participation Myth and Reality*, Oxford: Oxford University Press.

Hofstede, G. (1980) *Culture's Consequences: International Differences in Work-related Values*, Beverly Hills, CA: Sage.

Hofstede, G. (1983) 'National culture in four dimensions: A research-based theory of cultural differences among nations', *International Studies of Management and Organization* 13:46–74.

Huczynski, A. A. (1996) *Management Gurus*, London: Thomson Business Press.

Janis, I. L. (1972) *Victims of Groupthink*, Boston, MA: Houghton Mifflin.

Janis, I. L. (1982) *Groupthink: Psychological Studies of Policy Decisions and Fiascos*, Boston, MA: Houghton Mifflin.

Jenkins, A. (1994) 'Teams: From ideology to analysis', *Organization Studies* 15(6):849–860.

Jones, R. G. and Lindley, W. D. (1998) 'Issues in the transition to teams', *Journal of Business and Psychology* 13(1):31–40.

Jonsson, D., Medbo, L. and Engstrom, T. (2004) 'Some considerations relating to the reintroduction of assembly lines in the Swedish automotive industry', *International Journal of Operations and Production Management* 24(8):754–762.

Kanter, R. M. (1983) *The Change Masters: Innovations for Productivity in the American Corporation*, New York: Simon and Schuster.

Katzenbach , J. R. and Smith, D. K. (1993) *The Wisdom of Teams*, Boston, MA: Harvard Business School Press.

Kirkman, B. L. (2000) 'Why do employees resist teams? Examining the "resistance barrier" to work team effectiveness', *International Journal of Conflict Management* 11(1):74–93.

Kirkman, B. L. and Shapiro, D. L. (1997) 'The impact of cultural values on employees' resistance to teams: Towards a model of globalized self managing work team effectiveness', *Academy of Management Review* 22(3):730–757.

Kirkman, B. L., Shapiro, D. L., Novelli, L. Jr. and Brett, J. M. (1996) 'Employee concerns regarding self managing work teams: A multidimensional justice perspective', *Social Justice Research* 9(1):47–67.

Klein, J. A. (1989) 'The human costs of manufacturing reform', *Harvard Business Review* March–April: 60–66.

Kluckhohn, F. and Strodtbeck, F. L. (1961) *Variations in Value Orientations*, Evanston, IL: Row, Peterson.

Knights, D. and McCabe, D. (2000) 'Bewitched, bothered and bewildered: The meaning and experience of teamworking for employees in an automobile company', *Human Relations* 53(11):1481–1517.

Knights, D. and McCabe, D. (2003) 'Governing through teamwork: Re-constituting subjectivity in a call-center', *Journal of Management Studies* 40(7):587–619.

Laclau, E. (1990) *New Reflections on the Revolution of Our Time*, London: Verso.

Lammers, C. J. and Szell, B. (1989) *International Handbook of Organizational Participation, Vol. 1 Organizational Democracy: Taking Stock*, Oxford: Oxford University Press.

Lave, J. and Wenger, E. (1991) *Situated Learning: Legitimate Peripheral Participation*, New York: Cambridge University Press.

Levine, D. I. (2004) 'The wheels of Washington: Groupthink and Iraq', *San Francisco Chronicle*, 5 February, A23 [sfgate.com/article.cgi?file=/chronicle/archive/2004/02/05/EDGV34OCEP1.DTL].

Lewin, K. (1948) *Resolving Social Conflicts: Selected Papers on Group Dynamics*, London: Harper & Row.

Lipman-Blumen, J. and Leavitt, A. J. (1999) *Hot Groups: Seeding Them, Feeding Them and Using Them to Ignite Your Organization*, New York: Oxford University Press.

McCabe, D. and Black, J. (1996) ' "Something's gotta give": Trade unions and the road to teamworking', *Employer Relations* 1992:110–127.

McKinlay, A. and Taylor, P. (1996) 'Power, surveillance and resistance: Inside the "Factory of the Future" ', in P. Ackers, C. Smith and P. Smith (eds) *The New Workplace and Trade Unionism*, London: Routledge, p.p. 279–300.

Manz, C. C. (1990) 'Beyond self managing work teams: Towards self-leading teams in the workplace', in R. Glaser (ed.) *Classic Readings in Self-Managing Teamwork*, Pennsylvania: Organization Design and Development, Inc.

Manz , C. C. and Sims, H. P. (1987) 'Leading workers to lead themselves: The external leadership of self-managing work teams', *Administrative Science Quarterly* 32(1):106–128.

Manz, C. C. and Sims, H. P. (1991) 'Superleadership beyond the myth of heroic leadership', *Organizational Dynamics* 19(4): 18–35.

Manz, C. C. and Sims, H. P. (1992) 'Becoming a SuperLeader', in R. Glaser (ed.) *Classic Readings in Self-Managing Teamwork*, Pennsylvania: Organization Design and Development, Inc.

Manz, C. C. and Sims, H. P. (1993) *Business Without Bosses: How Self-Managing Teams are Building High-Performance Companies*, New York: John Wiley & Sons Inc.

Mayo, E. (1933) *The Human Problems of an Industrial Civilization*, New York: Macmillan.

Mayo, E. (1945) *The Social Problems of an Industrial Civilization*, New York: Macmillan.

Maznevski, M. L. and DiStefano, J. J. (1995) '*Measuring Culture in International Management: The Cultural Perspectives Questionnaire*', Working Paper, The University of Virginia: Charlottesville.

Metcalfe, B. and Linstead, A. (2003) 'Gendering teamwork: Re-writing the Feminine', *Gender, Work and Organization* 10(1):95–119.

Mills, P. K. and Ungson, G. (2003) 'Reassessing the limit of structural empowerment: Organizational constitutions trusts controls', *Academy of Management Review*, 28(1):143–151.

Monden, Y. (1983) *Toyota Production Systems*, Norcross: IIE Press.

Mueller, F. (1994) 'Teams between hierarchy and commitment: Changes strategies and the "internal environment" ', *Journal of Management Studies* 31(3):383–403.

Mulder, M. (1971) 'Power equalization through participation', *Administrative Science Quarterly* 16(1):31–40.

Nonaka, I. and Takeuchi, H. (1995) *The Knowledge Creating Company*, Oxford: Oxford University Press.

Oakland, J. C. (1996) *Total Quality Management: A Practical Approach*, University of Bradford Management Centre: European Centre for Total Quality Management.

Oakland, J. S. (1993) *TQM: The Route to Improving Performance*, Oxford: Butterworth-Heinemann.

Parker, M. and Slaughter, J. (1988) *Choosing Sides: Unions and the Team Concept*, Boston: South End Press.

Peters, T. (1988) *Thriving on Chaos: Handbook for a Management Revolution*, London: Pan Books.

Peters, T. and Waterman, R. H. (1982) *In Search of Excellence*, London: Harper and Row.

Pfeffer, J. (1998) 'The human equation: Building profits by putting people first', Boston, MA: Harvard Business School Press.

Plunkett, L. C. and Fournier, R. O. (1991) *Participative Management*, New York: Wiley.

Procter, S. and Mueller, F. (2000) *Teamworking*, London: Macmillan Business.

Pollert, A. (1996) ' "Team work" on the assembly line: Contradictions and the dynamic of union resilience', in P. Ackers, C. Smith and P. Smith (eds.) *The New Workplace and Trade Unionism*, London: Routledge, p.p. 178–209.

Poole, M. S. (1983) 'Decision development in small groups III a multiple sequence model group decision development', *Communications Monographs* 50: 206–232.

Reynolds, R. (1994) *Groupwork in Education and Training: Ideas in Practice,* The Educational and Training Technology Series, London: Kogan Page Limited.

Senge, P. (1990) *The Fifth Discipline: The Art and Practice of the Learning Organization*, New York: Doubleday/Currency.

Sewell, G. (1998) 'The discipline of team: The control of team-based industrial work through electronic and peer surveillance', *Administrative Science Quarterly* 43(2):397–429.

Sewell, G. and Wilkinson, B. (1992) ' "Someone to watch over me"; Surveillance, discipline and the just-in-time labour process', *Sociology* 26(2):271–298.

Shea, G. P. and Guzzo, R. A. (1987) 'Group effectiveness: What really matters?', *Sloar Management Review* 28(3):25–37.

Sinclair, A. (1992) 'The tyranny of team ideology', *Organization Studies* 13(4):611–626.

Starkey, K. (1996) *How Organisations Learn*, London: Thomson Business Press.

Tannenbaum, S. I., Beard, R. L. and Salas, E. (1992) 'Team building and its influence on team effectiveness: An examination of conceptual and empirical developments', in K. Kelley (ed.) *Issues, Theory, and Research in Industrial/Organizational Psychology (Vol. 82)*, Amsterdam: Elsevier Science, p.p. 117–153.

Thompson, P. and Wallace, T. (1996) 'Redesigning production through teamworking: Case studies from the Volvo Truck Corporation', *International Journal of Operations and Production Management* 16(2):103–118.

Thrift, N. (2001) ' "It's the romance, not the finance, that makes the business worth pursuing": Disclosing a new market culture', *Economy & Society* 30(4):412–432.

Tompkins, P. K. and Cheney, G. (1985) 'Communications and unobtrusive control in contemporary organisations', in R. D. McPhee and P. K. Thompkins (eds.) *Organizational Communication: Traditional Themes and New directions*, Newbury Park, CA: Sage, p.p. 179–210.

Trist, E. and Bamforth, K. (1951) 'Some social and psychological consequences of the Longwall method of coal-getting,' *Human Relations* 4(1):3–38.

Trist, E. L., Susman, G. I. and Brown, G. R (1977) 'An experiment in autonomous working in an American underground coal mine', *Human Relations* 30:201–236.

Tuckman, B. W. (1965) 'Developmental sequences in small groups', *Psychological Bulletin* 63(6):384–399.

Tuckman, B. W. and Jenson, M. A. (1977) 'Stages of small group development revisited', *Group and Organization Studies* 2:419–427.

Tushman, M. and Nadler, D. (1998) 'Organizing for innovation', in K. Starkey (ed.) *How Organizations Learn,* London: Thomson Business Press.

Van Amelsvoort, P. and Benders, J. (1996) 'Team time: a model for developing self-directed work teams', *International Journal of Operations & Production Management* 16(2):159–170.

Wall, T. D., Kemp, N. J., Jackson, P. R. and Clegg, C. W. (1986) 'Outcomes of autonomous workgroups: A long term field experiment', *Academy of Management Journal* 29: 280–304.

Wall, T. D., Kemp, N. J., Jackson, P. and Clegg, C. (1992) 'Outcomes of autonomous workgroups: A long term field experiment', in R. Glaser (ed.) *Classic Readings in Self-Managing Teamwork*, Pennsylvania: Organization Design and Development, Inc.

Wallace, T. (2004) 'The end of good work? Work organisation or lean production in Volvo organisation', *International Journal of Operations and Production Management* 24(8):750–753.

Waterson, P. E., Clegg, C. W., Bolden, R. and Pepper, K. *et al.* (1999) 'The use and effectiveness of modern manufacturing practices: A survey of UK industry', *International Journal of Production Research*, 37:2271–2292.

Weisbord, M. R. (1992) 'Participative work design: A personal odyssey', in R. Glaser (ed.) *Classic Readings in Self-Managing Teamwork*, Pennsylvania: Organization Design and Development, Inc.

Wellins, R. S., Byham, W. C. and Wilson, J. (1991) *Empowered Teams*, San Francisco: Jossey-Bass.

Wenger, E. (1998) *Communities of Practice: Learning, Meaning and identity*, Cambridge: Cambridge University Press.

Wenger, E. and Snyder, W. (2000) 'Communities of practice: The organizational frontier', *Harvard Business Review* Jan–Feb:139–145.

Wenger, E., McDermott, R. and Snyder, W. M. (2002) *Cultivating Communities of Practices*, Boston: Harvard Business School Press.

WERS – Cully, M., Woodland, S., O'Reilly A. and Dix, G. (1998) *1998 Workplace Employee Relations Survey*, London and New York: Routledge.

West, A. (2004) *Effective Teamwork: Practical Lessons from Organizational Research*, Oxford: Blackwell.

Wood, R. and Bandura, A. (1989) 'Social cognitive theory of organizational management', *Academy of Management Review* 14:361–384.

Womack, J. P., Jones, D. T. and Roos, D. (1990) *The Machine that Changed the World*, New York: Rawson Associates.

5 Knowledge and Learning: Consuming Management?

Andrew Sturdy[1]

Key concepts and learning objectives

- The very inclusion of the phrase 'learning objectives' in textbooks assumes that learning can be achieved from reading and thinking more or less on its own. It also assumes that learning can be planned by others and made explicit or codified. The first learning objective here then is to be able to critically assess the value of learning objectives in textbooks.

- To be able to illustrate different conceptions of knowledge, connect them with theoretical perspectives on learning and apply them to approaches that facilitate learning in organizations.

- To understand the different reasons why **management knowledge**, in the form of 'new' management ideas, is adopted in organizations and the implications this has for organizational effectiveness and organizational theories.

- To apply the idea that the relationship between power and knowledge is not simply associated with the view that those with knowledge have power, but that knowledge is power through delimiting what can be known and said and what is silenced, and that this has potentially both constructive and dangerous outcomes.

Aims of the chapter

This chapter will:

- Introduce the different perspectives and debates surrounding knowledge and learning and the importance of the subject to organizational analysis and experience. Using illustrations, including a mini-case study, exercises and core research work in the area, enable readers to reflect on their own learning, including through reading textbooks such as this one. Show how some common-sense views of knowledge as an object or commodity are challenged by both mainstream and critical perspectives, but that it is only through an understanding of the latter that a broader understanding can be developed – that knowledge and its use is essentially political.

Overview and key points

Until fairly recently, knowledge would not have featured as a core management textbook topic. Of course, learning might be covered in relation to organizational behaviour (OB) in terms of human development or the acquisition of skills through training for example. Equally, and as in this book, it might be discussed as part of an introductory chapter – how do we learn and what is the best way to use this text as a 'learning resource'? However, today knowledge has become fashionable, making it sometimes seem more like a commodity to be consumed, like a car or a new pair of trainers. Indeed, even though it has always been present and important, knowledge and its management are now seen as key to the competitiveness of organizations and even nations, and a whole 'knowledge industry' and set of associated concepts has emerged.

In this chapter we shall explore some of these concepts, but focus on the key concerns with knowledge in organizations, especially management knowledge – what it is and how and why it is acquired and, in particular, transferred from person to person and place to place. In one sense, we can address these questions quite easily – knowledge can be seen as one major source of a person's capability. It includes certain theoretical and/or practical skills, and is acquired and transferred through a process of education, learning, training and application. However, and as we shall see, it is not quite so simple, not least because, as with all phenomena, there are different ways of looking at knowledge and different aspects to it. Also, knowledge is not something peculiar to organizations, nor is it simply created and acquired to serve organizational ends. In the second half of the chapter, we shall explore some of these important, but neglected features of knowledge and learning.

Stop and think why you are reading this chapter. What do you hope to gain from doing so . . . a good assignment mark . . . a better understanding . . . avoiding the embarrassment of being seen as uninformed/ unprepared or . . . ? Note down your first few thoughts and return to them when you have finished reading.

Chapter structure

In the first part of the chapter, the mainstream approaches to knowledge and learning are explored in terms of the key perspectives and issues. In particular, we examine the different types of knowledge and the different theories of learning. We then focus on management knowledge and management ideas in particular, how they are promoted, selected, adapted and evaluated – how they are 'consumed'.

In the second half of the chapter, critical perspectives are introduced and explored. Here, alternative accounts of the nature of management knowledge and the reasons why management ideas are adopted are set out, suggesting that the popularity of an approach to management is no guide to its organizational effectiveness.

Finally, the importance of acknowledging the fact that knowledge is adapted according to context and political dynamics is highlighted. This suggests that knowledge and learning need to be understood in terms of the core concepts of the book, especially those of power, insecurity and inequality. In short, management knowledge can be seen to be used and abused, sometimes at the same time.

Mainstream approaches

Introduction

The most successful companies and the most successful countries will be those that manage **human capital** in the most effective and efficient fashion – investing in their workers, encouraging workers to invest in themselves, provide a good learning environment, and yes, include **social capital** as well as skills and training. (*Becker, 2001, p. 1*)

Why has knowledge begun to be seen as a new and important focus for organizations? Surely, knowledge has always been important in terms of producing goods and services, innovating and keeping up with the competition? It has. But even if we temper some of the hype or **rhetoric**, which is typical of those wanting to promote ideas, there have been some changes, in many Western markets at least, which warrant a change in focus:

- There has been a shift away from manufacturing industries in terms of the numbers employed. Here, manual skills were deemed of central importance. Many of these work processes have been either automated or exported (Braverman, 1974; Sennett, 2000). While, as we shall see, manual skills can be viewed as a form of knowledge, it is argued that the growth of service employment and 'knowledge-based sectors' (e.g. professional services, software and bioscience) are a source of greater competitive advantage (Cortada, 1998). They are comparatively more profitable partly because the knowledge they depend upon cannot easily be emulated and therefore new organizations find it difficult to enter the market in which they operate. This provides partially monopolistic conditions and those with even the faintest familiarity with economics will understand that this means higher profits.

- It is often claimed that the global economy has become more competitive, connected and dynamic. Therefore, information becomes more available and plentiful, but its advantages are short-lived. At the same time, pressures to innovate – to create and apply new knowledge – are more intense. Knowledge needs to be continually updated therefore.

- The boundaries perceived between organizations are becoming more fluid, giving rise to an opening up of sources of knowledge (from suppliers, customers, alliance partners and new or geographically distributed employees for example) and therefore also the danger of losing knowledge, or 'leakage'.

- While technology in the past was designed to mimic (control, cheapen and/or replace) the knowledge of many manual and office workers, it is now also being developed with the hope of capturing the expertise of professional and managerial individuals and groups and disseminating it selectively throughout the organization as quickly as possible. This is what is seen as 'knowledge management'. For example, in management consultancy, what has been learned from a client or project is often input into an IT database so that others in the consulting firm can draw on this information when working with the same or similar clients in future. But, and as we shall see shortly, knowledge is not the same as information.

This view of the emergence of knowledge-economies, knowledge-workers, knowledge-sectors, knowledge management and knowledge-intensive firms presents a potentially exciting (or frightening) scenario. Traditional practices of learning a trade or profession with great emphasis on early intensive and formal learning – a degree in business administration for example – followed by gradual personal development, sometimes through formal training, may now seem anachronistic or at least insufficient. Indeed, we are increasingly called upon to engage in regular and lifelong learning. Furthermore, traditional classroom-based instruction – first started because of a shortage of books! – is not only seen as of limited effectiveness (see Freire, 1972 for example), but inappropriate, given emerging, busy lifestyles and the declining 'shelf-life' of knowledge. Moreover, and as we shall see, it is not just the profile of knowledge that has changed, but also our views of it and how to develop it. For example, in a short space of time, it was hoped first that the limitations of the classroom would be addressed by the rise of self-directed and internet-based or e-learning (it was also seen as being cheaper), but the limitations of this soon gave rise to the importance of participating in communities of practice. Now, perhaps unsurprisingly, attention is focused on a mix of approaches or 'blended learning' (CIPD, 2002).

While knowledge is increasingly assuming a high profile for the success of businesses and organizations, it is not a new phenomenon. For example, it is inherent in activities such as innovation; organizational change; applying different management ideas or practices; crossing organizational and national cultures; learning new skills as well as other everyday organizational activities. Indeed, it can be argued that knowledge and learning are core human processes – 'all individuals and all organisations . . . are knowledgeable' (Blackler, 1995, p.p. 1022, 1026). It should certainly not, therefore, be seen solely as a topical area of study. Indeed, an understanding of knowledge in organizations and its mobility should be valuable in making sense of future developments, which we do not yet know about, such as new management ideas. Indeed, facilitating this type of understanding is one aim of this chapter. Before exploring knowledge and learning in more detail, however, the beginning of a short case is presented (see Case study 5.1), which should shed light on the issues raised in the rest of the chapter.

Image 5.1 Blended learning?

SOURCE: ©ISTOCKPHOTO.COM/NANCY LOUIE

Thinkpoint 5.2

If knowledge is changing so fast what are the implications of studying for a degree over three or four years or using textbooks, most of which change very little in terms of content? (When next in the library, pick a topic and compare it in two editions of the same textbook.) What type of knowledge is likely to have long-term relevance to the understanding and practices of organizations?

CASE STUDY 5.1 Learning to love the customer: Customer relationship management

Rohan Pryce is studying management at the 'College of Knowledge', or so it is jokingly known to the students there. His first piece of assessed work is an essay on learning.

His cousin Cathy has a new job in the local call-centre of a car insurance company, DK-Line, as a 'Learning Manager'. Rohan is curious about what this job means and thinks that, with a title like that, she should be able to help him produce an original and interesting essay.

It turns out that she is helping to set up an approach to service based on a new school of thought in marketing – **customer relationship management** (CRM). Cathy explains that the reason for this initiative is that the firm is losing their existing customers to cheaper competitors and so they want to develop good long-term relationships with their customers in order to retain their business. Her role is to ensure that the staff have the appropriate skills and knowledge to do this and then evaluate whether CRM was effective. Apart from trying to ensure that staff were motivated, the first part of this role involved staff recruitment, training and development.

Although most new recruits knew nothing about technical, insurance issues, this was quite easy to teach, not least because most recruits were quite literate and numerate and also had their own cars and so knew something about insurance already. Also, the more they knew, the higher (pay) grade they achieved. But even if staff often forgot things that were not used frequently when dealing with customers, the IT system had lots of information available at the press of a few buttons. It was more difficult to train other things like how to deal with people, to be generally sociable, and, with angry customers, calm and yet efficient. Indeed, Cathy knew from her own experience and from things that a group of managers she occasionally met up with at conferences had said, that some things were best learned from experience and through one's colleagues, especially the more experienced ones. Also, people should be given space to develop their own solutions. She had put these ideas into practice by introducing frequent team meetings for problem solving, assigning experienced mentors to new recruits and 'empowering' staff to create their own call scripts and coping mechanisms. The problem was trying to ensure that within the team meetings staff stuck to the agenda and produced solutions acceptable to their manager.

Rohan was beginning to see how he could use this account or 'case study' in his essay. He tried to bring the conversation to an end – the essay was due in the next day – but Cathy was so clearly 'into' her job and CRM, it was difficult to cut it short. He hadn't seen her like this before. She also seemed to get annoyed when Rohan said that it all seemed to fit with his lectures and books. She said that it was 'not that simple you know!' Rohan began to feel uncomfortable and made a sharp exit home to write his essay.

Key problems

Now that knowledge is seen to be so important to organizations, the difficulties in understanding what it means and how it can be captured and used are increasingly recognized. Indeed, paradoxically and as with so many phenomena, the more attention it receives, the less clear it becomes. There is nothing new in identifying types of knowledge, but distinctions have been quite basic and fail to recognize that knowledge is multiple and diverse. Therefore, there have been numerous attempts to **classify** knowledge and the relationships between different types. However, this runs alongside a more pressing and practical concern of how knowledge can be created, acquired and transferred to others.

Again, there is a long tradition in other fields such as education, **innovation** and training, and these have been drawn on in the field of management. But traditional approaches have been seen as lacking the necessary sophistication or the appropriate contexts for the kind of speed and flexibility seen as necessary in competitive and changing markets. Also, and as we shall see, there are different views on how people learn – which are the best methods and what are their practical implications? In addition, it is increasingly recognized that sources of knowledge are as likely to be outside the organization as inside and, either way, extracting and retaining knowledge is difficult to achieve. It is hoped by some that new communication technologies will be able to help in this regard as a repository, fast transmitter and editor or translator of information.

Finally, a more specific concern within the study of knowledge and learning is that of how management knowledge is promoted, adopted and evaluated. Here, there is some recognition that managers seem to be adopting the latest ideas in a **non-rigorous** way – as fashion victims – regardless of whether the ideas have been proven to be useful for the organization. Also, the transfer of ideas across cultures is seen to pose problems. How can **cultural barriers** to universally relevant management ideas be overcome, or is knowledge and learning more bound to particular contexts? Overall then, mainstream thinkers in management are seeking to help know, capture and transfer management knowledge to achieve organizational goals. We shall now explore some of these issues in more detail.

Key ideas and theories

What is knowledge?   In everyday talk, knowledge is often seen and treated as being like an object or **commodity**, something of value, which can be transferred from one place to another. For example, knowledge of different theories of learning might be gained from this text and applied in an assignment or in a seminar discussion. This view is also common in organizations, especially in knowledge management, where it is believed that experts' 'knowledge' of, say, a particular client or market, can be written onto an IT system (i.e. **codified** and captured), such as the customer database at DK-Line in the case study. However, and as we shall see, this view is problematic and can be misguided. For example, this book does not contain knowledge, but something more like codified information. Furthermore, reading it does not necessarily result in learning or an increase in knowledge. Learning may occur, depending on how you think about what you read, connecting it with things that you already know (not least your knowledge of the English language) and whether you try applying the ideas, even if only in your mind. Before going further into the nature of these processes, it is worth unpacking views of different types of knowledge, but note that this can reinforce the view of knowledge as being like an object.

KNOWLEDGE, INFORMATION AND DATA   Knowledge is often, especially in IT circles, distinguished from data (discrete facts) and information (categorized, summarized, contextualized data, used in decision making for example) in that it reflects a higher level of abstraction and ability. Data, and even information without knowledge, is meaningless. Think of the three different colours in a traffic light or those colours in the context of a crossroad. Without the knowledge of how they are there to direct the traffic so as to avoid accidents, the data and the information is meaningless. When information is infused with analysis, insights from experience, judgement, values and associated capabilities or skills, it may become knowledge (see Malone, 2003).

For example, say demand for OB textbooks in the United Kingdom is 30 000 copies (*data*). This is presented to a new marketing manager as 35 per cent of the total market of students studying OB. The manager uses this *information* to bid for a higher budget next year in order to grow sales. But this is rejected by her boss who *knows* from experience and a recent conversation with the production team that not only does the 35 per cent figure typically remain constant (most students do not buy the recommended text), but the production department is at full capacity for the next year. The point is that this is not necessarily the correct decision – production might be outsourced and more students could be persuaded to buy the book – but that it is based on a more developed and nuanced understanding or construction of the data and information.

KNOWLEDGE TO KNOWING A more common way of classifying knowledge is to distinguish between 'knowledge that' (or 'about') and 'knowledge how' (Ryle, 1949; see also Polyani, 1966). The typical example given is that of driving a car: *knowing that* you have to depress the clutch before changing gear does not mean that you *know how* to do it in practice. But it can be applied to all types of activity – knowing and applying types of knowledge for a start! This distinction is close to another, which distinguishes between knowledge that can be made *explicit* (e.g. described, written down) such as that suggested in textbooks and that which can be so only partially, which is implicit, elusive or **tacit** (see Lam, 2000; Chia, 2003). In the case study, for example, Cathy realized how some things could be taught quite easily, but others, such as social skills were more tacit.

These distinctions are very useful, but do not reveal some of the different characteristics of knowledge or the 'grey' areas between types. For example, some knowledge is clearly linked to individuals while other knowledge is also held in groups or networks of people and their activities – i.e. collective knowledge. Also, as knowledge has assumed greater importance in business, people have tried to capture it even more precisely (i.e. make knowledge of knowledge explicit). Blackler (1995) for example, identified five (overlapping) types of knowledge and Lam (2000) developed this schema in terms of whether they were primarily tacit or explicit and individual or collective:

- *embrained* (e.g. expertise in accounting principles): cognitive, individual and explicit
- *embodied* (e.g. craft skills): practical, individual and tacit
- *embedded* (e.g. who does what in a system of routines – beyond individual skills): collective, tacit and relational
- *encultured* (e.g. group norms): collective and tacit or explicit
- *encoded* (e.g. information in expert systems software): explicit and collective.

Thinkpoint 5.3

Take the knowledge involved in an occupation, job or activity (e.g. sport or playing a musical instrument) you are familiar with, and try and identify examples of Blackler's five knowledge types. How difficult is it to distinguish them?

The above classification of knowledge types is now commonly used in the literature and even some workplaces. Like categories generally, they help us feel as if we know something about the subject – knowledge itself in this instance – and we may feel reassured by this. They also help us have conversations about the topic and learn more (e.g. the difficulty in distinguishing them).

Paradoxically, after setting them out, Blackler himself shows them to be rather static and, ultimately, flawed. He opts for a focus on 'knowing as a process', something we (all) *do*, rather than knowledge as something we have (see Chapter 9 for the source of this distinction in organizational culture analysis). This is quite a complex and unconventional, but important, view of knowledge. It undermines or, at least, challenges the knowing–doing (knowledge that/how distinction mentioned above, and highlights the fluid, communal and emergent or contested nature of knowledge. In other words, knowledge is far from being tangible and fixed, but emerges in real time through social interaction, and this makes it subject to challenge and disagreement.

There are then two broad perspectives on knowledge. The **processual** view of Blackler and others can be contrasted with a more **objective, cognitive** (mental) and static *'structural'* perspective where knowledge types can be classified (see Newell *et al.*, 2002, p. 8). These views are evident in the different ways of understanding learning to which we now turn.

What is learning? People learn in a combination of different ways – from novelty, experience/doing and social interaction, for example. This may depend on the situation, including what they are learning (a foreign language, a poem, etc.). For example, learning to ride a bike or drive a car cannot be achieved through books or manuals alone. We acquire the skill largely through doing it, but we also rely on other knowledge, such as knowing that it will be possible, that the ground is solid (hopefully!) and that pushing the pedals makes the wheels go round. Also, and more generally, we may have personal/cultural inclinations or 'preferences' for particular types of learning, borne out of individual experiences – **learning styles**. This variation partly explains the range of different theories of learning, although perspectives also differ in their assumptions about people's behaviour in general and these rise and fall in popularity. We now examine groups of theoretical approaches to learning (see also CIPD, 2002).

LEARNING AS BEHAVIOUR This approach is associated with 'behaviourism', but is not restricted to this rather specific perspective in that the focus is on *learning by doing*. Behaviourism is a theory that explains human behaviour in terms of its pleasurable or painful consequences (Skinner, 1953, 1971). In responding to some stimulus in the environment, we learn which kinds of response have a pleasant effect and thereby seek to repeat such behaviour. Where a response has brought about pain, we seek to avoid it. Over time, 'appropriate' behaviour becomes automatic to us or habitual – it is then said to be **internalized** within us so that it is done without necessarily thinking of the consequences.

Image 5.2 B. F. Skinner – leading proponent of behaviourism

and that you should learn something from it or, even report back on what you learned while you were at lunch! Also, and with social learning more generally, while most would concede the learning potential of COPs, there are other pressures or constraints: work tasks need to be completed and, in particular, not everyone wants to share their knowledge or be in communities.

Thinkpoint 5.6

Think of how COPs relate to your learning about management and OB. How might you go about addressing the obstacles in order to cultivate your COP? Why might people be reluctant to share their knowledge or see their informal groups as something to extract knowledge from? What other obstacles might there be?

Exercise 5.1

As you did with the different types of knowledge earlier, reflect on how you learned how to do a particular job or activity (e.g. sport, playing a musical instrument, speaking a language) and connect this with the different approaches and perspectives on learning: as behaviour (practice and rewards), understanding (thinking, frameworks), knowledge construction and social practice/interaction. Can you make connections with all the approaches? Which seem most relevant? Are there any overlaps? What do your reflections imply for theories of learning and their changing popularity? Are we in the best position to assess how we learned something?

What is management knowledge?   The above discussion of knowledge and learning has been rather general. We now look at management knowledge specifically, and the different ways of classifying it, before exploring some of the processual issues associated with new management ideas. First of course, we need to be clear about the nature of management. This is being explored elsewhere in this book (see Chapter 7) and is, surprisingly perhaps, no easy task. If we focus on management as an activity, rather than as an occupation or hierarchical level for example (Hales, 1993), we can see that conventional views distinguish between the formal or 'espoused' views, and what happens in practice – knowledge *in use* (see Argyris and Schon, 1974). This gives rise to three dimensions of management activity (see also Watson, 1986):

- The 'art' of meeting organizational objectives through others.
- Systematic or rational planning and control.
- A messy, sometimes reactive, political, emotional and frenetic mix of activities.

We shall return to these later when considering the adoption of management ideas, but, for now, they suggest that the knowledge (and skills) involved in management is multifaceted. Alvarez (1998), for example, sets out a number of forms of management knowledge, which can be seen to roughly correspond to Blackler's classification discussed earlier. First, there is technical *or* **instrumental** knowledge such as specific marketing techniques (embrained and encoded). Secondly, there are habits and a sense of intuition such as that which might be involved in routine decision making (embodied). Thirdly, there is an understanding of what is acceptable, both formally ('professional' behaviour) and informally (e.g. who is in and out of favour) and, he argues, all types of knowledge are embedded in local (e.g. national) settings (encultured). This classification is also useful in that it combines both explicit and tacit forms of management knowledge. By definition, the latter is more difficult to unpack and transfer, as we have seen, and for this reason perhaps, attention is typically focused on explicit management knowledge or what might be described as 'management ideas'. These will now form the focus of our discussion, but it will become clear how this does not exclude more tacit and informal aspects of management activity.

EXPLICIT KNOWLEDGE: MANAGEMENT IDEAS   Studying management (and most other topics) we are faced with a mass of ideas, concepts, theories and prescriptions. Following the cognitive view of learning and the explicit view of knowledge, these are presented in lectures and textbooks in the form of lists, diagrams and written accounts. This is often experienced as overwhelming, not least because people are always updating, adapting and creating new ideas. In the same cognitive tradition then, it should be useful to construct classifications – 'mental pigeon holes' – of the ideas themselves. This should be helpful, not only as a way of organizing existing ideas, but making sense of (i.e. classifying, framing, comparing, understanding) seemingly new ideas as they come along after a formal period of study. The alternatives are to continue studying with further courses or reading, assume that nothing changes or ignore new ideas and continue to draw on and adapt those that we learned in the past. There are various ways to organize management ideas. These are informed by, and tell us something about, management, as well as the ideas themselves (see Huczynski, 1993).

First, management ideas are typically known in terms of the role they perform (e.g. change management, leadership) and therefore can often be grouped in terms of management functions (e.g. marketing, strategy, HRM, finance, etc.), although many of these ideas are relevant to all aspects of management. Sometimes similar ideas are combined or coalesce into a 'school of thought' or movement (e.g. CRM, HRM, entrepreneurship).

Thinkpoint 5.7

Many management ideas are represented as a three-letter acronym (TLA) (Grint, 1997). How many can you think of or find in the index of a management textbook, and why do you think TLAs are so popular?

These might be presented historically. For example, in OB, we might learn that bureaucracy (see Chapter 13) and scientific management (see Chapters 7 and 8) were followed by human relations, the more psychological 'neo-human relations' and culture management, and entrepreneurialism. Typically, each approach would be seen as incorporating, and/or an improvement on, the previous one (cf. Guillen, 1994). For example, in Case study 5.1, CRM is seen to be a development of customer service ideas more generally in that it focuses on developing long-term relationships.

An earlier and now less common form of classification in OB is on where the prescribed action is focused – organization, group, individual, customer. (Can you connect these with the above list of dominant OB schools of thought?) Similarly, specific ideas can be seen in terms of their level of impact. For example, personality testing is focused on the 'inner self'; speed reading on the 'outer self'; interviewing techniques on the interpersonal; teamworking on the group; and CRM on the organization as a whole (Huczynski, 1993, p. 211).

How else might management ideas and practices be classified?

How is management knowledge adopted and evaluated? While being aware of the different types of knowledge and of theories and approaches to learning can help in identifying and acquiring new knowledge, it does not help in assessing the value of that knowledge, nor does it reveal how management ideas are disseminated and adopted by managers. This is a huge topic, linked to studies of innovation and organizational change for example (see Rogers, 1995; Collins, 2000), but we introduce some key themes here. In particular we focus on the channels of knowledge transfer, the reasons for adoption and methods of evaluation.

DIFFUSION CHANNELS New ideas and, usually, their associated practices are introduced to individuals and organizations in many different ways:

- teaching/training/conference presentations
- alliances/joint ventures/relations with suppliers/mergers
- books, magazines, videos, training packages and other media
- new staff (e.g. CEO brings in new practice)
- management consultancy
- innovation/adapting existing practices
- compliance to professional/state requirements
- social networks (e.g. COPs)/word of mouth.

The ideas are then often implemented or applied – although typically only partially and with some difficulty – and eventually may become normal practice, taken for granted or 'institutionalized'. Then, of course, they may become inappropriate in new circumstances, or new improved ideas come along and the cycle starts again (cf. Strang and Macy, 2001).

SELECTION AND ADOPTION: THE RATIONAL APPROACH But why are new ideas of interest to organizations and their managers? If we take the first of the three themes of management activity outlined above – addressing organisational objectives – then the answer lies in issues such as solving organizational problems or improving organizational efficiency, effectiveness or competitiveness. For example, a company may be experiencing falling profits, be losing customers or suffering a costly level of staff turnover. In response, it will seek out solutions. This may involve thinking of different ways to adapt existing procedures, devising new approaches or seeking out solutions from a range of external sources or channels (as above). This was clearly the situation in Case study 5.1, where CRM was seen by Cathy as a way to solve the problem of losing customers.

If we take the second theme of management activity – systematic planning and control – then approaches and ideas such as CRM in the case study are selected and evaluated against these aims in a rational way. For example, evidence of its effectiveness will be sought and a quantitative cost–benefit analysis may be carried out to assess whether or not the returns are worth the investment compared to other possible solutions. Alternatively, if the solution is not known, management consultants may be asked to tender (compete) for a project and a choice is made on the basis of an 'objective' assessment of their bids and references. Such procedures are sometimes required by regulations, in the public sector for example. More generally, it has been argued that with increased competitive pressures and the potentially high costs of failure (Ramsay, 1996), organizations are becoming more 'objective' in their assessment of new ideas (Beer and Nohria, 2000).

SELECTION AND ADOPTION: 'SATISFICING' Such techniques and prescriptions fit with the view of management as seeking 'objective' solutions to specific organizational problems in a rational manner (i.e. by systematic measurement). In practice, and in keeping with more general critiques of managerial rationality (e.g. see Simon, 1960), the best that might be expected given limited time and/or available information, is 'satisficing' – making an acceptable, but not necessarily ideal decision/assessment. For example, in undertaking an assessment on the likely return on investment (ROI) in a new practice, it is often difficult to quantify some outcomes ('intangibles') such as employee innovativeness, and to isolate or control for the impact of the new idea from other influences on performance, including the experience of being measured itself (see Power, 1997; and Chapter 8 on decision making in this volume). For example, in the case study, customer retention might have increased after the impact of CRM, but this might have been due to the failures of a competitor and/or the fact that employees improved their performance while it was being measured.

Image 5.3 Systematic testing?

However, it is not simply the fact that making objective assessments is technically difficult or imperfect. If we take the third dimension of management activity – as being messy, sometimes reactive, political, emotional and frenetic – it becomes clear that in practice, selecting and evaluating ideas is not a completely rational process. We shall explore this more later in the chapter, but it is generally recognized that managers adopt ideas for a range of informal reasons, which can be classified as psychological (e.g. stress leads to adopting ideas impulsively), political (a new idea serves career or departmental interests) and cultural (ideas are adopted because they fit one's values). For example, in the case study, it appeared that Cathy was feeling under pressure and that this might influence her decision making and view of the success of CRM. What this means is that not only may effective ideas be rejected, but also flawed ideas may be adopted. This is clearly a real threat to the role and expertise of management. Indeed, this is not just true of management. There is a long history of inventions that were rejected despite technical and other advantages (e.g. see Rogers, 1995). What can be done then?

There is considerable attention being given to helping ensure that management can identify, adopt and implement the most effective ideas. One view is to improve the sophistication and implementation of objective assessment techniques. Another is to recognize such rational procedures as being flawed, but also as not only better than doing nothing, but serving an important function, providing some 'immunity' from pressures to adopt ideas in a non-rational way (e.g. Abrahamson, 1991). We shall return to this theme later in the chapter.

Thinkpoint 5.8

Compare the process of adopting new management ideas to that of buying a car or bike. You might be having problems with performance or a better model becomes available. To what extent do you adopt a rational and systematic approach to this process? For example, do you choose on the basis of technical evaluations in consumer magazines or on recommendations from friends?

Continuing debates

The above discussion set out why knowledge and learning have come to be seen as so important, and then explored some of the main views on knowledge and learning. The particular case of management knowledge and explicit ideas was then looked at, particularly in relation to how they are adopted and evaluated. These issues remain a feature of debates among and between academics and practitioners. Sometimes, however, the terms change. So, for example, the **transferability of knowledge** might now be seen in terms of its '**stickiness**' and the 'absorptive capacity' of the receiving organization or person, rather than a question of tacitness and motivation or cognitive ability. Also, while the above account is (hopefully) presented in quite a balanced way, there is sometimes fierce debate between people adopting different perspectives on knowledge and learning. At the same time, some perspectives are more pervasive and dominant in practice, even if the newer approaches receive more attention in articles and academic courses – a lecture or textbook chapter on social learning for example might be seen as a **paradox**. Why is this? Overall, behavioural and cognitive perspectives of learning continue to dominate, as does the view of knowledge as object-like and capable of transfer from one place to another.

Thinkpoint 5.9

Management ideas, theories and practices are like items in the daily news. Those that receive media coverage or academic attention do so because they are seen as relatively new or unusual. Hence, in the same way that it is easy to get the wrong impression about the likelihood of being murdered in your bed or the street, one can assume management innovations to be more common than they really are.

While debates continue, new ones are emerging or coming to the fore. In particular, it is increasingly recognized that knowledge is not easy to classify, capture, control and transfer, especially through information systems. Here, the social and constructivist theories have gained ground, but uncertainty remains as to how, and the extent to which, they can be applied or managed. For example, if knowing is preferred to knowledge, how can one assess learning outcomes? A related issue is that of aligning what individuals learn with the needs or demands of organizations (CIPD, 2002). For example, Cathy (in Case study 5.1) had this problem when she empowered her staff to develop their own solutions – they did not always stick to the agenda.

Within the realm of explicit management ideas, similar issues remain unresolved. For example, if the adoption of ideas by managers is not always wholly rational (in the sense of objective assessment against organizational objectives), how can this be achieved or improved in practice. Can managers become less prone to psychological and political influences? Similarly, with the continuation of globalization, a longstanding debate about the local specificity or embeddedness of knowledge continues to trouble and divide people. At one time, and for many, even currently, management knowledge was seen as of universal relevance, applicable everywhere (e.g. assembly line technology, CRM, KM). The adaptations that people made as ideas travelled to different sectors or countries were seen to distort or corrupt the idea and its associated practices. Now, such modifications might be seen, not as distortions so much as inevitable constructions of knowledge in action – as innovation. This might seem reasonable enough, but it raises a number of issues when it comes to ownership of knowledge or 'intellectual property rights', but also to the teaching and learning of management.

Selected studies

The use of references above illustrates some of the key names associated with different views of knowledge and learning for example. Here we highlight three particular studies that are commonly referred to.

Kolb's experiential learning cycle   Most of us would agree that we learn a lot through experience, but not all experience leads to learning. It depends on the extent to which we think about the experience. Kolb's (1984) model (see Figure 5.1) presents learning as an active (cognitive and experiential) process of perception and mental processing. Faced with direct (e.g. sensory) experience, we reflect on it and generate mental or visual concepts and conclusions, which we then test out in practice for feedback and, as we continually repeat this cycle, we develop our understanding. Think of an example of this process in the context of (a) travelling on a new foreign transport system (b) learning to play a new computer game.

Nonaka and Takeuchi: Learning as knowledge transformation   This integrative approach to learning emphasizes facilitating processes. Using the tacit-explicit distinction, Nonaka and Takeuchi (1995)

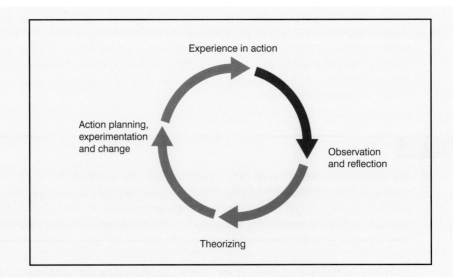

Figure 5.1 Kolb's experiential learning cycle

SOURCE: © KOLB, DAVID A.; EXPERIENTIAL LEARNING: EXPERIENCE AS THE SOURCE

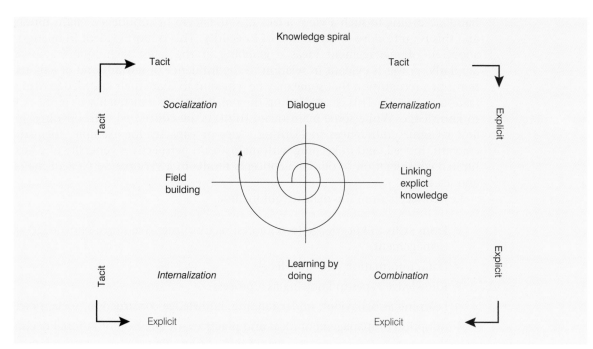

Figure 5.2 The Nonaka and Takeuchi SECI spiral

describe complex, independent, simultaneous or sequential processes through which knowledge is changed (see Figure 5.2). First, tacit-tacit knowledge transfer ('socialization') refers to the traditional 'master-apprentice' relationship where skills are learned through observation, imitation and practice.

Secondly, tacit-to-explicit transfer ('externalization') – the aim of much KM refers to attempts to unlock or capture knowledge through words, pictures or metaphors/analogies for example. It is, by definition, often impossible and always partial (e.g. writing golf coaching books). Thirdly, the opposite transfer of explicit to tacit knowledge ('internalization') relates to the application of representations of knowledge (e.g. manuals, diagrams and models) to develop abilities and understanding through practice and reflection. Finally, 'combination' is the use of existing explicit knowledge/s to create a 'bigger picture' such as is the case in formal learning situations like writing an essay and combining models.

Abrahamson's 'fads and fashions' Abrahamson (1991) is interested in helping managers make more rational decisions when adopting new management ideas. He recognizes that assumptions of rational management – free choice and clear organizational goals and criteria for assessing efficiency – are rarely appropriate or evident, especially in conditions of high uncertainty (cf. Simon, 1960). Rather, he shows how adoption of ideas can be 'forced' (e.g. government bodies requiring use of safety or quality protocols) or subject to the influence of 'fashion' (e.g. from consultants/gurus, media and business schools). Also, this can lead to copying others such as 'in-group' or peer companies. He calls this the 'fad' perspective, although most writers do not distinguish between fads and fashions.

Core concepts and the mainstream

Aside from the obvious case of knowledge, there has been little mention of our core concepts in the discussion so far. This does not mean that they are wholly absent in mainstream approaches. Indeed, if we had been able to go into more detail, some would have featured quite prominently. Identity, for example, is very important to social theories of learning in the sense of learning through significant others and of knowledge and interests being associated with what it is to be a consultant, plumber, etc. Similarly, freedom is evident in the notion of self-directed learning and empowering staff to develop their own knowledge, perspectives and approaches.

More generally, some learning theories are founded on a humanistic view whereby we develop and become 'free' and creative thinkers through life-long learning and self-improvement. On the other hand, according to such a view, a lack of self-esteem or confidence might hinder learning potential and this is quite close to the notion of insecurity. This is most evident in relation to the non-rational adoption of management ideas – grabbing at the latest technique for 'psychological' reasons. Similarly, power is evident in relation to the influence of rewards and of experts over others and in terms of a recognition that some may be reluctant to share their knowledge with others in the organization as a result. This clearly sets up the possibility of an inequality in terms of expertise and access to knowledge. While some mainstream thinkers are concerned with opening up access to learning, and recognize differences in learning styles or capacity for example, inequality is not a central concern. Indeed, and in keeping with mainstream perspectives generally of course, we shall see how limited consideration of our core concepts results in a very partial view of management knowledge and learning.

Key concepts from the mainstream include:

- From skills to knowledge (economies; sectors; intensive firms; knowledge-workers; and management).
- Data, information and knowledge.
- Knowledge types to knowing as a process.
- Learning as behaviour, understanding, knowledge construction, social practice/interaction.
- Adoption of management ideas and practices – a question of rational decision making?
- Knowledge as manageable and/or local and adaptable?

Using and abusing management knowledge

Introduction

How can one be critical of knowledge and learning? Surely they are to be valued? One might debate the direction in which they are channelled – what knowledge is to be learned and how – but they are unavoidable social processes or outcomes. Even if this is the case, the questions of:

- how knowledge and learning are conceived, prescribed and practised
- in whose name and interests
- with what consequences and
- who and what are silenced or marginalized through them are all of crucial importance.

They help not only in terms of our understanding of the subject and its contestability, but also as regards the way in which our lives are shaped and can be altered (Contu *et al.*, 2003) – how knowledge and learning can be used for particular ends that are seen as desirable or can be abused in the pursuit of undesirable or harmful ends. In this way, a critical view of learning can be seen as one that not only critiques learning theories and practices, but directs learning towards particular emancipatory goals (Freire, 1972). This is especially clear in the particular case of management knowledge, our focus here, and is evident even from a cursory look at the particular way in which our core concepts – power, identity, freedom, inequality and insecurity – are *absent* from much of the mainstream debate.

We have now seen how knowledge has become a key focus in mainstream studies of management and organizations. However, it is generally a particular view of knowledge that is used, one that is largely cognitive and suggests its transferability and market or commodity value for example. Implicit in the above account has been the fact that knowledge and learning have been directed at improving organizational performance. What of other forms of knowledge, such as that of the 'whistle-blower' who reveals unethical or illegal practices or knowledge that would be generally useful, but is withheld to protect the organization's interests – i.e. an abuse of knowledge by silencing it? And what of 'knowledge for its own sake' rather than that which is developed for particular instrumental motives?

Even in more sophisticated (e.g. processual) accounts, knowledge is largely divorced from a broader politics of **truth** or how reality is made (and silenced) by knowledge. For example, in relation to learning, the prevailing truth is that COPs are effective, but this may close off other approaches. Similarly with identity, where broader issues of power are neglected, self is seen as an individual possession rather than a partially shared story or narrative. And freedom also remains limited, as if achieved largely through self-knowledge and reflection or personal development – or as if we can all become who we want to be without constraint or consequences for others. Inequality is not an issue either, except in so far as management's primacy is taken for granted – the right to select people and set the parameters of, and access to, knowledge and methods of learning. Insecurity too tends to be seen outside of a political context, either as a universal trait or one induced by work pressures and 'curable' through training or insistence on rational procedures for the adoption of new knowledges. Indeed, emotion more generally has been marginalized or commodified in mainstream approaches. For example, it has been translated into something else, like motivation, or a measure such as 'emotional intelligence' (basically, social skills) rather than recognized as central to all processes, including the most 'rational' – scientists can be seen as having, or even needing, a *'passion'* for objectivity for example.

Overall then, the key point is that mainstream approaches tend to celebrate the rational and objective and underplay the political. Where the political is considered, it is only in terms of minor differences in individual or small group interests, say between different departments or teams, rather than in a more critical or fundamental sense. Sometimes, these themes are combined in the sense of legitimate power, such as in the view that the most powerful or influential ideas (or people) are so because they provide the most effective or rational solutions to organizational problems. We shall see how this view seriously distorts the practice of management. First however, we continue with our case study and present an alternative view of management learning with a focus beyond, but including, immediate cognitive and social interaction processes (see Case study 5.2).

CASE STUDY 5.2 Learning to love the customer: An alternative view of CRM

After hurriedly leaving Cathy's office, Rohan bumped into an old friend, John Melia. It turns out that John has worked at the DK-Line call-centre for a year or so. John knew all about customer relationship management (CRM) of course, but he had a different story to tell. His version, from the 'front-line' as it were, was that they weren't especially interested in developing relationships with customers as selling other products such as car breakdown and loans because these were more profitable. Also, they had only adopted this approach when it was realized that all their competitors were doing it. Most of them had used a firm of CRM consultants and they had come in to DK-Line after the CEO had seen a presentation of theirs promising all kinds of savings, especially staff costs. But there was no way that this could be checked now, as they didn't know what the output figures were before CRM at DK-Line.

As to the skills needed and the support given for this, John's view was that the mentors were effectively supervisors, checking up on mistakes and standards, and although staff had some leeway in the way they spoke to customers, this was quite restricted. For example, even if it was clear that customers didn't want any other service, staff had to offer the full range of additional products in every call. He agreed that much could be learned from colleagues, especially about how to deal with angry customers. The training on 'handling irates', as it was known, was useless, as it gave standard approaches that customers saw through and it used examples from what John called the 'have a nice day' approach. Also, being able to relate to customers was taken for granted in the firm. It was only technical insurance skills that helped get you promoted, and most didn't have the necessary time to study for the exams, especially those with family responsibilities. Finally, with the new IT system, although it was easier, having information available, you no longer needed to use your judgement. It was all set up for you in the 'frequently asked questions' page. They didn't need technically experienced recruits anymore . . . Rohan sat down at his computer to start his essay. It was going to be a long night!

Key issues/controversies

Beyond learning theories? In the first half of the chapter, we saw how mainstream approaches have become critical of traditional views of knowledge as objective. A range of perspectives were drawn upon including processual, learning as behaviour and understanding, and learning as the construction of knowledge in social practice and interaction. While this shift is evident in many written accounts, it was also noted how this is not always reflected in organizational and management practice. Indeed, this observation can be made more generally about management ideas and practices – espoused theories and theories in use (see above). Rather, knowledge continues to be seen as like an object or possession, which can be categorized into types, managed and acquired through the appropriate reward system and forms of instruction. However, there are more critical views of even the more **progressive** (and espoused) theories of knowledge and learning.

These critical views can be divided into two types (for a detailed outline of the literature see Grey and Antonacopoulou, 2004). First, there have been some sustained assaults on the detailed contents of mainstream learning theory. Thus, and in a similar tradition to more longstanding critiques of learning (e.g. Freire, 1972), Vince and Martin (1993) explore the way that conventional approaches neglect considerations of power, emotion and gender (see also *Management Learning*, 1997). By presenting or configuring individuals (us) as 'learners', the details of how such an identity is constructed and enacted are simply ignored. This is problematic because the 'learner' is a deeply individualized notion that marginalizes or silences the sociological and structural ways which – in other contexts – are widely recognized as configuring individuality. For example, individual assessment or appraisal encourages people to look upon themselves as separate from others and even in competition with them. It also encourages them to see their strengths and weaknesses and even their character or identity as of their own doing and making. It helps in a broader process through which we deny or play down our interdependence with others for who we are and what we do. It 'individualizes'.

This one-sidedness is most evident in the widespread invocation of the notion of 'learning style' (Honey and Mumford, 1986). Learning style is an unusual concept in that it simultaneously individualizes and classifies. The learner is indeed an individual with his or her own particular relationship with what is learnt: yet the learning style approach always parcels that individual into some kind of predetermined category – as a 'theorist' or 'pragmatist' for example – usually captured by a traditional two-by-two matrix. Such 'models' can be seen as abuse, not only of the empirical processes involved in learning, but of the individual learner as an object. Yet they are the staple of just about every management development course run in organizations or by consultants, as well as of academic learning models upon which they typically build. These comprise ever-more complex ways of linking learning to assorted 'variables' (e.g. work environment and personality), but this complexity can blind us to the underlying assumptions entailed by the paradox of the learner as individual and the learner as 'type' (see Reynolds, 1997, for a rare and systematic critique of learning styles within its own terms).

The second kind of critical view is less concerned with this or that detail of mainstream learning theory, but instead focuses on the general 'hoopla' or hype that infests writing on learning in organizations. One of the earliest and most incisive of these critiques was provided by Coopey (1995), where learning organizations are considered in terms of the way that they individualize and discipline their members. For example, by transforming *organizational* responsibilities for training into *individual* needs and responsibilities for (lifelong) 'learning', employees are pressured to develop such that any failures in development or even advancement are deemed to be solely of their own making. This is an important critique, not just for what it says about '**learning organizations**' or 'societies', but because it links the fad for learning with the rise of new organizational forms (see Chapters 4, 9 and 13 in this volume). In other words, preoccupations with learning cannot be separated from a much wider swathe of claims about organizations. More generally, it is simply invalid to divorce invocations of learning from their wider social and organizational context (see Contu *et al.*, 2003 in the 'Important studies within the empirical approach' section below).

Thus, mainstream learning theories and associated practices have begun to be critiqued, especially in terms of how the neglect of context results in a 'naturalizing' of particular approaches to organizing and being, making them seem inevitable. The individual becomes a 'learner' with a particular style and a personal responsibility for learning and the organization becomes an entity focused on the acquisition of knowledge. Here, we can see how learning is not unequivocally or unquestionably good. For does it not make a difference what is learnt? In this sense, any evaluation we make of learning cannot be separated from knowledge and/or its consequences, and it is to this theme that we now return.

Four alternative views of management knowledge   We have seen how management can be seen as an activity that, in the conventional view, is directed towards the rational achievement of organizational objectives, even if minor political, cultural or psychological factors may sometimes interfere with these processes. This gives rise to a particular view of management knowledge as that which achieves those ends. The means and ends are not questioned, but seen as neutral or legitimate.

Critical perspectives on management knowledge differ from this view. Needless to say, they do not appear in management guru presentations or most textbooks! (Why is this?) And even when they do appear in textbooks, they are often marginalized, labelled as being 'critical' and even separated off into a specific section in each chapter! In addition, the fact that they are less familiar means that they resonate less with our existing (learned) ways of seeing the world and this may make them seem less persuasive – they are 'too new'!

THE IDEOLOGY OF A PRIVILEGED MALE ELITE   All of us carry out activities that might be associated with 'management' (e.g. running a household; planning out tasks; organizing an event), but we are not all called 'managers'. While the activities of organizing are longstanding, management as an elite group is a comparatively recent phenomenon, derived largely from appropriating ('buying' or 'stealing') and monopolizing knowledge of how to do tasks from craft labour (Braverman, 1974; see also scientific management in Chapters 6, 10 and 13).

What is the basis of managers' 'right' to manage? Aside from formally acting on behalf of the legal owners of organizations (i.e. property rights gave rights of control), the authority and growth of management was founded on a claim to expertise, much like that of the professions such as lawyers and accountants, although without their formal associations and regulation. In this way then, management knowledge can be seen not only as associated with various activities, but as constructing and serving the interests of an elite, as *ideological* (Hales, 1993). Management qualifications are a good illustration – they help justify or legitimize expertise, higher salaries and positions in the hierarchy, while the majority are excluded (Willis, 1977). Would people study management in such large numbers if they were simply seeking a better understanding of business and organizations? What management ideas do you know that challenge the relatively privileged position of managers?

The notion of ideology is not solely a point about hierarchy, however, but about who occupies management positions. For example, the traditional emphasis in management on rationality, planning, measurement, competition and logical thinking can be seen as reflecting and favouring the male gender – management as masculine (see Morgan, 1988; Collinson and Hearn, 1996; Wilson, 1996). Women can, of course, emulate these masculine aspects of behaviour, but usually this involves a break with how they have been brought up and how broad ranging sexual identities reinforce more passive and less instrumental relationships. Instrumental behaviour is that which focuses on following the means to achieve a specific end. More generally as well, knowledge is valued differently according to whether it is associated with dominant groups. If not, it may be taken for granted, as natural and not warranting special reward. This has long been the case where jobs become gendered – seen as the domain of one particular sex. In the case study for example, John mentions how social skills are not recognized as highly as technical ability and that some groups are effectively denied access to the latter.

SOURCE: © ISTOCKPHOTO.COM/NANCY LOUIE

Image 5.4 Who is typically excluded from management?

NEO-IMPERIALISM AND/OR RELIGIOUS CONVERSION   Similarly, there is a cultural bias to management (and rationality more generally), founded, for the most part, on the economic dominance of the West. Here, the spread of North American management ideas and practices can be seen as 'neo-imperialism'. Indeed, Western consultants, managers and lecturers working in South-east Asia and Eastern Europe have been likened to missionaries, involved in a process of conversion to the *true* way of managing/organizing (e.g. 'free' market capitalism) (Kostera, 1995). This view draws attention not only to issues of power in terms of control over resources, but also claims to truth and whose knowledge is given voice and who are silenced or marginalized.

For example, it has been argued that a preoccupation with *explicit* management knowledge is a peculiarly Western notion and silences the wisdom and contribution of Eastern business practices (see Chia, 2003).

A DISCOURSE OF OUR TIME   The same issues are evident in the concept of management as a dominant discourse more generally. Here, in contrast to the above view that management knowledge is restricted to an elite few, recent critiques of hierarchy from within management and calls for de-layering and (limited) 'empowerment' suggest that 'we are all managers now' or should be (see Burrell, 1996; Chapter 13 on post-bureaucracy). Indeed, the legitimacy and relevance of management knowledge has spread way beyond business organizations into government and even how we personally 'manage' our health and personal relationships (Grey, 1999). In this way, management is political, not so much simply by association with having power and privilege, but by shaping the way we all think about, talk about and do things and silence other (e.g. more radical or traditional) ways of organizing (Parker, 2003).

We have seen how this is the case in relation to learning itself – we might see ourselves as having a particular learning style. But how management knowledge comes to shape how we think and feel, our identity, is evident more generally. For example, Rose (1989) shows how the organizational behaviour concepts of attitudes and personality were developed in the Second World War in public and private sector programmes to 'govern' citizens and employees. Now, we take for granted that we have a personality and attitudes and may see ourselves in this way. This highlights how what might seem to be a shared view is itself the product of power. For example, the idea of a sense of time discipline – a concern with punctuality or not wasting time – and, more recently, that of the consumer emerged and developed, partly to ensure greater work effort from employees (Thompson, 1967).

A MARKET COMMODITY   The combination of its importance, claimed universal relevance and its own focus on markets as key arbiters of value, makes management probably one of the most commoditized forms of knowledge. It is converted into an object-like form for transmission at a price in different markets – like 'milk into dairy products' (Huczynski, 1993). Although, as we know, explicit or codified knowledge may be merely the 'tip of the iceberg' when it comes to management, this view corresponds to many of the processes of managing knowledge.

SOURCE: © BETTMANN/CORBIS

Image 5.5 Popular discourses?

The 'products' are all very familiar from the management guru talk, text, training programme and DVD, through various graphical representations such as the classic two-by-two matrix used by consultants and management lecturers to the management degree and, of course, textbooks (see also Sturdy and Gabriel, 2000). In the latter case, it is important to note that they are seen by many publishers and authors as first and foremost a product in a market, just like any other (see Box 5.1).

Box 5.1: OB textbooks and the cost of packaged knowledge – Where does your money go?

The current market price for an introductory OB book such as this one in the United Kingdom is now around £40.00. From the first print run, say 5000, the income of £200 000 will be distributed approximately as follows:

Bookshop (c.35 per cent discount for university stores)	£70 000 (£14 per copy)
Author/s (commission at c.10 per cent receipts of £130 000)	£13 000 (£2.60 per copy)
Marketing and sales reps (c.5 per cent of receipts)	£6 500
Distribution and warehousing (c.5 per cent of receipts)	£6 500

Publisher overheads (e.g. staff) (c.30 per cent of receipts)	£39 000
Publisher (retained surplus)	£65 000 (£13.00 per copy)

Clearly, for the publisher, there is some risk that the book will not sell well and the above costs partly reflect an unknown investment. But costs will decline in subsequent years and print runs. For subsequent 'new' editions, profits will be greater still, not least because the price is likely to be higher and relative costs lower, especially as only minor changes to content are usually made.

How else might publishing textbooks be organized and rewarded? How can the value and ownership of knowledge be decided upon?

Four alternative views of the adoption of management ideas 'Management ideas do not work!' If this is the case, you may wish to stop reading at this point, and even stop studying management, certainly critically. You might also wonder about all the ideas in this and other texts. What is the point!? Alternatively, you might be intrigued about why some ideas become and remain popular and important and what some of their consequences are.

Of course, management ideas, when applied or even talked about, have numerous and often highly significant effects, but they can never work *exactly as intended*, and certainly do not meet the expectations and promises associated with them (see Kotter, 1995). They are, then, necessarily imperfect. This is one reason why there seems to be a constant stream of seemingly new management ideas or fashions. This transience of management ideas is typically explained by changes in the business environment – new ideas are needed for new times – or the need to keep ahead of rival companies. Alternatively, there are core dilemmas, in structuring organizations for example, which can never be resolved fully. For example, too much centralization of decision making can stifle creativity and too little can lead to a lack of focus (see Child, 1981). As a consequence, Mintzberg (1979) for example, compared the changing preferences for de/centralized organizations to the fashion in the hemlines of women's skirts! While there is some merit in these accounts, they cannot fully explain the apparent rate of change of management ideas.

A more radical view is that the demand for new ideas is almost constant because of the persistence of a forlorn hope that problems can be solved, enhanced by economic pressures on managers to achieve results. This hope might be described as a naive (unitary) view of everyone sharing the same interests in organizations, whereas ideas are often resisted by those who are subjected to them (Edwards, 1979). Conflict is inherent in organizations, not least because of the degrees of inequality. Here, unless the underlying causes of conflict are addressed, new ideas will never work and only treat the symptoms. Alternatively, it could be seen as a modernist faith (the power of rationality and scientific knowledge to control the world), which is especially problematic in relation to managing people's behaviour, values and emotions (e.g. their motivation) – the unmanageable organization (Gabriel, 1995). (Why is this the case?)

POWER In the first half of the chapter we saw how the adoption of new explicit forms of management knowledge matched two of the claimed dimensions of management activity – meeting organizational objectives and rational planning (e.g. evaluation) – although in practice an approximation or 'satisficing' might often occur. A more critical view would place greater emphasis on the third dimension of management, especially in terms of its emotional and political nature. We now take each of these in turn and then develop a more social approach to management knowledge in general.

While it is comforting to think that managers adopt ideas and use knowledge for the good of their organization (indeed, they are unlikely to admit otherwise), championing the latest idea in marketing, HR, finance or whatever, is likely to be helpful in getting noticed by superiors and helping advance one's career. Who gets promoted these days for saying that 'things are fine as they are. We don't need new ideas'? Given the difficulty in assessing the true impact of implemented ideas, this means that the emergence of ideas can be seen in terms of competition between different managers. Indeed, this can be seen at a broader level in terms of competition between management functions (e.g. accountants, consultants, marketers, etc.) both within individual organizations and generally (Armstrong, 1986 and Chapter 8 on decision making in this volume). Apart from pursuing personal or functional advancement, ideas can be adopted and (ab)used to legitimize or mask other, often sensitive, motives such as reducing headcounts or increasing control over employees (Braverman, 1974). For example, in our case study, CRM was adopted to increase cross-selling rather than improve relationships, and **mentors** were introduced, more to check up on than develop staff.

It is also important to consider those whose knowledge is not valued, whose voice is not heard and who are effectively denied access to valued (and valuable) ideas and practices. This raises the whole issue of how some knowledge is valued highly and the criteria against which knowledge is valued in society. For example, we have seen how management knowledge can be seen as a form of ideology that silences other (e.g. Eastern, feminine, **labourist**) views. This can be regarded as neo-imperialism in that, unlike imperialism based on the use of military force, colonization is achieved through ideas and market power.

Thinkpoint 5.10

Who decides which skills and forms of knowledge are valued most highly? Is this reflected in salaries and should it be? What other criteria might be used in assessing rewards?

Exercise 5.2

Rank the following skills in terms of their value (one is highest, eight is lowest): keyboard skills; prioritizing activities; driving a car; social skills; manual dexterity; memory; team leading; foreign language fluency. Now reflect on what criteria you used to value them. Using these criteria, compare two different jobs that you are familiar with. How do your evaluations compare the relative status and income of these jobs?

PSYCHODYNAMICS

Managers turn to management ideas in the same way that the Ancient Greeks turned to mythmakers and legends – to help them create a sense of order in the face of the potential chaos of human existence. *(Watson, 1994, p. 10)*

Psychodynamics refers to the 'anxieties, fears and yearnings' and corresponding psychological 'need' for a reassuring sense of order, *identity* and control, which underpins much behaviour.

Thinkpoint 5.11

Think of the release of anxiety if you were to know in advance what the questions in an exam were to be.

We have already referred to this in the sense of how managers act 'emotionally' and 'impulsively' in adopting or copying ideas in an effort to achieve psychological security, and that this may blind them to the organizational effectiveness of those ideas. The mainstream approach sees such 'non-rational' behaviour as pathological or something to be eradicated. Alternatively, it can be treated or 'immunized' against, by following systematic evaluation procedures (Abrahamson, 1991). However, more critical perspectives regard these issues as inescapable or, at least, as exacerbated by certain individualizing contexts, whether in terms of the organization (e.g. career hierarchies) or beyond (e.g. capitalism or consumerism). These conditions create underlying and sometimes overt pressures and anxieties, such as a fear of failure and a sense of isolation (see Jackall, 1988; Gill and Whittle, 1993). However, such dynamics do not only account for how managers might be seen as gullible victims of the latest fad, desperate to avoid being left out of the 'gang'. They also provide an important basis for energy and action – imagine an organization where there were no pressures or uncertainties about the future or our identity. Insecurity then, is a condition and consequence of management. But it is also reflected in managers wanting to be seen as innovators and leaders and as the creators of ideas (Huczynski, 1993; Jackson, 1996).

Explaining the adoption of management ideas and knowledge in terms of political and psychological motives and the inevitability of these dynamics provides an important counter to the mainstream rational view, but all three tend to generalize the processes. Why, for example, do some forms of management knowledge appear to spread (e.g. to different companies, sectors, countries) while others do not, or do so at a different time and sequence?

INSTITUTIONS AND NETWORKS There has always been knowledge diffusion across groups and societies (e.g. neighbouring interactions, exploration, colonization, trade, media) (see Rogers, 1995), often, but not always, from the most to the less powerful or 'effective'. (The crucifix and Coke bottle/McDonald's arch are said to be the two most recognized objects in the world.) This has been facilitated (and fuelled) by technologies (e.g. print, telegraph, telephone, TV, computer). However, working or travelling in different parts of the world clearly shows how business, organizations and management are both similar (e.g. bureaucracies; assembly lines) and different (see Chapter 12).

Institutional theory broadly seeks to demonstrate and explain the variety of societal influences on organizational/management structures and practices – their institutional 'embeddedness'. It is concerned with variations between contexts – why one management practice is adopted in

SOURCE: © BETTMANN/CORBIS

Image 5.6 Resolving anxieties through management ideas?

identity as a marketing manager, for example, you might point out that CRM is now a core element in the latest marketing qualification or course at a leading business school. Finally, you might consider the visual way in which the idea is presented (rhetorical) – a two-by-two matrix would be a good start, if a little clichéd – as 'the content (e.g. packaging) is itself part of the performance' (Grint 1997, p. 733).

Exercise 5.3

What rhetorical techniques are used in textbooks to persuade the readers of the validity or value of information (see also Fineman and Gabriel, 1994; Hackley, 2003)? How might promotion techniques be adapted to different learning theories?

Of course, much of this promotional packaging work may have already been done for you as management ideas are constructed and adapted at different stages (by consultants and academics for example) with their subsequent adoption by other managers in mind (see Huczynski, 1993). Indeed, it is important to highlight that management ideas are not simply invented by others (e.g. academics, consultants, gurus), but derived from the practice of managers and other employees (see Abrahamson and Fairchild, 1999). Indeed, this is a key criticism of the rhetorical approach. It presents managers as gullible victims of the clever tricks of management consultants and gurus – organizational 'witch-doctors' (Micklewait and Wooldridge, 1996) – rather than as a co-produced and more (inter)active process involving both insiders (managers, staff) and outsiders (e.g. consultants, academics) developing and applying ideas, techniques and practices.

Exercise 5.4

Promoting/selling a 'new' management idea Your task is to plan how to promote or market a new idea in a country (or sector) that you are familiar with using one or more of the frameworks and ideas discussed here, and others you can think of.

Table 5.1 Perspectives on the adoption of management ideas

Reason	Perspective
Organization effectiveness	Rational
Help career, function and/or control	Political
Relieve anxiety/fear	Psychodynamic
Provides legitimacy/ Imposed	Institutional
Fit values	Cultural
Well promoted	Rhetorical
Not sure there was one!	'Muddling through'

(See also Sturdy, 2004.)

Thinkpoint 5.12

Do the perspectives/reasons in Table 5.1 apply to your own interest in, or attraction to, particular management ideas? How would you rank them in importance? Why the differences?

Ideas, translation and practice   Outlining critical views of management knowledge and of the adoption of ideas by managers highlights how management is not a neutral, technical and objective process, but embedded in power relations, whether these are seen in psychological, institutional, cultural or rhetorical terms. However, the focus has been on management ideas more than management in practice. While there is a close connection between the two (see Sturdy and Fleming, 2003), not least in the promotion and adoption of practices, there is a danger of neglecting the application of ideas. For example, while ideas might be recognized by managers as being of value, this does not mean that others will be persuaded, or that the ideas will be applied in practice. In one respect we are considering the difference between cognitive/affective and behavioural learning or between espoused theories and theories in use – what people think and say and what people do.

We have noted how management practices (e.g. the assembly line) can sometimes be imposed on employees regardless of whether or not they 'buy into' them and the ideas that support them (Guillen, 1994). More generally, within all the management disciplines, there is a concern to identify whether or not the latest idea has been applied, regardless of how popular it seems (see also Kostova and Roth, 2002). Such an approach is useful, not least because it gets behind a media focus on the latest ideas to what is practised in organizations (Benders and van Veen, 2001), but it suggests that ideas do have *pure* ideational and practical forms. (Are the practices at DK-Line 'really' CRM?) This neglects the active and inevitable way in which both ideas and practices are amended for and in use – *translated*. Even relatively 'dogmatic' knowledge such as religion is adapted to local contexts and hybrids are formed (Lillrank, 1995). In other words what, say, BPR means, differs from one person/organization/context/OB essay to the next. More generally, and in keeping with social views of learning and processual views of knowledge, it can be argued that knowledge is never fixed, but always and necessarily interpreted so that it has meaning in a particular context (Latour, 1987). However, meanings are not simply free-floating and random, but channelled through power relations. This channelling is especially clear in relation to management knowledge as we shall see in the following section.

Translating the critical to the managerial   If a manager is persuaded of the utility of an explicit management idea it is simply one point in a continual process of adaptation. Clearly, if the idea is to develop in the organization an established practice, other managers and employees will need to be convinced, persuaded and taught. In doing so, the idea and its associated practices will change as we have seen. We have also seen how ideas are moulded and packaged prior to being presented to managers in written or verbal presentations. For example, think of the process of producing this text. Who decided the structure? How was it edited, by whom and with what thoughts or motives in mind?

A key difference with this text, compared to most others, is not that it breaks any convention in relation to the process whereby books are written, edited, marketed or produced. Its difference is largely based on the choice to include critical perspectives on management and organizations. As intimated when management was discussed as an ideology, management ideas will not explicitly challenge management interests. For example, imagine trying to make a management idea popular, however valid it was, which gave no role or status to managers. Indeed, this is a key challenge for this textbook, and critical ideas more generally – how can those interested in management (or being managers) be persuaded of ideas that challenge management and its privileges? Now, some cite empowerment as a popular idea, which appears to undermine management's role. However, it does not significantly challenge hierarchy and certainly not ownership patterns in industry, only the middle layers in an organization (Burrell, 1996). Moreover, there is good reason to do this for cost-cutting purposes because middle management has proliferated over recent years.

This does not mean that critical or challenging ideas do not emerge of course, for there are still other, albeit relatively marginalized, social contexts (e.g. universities and, in particular, political domains) or conditions that make them possible (see Parker, 2003). Indeed, numerous groups develop ideas that pose at least some challenge to management. Many of these are not heard (i.e. not published or read), but others are adapted in a way that silences or neuters that challenge, however slight. Indeed, Jacques (1996) shows how, when something genuinely novel and radical emerges, it tends to be adapted – or cut to size as in the Greek myth of Procrustes – to better fit current (modernist) arrangements and interests. For example, post-modern ideas might be more appropriate to present times. However, where they have been promoted, it is in a diluted, conservative form (e.g. Peters, 1992) and barely applied in practice. Hence, any potential challenge disappears in this abuse of ideas (Willmott, 1992).

The **neutering** of ideas may be quite explicit. For example, when you read case studies or research that names the organization/s in question, you are unlikely to see much criticism of the organization or its management unless they have left or heroically solved the problem at hand. This is partly an outcome of explicit censorship – who would allow such potentially bad publicity after all? But more often, it is self-censorship and author/publisher fear of litigation. But being critical is not pointing out that a particular individual or organization is managed badly; it is not so much personal, but potentially far more unsettling than that.

As the existence of this text suggests, critical ideas, if not practices, have some visibility. However, in textbooks for example, authors are constrained to present them in a largely commodified form (see Box 5.1 above) and alongside 'mainstream' approaches in order to reach large audiences. Equally, those with a commercial (e.g. consultancy) and, increasingly, academic interest tend to dilute or omit anything that is really critical. They may not even see it. This is evident generally, but also in the particular case of learning theory. For example, Contu and Willmott (2003) show how the situated learning theory associated with Lave and Wenger (1991) actually has important critical dimensions, which are lost in subsequent accounts of it by others and in its application. For example, power relations are central in their notion of 'legitimate peripheral participation' in terms of access of particular social groups to COPs and how seemingly consensual relations are produced **hegemonically** rather than naturally. These critical dimensions of Lave and Wenger's ideas are lost in others' adaptations and broader debate, such that situated learning comes to be known as a mainstream approach. Thus, the Procrustean process continues in translating the critical into the managerial. When this occurs in the realm of management writing, the possibility for translating critical ideas into critical practice becomes an even greater challenge.

Important studies within the critical approach

Braverman and de-skilling   Much of the above text has applied to managers' adoption and use of management ideas and the privileged status of management. Relatively little attention has been given to how management first came to acquire and apply this knowledge, and with what consequences for other employees. Braverman's (1974) classic study shows how both shop floor and office work in the 20th century was subjected to a rigorous process of de-skilling through the application of scientific management. This is quite a well-documented process whereby skills were effectively appropriated by management (and supporting academics) with the consequence that work became more intensive, poorly paid and alienating, if also often more productive. For example, in our case study, much of the judgement required on the job had been incorporated into the IT system. However, Braverman's key contribution was to place this in the context, not of improved efficiency, but the ideological nature of management. What was claimed as neutral, objective science was more about securing management control over labour and cheapening the costs of production, as a necessary condition for capitalism and continued growth in profitability – what many might see as an abuse of knowledge. This critique of capitalism has been itself criticized for focusing only on de-skilling, failing to recognize any re-skilling (e.g. use of computing) and ignoring gender divisions and the subjective experience of de-skilling. However, it remains important as a challenge to the **scientism** of management where its ideas and techniques are presented as objective and politically neutral. For example, and as already intimated, it could be argued that knowledge management is a contemporary approach to de-skilling, but further up the hierarchy. Now, it is professionals and managers whose knowledge is targeted for capture and abuse.

Guillen's models of management   Guillen's (1994) work combines a wide spread of research covering key streams of management thought (scientific management, human relations, systems theory, etc.), different countries (e.g. the United States, United Kingdom, Spain and Germany) and a critically informed recognition of the range of different factors involved in the adoption of ideas. It is an important counter to the rational-economic approach in that he showed how new knowledges and practices are not adopted universally, to the same extent, nor, necessarily, in the same sequence or for the same reasons across nations or sectors (see also Djelic, 1998). In Spain, for example, management elites and practitioners adopted the human relations ideology. However, only managers in large organizations (electronics and petrochemicals) implemented the practices because smaller companies

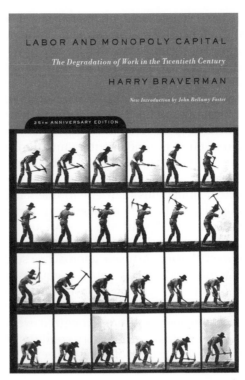

Image 5.8 *Labor and Monopoly Capital* (1974) – an important critique of management as control

did not have the necessary resources (e.g. training departments) and were less in need of more effective supervision and control. This **institutional approach** also places emphasis on the role of employee resistance to control in shaping how particular practices emerge.

Contu *et al*.: Against learning   Although only recently (2003) published, this is one of the few systematic attempts to critique learning, or, more accurately, the contemporary discourse of organizational learning. It uses the notion of a '**politics of truth**' in challenging hidden and explicit claims of this discourse, not least that learning is necessarily a good thing for all and is open to all. For example, contemporary learning discourse assumes that the content will not challenge managerial control and yet claims empowerment and post–bureaucratic structuring. Likewise, it shapes governmental agendas and broader politics in a manner that is difficult to contest as other voices are silenced. In short, learning organizations and societies enable one to learn only that which is good for them (rather than their members) and do not so much create knowledge as access it and seek to control it for **utilitarian** purposes (see also Fenwick, 2000).

Contribution to thinking about the field

This section of the chapter began by posing the question – how can one be critical of something as valuable as knowledge and learning? Hopefully, this has now been answered, at least in part. Critical perspectives overall place knowledge and power close together, but not simply in terms of knowledge as a commodity that brings power in the sense of influence over others. In the particular case of management knowledge, we have seen how a critical view challenges the idea of management as an objective, technical activity solely directed towards achieving organizational goals. At the same time, insofar as it does address and construct organizational aims, it is problematic in that these are also not **value-free**, nor without consequences in terms of inequality of resources and status, for example. Equally, regardless of issues of occupational privilege and management control over labour, management knowledge, like other forms, helps shape what we think and feel. In this sense, then, the issue, from a **pluralistic** or democratic point of view, is a concern over the increasing dominance of management as a **discourse** and the commodified or market form it takes (Chia, 2003). Such concerns are reinforced in the light of the association of management knowledge with other (e.g. Western, masculine, middle class) discourses of privilege.

Attention has been focused on management knowledge rather than learning as traditionally defined, but similar criticisms can be made of the particular form of knowledge surrounding management learning. For example, we have seen how approaches to learning that focus on relations of power are few and far between and continually censored, either by default or design. They tend to ignore the context in which learning shapes and individualizes identities, in terms of learning styles for example (cf. Contu *et al.*, 2003; Contu and Willmott, 2003). Overall, the principal contribution of critical approaches to management learning to date is in how management knowledge is engaged with or produced and with what consequences. Here, we have seen a number of approaches, that point to fundamental limitations of the mainstream, rational view of management knowledge as a universal and explicit tool that can be assessed and used for the control of organizations. For example, the continual emergence of waves of ideas are better seen as a reflection of their inherent limitations than environmental change, not least because there is little variation in the (modernist) nature of management ideas. Moreover, their limitations are extended by intended and unintended political outcomes such as resistance from those who are subjected to their application.

We have seen that mainstream approaches sometimes recognize that organizational life is not simple or 'rational' and that anxieties, identities, politics and culture are important. However, we have also seen that consideration of such issues tends to be couched in a unitary or consensus view, or fails to recognize power relations beyond local interpersonal or departmental conflicts. Moreover, even where such broader issues are recognized, we have seen how, over time, they may be edited out. Indeed, this abuse is almost a necessary condition for ideas to be disseminated beyond the confines of academic articles or 'critical' sections in textbooks. Nevertheless, we have also seen how culture, institutions and 'insecurity-identity' are not only important, but channelled within, and productive of, power relations. In particular, what is taken as normal and natural – the relative value of management knowledge or cultural values for example – is, on the contrary, historically and socially produced and, typically, distributed inequitably. It is therefore contestable and changeable. Likewise, what might be seen as abnormal, managerial anxiety or stress for example, could be regarded not so much as universal, but certainly not individualized or pathologized. In short then, a key element of the critical (and sociological) view of the world is scepticism or questioning things that are taken for granted, especially those beliefs that support inequitable relations of power. However, it should also be self-critical and, here, we can point to areas where critical approaches such as those outlined above are developing or may do so in future.

Much of the discussion of management knowledge centres on explicit ideas. There is a danger here that cognitive and commodified views of knowledge are reinforced and privileged at the expense of experiential and processual views. Moreover, there is a division between those who are interested in knowledge and its emergence and those who are concerned with practices and their consequences. For example, one might be concerned with the tension inherent in CRM, which was evident in the case study (establishing relationships versus extracting more sales) and not the consequences for employees in coping with this. This issue is a problem not just in terms of focus, but analytically. Here, mainstream theories might even be useful in drawing out how social practice and knowledge are intimately connected. This is also hinted at with a focus on how ideas are necessarily translated or 'in motion' and by a growing attention to knowledge as produced through action and social activity, including talk (Chia, 2003; Sturdy and Fleming, 2003).

Finally and relatedly, conceptual divisions may distort what is experienced. Recent critical approaches have sought to challenge some of these separations. For example, the above account of perspectives on the adoption of management ideas presents critical views in direct opposition to rational accounts. This clearly draws out some important limitations of the mainstream view, but perhaps goes too far conceptually. Thus, being rational is seen as *not* being anxious or emotional, or political or cultural for example. While this may conform to a common and classic distinction between emotion and rationality, heart and mind, informal and formal organization, in practice rationality is sustained (as well as threatened) by feelings, values and power. The crucial issue then is how these are channelled in particular directions and with what consequences. This returns us to some more basic questions that might act as a starting point for those wishing to pursue a critical view of knowledge and theories of knowledge: who makes claim to them; who is silenced or excluded; who assesses their value; what are their conditions and consequences, and how are these distributed or dispersed? In other words, what are the uses and abuses of management knowledge? Where such questions are directed at mainstream ideas and practices, they may go some way in reversing the typical translation process by converting the managerial to the critical.

Conclusion

Our core concepts – identity, power, freedom, insecurity, inequality and knowledge – have been evident to varying degrees throughout the chapter. Clearly, knowledge has been of central concern, but we have seen how this can be viewed in various ways. Similarly, power is recognized in some mainstream views, but in a very limited fashion, whereas a broader conception of power is what distinguishes critical perspectives. For example, insecurity and social identity are both important to some mainstream views of learning, but they are divorced from the power relations, which constitute, constrain and enable them.

Freedom and inequality have been largely implicit in the discussion, except insofar as access to valued knowledge is concerned and the ways in which critical approaches draw attention to those who are privileged and silenced. Nevertheless, both concepts are central to the subject of learning and knowledge. Indeed, both mainstream and critical approaches often present the pursuit and acquisition of knowledge as a route to freedom. However, they would differ in the view of knowledge and the ways in which it is valued and distributed in societies.

These are important distinctions, but those with opposing views often neglect what they may hold in common. Indeed, the structuring of the chapters in this textbook into mainstream and critical views serves to strengthen this limitation of both sides. For example, in the same way that mainstream views ignore or, at best, edit out critical knowledge, critical writers may readily dismiss the findings of mainstream research on the basis of their flawed or conservative assumptions. Also the assumptions and claims associated with behaviourism and cognitivism are highly problematic, but do have some validity and resonance with learning in practice. This is not necessarily to argue for some kind of middle ground or compromise, but more for the translation of mainstream into critical ideas and practices.

The aim of this chapter has been to present selectively both mainstream and critical approaches to knowledge and learning in the particular context of management. In the first part of the chapter, emphasis was placed on learning in general, while in the second part the focus was on learning in the sense of the adoption and translation of management ideas and practices. In both cases, different perspectives were presented within what have been organized as mainstream and critical approaches. Whatever position/s adopted, this is one of the most important issues – the plurality of available perspectives. This is important because it shows how an understanding of a topic is limited if it is restricted to a single approach. Indeed, in practice most researchers adopt a number of approaches or combine them. However, this does not mean that one gets closer to the truth the more perspectives one adopts. First, perspectives are sometimes quite incompatible and, secondly, there is no one truth. Indeed, an important lesson drawn from recent critical approaches, but with a long tradition, is that one should be sceptical of all claims to truth, even critical ones – the 'point is not that everything is bad, but that everything is dangerous' (Foucault, 1984, p. 343).

Discussion questions

1 Return to the notes you made at the start of the chapter about why you were reading it. Now that you have got to the end, have those aims been addressed? How would you now amend the learning objectives?

2 In a small group, agree and then list what you consider to be the main themes of the chapter. Then, take each one in turn and discuss what you understand them to mean, by thinking of examples. Note down any differences in views. Finally, discuss the implications of different understandings for the study of management.

3 Management ideas do not work as intended. Discuss/ consider the implications of this for (a) the practice of management and (b) studying management.

4 In what ways can one be critical of learning and knowledge? What practical implications does this have for organizations and for the design of courses and the presentation of ideas and theories?

Jacques, R. (1996) *Manufacturing the Employee*, London: Sage.

Kieser, A. (1997) 'Rhetoric and myth in management fashion', *Organisation* 4(1):49–74.

Kolb, D. A. (1984) *Experiential Learning*, Englewood Cliffs, NJ: Prentice Hall.

Kostera, M. (1995) 'The modern crusade: The missionaries of management come to eastern Europe', *Management Learning* 26(3):331–352.

Kostova, T. and Roth, K. (2002) 'Adoption of an organisational practice by subsidiaries of MNCs: Institutional and relational effects', *Academy of Management Journal* 45(1):215–233.

Kotter, J. P. (1995) 'Leading change: Why transformation efforts fail', *Harvard Business Review* 73(2):59–67.

Lam, A. (2000) 'Tacit knowledge, organisation studies and societal institutions: An integrated framework', *Organisation Studies* 21(3):487–513.

Latour, B. (1987) *Science in Action*, Cambridge, MA: Harvard University Press.

Lave, J. and Wenger, E. (1991) *Situated Learning: Legitimate Peripheral Participation*, New York: Cambridge University Press.

Lillrank, P. (1995) 'The transfer of management innovations from Japan', *Organisation Studies* 16(6):971–989.

Malone, S. A. (2003) *Learning About Learning*, London: Chartered Institute of Personnel and Development.

Management Learning (1997) 'Special issue: Emotion and learning in organisations', 28(1).

Micklewait, J. and Wooldridge, A. (1996) *The Witch Doctors: What the Management Gurus are Saying, Why It Matters and How to Make Sense of It*, London: Heinemann.

Mintzberg, H. (1979) *The Structuring of Organisations*, New York: Prentice Hall.

Morgan, G. (1988) *Images of Organisation*, London: Sage.

Newell, S., Robertson, M., Scarbrough, H. and Swan, J. (2002) *Managing Knowledge Work*, Houndmills: Palgrave.

Nonaka, I. and Takeuchi, H. (1995) *The Knowledge Creating Company*, Oxford: Oxford University Press.

Orr, J. (1996) *Talking About Machines: An Ethnography of a Modern Job*, Ithaca, NY: IRL Press.

Parker, M. (2003) *Against Management*, Cambridge: Polity.

Peters, T. (1992) *Liberation Management: Necessary Disorganisation for the Nanosecond Nineties*, New York: Knopf.

Piaget, J. (1950) *The Psychology of Intelligence*, London: Routledge.

Polyani, M. (1966) *The Tacit Dimension*, London: Routledge.

Power, M. (1997) *The Audit Society: Rituals of Verification*, Oxford: Oxford University Press.

Ramsay, H. (1996) 'Managing Sceptically: A Critique of Organisational Fashion', in S. R. Clegg and G. Palmer (eds.) *The Politics of Management Knowledge*, London: Sage.

Reynolds, M. (1997) 'Learning Styles: A Critique', *Management Learning* 28:115–133.

Robertson, M., Swan, J. and Newell, S. (1996) 'The role of networks in the diffusion of technological innovation', *Journal of Management Studies* 33(3):333–359.

Rogers, E. M. (1983/1995) *Diffusion of Innovations* (third/fourth editions), New York: Free Press.

Rose, N. (1989) *Governing the Soul: The Shaping of the Private Self*, London: Routledge.

Ryle, G. (1949) *The Concept of Mind*, Harmondsworth: Penguin Books.

Sennett, R. (2000) *The Corrosion of Character*, New York: W. W. Norton and Co.

Simon, H. (1960) *The New Science of Management Decisions*, New York: Harper and Row.

Skinner, B. F. (1953) *Science and Human Behaviour*, New York: Macmillan.

Skinner, B. F. (1971) *Beyond Freedom and Dignity*, Harmondsworth: Penguin.

Strang, D. and Macy, M. (2001) 'In search of excellence: Fads, success stories and adaptive emulation', *American Journal of Sociology* 107(1):147–182.

Sturdy, A. J. (2001) 'The global diffusion of customer service: A critique of cultural and institutional perspectives', *Asia Pacific Business Review* 7(3):73–87.

Sturdy, A. J. (2004) 'The adoption of management ideas and practices: Theoretical perspectives and possibilities', *Management Learning* 35(2):155–179.

Sturdy, A. J. and Fleming, P. (2003) 'Talk as technique: A critique of the words and deeds distinction in the diffusion of customer service cultures', *Journal of Management Studies* 40(5):753–773.

Sturdy, A. J. and Gabriel, Y. (2000) 'Missionaries, mercenaries or car salesmen? MBA teaching in Malaysia', *Journal of Management Studies*, 37(7):979–1002.

Thompson, E. P. (1967) 'Time, work discipline and industrial capitalism', *Past and Present* 38:56–97.

Vince, R. and Martin, L. (1993) 'Inside action learning: The psychology and the politics of the action learning model', *Management Education and Development* 24(3):205–15.

Vygotsky, L. S. (1962) *Thought and Language*, Cambridge, MA: MIT Press.

Watson, T. (1986) *Management, Organisations and Employment Strategy*, London: Routledge.

Watson, T. J. (1994), *In Search of Management: Culture Chaos and Control in Managerial Work*, London: Routledge.

Wilkinson, B. (1996) 'Culture, institutions and business in E. Asia', *Organisation Studies* 17(3): 421–447.

Willis, P. (1977) *Learning to Labor: How Working Class Kids Get Working Class Jobs*, New York: Columbia University Press.

Willmott, H. (1992) 'Post-modernism and excellence: The de-differentiation of economy and culture', *Journal of Organisational Change Management* 5(1): 58–68.

Wilson, F. (1996) 'Organisation theory: Blind and deaf to gender', *Organisation Studies* 17(5): 825–842.

Note

1 The author gratefully acknowledges the anonymous reviewers as well as those of Chris Grey, Karen Handley, Geraldine Lyons and the editors for their comments on an earlier draft of this chapter.

PART II
The Organizational Dimension

Part II covers a wide, though far from exhaustive, range of topics. Each chapter shows how they are examined in mainstream analysis, but also challenges the conventional assumption that organizations function as coherent and self-reproducing systems. In the mainstream, the consideration of politics, conflict or cultural diversity is fleeting and/or is seen as a disruptuive element that needs to be cauterized or contained. More critical approaches explore the recurrence and proliferation of such disruptions and the integral nature of their relationship to organizational and technological life, and their significance for its continually changing forms.

6 Organization, Structure and Design

David Knights and Hugh Willmott

Key concepts and learning objectives

- To develop an understanding of the assumptions and theories underpinning mainstream thinking.
- To show how ideas about the structure and design of organization are developed and applied in practice, with particular reference to a case study.
- To explore some alternative approaches and tensions associated with the design and control of organizations.
- To understand a number of key concepts that are relevant to mainstream and critical analysis, such as effectiveness and efficiency, and performance and control.

Aims of the chapter

This chapter will:

- Introduce key mainstream and critical contributions to the study of the structure and design of organizations.

- Explore the difference between classical and modern thinking about organization, highlighting the importance of open systems theory to contemporary organizational design.

- Clarify the nature of, and relationship between, 'formal' and 'informal' features of organizing.

- Explain and illustrate the basis of criticisms of mainstream thinking about organizational structure and design.

- Show how concepts of inequality, knowledge, power, freedom, identity, inequality and insecurity can provide a different way of considering issues of organizational structure and design.

- Review diverse contributions to the critical analysis of organization structure.

Overview and key points

> The concept of organization structure is at the heart of organizational studies, historically and contemporaneously . . . understanding organizational structure is central and the thrust of the discipline of organization theory is to understand effective and efficient organizing, through structural design. (*Hinings, 2003, p. 275*)

Suppose that you want to set up an organization. You might ask yourself: What exactly is it for? What difference do I want it to make? How do I go about it?

Very likely, you would base your organization on a familiar model. A dominant, common-sense way of designing an organization involves drawing a chart comprising a set of linked boxes, with the boxes indicating the positions or roles played and the lines identifying the main relationships – lines of authority and communication. As a first stab at a design, you might draw such a chart. When deciding on the number and type of boxes and the nature of the links between them, the chances are that you would more or less copy a model that you already know, such as a company you have worked for or your university, and then make a few modifications.

Whatever method you use, the outcome will be an organizational design with a distinctive structure. But what exactly does 'structure' mean? It is widely used to describe the *form* of an organization. For example, if in an organization of 100 members 99 report individually to one boss, then that would be called an extremely simple structure; but it is also one that is likely to overwhelm the boss because nothing is delegated. The boss probably wants to retain complete control by ensuring that s/he takes every decision, perhaps because s/he does not have the confidence or trust in anyone else taking them. A possible outcome is that s/he is worked into the ground and/or there are long delays while everyone waits for decisions to be made.

Have you ever been in such an organization, as a member or as a customer? What was it like? Why was it like that?

Alternatively, and still supposing that there is one owner-cum-boss, the other 99 people will be *grouped* in some way (e.g. by specialist activity, such as production or sales) and will report to a manager to whom the owner-cum-boss has delegated some authority/responsibility for overseeing that task. Here, then, we are moving towards a more elaborate, or less simple, structure. There is a horizontal division of labour into different specialist tasks (e.g. sales) and a vertical division that comprises three, rather than two, levels of a hierarchy – the big boss, some managers and the workers. Many decisions are now made by the managers to whom authority for their specialist areas of responsibility has been delegated. But the selection of the managers continues to be made by the boss who is accountable only to him or herself. The boss may continue to shape the organization (e.g. by making the hiring decisions or bullying the managers and workers) in ways that are inefficient or ineffective from the perspective of the workers and the managers.

Mainstream thinking can be grouped into its 'classical' and 'modern' variants. The classical variety believes in the possibility of identifying principles of organization that have universal applicability. By applying these principles, it seeks to replace non-rational, ill-disciplined, wasteful muddle – what is sometimes described as **custom and practice** – with more efficient and effective ways of mobilizing productive effort. So, for example, in an organization with 100 members, classical thinking would say that the **span of control** – roughly speaking, the number of people who report to the boss – is too great where there is no tier of managers. Classical theory, to repeat, assumes that the same, avowedly rational, efficient principles of organization can be successfully applied regardless of the context or environment in which the organization is situated. It does not contemplate the possibility that in some circumstances (e.g. where the 99 workers believe fervently in the superhuman powers of the big boss and/or refuse to take orders from anyone else) the creation of a tier of managers might be counterproductive. It could be counter-productive because, for example, they would be by-passed by workers, or because the specialist managers lack a broader overview of the implications of their decision making for other parts of the organization.

The modern variant of the mainstream approach retains the concern to make organizations more efficient and effective. But, crucially, it stresses the importance of adapting the design of organizations to the particular, *contingent* demands and opportunities of the context, or wider system, in which organizations are embedded. Additionally, it incorporates the understanding that some employees will respond positively to particular arrangements or styles of management (e.g. material incentives, the authority of 'experts') while others do not, and that these responses may themselves be reversed with changes of circumstance. Such considerations, modern thinking contends, should be built into the design of organizations so as to ensure their most effective operation.

Box 6.1: Diversity in mainstream thinking

It is a mistake to believe that classical (or modern) thinking is uniform. Some classical thinkers believed that a top-down approach to design would be effective so long as it included a more economically rational approach to the remuneration of effort. This belief assumes that people come to work primarily if not exclusively to earn a wage, and an improvement in wages would be made possible by the productivity gains achieved by imposing a more rational design of work organization. Other classical thinkers recognized that material compensation alone might be insufficient to secure productive cooperation, and therefore stressed the importance of creating an *'esprit de corps'* among employees. In short, managing the psychological 'engagement' of employees was given equal emphasis to their 'control' through incentives. Management was then charged with encouraging employees to identify with the workplace in a way going beyond a purely material, instrumental dependence upon it.

Exercise 6.1

Diversity and responsiveness From your own experience, identify some examples where particular arrangements or incentives have elicited a positive reaction (in terms of motivation and activity) from some people but a more negative one from others. You might, for example, think of the reactions of different students to contrasting styles of instruction and learning; or the reactions of different employees to particular management styles. (See also Chapter 3.)

Modern mainstream thinking is distinguished by its concern to take account of complexities in the organization–environment relationship that are ignored or inadequately appreciated by classical thinkers' uniform approach to the design of organization structures. The classical idea that there is a single, universal 'one best way' is replaced by a view that the effectiveness of an organization's structure depends upon adapting it to deal with the demands and opportunities of the situation.

When considering mainstream approaches, we have emphasized a basic difference between classical and modern variants. But it is perhaps more important to recognize similarities, especially as we are concerned ultimately to compare and contrast them to critical analyses of organization structure and design. Classical and modern mainstream thinking share (i) a rejection of traditional or haphazard ways of structuring economic organization that have no virtue other than familiarity, typified by the view that 'this is the way we have always done things around here'; (ii) a top-down approach in which it is assumed that those at the top of the hierarchy need only order things to be done and their expectations will be fulfilled; and (iii) a restricted way of appreciating the significance of the environment as an objective reality, but one that can be adapted to, as long as the appropriate organizational structure is in place.

Recap question What do classical and modern forms of mainstream thinking share? What makes them different? Construct a brief list to identify their common concerns and the differences between them.

Whether in its classical or modern form, mainstream thinking remains oblivious to how the structure of organizations reflects and often reproduces the distribution of power and the wider social inequalities in society. Little or no consideration is given to how history, culture, politics or economics are involved in conditioning an organization's design and development. In our example of the organization with 100 members, attention would be focused upon the horizontal and vertical divisions of labour, and not upon the cultural values or political struggles that have shaped its formation or guide its reform.

Critical analysis of organizations, in contrast, understands the theory and practice of organization to be deeply embedded in particular politico-economic social systems and for knowledge of organizations itself to be strongly influenced by this embeddedness. From this perspective, mainstream thinking does not approximate objectivity or neutrality. Rather, it is infused by dominant values and priorities, yet is largely blind to their influence and is incapable of acknowledging or examining their effects. Knowledge of organizations – including how concepts such as 'structure' are used to convey their reality in particular, limited ways – is itself understood to be conditioned by distinctive, mainstream and critical agendas.

Table 6.1 Comparison of mainstream and critical knowledge

Mainstream approach	Critical approach
Conceives structure and design as an impartial, rational process	Conceives structure and design as cultural and political process
Minimal attention to issues of power, inequality, etc.	Attentive to issues of power, inequality, etc.
Assumes consensus underpins organizations	Assumes conflicts are endemic to organizations
Preoccupied with improving control through better design	Concerned to illuminate and question control

Mainstream approach

Introducing structure and design

Mainstream thinking about organizations has been preoccupied with the design of their structure as a means of facilitating the efficient achievement of organizational goals, such as generating profits or providing public services. The idea of structure conveys cohesiveness and regularity. 'Structure' defines and maintains the form or identity of an institution, such as a family or an organization. A family is typically distinguished, and recognizable, by a structure of one or more parents and their children, which may extend to more than one generation.

An organization's structure comprises a set of hierarchical and/or horizontal positions and relationships. Its members might all be from the same family but more often there are few or no family ties. And their activities are generally divided and coordinated by more formal mechanisms, such as legal contracts of employment, written job descriptions and so on. So, for example, when it is announced that an organization is to 'restructure', there is an intention to reconfigure the vertical and/or horizontal divisions – perhaps by de-layering or by removing or rationalizing one or more of its areas of activity.

Components of the structure of organizations have been identified to include:

- The way people are grouped into teams or departments.

- The way activities and responsibilities are allocated.

- The line(s) of reporting from subordinate to superordinate (boss), and the number of subordinates that report to any one boss.

- The lines of communication between employees and the means of integrating different activities.

- The monitoring of performance and the design of reward systems.

As we shall see, there are differences of emphasis within mainstream thinking with regard to the importance of these elements. Some analysts concentrate primarily upon the design and allocation of tasks, while others take a broader view of the means of their integration, which may include, for example, reference to some basic values or to an *esprit de corps* that maintains motivation.

Consider the following definition of organization structure: 'The structure of an organization can be defined simply as the sum total of the ways in which it divides its labor into distinct tasks and then achieves coordination between them' (Mintzberg, 1979, p. 2).

In this definition of organization structure, it is *as if* organizations determine their own structure: we are told that '*it* divides its labor into distinct tasks' (our emphasis). It is also implied that the divisions are rational and functional. This definition of structure takes the division and coordination of labour as an established fact, rather than as something that is designed and continuously maintained or modified through a process of conflict and struggle in which managers as well as employees selectively accommodate or resist different pressures and forms of control. That, for us, is why we identify this definition as mainstream. The emphasis in the definition is upon tasks but, as our list of components of structure suggested, the meaning of structure can be extended to include such things as performance monitoring and systems of reward, which are likely to be areas of tension and stress. Even where these considerations are incorporated, however, mainstream thinking about organization, structure and design takes established structures of organization and power as given and necessary. It produces knowledge that operates to support, rather than question, prevailing organizational structures and designs. This understanding of the mainstream is developed further in the second half of the chapter where we consider critical approaches. For the moment, we further explore organization structure and design through a case study.

CASE STUDY 6.1 Bar Mar

In this and the following chapter on management and leadership, we draw on a case study of Bar Mar (a pseudonym). Bar Mar was established 20 years ago and has expanded to become an international chain of multi-award winning bar-bistros. This case is intended to help illustrate ideas and concepts as well as to demonstrate the relevance of ideas presented in these chapters.

Figure 6.1 shows the vertical and horizontal division of labour in the very first Bar Mar. Three staff are employed, each of whom has primary responsibility for a defined area of activity. The chart shows that selection and deployment of staff is determined and supervised by the owner-manager, Margaret.

To establish the first Bar Mar, Margaret took the risk of sinking her personal savings, together with a substantial windfall arising from the death of a relative, to set up and run a small bar – a dream she had nurtured for a few years. As the owner-manager, Margaret controlled key decisions, such as the nature and pricing of drinks and food, opening hours, working hours, furnishings and so on. One thing that had appealed to her about running a bar was the opportunity to create a total experience for her customers – a key part of which is their interaction with Bar Mar staff, herself included. She liked the idea of working with a small number of staff – co-workers and friends, as she thought of them – with whom she could provide and develop a distinctive atmosphere and a range of drinks, snacks and light meals.

Exercise 6.2

Linking theory and practice Thinking over the ideas that have been presented in this chapter so far, identify those that have relevance for analysing what you have learnt so far about the organizational structure of Bar Mar.

Margaret based Bar Mar on a familiar structure of organization – a hierarchical design with herself at the apex. She established how activities were to be allocated to her employees. Staff would report to her and she would ensure that their work was adequately coordinated. She would monitor and evaluate their conduct, and she decided how they were to be motivated and rewarded. At the same time, Margaret did not want to 'boss' her staff. Instead, she wanted them to learn

how to take responsibility for providing the quality of food and drink preparation and standard of customer service to which she aspired for Bar Mar. The last thing she wanted was to follow the example of McDonald's, where a highly detailed set of rules and procedures dictates how each activity is to be performed. What she had in mind was recruiting a type of employee who would *identify* with her vision for Bar Mar and 'automatically' work the way that she wanted, with the minimum

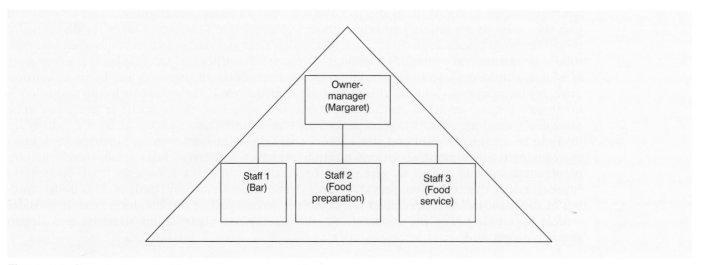

Figure 6.1 Organization chart for an owner-managed bar

Box 6.2: Control and commitment

An employee who does precisely and *only* what the rules permit – who 'works to rule' – is likely to be viewed as rather 'uncooperative' as well as inflexible. Much modern management theory is about developing styles of leadership among managers, and forms of commitment among employees, that incorporate productive elements of the 'personal' and 'informal' within a formal, impersonal contract of employment that ultimately demands compliance with instructions. There have been repeated efforts to find ways of softening a 'command-and-control' approach – for example, by shifting to a coach-and-empower philosophy, and by favouring flatter, less rigid forms of structure.

"The Organizational structure is pretty simple; We do the work; they take the credit."

Image 6.1

of surveillance and intervention on her part. Staff, that is, who would require very little supervision and who would care much more about the success of Bar Mar than they would about the (social) differences of ownership and control that distinguished Margaret and her staff.

In this respect, Margaret's thinking reflects the ideas of one of the classical writers on management, Mary Parker Follett (see Box 6.3), who believed that management must be 'depersonalized' in order to minimize frictions and, more specifically, to avoid problems of personal identity, such as the loss of dignity or status that may otherwise accompany being 'bossed around' (see Chapter 7).

What Follett terms 'depersonalization' does *not* mean impersonalization, where the relationship loses all personal qualities. Depersonalization occurs when employees respond to an instruction or request issued by a manager not as a casual favour or optional request but as an obligation or imperative arising from the functions performed by the respective, functionally necessary, positions, or offices, occupied by managers and managed. To put this another way, it means that there is an acceptance that the relationship is one of authority in which the superordinate (e.g. Margaret) is understood by the subordinate to have a legitimate right to have instructions or requests fulfilled.

Box 6.3: Mary Parker Follett on authority and civility

'Management is a responsible discharge of necessary functions, not the privilege of elites,' [Follett] maintained. Authority and responsibility derive from function, not privilege ... What was required was a reinstatement of civility, society, and fellowship in and through work and its organization if the corrosive effects of competitive individualism on the moral character of the employee were to be halted. People needed to think not just of themselves and the individual benefit to be gained through competition at work but how they fitted into an overall pattern of functions, responsibilities, and authoritative entitlements to command and to obey (Clegg *et al.*, 2005, p. 31).

Thinkpoint 6.2

Why is it that we are (often) willing to comply with, or obey, 'authorities'? When are we not so willing to comply?

In practice, 'depersonalization' may be difficult to establish and sustain, perhaps because managers are 'unprofessional' (for example, Margaret might ask a member of staff to do something, like clean her car, which lies outside contractual duties) or because their subordinates are 'bolshy' (for example, one of Margaret's staff ignores her requests or does not do anything unless told very specifically what is required). Establishing and maintaining such relationships requires a measure of willingness and cooperation that cannot be taken for granted. Often, it requires some inducement, which may take a symbolic (e.g. change of job title) as well as a material form. If Margaret did not pay her staff, it is unlikely that they would continue to work at Bar Mar. But even if Margaret paid them very well but treated them badly in other ways (e.g. harassing or bullying them) which led them to feel devalued and unappreciated, it is probable that they would look for work elsewhere. It is precisely the symbolic dimension of the employment relationship (e.g. making her staff feel valued and part of a team with a special *esprit de corps*) that Margaret sought to foster.

The first Bar Mar comprised a simple, hierarchical structure with a short span of control. Margaret had only three staff reporting to her, and she endeavoured to manage them with the minimum of rules by relying upon her ability to recruit and train staff who would identify with her vision. This simple structure can be compared to the structure of a much larger, multinational organization in which the differentiation is not only between factories (or business units comprising a cluster of operations) but also by product divisions and geographical area. The company is organized into several divisions, each of which is divided into sites or units within which a range of functions (e.g. production, accounting) and tasks (e.g. assembly, costing) are undertaken (see Figure 6.2).

At first glance, the organization chart of the multinational organization looks quite different to Bar Mar, but the basic structure remains – a hierarchy with a division of labour. In fact, as Bar Mar expanded and diversified as an international chain of bar-bistros, it came to resemble the structure of the multinational automotive company, with its separate but related areas of activity, each of which has become a division within the Bar Mar Group (see Figure 6.3; see also Chapter 12). The most significant difference between the first Bar Mar and the current Bar Mar structure is that there is now no direct reporting relationship between the CEO (e.g. Margaret) and the 'front-line' staff. Instead, there is an extended set of reporting relationships, or **chain of command**, in which areas of responsibility

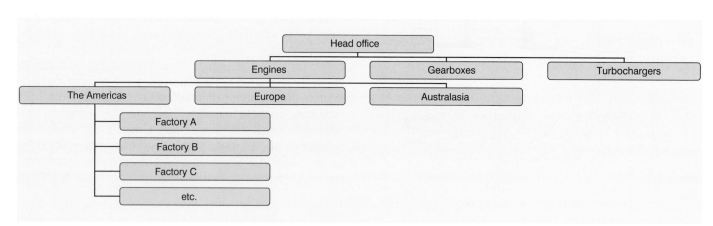

Figure 6.2 Structure of a multinational automotive company

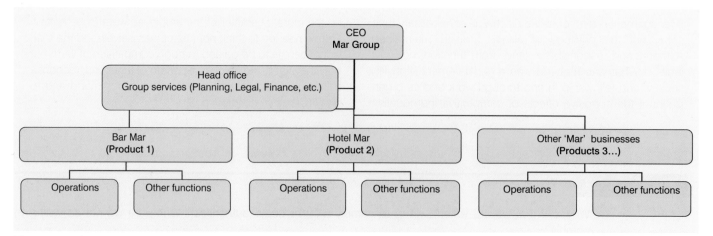

Figure 6.3 Bar Mar as one division within the Mar Group

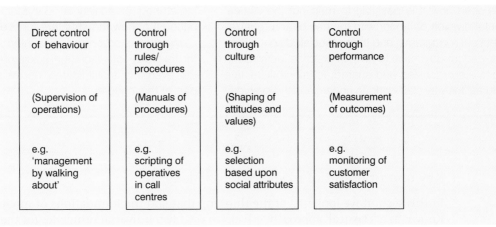

Figure 6.4 Four forms of control

are delegated, and then delegated again, through a series of layers of management.

In a hierarchy with numerous levels, it becomes impossible for the CEO to keep a direct eye on her, or his, staff. Margaret can no longer see what they are doing, or even know them personally or be responsible for their recruitment and training. Even if CCTV cameras were installed in each Bar Mar (assuming that this were compatible with the company ethos and acceptable to its staff), it would be impossible for Margaret to keep track on all of the branches all of the time. As a consequence, each manager in the hierarchy, from the CEO down, is obliged to rely upon more indirect forms of monitoring and control that increasingly are provided by information and communication technologies (ICTs) that, for example, track the revenues generated by each bar, or even each member of the serving staff. Unless the manager can depend upon those further down in the hierarchy to act as clones, doing precisely what s/he would do in the circumstances, s/he must depend upon other means of controlling their behaviour. That is where the introduction of (bureaucratic) rules, procedures and performance measures (see Chapter 13) as well as training programmes and forms of 'hoopla' (e.g. uniforms, catch phrases or party tricks) that encourage staff identification with Bar Mar provide substitutes for more direct forms of monitoring and control (see Chapter 9).

Even where a CEO attempts and succeeds in establishing a 'strong' culture – where employees are hired and trained who embrace a distinctive corporate vision – it is impossible to rely upon face-to-face ways of monitoring employee behaviour

(see Figure 6.4). That does not necessarily mean that there will be very detailed control of employee behaviour by introducing rules and procedures to cover every aspect of their work (e.g. 'McDonaldization') by using standardized procedures, including the scripting of interactions with customers, to produce standardized outputs so that everything is predictable. Instead, employees may be evaluated primarily by their outcomes (e.g. production targets; service quality levels). They may be allowed, and indeed encouraged, to exercise initiative and discretion in ways that are consistent with some overarching values. What is controlled is not task behaviour but the outcome of that behaviour. Satisfactory performance is rewarded through retention; unsatisfactory performance is punished through dismissal.

When Margaret set up the business, her preference was for something 'unique' and 'relaxed'. She wanted to create an organization in which 'the situation', rather than a rule book, would determine how, for example, staff would interact with customers. She would create 'the situation', and expected her staff to follow her example. Instead of giving detailed instructions about how each activity (bar, food preparation, food service) should be performed, Margaret preferred to pick the staff that she believed would do the right thing (in her eyes).

Margaret wanted a flexible, adaptable set of staff guided by a shared commitment to her vision of Bar Mar. She sought to inspire her staff with this vision so that they would exercise discretion in a way that was consistent with her dream – in terms of maintaining a distinctive atmosphere, helping each other out and so on. And, broadly speaking, Margaret succeeded.

Exercise 6.3

Comparing organization structures Compare and contrast the Bar Mar structure (Figure 6.3) with other organization charts (this may involve a little research but the web may provide most of the answers) with which you may be familiar (perhaps other bar chains such as Wetherspoons that you visit), or which you could draw on the basis of your knowledge of different organizations. Why do you think there are diverse organization structures, such as franchises? What are the advantages and disadvantages of simple, in contrast to more complex, designs of organization structure, and vice versa? Discuss and debate your views with student colleagues.

We have seen how it is possible to map out the vertical and horizontal division of labour with the use of an organization chart, but such diagrams, and their associated conception of structure, cannot do justice to how, in practice, activities in organizations are organized and shared, let alone illuminate what 'structures' the way staff work. To understand the everyday structuring of activity at Bar Mar, it is necessary to take account of how the structure functions in practice, how communication is organized, how information is shared, and how the exercise of discretion is circumscribed and monitored. But even this is still limited, as we shall show in the second part of this chapter.

Key contributions of mainstream thinking

In this section we look first at the thinking that laid the foundations of modern organization design. Known as a 'classical' approach, it seeks to establish universal principles for the design of organizations as well as the tasks undertaken with them. We consider the contributions of the two most influential advocates of this approach, Henri Fayol and Frederick Taylor, each of whom believed, in their own way, in methods of organizing that could be identified as having extensive applicability, summed up in the phrase 'one best way'.

Classical thinkers have been criticized by modern mainstream writers for the limited attention paid to the diverse and volatile demands placed upon organizations by their varied environments. It is asked: how can a single, classical design possibly be responsive to such different pressures? Yet others have questioned whether classical thinking takes adequate account, or fully realizes the potential, of the distinctiveness and diversity of the 'human element' as a uniquely creative and psychologically needy factor of production. Common to such doubts about classical thinking, which we explore later in this section, is a view that designs based upon classical thinking either fail to address the complexity of the contexts in which organizations operate and/or overlook the complexity of the people whose work is organized within them.

Classical thinking about organizational design We begin by examining some of the early writers on organization who now are regarded as leading 'classical' thinkers. We concentrate here on those that focused their attention on the structure of organizations.

Classical theorists of management developed a view of organizations as well-oiled machines. They sought to replace ways of organizing dominated by tradition and rules of thumb with what they considered to be a much more systematic and rational approach to organizational design and operation. To this end, universal principles were identified that, it was anticipated, would provide a comprehensive guide to management practice. One of the earliest and most influential writers was a Frenchman, Henri Fayol (1841–1925). Fayol was a practising manager whose writings have had an enduring impact on thinking about how best to structure and design organizations.

FAYOL'S PRINCIPLES OF ADMINISTRATION Henri Fayol had a direct and intimate knowledge of many aspects of work organization as he worked his way up through the company of which he became the managing director. His focus was upon administrative work, in contrast to Frederick Taylor who, as we shall see, directed his attention to the shop floor. Fayol became famous for turning around what had been a near-bankrupt company, and then for publishing a book that recorded his experience and drew out key lessons from it. In *General and Industrial Management* (1949, first published in 1916), Fayol distilled 14 key principles of organizational structure and design. These include, for example, the idea of a unified command structure in which each employee reports to one superordinate, and where attention is given to *esprit de corps* so as to ensure good morale and motivation. Huczynski and Buchanan (2001, p. 502) boil down Fayol's lengthy list of principles to five basic imperatives. We summarize these in Table 6.2, together with some reflections on their application in Bar Mar.

The classical interest in establishing principles of organization design and representing these in organizational charts is undiminished but there has also been a concern to overcome perceived shortcomings ('dysfunctions') in Fayol's thinking, such as those associated with the limited attention given to the *integration* of activities. It has been suggested, for example, that there are circumstances in which employees should report to more than one boss so as to ensure that adequate attention is given

Table 6.2 Fayol's key principles and their application at Bar Mar

Fayol's basic principles of administration	Bar Mar
● Functional division of work	Division into specialist activities. In the first Bar Mar, Margaret distinguished bar staff, food preparation and service
● Hierarchical relationships	Chain of command. Each of the staff at the first Bar Mar reported to Margaret
● Bureaucratic forms of control	Kept to minimum but increased as scale of operations made direct control an impossibility
● Narrow supervisory span	Initially limited to three staff. Later extended to more staff but deliberately kept narrow in order to facilitate direct forms of control
● Closely prescribed roles	Loosely prescribed roles not favoured when it leads to confusion and hampers accountability

to competing considerations (e.g. reporting to a product or service manager as well as to the head of the function that provides support to that activity). We examine this case when we consider the matrix design of organization.

Thinkpoint 6.3

The effectiveness of many of Fayol's principles has been questioned in recent years when the emphasis has been upon flexibility and agility. What do you consider to be the advantages and disadvantages or risks of *not* applying Fayol's ideas? Do you detect areas in which his principles are weak or could usefully be extended? Discuss with other students your distinctive lists and defend your choice.

Fayol's thinking has been influential in establishing some very broad principles for the overall structuring of organization. His principles were based upon personal experience and anecdote.

TAYLOR'S SCIENTIFIC MANAGEMENT By contrast, Frederick Taylor (1856–1915), the founder of 'scientific management', sought to demonstrate experimentally how a series of principles (see Table 6.3) could be applied to deliver increased productivity. He drew upon his experience as an engineer, manager and consultant observing factory work to devise a more rational system of organizing production. He was convinced that management had failed to gain adequate control of the division of labour and especially the detailed design and planning of work. In a sense, Taylor's focus was on the design of jobs rather than the grander concern with organizational structure. However, the application of his thinking has extensive implications for how organizations are structured and controlled. Taylor called for the design and structure of organizations to be dramatically changed, notably by dividing management into a number of specialized functions responsible for planning, monitoring and enhancing different aspects of productive activity.

FROM UNIFIED CHAIN OF COMMAND TO A MATRIX STRUCTURE One obvious limitation of classical thinking is the emphasis upon vertical, top-down reporting as this can pose problems for horizontal communication. In principle, a single chain of command means that there is no reporting relationship across organizations. For example, in a university management department or business school there are usually academic subject areas (e.g. organizational behaviour, finance and accounting) headed by a professor (in industry an equivalent is the head of specialist functional areas, such as production or marketing). There are also educational programmes headed by someone equivalent to a course or programme director (the industrial equivalent being a manager responsible for a product line). Lecturers within

Table 6.3 Taylor's principles and their application at Bar Mar

Taylor's scientific principles of organization	Bar Mar
● Separation of design and planning work from actually doing it	In the first Bar Mar, Margaret determined the structure, and planned activities
● Detailed division of labour	After the expansion into an international chain, there was a division into specialist areas of activity such as operations, marketing, etc.
● Based on observation of working practices	Identification of 'best practices' and training of staff to adopt them

subject areas provide services (e.g. lecture courses) to programmes. But lecturers report to their 'line manager', the professor who heads the subject area. So, what does the programme manager do if s/he is concerned about the contents of a lecture course being delivered by a member of staff? Recall that the lecturer does not report to the programme director but to the subject area head. The lecturer may, indeed, refuse to be 'bossed around' by the programme director, arguing that the programme director lacks the formal authority to determine course content. In principle, then, the programme director must speak to the head of the subject area who then raises the issue with the lecturer concerned.

This is a simple example of how a unity of command comprising a single, vertical chain encounters limitations with respect to *horizontal* forms of communication. It is this limitation that has been addressed by an innovative, matrix structure of organization where there are two reporting lines – one to the manager of the specialist function (e.g. the subject group head) and the other to the user of this function (e.g. the programme director). This is illustrated in Figure 6.5

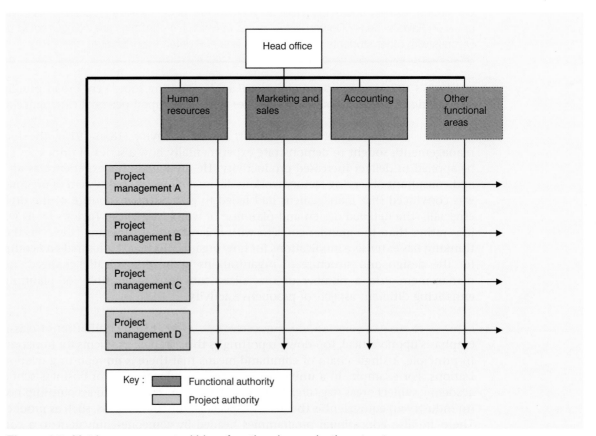

Figure 6.5 Matrix arrangement within a functional organization structure

with the example of a series of projects (equivalent to teaching programmes) to which different specialisms (equivalent to subject groups) contribute. The basic difference is that an employee (e.g. a lecturer) occupying a position at the intersection of the vertical and horizontal lines is required to report to both the functional (e.g. subject area) and project (e.g. programme director) heads. The intention is that the delivery of products/services/projects receives as much attention as the development of functional expertise (and vice versa), thereby securing greater integration.

The matrix design runs counter to Fayol's principle of a unity of command. Likewise, current trends towards flatter organizations (at least in principle and as presented in organization charts), where hierarchical layers are removed, requires an extension of a span of control beyond the optimal number recommended by Fayol. Managers, consultants and academics have challenged the claim of classical thinking to provide a *universally* relevant and effective means of maximizing productivity. When it has not been shunned on moral or religious grounds for its tendency to treat employees like imbeciles, robots or machines, scientific management has been criticized for provoking resistance by de-skilling work and robbing staff of their dignity, or for failing to fully harness human beings' unique capacity to be creatively involved in the production process in order to make continuous improvements. In short, modern thinking has questioned the capacity of its classical predecessor adequately to appreciate and address the complexity and diversity of issues confronted by the designers and adapters of organizational structures.

Modern thinking

A modern approach to organization design and structure abandons the idea of finding the ideal, universal, one best design. The consistent application of principles is replaced by a concern to adapt the design of the organization to the contingencies of the context, such as the stability or volatility of the market for its goods or services. Organizational designs and structures are then expected to ensure a good fit with the demands or constraints of the environment.

Thinkpoint 6.4

What ideas and arguments would you use to justify abandoning Fayol and Taylor's classical principles? Once you have identified these ideas and arguments, try to distinguish the values that render these ideas coherent and the arguments credible.

Systems thinking Systems thinking analyses organizational activities in terms of inputs, conversion processes and outputs. For example, at Bar Mar inputs include labour and raw materials (foodstuffs); conversion processes involve cooking and serving, etc.; and the outputs include prepared meals and potentially satisfied customers. Classical thinking assumes a closed system in which no attention is given to any factors such as changing lifestyles or customer tastes that are external to the system. Such thinking commends the continuous perfection of what is assumed to be a universally effective formula of organizational design and operation. This is rather like a car producer developing a single model that is intended to be suitable for any customer, terrain or climate.

Open systems thinking analyses activities in terms of inputs, processes and outputs and takes account of how each system is interdependent with others in the wider system. Organizations are seen as similar to organic bodies where all the parts (e.g. brain, heart and lungs) are functionally integrated to secure stability or equilibrium in relation to external conditions. Consequently there is sensitivity to how changes external to one system impact upon its operation and effectiveness. Returning to the car producer, a variety of models, including hybrids, would be developed to take account of diversity and change in relation to customer taste, running costs, climates and regulations. Open systems thinking favours greater experimentation and innovation as a way of adapting to changing circumstances.

Exercise 6.4

Comparing closed and open systems thinking Can you draw up a list of points that support a modern, open systems view of organization in contrast to a more closed, classical approach?

Modern open systems thinkers adapt the design of organizations to the contingencies of the situation (see Box 6.4). Partly, variation is understood to come 'internally' with the increasing size of the modern corporation that arises from mergers and acquisitions as well as growth. The *simple* hierarchical structure favoured by the classical theorists makes little allowance for such contingencies. But conglomerates (combinations of different kinds of businesses) and multinationals have tended to allow their constituent companies and divisions a greater level of independence than allowed, for example, by classical thinking. Adherence to Fayol's principles is selective as contingencies are encountered and accommodated.

Different product or regional divisions may exercise discretion as to which markets they enter and the products they develop but they are also accountable to the centre for results that flow from their decisions (see Chapter 12). In the multi-divisional form, each national, regional or divisional operation may become a 'business unit' with its own cost and profit centre. Each operation is required to make profit from its operations as if it were an independent company; it is 'however' accountable to the head office for its performance and, of course, dependent on it for future investment resources unless allowed to retain some of its profits for that purpose. In short, there are recurrent attempts to manage complexity in ways that harness the benefits of diversity (of product or location) and integration (e.g. centralized setting and monitoring of performance targets). The earlier chart (Figure 6.3) that sets out Bar Mar's product divisions illustrates this approach. Other criteria that are used for structuring larger organizations, whether of a regional, national or international form, include those based on product differences, process or function, project, or some hybrid variation such as a matrix design where there are two or more lines of authority rather than one.

Another way in which a correction to the disadvantages of classical organization design may be attempted is by reducing the number of levels in the hierarchy through creating what is called the

Box 6.4: Applying systems thinking to team sports

In a sports team, such as in netball or football, a closed system view assumes the possibility of selecting and training players according to one method of organization that can beat all challengers. It assumes the possibility of identifying the perfect approach for outwitting the opposition, irrespective of their strategy and tactics. An open system approach, in contrast, considers the specific qualities of the competition, and then decides upon the choice of team members and relevant formations. In principle, open systems thinking can enable a team of players with a limited stock of individual talent to outsmart teams that possess more talent on paper, yet struggle to respond to the challenges presented by resourceful opponents.

In the world of football, Nottingham Forest are renowned for having won two European Cups in successive seasons with 'underperforming' players that top clubs at that time were not interested in acquiring. With the benefit of hindsight, it is clear that these players had potential but this potential

was realized only though their development and operation as a team. The approach to training and team play favoured by the manager, Brian Clough, was extraordinarily successful, but it did not continue to produce the same magic in changing circumstances. A more recent example is Liverpool beating Chelsea in the semi-finals of the European Cup in 2005. Clearly Chelsea was the much better footballing side but their superiority did not clinch the result. Liverpool's capacity to adapt was dramatically demonstrated in the final of this competition against a better AC Milan where at half time they were three goals down. By changing their formation they clawed back all three goals to force a penalty shootout in extra time, which Liverpool went on to win. Open systems theory helps to explain why AC Milan's formula or system that succeeded brilliantly in the first half was less effective in the second once Liverpool had changed their formula. A system does not necessarily produce the same level of performance when applied in a different place and/or time.

'flatter' organization. Here, not only are there fewer middle managers to whom employees are accountable, but also power is seen to be delegated to the operational functions in what has been called **empowerment** (see Chapters 2, 3, 4 and 11). This process of empowerment means that lower hierarchy staff are able to take the initiative and make decisions without seeking permission from more senior staff. Yet they are also responsible for the decisions made and therefore have to engage in a greater degree of *self*-management. Often the organizational structure is 'softened', not merely by flattening the hierarchy and empowering the workforce but also by mediating the flows of management control with the introduction of teams of workers that have a degree of autonomy for particular tasks or specialisms in the production process (see Chapters 2 and 11). Teams provide for a more intimate set of work relations and sources of identification with the team and its leader (see Chapter 7) thus enabling members to feel a sense of identity that is more difficult in relation to the more remote organization as a whole. Structuring an organization around teams also facilitates internal cooperation within the team and possibly a competitive rivalry between teams that may have positive productive outcomes for the organization as a whole. Just as with the league tables in sport (e.g. football), striving to be higher up the league stimulates extra effort and dedication.

Some modern thinking also begins to contemplate the possibility that eradicating conflicts, including those that result in waste and unproductive expenditure of effort, will not necessarily follow from the application of classical principles. It may even acknowledge that conflicts of values and competing priorities can be very difficult, and perhaps impossible to reconcile and eliminate.

Take 'human resources' (see Chapter 2). People are recruited from diverse backgrounds with differing values and aspirations. People have different ways of looking at the world, including the opportunities and problems encountered in organizations. Considerable efforts may be made to deter the most blatant forms of discrimination and prejudice. But modern, open systems thinking may also accept that effective organization is about managing conflicts in ways that are effective, rather than attempting to eradicate them (which may provoke a degree of resistance that is counter-productive). Within a systems approach, there may be some recognition of how competing demands find accommodation through processes of negotiation and mutual respect – for example, by developing institutional means of bridging differences between management and trade unions. Trade unions may become 'partners' rather than enemies of management; and managers may endeavour to develop a language and employee policies that appease or placate, rather than provoke and anger, actual and potential union members. Otherwise, systems thinkers anticipate, the organization will experience disruption and this could threaten its effectiveness and even its survival.

Like bodies, organizations are conceived by open systems thinkers to maintain themselves in 'good health' by being adaptive to changes in the environment. They tend towards equilibrium, with each part working cooperatively to maintain the whole, with each member or department sharing similar values and objectives. Consensus is an assumption common to both classical (closed) and modern (open) systems thinking. Classical thinking conceives of organizations as closed systems in which the environment would be controlled or conquered by ensuring that organization design followed its universal principles. Modern, open systems thinking, in contrast, gives much more attention to the organization–environment interface, arguing that design must be adapted to secure a productive

---

Box 6.5: Open and closed systems – spans of control and organization methods

Classical theorists sought to identify the optimal span of control – that is, the number of people reporting to a given manager. The contemporary view is that there is no universally applicable optimal number. What is optimal will depend upon so many factors, including the environmental demands, the nature of the activity and the skills of the manager. Where behaviour is already well disciplined and/or where there is much regularity and predictability, extended spans of control may work well and be cheaper in terms of managerial overheads. Conversely, in more volatile and uncertain conditions, control is more problematical and a wide span may become unmanageable. Alternatively, other arrangements may be favoured, such as a matrix structure (see Figure 6.5) where integration is accomplished through more than one reporting line.

exchange. Organizations are not closed to the world and they cannot be fully protected or isolated from its influences. And, crucially, employees' values are not necessarily identical to the expectations, values and assumptions that are given priority within work organizations. This is the basic insight of open systems thinking, and it presents a direct challenge to classical theory, which assumes that universal principles can be applied irrespective of the *specific* circumstances.

Thinkpoint 6.5

Consider an experience of your own as a participant in or supporter of a group activity, such as sports, music or drama.

- Can you identify elements of 'closed' and 'open' systems thinking in how the activity was organized and performed?
- What benefits and what costs were associated with each type of thinking?
- In what circumstances might 'closed system' thinking be effective, and 'open systems' thinking be counter-productive, in terms of formulating aims and achieving objectives?

CONTINGENCY THEORY Open systems thinking underpins various forms of contingency theory. This thinking conceives of organizations as engaged in processes of continuous and somewhat experimental adjustment (e.g. through restructuring) to changing circumstances or contingencies. Organizations are seen as adaptive systems not unlike the human body (see above) where changes in the 'environment' are accommodated to ensure their effective functioning. Each organization is regarded as a sub-system of a wider system that comprises all the systems that make up its environment (see Figure 6.6). As indicated by the dotted line between the organization and its environment, the boundary is regarded as permeable and shifting. Superior performance is attributed to the goodness of 'fit' between the elements of sub-systems (e.g. people, technology, etc.) and the environment in which they are located.

Contingency theory seeks to take account of changing environmental demands and opportunities – such as legislative requirements (e.g. employment regulations), availability and costs of people and natural resources (e.g. energy), developments in technologies, etc. – when acquiring and matching

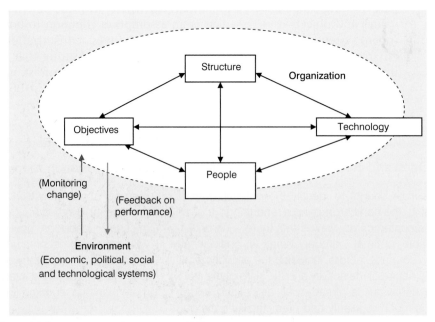

Figure 6.6 Organizations as complex open systems

all the parts of the system (e.g. technology, people, objectives) and designing the structure to ensure their effective interdependence. Note how people and technology span the organization and its environment.

Attention is paid in contingency theory to the interdependence of system components. For example, the identification of appropriate or realistic 'objectives' is conceived to depend upon the capability of people, technology and the available means of their combination. In turn, the attainment of these objectives is considered to be conditional, or contingent, upon combining people, technology and structure in ways that effectively match and address the opportunities and demands – economic, political, social and technological – presented by the environment. This is indicated by the blue arrow, which points to the organizational monitoring of change in the environment and the red arrow that shows the feedback on performance provided by the organization (e.g. through annual reports).

Exercise 6.5

Draw a diagram that presents a view of a university lecture as a system.

- How do its components interact?
- What are its input – output interfaces?

Compare and contrast this with a similar diagram of a seminar or tutorial. Which is closer to a closed system and which to an open system?

Summary Open systems thinking examines the design and operation of conversion processes within organizations in relation to the environment from which resources are drawn, opportunities arise and constraints are imposed, and from which demands for goods or services are derived. The effectiveness of the conversion processes is assessed in terms of the capacity to secure the necessary resources and exploit the available opportunities while operating within the constraints of legislation, economic climate, technology, etc. and the behaviour of competitors whose strategies and methods they seek to emulate or discredit. Structural contingency theory is based upon the insights of open systems thinking. It argues that structure must be designed and continuously adapted not only to the objectives, technology and people in the organization but to the various sub-systems that comprise the environment. By definition, however, structure is concerned with the specification of positions and reporting relationships that have official or administrative legitimacy (e.g. they are in job specifications), rather than with all manner of practices and processes that, in comparison, are 'informal' and which may be tolerated or even encouraged but lack *official* recognition and sanction.

From structure to process: Informal understandings and practices

Classical and modern thinking tends to be preoccupied with establishing formal order, which requires the substitution of rational planning for the chaos of custom and practice. What is largely excluded from such thinking is recognition of informality in organizations. The term 'informality' is potentially confusing as there is often a mixed view of its value. In principle, any valued 'informal' practice should be incorporated into officially agreed, formal arrangements and procedures. In which case, remaining forms of 'informality' are, at best, of dubious legitimacy. In practice, however, elements of informality – such as a preference for casual forms of communication and the designing-in of networks and ad hoc groups – may be tolerated and perhaps actively encouraged by some designers of organizational structures. Indeed, even in a rigid bureaucracy, there will be a degree of dependence upon informal understandings and practices in order to 'get the job done'. So, invariably organizations depend upon 'informal' understandings and practices that exist alongside officially sanctioned rules and procedures, even where strenuous efforts are made to design them out.

Classical thinkers wanted to replace fuzzy, 'informal' arrangements with clear reporting lines and detailed job descriptions. They wanted to remove ambiguity and replace loosely negotiated agreements with clearly demarcated boundaries and precise rules and procedures. Such formalization,

Table 6.4 Formal and informal aspects of organization

Formal	Informal
Planned, procedural	Emergent, pragmatic
Officially sanctioned	Officially illegitimate but may be unofficially tolerated or encouraged
Comparatively fixed and rigid	Comparatively dynamic and flexible
Based on authority	Based on trust or reciprocity
On the record	Off the record
Reliant upon position	Reliant upon personal affinity or political allegiance

however, is often accompanied by rigidity. Rigidity occurs as action becomes dependent upon a rule or procedure that permits it. Behaviour that does not comply with a rule is, in principle, illegitimate. A consequence of this rigidity is that employees may become demoralized or demotivated as they experience themselves as a part of the (bureaucratic) machinery over which they can exert little or no control (see Chapter 14). Alternatively, greater informality may be commended as a key resource for securing the effective functioning of organizations. For it can assist in removing or avoiding **red tape** and cumbersome procedures (see Chapter 13) and thereby minimize unproductive effort and waste. (See Table 6.4.)

Box 6.6: Working to rule

When, instead of going on strike, union members engage in industrial action by **working to rule**, the shortcomings of formally endorsed methods of working rapidly becomes apparent. Reliance upon various tacit skills and informal understandings is evidently normal and necessary. Deviation from the letter of formal rules is routine because, when employees comply fully with the rules, productive activity is impeded rather than enabled.

You might expect that the formal rules would be changed to reflect actual practice. That would remove the legitimate means of working to rule that can cause so much disruption. But this would require a further elaboration of the rules that, in all likelihood, will hamper productivity and, of course, reduce flexibility and responsiveness to changing conditions. Here we encounter a contradiction of formalization. Greater formality is introduced to eliminate the uncertainties and inefficiencies of custom and practice. But, in the process, it creates some of the problems that it is intended to overcome.

A recognition of informality points to the limitations of a predominantly formal approach to design. For one thing, officially sanctioned methods are rarely sufficiently comprehensive to cover every possible eventuality. In practice, employees may ignore them, overlook them, short-circuit them, or even find better – more acceptable and/or efficient or effective – alternatives to them.

Formal rules are rarely applicable in *every* situation as they demand standardized responses to diverse circumstances. This limitation is frequently addressed through informal practices. Take the submission of course work. A formal procedure or channel of communication may require you, as a student, to submit a piece of course work by a certain date. Informally, however, you have discovered 'through the grapevine' that it is possible to 'negotiate' some extra time with certain lecturers. Such informal arrangements may facilitate or impede effectiveness in organizations. It may enable you to write a better essay as you have more time to prepare it. But it may also make it more likely that a lecturer's time is taken up negotiating extensions with students who, in any event, will often leave writing their essays until the last minute and, as a consequence of being granted an extension, do not acquire the discipline to meet deadlines. On the other hand, rigidly imposing deadlines may be regarded by some students as overbearing and demotivating, especially when the hand-in date seems to be rather arbitrary.

Supposing that you were a lecturer (or any other person in authority, such as a policeman, who is expected to enforce rules), how would you ensure that students comply with formal rules in relation to, for example, attendance at classes, course work submission dates, chatting in lectures, participating in seminars, etc.?

In considering this question, think about the *practicalities* of different courses of action.

From a classical perspective, the informal realm may be viewed as a threat to the sense of order and predictability provided by a formally designed set of positions and procedures. Sometimes, a blind eye may be turned to informal practices, but they are implicitly a challenge to formal authority and the values, including a sense of security, that this provides. The substitution of informality for formality also runs the risk of allowing those who occupy a superordinate position in the hierarchy to abuse their position by stepping outside what is officially allowed (see Chapter 13). Without formal rules and procedures, subordinates may be in a weaker position to take issue with the inappropriate exercise of authority – for example, in the form of bullying and harassment.

Box 6.7: In defence of formality

'I want formality back so that we can all regain some dignity. Besides, employees were never taken in by all that talk about informality. On the one hand, the boss was firing people; on the other hand, he was saying, "Oh, we're just like a family". And employees thought: "Oh no we're not!" . . . let's face it: It isn't etiquette that keeps people from telling the truth to the boss, it's the fear of losing their job.'

Source: 'In Praise of Boundaries: A conversation with Miss Manners', *Harvard Business Review*, December 2003, Volume 81, Issue 12, p. 3.

Summary   Our consideration of mainstream thinking has concentrated, first, upon the 'closed system' approach favoured by classical thinkers and, second, upon the contingency approach developed by modern thinkers who have been influenced by 'open systems' theory. Closed system thinking seeks to identify and promote universal principles of organizational design that are effective independently of their context. By contrast, open systems theory is distinguished by its attentiveness to the interface between organizations and their environment (including other organizations). One kind of dependence is upon people who bring aspects of the environment with them to work, in the form of their values, expectations and so on. Imposing formalization, in the guise of rules and procedures, in order to eliminate culturally specific, 'informal' understandings and practices can be counterproductive when, for example, it estranges and demotivates employees, and when it creates rigidities that impede rather than facilitate effectiveness. Classical organization thinking suggested that organizations could be improved by adopting more rational, formalized ways of dividing labour and ensuring its integration. Modern mainstream organization theory continues to be preoccupied with performance but suggests that an over-reliance upon universal principles of design based upon increased formality can be self-defeating, and that performance improvement depends upon a careful assessment of the environment and then a development of the organization to match its opportunities and constraints.

Other perspectives: Organizations as complex institutions

We now briefly review a number of other important but rather less influential contributions to mainstream theory. In different ways, these contributions further develop or illuminate a number of the ideas found in classical and contingency theory. While in some ways stretching the mainstream, they broadly endorse rather than challenge the status quo. These contributions are:

- institutional economics
- institutional theory
- resource dependency theory
- population ecology theory
- network theory
- virtual organization.

Institutional economics: Markets and hierarchies   Institutional economists developed a theory of **transaction cost economics** to explain the existence of organizations in terms of their comparative cost-effectiveness in relation to market-based ways of doing business. According to institutional economists, organizations come into existence when the cost of business transactions conducted through buying and selling in markets becomes greater than can be achieved through the alternative structure of an organizational hierarchy. A preference for transferring transactions to organizations occurs when, as a consequence of price volatility and/or problems of reliability and quality, costs of transactions in the market-place become excessive. Hierarchies of control in organizations emerge and survive by competing successfully against markets in providing economic returns that are greater than the costs of managing, producing, controlling and distributing their outputs. Conversely, the demise of organizations is understood to occur when the costs of internal hierarchical transactions exceed those of market exchanges.

Institutional economists, such as Williamson (1975), who draws upon the earlier work of Coase (1937) in economics and Chandler (1962) from business history, believe that the key to understanding the formation and adaptation of organizations resides in their capacity to operate more cost-effectively than market-based forms of economic activity. Implicitly, this echoes the view of classical theorists who assumed that the formalization of economic relationships within hierarchies would, in many circumstances, provide the most competitive, cost-effective way of organizing economic activity.

Returning to our case study of Bar Mar (see p.p. 198–202), Margaret could have hired staff on a casual, market basis – for example, on an hourly or daily rate, employing the very cheapest available. Such a market-based approach would have been highly risky. Some days many people might arrive seeking work; other days there might be no one. And even if there had been a reliable supply of casual labour, Margaret might not be able to select anyone who she believed would share her vision for Bar Mar. She might have hired the kind of employees that she wanted but it would have been a matter of chance. In short, the transaction costs – in the extreme case, she would have all the costs of the business but no staff to generate revenues – would have been prohibitively high. So, an alternative economic institution, in the form of a hierarchy, was adopted as a means of addressing the issue of labour supply. In fact, as we noted right at the beginning of this chapter, the very normality of a simple hierarchical design probably meant that Margaret did not even consider the market alternative.

Markets become a comparatively inefficient method of transacting business when, for example, buyers or consumers have limited or imperfect knowledge, and so behave in ways that do not exert competitive pressure on prices and efficiency. Organizations emerge to control the transaction costs associated with, for example, poor product quality or reliability of supply. This control process has been conceived of in terms of 'asset specificity', 'uncertainty' and 'repetitiveness' (see Table 6.5).

Alternatively, organizations may shift some parts of their operation to the market-place. Changes in structure associated with **outsourcing**, involving the transfer of some activities to an external supplier, are often prompted by the calculation that the organization can find a more cost–effective, market-based way of securing particular goods or services. In recent times, for example, many corporations have chosen to buy in services from overseas where labour can be as low as 10 per cent of the costs at home.

Exercise 6.7

Think of some product or service examples where an organization has turned to the market to buy services from the cheapest supplier rather than provide them in-house. Discuss these with members of your seminar group.

Table 6.5 Elements of the control process

Asset specificity

This refers to the extent to which assets (e.g. machinery, buildings, labour, skills) are easily substitutable – for example, by transferring raw materials to or from other ventures. When a high degree of 'asset specificity' is unavoidable, an organization or institution will tend to emerge in place of market relations. Where labour is highly specialized and necessitates a long training period (e.g. skilled machinists), for example, it is managed through organization because the costs of acquiring and retaining the skills will be lower than in market transactions.

Thinkpoint: How would you describe different types of university degree in terms of asset specificity?

Uncertainty

Conditions of uncertainty also favour an organizational or hierarchical solution. This solution provides a way of intervening in markets to reduce uncertainty, partly through introducing some asset specificity (e.g. a brand image for a product; a 'professional' service supplied by labour) and management of repetitive activities (see below). 'Professionalism', however, can be a mixed blessing since it adds another layer of uncertainty as to whether the professional worker will be loyal to the organization or to the profession.

Thinkpoint: What does your university or department do to manage students' uncertainties about the content and quality of its degrees?

Repetitiveness

When the same activities are repeated on a routine basis, the advantage of organized relationships become obvious as knowledge and skill accumulate rather than having to be constantly negotiated or learned in each transaction. However, these relationships have to be managed since organizations can be subjected to exploitation and opportunism. Highly trained labour, for example, may exploit its specific skills or contacts through opportunistic offers of these assets to competitors.

Thinkpoint: How does repetitiveness reduce the costs of education in the context of universities?

Economic self-interest is assumed to be the basis of transactions in institutional economics. It is taken for granted that unless these transactions are managed or constrained by structures, individuals will be opportunistic, devious and manipulative. In pursuing their interests, they will create risks and costs. Organizational structures are intended to control or channel their members' individual economic self-interests towards the goals of the organization. What institutional economics tends to ignore – an oversight seized upon by critical thinkers – is that organizations can be established or developed to control markets (at least in the short-to-medium term and possibly in the longer term too) by creating various barriers to market entry.

There is an assumption that organizations are established to overcome limitations of markets but they may be created and maintained to exploit such limitations. Once in a dominant position, organizations may extend their domination by, for example, discounting goods in order to undercut and destroy weaker competitors, and thereby secure their own growth. This logic is reflected in the widespread existence of **oligopolistic** markets in which a few large firms are dominant, and where smaller firms struggle to survive, let alone grow. Institutional economists also assume that markets in some pure form did once, or could, exist independently of organization – as if even town markets or commodity exchanges could prevail without some degree of organization, however limited.

Institutional theory Institutional theory offers an alternative to an economics-led approach, which, as we have seen, conceives of the existence, design and survival of organizations primarily in terms of minimizing transaction costs (DiMaggio and Powell, 1991; Rowlinson, 1997, Chapter 4). Institutional theory conceives of organizations as embedded in, and emergent out of, broader

Population ecology theory Population ecology theory is concerned with the birth and death of populations of organizations, and contends that their structures largely reflect what is supportable within (changing) environments (Hannan and Freeman, 1989). At the risk of oversimplifying, the nature and fate of organization structures is seen to depend primarily upon the environment, which is seen to have the decisive influence. Compared to other mainstream thinking, such as institutional theory (see above), a negligible role is ascribed to managers' powers of interpretation and adaptation. Instead, it is the ecology of the environment that promotes the development, and seals the fortune, of organizations.

Of the diversity of structures that are developed, only those found to be supportable by the (changing) environment survive. Unless it matches environmental requirements, the structure of an organization and indeed the organization itself will disappear much like a species (e.g. the dinosaur) that has been rendered extinct through evolutionary processes of natural selection (e.g. inability to adapt sufficiently quickly to a changed environment). As environments alter, the attributes favoured also change, resulting in the demise of some organizations and the flourishing of those with the more congruent features. If the environment changes in such a way as to select and support a new form of structure for reliably and conveniently delivering a product – such as Amazon as contrasted with the local bookstore or music shop – then the new business model will flourish and the outmoded approach will decline.

Population ecology also points to the difficulty for organizations adapting to new circumstances – for example, the challenge faced by bookstores that attempt to copy and compete with the likes of Amazon, or airlines struggling to compete with the 'no frills' operations of budget providers – since they will suffer from the legacy of structures (e.g. limited electronic infrastructure, inflexible bureaucratic rules, generous pay and conditions packages) that lack congruency with the changed environment and the ability to respond to it.

As environments change, new entrants to markets create new populations but, in turn, this leads to intensified competition between these entrants when there are insufficient growth opportunities to support the entire population. In turn, this results in the death of some organizations as they either go out of business or are targets of acquisition. But those that are selected for survival by the environment are themselves vulnerable to future environmental changes that will render their structures inadequate in comparison to as yet unimagined alternative organizational designs.

From a critical standpoint, population ecology is one-sided in that it simply ignores or by-passes key questions concerning how organizations might not just respond to, but also be active in, the creation and shaping of, environments. In population ecology theory, environments appear to exist and change independently of the organizations that make them up. Population ecology focuses upon outcomes – births and deaths – without consideration of the processes that select or reject certain structures. What from a critical perspective are viewed as politically charged processes of organizational reproduction and transformation are represented by population ecology as largely impersonal and inevitable outcomes of environmental selection.

Network theory Powell (1990) describes network theory as follows:

> In network modes of resource allocation, transactions occur neither through discrete exchanges nor by administrative fiat, but through networks of individuals [or organizations] engaged in reciprocal, preferential, mutually supportive actions . . . the basic assumption of network relationships is that one party is dependent upon resources controlled by another, and that there are gains to be had by the pooling of resources.

Network theory introduces a form of economic organization that departs from the classic, hierarchical, vertically integrated model but avoids the uncertainty and potential anarchy of exclusively market transactions (Castells, 1996). The network notion emphasizes the importance and potential of interdependencies within and between organizations. It takes a more modular view, with organizations forming more or less temporary alliances or partnerships to develop or produce services and products in ways that are more cost-effective than undertaking the equivalent activities in-house. Structures are understood to permit and support arrangements that are more or less transitory.

Networking is therefore something of a hybrid between the flexibility of 'markets' where, in principle, an alternative supplier can be found, and the reliability of 'hierarchies' where dependence on suppliers is replaced by direct, internal controls. Like market relations, alliances and partnerships can be replaced if they prove unsatisfactory; but like hierarchical relations, they offer greater certainty than purely market relations. Increasingly, larger companies (e.g. vehicle assemblers, hypermarkets) are creating networks of preferred suppliers with whom they 'cooperate' to supply at the price and to the specification that they demand. In return, the supplier receives some 'assistance' to ensure that deliveries to the required specification arrive just-in-time, and they have a guaranteed trade rather than having to rely on the precariousness of sales in the market-place. In this respect, such networks can also be analysed using resource dependency theory to argue that they provide a more effective means of reducing uncertainties and/or a means of squeezing out competitors who lack the resources to attract the premier suppliers. Powell (1990) draws on institutional economics and resource dependency theory to characterize the distinctive features of networks (see Table 6.6)

Table 6.6 Comparing markets, hierarchies and networks

Key features	Markets	Hierarchies	Networks
Tone or climate	Precision and/or suspicion	Formal, bureaucratic	Open-ended, mutual benefits
Methods of conflict resolution	Haggling – resort to courts for enforcement	Administrative fiat – supervision	Norm of reciprocity – reputational concerns
Degree of flexibility	High	Low	Medium

Source: Adapted from Powell (1990)

Networks illustrate how organizational dependencies are actively organized and managed – for example, through the creation of alliances and partnerships. The equivalent form within organizations is an 'organic' model in which groups form and reform on the basis of the relevance of their members' expertise and anticipated contribution, rather than through their allocation by a more senior person in the hierarchy. Reliance upon such spontaneously forming and reforming 'networks' is associated with a more fluid and seemingly chaotic approach in which boundaries between positions and activities are extremely fuzzy and honoured in their breach. At its most extreme, a network structure promotes and supports an approach where 'everyone pitches in' to make their distinctive contribution, and to learn from each other as rapidly as possible. The network conveys and commends the idea of more mobile and agile intra and inter-organizational relationships in which diversity of knowledge, skill, creative power and responsiveness are harnessed to out-compete more traditional forms of economic institution.

A problem that can arise with networks concerns the comparative absence of some form of centralized control and monitoring of their governance and progress towards specific targets. This may result in the withdrawal of investors who are unwilling to fund or support an organization without detailed business plans and key performance measures. Such pressures are likely to produce a shift from network relationships, at least internally, towards a more hierarchical, bureaucratic approach in which control is centralized and performance continuously monitored. In the case of small to medium-sized enterprises, it is worth emphasizing that this shift is not just about the 'routinization of charisma' – where a creative and inspiring founder or leader has to be replaced by more mundane procedures and routines. This may occur when key individuals 'burn out' or leave – although the positive contribution of a founder or charismatic leader may be time-limited if only by their disinterest in managing the organization as contrasted with the initial excitement of working as an entrepreneur to get the venture off the ground. In start-ups, the shift towards hierarchy tends to occur when investors seek (that is, demand) reassurances about the security of their capital and, therefore, endeavour to introduce (control) measures that are intended to minimize the risk of its loss. In the case of larger and more established organizations, the emphasis upon hierarchical accountability and performance measurement is likely to be even greater.

From a critical perspective, network theory neglects to examine the political and career processes that lie behind the development and maintenance of alliances and how the power and dominance of an alliance might result in inefficiencies for the economy as a whole. An example would be the big supermarket or hypermarket retailers who control their suppliers by making 'alliances' with them; and because of their dominant (oligopolistic) position chase out other sources of supply. They also squeeze the margins of the suppliers that are dependent on them. Because they occupy a dominant position, supermarkets are able to avoid passing on the lower prices to consumers except through single-item loss leaders that are promoted to attract customers whom they know will buy non-discounted items as well.

Virtual organization Electronic technologies are commonly viewed as enabling (and even requiring) innovation and experimentation with new forms of organization. The role that technologies of 'virtual distribution' may play in facilitating new practices of organizing and management is frequently apprehended in the literature through the loosely defined concept of the virtual organization (Handy, 1996; Mowshowitz, 2002) that can be summarized as follows:

- Coordination across time and space through continuous electronic connectedness between suppliers, employees and consumers.
- Ability to 'switch' between resources via vertical **disintermediation** and outsourcing of facilities, and fluid participation of personnel.
- Freedom from constraints imposed by time and distance – 'time–space compression' – making possible:
  - an ethos of flexibility and adaptability though permanent innovation, that is further enabled through
  - 'flattened hierarchies', employee empowerment and an organizational culture of trust and responsibility.

In this (largely anecdotal) literature, organizations are identified as close to the 'virtual' ideal by virtue of their possession of some or all of these characteristics. There is little question that the internet and information and communication technologies have broken down the time – space distances between people in the electronic age, but these new channels do not seem significantly to undermine 'traditional' channels. Internet banking, in particular, is supplementary and often stimulates dependence on, and an increase in business through, other channels, especially the telephone. Rather than a movement towards the virtual organization, we encounter a multiplication of **hybrid** forms.

Box 6.9: Virtual organization

'If one ignores the technology, there is nothing new, conceptually, in the idea of an activity without a building as its home. Where information is the raw material of work, it has never been necessary to have all the people in the same place at the same time. *A network of salespeople is the most common example – so ordinary and everyday an example that we would not think of giving it such a grandiose title as a virtual organization.* Yet salespeople operate on their own, out of no common place – out of

sight but not, one hopes, out of touch or, for that matter, out of line.

Journalism provides other examples. I myself fill an occasional slot on the BBC morning radio program Today. For many years, I did not meet my director, nor have I ever met any members of the production team. I communicate by telephone from wherever I happen to be, and my contributions are often broadcast from remote, unmanned studios. It is not in any way unusual.'

Source: C. Handy, *Trust and the Virtual Organization* (2000).

Morally charged notions such as flexibility, adaptability, etc., certainly figure prominently in the promotional discourses of technology companies, consultants and other purveyors of 'virtuality'. Despite this encouragement, examples such as the (short-lived) purely internet-based Security First Network Bank (SFNB), which had no branch network for its customers, are infrequent. Instead, many established institutions have created independent, stand-alone 'virtual' operations and others have sought add-ons at minimal cost. Here there is often little, if any, integration between remote distribution and traditional 'bricks and mortar' operations. The establishment of stand-alone organizations for new channels gives more freedom to experiment with developing the special skills and competencies required without the encumbrance of **legacy systems** and traditional culture. It also means that the traditional brand can be protected if the new channel fails or has teething troubles. However, perhaps the most important reason is that the new operation can provide discounted (and usually unprofitable) rates in order to attract a particular segment of the market without having to make the same offer to their existing customers:

'The last thing we want is someone coming in to a branch to tell us "I saw this internet rate advertised on TV. I have been with this bank for 20 years. Give me or I walk"' (interviewee technology manager in a 'big 4' bank).

Those adding on a new channel have largely been operating defensively against the erosion of quality business by new entrants. Internet operations like phone banks, for example, have lower costs and a more progressive image so that the traditional banks see no alternative but to emulate them. However, this increases their cost structure in the medium term as they still have a costly branch network. Consequently, they have sought to avoid excessive costs and this precludes either the strategy of setting up a green-field site or fully integrating the operations within the business. Technological integration has typically proved both difficult and expensive, with each new operation, merger and acquisition often contributing not to the seamless and frictionless electronic traffic prophesied in the virtual organization literature but rather to legacy systems almost baroque in their complexity.

The criticisms levelled against the other types of analysis presented in this section are also applicable to network theory. In addition, virtual organization can be criticized for exaggerating the difference between established and virtual forms of organizing. So, for example, telephone communications and even memos that are commonplace in established organizations could be characterized as 'virtual' in the sense of having no face-to-face encounter. It is probably best to conceive of 'virtuality' as a way of signalling the presence and influence of ICTs (information and communication technologies) in organizations and their use to communicate between organizations, rather than think of particular, novel organizations as 'virtual' (Woolgar, 2002).

Thinkpoint 6.8

Reviewing criticisms that have been made of the five other kinds of organization theory sketched in this section, consider how they apply to network theory.

Reinvention of 'one best way': Business process re-engineering and total quality management

Elements of network structures may develop *within* areas of organizations where the demand for innovation or pressures for rapid results are stronger than demands for hierarchical accountability and control. Networks may also develop within the interstices of organizations where horizontal communication and collaboration do not map on to formally prescribed hierarchical roles and relationships. In the main, however, network structures are subordinated to more familiar, hierarchical arrangements and associated lines of authority. Business process re-engineering (BPR) and total quality management (TQM) are two influential examples of techniques that have been developed to bring improvements to established, hierarchical forms of organizational design.

The history of mainstream thinking has been preoccupied with the question of how the benefits of a more rational, or rationalized, approach to the design of work and organization can be enjoyed without provoking individual and collective forms of resistance to its demands. In essence, this history has taken two intersecting paths. First, there have been recurrent efforts to reinvent Taylorism by introducing 'hard' methods of measurement and control, in the form of performance indicators, benchmarking, scorecards and so on. Here structures and designs of organizations, functions and tasks predominate. The emphasis is upon getting the design right. In common with Taylor's thinking, these methods pay minimal attention to questions of how their presence and application are likely to be received and interpreted by employees. In contrast, a second path implicitly challenges the assumption that the application of 'hard' methods will mechanically improve performance by inducing more productive behaviour. Instead of designing a technically perfect system into which people are expected to fit, the second path pays greater attention to existing arrangements and expectations and considers how, by going 'with the grain', these can be adapted and managed to improve performance.

Business process re-engineering (BPR)   BPR, the dominant fad of the 1990s, followed the first path, promising to transform the internal structures of businesses using information and communication technologies to convert sequential into parallel processing of tasks (see Box 6.10).

Central to BPR thinking is the destruction of the '**silos**' that are seen to result from the organization of work around specialist departments. Silos are seen to organize employees' activities around the expansion and preservation of their specialisms rather than the processes necessary to produce competitive products and services. Information and communication technologies (ICTs) are identified as providing the means of ensuring horizontal coordination and vertical control (through remote monitoring of activity). Notably, ICTs facilitate a process of self-managing in which unproductive, non value-adding activities are stripped out, with the attendant gains in profitability and losses of jobs.

In the majority of cases, BPR failed to deliver, principally because insufficient attention was given to the human dimension of bringing about radical, step change (although it may also be doubted whether simply giving this greater attention would have made a bitter pill of lay-offs any more acceptable). Management often lacked the capability and authority, and sometimes also the inclination, to impose BPR upon employees who regarded it as disruptive of their established routines and positions, and threatening insofar as it openly advertised its capacity to cut costs by downsizing – which is polite language for axing jobs, including the jobs of many managers who, in principle, also face redundancy as a consequence of the promotion of empowered, *self-managing* teams (see Chapter 4).

Difficulties are encountered in implementing BPR's demand that organizations transform their familiar silo-logic to a loss of confidence and support from consultants, practitioners and academics. Insofar as aspects of BPR have been adopted, organizations have invariably customized it to their own distinctive circumstances and this has meant that its influence has been partial rather than total. At the very least, the threat of more radical action has eased the introduction of more incremental forms of change, such as TQM (see below), although many of these less radical innovations were adopted before the emergence of BPR. Of course, there remain those who believe that only wholesale change will be sufficient, in the longer term, to remain competitive; and, relatedly, who believe that the power and falling cost of ICTs will eventually bring about a transformation. For its advocates, failures of BPR to deliver on its promises, are attributed to its partial or bungled application rather than its limited or negative and mechanistic understanding of the complexities of organizations as institutions.

The second path takes fuller account of the social dimensions of organizations as systems, such as their members' values and habitual concerns with social recognition and identity. This path stresses that no matter how well an organization is designed or structured, it is only people, not organizations, who 'behave' – that is, engage in activities that may be more or less 'productive'. As discussed in Chapter 2, 'human relations' has been an influential variant of this thinking. It appeals to the common-sense view that all human beings have 'social needs' for recognition and value a sense of belonging to a wider group (thereby excluding consideration of how it ignores the variability of such 'needs' and the extent to which group membership can be oppressive rather than affirming).

Box 6.10: What is business process re-engineering?

Three key features of BPR that differentiate it from other contemporary recipes for business transformation are:

- *From function to process.* BPR aspires to produce radical, quantum-leap change by reorienting businesses around key processes. It demands the complete replacement of bureaucratic and functional silos by units organized around delivering customer requirements.
- *Entrepreneurialism.* The aim is to transform organizations so that all staff are driven by a

competitive desire to provide the 'best' and most profitable customer service.

- *Information technology.* Advocates the widespread use of information and communication technologies to enable the shift from function to process, combined with some, apparently universally applicable HRM techniques that are intended to empower employees and facilitate teamworking.

Total quality management (TQM) A version of this thinking is present, in a more focused and self-managing form, in the quality management movement, which became full-blown in the development of TQM, where individuals or teams of employees cooperate to identify where there is scope for improving their practice.

Box 6.11: Focus on quality

The focus on quality came out of Japan, although by way of the United States since its originator – Ishiwaka (1985) – had brought it to America but then re-exported it to Japan before it took off as a global phenomenon. Its earliest introduction was concerned with both qualitative and quantifiable quality issues. As quality management evolved into total quality management, the concentration on the 'hard' techniques of statistical process control and 'sixth sigma' were supplemented and even overhauled by broader attempts to change organization cultures to secure continuous improvement in the direction of quality (Tuckman, 1995).

The qualitative aspects of the early quality management programmes revolved around 'quality circles' (Hill, 1991) where teams of employees meet regularly to discuss work and production problems and to suggest practical ways of improving the quality of process and output – a kind of 'live', interactive suggestion box (which had been the previous, bureaucratic version of how to capture the knowledge of employees who had the greatest familiarity with the organization of work and its limitations of design). In contrast to BPR, which advocates a more radical transformation of established practice, quality management, including TQM, favours a process of incremental change. Although there is always room for improvement, TQM assumes that the basic design of work and organizations is sound. It does not seek to substitute its own 'one best way' of reforming existing practice but, rather, aspires to work with the grain of the particularities of such practice with the aim of removing unnecessary impediments to the quality as well as the quantity of productive activity. Instead of a 'one best way' approach, TQM is based upon a set of broad points of reference (see Box 6.12).

Box 6.12: What is total quality management?

- *Continuous improvement.* TQM is concerned with improving internal processes through, for example, quality circles, where groups of employees are brought together to discuss how working practices can be improved. Various technical means have also been devised to achieve the improvements, including statistical process control and 'zero defects', which involve the quantification and monitoring of quality outputs to remove all obstacles to perfection.

- *Customer orientation.* The aim of TQM is to transform the culture of an organization such that products or services will be characterized by their 'fitness for use' and thus 'meet the expectations of the customers'.

- *Teamworking.* Combined with a notion of employee empowerment and participation, which involves assigning greater discretion to team members, teamworking has become a central means of securing quality objectives.

A broad based quality approach has enjoyed a long period of widespread managerial support and continues to attract management practitioners. This may well be because it is an amalgamation of a number of moderate and incrementalist innovations – culture change, empowerment, quality circles and teamworking – and it is permissive in the sense that it does not dictate to managers that all its elements must be simultaneously and fully adopted. It also gives encouragement to managers to involve employees in its implementation, in contrast to BPR where there is insistence upon its relentless top-down application, with the anticipation that employees will be automatically empowered as a result. With TQM, it is more likely (but by no means inevitable – see Chapter 10), that employees will interpret aspects of the changes as bringing some benefits to them, and for this reason there is rarely much resistance, whether in the form of covert withdrawal of cooperation or open hostility to its introduction.

Many of the difficulties of applying business process re-engineering (see above) could be interpreted within a socio-technical systems framework. It would suggest that the architects and implementers of BPR were often insufficiently attentive or sensitive to the social dimensions of organizational life. That is to say, they treat organizations as if they are purely technical systems, without adequate regard for the norms and sensibilities of employees. But equally, this observation suggests the cautious and conservative quality of socio-technical systems thinking is derived from the human relations philosophy (see Chapter 2) that is its guiding light. Here the maintenance of balance is given priority over the more radical kinds of proposals favoured by root-and-branch reformers such as advocates of scientific management or champions of BPR. While the systems theorists were perhaps too cautious and conservative, the radical reformers had little hesitation in throwing out the baby with the bathwater, particularly with respect to displacing the tacit skills and knowledge on which organizations so depend.

Box 6.13: The importance of 'tacit knowledge' and 'user involvement'

'Tacit knowledge', although having no formal standing or recognition, is the lifeblood of an organization. Tacit knowledge consists of the numerous routine, sometimes idiosyncratic, and often subconscious ways through which we carry out work tasks and that we have acquired through long periods of familiarity with those tasks. These ways may not comply with any rational model of how things should be done, and indeed it is this 'idiosyncrasy' that the advocates of BPR and similar programmes seek to eliminate. The problem, however, is that their removal is highly disruptive, and the various contingencies and eventualities that they have grown up to address cannot be readily appreciated by the designers of (re-engineered) systems that are their intended replacement. It is the implicit understanding, often ignored by engineers or those seeking to re-engineer, that results in the mantra of 'user-involvement' and 'user-friendliness' being increasingly rehearsed. But even if this mantra is heeded and followed, it is often extremely difficult for the users themselves to articulate their tacit knowledge or to communicate effectively with consultants and (re)designers whose temporary and transient status is not conducive to generating the kind of trust that would be necessary to elicit such revelations. And, of course, users may also be reluctant to share this information if they fear that it will enable others to appropriate responsibility for designing their jobs, making their jobs more demanding, less interesting or even surplus to requirements.

If, following a redesign, the tasks and/or personnel carrying them out change dramatically, the informal culture and tacit skill disappears, with attendant difficulties for addressing unforeseen problems. In such circumstances, and in the absence of their control over the process of change, employees may well become fearful and insecure, or at best resigned and disaffected, about their jobs and the material and symbolic security that they ordinarily provide. In short, their identities will be more vulnerable than before, leading to highly defensive behaviour in response to management power. They are much less likely to trust managers and in this sense a greater polarization between them may result in which power and inequality, rather than productive collaboration, frames the relationship.

The kinds of criticisms levelled against the study of technology in organizations can be generalized to many mainstream studies, which attempt to isolate and measure variables, including structure. These studies disregard how the very identification and specification of the variables, quite apart from the (determining) effects attributed to them, are the constructions of, and are mediated by, organizational members and/or social scientists. 'Technology', for example, cannot be known except by identifying it in particular, interpretation-dependent ways. Its effect upon other 'variables', such as structure or performance, depends not upon the technology in itself but upon the specific, favoured meaning or interpretation of technology. And this meaning is mediated by organizational members as well as by researchers. Unfortunately, much mainstream thinking excludes consideration of this process. As a consequence, statistical correlations are frequently spurious in the sense that they register outcomes that are a consequence of something (e.g. cultural, social, political or economic relations) outside of the variables that are being considered. Mainstream thinking operates routinely to deflect attention from a host of important human and relational issues that critical organization studies aspires to understand better.

Contributions and limitations of the mainstream

Contributions We can summarize the contribution of the mainstream as follows:

- The structure of organizations is seen largely to determine behaviour so that it is vital to ensure that it is designed, redesigned or re-engineered to be compatible with its environment.

- The analytical framework most commonly drawn upon is some variant of systems theory (closed or open) where inputs (labour, resources, policies) are processed to produce the required outputs (profitable or efficient products and services).

- Generally, a consensus is presumed to exist within organizations and it is just a matter of creating and sustaining a rationally defensible ordering of hierarchical work relationships.

- Structures define roles and responsibilities but they reflect and reproduce the existing organizational arrangements.

- Although there are a wide variety of different analytical approaches, they all are concerned to indicate how the organization has to adapt to, or is determined by, the environment.

- A diverse range of innovations or technologies of intervention exist but they share in common a belief in having discovered the one best way to structure and organize activities.

Mainstream thinking about management and organization is firmly wedded to the view that knowledge that has any relevance and value is properly and exclusively concerned with *enhancing performance within the ideological and political parameters of the status quo*. Performance is therefore closely coupled to profitability and growth rather than to any wider measures of human advancement. Knowledge that challenges the status quo or is not perceived to be relevant for its functional reform is identified as irrelevant if not outright dangerous. Yet, despite its rather narrow focus, the mainstream agenda enjoys credibility and legitimacy – precisely because it seems so sensible and acceptable to seek out those organizational structures that are assessed to be the most efficient and productive for maintaining and renewing the status quo – in terms of preserving established hierarchies of power and inequality. Yet, questions of whether pursuit of the mainstream agenda is necessarily beneficial or sustainable for people (e.g. work–life balance; exploitation of Third World labour that lacks basic legal protections in terms of working conditions, age restrictions, hours worked, etc.), non-human life (e.g. factory farming) or the future of the planet (e.g. global warming) tends to be marginalized or dismissed as 'moral' or 'ethical' matters beyond the technical domain of management. At best, these questions are placed in the domain of government, and the 'efficient' organization has to find ways of accommodating restrictions upon their operations when legal intervention forces them to do so. Even then, it is often more a matter of being seen to conform to the letter of the law or even calculating the business risk of deliberately evading regulations, rather than actively welcoming reforms that place quality of life before profitable production.

In *The Organization of Business*, Stephen Ackroyd (2002) concludes that the orthodox approach to organizational structure should be discarded because it is incapable of understanding contemporary patterns of organizational change. The argument that designs or structures are simply functional for organizations to survive by facilitating their adaptation to the environment is, he contends, a one-sided and highly partial view. It deflects attention from the power relations that underlie such structures and precludes any understanding of how organizations constitute and enact their environments rather than simply respond to them. To this, we would add that organizations are historically and culturally embedded so that their design and operation necessarily reflect, or at least articulate, the values and priorities of their particular contexts.

We may recall that an important part of the mainstream – institutional theory – also rejects the systems or contingency approach insofar as the latter sees the organization as adapting to, rather than enacting, its environment. Institutional theory also invites us to appreciate how non-rational considerations colour the design of organizational structures, in ways that may enhance their effectiveness as well as their legitimacy. Once again, this demonstrates the permeability of boundaries between 'mainstream' and 'critical' approaches. Indeed, there are some who would argue that not only has the mainstream prepared the ground for a critical approach but that the latter is gradually becoming accepted as part of the mainstream. For example, the most mainstream of institutions – the American

Critical approaches begin by inverting these ideas by arguing that within mainstream thinking:

1. Systems thinking produces an abstracted set of concepts about organization that marginalize the human, political and process dimensions of organization and management.

2. Even when some idea of the human, political and process dimensions (e.g. through the distinction between formal and informal elements) is introduced, this is limited by a belief that these need to be eradicated or contained to prevent them disrupting the formal system and managements' goals.

What fundamentally distinguishes these contrasting approaches is a different perception and attitude towards consensus and conflict in organizations and society.

Mainstream thinking tends to assume consensus and social balance as the norm in organizations. Conflict is regarded as an aberration that managers or leaders must remove or divert and direct into productive channels. Dominant in mainstream thinking is an adherence to closed or open systems theory in which organizations are represented as interdependent elements that seemingly develop and operate independently of the processes through which organizational members (re)produce organizational realities. From a critical perspective, systems theory 'neglects the ways in which [members'] purposes and perspectives intervene in the interpretation and contesting of goal-related prescriptions for action' (Elger, 1975, p. 94).

Neglect of how organizational realities are an ongoing outcome of processes of contest and negotiation is reflected in the assumption that 'an over-arching consensus informs all organizational processes' (ibid.). The assumption of consensus (and equilibrium) is justified by an absence of overt conflict in organizations. Or, where it is difficult to ignore certain tensions, consensus is assumed to be latent, simply waiting to be actualized by judicious managerial interventions that will remove obstacles and allow it to flourish. Critics, in contrast, are sceptical about such claims, arguing that consensus is often *forced*, rather than determined through informed debate under conditions of an equality of participation, and that the absence of tension and conflict is more credibly interpreted as a product of effective control rather than a sign of underlying harmony.

Thinkpoint 6.11

Consider an occasion where, beneath the surface, there were major conflicts brewing but there was very little visible evidence of these. How would you account for their invisibility? Were there any tell-tale signs of the conflicts? If your example was drawn from outside the sphere of organizations, can you think of some examples within them, again drawing upon your experience?

Once the presumption of consensus is challenged, the notion that organizations have a single, shared goal is also placed under critical scrutiny. For it is understood that different groups and individuals have *diverse* agendas and 'goals', and that these cannot sensibly be equated with a *single* organizational goal. Accordingly, the notion that organizations, rather than their members, have goals is no longer conceived as a self-evident fact but, instead, is viewed as a misleading fantasy of a dominant group that has acquired widespread commonsensical plausibility. For ideas are now linked to groups or individuals within organizations, not to organizations themselves.

That such a (selective and potentially misleading) view becomes deeply ingrained in commonsense thinking is explained, from a critical perspective, by the differentials of power between individuals and groups. For some groups – those who have access to channels of communication within organizations or the media more generally – are able to exert greater influence upon the formation of what becomes received wisdom or commonsense. In this way, a questionable claim – such as the idea that organizations have goals or that roles within organizations are determined by functional imperatives 'untouched by personal concerns or collective interests' – comes to be taken-for-granted as a 'common normative standard' (ibid.). According to Elger (1975, p.p. 103 and 114):

Systems perspectives identify roles [within organizations] as consensually defined clusters of rights and obligations, unambiguously linked with 'organizational tasks' and untouched by personal concerns and collective interests . . . [The] processual perspective emphasizes that the social structures of industrial concerns are patterned by negotiation and interpretation among participants with diverse interests and resources, so that analyses of variations and changes in such structures must attend to those sustaining and transforming processes.

One way in which the presumption of consensus can be sustained without challenge is through the design and structure of an organization. This is so especially where the structure is represented and accepted as the most rational, cost-effective and even 'one best way' of organizing. The idea of questioning the legitimacy of the design and structure of an organization is troublesome, if not taboo. Only at times of crisis or when there are major disruptions – due perhaps to a takeover, a change of government or regulatory reform – is it likely that the structure of an organization becomes a focus for critical re-examination or radical redesign. And, for this very reason, it becomes an important target for critical approaches. From a critical perspective, mainstream approaches do not provide impartial or neutral knowledge as they reflect senior management's interest in control by assuming the legitimacy and functionality of the structure of inequality. Mainstream approaches lend credibility to knowledge that supports the status quo by presuming, rather than interrogating, organizational consensus.

Critical approaches challenge the mainstream view that organizational consensus is the normal and established state of affairs. They also question the presumption that consensus is always and everywhere to be preferred. They do so by casting a critically reflective eye upon the design and structure of the organization. Critical approaches identify how organizational structure is a condition of, but also has consequences for, the reproduction of power and inequality.

A fundamental aspect of economic organizations is that a majority are privately owned and thereby designed principally to make profit for their owners. In speaking about the structure and design of organizations, mainstream texts rarely mention that our economy is capitalist, let alone discuss the implications of it being so. Even when considering the public sector, there is a concentration upon the efficiency of the means of attaining objectives rather than any questioning of them. Mainstream texts simply take for granted that profit and/or efficiency are the key drivers of organizations and assume a managerialist focus where the major purpose of studying organizations is to discover ways of facilitating the achievement of efficiency and/or the attainment of profits. How far

Image 6.2

From a critical standpoint, capitalist economies systematically disadvantage a *majority* of people – consumers as well as employees. How can that be, since over recent years a majority of the population, in developed economies at least, have normally experienced a progressively improving material standard of living? Excluding pensioners and members of the so-called 'underclass', people find that their spending power is increasing. In most cases, they consider themselves to be paid appropriately for the work that they do; and do not regard themselves as exploited by their employers. And yet, at the same time, many feel little enthusiasm for, or have a sense of control over, the work they do or their long-term future. There is a feeling of being a cog in a machine whose work is continuously measured and evaluated, and where the primary meaning of work is to become a bigger, better paid cog (see Box 6.15) – just as Taylor advocated (see Chapters 13 and 14).

Box 6.15: Performance measurement and becoming a cog

'The performance of each individual worker is mathematically measured, each man becomes a little cog in the machine and aware of this, his one preoccupation is whether he can become a bigger cog . . . as if were to become men who need "order" and nothing but order, who become nervous and cowardly if for one moment this order wavers, and helpless if they are torn away from their total incorporation in it.'

Source: Max Weber, quoted in Mayer (1956, p.p. 126–127).

The structure of work organization

How, then, is sense to be made of this? The form of critical analysis that responds to this challenge draws originally from Marx's ideas and, more specifically, from his analysis of the organization of labour processes in the distinctive context of capitalist economic organization.

In examining how work is organized in capitalist enterprises, Marx shifts analysis away from the idea that every commodity, including labour, secures its fair price in the market where demand and supply find their equilibrium. That is the assumption that underpins so much of mainstream thinking, particularly analysis that takes its lead from neo-classical economics. In its place, Marx seeks to understand the status of labour in capitalist economies and, in particular, how it is organized within workplaces to ensure that an adequate surplus, or profit, can be willingly extracted from the productive efforts of labour.

In Box 6.16, Marx illustrates the capitalist–worker relationship by giving it a personal dramatization. His point is that when each party is involved in agreeing a payment for the worker's productive capability (i.e. 'labour power'), the contract is 'freely' entered into. It is based upon agreement, rather than feudal obligation, slavery or some other form of overt coercion. As a market transaction, the worker is at liberty to terminate the contract, just as 'he' freely accepts it. Or, so it seems, at least, from what Marx identifies as a *particular*, 'bourgeois', mainstream perspective where the freedoms associated with market relations are abstracted from a wider structure of (capitalist) social relations in which markets are promoted and supported as their key and dominant institution. So, why, as the workplace is approached, does 'the possessor of labour power become timid and 'hold back'? Marx's answer is that with the exchange of this power for an agreed wage, the worker effectively *surrenders control* – that is, s/he becomes enslaved and subordinated to the employer – for the duration of employment.

Box 6.16: The capitalist and the worker

'When we leave the simple sphere of circulation or the exchange of commodities . . . a certain change takes place . . . He who was previously the money-owner now strides out in front as a capitalist; the possessor of labour power follows as his worker. The one smirks self-importantly and is intent on business: the other is timid and holds back, like someone who has brought his own hide to market and now has nothing else to expect but a tanning.'

Source: Marx, K. (1973) *Capital, Vol. 1*, Harmondsworth: Penguin, p. 280.

The worker enters a situation where, in principle, s/he is obliged to work in ways that will secure an adequate level of profit for the employer.

Such subordination, Marx contends, is integral to the structure of capitalist economic organization. It may be more or less relaxed or tightened – some employees receive training or education sufficient to become (internally) self-disciplined and therefore require less direct supervision, whereas others will apply themselves only if they are coerced or closely monitored. Others may successfully resist efforts to control them; and others may be too important to the employer – because their labour is so scarce and/or because the added value that they create is so great – to risk losing them by imposing counter-productive controls. So, in some cases, the subordination may be mainly what Marx calls 'formal' (see Box 6.17). A relationship of exploitation exists but it is something of a formality. The employer does not directly exercise control over the employees' labour process. The planning and organization of work on a day-to-day basis remains the responsibility of the employee. With the development of scientific management, however, the subordination changes from being formal to becoming increasingly 'real' as the employer intervenes to organize and control the detail of how employees work such that they are required to execute tasks strictly designed and monitored by management.

Box 6.17: Subordination – formal and real

In many situations, there is a difference between what is formally required (e.g. the requirement to attend the workplace between certain hours) and what control over labour is 'really' secured.

- *Formal subordination of labour*, where the working day is lengthened or cheap labour (e.g. children, women, immigrants, students) is introduced.
- *Real subordination of labour*, where there is an intensification of production (e.g. capital investment,

new technology, strict job specifications, productivity schemes, targets, bonus systems, etc.).

This difference is illustrated by the quip-cum-slogan: 'We are employed here 9–5, you surely don't expect us to work as well!' What this signals is how formal subordination, in terms of the obligation to be at the workplace, is bad enough without adding insult to injury by forcing them to work hard (e.g. on the assembly line) while there.

As subordination becomes progressively 'real', the employee is told what to do, how to do it and when to do it. There may then be some relaxation of control as the employer becomes more trusting of 'loyal' employees and/or calculates that the production process is adequately profitable only if employees are allowed to exercise greater discretion within boundaries that continue to be set and policed by employers. But this situation is understood to remain one of 'real' subordination of labour, rather than to be a return to a formal position, as the control logic of the employer is now internalized by the employee (see Chapter 10).

Box 6.18: Exploitation at Bar Mar?

What might an analysis of Bar Mar focusing upon exploitation look like? Suppose that Margaret's staff were working overtime but not being paid the extra hours worked. In common-sense terms, that would be viewed as 'exploitative'. Why? Because it breaks the formal or informal contract that Margaret has with her employees. She agreed to pay them so much per hour and she is now expecting them to work for nothing. But, from a more critical standpoint, it would be argued that Margaret's staff are exploited *every hour that they work*, and not just when they put in overtime without extra pay. That is because the very structure of their relationship is seen to be exploitative, regardless of how well staff are treated and how promptly they are paid. For Margaret is understood to be

extracting money from the labour of her staff by paying them less than the revenues that she derives from their work. The difference between the revenues and the costs of her business are not distributed among those whose labour has produced this surplus. Instead, the surplus is appropriated and accumulated by Margaret as her (personal) capital.

Margaret treats her staff well. She pays them more than the market rate. She does her very best to accommodate their family responsibilities. She has always paid them a handsome Christmas bonus. So, how can she possibly be exploiting them? They are content; they would not dream of working for anyone else. But, that, arguably, is because they have come to normalize and accept the capitalist basis of contemporary economic organization. They take it for granted, and do not mind, that Margaret hires them and tells them how they should behave, not the other way around. Should they become unhappy with the way Margaret is running the business, they have no basis for sacking her. They are in no position to do so. It is difficult for them even to approach her to object to her attitude, tactics or strategy. At base, it would be suggested, the relationship is one of domination and exploitation, based upon Margaret's ownership of Bar Mar and the dependence of staff upon her for their employment. It is this basic structure, above all, that is understood to condition how they relate to each other.

Prior to the intervention of the state, capitalist economies endorse 'free' markets where everything is viewed as a commodity – art, education; even religion, air or water – that has its price and/or becomes a business (see Box 6.19). Such thinking defined by Marx as **bourgeois** is so widespread and institutionalized, as a common-sense truth, that it becomes embraced by the sellers of labour (i.e. employees) as well as by its buyers (i.e. employers). Jobs become valued primarily on the basis of the economic wage, not whether they are meaningful or rewarding either for the worker or for the wider community. It is the credibility and authority of this thinking that Marx challenges as he invites us to turn our attention from the market-place to the workplace. And, in doing so, he seeks to show why the institution of the market and its associated ideology of freedom, to which many workers commonsensically subscribe, is so important for the development and maintenance of capitalist economies.

Box 6.19: The commodification of everything

'It would be hard to deny that a central pressure of modern life is the always potential commodification of any object, event or action . . . Marketization spreads through inventive ways of commodifying things that are normally viewed as alienable (water, air), and by transforming into saleable objects social phenomena which were not previously framed in that manner (advice, love, care).'

Source: Slater, D. and Tonkiss, F. (2001) *Market Society*, Cambridge: Polity Press, p. 24.

What, then, does Marx have to say about the organization of labour processes within capitalist workplaces? The analysis hinges upon the understanding that wealth is fundamentally dependent upon the application of workers' productive capability, or labour power. But, in the context of capitalist workplaces, workers are denied control of the application of this labour because, above all, the capitalist must ensure that an acceptable level of profit is generated by the activities that create products or deliver services.

The factory system The growth and development of capitalism in the 19th century depended on the success of the factory system and this was attributed to its greater efficiencies – workers could be trained and supervised more effectively and could also be harnessed to the most productive technologies. However, this interpretation tends to overlook or underplay how, for its architects and investors, the appeal of the factory system resided in its promise, and its subsequent demonstration, that it could be a reliable and sustainable means of *controlling* labour so that greater and more dependable profits could be extracted from its productive activity.

Often, draconian measures and penalties were introduced to force and contain workers within the factory system. Abject poverty drove many reluctant workers into the factories where they would find themselves corralled like cattle. But with the rise of trades unions and an associated labour movement, workers were able to mobilize some resistance or at least a voice of opposition to the worst exploitative excesses of their employers. As Hobsbawn (1975, p. 214) observes, collective action through the union was for many more than a 'tool of struggle: it was a way of life'. For it enabled them to construct an alternative identity to that of the disposable commodity that was treated by most employers in a manner directly comparable to other, inert factors of production, such as cotton or machinery. This way of life was 'collective, communal, combative', where a sense of **agency** was recovered and asserted, giving their lives a renewed sense of 'coherence and purpose' (ibid.). Today, this struggle continues as employees working in diverse organizations organize to resist efforts to de-skill or to intensify their work.

Box 6.20: Workers struggle at Critchley Labels

Critchley sacked 31 Communication Workers Union members in February 1997 while they were taking part in balloted, legal industrial action. The company derecognized the union despite over 70 per cent of its employees being members.

Marches, rallies, petitions, a cyber picket of the company worldwide (using e-mail and faxes), lobbying, an international campaign – all were tried. A great wave of sympathy for the strikers flowed from all over Wales, the rest of the United Kingdom and many other parts of the world.

Source: http://www.waleswatch.welshnet.co.uk/rarebits/critchley.htm

---

For employers, ensuring the attendance of workers in workplaces was and remains only part of the challenge. The larger part is to *convert the potential* of labour to be productive into products and services that can be sold for a profit. For it is one thing to buy the labour, it is quite another to organize it in ways that renders its production adequately profitable. It is the challenge that continues to face the designers and managers of organization who are employed to ensure that labour is marshalled and controlled in ways that secure this surplus.

Box 6.21: The workplace as a contested terrain

'The task of extracting labour from workers who have no direct stake in profits remains to be carried out in the workplace itself. Conflict arises over how work shall be organized, what work pace shall be established, what conditions producers must labour under, what rights workers shall enjoy, and how the various employees of the enterprise shall relate to each other. The workplace becomes a battleground, as employers attempt to extract the maximum effort from workers and workers necessarily resist their bosses' impositions.'

Source: Edwards, R. (1979), *Contested Terrain: The Transformation of the Workplace in the Twentieth Century*, London: Heinemann, p. 13.

It is here that we return to the earlier examination of classical thinking about organization and, more specifically, to Taylor's ideas about scientific management. It should be acknowledged that few if any factories or offices have adopted Taylor's ideas in their entirety. As we noted earlier in this chapter, 'pure' Taylorism encounters the virtually insuperable obstacle of established social practices and traditions. While it aspires to sweep these aside, it necessarily relies upon people – notably managers – who are themselves steeped in these traditions. More obviously, its demands for change encounter resistance from workers who fear that more efficient production methods will bring redundancies and/or are not convinced that complying with design requirement imposed by management will be adequately compensated by higher wages. So, the importance of Taylorism lies less in its direct application than in its distillation and articulation of a particular mode of thinking that has shaped the development of industrial capitalism. More specifically, Taylorism has served to justify the exclusion of workers from participation in key design decisions that affect their working lives.

Braverman's *Labor and Monopoly Capital* The major contribution to a critical analysis of work organization has been Harry Braverman's *Labor and Monopoly Capital* (1974). Just as Taylor's thinking had had the greatest influence upon the design of work in the 20th century, Braverman's critique of Taylorism inspired and provoked critical analysis of its effects. Braverman identifies Taylor's writings on scientific management as the key to understanding the transformation of work that has occurred over the past two centuries and, more specifically, within industrialized economies. What Braverman singles out, and finds to be the pivotal feature of Taylorism, is the progressive separation of 'thought and action, conception and execution, mind and hand' (Braverman, 1974, p. 171).

Braverman's view is that the determination of the structure and design of work has transferred to managers and 'experts' who have then been able to justify their monopoly of the procedures of control in the name of science. In this process, work has been widely de-skilled and degraded as workers are left

Table 6.7 Key ideas in Braverman's (1974) *Labor and Monopoly Capital*

Braverman believed that applying the principles of scientific management demanded:

1 A separation of conception (i.e. design, planning, organization of work) from its execution (i.e. carrying out the work tasks). Braverman described this as de-skilling.
2 A detailed division of labour which Braverman described as job fragmentation and simple, 'monotonous', repetitive work tasks. Braverman labelled this the 'degradation' of work.
3 Payment-by-results, often, though not necessarily, taking the form of piece-work rates of pay based on time and motion studies.

with the execution of highly specialized, repetitive tasks designed by those senior in the hierarchy. Workers have progressively been subordinated to designs created by managers and other experts. Managers have become 'the sole subjective element', in the sense that they alone are active in making the decisions about organizational structure and the design of jobs. Workers are expected to be compliant and passive but are often also smoulderingly resentful in simply having to execute what managers and other self-styled experts have planned. It is this sense of oppression and unfairness that can ignite into individual and collective forms of resistance and ultimately into workers movements, general strikes and revolutionary change.

Exercise 6.9

Think of an occasion when, in no uncertain terms, you were told what to do, and reflect on what it felt like and how you responded or might have responded if you had not been concerned about the consequences of contradicting the command. Discuss your own experiences of this with those of other students to see whether there are any common features.

Of course, the exact opposite can also occur. Where employees have been used to undertaking routinized tasks designed by others, and are then asked to engage their mind in some redesign of work, they may refuse to assume greater responsibilities. They may resent the imposition of such demands, arguing that they are not paid to think and/or to do management's job for them. Management innovations such as teamworking, quality initiatives or re-engineering that have been introduced into a previously Taylorized work regime have come unstuck because of such attitudes.

It is not difficult to find examples (of repetitive, closely supervised, assembly line work or the scripting and electronic surveillance of some contemporary call-centres) that lend instant relevance and credibility to Braverman's analysis. More generally, it is possible to see how all kinds of supervisory, managerial and professional work is subjected to disciplines of the kind commended by Taylor – specialization of tasks, work measurement, payment by results, etc. Take, for example, the labour process of leading accountancy and law firms. There is a specialist division of labour including a 'managing partner', there are time sheets for charging customers with targets for billable hours, and there are bonuses for meeting and exceeding targets. So, even the most prestigious and ostensibly unindustrialized work exhibits key features of Taylorism. On the other hand, many who are broadly sympathetic to Braverman's analysis have identified a number of its limitations:

1. By suggesting that management has become 'the sole subjective element', Braverman minimizes the extent to which managers have had to address the 'subjectivity' of labour. Historically, managers have had to anticipate, and to a degree accommodate, the values and priorities of labour in order to transform the potential of labour power into productive activity. As Burawoy (1985, p. 48) notes, 'the advance of mechanization must be seen as a response not just to increasing costs of labour but also to labour's increasing power' as machines offered a means of employing less skilled workers of which there was a greater supply and also using machines to pace their work. Workers' values and priorities have included social divisions of gender, ethnicity, age, etc., and employers have sought to exploit these differences. But Braverman has rather little to say about the presence and influence of these divisions. However, precisely because managers rely in numerous ways upon the subjectivity of labour, they are obliged to respect this dependence – for example, by acting to

preserve ethnic and gender inequalities even when they personally disagree with them – if conflicts are to be minimized and cooperation is not be withdrawn by significant (e.g. white/male) sections of the workforce. Management never has been all-powerful, nor can managers expect to become so, as they are constrained by values and priorities that extend into the wider society. For this reason, the forms of capitalist work organization exhibit considerable variation across sectors and economies around the world.

2. A highly specialized, fragmented division of labour is not necessarily the most effective or even the most controlled way of organizing work. Allowing employees to exercise a degree of discretion, rather than subjecting them to close, direct control, can bring benefits of commitment and motivation as well as flexibility, thereby limiting the requirement for, and cost of, managerial oversight. Management innovations (e.g. quality, teamworking, computer-assisted design) may be introduced in ways that facilitate a *reintegration* of conception (i.e. organizing production) and execution (i.e. completing well-defined tasks) rather than its further separation.

3. Managers *continue to rely* upon labour as a 'subjective element'. In order to ensure the optimum quality of the product or a more effective method of production (or service delivery), it may be necessary to involve employees (e.g. through quality circles) in decision making about the structure and design of their work. Workers and 'users' at the 'coal face' or 'sharp end' of the business are increasingly seen as sources of tacit knowledge about the complex practicalities of work that are alien and/or inaccessible to managers remote from day-to-day practices.

4. The structure of work organization in capitalist economies is not designed to maximize control per se but, rather, to ensure an acceptable level of profitability in the face of numerous issues, including the cooperation and productivity of labour, that can derail it. An important element of this cooperation is the legitimation of capitalism through its regulation and redistribution of wealth by the state, in the form of public services (e.g. education) that are provided through the taxation of economic activity. Legitimation is by no means automatic as there are frequently tensions between what people want and what employers and politicians are able to deliver. Braverman has a rather romantic view of the skills of the craft worker that skates over the operation of guilds as monopolies and their creation of an aristocracy of labour that has often been hostile to the aspirations of, and dismissive of, the importance of non-artisanal skills. He pays only passing attention to how the level and value of a skill is socially defined through a series of historical and cultural evaluations and legitimations, rather than simply given by its exercise. He does not, for example, appreciate how, historically, the association of skill with masculinity has tended to raise its value; and how work predominantly carried out by women (e.g. nursing, secretarial, teaching) tends to be devalued at least in terms of economic reward if not status as well. But he also overlooks how 'unskilled' and 'semi-skilled' work generally involves the application of considerable tacit knowledge and unacknowledged skill.

5. Braverman implies that managers are unified in their intent to de-skill and degrade labour. But they are divided by their own specialisms as well as through hierarchical differences (see Box 6.22). While Braverman recognizes that middle management are increasingly subjected to Tayloristic forms of accountability and control (e.g. management by objectives, payment by results), he does not consider how divisions within management are reflected in differential degrees of enthusiasm for varying aspects of Taylor's thinking.

Box 6.22: Divisions within management

' . . . managers themselves do not form a monolithic group . . . different levels of management will be preoccupied with different aspects of the labour process. Lower-level management, in daily contact with the worker, might oppose the introduction of Taylorism in an attempt to prevent conflict, while middle levels of management might be responsible for instigating such changes with a view to cheapening the cost of labour power. The highest level might be concerned only with profits and efficiency and express little interest in how these are realized.'

Source: Burawoy, M. (1985), *The Politics of Production*, London: Verso, p. 46.

Empirical case studies: Inequality, identity and insecurity

The thrust of Braverman's analysis is that management has broadly succeeded in securing control over the design of organization structures, as commended by classical thinkers like Taylor and Fayol. Labour is presented as a progressively powerless and passive pawn in this process. There is little interest in how the new structures become normalized and institutionalized, or in workers' active participation in this process. Instead, it is assumed that workers are cowed into submission by the overwhelming inequality of resources and therefore the force of management to impose its power. In order to ensure that employees cooperate to the maximum, managers are seen to have introduced psychological enticements, in the form of 'human relations' techniques targeted primarily at the sentiments of, and the desire for social recognition among the workforce, and thereby only indirectly at their actions (see Chapters 2 and 7). These techniques exhort managers to treat employees as junior colleagues rather than simply as subordinates, and to encourage employees to develop a sense of solidarity involving mutual obligations.

'Human relations' techniques have promised to release management and workers from the vicious circle of material compensation (wage increases) as a single solution to all disputes that simply raised future (often wage inflationary) expectations without necessarily bringing about a compensating increase in productivity nor a reduction in grievances. Ensuring the development of a supportive supervisory relationship that could engender a productive, psychologically balanced, work group culture is regarded as a key task for 'enlightened' management. Supported by the Hawthorne experiments (Roethlisberger and Dickson, 1939) and later neo-human relations research (see Chapter 2), the seductive idea is that human beings are naturally, spontaneously cooperative and that this is evident in their own, informal behaviour where there is a strong tendency to establish and respect group norms. The task of management, according to advocates of such thinking, is to shape work group norms so that they are aligned to corporate priorities. Once established and rooted, it is anticipated that such a culture would be largely self-maintaining. Each member of a harmonious group will seek to preserve positive relations among its members; and will therefore intervene to censure, and ultimately to isolate, disruptive colleagues. The challenge for managers, then, is to intervene in unobtrusive, friendly ways so as to steer the development of work group culture away from informal norms and expressions of solidarity that are anti-management – such as the restriction of output or punishing workers who work too hard – towards those that are congruent with managerial objectives, such as cooperating with management to raise output or restraining 'troublemakers' who disrupt the harmony of the group (see Chapters 4, 7 and 10).

Managing the Shopfloor: Gendering the structure of work organization   In *Managing the Shopfloor*, David Collinson (1992) develops an illuminating analysis of power and identity through his ethnographic study of workplace culture in a motor manufacturing corporation. It departs radically from the mainstream attempt to relate the design and structure of the organization simply to performance variables. Nonetheless, while focusing primarily on cultural issues of masculine identity, power and inequality, it has significance for the performative aspects of organization. At the time of the research, the organization had just been taken over by a US international corporation and the new management had become persuaded of the importance of a humanized management style and structure as advocated by the human relations school of organization (see Chapter 10).

Open and friendly management was the new style, so that managers could be spoken to on first name terms regardless of hierarchical position and this was to be encouraged. 'Call me Barney' and 'my door is always open' was the mantra of the new managing director from the United States. But this did not go down well with the manual workers who quickly caricatured the message as 'bullshit from Barney'. The 'softer' managerial approach was not something they respected because they were not steeped in the middle class culture of humanism and therefore preferred the straightforward and 'down to earth' policies of a 'harder' management system. For that was closer to their masculine self-images (i.e. identities) and associated view of their work as 'tough', physical, material and predictable.

The more 'open', 'softer' and symbolic aspects of this new managerial culture they regarded as effeminate. It belonged in the office culture where predominantly 'pen pushing' women went around in circles, as the men saw it, not contributing anything to the actual production of physical output. Surprisingly, perhaps the shop floor men were much more respectful of the 'hard' figure work

Image 6.4

performed by accountants, even when their accounts were the basis for a redundancy programme. The shop floor seemed to identify with figures more like they did with physical and material reality; numbers were perhaps more 'real' because of their association with mathematics and the natural sciences. Masculine identity could be reinforced by the certainty of physical and mathematical reality but its reproduction depended on its ability to undermine that which it is not – effeminate symbolic reality.

Exercise 6.11

The UK labour market is among the most segregated in Europe: Scott (1994) found that 66 per cent of men worked exclusively or mainly with other men, and 54 per cent of women worked exclusively or mainly with women. Half of women in employment are in just three occupational groups: clerical and secretarial, personal and protective services, and sales, as compared to about one-fifth of men. On the other hand, women are very under-represented in areas such as engineering and sciences (Knights and Richards, 2003).

Provide a brief explanation of this from your own point of view. Compare your account with those of other students carrying out the same exercise. Are there any patterns in the explanations, particularly in relation to the gender of the student providing the explanation?

The irony, of course, is that the men on the shop floor were using material certainties to defend and sustain a symbolic reality – masculine identity. Moreover, in accepting the accounting numbers, these workers participated in their own labour demise (i.e. redundancy), thus removing one of the principal sources of masculine identity – physical work and 'breadwinner' wages. We cannot ascertain the extent to which the redundancy pay and the escape from work might have been seen as adequate compensation for the loss of employment. There is little doubt that their experience of inequality and insecurity makes such payouts seem large *but*, when spread over the period that they might suffer unemployment, they are miserably small.

A classical approach to organizational design, structure and management style might, perhaps, have been the most appropriate for this factory. But this was not due to some universal sense of a 'one best way' (Taylor, 1911) or because it necessarily correlated with effective performance for a mass assembly line production system (Woodward, 1958). Rather, its appropriateness would have been its fit with the shop floor culture where workers appeared to be preoccupied with sustaining or embellishing their masculine identities. What remains in doubt, of course, is whether this classical approach was compatible with the ideology of the company or indeed with the demands of a changing product market in which flexibility of response through close cooperation, relying upon 'soft' skills, between managers and workers was becoming of increasing importance.

What Collinson's study shows is not dissimilar to Paul Willis's (1977) research on working class kids who were found to distance themselves from education because it failed to support their masculine identities. Ending up with no qualifications and few aspirations, these kids enthusiastically reproduce the conditions of their own deprivation as unskilled workers. Partly because it helped to reinforce their masculine identities, Collinson's shop floor workers accepted the 'hard' figures of the accountants as if they could not be challenged. In doing so, they participated in their own eventual redundancy. Which is not to say that challenging the figures would have resulted in them keeping their jobs. But the union would not have been placed in such a weak position to fight the redundancy. In short, it can be argued that the insecure masculine identities of these shop floor workers contributed significantly to the legitimacy of power-knowledge relations (accounting and management) that reproduced the conditions of their own inequality and loss of economic freedom. In a way that parallels these observations, critics of 'human relations' have argued that its emphasis on cooperation glosses over deep-seated differences of power and inequality, and that improving labour prospects and influence over the design of organizational structures rests 'not on spontaneous cooperation but upon the legitimization of industrial conflict through collective bargaining and strikes' (Perrow, 1972, p. 72).

Box 6.24: What about 'industrial relations'?

From mid-century until around the late 1970s the more common practice was one of accommodating conflict through collective negotiations rather than suppressing it. During this period, conflict was viewed less as an aberration to be removed than understood as an expression of incompatible interests and demands for change, especially in relation to inequities in the distribution of material (e.g. income) and symbolic (e.g. status) goods.

Attention to conflict coincided with the challenge to forms of functionalist theory, including closed and open systems theory, structure is understood in relation to the functions that it performs in securing organizational survival, health and development. Students of work organizations who questioned whether open systems theory adequately appreciated the contested nature of productive activity and the structures that supported it began in the 1950s and 1960s to research industrial conflict. Especially in the United Kingdom, studies were often informed, and perhaps politically motivated, by a Marxist or neo-Marxist (see earlier discussion) perspective that sought to expose and challenge the inequalities, injustices and the constraints on freedom perpetuated by corporate capitalism.

The emergence of a discipline called 'industrial relations' coincided with the increasing legitimacy of left-of-centre political parties, which identified collective negotiations as a solution to the problems of managing large public bureaucracies. In this process, and regardless of their neo-Marxist sympathies, many industrial relations 'experts' became part of 'the establishment'. This illustrates the shifting nature of the boundary between critical and mainstream thinking, where elements of the former become incorporated into the latter. What was once critical is appropriated and perhaps also varnished so that it becomes fit for mainstream consumption. Earlier, we referred to the initial exclusion from mainstream thinking of 'informal' activities and environmental contingencies. But these were later accommodated within open systems thinking, which began to encompass consideration of the human, political and process dimensions of organization. As in other spheres (e.g. art, drama, music), what is at one time threatening if not intolerable becomes insightful, relevant and valued.

Collective bargaining in which conflicts between employers and employees (e.g. over pay, conditions of work, etc.) can be placed in a mutually acceptable framework of negotiation involves a modification to organizational structure. Instead of the authority of management simply passing down the line through decisions that eventually affect all employees, a mediation of these decisions occurred at the highest level between representatives of management and representatives of labour. Many management decisions, especially those relating to the quantity and quality of available work then had to be negotiated rather than dictated. Collective bargaining became a new means of management control with unions securing the consent of the workforce in return for hard-fought negotiations on wages and other terms and conditions of employment. And unions were thereby enlisted into ensuring that agreements were honoured by their members – and thus became like an arm of management.

Manufacturing consent: Obscuring exploitation Distancing himself from the analysis provided by Braverman, and drawing upon his experience as a machine operator working in a multinational corporation, Michael Burawoy argues that the key to understanding the development and reproduction of capitalism is not the separation of conception (organizing work) from execution (work practices). Rather, it is workers' involvement in the practices (e.g. piece-work machining of diesel engines) through which organizational structures are reproduced that obscures the extraction of surpluses (i.e. profit) from employees (see Box 6.25). As we noted earlier, Burawoy's analysis stands as a corrective to Braverman's deliberate exclusion of the role of workers' consciousness in reproducing as well as resisting forms of organizational structure and control. Whereas Braverman concentrates on evidence of what he regards as an inevitable trajectory of de-skilling and degradation, Burawoy examines how the same shop floor activity is simultaneously an articulation of an imperfect form of management control and a compromised expression of workers' resistance (see Chapter 2).

At the centre of Burawoy's analysis is the notion that shop floor resistance to management control rarely turns into revolt because the exploitation of their labour is obscured from workers by their absorption in the realities – for example, the activities and 'games' that make working life more meaningful and less oppressive – that they construct in the process of participating in their own subordination. To explain their importance, Burawoy contrasts the situation of the employee with that of the serf. For serfs, the extraction of a surplus from their labour to maintain the materially and symbolically privileged lifestyle of the feudal lord is comparatively transparent. For feudal relations of production require a proportion of what the serf produces to be physically handed over to the lord. What justifies this *social* arrangement and holds it in place is the ideology that presents it as a *natural* order ordained by God in which the lord has an obligation to ensure a minimum level of well-being for the serfs in return for their service and loyalty.

In capitalist societies, in contrast, comparatively underprivileged groups have struggled to establish democratically elected governments through which basic public services and welfare provisions are funded by taxation revenues. For most people, the gravest impacts of inequality are averted, and this is facilitated by the free exchange of labour for a wage. Unlike the serf, the worker is in principle free to sell his/her labour to whichever buyer (i.e. employer) that s/he chooses.

According to Burawoy, however, it is at the very point of production or of service delivery – where people are engaged in productive labour – that the extraction of surplus value from the labour of working people is obscured. Forms of 'making out' at work, including participation in competitive, productivity games among workers, 'had the effect of generating consent and of obscuring the conditions that framed them . . . as we slaved away on our machines trying to make our quotas we

Box 6.25: Obscuring surplus value and the significance of the 'subjective' aspects of work

'[Braverman] assimilates the separation of conception and execution to the fundamental structure of capitalist control. In so doing he treats what is but a single expression of capitalist control as its essence. . . . I have tried to construct the features common to all forms of the capitalist labour process. I have defined these in terms of what has to be accomplished – namely, the obscuring and securing of surplus value . . . Braverman's restricted attention to the "objective" elements of work does not allow us to understand the nature of control – for, by definition, control involves what Braverman would refer to as "subjective" aspects of work and what I will refer to as political and ideological processes.'

Source: Burawoy, M. (1985) *The Politics of Production*, London: Verso, p. 35.

"We offer competitive pay, good benefits and an attractive severance package."

Image 6.5

manufactured not only parts of diesel engines, not only relations of cooperation and domination, but also consent to those activities and relations' (Burawoy, 1986, p. 11).

In such ways, the exploitative nature of capitalist relations *of* production are seen to be routinely obscured by employees' lived experience of relations *in* production. Much industrial work is unpleasant as it is physically demanding (e.g. tiring) or mentally draining (e.g. monotonous). But, even in the most physically and emotionally demanding conditions, employees are creative and skilful in developing diverse coping and compensating mechanisms that render such work minimally bearable and provide relative satisfactions in the sense that they offer a degree of 'temporary relief from the discomfort of certain work realities' (Baldamus, 1961 p. 53, cited in Burawoy, 1985, p. 37). In short, Burawoy follows Marx and Braverman in conceiving of capitalist relations of production as inherently oppressive and exploitative, but emphasizes that it is necessary to appreciate what happens in the very process of production in order to arrive at an adequate understanding of how this structure of work organization operates and is maintained.

Thinkpoint 6.14

Think of a time when immersion in some aspect of an activity diverted or distracted your attention from appreciating the bigger picture and the place of such activity within it. To what extent did others encourage your involvement in this activity? And what were the consequences?

As an illustration of this argument, Burawoy (1979) highlights the importance of various 'games' devised by workers to gain relative satisfactions, generally by carving out a sphere and/or sense of control, however partial and limited. Such attention to workers' games and related 'informal practices', Burawoy notes, is usually considered to be of marginal interest to mainstream and especially to critical students of work and organization, who have tended to interpret them, respectively, as more or less functional for worker retention and productivity or irrelevant to understanding workers' struggles and the development of collective forms of resistance.

In mainstream analysis, games are associated with restrictions of output as workers police each other's productivity or they are understood to counter demoralization and disaffection, and thereby limit psychological withdrawal, unproductive time and labour turnover. For Burawoy, however, the games and other practices that generate 'relative satisfactions' are absolutely central. Participation in them, he argues, 'generates the legitimacy of the conditions that define [the] rules and objectives' (Burawoy, 1986, p. 38) of capitalist economic organization. In other words, they are fundamental to the process of reproducing organizational structure. They are not deliberately 'designed in' to this structure but, nonetheless, they are critical for analysing its operation. By valuing and pursuing such games and practices, employees routinely and unintentionally take as given and reproduce the wider set of production relations in which capital systematically extracts surplus from labour.

An unintended consequence of engaging in games, etc. – in which management may often collude when they are either powerless to intervene or assess that the games assist their own objectives – is maintenance of the 'conditions' that make possible the activity of game playing. What are those conditions? Burawoy answers: 'having to come to work, the expropriation of unpaid labour' (ibid., p. 38). So, it is through employees' creative efforts to make work more bearable or even enjoyable that, according to Burawoy, the obscuring as well as the securing of surplus value is accomplished. Consent does not proceed, and is not a precondition of, employees' participation in production relations, nor is it engendered by the skilful interventions of management. Rather, employees' consent is generated through the process of participating in the games that they create.

Burawoy's analysis is valuable in drawing attention to how employees' participation in games reproduces the organizational structures without any necessary intention to do so. His assumption is that this is simply an unintended consequence of employees' concerns to transform the grinding routines of shop floor work into something more pleasurable and minimally bearable. Here we can see some similarities with Collinson's study of shop floor workers who participated in a subculture that had the effect of enhancing their masculinity, but Burawoy sees no gender element in the preoccupation of his workers with competition, even though this is a feature of so many aspects of contemporary capitalist economic organization. Nonetheless, Burawoy does point to, although he does not elaborate upon, the extent to which employees '*develop a stake* in those rules and objectives' (ibid., p. 38) that form part-and-parcel of game playing and related informal practices, 'as can be seen when management intervenes to change them or somehow infringes them' (ibid., p. 38). In other words, it is not simply the existence of the games but employees' *identification* with their rules that ensures their contribution to the maintenance of organizational structures, which dominate them, and, if the thinking of Marx or Braverman is accepted, exploits them.

The limitations of Burawoy's analysis stems from the assumption that extraction of surplus is *obscured* as well as secured through relations in production. Equally possible, and arguably more likely, is the view that (1) the issue of exploitation per se is not a live one for most employees; and (2) that, in many cases, employees are aware of how investors and managers systematically organize productive activity to ensure that an adequate profit is appropriated. They may also calculate that their own earnings power, and the material standard of living that accompanies this, is likely to be greater within a capitalist economic system than in any system that replaces it. As Burawoy (1986) himself acknowledges, there is no *imperative* that workers will come to regard themselves as economically exploited (rather than, say, psychologically dissatisfied) as their understanding of themselves and their situation is mediated and organized through 'political and ideological processes' (ibid., p. 35). As a consequence of these processes, in which employees actively participate, they *may* come to regard the structures of capitalist economic organization, including competition, as normal and broadly beneficial.

Controversies and debates

Self-discipline and the panopticon It is relevant to appreciate how efforts to address feelings of insecurity and the associated desire to maintain or reinforce an established sense of identity serve to reproduce the status quo. Any identity is precarious and vulnerable to challenge, a precariousness that produces insecurity. From this perspective, it is not simply game playing or other broad political and ideological processes that serve to explain how organizational structures are reproduced. In addition, and perhaps more fundamentally, it is the process of stimulating and then addressing feelings of insecurity that holds the key to maintaining the status quo. Identification with the disciplines of organization, to which Michel Foucault's analyses have made a lasting contribution, provides the practical means of holding insecurity in check.

It is impossible to do justice to the scope and depth of Foucault's contribution to the contemporary analysis of social relations. It is possible only to provide a sketch of his thinking as it applies directly to the study of organizational structure. Most relevant and accessible are his ideas about discipline and his discussion of the panopticon as a dramatic way of conveying how control operates in modern organizations.

The panopticon (all-seeing apparatus) was a design for a prison developed in the 19th century by Jeremy Bentham in which guards occupied a central tower so that they were able to see into the prisoners' cells without themselves being seen. In this way, prisoners had to assume that they were continuously under surveillance, rather than only when a guard checked their door. The broader significance of this arrangement is that it encourages individual prisoners to engage in a process of continuous self-surveillance and related self-discipline as they anticipate that they may be being watched. A contemporary equivalent is the use of CCTV cameras, which have proved effective in deterring crime within their sphere of operation, just as open plan offices deter unproductive activity. The panopticon example has direct parallels for work organizations in which direct control by gang bosses or supervisors is replaced by other, less personal and immediate forms of surveillance and discipline that operate at a distance. So, for example, even when behaviour cannot be directly observed, the development of performance measures and targets enables managers to make outcomes visible and, of course to compare performance levels. However, and crucially, the significance of such measures does not reside in their existence per se but rather it depends upon the amenability of employees to internalizing their direction.

Box 6.26: Designing today's prisons – Los Angeles twin towers jail

'While direct supervision was the hot new trend 15 years ago, today, high-tech circular designs dominate the punitive cutting edge. Chief Barry King, who runs Twin Towers, is convinced that the round design of the jail, coupled with its reliance on technology, is the only thing that makes the 4000-bed, maximum security jail affordable to operate. "In an old jail, everything was designed in blocks – you needed more people to walk the rows of cells. Over here, you can have one guard watch the whole area," he says, gesturing at the stylish new jail that rises outside his window.

To develop efficient plans for people like King, designers have looked all the way back to Jeremy Bentham, the 18th century British utilitarian philosopher and grandfather of the hottest trend in prison design today. Bentham, a social reformer, drew up plans for his ideal prison, the panopticon – a circular cell-house with a central guard station where a few officers could watch over hundreds of inmates stacked many stories high. Prison administrators following Bentham believed that the specter of constant surveillance would make prisoners more apt to follow rules and help them integrate into society when they were released. Bentham's plan also required fewer guards – a fact that has not been lost on today's prison designers.'

Source: Rendon, J. (1999) *Inside the New High-Tech Lock-Downs* (http://archive.salon.com/21st/feature/1998/09/cov_08feature.html).

The panopticon is an example of what Foucault (1977) terms 'hierarchical observation', whereby a privileged group exercises power through its surveillance of a subordinate group. The relationship between management as observers, and workers as the target of surveillance, illustrates this phenomenon. It is accompanied by 'normalizing judgement' involving the punishment of those who stray from the norm and the rewarding of those who respect it. Finally the 'examination' combines 'hierarchical observation' (the difference between the examiner and the examined) and 'normalizing judgement' that is exercised by the examiner who assesses and classifies the examinees in a series of reports. Its intent is to produce particular, *self-disciplining* individuals whose very perceptions of reality are governed by such discipline. Discipline, however, is not conceived as inherently negative or repressive, or as something that individuals would necessarily avoid or resist. Instead, it is recognized to be enabling as well as constraining, as something that is as much welcomed by individuals as they bemoan it. Even prisoners might regard panoptical control as less intrusive than the closer and less predictable form of attention provided by a guard's tour of the cells. To the extent that discipline is internalized, it is far reaching in its effects as it 'resides in every perception, every judgement, every act. In its positive sense it enables and makes possible; and negatively it excludes and marginalizes' (Deetz, 2004, p. 29). So, for example, it enables prisoners to escape the *personal* attentions of their guards by making surveillance a more distanced, impersonal process. But it also reduces, if not excludes, the possibility of influencing how they are treated.

Box 6.27: The power of the panopticon

'He who is subjected to a field of visibility, and who knows it, assumes responsibility for the constraints of power; he makes them play spontaneously upon himself; he inscribes in himself the power relation in which he simultaneously plays both roles; he becomes the principle of his own subjection.'

Source: Foucault, M. (1977) *Discipline and Punish: The Birth of the Prison*, Harmondsworth: Penguin, p. 203.

One thing that such discipline tends to 'exclude and marginalize' is forms of knowledge that encourage critical reflection upon the presence and pervasiveness of disciplinary power. Foucault (1980) describes this as 'subjugated knowledge' – it occupies the margins of visibility in a society and only surfaces once it has already begun to be taken account of by the established powers. Examples of such knowledge, which have now assumed a less than marginal status, include knowledge of the ecological damage perpetrated by industry, and feminist perceptions of the gendered aspects of management and organization. Consideration of how discipline operates therefore offers a possible way of understanding how it is that capitalist relations of production and, more specifically the routine extraction of surplus from labour, come to be so widely normalized and taken for granted.

Such analysis suggests that it is through the institutionalization of disciplinary power – in the form of hierarchical observation, normalized judgement and the examination – that the structures of contemporary work organization have been determined and are maintained. In modern organizations, Deetz notes how, for example, HRM specialists exercise disciplinary power insofar as they 'create "normalized" knowledge, operating procedures, and methods of inquiry, and suppress competitive practices' (Deetz, 2004, p. 36).

The account of disciplinary power presented in Box 6.28 illustrates how mainstream thinking, in the form of 'soft' HRM principles, aspires to achieve the full, self-disciplined identification of the individual with the role that they are allocated to fulfil as an employee within the organization. However, this aspiration is rarely if ever met, if only because employees frequently have numerous identifications (e.g. with family, hobbies, community, religion, etc.) that are not necessarily easily reconciled with 'the vocabulary and divisions of the work function' (ibid., p. 38). For example, family commitments may conflict with work obligations. Identification with the values and traditions of a particular ethnic community may sit uneasily with secular, corporate expectations of behaviour. In the language of mainstream thinking, organizations are 'open systems'.

Box 6.28: Human resource management in Foucauldian perspective

'Core to the human resources function is to provide and police the vocabularies of attention and division in the workplace. This includes partitioning the organization into functions, ranking, differential pay and job classification . . . The implicit values and hierarchies become reified and suppress potential discussions and conflicts . . . The individual's identity in this discourse becomes connected to the vocabulary and divisions of the work function in the organization . . . The individual is given a vocabulary for self-management. The individual with the help of this new knowledge can now monitor and act on the self, thereby working to remove the defects and acquire the capacities to match the qualities of the job.'

Source: Deetz, S. (2004) 'Disciplinary power, conflict suppression and human resources management', in M. Alvesson and H. Willmott (eds). *Studying Management Critically*, London: Sage, p.p. 37–39.

HRM policies are frequently intended to smooth out tensions arising from employees' competing identifications – by establishing work–life balance policies, by recognizing and supporting diversity in workplaces or by taking steps to minimize the risk of employees concerns being represented by a union rather than an in-house staff association, for example. But HRM inevitably competes with the priorities and expediency of other specialists – in production, accounting or marketing – who promote their own, distinctive judgements in relation to the management of their staff. Production managers, for example, are more interested in getting staff to hit targets than in applying HRM policies in a consistent manner.

Box 6.29: Sex discrimination in recruitment

In some research conducted on sex discrimination in recruitment (Collinson et al., 1990), the HRM Department had begun to distribute its functions to line management but there was some tension when it came to equal opportunities because line managers wanted simply to recruit, promote and develop staff quickly so as to limit any disruption to production. Complying with equal opportunities legislation was the last thing on their minds, but HRM felt they were shirking their professional responsibilities if they did not interfere in decisions. Conflict was greater as a result of distributing the functions down the line than when previously HRM had assumed control of all matters connected with personnel. Yet assuming control had resulted in tensions and resistance from line managers, especially relating to the delay in reaching decisions, and the lack of knowledge that HRM had of the work tasks and jobs to which they were recruiting.

Questions

- Why do you think HRM distributed their functions and responsibilities to line managers?
- What is the relationship between these developments and broader issues in society?

HRM policies and practices also compete with other spheres of life where employees may prefer or be encouraged to identify with, and assess themselves in terms of, the 'devoted parent', the 'loving partner', the 'dutiful sibling', feminist, race or minority protest, the 'pillar of the community', 'one of the lads', etc. For this reason, attempts to 'provide and police the vocabularies of attention and division in the workplace' (ibid., p. 37) are likely to prove partial and fragile. Achieving the full and *unreserved identification* of employees with such demands can be expected to be more difficult than securing their *pragmatic compliance*. Nonetheless, compliance may well be sufficient to ensure that conflicts are adequately, if not completely, suppressed for the practical purpose of securing (at least minimal) employee participation in the maintenance and renewal of established organization structures. The suppression of conflict associated with mainstream organization studies and managerial practice has not always been the pre-eminent strategy for managing labour.

Diversity studies Studies of conflict have tended to focus most of their attention on class conflicts and workplace struggles between labour and management over terms and conditions, and to rather ignore other fundamental divisions such as gender, race, religion and capacity limitations. These were generally seen as the terrain of those focusing on equal opportunity and other personnel issues within personnel management, or what is now termed human resource management (HRM). More recently, the interest in different social divisions at work has coalesced around diversity studies that, like industrial relations, lie on the boundary of mainstream and critical approaches. While deriving from fairly radical and critical studies of gender, race and other discriminations within organizations, their recombination and renaming within diversity studies hare resulted in their modification to make them more compatible with managerial concerns (Konrad, Prasad and Pringle, 2005). In addition, as Blommaert and Verschueren (1998, p. 3) have argued, diversity studies and the debate they stimulate 'may be more of a problem than diversity itself. In other words, a major part of the problem consists precisely in viewing diversity as a problem'. This understanding of diversity as a problem can generate some of the most efficient practices of discrimination, albeit subtly concealed by rhetorics of tolerance (ibid., p. 4). We have seen this development in the ascendancy of concerns about, if not a demonization of, asylum seekers, migrant workers, and especially illegal immigrants in many European countries – a threat presented in the popular media as apparently equivalent to the now defunct communist domino effect. In the name of stability, there is an attempt to preserve an equilibrium of established organizational structures for those who feel threatened by new entrants who are perceived to lack a legitimate claim to available resources, including employment.

Exercise 6.12

In Bar Mar, women represent around 70 per cent and ethnic minorities around 20 per cent of the staff in the chain, but there are only two women on the board – Margaret (the CEO) and Sally (Director of Human Resources) and no ethnic minorities. Also the next layers down of senior managers responsible for the areas and all white men.

Given a woman in charge and the gender distribution of labour being so skewed towards women, how would you go about understanding the absence of both women and minorities in the senior ranks of management? Discuss your accounts with other students and ask each other to justify the arguments.

Early studies of inequality at work sought generally to frame their analyses within the overall legislative framework around equal opportunity or anti-discrimination laws. Diversity studies, in contrast, seek to incorporate managerial thinking by showing how diversity is a problem that can be transformed into a resource if only it is managed properly. One way in which diversity can be seen as a resource is by focusing on its potential contribution to providing customer service (clearly one of the major concerns of Margaret at Bar Mar). Since the customers of most companies reflect a diversity of age groups, the lesser able, social classes and occupational groups, ethnic and racial minorities, gender, religious identifications and sexual preferences, it is commercially prudent to ensure that some of these same diversities are present among staff who deal with them.

Box 6.30: Diversity statement of the University of California, Berkeley

'Educating managers and staff on how to work effectively in a diverse environment helps the University prevent discrimination and promote inclusiveness. There is evidence that managing a diverse work force well can contribute to increased staff retention and productivity. It can enhance the organization's responsiveness to an increasingly diverse world of customers, improve relations with the surrounding community, increase the organization's ability to cope with change, and expand the creativity of the organization. In addition to contributing to these business goals, diversity can contribute to goals unique to the University as a public institution, such as increased accessibility and accountability to all residents of the state. Good management of a diverse work force can increase productivity and enhance the University's ability to maneuver in an increasingly complex and diverse environment.'

Source: http://hrweb.berkeley.edu/aaeeo/diverse.htm

In the past, the divisions associated with diversity were assessed to be a problem to be managed by equal opportunity policies, grievance procedures and by managing with sensitivity to difference. Increasingly, 'diversity' is invoked as a previously unrecognized resource. The existence of diversity is understood to make it more likely that customers will encounter a response that is more attuned to their preferences and expectations even if it is not always possible to achieve a perfect match between customers and company representatives. When thought of in this way, diversity policies are seen to have a commercial pay-off insofar as they facilitate interactions with customers as well as protecting companies from current anti-discrimination laws; and, of course, they are also more congruent with broader human rights legislation and contemporary social and political moralities.

But there are reasons other than commercial prudence or 'progressive' morality for establishing diversity employment structures and practices. Some Western economies are experiencing rates of full employment and/or shortages of labour in certain areas (e.g. healthcare) even before taking into account the demographics of longer life spans and lower birth rates, which are having the effect of reducing the proportion of the population that is economically active. By 2025, 16 per cent of the world's population will be over 60 (*Start the Week*, BBC Radio 4, 16 January 2004) and, in the advanced countries, more skewed since in a majority there are already over 20 per cent of the population over 60. By 2045 this is expected to rise to 30–45 per cent and by 2050 in the United Kingdom 20 per cent of the population will be over 70 – an age that is considered by most to be beyond active employment (*Observer*, 25 January 2004). Despite this, government policies are only just beginning to recognize that their 'ageist' retirement policies may not just be discriminatory but also economically damaging, as the dependent population increases precisely at a time that the number of active

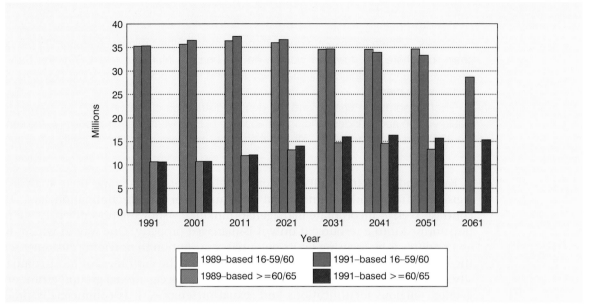

SOURCE: © STATISTICAL SOURCE: GOVERNMENT ACTUARY DEPARTMENT

Figure 6.8 UK working and pensioner populations, 1991 to 2061 (1981 and 1991 based population projections)

workers is falling dramatically. Government actuaries have predicted that the number of economically active individuals per dependent will fall from 3.3:1 in 1991 to 2.2:1 by 2030, representing an increase in the dependency support ratio of 50 per cent (see Figure 6.8).

Exercise 6.13

What are the implications of this situation for management given the existing structure of organizations? Can you think of any solutions that you would recommend were you in a position to advise employers?

Despite demographic knowledge providing us with fairly accurate predictions of future age distributions of the population, until quite recently the downsizing policies of many corporations meant a shedding of numerous workers in their 50s with early retirement incentives or simple redundancy packages. Given the imminent demographic explosion of the economically inactive, this policy was clearly short-sighted and, of course, the EU has now sought to reverse these trends even to the point of introducing a more flexible state retirement age. From 2006, workers will be given financial incentives to defer taking their state pension at age 65 and continue working perhaps until 70 or later. It is interesting to recognize that ageism is now beginning to be taboo, yet age has never been an obstacle to the elite in society. Political and corporate leaders and even media superstars have often worked well into old age.

It has long been an argument of equal opportunity supporters that the discriminatory leadership and management of organizations is counter-productive since it precludes taking advantage of the best talents within their workforces. The most classic examples are given by the women in management movement who indicate that in large numbers of organizations (e.g. banks, supermarkets) women are often more than 50 per cent of the workforce yet have minimal representation in the senior ranks, especially on the board of directors.

Exercise 6.14

List as many names as you can of people who have continued working beyond what in the past has been the normal retirement age (65 for men and 60 for women). Discuss your results with other students and seek to explain why the list is distributed in the way that it is in terms of class, gender and race.

Diversity theorists challenge this approach to promoting equal opportunity since they believe that demanding reverse discrimination inevitably creates resentment among white male employees and managers. Instead, they argue that the organizational culture needs to be changed (Mullins, 2002, p. 301) so that everyone believes in equal opportunity, thus avoiding any resentment when minorities or women climb the hierarchy. This, however, reveals how the diversity approach is on the boundary of the mainstream, seeking to drag the more critical approaches of, say, feminists or race relations theorists with them but offering what, from a critical perspective, is comparatively naive. Critical approaches perceive culture as something an organization *is*, not what it *has* (see Chapter 10) and, if this is the case, it is not possible to change it by fiat.

Indeed, after over 30 years of legislation against sex and racial discrimination, the distribution of women and minorities in the higher echelons of organizations has changed only marginally. It could, of course, be argued that laws provide the conditions that make it possible for cultural change and it is now less legitimate to be openly discriminatory (e.g. sexist or racist), but there is often a gap between what people 'say' and what their policies require, and what is done. Consequently, few managers or leaders would openly declare their prejudices in public, but the statistics on the distribution of women and minorities in organizational hierarchies suggests that inequality of opportunity is still rife. Only very slowly are organizations recognized to be 'institutionally' – that is, structurally – racist or discriminatory so that the introduction of diversity policies is found to be ineffective, and simply provides a convenient smokescreen when responding to critical observers.

Box 6.31: The MacPherson Report on the Metropolitan Police Force (London)

In 1999, the MacPherson Report presented its evidence following an investigation of the unsolved murder of a black youth, Stephen Lawrence, in an unprovoked attack allegedly by a white gang. It concluded that the British Police Force suffered from institutional racism, which it defined as 'the collective failure of an organization to provide an appropriate and professional service to people because of their colour, culture or ethnic origin'. Despite individual police officers not meaning to act in a racially discriminatory way, the outcome was racist. The reason for this is that the institution was found to be steeped in practices insensitive to racial and ethnic differences. After the publication of the Report, the Metropolitan Police set up an independent advisory group to advise it on race issues. Four black members of this group subsequently resigned, saying they had been reduced to 'nodding dogs'; that the group was controlled by the police; and that they had lost confidence in the independence and credibility of the advisory group.

Source: BBC News (at bbcnews.com).

A more critical approach to discrimination draws on feminist, post-colonial and post-modernist analyses of gender, ethnicity and other diversities. The comparatively small number of such studies that are relevant to an analysis of organizational structure indicate a major chasm between the equal opportunity literature that generally takes a liberal political position and seeks to enhance women's role in management and a more radical re-examination of the conditions and consequences of sex and race discrimination. At its most critical, advocates of equal opportunity favour 'positive discrimination', which, for example, would seek to displace men from senior positions and replace them by women but leave the structure of hierarchical inequality unchanged.

By contrast, more radical commentators seek to theorize notions of gender and race in order to understand and then perhaps disrupt the resilience of organizations to social transformation. It is argued that far from generating a more open view of the relations between the sexes and races within organizations, the equal opportunity literature simply reinforces and renders more legitimate the hierarchy of power and privilege. Feminist, post-colonial and post-modernist analyses, on the other hand, seek to understand the reproduction of various inequalities in terms of historical and contemporary relations of power and subjectivity, drawing on notions of, for example, feminine and masculine identities, and post-colonial conceptions of knowledge. The approach taken here is similar but complements their analyses with further discussions of identity, insecurity and freedom.

Conclusion

Contributions The critical approach differs from the mainstream in refusing to reproduce the taken for granted view that organization studies is only valuable if it contributes to the productivity, performance and/or profitability of administration or business. In contrast, it makes the human, political and process dimensions of organizations central to its pursuits. It:

- Demonstrates how power and knowledge as well as concepts of inequality, insecurity, identity and freedom can help us to understand the way that organizations are designed and structured.
- Focuses on the relationship between society and organization.
- Resists legitimizing the status quo.
- Develops an awareness of how ideas about organization and management help to shape the world that organization theorists aspire to analyse.

While focusing on matters other than productivity and performance in order to compensate for the dominance of these ideas in the mainstream, the critical approach generates insights that indirectly may not be unhelpful to practitioners in securing their objectives. For example, it may help them to avoid too myopic a concentration on profit and efficiency that can be self-defeating. It is clear from critical research that organizations are much more complex than the mainstream literature, in its search for 'quick fixes' or simple causal patterns, presumes. Understanding, for example, the part that identity plays in employees' lives or how some level of insecurity can be productive, yet incapacitating if excessive, is probably of more value than misleading beliefs about the perfect organizational design. Employees are more likely to be creative when they are not resentful about the levels of inequality or discrimination, and where their every movement is not constrained by the structures of management control.

Clearly the design and structure of an organization is not independent of wider economic, social and political relations. Mergers and acquisitions affect organizations not just when they occur but, in a capitalist society, by their very possibility, presenting a continual threat to organizations. Going international or even global (see Chapter 12) can be a strategy that challenges organizational designs and structures. Since organizations are so dynamic it makes sense to challenge conventional thinking about them. We also need to be aware that while the direct relationship between theory and practice or ideas and their adoption, is not always obvious, academic research and writing indirectly and perhaps quite slowly filters into the consciousness of those who are studied.

Indeed, it is possible that organizations – principally in the form of industrial and commercial corporations – have become more powerful in their effects upon societies than the other way around (Ackroyd, 2002). Two explanations are offered for this: first, organizations are in the direct control of wealthy elites as a consequence of the domination of economic activity in what is rapidly becoming a global capitalist economy; and, secondly, those who do not have access to, or are excluded from powerful work organizations become, in effect, second class citizens. These developments are linked to broad-ranging changes in the socio-economic structure of society in which there is an 'increase in

---

Box 6.32: Corporate lobbying of governments

'The complex, often unaccountable EU decision-making procedures and the lack of a truly European public debate are obstacles to democracy, but provide fertile ground for corporate lobbyists,' says the Corporate Europe Observatory (CEO), an Amsterdam-based campaign group that monitors the political influence of business.

'Lobby groups succeed all too frequently in postponing, weakening or blocking sorely needed progress in EU social, environmental and consumer protections,' Olivier Hoedeman,

research coordinator at the CEO told IPS. 'We believe such groups are leading the EU to becoming self-centred in international negotiations, including the EU's negotiating strategies within the World Trade Organisation (WTO) trade talks.'

The European Parliament website lists 5039 accredited lobbyists working for a range of familiar names such as McDonald's and Visa. The CEO puts the total number of lobbyists at somewhere between 15 000 and 20 000, and says two-thirds of these represent big business.

Source: Stefania Bianchi, 'EU: Corporate lobbying grows', *Inter Press Service*, 22 December 2004.

the importance of the economic, as opposed to the political or civil, institutions in shaping the life-chances of people' (ibid., p. 250). In this context, it is those who occupy the top positions in the largest corporations who are seen to shape our destiny by, for example, deploying their resources to fund political parties and/or lobbying governments so that policies broadly supportive of corporations are pursued.

In a mainstream approach to the study of organizations, little attention is given either to the wider politico-economic context, such as the lobbying of governments, that conditions the formation and reproduction of organization structure or to the significance of the micro-politics of 'game playing' in the workplace that serves to reproduce employees participation in the maintenance of established structures. The critical approach is concerned to take analysis beyond these boundaries as it examines the design and structuring of organizations as an historical and political process. This process is understood to involve struggles between groups pursuing differing priorities, and accruing benefits and penalties – consequences that are themselves widely promoted and delivered through the medium of organizations. The critical approach is concerned with scrutinizing what mainstream thinking either takes for granted or excludes from its field of vision. It favours an opening up and problematizing of what we commonsensically know and value about organizations, with the possibility that their design and priorities might be radically changed for the better.

Limitations As supporters of critical approaches, our inclination is to defend rather than to attack them. But if we are to be consistently critical, then we must be self-critical. Here then are some of the limitations of critical approaches:

- Can be too human-centred.
- May neglect the global nature of capitalism.
- May neglect the domination of financial power.
- Can be theoretical and idealistic rather than practical and applied/pragmatic.

Because critics are seeking to challenge the domination of concerns with productivity, performance and profitability found in the mainstream, they may tend to focus too heavily on human-centred and environmental issues. Of course, the focus of this chapter on the structure of organizations leads necessarily to a critique that demonstrates how formal structures depend upon human beings for their design, development and implementation. Neglecting the human dimension must, as a consequence, be self-defeating. Much mainstream thinking has gradually incorporated an appreciation of this insight – from human relations to more contemporary attention as forms of 'empowerment'. But it does so by modelling human nature in a way that is malleable to 'enlightened' forms of management control. It is assumed that there is an essential underlying consensus within organizations, and that applying progressive techniques will ensure employee commitment. Critical approaches have regarded such techniques as manipulative – an assessment that has often been based upon an inadequately examined humanistic philosophy. There has been insufficient appreciation of how humanism, and especially its preoccupation with the autonomy of the individual, can be oppressive, or what Foucault (1984) termed the 'greatest confinement'. Humanism, it has been argued, forces individuals back on themselves, makes them reliant on their own devices for a sense of self, and it is this that fuels the insecurity we all tend to have about our identity.

Focusing on the human dimension also may lead us to neglect broader structures of power such as global capitalism, international regulation and finance capital. Recent protests about global capitalism have proliferated. International economic and political events have been skilfully targeted and lampooned, thereby generating massive media coverage and considerable public sympathy. Effective use of global communication has been made through the internet, which has probably served the cause of anti-globalization protesters and sympathizers better than it has the corporations and international institutions that they seek to criticize for their exploitation of developing countries, labour and the environment. Global corporations and the finance capital that sustains them have been depicted as exploitative of the comparatively weak, and as dominators of other organizations, especially suppliers and distributors. To the extent to which governments have sided with the largest corporations, established party politics has become discredited and activists who pursue single issue politics, have become increasingly linked together by a common antagonism towards the divisive and damaging policies of global corporations. Critical approaches have yet to rise to the challenge of developing analyses that resonate with, and provide academically credible studies of, these contemporary issues and movements.

Despite what has been claimed above regarding the indirect and often unintended benefits of critical analyses to practitioners, another problem is that there is a tendency to be abstract, idealistic and over-theoretical. This is partly because the immediate audience for critical research is more likely to be other academics rather than practitioners.

To conclude, the design and structure of organizations is discussed in mainstream texts predominantly through the lens of a systems model where the parts of an organization are seen as similar to the parts of a body or a machine. Like a car, the organization is seen to work most efficiently when designed properly. Hence, even when it is recognized that designs and structures are contingent on the context in which they are to be applied, theorists find it difficult not to search for the holy grail of a technique, or set of techniques, that will remedy organizational problems. Notably, the mainstream literature does not give much attention to how power is relational. Instead, senior managers are seen to possess power, much like someone owns a house. When others are seen to exercise power, such as subordinates or unions, this is not a trigger for appreciating its relational quality but, rather, a stimulus for seeing how it can be either suppressed (scientific management) or harnessed (human relations) to managerial ends according to the circumstances (contingency theory). There is an associated tendency to believe that decisions at the top will, and should, be automatically executed lower down the hierarchy, much like we expect the car to move once it is switched on and we press the accelerator.

To avoid such simplistic thinking, it is necessary to conceptualize power as a relationship, and thereby to see it as only fully effective when its exercise transforms individuals (e.g. other managers and subordinates) into subjects that secure a sense of their own purpose, meaning, identity and reality through behaving in accordance with its demands. A critical approach fills that vacuum as well as identifying a range of other concepts that help us to understand how organizations are more than the sum of their structural parts.

Since almost all organizations in contemporary society are designed or structured around a hierarchy, there is no escape from power. But it has been argued throughout this chapter that the structure of an organization can never guarantee to deliver what it is designed to do. This is because, as was discussed in the introductory chapter to this book, power is a relationship and depends on those subjected to it consenting or complying with its demands. Often the structure of an organization will be sufficient to command consent or compliance since it embodies authority and legitimacy, or simply because there seems to be no realistic alternative. Of course, subordinates benefit from their membership of an organization as well as superordinates. Mostly this takes the form of some economic benefit in the form of wages or salaries but work is far more than a mere economic activity – it is also social. As members of organizations, we also derive meaning and purpose from our work and this provides us with a sense of identity and security. While our knowledge is important to an organization and will help us in gaining employment, we also learn a great deal from work; and this practical knowledge enhances our sense of freedom or self-determination, for example, to advance in the hierarchy or to move elsewhere.

Although there is much inequality in organizations and this is reflected precisely in the hierarchical design and structure, it is constrained by the necessity to secure the consent, cooperation, creativity and collaboration of those engaged in production. This is made easier because of hegemonically inscribed values such as respect for authority and property, the law, the legitimacy of management, and the belief that inequality is a function of just rewards for ability and effort, etc. Mainstream organization theory trades on these values without ever discussing their influence and significance. A critical approach raises them as important issues to understand, challenge and debate – with the prospect of contributing to a process of more informed and democratic change.

Discussion questions

1 How does the design and structure of an organization affect people?

2 Are the main assumptions underlying a systems approach valid?

3 What are some of the contingencies that need to be considered in relation to an appropriate organization structure?

4 What are the main differences between a classical and an open systems approach to organizational design and structure?

5 What does a critical view of organizational design and structure add to our understanding of organizations?

Further reading

Important empirical studies

Barker, J. R. (1999) *The Discipline of Teamwork*, London: Sage.

Barnard, C. (1938) *The Functions of the Executive*, Cambridge, MA: Harvard University Press.

Beynon, H. (1973) *Working for Ford*, Harmondsworth: Penguin.

Burawoy, M. (1979) *Manufacturing Consent*, Chicago: Chicago University Press.

Frankel, S., Korczynski, M., Shire, K. and Tam, M. (1999) *On the Front Line: Organization of Work in the Information Economy*, New York: Cornell University Press.

Kondo, D. (1990) *Crafting Selves: Power, Gender and Discourses of Identity in a Japanese Workplace*, Chicago, IL: University of Chicago Press.

Kunda, G. (1996) *Engineering Culture*, Philadelphia: Temple University Press.

Nichols, N. and Beynon, H. (1977) *Living with Capitalism*, London: Routledge.

Annotated texts

Daft, R. L. (1995) ***Organization Theory and Design***, **New York: West Publishing Company.** A mainstream textbook that has gone through several editions, this book provides a useful summary of the different theoretical frameworks and models in relation to empirical findings and cases about changes in the design and structure of actual organizations. As well as using a diverse range of pedagogical (teaching) techniques, the book also seeks to provide an integration of different perspectives rather than treating them discretely.

Ackroyd, S. (2002) ***The Organization of Business: Applying Organizational Theory to Contemporary Change***, **Oxford: Oxford University Press.** This book summarizes the mainstream approaches to the diverse ways in which British organizations are designed and structured. Identifying these approaches as informed by contingency theory where there is an absence of any focus on the human dimension, the author offers an alternative view of organizations as designed and structured through processes of negotiation between individuals and groups.

Kanter, R. Moss (1993) ***Men and Women of the Corporation***, **New York: Basic Books.** Based on concrete observations of organizations in action, this book examines the structure of US corporate organizations as a reflection of white male dominated power relations. In this sense, it is an empirical example of how the design and structure of an organization are an outcome of negotiations and career struggles largely between men, but it also pays attention to the increasing demands of the global economy.

Du Gay, P. (2001) ***In Praise of Bureaucracy***, **London: Sage.** Most modern texts have been critical of bureaucratic organizational structures on the basis that they are too inflexible and rule-bound to respond adequately and speedily to the dramatic levels of change in contemporary society. This book bucks the trend, defending bureaucratic forms of organization design and structure as necessary to good government in democratic societies. Following Weber, the author contends that the bureaucratic ethos encompassing impersonal and detached, rule-based decision making can be defended as the most ethically and technically appropriate mechanism for managing responsible public organizations.

More general reading

Ackers, P. and Wilkinson, A. (eds.) (2003) *Understanding Work and Employment: Industrial Relations in Transition*, Oxford: Oxford University Press.

Barley, S. and Kunda, G. (1992) 'Design and devotion: Surges of rational and normative ideologies of control in managerial discourse', *Administrative Science Quarterly*, 37:363–399.

Burrell, G. and Morgan, G. (1970) *Sociological Paradigms and Organisational Analysis*, London: Heinemann.

Dawson, P. (2003) *Understanding Organizational Change*, London: Sage.

Hancock, P. and Tylker, M. (2001) *Work, Postmodernism and Organization*, London: Sage.

Jacques, R. (1996) *Manufacturing the Employee: Management Knowledge from the 19th to the 21st Centuries*, London: Sage.

Kanigel, R. (1997) *One Best Way: Frederick Winslow Taylor and the Enigma of Efficiency*, New York: Viking.

Knights, D. and Willmott, H. C. (eds.) (2000) *The Reengineering Revolution? Critical Studies in Corporate Change*, London: Macmillan.

Lennie, I. (1999) *Beyond Management*, London: Sage

Littler, C. (1982) *The Development of the Labour Process in Capitalist Societies: A Comparative Study of the Transformation of Work Organization in Britain, Japan, and the USA*, London: Heinemann.

Marchington, M., Grimshaw, D., Rubery, J. and Willmott, H. C. (2005) *Fragmenting Work: Blurring Organizational Boundaries and Disordering Hierarchies*, Oxford: Oxford University Press.

McDowell, L. (1997) *Capital Culture*, Oxford: Blackwell.

Roberts, J. (2004) *The Modern Firm: Organization Design for Performance and Growth*, Oxford: Oxford University Press.

Rowlinson, M. (1997) *Organizations and Institutions*, London: Macmillan.

Salaman, G. (1979) *Work Organizations: Resistance and Control*, London: Longman.

Thompson, P. (1983) *The Nature of Work*, London: Macmillan.

Willmott, H. C. and Wilkinson, A. (eds.) (1995) *Making Quality Critical*, London: Routledge.

References

Ackroyd, S. (2002) *The Organization of Business: Applying Organizational Theory to Contemporary Change*, Oxford: Oxford University Press.

Blommaert, J. and Verschueren, J. (1998) *Debating Diversity: Analysing the Discourse of Tolerance*, London: Routledge.

Braverman, H. (1974) *Labor and Monopoly Capital*, New York: Monthly Review Press.

Burawoy, M. (1979) *Manufacturing Consent*, London: Routledge.

Burawoy, M. (1985) *The Politics of Production*, London: Verso.

Burawoy, M. (1986) *The Politics of Production*, London: Verso.

Castells, M. (1996) *The Rise of the Network Society*, Oxford: Blackwell.

Chandler, A. D., Jr. (1962) *Strategy and Structure: Chapters in the History of Industrial Enterprise*, Cambridge, MA: MIT Press.

Clegg, S. and Dunkerley, D. (1980) *Organization, Class and Control*, London: Routledge.

Clegg, S., Kornberger, M. and Pitsis, T. (2005) *Managing and Organizations: An Introduction to Theory and Practice*, London: Sage.

Coase, R. (1937) 'The nature of the firm', *Economica*, 4:386–405.

Collinson, D. (1992) *Managing the Shopfloor: Subjectivity, Masculinity and Workplace Culture*, Berlin: de Gruyter.

Collinson, D., Knights, D. and Collinson, M. (1990) *Managing to Discriminate*, London: Routledge.

Deetz, S. (2004) 'Disciplinary power, conflict suppression and human resource management', in M. Alvesson and H. Willmott (eds.) *Studying Management Critically*, London: Sage.

DiMaggio, P. and Powell, W. (1991) *The New Institutionalism in Organizational Analysis*, Chicago: University of Chicago Press.

Elger, A. (1975) 'Industrial organizations: A processual perspective', in J. B. McKinlay (ed.) *Processing People: Cases in Organizational Behaviour*, New York: Holt, Rinehart and Winston.

Fayol, H. (1916/1949) *General and Industrial Management*, London: Pitman.

Feigenbaum, A. (1983) *Total Quality Control*, New York: McGraw-Hill.

Foucault, M. (1977) *Discipline and Punish: The Birth of the Prison*, Harmondsworth: Penguin.

Foucault, M. (1980) 'Power/knowledge: Selective interviews and other writings 1972–1977', ed. C. Gordon, Brighton: Harvester Press.

Foucault, M. (1984) 'What is enlightenment?', in P. Rabinow (ed.), *The Foucault Reader*, Harmondsworth: Penguin.

Handy, C. (1996) *Beyond Certainty: The Changing Worlds of Organizations*, Boston: Harvard University Press.

Hannan, M. T. and Freeman, J. (1989) *Organizational Ecology*, Cambridge, MA: Harvard University Press.

Hill, S. (1991) 'Why quality circles failed but total quality management might succeed', *British Journal of Industrial Relations*, 29(1):541–568.

Hinings, B. (2003) 'Organizations and their structures', in R. Westwood and S. Clegg (eds.) *Debating Organization: Point-Counterpoint in Organization Studies*, Oxford: Blackwell.

Hobsbawn, E. (1975) *The Age of Capital 1848–1875*, London: Weidenfeld and Nicholson.

Huczynski, A. and Buchanan, D. (2001) *Organizational Behaviour: An introductory Text*, London: Prentice Hall/FT.

Ishiwaka, K. (1985) *What is Total Quality Control?: The Japanese Way*, Englewood Cliffs, NJ: Prentice Hall.

Knights, D. and Richards, W. (2003) 'Sex discrimination in UK academia', *Gender, Work and Organization* 10:2.

Konrad, A. M, Prasad, P. and Pringle, J. (eds.) (2005) *Handbook of Workplace Diversity*, London: Sage.

Mayer, J. P. (1956) *Max Weber and Germany Politics*, London: Faber and Faber.

Mintzberg (1979) *The Structuring of Organizations*, Englewood-Cliffs, NJ: Prentice Hall.

Mowshowitz, A. (2002) *Virtual Organization: Toward a Theory of Societal Transformation Stimulated by Information Technology*, New York: Quorum Books.

Mullins, L. J. (2002) *Management and Organizational Behaviour*, sixth edition, London: Pearson Education Financial Times/Prentice Hall.

Perrow, C. (1972), *Complex Organizations: A Critical Essay*, Glenview, IL: Scott, Foresman and Company.

Pfeffer, J. and Salancik, G. R. (1978) *The External Control of Organizations: A Resource Dependency Perspective*, New York: Harper and Row.

Powell, W. W. (1990) 'Neither market nor hierarchy: Network forms of organization', *Research in Organizational Behaviour*, 12:295–336

Powell, W. W. and DiMaggio, P. J. (1991) 'Introduction', in W. W. Powell and P. J. DiMaggio (eds.) *The New Institutionalism in Organizational Analysis*, Chicago: University of Chicago Press.

Prasad, P., Mills, A. J., Elms, M. and Prasad, A. (eds.) (1977) *Managing the Organizational Melting Pot: Dilemmas of Workplace Diversity*, London: Sage.

Pugh, D. and Hickson, D. (1968/1973) 'The comparative study of organizations', in D. Pym (ed.) *Industrial Society*, Harmondsworth: Penguin. Reprinted in Salaman, G. and Thompson, K. (eds.) (1973) *People and Organizations*, London: Open University Press, p.p. 50–66.

Roethlisberger, F. J. and Dickson, W. J. (1939) *Management and the Worker*, Cambridge, MA: Harvard University Press.

Rose, M. (1975) *Industrial Behaviour*, Harmondsworth: Penguin.

Rowlinson, M. (1997) *Organizations and Institutions*, London: Macmillan.

Scott, A. M. (ed.) (1994) *Gender Segregation and Social Change*, Oxford: Oxford University Press.

Selznick, P. (1949) *TVA and the Grass Roots*, Berkeley: University of California Press.

Selznick, P. (1957) *Leadership in Administration*, New York: Harper & Row.

Taylor, F. W. (1911) *The Principles of Scientific Management*, New York: Harper.

Tuckman, A. (1995) 'Ideology, quality and TQM' in A. Wilkinson and H. Willmott (eds.) *Making Quality Critical*, London: Routledge.

Williamson, O. E. (1975) *Markets and Hierarchies: Analysis and Anti-Trust Implications – A Study in the Economics of Internal Organization*, London: Macmillan.

Willis, P. E. (1977) *Learning to Labour*, London: Saxon House.

Woodward, J. (1958) *Management and Technology*, London: HMSO.

Woodward, J. (1965) *Industrial Organization: Theory and Practice*, Oxford: Oxford University Press.

Woolgar, S. (2002) *Virtual Society? Technology, Hyperbole, Reality*, Oxford: Oxford University Press.

7 Management and Leadership

David Knights and Hugh Willmott

Key concepts and learning objectives

- To show how ideas about organization, management and leadership are developed and applied in practice, with particular reference to a case study.
- To explore some of the tensions associated with managing and leading staff.
- To present and define a number of key concepts that are relevant to mainstream and critical analysis, such as types of leadership and styles of management.
- To develop an understanding of the assumptions and theories underpinning mainstream thinking on management and leadership.
- To understand some important concepts relevant to mainstream and critical analysis, such as effectiveness and efficiency, and performance and control.

Aims of the chapter

This chapter will:

- Introduce the nature and significance of management and leadership and explore the linkages between them.
- Identify the assumptions and values underpinning and framing mainstream thinking about management and leadership.
- Consider personal and impersonal modes of control, and the use of forms of 'mutual adjustment' within both.
- Provide an overview of the diversity of mainstream thinking about management and leadership.
- Explain and illustrate the basis of criticisms of mainstream thinking about management and leadership.
- Show how concepts of inequality, knowledge, power, freedom, identity, inequality and insecurity can provide a different way of considering issues of management and leadership.
- Examine different strands of a critical approach for analysing organization management and leadership.

Overview and key points

This chapter is concerned with an appreciation of the overlaps, interconnections as well as the differences between management and leadership in both a conceptual or theoretical and a practical or empirical sense. In everyday conversation, in the media, in workplaces and even among academics, the terms are often used interchangeably and this is acknowledged, but the chapter also documents their difference and distinctiveness. In developing this knowledge, we seek to understand the development of thinking about management from closed to open system theory and from the control of factors of production to the shaping of culture and values. By contrast, the chapter examines thinking about leadership where the emphasis is upon directing others through inspiration and motivation, rather than through hierarchical control. Leadership is understood in terms of personal(ity) qualities. In the second part of the chapter these mainstream views of both management and leadership are examined critically to reveal the assumptions that they take for granted.

Mainstream approaches to management and leadership

Management and leadership are central to studying behaviour in workplaces (see Box 7.1). Both concepts have been adopted and elaborated to make sense of, and also to control, what goes on in work organizations. As a concept, 'management' identifies responsibility for maintaining the division and coordination of tasks, often through the development of a hierarchy to regulate the allocation and flow of work. Leadership is concerned less with allocating work tasks than with energizing staff with a sense of direction and commitment. It promotes a collective sense of purpose to which members of the organization commit their 'hearts and minds'. The role of management in organizing and controlling the labour of others is said to account for 'the proportion of output that cannot be explained by the growth of input' (Chandler, 1977, p. 490). 'Management' supplements and may even replace 'leadership' to the extent that a hierarchy, whether formal or informal, develops. Responsibility then passes from the founder or leader to a group of 'professional' managers who sustain the continuing division and coordination of productive effort.

Box 7.1: The importance of management

Management has been celebrated as a modern invention whose importance and impact is equivalent to the most influential of world-changing technologies: 'What were the most important innovations of the past century? [Make your own list – antibiotics, contraceptives, computers, etc.]. All of these innovations transformed our lives, yet none of them could have taken hold so rapidly or spread so widely without another. That innovation is the discipline of management,

the accumulating body of thought and practice that make organizations work. When we take stock of the productivity gains that drive our prosperity, technology gets all of the credit. In fact, management is doing a lot of the heavy lifting' (Magretta, 2002, p. 1). In short, it can be claimed that management is crucial in turning gizmos into gadgets, inventions into necessities, or innovations into taken for granted everyday realities.

Distinctions have their limits. At what point does black become white? In the case of management and leadership, it might be argued that the 'leader' who founds an organization probably exercises some 'management' skills, such as the ability to plan effectively. Equally, management involves some of the skills associated with 'leadership', such as the capacity to inspire respect. It would be a mistake to think of 'leadership' as *simply* coming before 'management'. Following the introduction of more management and the formalization of procedures, the initial sense of direction and inspiration may diminish – something that makes 'leadership' a recurrent concern (see Box 7.2).

It has become fashionable recently to elevate leadership over management. An interest in, and preference for, 'leadership' often indicates a desire to move away from 'bureaucratic', command-and-control approaches associated with 'management' (see Chapter 14). Leadership is therefore linked with a process of organizing in which (in principle) greater emphasis is placed on inspiring, listening, facilitating and involving people, rather than instructing them to act. Leadership is linked to communication and innovation. Grint (2005) has associated management with the solving of 'tame' or routine problems, whereas leadership is required for more difficult, 'wicked' problems that defy any

Box 7.2: Management is 'Out', Leadership is 'In'

'. . . the world's most admired manager, GE's legendary leader Jack Welch . . . consciously rejected the word *manager*. It carried too much bad baggage. It smacked of control and bureaucracy. Welch was on a crusade. His call for *leaders* struck a responsive chord' (Magretta, 2002, p. 5). What might Welch do with managers who were

unresponsive to this call?; and what does that tell us about the standing of most managers in such organizations? For those of you who may be interested in reading more about Welch and GE, see N. M. Tichey and S. Sherman (1993), *Control Your Destiny or Someone Else Will*, New York: Doubleday.

clear-cut solution. An example of a comparatively tame problem, which can also be complex, is teaching a young adult to pass the driving test. Being a good or 'successful' parent of this young adult is, in contrast, an ill-defined and recurrently tricky endeavour. 'Management might be focussed on solving complex but essentially tame problems in a unilinear fashion: applying what worked last time; but leadership', Grint suggests, 'is essentially about facing wicked problems that are literally "unmanageable" ' (Grint, 2005, p. 9).

There is, of course, a difference between preaching an approach to leadership and practising it. As we shall suggest when considering more critical studies of management, what accounts for this difference is the politics of organizing (see Chapter 8) where issues of identity, inequality, power and insecurity are entangled in the advocacy of leadership (and management) as well as resistance to its realization. A self-aware, facilitative approach to leadership may sound like a good idea, only to be rejected by managers who have invested their careers, and their very selves, in a 'bossier' kind of relationship with their 'subordinates'. Or these managers may be deeply sceptical about the value of a participative style in highly demanding and contradictory contexts where it is difficult to maintain a consistent approach, and where greater participation seems to risk loss of control. They may believe that effective leadership demands a more 'hard-headed', aggressive and coercive approach – one that has been emphasized in a number of recent business-related TV shows, such as *The Apprentice* (http://www.bbc.co.uk/apprentice/) where Alan Sugar celebrates an autocratic style that scores points at the expense of his subordinates. In the United States, where the show originated, it was Donald Trump who took on the role of the business 'master' (see http://www.nbc.com/nbc/The_Apprentice/).

Those wedded to an autocratic style are likely to experience great difficulty in shifting from a 'hire and fire' mentality to one in which 'coaching' and engaging staff is seen as more appropriate to the idea of leadership. At best, the security provided by charisma and charm may make bullying tolerable. And, in the effort to 'change their spots', autocratic managers may lose their capacity to lead. That is because their ability to provide a degree of certainty and security in confusing and contested situations is what, despite their bullying tendencies, can make them seductive, if not necessarily particularly attractive, figures of authority.

Fuzzy boundaries: Management and leadership

We have noted how definitions of, and boundaries between, management and leadership can be useful but also somewhat loose, arbitrary and potentially misleading (see Box 7.3). Each tends to be defined in relation to the other, and a notion of 'good management' may well incorporate leadership skills. There are further complications. 'Management' is a term used to describe a comparatively privileged (in terms of pay and status) occupational group or elite, as well as an organizational function or role. This not only adds a layer of complexity in terms of developing an analysis but also it creates difficulties in practice, as the issue of privilege can undermine the 'legitimacy' of management decisions. However, the meanings attributed to the concepts of management and leadership are fluid, and vary with the contexts in which they are used and, indeed, the terms may be used almost interchangeably, as in the lament or exhortation: 'There is a need for better management/leadership around here'.

A recurrent complaint of senior executives is the lack of 'leadership' in middle and supervisory levels of management. Because they are judged ultimately on the basis of their subordinates' performance, executives generally want to see more productivity, effectiveness and innovation within 'their' organizations; and they often regard 'better leadership' from their subordinates, including middle managers, as the key to such change (see Chapter 11.) This desire is understandable but it fails to appreciate how identification with, and commitment to, the organization often declines lower down the hierarchy.

Box 7.3: Manager or leader?

At DipPep (a pseudonym), the meanings of 'manager' and 'leader' were virtually interchangeable. Leadership was regarded as an integral and essential element of management (even if, in practice, the motivation and scope for 'leading' was restricted by the manager's position in the hierarchy). At BoxCo (a pseudonym), in contrast, the CEO repeatedly emphasized the difference between management and leadership in order to highlight what he perceived to be missing (i.e. 'leadership') from his management team.

Securing commitment is by no means straightforward. Lower levels of staff are generally much less well paid and provided for; they also lack any direct accountability to the owners or senior executives Whether the organization performs especially well is of limited consequence to them, in terms of their sense of self-esteem, career prospects or returns on stock options. Employees may therefore be rather unresponsive to calls to exercise greater leadership (for example, in teams, see Chapter 4), or to commit themselves beyond the call of duty (i.e. to do more than is formally written into their job description). Where employees are fearful of losing their jobs, they may comply superficially with new expectations without being committed to them. In conditions where staff lack a strong identification with the organization for which they work, qualities characterized as 'leadership' are less likely to emerge among them. Here managers may also find it more difficult to be effective leaders. In other words, issues of power, inequality, identity and insecurity (i) shape how we organize, (ii) stimulate calls for and (iii) prompt different responses to, demands for more or better 'management' and 'leadership'.

To summarize:

- 'Management is associated with the maintenance of existing organizational arrangements, whereas 'leadership' is associated with their establishment, revitalization or transformation.
- The meaning of the terms 'management' and 'leadership' is often fluid – for example, the latter may be incorporated into the former.
- Issues of inequality and limited commitment to the organization can frustrate as well as stimulate efforts to improve management and/or leadership both among managers and staff.

Thinkpoint 7.1

Management and leadership: Your experience Think of an example of leadership drawn from your own experience – perhaps a job you have worked in, participating in a collective activity, playing a sport, or simply going out with mates.

- Can you identify elements of this experience that comprise some part of 'management'?
- What singled out certain people as 'leaders' or distinguished their behaviour as having the characteristics of 'leadership'?

Reflecting upon your experiences of leadership (see Thinkpoint 7.1) has probably shown you how ideas about leadership, and what we think of as management (and organization), overlap. For example, a person identified as a leader, or as exhibiting leadership behaviour, may also be regarded as a good organizer or manager – someone who is able to 'pull together' or harness the diverse skills of a group. Without this leader, the group may become 'dis-organized', perhaps resulting in the quest for a replacement leader. Or the failure of a particular leader may demand a different way of organizing that reduces the risk of dependency upon a single leader. One way to limit this risk is for rules and routines of organization to emerge, and for a managerial hierarchy to be created, whereupon conformity to the bureaucracy substitutes for leadership (see Chapter 10). Behaviour is then organized without such heavy reliance upon leadership that recurrently provides inspiration and direction, but with possible adverse consequences for harnessing the energies of those involved.

Exercise 7.1

Identify some of the different ways in which management and leadership overlap, interconnect, or are substitutes for each other.

Needless to say, activities identified as management and leadership extend well beyond the world of work. In other spheres – at home or in leisure pursuits – we often find ourselves being 'managed' by, or we end up 'managing' others, such as our partners, close relatives, friends and acquaintances. We also identify, and perhaps more readily admire, 'leadership qualities' in others and occasionally have these qualities attributed to our own actions. On reflection, we recognize that management and a slight premium for the special experience and treatment they received.

Ideally, Margaret wanted to recruit a set of 'carbon copies' of herself as managers of each newly opened Bar Mar, who would then lead and inspire by example as she had always done She wanted Bar Mar staff, and especially the managers, to be as enthusiastic about, and committed to, the Bar Mar concept as she was herself. She expected Bar Mar managers at all levels of the organization to provide a broad sense of direction for their subordinates. They would then know what was required in every area of activity without having to be given a very detailed set of instructions, comply with a series of procedures or even achieve a set of financial targets. Margaret believed that commercial success would inevitably follow from upholding and refining the basic Bar Mar concept and ambience, eventually condensed in two, low-key and somewhat up-market slogans: 'Meet, Absorb and Recharge' and 'Lively Ambience, Exciting Food, Affordable Prices'.

Instead of hiring managers to act as trainers who would drill their staff to obey the commands set out in the corporate rule book, Margaret wanted managers to recruit and train staff who would enthusiastically embrace and live out the basic, guiding values of Bar Mar. She wanted and expected all Bar Mar staff to use their initiative and act with discretion to ensure that these values were communicated and fulfilled in every aspect of its operations. Margaret discovered, however, that it is not easy to find or retain staff showing the degree of dedication and commitment required of them. It seemed to Margaret that Bar Mar staff – managers at different levels as well as their staff – were often going through the motions of embracing Bar Mar values without fully grasping, or indeed caring, how to put them into practice. When asked about the company's values, they said 'all the right things' but they did not necessarily or faithfully act them out when serving drinks or interacting with customers. Instead of showing that they could not be more concerned for the customers, they unintentionally communicated an attitude of not caring less.

Thinkpoint 7.3

What dilemmas is Margaret facing? As Margaret expands the Bar Mar chain, she encounters a number of unforeseen difficulties of organization, management and leadership. How would you describe and diagnose these problems? What remedies would you consider in similar circumstances?

Margaret believed that more careful selection and training of staff could solve the problem. The human resources (HR) budget in these areas was substantially increased. This had mixed but generally disappointing results, however. According to reports from 'mystery shoppers' who regularly visited each Bar Mar, little difference could be detected between the experience of visiting bars where staff had been given additional training compared to staff in bars who had yet to receive it.

Thinkpoint 7.4

The limits of training Margaret believed that training would solve what she identified as a key problem for the reputation and future of the Bar Mar chain. What might have led her to place her faith in this remedy? What might explain its limited success? What solutions would you suggest?

Margaret was reluctant to abandon her faith in the Bar Mar concept. She believed that there must be some way of managing the staff that would enable them to 'do things right'. She continued to give much thought to this issue but, at the same time, she conceded that an alternative approach was required if the standards she had set for the company were to be realized and, ideally, surpassed. Against all her instincts, Margaret accepted that exemplary leadership was insufficient, and that it would have to be supplemented, and perhaps partially

displaced, by a closer specification of requirements, more effective forms of surveillance and ultimately by disciplinary procedures for staff found breaching company rules. She comforted herself with the thought that this was simply a 'stop-gap' measure that could be dropped, or at least trimmed back, once the HR specialists identified a more effective way of training staff to embrace Bar Mar's defining values. But, half-consciously, she had her doubts about whether a 'magic bullet' would ever be found.

Thinkpoint 7.5

Additional information required? In considering this case and the series of 'thinkpoints', what additional information or knowledge about Bar Mar did you feel you needed? How might this have influenced or changed your views or assessments?

The mainstream agenda

The mainstream agenda is preoccupied with how to manage and lead in order to maximize performance; and it tends to assume an underlying consensus of values and objectives between members of society and organizations. Where there are some difficulties of alignment, it is assumed that a technical remedy, such as improved staff selection or training, will resolve the problem. Organization, management and leadership are conceived as three distinct but interrelated elements of a system that is routinely and legitimately treated as an object of manipulation and control. The mainstream is 'managerial' in the sense that it *assumes* the legitimacy of management and is focused on how to help managers in organizations meet their existing goals rather than reflect critically upon how these goals are identified and pursued. This is typically the *exclusive* focus of management textbooks, such as Laurie Mullins's *Management and Organizational Behaviour* (see Box 7.5).

In common with other chapters of this book, the first part of this chapter presents an overview of key elements of the mainstream approach before complementing this with a more critical approach in the second part.

Box 7.5: The purpose of mainstream thinking

'This book presents a managerial approach to organizational behaviour . . . The underlying theme of this book is the need for organizational effectiveness and the importance of the role of management as an integrating activity.'

Source: Laurie Mullins (1999) *Management and Organizational Behaviour*, fifth edition, London: Financial Times, p. 4.

Management: Discipline, function, social group As a discipline, the term 'management' is used to indicate a measure of responsibility, deliberate planning and control. This discipline was developed in work organizations – church, army, factory, etc. – but has increasingly become an integral part of modern everyday life. For example, the idea of self-management suggests the acquisition of a discipline that enables the individual to take responsibility for their own life (e.g. career choices and development), which they plan, review and control. Margaret's decision to establish the first Bar Mar and her continuing efforts to retain her vision during its expansion into an international chain requires considerable skills of self-management, such as allocating her time and focusing her effort. This effort to manage activities and processes occurs at all levels within organizations. The shop floor worker or the clerical assistant may have minimal formal authority and exercise little discretion, but they have some involvement in managing themselves and others to perform tasks that have been identified, but not exhaustively specified, by superiors within the hierarchy. Today, management as a discipline has been disseminated into almost every institution (e.g. charitable foundations, voluntary groups, personal health, etc.) in advanced capitalist societies. As a discipline and way of thinking, management is advocated to deal effectively with all kinds of personal and social problems, including the control of scientific work (see Box 7.6).

As a function, management is conceived in relation to an understanding of how collective forms of activity are organized. 'Management' is thought of as an essential and necessary component of such activity. Without this function, there is the prospect of chaos or, at least, a sub-optimal use of

---

Box 7.6: Management to control science

'Keith Waldron of the Institute of Food Research suggests a more balanced approach to managing research establishments could be developed through a closer relationship with business schools . . . Dr Waldron writes that the expertise to tackle the problem [of performance] could be found in business management schools. "Perhaps now is the time to exploit these with a view to clarifying the roles and responsibilities of scientists in relation to organizational management and strategic intent." '

Source: *Times Higher Educational Supplement*, 30 January 2004, p. 6.

Table 7.1 Summary: Three common meanings of management

Management as discipline	Practices directed to increasing output for a given input. Employed by many people but institutionalized in work organizations
Management as function	Conceived as an essential and universal component of organized activity
Management as a social group or elite	A social and organizational stratum that is positioned between a small number of major owners of property and land and a mass of comparatively unqualified and unskilled employees

resources involving unnecessary wastage of human and/or material resources. The function of management is understood to ensure effective forms of division and integration of tasks among elements – people and technologies – that comprise organization. It may be identified as a function for which there is collective responsibility (e.g. through mutual adjustment or a democratic election of managers) but it is more often conceived as an area of specialist expertise to be undertaken by those with relevant qualifications who are appointed by an elite. In the Bar Mar example, the management function was assessed to be weak by the venture capitalists who made their investment conditional upon the recruitment of senior executives with specialist knowledge of key areas.

Finally, management is conceived of as a social group that acquires and applies specialist expertise, and to which differential power and privileges are often attributed. The term 'management' is used to identify a stratum of people who occupy positions of comparative seniority and advantage within work organizations. Initially, Margaret was the sole member of this group, though she was reluctant to identify herself as hierarchically distanced from 'her' staff. Later, as the chain expanded, more managers were appointed (by Margaret) and eventually an elite group of executives joined the business as a condition of obtaining the financing for further expansion (see Table 7.1).

Thinkpoint 7.6

Consider the case of Margaret, the founder of the Bar Mar chain of bar-bistros. In what ways does she embody management as a discipline, function and social group?

In what ways does 'management' as a discipline shape your experience and how you act? Consider, for example, how notions of 'planning', 'budgeting' and 'scheduling' influence your everyday behaviour.

Exercise 7.2

Work in a small group to construct a table in which you list and illustrate some key elements of management as a discipline, as a function and as a social group.

Central to the mainstream view on management is an assumption that, as a function, as a discipline and as a social group, management plays an essential, impartial and legitimate role in improving human welfare. Those who are most closely identified with 'management' – as a discipline, function and/or social position – are understood to apply their specialist expertise in an impartial manner for the common good. Disciplined expertise is a hallmark of their functional contribution that is manifest in the strategies, structures and systems devised by them to transform raw materials and human labour into needed outputs (see Chapter 6); and it is the scarcity of this expertise that accounts for their formation as an elite social group. A rather different view of management is explored in the second half of this chapter, where we suggest that their expertise is shaped and applied in specific ways that are valuable for maintaining capitalist enterprise and/or the comparatively privileged place of managers within it.

Management as ever-present? The capacity to 'manage' – to plan, review and control – *may* be seen as a universal human capability that has been applied, more or less systematically and widely, in all societies. In pre-modern societies, however, other influences, notably, the weight of tradition or the dominance of myth, were more powerful in directing and legitimizing human behaviour. An acceleration of the discipline of management, involving the spread of calculating, secular, this-worldly reasoning, occurred during the 19th and 20th centuries when it was harnessed to the development of capitalist organizations (see Box 7.7).

Prior to the emergence and consolidation of capitalist economic organizations, management as a discipline had been developed, in comparatively embryonic form, in religious, military and governmental forms. It was then augmented, further rationalized and embroidered in the process of developing and governing commercial as well as public sector organizations so that, today, it is a pervasive discipline that extends well beyond work organizations and into everyday life (see Box 7.8).

CLASSICAL THINKING ABOUT MANAGEMENT We have noted how, in mainstream considerations of management, there is an assumption that the objectives or 'goals' of organizations are readily identified, understood and shared; and that the responsibility of management is to establish a framework of policy and practice that ensures their effective realization. Mainstream knowledge of management also assumes the value and legitimate place of management as a social elite. We will consider an alternative, more critical view of management, summarized in Box 7.9, on p. 268 of this chapter, but it is worth bearing it mind as we consider the mainstream approach.

Box 7.7: Management in modern society – what's new?

'Like generals of old [managers in 18th century Britain] had to control numerous men, but without powers of compulsion . . . Again, unlike the builders of the pyramids, they had not only to show absolute results in terms of certain products of their efforts, but to relate them to costs, and sell them competitively. While they used capital like the merchants, yet they had to combine it with labour, and transform it first, not merely into saleable commodities, but also into instruments of production embodying the latest achievements of a changing technology. And about it all there lay the heavy hand of a hostile State and an unsympathetic legal system, which they had to transform, as they had to transform so much of the rest of their environment, in the process of creating their industrial capitalism.'

Source: S. Pollard (1965) *The Genesis of Modern Management*, London: Edward Arnold, p.p. 6–7.

Box 7.8: The development of management in capitalist economies – a two-stage process

Historically, owners of capital – in the form of buildings, tools and machinery – emerged as a distinctive group who used skilled labour that previously worked in guilds and owned their own means of (craft) production but did not employ it directly. These owners developed and applied some basic management disciplines as they decided which tools and raw materials to purchase, what outputs would be required and where these would be sold. But these owners did not hire labour directly or take responsibility for how it was organized. Instead, they paid 'gang masters' who gathered together groups of workers. The gang masters were paid by the owners for whatever output they produced that met the agreed standard. In effect, during this first stage, owners 'outsourced' responsibility for work organization to the gang bosses. There was minimal direct intervention by owners in the organization of production, largely because this was contracted out to an external supplier of labour.

During the second stage, owners took a closer inerest in how production was organized. The owners employed their own staff – managers – to undertake the task of deciding when, where and how labour was to be deployed, in an effort to improve its reliability and productivity. Employees were hired directly by managers who decided how their effort was to be deployed and rewarded. Today, this second stage has become so institutionalized as to be largely taken for granted. Increasingly, this system of 'managerial capitalism' (Chandler, 1977) renders the owners almost invisible, in part because ownership has been extended through wider participation in savings and pension schemes. Despite their withdrawal from day-to-day management, the interests of owners has rarely suffered partly due to managers' legal obligations to shareholders but also because profit is the clearest measure of managerial competence.

A distinguishing feature of 'classical thinking' in management is its belief in the possibility of specifying a single way of organizing, managerial style or mode of leadership that would have universal efficacy. Conceived as a system of expertise that is technically adept, politically neutral and morally benign, classical thinking about management assumes the existence of a set of principles whose application will ensure the smooth operation of any collective endeavour. The possibility that management could be, like anything else, a manifestation of its time and place – a product of struggles between those who believe in, and value, its claims and those who are neither convinced nor seduced – is unacknowledged or brushed aside. Instead, it is assumed that more management – as discipline and/or function – inevitably produces a better world. With extraordinary self-confidence, its champions have urged its adoption in every sphere of human activity.

One of the most celebrated efforts to catalogue its constituent parts was produced by Henri Fayol (see Table 7.2); and versions of this list have reappeared in numerous guises (e.g. Barnard, 1936; Drucker, 1974; Koontz *et al.*, 1984) since its publication in *General and Industrial Administration* (1916/1949).

Table 7.2 Fayol's principles of management

1	Division of work	Reduces the span of attention or effort for any one person or group. Develops practice and familiarity.
2	Authority	The right to give orders. Should not be considered without reference to responsibility.
3	Discipline	Outward marks of respect in accordance with formal or informal agreements between firm and its employees.
4	Unity of command	One man, one superior!
5	Unity of direction	One head and one plan for a group of activities with the same objective.
6	Subordination of individual interests to the general interest	The interest of one individual or one group should not prevail over the general good. This is a difficult area of management.
7	Remuneration	Pay should be fair to both the employee and the firm.
8	Centralization	Is always present to a greater or lesser extent, depending on the size of company and quality of its managers.
9	Scalar chain	The line of authority from top to bottom of the organization.
10	Order	A place for everything and everything in its place; the right person in the right place.
11	Equity	A combination of kindliness and justice towards employees.
12	Stability of tenure of personnel	Employees need to be given time to settle into their jobs, even though this may be a lengthy period in the case of managers.
13	Initiative	Within the limits of authority and discipline, all levels of staff should be encouraged to show initiative.
14	*Esprit de corps*	Harmony is a great strength to an organization; teamwork should be encouraged.

Box 7.9: Thinking critically about management

Critical analysis questions how institutions become established, and are maintained, through the exercise of power and everyday acts of domination. Its analysis of management focuses upon fundamental conflicts of interest or paradoxes that recurrently undermine efforts to 'police' delegation, while mainstream analysis examines the obstacles in terms of personal foibles ('I know best') and interpersonal tensions ('let the boss carry the can'), and assumes that difficulties can be overcome by building confidence, and learning to trust and support others who will inevitably make mistakes and undertake delegated activities in a way that departs from the approach taken by the manager. The question, from a critical perspective, is whether the very organization of modern organizations – in terms of the divisions between ownership, management and subordinates – is conducive to establishing enduring relationships of trust and confidence; or whether such relations are repeatedly eroded by pressures that recurrently disturb and disrupt their formation.

Classical theory presupposes that any institution can benefit from attaining its objectives by identifying and enhancing its methods in five respects – planning, organizing, coordinating, commanding and controlling. The discipline of management subject the five components to systematic analysis so as to pinpoint current deficiencies and devise a remedy for their imperfect design. The role of management, as a discipline, is to identify and rectify weaknesses – influences and limited effectiveness – in institutions, and thereby secure their productive operation. Fayol and other 'classical' theorists believed that the application of universal principles of management would serve to transform institutions based upon custom, prejudice and favouritism into rational, balanced, well-integrated entities from which unproductive frictions, misunderstandings and conflicts are progressively eliminated.

Thinkpoint 7.7

Consider again the case of Margaret, the founder of the Bar Mar chain of bar-bistros. In what respects does her work illustrate Fayol's basic components of management? Are any aspects missing from Fayol's overview of components?

One absentee from Fayol's catalogue of components of management is any direct reference to motivation and to related, human aspects of work organization. Motivation is something that more recent management writers have repeatedly considered; and which is central to the study of leadership (see Chapter 2) where the focus shifts from functions to relationships. In Fayol's thinking, motivation is apparently assured by the smooth operation of the five components. He commends forms of 'good practice' that may be associated with the positive motivation of staff, such as equality of treatment and developing an '*esprit de corps*' so that strife and division is minimized. Other related elements marginalized by Fayol, though emphasized by later, 'modern' thinkers, include the development of staff, the importance of communicating with them and, finally, the wider social responsibilities of management. (See Chapters 10 and 14.)

Of the classical theorists, Mary Parker Follett was more conscious of the human dimension of management and how, at least within her own US culture, subordinates dislike being 'bossed about'. She proposed that management and leadership should be depersonalized so that authority is related to its context, and compliance is contingent upon what she represents as *the demands of the situation*, not of a manager or leader. As we shall see later, modern management and leadership has sometimes achieved this state of affairs – for example, by securing consent to some activity or set of symbols, such as achieving a bonus or identifying with the culture, thus obscuring the management control that lies behind them.

MODERN THINKING ABOUT MANAGEMENT   More recent thinking emphasizes the particular circumstances (of culture, technology, history, etc.) in which management disciplines and functions are applied. Notably, open systems thinking (see Chapter 6) indicates, for example, that a style of leadership that 'fits' and performs well with one particular combination of people and technologies will not necessarily succeed when applied in a different context. There is greater attentiveness to how cultural differences and established ways of doing things – comprising practices of organizing, managing and leading considered 'normal' and 'acceptable' within particular environments – exert an influence upon people as they work. Employees are recognized to bring diverse elements of their 'environments', such as their habits, prejudices and expectations, to work; and open systems thinking suggests that such elements have to be managed in ways that are sensitive to, and appropriate for, the particular organization. In this way, open systems thinking can, in principle, incorporate some awareness of the 'importation' and influence of norms and values within organizations – ways of thinking and acting that can enable, but also may constrain, efforts to impose universal, formal rules and procedures.

Thinkpoint 7.8

Think of an occasion on which a person in authority (e.g. a teacher or manager) was insensitive to the particular circumstances of their actions. How was their behaviour received? What difference might appropriate preparation or skills 'training' have made?

In lay terminology, open systems thinking prompts consideration of a wide range of factors that interact to influence the situation and, therefore, the rational choice of 'strategies', 'structures' and 'processes' for managing it. Open systems thinking may extend to include 'flexibility' in which certain teams or players are managed and led, depending upon variations in the way in which they respond to different approaches. Simultaneously, it attends to the negative effects upon morale if such flexibility is interpreted as favouritism or inconsistency rather than an effective means of improving performance. It commends the scanning of environments to select a philosophy and design that matches what the environment has to offer (e.g. technologies, levels of skill) with what is demanded by it (e.g. speedy responses, reliability). So, even when a generic formula or prescription is embraced – such as 'strong corporate culture' (Chapter 9) or 'lean production' (Chapter 14) – modern thinking stresses how the particularities of the context should be taken into account and the formula thereby adjusted or modified to fit with the specific conditions in which it is being applied. But, at the same time, modern management thinking continues to hanker after guidelines that are conceived to have widespread efficacy, sometimes described as 'best practices'.

Modern management guidelines include being attentive to customers and anticipating, or even initiating, shifts in demand (e.g. through branding and associated customer loyalty schemes); paying attention to current and potential competitors so as to establish a distinctive market position where better profits can be made; attending to costs through careful monitoring and control (e.g. by harnessing the power of information and communication technologies), contracting out activities that can be done more cheaply elsewhere and establishing closer relationships with suppliers. It also involves attending to processes as much as outputs so as to achieve continuous improvements in quality and productivity; and paying attention to staff (e.g. by fostering greater openness and trust) especially in knowledge-intensive industries where their knowledge and skills are critical to performance. While these guidelines do not necessarily depart markedly from classical principles, they suggest a more holistic approach that is simultaneously mindful of the immediate (business) and wider contexts of its operations. Such 'modern' thinking has been applied in the private sector but is increasingly being introduced into public sector organizations – in the form of 'new public management' where 'business disciplines' drawn from the private sector are applied in an effort to 'modernize' and 'streamline' what are viewed as inefficient, excessively labour-intensive, customer-unfriendly and inflexible practices (see Box 7.10).

Major issues/controversies in this field: Mainstream debates

The human dimension of work   Classical thinkers paid minimal attention to complex issues of motivation. They focused upon structures and systems (see Chapter 6) without much consideration of how employees would respond to such methods and measures. It was believed that a positive – cooperative, productive – response would follow naturally from the application of classical principles of 'good management'. In Frederick Taylor's *Principles of Scientific Management*, for example, it was assumed that better pay would compensate for the imposition of narrowly drawn and repetitive tasks. Taylor believed that economic reward is the primary, if not, sole purpose of going to work. From this

---

Box 7.10: Modernizing manufacturing – from mass to niche production

[A Japanese] company had realized by 1984 that demographic changes would soon fragment its market into niches. That implied a need to switch from producing a few washing machine models in high volumes to making a broad selection of models, which would sell at lower volumes. The challenge was to accomplish that without threatening profits. The company created a flexible production system designed to respond directly to the ebb and flow of sales. In five years it tripled the number of new washer models it introduced. The washer factory became accustomed to 11 model changes per day, versus 2.5 daily in 1985. Spending only US$2 million to US$3 million per year to make all these changes, the business doubled both its manufacturing capacity and the dollar amount of sales per employee. At the same time, quality dramatically improved.

Source: N. M. Tichy and S. Sherman (1993) *Control Your Destiny or Someone Else Will*, New York: Doubleday, p. 206.

assumption it followed that any change in working practices would be accepted as long as earnings increased as a result. It is questionable, however, whether Taylor's assumption about work and industrial workers' purely economic interest in wages is universally correct or merely a 'self-fulfilling' prophecy in the sense that more money is what workers demand if there is no other available means of compensating the deprivations experienced at work (see Box 7.11).

Box 7.11: Self-fulfilling prophecies

The notion of the self-fulfilling prophecy applies to large parts of human behaviour where those exercising power strongly condition the framework of meaning by their decisions. When managers believe that workers are only motivated by money, they devise the workplace in such a way as to virtually remove any other possible meaning or interests (e.g. planning the work, innovating methods, social recognition, camaraderie between workers) such that only the size of the wage can matter. Lo and behold, the assumption about economic interests is confirmed. But this is a self-fulfilling prophecy because scientific management has generated the conditions through which it would become true. Of course, an understanding that the prophecy is self-fulfilling does not make the basic belief incorrect, but, rather, suggests that its effectiveness depends upon the situation that acts either to confirm or to deny its claims.

That said, it should be noted that Taylor, in common with Fayol and others (e.g. Urwick), believed that employees should be treated 'decently' by training them to acquire the work methods that were 'scientifically proven' . They were adamantly opposed to reliance upon some arbitrary (e.g. personal threat) basis for giving instructions. This, of course, placed a significant burden of responsibility upon those managers who had previously relied upon their power to hire and fire to simply pressure and coerce (i.e. bully) employees to 'work harder "or else" '. Not surprisingly, there was considerable resistance from managers to Taylor's principles. Applying the principles placed new demands upon them. Previously, they had not been burdened by the responsibility of introducing new methods but, instead, habitually relied upon personal (e.g. favouritism) and despotic (e.g. punishment-based) ways of securing employee productivity.

Largely absent from both despotic and 'scientific' approaches to management was any careful or close consideration of employee psychology. When Taylor challenged custom and practice, he did so by assuming a direct relationship between productivity and reward, in the form of payment by results. It did not occur to him that employees might place a greater value upon other concerns, such as solidarity with their fellow employees, their dignity or the comforts of habitual ways of working. Resistance to classical methods of organization, and especially to the demands (and privations) of scientific management, resulted in this assumption being questioned.

Thinkpoint 7.9

If Taylor were considering the work of students, how might he seek to apply his principles? To what extent do you think that academic credentials (i.e. degree results) have a tendency to perform the same function in university as money in scientific management? Can you identify areas of higher education that have been 'Taylorized' (some commentators have described contemporary universities as McUniversities)? Why might Taylor's ideas have limited application in this context? Can you identify areas in which Bar Mar has tended to become 'Taylorized'? In what ways has Margaret sought to resist this tendency?

Resistance to the application of the principles of scientific management was both individual and collective. As individuals, many workers disliked and resented the redesign of their jobs, which removed any scope for imagination or personal identification with the task. They often experienced the uniformity of the new methods as alien and degrading as these sought to eliminate all individuality and differences between workers and to minimize the scope for exercising discretion or creativity. Employees may have strongly disliked the 'irrationality' of 'unscientific', tyrannical bosses who managed according to personal whims and arbitrary prejudices, rather than by the seemingly impartial logic of 'scientific' principles. However, their disinclination to manage consistently and closely always creates space and scope in which employees can more readily develop and control meanings about their work (that is 'sub-cultures') that are not reducible to a calculation about output and wages (see Chapter 6).

Collectively, workers subjected to classical principles of management became homogenized and fragmented as their jobs were mechanized and de-skilled through a process of specialization that made each task narrower and more repetitive. A sense of control over the nature and pace of work was lost as 'scientific' experts applied the new disciplines of management. In addition, workers feared that increases in productivity arising from the implementation of forms of scientific management would result in major lay-offs. By design, its 'scientific' principles exclude workers from involvement in the development and application of this instrument of management control. They are entirely its targets or objects, not its architects or subjects. Not surprisingly, then, for many workers, the classical principles of management were not experienced as a neutral and progressive technology but as a political and socially divisive instrument that posed a threat to their sense of identity, solidarity and interests. To the extent that forms of scientific management encountered increasingly organized resistance, it had the effect of provoking opposition to its aim of rationalizing the workplace rather than exposing and removing irrational deviations from it.

THEORIES 'X', 'Y' AND 'Z'   Throughout the history of management thinking and practice, there have been recurrent efforts to understand and manage the 'softer', more complex aspects of organizational behaviour. The emphasis here is upon getting employee motivation right. The underlying assumption is that properly motivated staff, from the bottom to the top of an organization, will develop the most appropriate and effective ways of organizing, including the appropriate use of 'harder', more rational and quantitative methods of assessing and rewarding staff. It is believed that the complexity of human motivation can, if managed effectively, enable organizations to be more productive as well as less heartless.

Thinkpoint 7.10

In what ways did Margaret attempt to manage the 'softer' aspects of the Bar Mar operation?

The introduction of more 'enlightened' or 'humanistic' management is understood to require a deep appreciation of individual and especially group psychology. It necessitates, for example, an understanding of how the norms of work groups can exert a stronger influence upon worker identity and behaviour than the rules and incentives imposed by managers. This is the central message of human relations thinking popularized by Elton Mayo, a Harvard academic, who studied the influence of social factors, such as recognition of contribution and the operation of group norms (e.g. the socially acceptable level of effort and cooperation) upon the productivity of factory workers (see Box 7.12).

Box 7.12: Mayo's human relations thinking

'Human collaboration in work . . . has always depended for its perpetuation upon the evolution of a non-logical social code that regulates the relations between persons and their attitudes to one another.'

Source: E. Mayo (1933) *The Human Problems of an Industrial Civilisation*, New York: Macmillan, p. 120.

So, even when there is a strong material incentive to produce more (e.g. payment by results), Mayo observed that the effectiveness of such inducements may be dampened by the strength of a group norm about the acceptable level of output. In such circumstances, the material incentive does not elicit a high level of productivity if there is a strong desire to avoid being excluded or stigmatized by fellow workers. Instead of operating against the grain of such work group norms and values – a stratagem that is seen to risk a loss of morale and/or increased opposition to management – the 'humanizing' approach pays close attention to employees' 'non-logical' or 'irrational', psychological 'needs'.

They are termed 'non-logical' or 'irrational' because, in purely economic terms, they are seen to obstruct the individual's maximization of earnings. Instead of ignoring or dismissing such 'needs', managers are encouraged to acknowledge, address and, indeed, 'exploit' the 'need to belong' – for example, by making the organization, and not the work group, the primary source of satisfaction of workers' 'irrational' needs (e.g. by developing schemes and styles of management that demonstrated how the corporation and their supervisors were taking care of their psychological as well as their material welfare). Human relations thinking suggested that while economic incentives could not be ignored, employees also seek to have their sense of identity developed and confirmed at work. For the advocates of human relations thinking, worker resistance to management control is surmountable by training managers in interpersonal, leadership skills. To put this another way, employees were no longer to be treated as mere 'hands' but were complex elements within an 'open system' – elements that imported values into the organization that managers would ignore at their peril, but, with the benefit of social science, might harness to their advantage.

Building upon the insights of human relations ideas, 'modernist' thinking shifts from a model of the worker as an appendage to the machine – writ large in Fordism (see Chapter 6) where the pacing of the assembly line was deployed to dictate the speed of each worker's task (see Chapter 11) – to an idea of the worker as a more complex creature who is malleable and, returning to our point about the self-fulfilling prophecy (see Box 7.11), comes to resemble how s/he is treated. That is to say, the worker is a person with diverse needs who, if treated like a machine, will tend to feel frustrated and resentful, and therefore become the mulish, inflexible individual who is motivated to work harder only by the incentive of more pay. Conversely, if the complex and diverse character of workers' interests, motives or orientations is recognized and met, the worker feels appreciated, grows in confidence and self-esteem, becomes more cooperative and therefore more productive.

McGregor (1960) summarized this difference between classical and modern thinking about management by coining the terms 'Theory X' and 'Theory Y' (see Table 7.3). Common to variants of Theory Y is the understanding, or assumption, that the need to belong enables the integration of individual and organizational goals; and that organizations can be managed in ways that motivate individuals by providing opportunities to fulfil their other needs, such as self-esteem and self-actualization (see Box 7.13).

Table 7.3 Comparison of Theory X and Theory Y

Understanding of	Theory X classical	Theory Y modern
Human nature	Lazy. Must be induced or coerced into productive activity	Potentially self-motivating. Will respond positively to opportunities to take responsibility and exercise discretion
Employee's attitude towards work	Negative. Extrinsic rewards (money) compensates for effort expended	Positive. Intrinsic rewards (enjoyment, fulfilment), such as the opportunity to learn and develop, are important
Role of management	Supervise and direct to ensure that work is done	Support to enable learning and development

Box 7.13: Theory Y in practice: 'Management by objectives'

Management by objectives (MBO) is a widely used technique in which common goals and targets are mutually agreed between superior and subordinate, and then subsequently reviewed to assess performance and identify changes (e.g. in systems or personnel) necessary to make further improvements. This is consistent with Theory Y insofar as subordinates are not given detailed instructions for performing their tasks but, rather, are permitted to use initiative and discretion to achieve the agreed goals.

Only then, advocates of Theory Y contend, is it possible to design the content of jobs and the activities of work groups, as well as relevant systems of reward, that harness human potential to the realization of organizational goals. In effect, a psychological remedy is advocated, which, it is claimed, can reconcile the 'needs' of the individual worker with the 'needs' of the organization. We have placed these terms in inverted commas because it is far from clear that needs can be so readily identified or taken for granted – an issue to which we will return in the second part of this chapter.

Exercise 7.3

Complete the following table by listing some of the key differences between 'X' and 'Y' theories of management

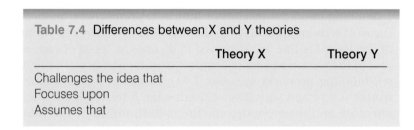

Table 7.4 Differences between X and Y theories

	Theory X	Theory Y
Challenges the idea that		
Focuses upon		
Assumes that		

Theories X and Y have their parallels in management styles. A 'managerial grid' (see Figure 7.2) constructed by Blake and Mouton' (1964; see also Blake and McCanse, 1991), which takes as one of its axes the results-orientation, is largely indifferent to human psychology and therefore a variant of Theory X but combines it with a people-centredness approach that is very reminiscent of Theory Y. This grid produces five distinctive styles and, of course, numerous less extreme mixes of them:

- low X, low Y = impoverished management
- high X, high Y = team management
- high X, low Y = country club management
- low Y, high X = authority-compliance management
- medium X, medium Y = middle-of-the-road management.

Management is described as 'impoverished where there is a lack of attention both to people and production. In effect, management is 'hands off'. Both managers and workers exert the minimum of effort to sustain the organization. 'Team management' combines maximum concern with employees and production by ensuring that individual needs and organizational goals are fully integrated. There is an emphasis upon building trust and mutual respect. 'Country club management' describes an approach where there is much attention to employee needs, but limited attention to production. The atmosphere is relaxed, and maintaining harmonious relationships is more important than raising output. Finally, high concern for production combined with minimal concern for people is described as an 'authority-compliance' approach. It is a form of management associated with arranging work in ways that are designed to minimize human intervention.

Not surprisingly, the 'team management' combination of concern for people with a concern for production is viewed as the most desirable. Blake and Mouton's 'team management' is similar to Likert's 'System 4' (see Table 7.5) where management develops and welds the contributions of individuals into an effective, mutually supportive and productive (synergistic) group.

For champions of modern Theory Y, the primary task and responsibility of managers is to enable and educate employees into seeing how the desire to satisfy their own needs can be aligned with the attainment of organizational goals. Managers might be invited, for example, to locate their 'style' on the axes of the 'managerial grid', and then to reflect upon how they can develop themselves to move in the direction of the optimal 'team management' approach. Blake and Mouton developed their grid in the early 1960s but it took another 20 years before the value of 'teamworking' became widely applauded and applied in forms of leadership (see below), total quality management (TQM), business process re-engineering (BPR) and culture management (see also Chapters 2, 4 and 7).

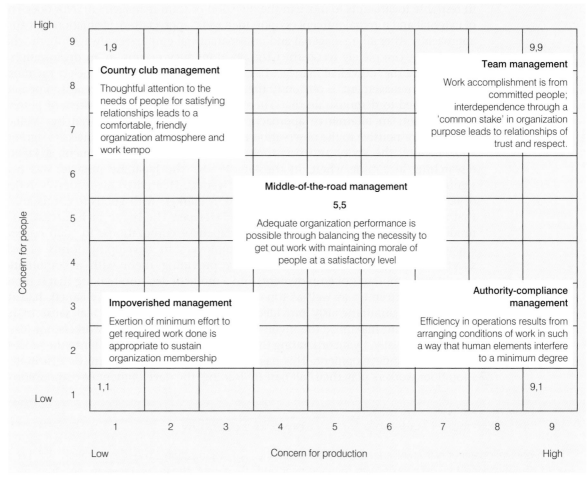

Figure 7.2 A management grid

Table 7.5 Likert's 'System 4' approach to management: Key features	
Management characteristic	**Management behaviour**
Share knowledge and insights	Be attentive and approachable
Acknowledge and reward success	Provide guidance and coaching
Recognize and address personal issues	Support career advancement

Source: Adapted by the author from Likert, 1961.

Thinkpoint 7.11

● How would you describe Margaret's changing approach to management, using the categories developed by Likert?

● What limitations do you detect in the Theory Y prescriptions for improved employee motivation and productivity?

One limitation of a focus upon the needs of individuals as the key to motivation is the scant attention paid to the wider context of managing people in organizations. It does not consider, for example, how national culture or dominant organizational values may strongly condition not only the response of employees to different styles of management but also to the very construction or development of those styles in the first place. So, for example, employees who are used to 'authority-compliance management' may simply be less productive and/or less disciplined (i.e. 'slacken off'; 'take advantage') in response to attempts to move in the direction of team management. Nor does Theory Y take account of external and internal influences upon managers' appreciation, evaluation and application of different approaches. After all, managerial and non-managerial employees always inherit what has gone before – they do not completely reconstruct the positions they occupy in an organization. The theory simply assumes that the individual manager has the power and discretion to select the most effective style, and that 'team management' is obviously the best as it combines attentiveness to people and production.

Concerned to demonstrate that Theories X and Y are not exhaustive of potential philosophies of management, an alternative approach, labelled Theory Z, advanced by William Ouchi (1981) is somewhat responsive to the observation that wider organizational values are significant in constraining and enabling the styles and decisions of individual managers. Ouchi, a Japanese American, was researching at a time when, in the late 1970s, 'the Japanese miracle' was beginning to make a significant impact upon global US competitiveness. He invited his readers to reflect upon the success of Japanese companies in penetrating Western markets with goods (e.g. cars and electrical products) that were of better quality, more reliable and cheaper. The key to such success, according to Theory Z, resides in the distinctive culture of large Japanese corporations. In such corporations, the culture encouraged the active involvement of employees in developing forms of lean production and shortened design-to-manufacture times by providing them with a combination of job security (e.g. lifetime contracts of employment) and a mode of decision making that is more inclusive by being somewhat bottom-up as well as top-down. The Japanese, it was claimed, had developed corporate cultures that simultaneously provided economic security and a real sense of belonging. This had enabled them to maximize the involvement and contribution of workers not just through their hard work but, crucially, by incorporating their ideas, knowledge and skill into the process of innovation and manufacturing development. This has also been described as a form of 'distributed leadership' where shop floor workers play their full part in 'leading' the development of corporations (see Box 7.14).

Box 7.14: Distributed leadership for the networked economy

'The organizational theory that will successfully dominate the world of networking has less to do with management and more to do with leadership – not leadership in the charismatic sense that comes from the top, but leadership that exists and operates all throughout the organization. Such leadership is frequently not "scientific," nor the result of a formal planning process, but more results from a "hands-on" relationship with particular work processes – what Shoshana Zuboff has called informating the workplace.

The information age demands, and will enforce, a transition to empowered employees all throughout the organization. The organization will be successful to the extent those employees are free to, and capable of, exercising leadership. The organizations faced with the most difficult transition to the information age are likely to be those that never really bought into the industrial age management paradigm – the public sector, with higher education and health care being the two most obvious examples . . . they tend to be far more inertia-bound than their aggressive private sector cousins, particularly than the high-tech industries that currently drive the economies of developed countries.'

Source: Robert C. Heterick, *Getting Organized* (http://www.educause.edu/pub/er/review/reviewArticles/31260.html).

Theory Z suggests the importance of the context of management. The limited duration of the Japanese success story and its subsequent 'unravelling' also confirms the view that any 'best way' is limited by time as well as place. 'Fordism', founded primarily upon Theory X with a gloss of paternalism, is another example. Fordist manufacture, which was adopted by all the mass automobile manufacturers, combined Taylor's philosophy of job specialization and simplification with an automated line that effectively paced the work (see Chapter 11). This proved to be a highly successful approach until the system developed by Toyota, which unified elements of Theory Z with a greater responsiveness to consumers' developing interest in greater customization and better quality, demonstrated that Fordism was not, or was no longer, the 'one best way'.

Thinkpoint 7.12

Consider a situation in which you have been strongly motivated to perform a task or achieve a goal. How might Theories X, Y and Z be applied to account for the strength of your motivation?

It was not just Theory Z but a whole range of management thinking – including innovations such as culture management, teamworking, the learning organization, TQM, BPR and knowledge management (KM) – which embraced and promoted the view that employees responsible for daily production have numerous skills and tacit knowledge. These largely discounted by Theory X mass assembly automation, although could, in principle, be transformed into a resource for improving productivity and achieving greater profitability. In a market for mass produced goods that was reaching saturation point, it is also becoming increasingly important to develop ways of differentiating products in terms other than mere functionality. It was recognized that cars and other consumer goods could be a status symbol – an expression of one's place in the social order (see Exercise 7.4) or a statement of a particular lifestyle; and it also has became clearer that product competition is less likely to be successful if customer service fails to be of a high standard.

Exercise 7.4

Take a car manufacturer like Mercedes or some other of your choice and note one of its models that appeals to you, and how it differentiates itself from the equivalent models of other manufacturers. In the case of Mercedes, explore how surveys of reliability and customer satisfaction compare with the image projected by the manufacturer and reflect upon how any discrepancies are managed.

Technological developments in general, but information communication technology in particular, have also created the conditions in which the advantages of mass production can be combined with making products unique to individual, or groups of, customers (see Chapters 11, 12 and 14). Tailoring products to niche markets and 'mass customization' offer ways of combining economies of scale (thereby minimizing unit cost) with economies of scope (by enabling the same production line to create different models).

In *The Art of Japanese Management*, Pascale and Athos (1982) present a '7-S' framework, devised by the consultants McKinsey, that combines elements of Theories X, Y and Z. The '7-S' framework retains a classical emphasis upon structure, systems, skill and strategy but incorporates, and makes central, an attentiveness to staff, style and, most importantly, shared values. As with Theory Z, the focus in the '7-S' framework, which is also central to Peters and Waterman's (1982) highly influential *In Search of Excellence* (see Box 7.15), is upon developing a strong organizational culture. As we have seen, Theory Y anticipates that individual and organizational needs will be reconciled if individuals are given the opportunity to fulfil their needs. Theory Z, and especially *In Search of Excellence*, makes no such assumption. Instead, management is urged to 'create a broad, uplifting, shared culture' (Peters and Waterman, 1982, p. 51) where 'the real role of the chief executive is to manage the values of the organization' (ibid., p. 26), and where employees 'either buy in to their norms or get out' (ibid., p. 77). While some might want to describe the ideal Theory Z worker (see Box 7.15) as displaying obsessive behaviour that requires psychiatric attention, advocates of strong cultures seek to make all workers as devotional and obsessive about their companies as cult members are about their values.

In a chapter entitled 'Man Waiting for Motivation', Peters and Waterman (1982) contend that the key to delivering 'better relative performance, a higher level of contribution from the "average" is to establish a "strong culture" reinforced by "transforming leadership" '. It is this combination of culture and leadership that, according to Peters and Waterman, differentiates the 'best-run companies' from the also-rans. Their claim is that a strong culture provides the final solution to the long-lamented

---

Box 7.15: The ideal Theory Z worker

'One of our favourite stories is about a Honda worker who, on his way home each evening, straightens up windshield wiper blades on all the Hondas he passes. He just can't stand to see a flaw in a Honda! Now, why is all of this important? Because so much excellence in performance has to do with people being motivated by compelling, simple – even beautiful – values.'

Source: Peters and Waterman (1982), p. 37.

Table 7.6 Key findings of contemporary empirical studies of managerial work

Character	Behaviour
Frenetic, fragmented and disjointed	Reactive rather than initiating
Preoccupied with ad hoc, immediate matters	Much negotiating and bargaining
Decisions and plans emergent in process of dealing with immediate matters	Preference for working with practicalities rather than abstractions

Source: Adapted from Hales, 1993, p. 14.

it is to manage using any single formula as, in practice, any consistent approach is routinely compromised by pressures to act in ways that contradict it.

Recent empirical studies show how normative theories of management tend to be highly idealized. That is to say, they abstract 'management' – as a set of principles, functions or roles – from the specific context in which the practice of management occurs. Even when they stress the importance of taking account of context, they underestimate the importance of the institutions and sets of relations that have been both a condition and consequence of the development of management and which continue to compel and shape the ongoing process of its operation and transformation. These institutions are also downplayed in studies that directly address the question of 'what managers do'. In the studies of Mintzberg and Kotter, there is little consideration of the wider context – politico-economic as well as cultural – in which, and through which, managerial work is undertaken. These studies do not, for example, consider how the very meaning of 'management' and aspirations of 'managers' have emerged through struggles to establish their credibility and exert influence in the teeth of opposition – for example, from owners who have been reluctant to trust them; from employees who have been unwilling to obey them; from politicians who think they fail to deliver on expectations for the economy; from regulators who seek to constrain them; and from a wide range of commentators, such as journalists, academics and various special interest groups, who alternatively idolize or harass them.

Thinkpoint 7.13

Consider the work of a CEO like Margaret at Bar Mar. In what ways would you expect their activities to illustrate the findings of studies undertaken by Mintzberg and Kotter?

Key ideas and contributions on leadership

We noted earlier how the idea of 'leadership' is distinguished from 'management' by a greater emphasis upon directing others through inspiration and motivation, rather than command-and-control reliance upon hierarchical position. Leadership also tends to be associated with personal qualities, such as drive, determination, focus, dedication, etc.; but it has also been associated with ruthlessness, obstinacy, autocracy and obsessiveness. In any event, ascribing the virtues of leadership to an individual suggests that their influence or capacity to 'get things done' does not depend purely, or even primarily, upon the occupancy of (managerial) position but, rather, upon qualities summed up as 'leadership' that may take a variety of forms and 'styles'.

Thinkpoint 7.14

Identify a person whom you have known and you regard as a leader. Attempt to create a list of characteristics that distinguish this person from other people. Would *anyone* exhibiting these characteristics be viewed as a leader? Can you think of situations in which such characteristics would be viewed negatively rather than positively?

Classical thinking about leadership

Leadership as a personality trait The traits approach to leadership concentrates upon identifying the qualities attributed to individuals who are widely viewed as leaders. Traits of leadership have included such qualities as initiative, intelligence and self-assurance. The difficulty is that few leaders have been found to share many of these traits and/or non-leaders are also deemed to possess them in equal measure. Such traits do not appear to discriminate sufficiently between leaders and non-leaders to be of analytical use. Nonetheless, a variant of the traits approach has resurfaced in the form of 'transformational' leadership (Burns, 1978; Bass, 1985) – a kind of leadership capable of meeting the challenge of re-energizing or reinventing organizations or departments during periods of turbulence and uncertainty. 'Transformational leaders' are conceived to possess the qualities needed to inspire and redirect staff to solve problems and attain ambitious objectives – objectives that are rarely achieved by relying upon a 'transactional' approach where cooperation relies upon narrow calculations of self-interest ('if you do/don't do this, you will/won't get this', as exemplified by bonus schemes, promotion systems, etc.). In contrast to mere managers who lack transformational traits and, as a consequence, fall back upon more mundane, transactional techniques to secure compliance, transformational leaders are seen to exhibit behaviours that energize and enthuse others so that their followers come to care as much and more about realizing the visions or mission of the leader as they do about any personal gain that they may derive from their fulfilment. Key features attributed to transformational leaders are set out in Table 7.7.

In common with trait theories of leadership, the idea of transformational leadership assumes that exhibiting its key features delivers the intended results irrespective of the circumstances, such as the nature and scale of the task at hand, the established systems and culture of the organization, or the readiness of followers to respond to the calls of a leader who aspires to be transformational.

We can conclude that classical approaches perceived leadership broadly to be an attribute of the individual – an individualized and therefore bastardized version of the ancient Greek image of leadership as honourable and heroic, so well represented by Odysseus in Homer's narratives. By contrast, modern approaches begin to see leadership more in relational terms and in the context of followers or with respect to the contingencies that are the medium and outcome of its impact.

Modern thinking about leadership In modern, contingency thinking, leadership is a product of an interaction between a number of variables. Contingency thinking also allows for the possibility that leadership is a function of collective activity comprising diverse elements that may be shared by, or passed among, various people at different times, rather than a role that is played by individuals who possess the appropriate traits or display the relevant behaviours. When leadership is conceived of as a function that occurs within any group engaged in a task, it is no longer seen as the preserve of a single individual but, rather, may be spread across a number of group members or simply executed as part of a group process. Numerous components of leadership as a function have been suggested (see Table 7.8), many of which bear a marked resemblance to the set of roles ascribed by Mintzberg to managers (see Figure 7.3), except that they are conceived as

Table 7.7 Transformational leaders

- Clear and compelling sense of vision
- Capacity to provide and stimulate creativity and innovation
- Admiration and/or respect from followers
- Clear linking of strategies to vision
- Ability to communicate and persuade
- Engendering of confidence and optimism

Table 7.8 Elements of the leadership function

- Father-figure
- Role model

- Expert
- Purveyor of rewards and punishments

- Opinion shaper
- Policy maker and implementer

- Arbitrator and mediator
- Distributor of tasks and responsibilities

- Planner
- Anxiety absorber

- Figurehead
- Scapegoat for failure

Source: Adapted by the author from Krech, Crutchfield and Ballachey, 1962.

a property of a group and may therefore be undertaken by one or more individuals at different points in time.

Situational theories conceive of different elements or aspects of leadership – such as the provision of expertise or the implementation of policy – shifting between individuals over time. Considered in this way, a person who emerges as a leader, and may be identified by the group as their leader, is the one who is perceived by others to perform the most significant of these elements or to be the best exponent of key leadership tasks, the importance of which may itself shift with changing circumstances. In short, leadership needs to reflect the situation in which it finds itself.

According to Adair (1979), the function of leadership, whether undertaken individually or collectively, involves not only the achievement of tasks but also the maintenance of group processes (e.g. building morale, maintaining focus) and addressing the particular needs of group members (e.g. self-esteem). Individuals are understood to exhibit leadership characteristics whenever they take

CASE STUDY 7.2 Cornerville street-corner society

In his classic **participant observation** study of street corner gangs in Cornerville (a pseudonym – an American slum), Whyte (1943/1993) demonstrated the centrality of leadership and organization regardless of whether the activity has a purpose in relation to work or the formal economy. The study concentrated on one of the gangs and discovered that unemployment, poverty and marginality were no obstacles to a highly organized life based on hanging around with the gang. These gangs were formed on the street where they can be found almost every night of the week. Membership continued well beyond teenage life into adulthood, even after marriage. Doc, the leader of the gang with whom Whyte spent most of his time, was either more proficient in all the activities (e.g. alley bowling, fighting, gambling, womanizing) or at least made to appear so. For he would promote those activities where he excelled and discourage those in which he was less skilled. Whyte (ibid., p. 23) found a 'very close correspondence between social position in the gang and bowling performance': bowling had become the main activity of the gang and, more importantly, the vehicle for maintaining, gaining or losing prestige. Several other social psychological regularities or norms were discovered relating to group behaviour. Among these were that: the leader spends more money on his followers than they on him; the gang has little collective coherence in the absence of the leader; the leader is more decisive and his decisions are more satisfactory to the group and therefore usually considered 'right'; and he is better known and more respected outside his group than any of his followers, and is expected to represent the interests of the group externally whether in conflict, competition or cooperation (ibid., p. 260). Whyte concludes that a major benefit of his study is to help inform social workers about leadership. Rather than relying on the so-called leading figures in the community – those middle class 'respectable business and professional men' – Whyte recommends that social workers mobilize the informal leaders in street-corner gangs that Cornerville people recognize. Potentially, these leaders could be harnessed to forms of community development – an orientation that has its parallels in the appropriation of informal shop floor behaviour for managerial purposes.

opportunities to practice the skills associated with delivering the elements of the leadership function. This understanding challenges the view that leadership is a manifestation of personality traits possessed by individuals. Instead, it is seen to be an outcome of opportunities, willingness and capacity to master its constituent elements. In this sense, leaders like Doc in Case study 7.2 are considered to be made in this process of 'mastery', not born.

Leadership *style* characterizes differences in how elements of leadership are undertaken. One possibility is for all members of a group to refuse to take responsibility for the leadership function such that no single leader arises – in effect, the style of 'abdication'. Another possibility is for the group or a leader to decide that each member will assume responsibility for all elements of the leadership function. Rather confusingly, this has been described as '*laissez-faire*', which implies that each individual is left to 'do their own thing', whereas it is clear that very considerable responsibilities are imposed upon each individual by a leader or actively embraced by all members of a group.

Leaving aside the rather rare and exceptional options of abdication and *laissez-faire*, a basic division in styles of leadership is generally between those that are consultative or participative (widely described as 'democratic'), and others that are imposing and dictatorial (widely called 'authoritarian'). A dictatorial style generally relies exclusively upon personal conviction, the force of personality and the power to favour, or to dispense with, followers. This may be accompanied by giving trusted lieutenants considerable discretion to act in ways that realize the broad direction and goals set by the leader as well as unqualified confidence in the ability of the mass of followers to excel in their work. Churchill, and more especially Hitler, provide examples of what House (1971) terms a 'path–goal theory' of leadership in which the central function of leadership involves identifying a route to the achievement of desired goals but does not necessarily include any detailed specification of how the goals are to be realized. While authoritarian leaders may not always be 'control freaks', they often get by with a minimal degree of cooperation from followers. Unconditional commitment may be the desired outcome but lip service rather than active consent or devotion to the leader may be sufficient to sustain their leadership. An authoritarian style is, however, more vulnerable to disenchantment and rebellion if the leader's grip on power is seen to slip – ironically in Churchill's case by his strategic role in winning the war and in Hitler's case by losing it (see Box 7.16).

Box 7.16: Hitler and Churchill: Born leaders?

The association of inspiration and direction with leadership explains why Hitler and Churchill are widely identified as leaders. Were Churchill and Hitler born leaders or did they learn to master key elements of the leadership function? Would they have emerged as leaders at any time or place, or did circumstances 'conspire', as it were, to identify them as popular, and seemingly 'natural', leaders? Especially through their speeches, each articulated a set of beliefs and policies that served to remove doubts and establish resolve in the masses who became their followers. Churchill and Hitler depended upon the cooperation of others – not only for the organization and management of the political and military apparatus they commanded, but also for a continuing belief in their leadership capabilities – something that was greatly tested when war propaganda was unable to conceal defeats and setbacks. In Churchill's case, qualities of leadership that were an inspiration to most of the population during a period of national crisis (i.e. the Second World War) were shown to lack popular appeal and relevant direction during the subsequent period of reconstruction, as evidenced by the rejection of his party at the general election of 1945. Hitler was seen as a charismatic leader but chose to consolidate his power through totalitarian methods intended to scare any doubters into submission. Yet had he not entered political life at a time of economic crisis due to hyperinflation in Germany, his message would probably have secured support only from a fringe of ultra-nationalists and racists. Followers can readily destroy as well as make leaders, since each process is dependent upon the situation or circumstances that render ideas (e.g. fascism) credible or at least supportable, and thereby confer leadership upon their most articulate and persuasive champions.

Thinkpoint 7.15

How would you characterize Margaret's style of leadership at Bar Mar?

A consultative style or mode of leadership necessitates a process of discussion in which followers participate in shaping opinions, making policies and making decisions about the distribution of tasks and responsibilities. In principle, the consultative style harnesses the collective wisdom of the group, rather than assuming that an individual leader possesses a monopoly of truth and good judgement. The consultative style risks paralysis induced by endless discussions resulting in costly delays, procrastination and compromises. Discussion may ensure a degree of harmony, but at the expense of dealing effectively with issues faced by the group. Styles of leadership can be related and contrasted by considering the extent to which group members take responsibility for the leadership function and the extent to which they rely upon a leader to perform this function.

Exercise 7.5

Above we have discussed the various approaches to leadership. Respectively, leadership is seen as consisting of:

- personality traits
- transformational capacities
- functions and styles.

In a seminar or tutorial group divide into three groups each of which is required to support and defend the merits of one of the three approaches. Each group should elect a spokesperson at the beginning of a discussion in which you seek to develop arguments to defend the approach designated to you. This is a role-play exercise so you do not necessarily have to be actually committed to the approach you are supporting, except for the purpose of this exercise. It will help to support your arguments with examples of leaders from the case studies of Bar Mar and Cornerville, the world of politics, sport, the media, soaps, history or whatever else may help to render your case more convincing. When you return to the whole seminar group, the spokesperson should present the defence after which there will be space for questions and comments from the group as a whole.

Leadership and contingency Contingency theories relate the effectiveness of leadership behaviours to the demands and possibilities presented by a specific situation or context. The success of a leader or leadership style is understood to be contingent upon the circumstances that support its effectiveness. Hickson *et al.* (1971) found that the power of a leader increases in direct proportion to their indispensability (difficult to replace) and their ability to manage uncertainty (see also Chapter 9). Other aspects of the situation that are regarded by Fiedler (1967) as influential include the nature of the task, the make-up of the followers including their assessment of the leader, the culture of the group and the formal position occupied by the leader. Fiedler's contingency model of leadership suggests that the effectiveness of a leader depends upon the adoption of a style that is appropriate to (i) the status of the task – is it structured or unstructured?; (ii) leader–member relations – is the leader trusted and respected? and (iii) position power – does the leader occupy a formal position of authority? (See Table 7.9.)

Table 7.9 Fiedler's contingency model of leadership

Style of leadership	Leader–group relations	Task	Position power
Authoritarian	Good	Structured	Strong
Authoritarian	Bad	Unstructured	Weak
Participative	Mixed: Not consistently or unambiguously positive or negative		

Fiedler distinguishes between styles of leadership that are more or less participative. A directive style, he contends, is more effective when there is little inconsistency and ambiguity about these three contingencies: they are either highly positive or completely negative. A directive, authoritarian style is said to deliver results in situations where the task is either highly structured or completely unstructured; where the leader is highly respected or totally disparaged; and where there is very strong or very weak position power. Conversely, where there is greater ambiguity or inconsistency in the contingencies – for example, where position power is high and the task is structured but trust in leader–group relations has not been fully established – then a more participative style is conceived to have a better chance of success. In turn, this suggests that for maximum effectiveness, the selection of a leader by an organization or a work group should be made on the basis of the contingencies of the situation. For example, only where there is ambiguity and inconsistency is it recommended that a person with a participative style be selected.

Thinkpoint 7.16

On what basis is Fiedler's assessment and recommendation of the appropriateness of different leadership styles being made?

A recurrent theme of contingency theories of leadership is the relationship between the leader and the group, and students of follower behaviour take up this aspect. They focus upon the readiness of followers to be led – are they willing, able and/or confident in their leader? Hersey and Blanchard (1993) suggest that the effectiveness of a leadership style depends critically upon its compatibility with followers' preparedness to accept and respond to it (see Table 7.10).

When followers are unable, unwilling or insecure about the task, then 'telling' by giving strong guidance on tasks is the most effective style. This coincides with the view, sketched earlier, of a leader being more powerful when s/he demonstrates an ability to manage uncertainty (see Chapter 9). At the other end of the continuum of 'follower readiness', 'delegating' is most likely to succeed when followers are able, committed and confident. In between, there are followers who have the ability to follow (e.g. to perform a task) but are unwilling or insufficiently confident to have the task delegated to them, and who therefore require support through 'participating' but need little guidance on the task. Another group in the middle are those with low to moderate readiness but lack the ability to perform a task independently of the leader. Nevertheless, they are willing and (over)confident so that 'selling', in the form of guidance on the task, justifying the instruction and providing support for its accomplishment, is advised.

Major issues/controversies in this field: Mainstream debates

Contingency theories of leadership, including Fiedler's, are based upon matching a style of leadership to the demands attributed to the current situation – in respect of the task, the relations with the group, the environment and so on. Vroom and Yetton (1973) and Vroom and Jago (1988) develop the contingency model to incorporate a consideration of the future consequences of adopting a particular style – an approach that extends beyond an assessment of its probable effectiveness in

Table 7.10 Hersey and Blanchard's contingency model of leadership style

Followership readiness	Leadership style
High (able, willing, confident)	Delegating
Moderate to high (able yet unwilling; able but insecure)	Participating
Low to moderate (willing and confident yet unable)	Selling
Low (unable, unwilling, insecure)	Telling

What are the key similarities and differences between Fiedler's and Hersey and Blanchard's ideas about leadership?

achieving a current goal. The choice of leadership style, this theory suggests, should take account of its longer-term effects upon the motivation and commitment of individual employees and/or group members (see Chapter 2), such as the development of competencies and capacities to undertake future tasks. Balanced against this, the theory includes consideration of the time available to address a problem, which may, for example, make a more consultative approach untenable. Different types of problems are conceived to be best addressed with different leadership styles – autocratic, consultative or 'group', the latter being descriptive of a style where the leader acts as a chairperson or facilitator of a group discussion in which the objective is to achieve consensus among its members (see Chapter 4).

Vroom and Jago's (1988) contingency approach seeks to link particular styles of leadership (revolving around the autocratic–democratic polarity) to different contexts (see Table 7.11). Three kinds of context have been discussed:

1. Where democratic/participatory styles of leadership are presumed appropriate, there is generally uncertainty and ambiguity regarding relations with the led, the task structure and/or the power of the leader. An autocratic style is suited to all other situations, where the dimensions are clear-cut either in a positive or negative direction.

2. Followership studies concentrate more on the relations with the led, simply providing more detail as to the capability, willingness and confidence of followers to carry out tasks independently of the leader. These should inform the selection of the style of leadership.

3. Attention to personal and organizational development extends consideration of the context beyond the present to anticipate the consequences of a style of leadership for the future motivation, commitment, capability and competence of followers.

Table 7.11 Vroom and Jago's (1988) contingency model of leadership style

Type of problem	Leadership style
Principally affecting a single individual: tough time constraints	Autocratic Leader makes decision for subordinate or obtains information from subordinates and provides a solution
Principally affecting a single individual: manager wishes to develop employee	Consultative Problem explored with individual subordinates: decision taken by leader which may reflect influence of subordinates
Principally a group-level problem: tough time constraints	Autocratic Leader makes decision for subordinate or obtains information from subordinates and provides own solution *or* Consultative Problem explored with subordinates as a group, then takes decision
Principally a group-level problem: manager wishes to develop employees' capabilities	Group Problem explored with subordinates, with leader facilitating this exploration to achieve consensus

CASE STUDY 7.3 Management and innovation

Burns and Stalker (1961) conducted empirical case studies of management and organization. One of these concerned a rayon factory and the other an electronics company. In the rayon factory formal bureaucratic rules and relationships were dominant, interactions tended to be vertical and decision making was also strictly hierarchical – a method of organizing that, in the authors' view, is somewhat discrepant with modern thinking about management. Much to their surprise, however, the company was efficient and successful and appeared not to generate dissatisfaction or protest on the part of employees. By contrast, the electronic company exhibited what the authors called an organic system of highly informal and non-hierarchical procedures where face-to-face interpersonal relations rather than formal rules and methods determined working practices.

Since the 1950s, Peter Drucker (1974), the celebrated management guru, had criticized bureaucratic organization for its mechanistic, over-prescription of work processes where managers are reduced to mere administrators rather than 'dynamic, life-giving elements' (ibid., p. 3), stimulating businesses to creative growth. In common with other gurus, Drucker's prescriptions are an expression of his beliefs: for him, management is not a science or a technical and professional skill but, rather, a creative practice. Managing organically is, for Drucker, an imperative for all modern organizations. However, Burns and Stalker's research suggests that it is effective in some (comparatively uncertain and turbulent) environments, and for certain technological processes, but perhaps not for others. Their findings suggest that organic systems of management are best suited to situations of environmental and/or product market instability where a speedy and flexible response to change is critically important. Where the technology and the market for products are stable and more predictable, as in the case of the rayon factory, a mechanistic system of management is seen to work perfectly well.

Exercise 7.7

Return to the management Theories X, Y and Z discussed earlier and apply them to this case study. Which of the theories is most appropriate to managing an organization in a stable environment and which in a turbulent environment?

CASE STUDY 7.4 Qualbank (adapted from Knights and McCabe, 1999)

In 1989 operating costs were rising rapidly and rising faster than income. Between 1986 and 1989 the cost/income ratio for Qualbank, a leading UK bank, had risen from 65.5 per cent to over 75 per cent. The CEO described the organization at that time as having a 'many-layered management' that was in need of substantial rationalization. A strategy was put in place in 1989 to 'drive costs down and increase quality and sustainable income'. Between 1990 and 1995, 8500 jobs were removed following substantial restructuring. The company closed 19 per cent of its branches between 1989 and 1994 against 16.8 per cent for all banks; the company lost 37 per cent of its 1989 staff complement against 20 per cent for all banks (source: *Annual Abstract of Statistics*, British Bankers' Association). As well as downsizing, this entailed removing 15 per cent of in-branch work from the branches to back-office processing centres.

Homeco was a wholly owned but comparatively small subsidiary of Qualbank specializing in mortgages and had a staff of 320 organized around teams of workers each headed by a team leader. Alongside the rationalization of the bank, Homeco was also centralized and was expected to deliver a 25 per cent improvement in productivity in three years assuming no investment in technology. It was decided that the customer interface would remain at the branch level of Qualbank and therefore Homeco would regard the branch as its customer. With the principle of 'customer service' it was felt important that customers (branch staff) contacting Homeco should be able to fulfil all their requirements through a single communication. Productivity at Homeco for application processing increased by 103 per cent from 1990 to 1993 with a policy of fixed staffing levels. Under the regional structure, mortgages often took five days to be offered following receipt of an application. Now Homeco provides service levels of the same day issue upon receipt. However, there were considerable tensions if not ill will between Homeco and the bank branches of Qualbank.

'Partnership' meetings were introduced so as to reduce these tensions, which related largely to mortgage applications and processing. The basic objective was to encourage Homeco to be less restrictive in its lending policy and more flexible in administering mortgage business so as to enable the bank to reverse the loss of business to competitors now the market had moved against them. The Partnership had been initiated by three senior branch representatives and they attended alongside two less senior team leaders nominated by a Homeco senior manager whose absence reflected his belief that the issues were relatively trivial, not a view shared by the branches. In addition, there was a facilitator from the quality department of the bank, who established the purpose of the meeting as one of 'agreeing and prioritizing an internal customer/supplier improvement plan'. The facilitator continued to establish the ground rules as follows:

- participation on the basis of equality, not rank
- be objective rather than subjective
- it should be fun
- there should be no personal attacks.

Without questioning the validity of some of these ground rules, at a common-sense level many of them were breached within a very short period of time. While criticisms about Homeco from the branches may not have been directly personal, they did appear to be taken so. The opening discussion revealed that some managers in the branches felt that a polarized attitude of 'us' and 'them' had arisen between the branches and Homeco. These branch managers believed that Homeco followed a 'narrow interpretation of quality'. For example, they complained that under the auspices of the TQM programme, Homeco had instigated a scheme whereby 'junior' staff were measuring the errors on mortgage applications and, as a result, applications were being rejected. Complaints from branches particularly focused around being appraised by 'lowly' clerical workers at Homeco, the pedantic approach towards measuring errors, and also the loss of business due to mortgage delays.

Participation was very hierarchical throughout the meeting in that the more senior branch managers tended to dominate while aggressively outlining the problems and concerns as they saw them. Certainly, the meeting did not seem to be much fun, and did not come alive until the group moved outside of the highly mechanistic framework created by the facilitator. This framework involved each member listing the services that they believed themselves to provide for their 'internal customers'. These were then listed on a flip chart and everyone was asked to rank them in terms of importance and how well the service was performed. When this rigid framework for participation broke down, Homeco staff began to retaliate and defend themselves against the criticisms of the branch

members. The initial and ongoing passivity of Homeco staff, however, seemed to reflect their junior status as team leaders vis-à-vis the more senior branch managers. But while junior, because of their power of veto, they were still in the driving seat.

Three areas of importance for improvement were eventually agreed upon:

1 *Decisions on mortgage applications*. The branches suggested that decisions were often arbitrary or certainly not sensible in terms of the current competitive market for loans. For this reason the second area of importance was

2 *Appeals*. Here branch personnel considered that anomalies were occurring that did not secure adequate treatment in appeals.

3 *Telephone communication*. Homeco required accurate mortgage information from the branches, and the branches needed to be kept informed as to the progress of applications.

Analysis

The Partnership was both a consequence and occasion for the exercise of power as well as generating certain resistant responses. One example of this exercise of power was the way that the branches largely set the agenda, despite apparently following the equal participation procedures laid down by the facilitator. In the Partnership, the facilitator stressed that he should be acting 'very much as an observer and allowing for far more autonomy within the group'. At one point, he noted that he was actually steering the group more than he should (understatement). But had he not done so, it seems unlikely that the Partnership would have progressed. Individuals were so preoccupied with their own idiosyncratic problems and anxieties that they were unable, or unprepared, to set them aside. The Partnership members looked for guidance, structure, motivation and leadership from the facilitator. Yet in terms of the philosophy and spirit of empowerment, this should have been continuously refused, thus encouraging the members to take full ownership of the problems they were attempting to handle, including those of how to work together in resolving them. This, of course, ignores the threat that such an approach would pose to the individual career identities of the Partnership members, for 'failure' of the Partnership could reflect badly on them, especially those branch managers who had initiated its development. Moreover, this empowerment would have more than likely increased the tensions between Homeco and the branch management. At the end of the second meeting the 'decision-making' team proposed that an agreement-in-principle (AIP) form be designed so that speedy acceptances of mortgages could be offered to clients at the branches. After a couple more meetings, however, the Partnership collapsed due to the failure to secure a response to a summary of the AIP problem (i.e. a single page of A4 which was little more than a record of what had been decided) that had been distributed to the Partnership members.

The person who had originally proposed establishing an AIP form commented on the Partnership's failure:

We've had to re-look at the Partnership because of the people we've got involved from the Homeco side . . . we're pulling together a more high-powered meeting. They're looking at bringing on board the Homeco general manager . . . the decision maker . . . the meetings have very much been going round in circles, and I was a little bit frustrated because I had done about a three-page document . . . and I discovered that that hadn't gone up the line to the regional director. So straight away, you know, I flagged up – things aren't happening . . . we need more senior people . . . it's purely the bureaucracy and the structure, through no fault of our own.

Another branch representative commented upon the failure of the Partnership and, regarding Homeco, he remarked:

They seem a bit intransigent or reluctant to change . . . There are still major problems . . . I found it incredible that the facilitator sat-in on the meeting where they started doing these AIPs, and then at the next meeting said that 'this is wrong, why didn't you measure the problems first' . . . why didn't he say that the first time? . . . we can do our part in this . . . but we're getting inconsistencies within Homeco . . . in terms of how they respond . . . we've done our bit.

Exercise 7.8

Examine this case from the point of view of the leadership studies discussed above. Which of the theories is most appropriate in seeking to understand the events of this case? Explain how the theory you have selected provides insights into the case.

Contribution and limitations of the mainstream approaches

The mainstream approaches to management and leadership are extremely varied and provide numerous insights. We can summarize our review as follows:

- 'Management' and 'leadership' are often used interchangeably and their meaning changes in accordance with circumstances and fashion. Currently leadership has had a new lease of life among both practitioners and theorists, which we will examine in the second part of this chapter.
- Management is generally associated with the maintenance of existing organizational arrangements whereas 'leadership' is more linked to change, innovation and transformation.
- Management can be seen as a discipline of modern society, an organizational function and a privileged social group, whereas leadership is seen either as an individual attribute, or a style appropriate to particular contingencies or contexts.
- While management is associated with planning, administrative coordination and control, leadership is linked with inspiring and motivating people, whether by autocratic or democratic means, to develop and realize their individual and collective capabilities.
- Most modern approaches to management and leadership have drawn on some variant of open systems or contingency theory.

The limitations of the mainstream approaches to management and leadership stem from taking for granted the prevailing form, structure and knowledge of organizations. The sense that mainstream thinking makes of management and leadership tends to assume and reinforce ways of organizing that have developed within this structure, even when they aspire to challenge them.

For example, more participative styles of management and leadership may be prescribed but basic inequalities of earnings are maintained or increased. Hierarchies are preserved even if they are de-layered. Leadership is associated with preserving, or bringing reform to, established forms and structures, not with their transformation in any radical sense. Managers are largely unaccountable to their subordinates even if subordinates are 'empowered'. The very term 'transformational' when applied to leadership (or management) is an oxymoron as its intent is to renew or streamline established practices, not to transform them. While democracy in society is trumpeted as a defining feature of modern, civilized societies, democracy in organizations is usually absent from the agenda. Forms of participation and involvement that operate within the framework of prevailing hierarchies, with management at the helm, effectively displace their substantive realization. In short, mainstream thinking implicitly endorses and legitimizes the values of the status quo and the distribution of material and symbolic (e.g. status) goods that flow from it. It plays upon, rather than addresses the roots of, the insecurities that are engendered by patterns of domination – with regard to gender and ethnicity as well as wealth.

We have noted how modern thinking about management and leadership is inclined to favour an open systems or contingency approach. By conceiving of organization, management and leadership in such terms, the existence and necessity of the 'system' and its sub-systems is taken for granted. The challenge is to control or manipulate its elements in ways that achieve existing objectives and priorities even more effectively. Disregarding the presence of inequalities and power in the formation of practice and theory, consensus is assumed, and attention is concentrated on adapting the organization to its environment. The problems with it are numerous. It assumes, for example, that:

- Managers or leaders are rational actors effectively applying their knowledge of the organization and its environment in pursuit of a consensual set of goals, yet knowledge is not only imperfect but often unavailable, behaviour is diverse and unpredictable and goals are variable and often conflicting between different members of an organization.

- Managers or leaders possess the power to implement their decisions and have them executed by lower hierarchy staff without leakage or even disruption, yet these staff frequently have a very low regard for the competence and integrity of their subordinates.

- Managers or leaders focus exclusively upon the goals of the organization and not upon their own personal interests in power and identity, or a concern with freedom and/or security that might conflict with such goals.

- Managers or leaders tend to adopt a linear causal understanding wherein one or a small number of determinants of desired behaviour can be discovered. This relies upon sharp boundary distinctions between so-called independent variables (e.g. managers or leaders) and dependent variables (e.g. the managed or led) since these are necessary if one factor or variable is seen to cause another. Yet this can presume the knowledge that there is a clear-cut boundary between the organization and the environment rather than understanding both as constructions that reflect and reinforce the power, interests, knowledge and identity of those that construct them.

- Managers or leaders need not concern themselves with a whole range of 'environmental', social and other interests and pressures that might conflict with the straightforward preoccupation with the economic goals of performance, productivity and profit.

Critical approach

Introduction: Overview of a critical approach to management and leadership

Critical analysts are sceptical about the assumptions upon which mainstream accounts of management and leadership are based. Major parts of the critical analysis of management were covered in the chapter on structure and design (Chapter 6) so here we will concentrate primarily upon the area of leadership. In any event, as we noted earlier in this chapter, there is considerable overlap between 'managing' and 'leading', with the term leadership being used to identify the more dynamic and innovative features of management.

The assumptions made in mainstream leadership and management literatures are generally so taken-for-granted that they are not explicitly made. Take, for example, the assumption of consensus. Few, if any, mainstream thinkers directly acknowledge that they assume consensus in organizations. They simply proceed as if this is the case. How do we know that? We deduce it from the fact that little attention is given to conflicts; and when conflict is addressed it is analysed as something pathological or attributed to something like 'resistance to change'. The possibility that there might be underlying, endemic conflicts, associated with inequalities of wealth, status or power or the incorporation of managers to deliver what is expected of them, is simply not contemplated.

The assessment of critical analysts, in contrast, is that organizations may *appear* to be consensual but this is because managers occupy positions in the hierarchy that enable them to suppress conflict and/or because subordinates have a 'realistic' understanding that compliance or consent is in their own 'best' interests. In other words, the absence of overt conflict is a consequence of relations of *dependence*. Subordinates are usually dependent on managers for a variety of workplace terms and conditions – for example, retaining their jobs, the allocation of tasks and responsibilities, increments in pay, overtime, promotion, future employment references, etc. Given this relative dependence, it is perhaps surprising that there is ever any conflict, especially of the kind that directly challenges management.

Thinkpoint 7.17

Think of an occasion – at home or university – where conflict has been suppressed; that is where a potential antagonism has not surfaced or been expressed. Does that mean that it does not 'come out' in other ways? Think of examples of how 'buried' conflicts are articulated, more or less consciously, in a covert or subtle manner.

The suppression of something does not mean that it is eradicated. Instead, it is driven 'underground' and manifests itself in acts of more or less subtle subversion. Often dissent and opposition are expressed in the form of humour directed at management practices. In 'Bullshit Bingo' (see Figure 7.4), it is the very basis of managerial expertise that is challenged. Management's self-importance – manifest in the obsession with holding meetings that often make little contribution to productive activity – is lampooned by redefining the content of its communications as 'bullshit'. Managers are seen to be slaves to, and mindlessly dependent upon, demonstrating their credentials as managers by puffing themselves up with self-serving platitudes and vacuous catchphrases.

At the very least, 'Bullshit Bingo' offers a form of tension release from the boredom and hypocrisy of routine managerial work where managers often either fear to say what they think, deliberately

Do you keep falling asleep in meetings and seminars? What about those long and boring conference calls? Here is a way to change all of that!

How to play: Check off each block when you hear these words during a meeting, seminar, or phone call. When you get five blocks horizontally, vertically, or diagonally, stand up and shout **BULLSHIT**!!

Synergy	Strategic fit	Gap analysis	Best practice	Bottom line
Revisit	Bandwidth	Hardball	Out of the loop	Benchmark
Value-added	Proactive	Win-win	Think outside the box	Fast track
Result-driven	Empower [or] Empowerment	Knowledge base	Total quality [or] Quality driven	Touch base
Mindset	Client focus[ed]	Ball park	Game plan	Leverage

Figure 7.4 'Bullshit Bingo'

mislead or are highly selective in what they communicate in order to gain some kind of tactical, competitive advantage. Problems of management are frequently described and diagnosed in terms of 'poor communication'. Yet communication is so often poor because there are games being played (i.e. monopolizing information; keeping others in the dark because they 'don't matter') and other priorities being pursued. Critical analysis assumes that conflicts of priority and 'interest' are endemic and deeply engrained, not sporadic or superficial. Forms of humour and gossip frequently are understood to expose the underside of organizational life by articulating a sense of grievance or absurdity that is felt but unexpressed on a day-to-day basis. Humour – notably, irony and satire – can be a comparatively subtle and ambiguous way of signalling issues and grievances that are otherwise difficult or dangerous to express. They are difficult and dangerous precisely because of relations of dependence that make the anticipated sanction or punishment following an overt challenge (in terms of employment prospects or reputation) too great. In effect, there is a climate of fear, often masquerading as one of openness (e.g. the 'open door' policy that no one dare take up) that operates to suppress dissent, and thereby produces the impression that no significant conflict exists.

A critical analysis of management and leadership also assumes that manifestations of conflict cannot be adequately explained away in terms of awkward, militant or pathological 'personalities'. Individual differences (see Chapter 3) are not denied, but their 'positive' (e.g. 'Sam(antha) is a brilliant, charismatic leader/manager) or 'negative' (e.g. 'Sam(antha) is an incompetent, indecisive manager/leader) evaluation is related to the particular social situations in which such differences are shaped (socialization) and assessed (organizational setting). From a critical analytical standpoint, Sam(antha) is not essentially 'charismatic' or 'indecisive' but is understood to have developed ways of interacting with other people (i.e. she has been socialized). And, *in the present context*, mainstream thinking often equates such ways of interacting with personality differences. This kind of thinking is itself a potent way of glossing over social differences and conflicts by attributing them to *essential* personality differences. In doing so, it takes for granted and acts to solidify and sanctify the *particular*, circumstances that, in principle, could be changed.

Yet, despite the best efforts of managers to suppress tensions, remove 'troublemakers' and placate dissenters, collective industrial action occasionally erupts as employees withdraw their labour or refuse normal cooperation in attempts to have grievances settled. Or, more frequently, individuals simply decide to seek employment elsewhere or become self-employed. For employees, the existence of a trades union can provide a degree of legitimacy and some protection against managerial victimization of activists. One task for the critical researcher is to expose the extent to which an apparent consensus conceals or diverts attention from seething discontent, dissent and disarray that bubbles beneath the surface of organizational serenity. This is to express the point rather colourfully. Yet most of us would recognize that organizations breed forms of antagonism, resentment and fear that are either unknown to, or are ignored or exploited by, management. Mainstream analysis is, of course, not unaware of imperfections of morale and motivation in the informal system of organizations. Efforts to build 'strong cultures' (see Chapter 9) or 'cohesive teams' (see Chapter 4) are responses to this. But the response is limited to developing 'better' styles of 'professional' management (as designers of effective cultures and teams) that, in principle, remove the sources of disaffection (e.g. by eliminating favouritism, bullying, sexism, racism, etc.). The critic, in contrast, is more likely to interpret conflict as an indication of employees' capacity to challenge, or at least subvert, the imposition of self-serving management control, including its seemingly benign forms (e.g. programmes of 'empowerment') rather than seek instantly to repair or eliminate it.

Thinkpoint 7.18

Think of your experience of working in an organization or simply being a student. How often have you been (or have you noticed others being) polite and cooperative to your (their) 'boss' or your teacher, and thought secretly – 'what a "bastard"'? Reflect on what made you or others have thoughts that were inconsistent with your (their) actual behaviour. What were their source – were they related to problems concerning managers as people, inadequate leadership, inequality at work, the nature of authority or something else?

CASE STUDY 7.5 Strife at the Dog and Duck

Conflict that is evident in organizations is often a reflection of the inequalities of income, status, hierarchical position and gender, ethnic or other diversities (see Chapters 2 and 7), but this is not always obvious. To illustrate this, we will return to our introductory chapter and the case of Jackie and Christine falling out behind the bar at the Dog and Duck. Jackie a student, is asked by the landlord to act as manager for an evening. This upsets Christine because she has worked at the pub for much longer and regards Jackie as an upstart. In everyday language, Christine feels snubbed. Feelings of injustice and resentment boil over into overt conflict between them.

Someone coming into the pub for the first time that evening who witnessed the dispute between Jackie and Christine may have reasonably concluded that this was a conflict between staff of similar status. Yet, as we know, Christine was angry with Jackie having been given the temporary management position when she felt that her experience and career ambitions in bar work qualified her better for the role. The situation was clearly explosive, just waiting for an 'accident to happen', and the ensuing row could have been anticipated, assuming knowledge of the background. Without this knowledge, it would be easy to describe this, and many other disputes, as just personality conflicts and therefore relatively trivial. Such descriptions are often favoured in mainstream thinking because they do not represent a threat to the often taken-for-granted presumption of an underlying consensus within organizations. In these accounts, conflict is represented simply as a clash between individuals that is seemingly unrelated to differences of values, priorities, politics and so on. Analysis of this kind pays limited attention to the social context of a behavioural event, such as the conflict discussed here.

Thinkpoint 7.19

Do you think it would have made any difference if Jackie had been Jack or Christine had been Christopher? What if Jackie and Christine had been from very different ethnic backgrounds? Would such differences have been irrelevant, or would they have made the conflict less or more likely, or take a rather different form? Of course, we cannot know. But such questions can encourage us to reflect upon how everyday working relationships are conditioned by wider social contexts, expectations, 'prejudices' and power relations.

What do you think a mainstream management view would be of this conflict, and of the landlord's decision to ask Jackie to manage the pub? Is it possible to act objectively or impartially in such situations?

CASE STUDY 7.6 BoxCo and leadership

Here we return to BoxCo (pseudonym) presented briefly earlier in this chapter. At BoxCo, the CEO emphasized the difference between management and leadership in order to highlight what he perceived to be missing (i.e. 'leadership') from his management team. He subscribed to a view of leadership that he had learned on a management course in which leadership was understood to be synonymous with personality traits or qualities, which though possible to improve, are broadly inherited characteristics. Consequently, most attention had to be focused on recruiting 'good' leaders – that is, people who were assessed to have natural talent as leaders.

Some more junior managers whose management training was more recent were highly sceptical of this approach to leadership. They recognized that the trait approach produces an almost endless list of leadership characteristics (e.g. extraversion, vision, initiative), which have little correlation with one another or with 'successful' practice. The trait approach attributes essences to individuals, thus ignoring the social context and the importance of followers in any leadership practice. Being convinced of the correctness of his views, the CEO as the leader of BoxCo was in a position to ignore the views of his subordinates. Fear of contradicting their 'leader' led the junior managers to comply with his views, thereby confirming the CEO's false belief that consensus prevailed. The cartoon here illustrates both the normality and absurdity of claims that difference of pay and status are largely irrelevant because each person has an equally important role to play in ensuring the success of the organization (see Box 7.17).

BTW111-TS

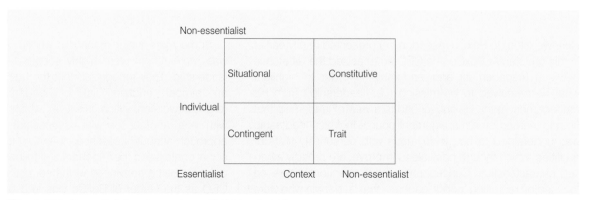

"Now, Dan, we're all equals here. Have a seat."

Image 7.2

Box 7.17: Blurring any distinction between self and organization

' . . . more leaders are attempting to bind employees to the corporate ideal, while curtailing forums of debate. They project an image of charismatic leadership, stress a compelling vision, depict their companies as surrogate family and attempt to blur any perceived difference between the interests of managers and non-managers . . . Such approaches seek to re-engineer the most intimate beliefs of employees, so that they are aligned with whatever the leader deems is helpful to the corporate enterprise. It makes it even less likely that employees will ask awkward questions of their leaders, and so be capable of correcting their inevitable misjudgements. These may constitute fertile conditions for the emergence of other Enrons in the future.'

Source: Tourish and Vatcha, 2005, p. 476.

A critical perspective on leadership

Before he became an academic, Keith Grint (2000) was a senior representative of a trade union. In that capacity, he had been practising leadership at least 10 years before he began studying it. His conclusions, after some 14 years of study and having written many books and research articles on the subject, was that his understanding had 'decreased in direct proportion to his knowledge' (ibid., p. 1). The more he read, the less he felt he understood. Instead of enriching or extending his insights, the literature was dulling and diffusing them. In this assessment, Grint echoes sentiments that had been expressed almost half a century earlier by Warren Bennis (1959), one of the top researchers in leadership studies. He suggested that 'probably more has been written and less is known about leadership than any other topic in the behavioural sciences' (ibid., p. 259). Having become critical of the mainstream approaches, Grint offers an alternative, constitutive approach. This approach contrasts with the three mainstream approaches – trait, contingent and situational – each of which is understood to have a distinctive identity in relation to whether leadership was *essentially* an individual matter or one that was *essentially* determined by the context (see Figure 7.5).

Non-essentialist

	Situational	Constitutive
Individual	Contingent	Trait

Essentialist   Context   Non-essentialist

Figure 7.5 Essentialist and non-essentialist leadership

Before discussing these approaches from a critical perspective, the term 'essential' is in need of clarification. In essentialist thinking, it is assumed that the world comprises a series of 'essences', and that the purpose of reflection is to discover the fundamental or universal aspects of whatever is being examined. So, for example, it would seek to identify what is *essential to human nature* as the basis of all human and social life. Take the phrase 'its just human nature'. It is frequently used as an explanation of a person's behaviour when nothing more specific comes to mind. It may, for example, be used to excuse a person or an action of which you disapprove, often because they behave in a way that is irresponsible or is seen to exhibit extreme self-interest. The excuse is built into a notion that it is natural, and therefore perfectly normal if not necessarily commendable, to look after yourself first. It is clearly a universal explanation. But it is developed within a particular context. In other words, its plausibility as a universal explanation is context-dependent but it is precisely this dependence that is unacknowledged by such explanations. That is why 'it's just human nature' can appear to be a self-evident truth when, arguably, it is a *claim* that acquires the status of truth only because it resonates with deeply ingrained, individualistic and Judeo-Christian attitudes. Such attitudes are tied up with notions of original sin and Darwinian ideas about the survival of the fittest. They take no account of either the awesome openness of human existence (as the New Testament puts it: the birds have their nests but the son of Man has no place to rest his head); and, relatedly, they disregard the deeply social quality of human development.

Exercise 7.9

The following questions could provide a focus for discussion in a small student group:

- If self-interested behaviour is 'human nature', does it mean that someone who sacrifices their own interests to the interests of others is not human?
- Would it ever be possible to disprove an explanation of behaviour that resorts to the notion of human nature?

Hint: There is always a danger of replacing one essentialism (human nature is 'X') with another essentialism (human nature is 'Y'). Think for example of McGregor's distinction between Theory X and Theory Y conceptions of management. Is there a way of avoiding such essentialist thinking?

COMPARING APPROACHES TO LEADERSHIP When we revisit the trait approach in the light of our reflections upon essentialism, we can better see how the context is ignored in favour of a more universal individual 'essence' – a personality or character that is seen to be the foundation of their leadership and/or transformational powers. The trait approach emphasizes selection as most crucial since if you get it wrong at that stage then there is no escape short of dismissing the leader. By contrast, the situational approach perceives the context as essential. It assumes that there are no universal modes or styles of leadership but only ones appropriate to different contexts or situations. The situational approach commends the training and development of leaders by developing and applying the appropriate skills for the specific context in which they lead. It assumes that the characteristics of the context can be pinned or boiled down into their essential features. Managers or leaders 'grow' into the job when they make a competent analysis that discloses the essence of the situation and act accordingly. Wherever an essence is sought – whether it be in the person or in the context – a deterministic stance is implicitly taken. That is, leadership is seen to be caused or determined by some essential factor – the personality (trait approach) or the environment (situational approach) (see Box 7.18).

Box 7.18: From traits to control reluctant followers to contexts to create willing followers

'Whereas the leader-centric perspective favours the rather direct control of followers . . . this (m)anipulation of contexts and constructions, rather than of leader behaviours, would, in a sense, constitute the "practice" of leadership. Rather than searching for the right personality, one would search for the opportunity to create the right impression.'

Source: J. P. Meindl (1995) 'The Romance of Leadership', *Leadership Quarterly*, 6(3):329–341, p. 333.

DON'T THINK OF YOURSELF AS JUST ANOTHER SMALL COG IN A VAST BUREAUCRATIC MACHINE ... BUT RATHER AS A QUITE IMPORTANT COST CENTRE !

FRAN

SOURCE: © FRAN/CARTOONSTOCK.COM

Image 7.3

The contingency approach seeks to combine both the trait and the situational approaches in one position and thereby believes both individual characteristics and the context are equally important elements of an adequate explanation, and associated technology, of good leadership. Here, certain types of leaders are appropriate to certain contexts and it is just a matter of matching the two. A major limitation of mainstream thinking is its reliance on open systems or contingency theory where a number of assumptions go unchallenged. For example, as we noted earlier, a linear conception of causation is favoured where one, or at least a small number, of prime determinants of the object ofstudy can be established. In order to deliver on this model of causation, hard-and-fast distinctions – between say leaders and the led and between the organization and the environment – are sustained so that clear-cut causal relationships can be made between them. So, in contingency approaches, the environment is depicted as the source of uncertainties, the reduction of which determines the effectiveness of leadership. Yet the environment, let alone the uncertainties that it is seen to create, is not a self-evident, transparent or readily accessible entity. Rather, its existence is defined, described or constructed by members of organizations and therefore the uncertainties are not independent of the interests, identities and politics of those that mobilize them as resources in their organizational pursuits. The same point is illustrated in the 'Small Cog' cartoon where the subordinate is encouraged or instructed to think of himself in a distinctive way – not as someone who occupies a small but key part in the bigger machine but, instead, as someone who costs the organization and therefore is a key, 'important' target of cost reduction. Here it is the worker rather than the environment that is being assigned an identity. In this case, the message is intended to concentrate the minds of employees to demonstrate how their production of benefits, or value, is at least equivalent to the costs, or drain, they impose on the organization.

This takes us to a more recent 'constitutional' approach (see also Knights and Willmott, 1992; Knights and Morgan, 1992), which not only questions the idea of essential leadership qualities or traits but also the idea that the context or environment is a self-evident, readily accessible truth or 'objective' reality. Both are understood to be constituted socially. What is seen as a 'good leader', or what the context or environment is, is conceived to be unavoidably open to interpretation, and any shared view, or 'consensus' about this is not independent of the exercise of power. Crucially, those who fill leadership positions or functions are expected to provide definitions of the context – indeed that is one of the common sense tests of a 'real' leader – and therefore have the opportunity to exert greater influence over others, including others' propensity to accept, in public at least, that they are suited to lead. From this standpoint, 'leadership' is less a matter of matching a style with a context than about 'the management of meaning' (Pfeffer, 1981; Smircich and Morgan, 1982) – of educating potential followers about (the 'real' or 'objective' naming of) the context so that they accept this definition of the situation and therefore, come to identify its author as their leader. The constitutive approach suggests that the very acquisition of positions of leadership involves managing others' definitions of reality, particularly those of potential and existing followers. Gaining the support of followers is about power and identity but this is often presented in the language of leadership.

If a manager can mobilize resources (e.g. finance, material artefacts or other organizations) and enrol people (e.g. politicians, celebrities or the public), s/he is likely to assume a leadership position but is also better placed to sustain this position once it is attained (the actor-network perspective discussed in Chapter 12 shares this view). Interpretations of reality tend to be more appealing and convincing when they facilitate people in maintaining their identities or making them feel free, less insecure and more respected (less unequal).

Exercise 7.10

Identify examples of leaders that you know, and examine them in terms of the four approaches discussed above. What is distinctively critical about the constitutive approach?

So far we have sought to elaborate the distinction between a critical and a mainstream approach. In the process, we confess to having committed one of the sins that critics often direct towards the mainstream. For we have tended to treat complex, diverse and multiple forms of knowledge (of leadership, for example) in a universal fashion as if all studies converged upon the four, readily identifiable conceptions of leadership – trait, contingency, situational and constitutive. But it would be more consistent with our critical thinking to conceive of the division of research on leadership into four types of approach as *itself* constitutive. Like any other schema, it is inviting you to adopt its definition of the situation. It is asking you to see the world through this lens. Implicitly, it is encouraging you not only to think about leadership in a particular way but also to engage in the practices associated with leadership in a different way as a consequence of being subjected to this knowledge. This process of influence forms part of what Gramsci (1891–1937) called 'organic' intellectual leadership, which is where thinkers do not simply describe social life in accordance with scientific rules, but rather 'express', through the language of culture, the experiences and feelings that others (who do not have the education, time or inclination) are unable to articulate for themselves. Critical scholarship offers an alternative to the content and form of intellectual leadership supplied and supported by those who are wedded to the status quo.

The example of ethics and leadership   Various corporate scandals and disquiet about the trustworthiness and propriety of top corporate leaders has stimulated interest in the relationship between ethics and leadership. The mainstream response to major scandals such as Enron in the United States, where corrupt accounting practices led to the collapse of the corporation and the imprisonment of its chief executive, has sought to combine literatures on leadership traits and transformational leadership with those mainstream literatures on business ethics (where the latter is invariably perceived as a competitive, brand-image management tool) (see Chapter 15). Minkes *et al.* (1999, p. 328) argue that conformity to ethical requirements is a responsibility of, and depends on, leadership in the organization[1]. Drawing on the case of the Salomon Brothers, Sims and Brinkmann (2002) blame the leader John Gutfreund for moulding an organizational culture that resulted in unethical and illegal behaviour by its members. The focus of their research is on the character of Gutfreund, his absolute attention to a short-term business focus, his alleged willingness to cover-up illegal behaviour and the ease with which he allegedly betrayed his mentor in his rise to power.

A basic assumption of such contributions is that 'poor leaders' are a primary cause of current problems and therefore that better leadership will restore confidence. Treviño *et al.* (2003) are also concerned at the absence of empirical studies of ethical leadership and are critical in the sense that they wish to understand how ethical leadership is 'perceived and attributed to executives' (ibid., p. 7). But their concerns are voiced from within a taken-for-granted, common-sense notion of leadership. They favour an attribution theory approach that seeks to show how the qualities of ethical leadership are defined and attributed to managers by other members of the organization. This may *reveal* the dependence of such attributions on common-sense reasoning but it fails to problematize this dependence, as would a critical perspective. A main problem is that it tends to attribute leadership to managers of organizations that are deemed to be conventionally successful, and a lack of leadership to organizations that fail in some way. In other words, if an organization is deemed to be successful in common-sense terms, then it is conceived to be 'well led'. You may see parallels here with the mainstream systems approach discussed earlier in the chapter, where parts of an organization were explained in terms of their consequences for, or function in, maintaining its stability. It fails to focus on how the very topic of leadership and methods of researching it are socially constituted.

Feminist scholarship and leadership   What is meant by the topic of leadership and methods of researching it being 'socially constituted' has been explored by feminist scholarship. Sinclair (2005, p. 1), for example, contends that there is a 'close connection between constructs of leadership, traditional assumptions of masculinity and a particular expression of male heterosexual identity'. The basic idea here is that what we understand as 'leadership' is deeply conditioned by its development over the past several hundred years in patriarchal societies where (commonsensically identified) positions of leadership have been occupied by men. Indeed, the very identification of only some positions (those generally occupied by males, such as president and CEO) as exhibiting qualities of 'leadership' downplays the possibility of women being leaders (e.g. in the domestic sphere). This effect is illustrative of how leadership has been socially constituted. Conversely, the very possibility of women, such as Amanda Sinclair, assuming a position of authority/leadership as a business school professor indicates that the-times-they-are-a-changing. That is to say, women are assuming positions in which they are able to give voice to alternative conceptions of management.

For Sinclair, an alternative way of 'doing leadership' involves an avoidance or renunciation of a 'macho' view of leadership, where the leader feels compelled to be 'hard' and 'controlling' so that respect is based upon fear and blind loyalty rather than a sense of mutual valuation and trust. This 'macho' approach, Sinclair suggests, is not only often counter-productive in terms of winning the trust and full cooperation of subordinates. It is also damaging, emotionally and spiritually, for the leader who is obliged to repress or hide those impulses and aspects of identity that are incompatible with being, or at least giving the appearance of being, 'macho'. And, of course, this applies as much, if not more, to women who feel pressured by the dominant expectations of leaders to be tough, combative and 'Thatcher-like' in their relationships with subordinates. Interestingly, leaders may often be gentle, subtle and even seductive, but it has been suggested by Marta Calas and Linda Smircich (2001) that such features are often made to appear invisible in the literature on leadership since they are rarely discussed. Their suggestion is that acknowledging the presence of seduction, for example, can facilitate the development of innovation in leadership theory – something that is evident in Sinclair's theory of leadership and sexuality (2005, Chapter 9) where she explores the varied ways in which sexual identities are brought to leadership.

Doing leadership differently

> For men and women in organizations, being different as leaders means asking what their leadership work is for. It involves standing up for work that is valuable and important, and insisting on doing it in a reflective and compassionate way, not simply capitulating to the imperatives generated by an overpowering boss, truculent client or invented sense of urgency. Leadership of this kind risks the individual being used as a scapegoat, being singled out as 'not a team player' or not 'on board' with the interests of the organization. Yet, in a wider sense, taking such a position is exactly what leadership is often about. *(Sinclair, 2005, p. x)*

Sinclair cautions about the appropriation of elements or trappings of this alternative conception of leadership to 'strengthen the status quo'. She foresees the way in which people, especially men, who are captivated by the idea of *'life as a contest'* will mouth 'the language of care and consultation' in order to sound fashionable and/or advance their careers. This is a manipulative use of the alternative conception of leadership as a weapon for managing a favourable impression so as to secure or advance their position.

More generally, as individuals, managers (men or women) may privately harbour doubts about the moral value and integrity of their actions. But, in order to hold down their jobs and/or meet their family responsibilities, they tell themselves and others, with greater or lesser conviction, that it is necessary to dilute or suspend personal values. They are encouraged in this by the tendency of corporate managers to punish those who take issue with their corporate practices, such as 'whistle-blowers' who are instantly removed and disowned.

Exercise 7.11

Can you think of people or occasions that illustrate an alternative form of leadership? Were there 'risks' and how were these dealt with?

CASE STUDY 7.7 Leadership at the Football Association

In 2004 the football governing body for England, the FA, went through a major crisis when the Chief Executive, Mark Palios and the England team manager, Sven Göran Erickson were discovered to have both had an affair with the same FA secretary, Faria Alam, who subsequently appeared on *Celebrity Big Brother*. Later, at a tribunal held to consider if her dismissal from her job had been unfair, she recalled how she had sat between her two suitors as they vied for her attention at the office Christmas dinner.

For the England manager, this was the second occasion that he had been caught up in a 'sex scandal'. That alone might have been sufficient reason to cast doubt upon the manager's leadership qualities or, at the very least, his judgement and character. The context of the England's team disappointing performance in the Euro 2004 tournament was the touchpaper for favouring such an interpretation, and critical elements in the media were not slow to play this card. However, an unexpected,

and arguably more scandalous turn of events came to Sven's rescue. First of all, the FA denied that any affair had taken place and then, when this seemed implausible, the public relations people tried to protect their Chief Executive by promising the full detail on Sven to the *News of the World* in exchange for silence on Palios. The *News of the World* reported that 'The men who run football were even ready to bully top FA secretary Faria into giving details about her affair with Eriksson just to save Palios's neck.' Alam was reported to have refused to cooperate with the FA plan, so the *News of the World* ran its story exposing Palios's fling (see Box 7.19).

Box 7.19: Profile of Mark Palios (on the eve of becoming Chief Executive of the Football Association)

'As a restructuring expert, Palios understands the financial aspects of running a business and has experience of getting a troubled business out of the red. And as a football player, he has a deeper insight than most into the problems facing football.

Originally from Birkenhead, Palios joined Tranmere Rovers at the age of 16. During the 1970s and early 1980s,

he was one of the club's best players, playing in mid-field and scoring 33 goals. He was also Tranmere's representative at the Professional Footballers' Association.

Palios joined Price Waterhouse Coopers in 1989 as a partner from Ernst & Young. He worked his way through the ranks and is currently a business regeneration leader, which many believe is exactly what the FA needs at the moment.'

Source: http://www.accountancyage.com/accountancyage/features/2040141/profile-footballer-turned-accountant-mark-palios.

Not surprisingly, given this revelation, Palios resigned. In the meantime, Sven's position hinged on whether or not he had lied about the affair with Alam. His position was that he had neither confirmed nor denied the affair. An FA investigation concluded that he had no case to answer. He retained his job as manager of the England team and it was the FA as an

organization that was heavily criticized by the media. Management experts called upon by the media declared that the FA needed both reform and strong leadership. The irony of this suggestion was that prior to the 'sex scandal' Palios – the footballer turned accountant – had been widely praised for his reforms and strong leadership.

Thinkpoint 7.20

Do you think that reform and strong leadership would have been the answer to these problems or is there something else that might have been needed?

Leadership and management development One area in which management and leadership come together is in the sphere of management development where good management is conceived to rely upon the honing of interlinked mindsets. Jonathan Gosling and Henry Mintzberg (2003, p. 2) suggest a framework of management development that comprises five interventions that are necessary for improving the leadership of managers and the managing of leadership:

- Managing self: the reflective mindset.
- Managing organizations: the analytic mindset.
- Managing context: the worldly mindset.
- Managing relationships: the collaborative mindset.
- Managing change: the action mindset.

The identification of five mindsets emerged mainly through the authors' own practice in developing and delivering management programmes and it is not intended to be exhaustive. The emphasis upon managing rather than leading is intended precisely because 'nobody aspires to be a good manager anymore, everybody wants to be a good leader' (ibid., p. 1). Echoing our earlier discussion of how the meanings of management and leadership are differentiated, Gosling and Mintzberg argue that management without leadership is uninspiring but that leadership without management produces a disconnected style. This view of leadership nonetheless is somewhat unconventional as they believe that 'leaders don't *do* most of the things that their organizations get done, they do not even make them get done. Rather they help to establish the structures, conditions, and attitudes through which things get done' (ibid., p. 7, original emphasis). In other words, what they are suggesting is that leadership comprises that element of management which is concerned with establishing and enabling ways to get things done – with respect to creating 'structures', nurturing conditions and shaping attitudes. This requires the interlocking of the various mindsets. The action mindset is alert to, and facilitative of, change. In order to develop an effective patterning or structure of activities or to manage change, contexts and relationships are examined analytically. Finally, Gosling and Mintzberg's framework recalls that every intervention by the manager/leader is contingent upon the managing of self, which involves a reflexive mindset capable of reviewing, challenging and developing the other mindsets.

This is a potentially useful way of framing key aspects of activities identified as managing and leading. It locates these activities in a wider context that is attended to by the worldly mindset. It also appreciates that leading and managing in the context of organizations involves collaboration that necessitates the managing of relationships. But perhaps the key question concerns the boundaries of the knowledge that inform this process. Does the 'analytic mindset', for example, encompass the kinds of critical ideas about leadership and management that have been discussed in this and other chapters? To return to Amanda Sinclair's assessment of the boundaries of mainstream thinking about leadership, does the Gosling and Mintzberg framework itself exemplify a rather masculinist, if not macho, approach? How far does their reflective mindset stretch – just as far as is thought functional for getting the job done, or does it allow for the possibility, even if it does not commend it, of reflection resulting in the rejection of mainstream thinking and methods of leading and managing?

Exercise 7.12

Returning to Case study 7.7 on the English Football Association, do you think these five mindsets could help us to understand the problems that were experienced?

To take up the focus of the reflective mindset, it is relevant to acknowledge how managers are not unaware or unreflective about the pressures and contradictions of their work (Watson, 1994). Notably, they detect the tensions between the official, formally stated objectives and policies of their employing organization and the demands and evaluations of them from those immediately above them in the hierarchy. Needless to say, the obvious way to survive and succeed is to pay closest attention to the immediate priorities, expectations and criteria of evaluation applied by superiors (see Jackall, 1988; Dalton, 1959), and not to risk the emotional and financial penalties of being scapegoated or ostracized for 'rocking the boat' and failing to be a 'team player'. Here is another instance of how conflict is suppressed through self-censorship occasioned by reflection upon the likely consequences of being genuinely open and communicative. Not surprisingly, managers frequently feel frustrated and abused by the systems that they supposedly control, and bemoan the difficulties encountered in gaining unequivocal cooperation and commitment from their staff.

Managers routinely experience these contradictions and problems, but mainstream knowledge provides them with very limited resources for making sense of their situation. Management education and development tends to substitute prescription for diagnosis. That is to say, it rushes to provide a five bullet point plan of action without first examining in depth the nature of the problem for which the plan is presented as a solution. Such lists may supply managers with some reassuring prescriptions as well as a comforting sense of their own importance. They may even believe that, on the basis of this knowledge, they can develop or enhance a mindset for (strategically) analysing contexts or (operationally) managing change. Insofar as mainstream thinking marginalizes or trivializes discussion of the complex politics of managerial and leadership work, however, the consumers of mainstream knowledge are denied access to critical thinking that, arguably, would enable them to make more incisive sense of their predicament. In particular, it would challenge the tendency to diagnose difficulties in terms of personal failings (for which attendance at management development seminars is the recommended solution), and place in doubt any inclination to address these difficulties by redoubling their efforts (e.g. by becoming even more calculating or macho). In general, a major problem with management development courses that are intended to improve managerial or leadership skills is that they do not adequately address the conditions that impede their development and application. Their contents may be plausible enough in principle, but within a couple of weeks of taking the course, the pressures of work frustrate or overwhelm any good intentions to put them into practice.

Managers find themselves juggling competing demands for resources (e.g. jobs) and recognition – demands that come as much from other managers as from their subordinates. In mainstream thinking (e.g. Kotter, 1982), this is interpreted as inter-group politics as if such conflicts are unrelated to deeper social divisions, which include those of gender and ethnicity as well as those between employers and employees and managers and workers. It makes *ideological* sense to exclude from critical scrutiny the view that managerial authority is firmly founded upon objective expertise that is uncompromised by a concern to maintain the status quo and the distribution of privileges associated with it, including the lack of accountability of the managers to the managed. In this way, management is sanitized as it is distanced from the political conditions of its own formation and development (see Chapter 6).

CASE STUDY 7.8 In search of critical reflection

Tony Watson (1994) studied a group of senior managers. Following interviews with their new Managing Director, Paul Syston, these managers suspected that Syston had been hired as a hatchet man and feared for their jobs. In principle, such unsettling situations can stimulate a process of reflection on the conditions that make such episodes and responses possible. The managers might have reflected upon the rationality of an economic system that results in its participants, even its more privileged members, feeling deeply mistrustful and threatened. However, for this process of reflection to develop, there must at the very least be access to a (critical) theory that provides an interpretation of such episodes that gets beyond the personalities involved and the probable consequences for the individuals concerned, significant as they may be (see Willmott, 1997). Given their lack of access to such knowledge, it is understandable that the managers concerned were exclusively preoccupied with discussing Syston's motives, his personal style and inclinations, and were uninterested in analysing the conditions that make it possible for a boss to treat subordinates in a distant, intimidating manner. Had they avoided personalizing the problem – in terms of Syston's distant personal style or his appearance as 'a bit of a miserable sod' (Watson, 1994, p. 103) – they might have reflected on how the hierarchical relationship between managing directors and senior managers

as well as between managers and their subordinates tends to produce such disorientating and demoralizing encounters.

Syston's coolness might be read as the nervousness or defensiveness of an outsider who is brought in by his own superiors, perhaps against his own preferences, for such a job but in order to secure his position or fulfil his ambitions. In other words, Syston's distant, non-communicative style can be interpreted as symptomatic of how the wider system of employment relationships is organized. By declining to enter into any kind of personal relationship with his senior managers, Syston minimized his moral relationship to them. It was probably this impersonal distance, above all else, that made the senior managers anxious as they experienced Syston as a cold fish and a closed book; and they anticipated that they would encounter great difficulty in exerting any personal influence over such a 'miserable sod'. The outcome of this anxiety was inaction, rationalized by the comforting idea that perhaps Syston would be willing to listen to them and therefore that they would 'wait and see' rather than, say, resolve collectively to defend and develop more open and democratic processes of corporate governance where, in principle, those occupying positions of authority, such as Syston, would be under much greater pressure from below to communicate the plans of the company with regard to job losses.

executives in board meetings seeking to construct their own reality but often having their reality constructed for them by the CEO. We drew on different analytical frameworks to examine leadership practice as a lived-experience but one that is embedded in the CEO's construction of reality. To sustain this reality the CEO stigmatized any signs of divergence as evidence of individual incompetence, if not disloyalty. The CEO made effective use of his structural position at the apex of the hierarchy to assert his definition of the situation and to undermine the identity of anyone who sought to challenge it. Take the following extract from a board meeting where the Assistant General Manager of Customer Services (CS) challenges the CEO:

> CS: 'I think the point that I would like to make is that I think that one needs to distinguish between direction, which is clearly your prerogative and the more detailed decision-making, and I've felt that there's been a tendency to move down to a more detailed decision-making . . . '

> CEO: 'Oh, certainly, I think the idea of being in the City office and taking everything that is going just isn't on. Not with me and my temperament. I intend to be right there and I will stay there as long as I find, taking New Business as an example, that there have been "hot line" cases for two and half weeks and they still haven't left the office. That sort of thing will just drive me mad. And if anybody wants to get rid of me on jobs like that, there's a simple answer: don't let me see . . . '

In this transcript, the CS finds himself reprimanded for his rather mild attempt to persuade the CEO to focus less on the detail and more on the bigger picture of overall 'direction'. In response, the CEO picks on precisely a weakness in the area that the CS is responsible for – processing New Business so that clients have their policies speedily. He argues afterwards that while he is prepared to listen to those who think he is interfering too much (yet clearly he was not prepared to listen to the CS), 'my interests are quite calculated. They're not random.' But there is a broader context to the CEO's interventions, which is his concern to make decision making more sensitive and responsive to its strategic significance for the company's competitive position. That is why he is unwilling to tolerate New Business taking more than two and a half weeks to process.

Mainstream analyses of traits, styles or the characteristics of followers have proven less than informative since they fail to capture the lived experience and the politico-economic and cultural contexts of leadership as a practical accomplishment. A more critical approach is less concerned with providing technical prescriptions of leadership than highlighting some of the hidden processes to show how leadership is accomplished in daily encounters such as the brief excerpt illustrated above.

'Making out' We examined in Chapter 6 the ways in which productivity targets and bonus schemes were transformed by shop floor engineering workers into a competitive game whereby their function as a management control was obscured (Burawoy, 1979, 1985). Of course, management designed the bonus scheme with its targets and rewards for achieving them and did not anticipate how it could provide a framework for a game called 'making out'.

> 'Making out' can be seen 'as comprising a sequence of stages – of encounters between machine operators and the social or nonsocial objects that regulate the conditions of work. The rules of 'making out are experienced as a set of externally imposed relationships. The art of making out is to manipulate those relationships with the purpose of advancing as quickly as possible from one stage to the next'. . . 'The games workers play are . . . played within limits defined by minimum wages and acceptable profit margins. Management, at least at the lower levels, actively participates not only in the organization of the game but in the enforcement of its rules' (Burawoy, 1985, p. 80). Much of the stimulus to engage in such games 'derives from the inexorable coercion of coming to work, and subordination to the dictates of the labor process once there' (ibid., p. 81). In short, turning work into a game relieves workers of the numbing routine and the indignity of subordination; it almost becomes fun. It is also what best accounts for the huge amount of humour and practical joking that occur in factories (Collinson, 1992).

In short, game-playing displaced the need for managers as leaders because the workforce led itself – there was a kind of collective self-discipline that removed any necessity for management or leaders to intervene. According to Burawoy, the significance of creating a game out of the labour process extends well beyond the particularities of making out: 'The very activity of playing a game generates consent with respect to its rules' (Burawoy, 1979, p. 80). Management no longer needed to be visible as leaders or as the embodied manifestation of control and direction for the workforce. Involvement in the competitive game of achieving targets and bonuses meant that the workers managed themselves, thus removing what the classical writer Mary Parker Follett (see page 269) saw as the greatest vulnerability of managers – having to tell employees what to do. The case study demonstrates how the 'trick' of management or leadership is to dissolve into the background as those whom it seeks to manage are enabled to become self-managing.

Gideon Kunda (1991) also advances a thesis about how management seeks to develop a culture in which the workforce become self-disciplining because of having internalized the values of the company. In the company he studied, there was a comprehensive system of 'normative control' wherein employees were symbolically entrapped within the reality defined by management in terms of the corporate interests (ibid., 219–20). Management recognizes the importance of identity for employees and thereby seeks to map these concerns onto a sense of the organization as a community. Management and leadership is focused on managing identity through sustaining a strong organizational culture (see Chapter 9) whereby the norms and values are deeply internalized. However, Kunda finds that employees remain fairly ambivalent and relate to these attempts at internalizing an identity tied to the company with some irony and symbolic distance. But, of course, this can also be a safety valve or a means of boosting the egos of staff who consider themselves smart enough to see through, and poke fun at, the corporate culture. The generation of a corporate culture that seeks to secure the commitment and loyalty of employees through appropriating their identities can, argues Kunda (ibid., p. 222), also create the very conditions of its own demise. That is to say, by providing the conditions through which employees generate a sense of community, such solidarity can in principle be turned against the corporation and management interests just as easily as in support of them.

Contributions and limitations to thinking about the field

Contributions Critical thinking is concerned to link larger social and political issues with the theory and practice of managing, leading and organizing. It also focuses more directly on human, political and process dimensions of management and leadership. While the mainstream has recognized these aspects of life in organizations, the human, political and process dimensions of organization are domesticated by treating them as an informal system either to be manipulated to secure more effective management control, or, if this proves too difficult or costly, to be viewed as an aberration to be eradicated. By contrast, critical studies see human and political processes as integral to the 'lived reality' of organizations and view attempts to eradicate them as self-defeating.

Critical analysis of management and leadership may provide practitioners with insights into how management and leadership are possible since it is only through their acceptance as legitimate activities by the managed and the led that they can be in the least effective. In particular it:

- Gives close consideration to the political and processual character of (practices that are identified as) 'management' and 'leadership'.
- Applies a number of key concepts, including identity, inequality, insecurity and freedom to explore management and leadership as problematical *social* phenomena rather than taking them as self-evident objects of examination and improvement.
- Gives attention to the historical formation of management and the way leadership involves the management of meaning, including the meaning of management.
- Moves away from knowledge of management as assuming the adequacy of common-sense thinking and the legitimacy of the status quo.
- Invites a more sceptical assessment of the claims made in the name of management and leadership and thereby opens up a space for different notions of what they could mean.

In mainstream thinking, 'management' and 'leadership' tend to be widely viewed as unquestionably valuable and therefore desirable. Leadership, in particular, has a very seductive appeal. It is assumed to be something that is obviously 'needed' and, in principle, easily identified and improved. Books and courses on leadership instantly attract attention and gain a large audience. Critical analysis contributes to a stripping away of the gloss and hype that surrounds leadership. In this chapter we have concentrated on issues less connected with productivity, performance or profitability than is usual in the mainstream. Critical approaches, we believe, can provide managers and leaders with knowledge and insights that they would not secure elsewhere. This is particularly relevant when there is a proliferation of stakeholders making demands on organizations. Organizations exist within society and increasingly managers find themselves harried by predatory competitors, let down by unreliable suppliers, rebuffed by discriminating customers and deserted by footloose staff, not to mention pressured by fund managers who demand the impossible of 'above average' performance from all companies. And a parallel picture applies to public and not-for-profit sector managers who are under relentless pressure to introduce changes that promise to produce more for less. Today, managers probably have less discretion to pursue a narrow range of interests, especially as the media will expose any management that is discovered or deemed to behave dangerously or without due care and attention. Many organizations are caught up in increasingly global relations (see Chapter 12) where an apparently insignificant local action can have massive world-wide repercussions, much like a whisper turning ultimately into a hurricane. This goes for academic analyses every bit as much as practitioners, since actions and words are always affecting the actions of others and this can multiply into global proportions.

While we cannot ultimately control for the unintended consequences of our actions, we can endeavour to think ethically and to be as responsible as possible for what we say and do. It is clear from critical research that organizations are much more complex than the mainstream literature, in its search for 'quick fixes' or simple causal patterns, presumes. Understanding, for example, what part that identity plays in managers' and employees' lives, or how some level of insecurity can be produc-tive yet incapacitating if excessive, is of greater value than fantasies about perfect leadership or profound management. Since organizations are dynamic, it makes sense to challenge conventional thinking about them. While the direct relationship between theory and practice or ideas and their adoption is not always obvious, academic research and writing indirectly and perhaps quite slowly filters into the consciousness of those we study. At the time of writing, there has been a fashion for leadership, and this is why we have sought to question and counter any tendency for management to become neglected. A critical approach tends to foster scepticism about panaceas or fashions, which is no less relevant to the fashionable advocacy of 'leadership' than it is to the longer established preferences for 'one best way' approaches to management, such as Theories X, Y and Z.

Limitations   One of the strengths of a critical approach is that it is self-reflexive as well as reflexive about broader relations both internal and external to organizations. It follows that it is self-critical about critical approaches as well as the mainstream both in terms of the value of our theory and its implications for practice. We offer the following limitations of critical approaches, which are often excessively centred on managing people and may, as a consequence:

- Neglect the global nature of capitalism.
- Neglect the domination of financial power.
- Be theoretical and idealistic rather than practical and applied/pragmatic.

Insofar as we compensate for the domination of concerns with productivity, performance and profitability in the mainstream, one problem of the critical approach is to be over-concerned with issues of managing people or, to be more accurate, managing relations between people. Also we should beware believing that relations can be managed or controlled since that is rarely the case. Managing or leading is about facilitating the conditions that enable people to manage their own relations in ways that benefit one another and ultimately the productive power of an organization, but in ways that are responsible and ethical for others (e.g. customers, the public, environmentalists, the devel-oping world, minorities or government) who are not direct stakeholders. Of course, the focus of this chapter on management and leadership necessarily means that we cannot avoid a strong focus on the human dimension as it is impossible to manage and lead without inspiring, engaging, motivating or driving human beings to pursue their tasks creatively, collaboratively and competitively.

The human dimension outside of organizations might lead us to focus on the broader structures of power such as global capitalism, international regulation and finance capital, particularly given the success of recent protests about global capitalism that have captured media attention. It is interesting to note how radical movements have made as much use of global telecommunications as have the corporations and the international institutions that they seek to criticize for their exploitation of developing countries, labour and the environment. Not only are the global corporations and the finance capital that sustains them exploitative of the comparatively weak, but also they tend to dominate other organizations, especially suppliers and distributors. Their power as both buyers and providers can force suppliers and distributors into uneconomic exchanges that render them ultimately vulnerable to cheap takeovers.

Finally, despite what has been claimed above regarding the indirect and often unintended, benefits of critical analyses to practitioners, much of it remains abstract, idealistic, and over-theoretical. For example, many critical theorists are prone to draw on esoteric theories drawn from philosophy partly perhaps to display their intellectual credentials and scholarly credibility. Whereas the mainstream justifies itself on claims to advancing a science of behaviour, the critics seek a philosophical self-justification.

Synopsis and conclusion

Theories of 'leadership', it is believed, enable us to identify 'leaders' and perhaps train them and others to become better leaders. For many practitioners and theorists of leadership, this way of understanding leadership makes good sense. The challenge is to develop or identify a way of conceptualizing and studying leadership (or management) that detects its existence and, if possible, enhances it. This process of detection and prescription necessitates developing a view or concept, or *theory*, of leadership (or management) that accurately reflects the realities of leadership 'out there'.

Can 'leadership', etc. be understood in another way? Attempting to do so is not easy as it necessitates some bracketing or suspension of belief in common-sense ways, or habits, of thinking. How else might 'leadership', etc. be understood, if not as an effort to capture and upgrade the realities that it aspires to reflect? To develop a different understanding requires the questioning and abandoning of the assumption of a neat *separation* between, on the one side, thought (or theory) and, on the other side, the reality (or practices) that concepts of organization, etc. are assumed to reflect, more or less adequately. For it is on this basis that established thinking, and knowledge, about organization, management and leadership is founded. If an alternative approach is to be advanced and appreciated, then the assumption of this separation must be set aside (see Box 7.21).

Rarely do we find organizations, other than families and friendship groups, not organized through a division of labour in which managers and leaders are in the senior hierarchical ranks enjoying the power to allocate scarce rewards and resources (e.g. wages, bonuses, promotions, status, etc.). In

Box 7.21: Disrupting the theory–practice division

If the separation between thought and reality is rejected, and the 'acid test' of an independent reality against which to assess competing theories is denied, how are we to assess the credibility of different theories, except against the claims of other theories?

In response to this concern, it can be suggested that the difficulties associated with rejecting the thought-reality separation are not a compelling reason for continuing to harbour the illusion that reality exists in an external relation to thought, and that reality can be reflected, rather than constructed, through theory. Accepting this argument does not mean that reality ceases to exist. It means, instead, that claims about 'knowing' this reality must be treated sceptically and *viewed as political rather than as disinterested (or 'scientific') claims*. Such claims are neither provable nor falsifiable by testing them against reality because access to this 'reality' (practices) is inescapably mediated or interpreted by value-based thought (theories).

This perspective, which itself should be treated as comprising a number of political rather than disinterested claims, or assumptions, has a number of implications:

1 Theories in management and organization studies are understood to be embedded in, and indelibly coloured by, the practices that they endeavour to represent. They do not stand apart from these practices. Nor can they ever reflect these practices, or even capture some element of them. They simply offer competing ways of making sense.

2 Theories should be viewed as comprising truth *claims*, the plausibility of which depends not upon their approximation to workplace reality, since this is inaccessible in any unmediated way, but upon how these claims are accepted and legitimized by different practitioners.

3 Truth claims in certain management theories (e.g. popularized accounts of Maslow's hierarchy of needs or notions of democratic leadership) may be enthusiastically received by managers while they are treated with extreme scepticism and even disdain by many management academics. Their credibility does not depend upon the accuracy of such claims but, rather, their plausibility, as interpreted within competing (discursive) frameworks of meaning.

4 When truth claims are endorsed, they are then actively drawn upon by those seeking to construct or define reality for others (e.g. the CEO in the Pensco example discussed above). In short, truth claims are an inescapable part of, or serve to construct, the very same reality that we claim to know.

addition, these managers and leaders enjoy several of their own material (economic) and symbolic (status) privileges associated with their position. We live in a hierarchical and competitive society that is grounded in an ethic of success and achievement. In Chapter 6 the ideology of equal opportunity was critically challenged as providing legitimacy to existing inequalities and a faith in *reason* for the mainstream simply to take them for granted. In this chapter, we have focused more on the difficulties that managers and leaders have in securing the consent or compliance of employees that are partly a result of major inequalities. While the mainstream takes this consent and compliance as unproblematic, the critical literature has sought to demonstrate how it may be secured by management appearing *not* to manage and lead as then, the extent to which they coerce and control employees is obscured. Sometimes this occurs accidentally as when employees become preoccupied with achieving their bonuses as a competitive game; at other times, managers foster and facilitate forms of employee collective and individual self-discipline as the most effective managerial and leadership strategy. Conditions are created in which subordinates find their work sufficiently meaningful for the sense they have of themselves (i.e. their identity) as to secure a self-disciplined commitment in fulfilling their tasks that displaces feelings of subjugation and grievances associated with exploitation.

Management and leadership are discussed in mainstream texts predominantly through the lens of a systems model where the parts of an organization are seen as similar to the parts of a body or a machine and/or through individualistic conceptions of the leader who possesses appropriate personality traits, is constrained by the situation or adapts to contingent factors. The organic or mechanical analogy largely remains unquestioned in the mainstream despite the fact that the parts of an organization are human beings who think for themselves, interpret their experiences and may challenge or contest, just as well as collaborate and comply with the demands made of them. Similarly, the ways in which the context and attribution of leadership are both constituted through relations of power and knowledge is not considered by the mainstream. Of course, these critical ways of understanding management and leadership completely undermine any possibility of there being a 'one best way'. Consequently, management and leadership have to survive and thrive as untidy and unpredictable activities within uncertain and continually changing circumstances. By focusing on power, knowledge, identity, insecurity, freedom and inequality, we are continually confronted by the precarious and unpredictable aspects of management and leadership. This makes it all but impossible to accept the mainstream in its presumptions of a general consensus regarding managing and leading members of their organization.

The critical approach does not follow the mainstream in legitimizing the status quo or providing managers with ready-made solutions designed to make organizations more efficient or profitable. This is what throughout this book we have called a narrow managerialism in the approach to studying organizations. Rather, the critical analyst is concerned to incorporate consideration of much broader issues in society such as equality, justice and freedom and the extent to which managers, leaders and their work organizations contribute to, or constrain and deflect attention toward, such ideals. It has to be said, however, that even though it is not their direct intention, critical studies of organization can be beneficial to management in providing alternative insights and visions that would be unlikely to arise from the mainstream. Indeed, an unintended consequence of critical work may be that it helps managers pursue their performance and/or profit objectives more effectively than the mainstream if only because its examination of issues – from motivation to governance – provides managers with a broader and fresher perspective that enables them to develop innovative approaches and/or avoid self-defeating methods of management control. Its effect may be to enable managers to think beyond the current conventional wisdom.

Discussion questions

1 How do managers and leaders make a difference to organizations?

2 Are the main assumptions underlying a mainstream approach to management and leadership valid?

3 Is management likely to be effective in the absence of leadership, and vice versa?

4 What are some of the contingencies that managers and leaders have to consider in carrying out their work?

5 What are the main differences between a classical and an open systems approach to organizational design and structure?

6 What does a critical view of management and leadership add to our understanding of organizations?

Further reading

Empirical studies

Burawoy, M. (1979) *The Manufacture of Consent*, Chicago: Chicago University Press.

Burns, T. and Stalker, G. (1961) *The Management of Innovation*, Oxford: Oxford University Press.

Collinson, D. (1992) *Managing the Shopfloor*, Berlin: de Gruyter.

Kanter, R. M. (1977/1993) *Men and Women of the Corporation*, New York: Basic Books.

Kidder, T. (1981) *The Soul of the New Machine*, Harmondsworth: Penguin.

Knights, D. and McCabe, D. (2003) *Organization and Innovation: Gurus Schemes and American Dreams*, Milton Keynes: Open University Press/McGraw Hill.

Kondo, D. (1990) *Crafting Selves: Power, Gender and Discourses of Identity in a Japanese Workplace*, Chicago, IL: University of Chicago Press.

Kunda, G. (1991) *Engineering Culture*, Philadelphia: Temple University Press.

Annotated readings

Yukl, G. (2002) *Leadership in Organizations*, Upper Saddle River, NJ: Prentice Hall.

Presents a comprehensive review of mainstream approaches to leadership in organizations. Also includes a chapter on the nature of managerial work and a final chapter that overviews a number of 'biases' and 'controversies' in the field. For students who want to gain a close understanding of what 'mainstream analysis' looks like, this is to be strongly recommended.

Grint, K. (2005) *Leadership: Limits and Possibilities*, London: Palgrave.

A text that takes a more critical approach to the claims made by theories of leadership.

Sinclair, A. (2005) *Doing Leadership Differently*, Melbourne: Melbourne University Press.

Takes an explicitly feminist line on leadership. Connects with mainstream preoccupations but addresses them in a more critical way. Provides something of a bridge between mainstream and critical approaches. Written in a more personal and engaging manner.

Alvesson, M. and Willmott, H. C. (1996) *Making Sense of Management*, London: Sage.

Reviews critical contributions to the study of management including its specialist areas of activity such as marketing and accounting. Illustrates how critical analysis can be applied to

develop an alternative way of making sense of the development of management.

Anthony, P. (1986) *The Foundations of Management*, London: Tavistock.

An accessible and thoughtful reflection upon the basis of management's claim or prerogative to manage. Pays close attention to the morality of management.

Parker, M. (2002) *Against Management*, Oxford: Polity Press.

An entertaining polemic that draws together the numerous strands of criticism that can be levelled against management. Includes a critique of 'critical management'.

More general reading

Academy of Management Executive (2003) 'Retrospective: The practice of management', 7(3):7–23.

Ackroyd, S. and Thompson, P. (1999) *Organizational Misbehaviour*, London: Sage.

Bryman, A. (1999) 'Leadership in organizations', in S. R. Clegg, C. Hardy and W. R. Nord (eds.) *Managing Organizations*, London: Sage.

Burnham, J. (1941) *The Managerial Revolution*, Harmondsworth: Penguin.

Casey, C. (1995) *Work, Self and Society: After Industrialism*, London and New York: Routledge.

Fulop, L. and Stephen Linstead, S. (eds.) (1999) *Management: A Critical Text*, London: Macmillan Business.

Hales, C. (1993) *Managing Through Organization*, Routledge: London.

Harding, N. (2003) *The Social Construction of Management: Texts and Identities*, London: Routledge.

Jackson, N. and Carter, P. (2000) *Rethinking Organizational Behaviour*, London: Financial Times/Prentice Hall.

Knights, D. and Morgan, G. (1992) 'Leadership and corporate strategy: Toward a critical analysis', *Leadership Quarterly* 3(3):171–190.

Pollard, S. (1965) *The Genesis of Modern Management*, London: Edward Arnold.

Rhodes, C. (2002) 'Coffee and the business of pleasure: The case of Harbucks v. Mr Tweek', *Culture and Organization* 8(4):293–306.

Shotter, J. (1992) 'The manager as a practical author: Conversations for action', in J. Shotter (ed.) *Conversational Realities: Constructing Life Through Language*, London: Sage.

Willmott, H. C. (1984) 'Images and Ideals of Managerial Work', *Journal of Management Studies* 21(3):349–368.

References

Adair, J. (1979) *Action-Centred Leadership*, Aldershot: Gower.

Anthony, P. (1977) *The Ideology of Work*, London: Tavistock.

Barnard, C. (1936) *The Functions of the Executive*, Cambridge, MA: Harvard University Press.

Bass, B. (1985) *Leadership and Performance: Beyond Expectations*, New York: Free Press.

Bennis, W. G. (1959) 'Leadership theory and administrative behaviour: The problem of authority', *Administrative Science Quarterly* 2:42–47.

Blake, R. R. and McCanse, A. A. (1991) *Leadership Dilemmas: Grid Solutions*, Houston, TX: Gulf Publishing.

Blake, R. R. and Mouton, J. S. (1964) *The Managerial Grid*, Houston, TX: Gulf Publishing.

Burawoy, M. (1979) *The Manufacture of Consent*, Chicago: Chicago University Press.

Burawoy, M. (1985) *The Politics of Production*, London: Verso.

Burns, J. M. (1978) *Leadership*, New York: Harper & Row.

Burns, T. and Stalker, G. M. (1961) *The Management of Innovation*, Oxford: Oxford University Press.

Calas, M. and Smircich, L. (2001) 'Voicing seduction to silence leadership', *Organization Studies* 12(4):567–602.

Chandler, A. D. Jr. (1977) *The Visible Hand: The Managerial Revolution in American Business*, Cambridge, MA: The Belknapp Press of Harvard University.

Child, J. (1984) *Organization*, second edition, London: Harper and Row.

Collinson, D. (1988) ' "Engineering humour": Masculinity, joking and conflict in shop floor relations', *Organization Studies* 9(2):181–199.

Collinson, D. (1992) *Managing the Shopfloor*, Berlin: de Gruyter.

Dalton, M. (1959) *Men Who Manage*, New York: Wiley.

Drucker, P. (1974) *Management: Tasks, Responsibilities, Practices*, London: Heinemann.

Fayol, H. (1916/1949) *General and Industrial Management*, London: Pitman.

Fiedler, F. E. (1967) *A Theory of Leadership Effectiveness*, New York: McGraw-Hill.

Gosling, J. and Mintzberg, H. (2003) 'The five minds of a manager', *Harvard Business Review*, Nov., 1–9.

Grint, K. (2000) *The Arts of Leadership*, Oxford: Oxford University Press.

Grint, K. (2005) *Leadership: Limits and Possibilities*, London: Palgrave.

Hersey, P. and Blanchard, K. H. (1993) *Management of Organizational Behaviour: Utilising Human Resources*, sixth edition, Englewood Cliffs, NJ: Prentice Hall.

Hickson, D., Pugh, D. and Pheysey, D. (1971) 'Operations technology and organisation structure: An empirical appraisal', *Administrative Science Quarterly* 14:378–397.

House, R. J. (1971) 'A path–goal theory of leadership effectiveness', *Administrative Science Quarterly* 16:321–338.

Jackall, R. (1988) *Moral Mazes: The World of Corporate Managers*, New York: Oxford University Press.

Knights, D. and McCabe, D. (1999) 'There are no limits to authority?: TQM and organizational power relations', *Organization Studies* 20(2):197–224.

Knights, D. and Morgan, G (1992) 'Leadership as corporate strategy: Towards a critical analysis', *Leadership Quarterly* 3(3):171–190.

Knights, D. and O'Leary, M. (2006) 'The possibility of ethical leadership', *Journal of Business Ethics*, forthcoming.

Knights, D. and Willmott, H. (1992) 'Conceptualising leadership processes: A study of senior managers in a financial services company', *Journal of Management Studies* 29(6):761–782.

Koontz, H., O'Donnell, C. and Weihrich, H. (1984) *Management*, eight edition, Tokyo: McGraw-Hill.

Kotter, J. (1982) *The General Managers*, New York: Free Press.

Krech, D., Crutchfield, R. S. and Ballachey, E. L. (1962) *Individual in Society*, New York: McGraw-Hill.

Kunda, G. (1991) *Engineering Culture*, Philadelphia: Temple University Press.

Likert, R. (1961) *New Patterns of Management*, New York: McGraw Hill.

Magretta, J. (with N. Stone) (2002) *What Management Is*, London: Profile.

McGregor, D. (1960) *The Human Side of Enterprise*, New York: McGraw Hill.

Minkes, A. L., Small, M. W. and Chatterjee, S. R. (1999) 'Leadership and business ethics: Does it matter? Implications for management', *Journal of Business Ethics* 20:327–335, cited in Knights and O'Leary (2006, op. cit., p. 12).

Mintzberg, H. (1973) *The Nature of Managerial Work*, New York: Harper and Row.

Mintzberg, H. (1979) *The Structuring of Organizations*, Englewood Cliffs, NJ: Prentice Hall.

Mullins, L. J. (2002) *Management and Organizational Behaviour*, sixth edition, London: Financial Times/Prentice Hall.

Nichols, T. and Beynon, H. (1977) *Living with Capitalism*, London: Heinemann.

Ouchi, W. (1981) *Theory Z*, Reading, MA: Addison-Wesley.

Pascale, R. T. and Athos, A. G. (1982) *The Art of Japanese Management*, Harmondsworth: Penguin.

Peters, T. and Waterman, R. H. (1982) *In Search of Excellence*, London: Harper and Row.

Pettigrew, A. (1973) *The Politics of Organizational Decision Making*, London: Tavistock.

Pfeffer, G. (1981) 'Management as symbolic action: The creation and maintenance of organizational paradigms', in L. L. Cummings and B. M. Staw (eds.) *Research in Organizational Behaviour, Vol. 3*, Greenwich, CT: JAI Press.

Pfeffer, J. (1981) *Power in Organizations*, Massachusetts: Marshfield.

Sims, R. and Brinkamann, J. (2002) 'Leaders as role models: The case of John Gutfreund at Solomon Brothers', *Journal of Business Ethics* 35:327–339, cited in Knights and O'Leary (2006, op. cit.).

Sinclair, A. (2005) *Doing Leadership Differently*, second edition, Melbourne: Melbourne University Press.

Smircich, L. and Morgan, G. (1982) 'Leadership: The management of meaning', *Journal of Applied Behavioral Science* 18:257–273.

Tourish, D. and Vatcha, N. (2005) 'Charismatic leadership and corporate cultism at Enron: The elimination of dissent, the promotion of conformity and organizational collapse', *Leadership* 1(4):455–480.

Treviño, L. K., Brown, M. and Pincus, L. (2003) 'A qualitative investigation of perceived executive ethical leadership: Perceptions from inside and outside the executive suite', *Human Relations* 56(1):5–36.

Vroom, V. H. and Jago, A. G. (1988) *The New Leadership: Managing Participation in Organizations*, Englewood Cliffs, NJ: Prentice Hall.

Vroom, V. H. and Yetton, P. W. (1973) *Leadership and Decision-Making*, Pittsburgh: University of Pittsburgh Press.

Watson, T. (1994) *In Search of Management*, London: Routledge.

Whyte, W. F. (1943/1993) *Street Corner Society: The Social Structure of an Italian Slum*, fourth edition, Chicago: University of Chicago Press.

Willmott, H. C. (1997) 'Critical management learning', in J. Burgoyne and M. Reynolds (eds.) *Management Learning*, London: Sage, p.p. 161–176.

Note

1 The following paragraphs draw heavily on Knights and O'Leary (2006).

8 Political Organizations and Decision Making

Pamela Odih and David Knights

Key concepts and learning objectives

By the end of this chapter you should understand:

- The key conceptual and theoretical ideas that form the pluralist model of organizational decision making.

- The disputes about their value with regards to effectively explaining the power dynamics of decision making, conflict resolution and goal achievement.

- The ideological issues that inform mainstream perspectives.

- The contribution of a critical perspective in outlining the importance of problematizing power and its operation in decision making.

Aims of the chapter

This chapter will:

- Give an account of pluralist models of political organizations and decision making as part of the mainstream perspective.

- Examine several significant mainstream studies.

- Discuss a selection of major critical studies.

- Explore the strengths and weaknesses of critical approaches.

Overview and key points

The chapter examines a familiar concept – politics. A political analysis highlights organizations as systems of government, inclined either towards authoritarian or democratic forms of rule. It is a valuable focus enabling researchers to understand how organizations become orderly or not and how diverse individuals and groups may be directed to follow common organizational pursuits. Yet insofar as mainstream writers have (and often they do not) acknowledge organizational politics, they (e.g. Pettigrew, 1973a) tend to comprehend it pejoratively as something negative that needs to be eradicated (Knights and Murray, 1994). The primary benefit of politics is that of 'sorting it out'. Writers and researchers struggled to come to terms with the fact that organizational life has as much to do with differences as with similarities. And yet classical theorists frequently made reference to authority and power without recognizing them to be political issues, which establish specific forms of superior–subordinate relations.

Mainstream approach

Introduction to the mainstream approach

People are recruited into work as individuals but they bring with them a collection of social experiences, attitudes and values that help define their informal relations with other organizational members. Although individuals might not formally be aware of their links to groups, they will inevitably share a sense of commonality with certain colleagues. Imagine that you have been recruited, on a temporary basis by a local council office. The council office is currently actively lobbying for an expansion of its administrative capacities. Given the complexity of local council resourcing, the initiative is likely to generate disagreements. Indeed discussions during lunchtime and around the water cooler are rife with speculation and counter speculation of redundancies and promotions. While you might wish to remain blissfully oblivious to the wider processes of recruitment, your appointment has already aligned you with the interests of those that recruited you.

Chances are that your appointment is an outcome of competition between groups for limited organizational resources, power and influence. The employment of an additional administrator might provide key personnel with the freedom to use their expertise more strategically. Alternatively, your appointment as a temporary administrator might highlight the performance of the group and their contribution to the overall goals of the organization. Your employment could pave the way for others to secure pay increases or other rewards. Yet disparities in pay often fuel divisions between different groups of workers. This diversity of views and their implications concerning an individual appointment illustrate how decisions in organizations are always steeped in politics – that is, differences about their consequences in terms of security, rewards, status and prospects for individuals and groups. Indeed the concept of organizational politics stems from the view that conflicts and power occupy centre stage in the ebb and flow of organizational decision making (Knights and Murray, 1994).

A definition of political behaviour in Box 8.1 is intended to draw your attention to key conceptual ideas. First, that political behaviour extends far beyond the formal authority of one's specified job requirement (Robbins, 1998). Secondly, that political behaviour involves cultivating influential allies, controlling the flow of information and influencing decisions through the informal use of one's power basis (ibid.). And finally how political behaviour is directly linked to decision making. Organizational decision making is entwined with the political strategies of bargaining, compromising and trading support for information and other scarce resources.

Classical theory, ideologies and the emergence of the mainstream approach　The earliest writers on organization theory, like some managers today, assumed a complete consensus about the overall goal of the organization as the achievement of common objectives (Fincham and Rhodes, 1996). This is what has been termed a **unitary** perspective on organization (Fox, 1974) – one in which the views of top management are assumed to be shared by everyone and conflict simply treated as **pathological** rather than a reflection of different interpretations and interests. These writers dedicated their academic activities to identifying the rules or principles that should be used in designing the operation of organizations. Such principles were assumed to be relevant to all types of formal organization. These writers formed the **classical school** and were characterized by a focus on the formal organization of work. They were particularly concerned with specifying the relationship between line managers and staff. Their chief contribution here was to emphasize the importance of defined authority structures and clarity in role specification. The organizational structure formally unites organizational members into a well-integrated team dedicated to the pursuit of common goals. Conflicts are rare,

Box 8.1: 'Political behaviour' – a mainstream definition

Political behaviour is defined as those private activities, which may not be consistent with the interests of the organization, but that influence, or attempt to influence, the distribution of advantages and disadvantages within the organization (Robbins, 1998, p. 410).

transient dysfunctions, which can be effectively removed through appropriate managerial action. And organizational life is best served through the principal of 'top-down' decision making where senior management make decisions that they expect subordinates to carry out automatically and without any kind of discontinuity or diversion.

More recent mainstream orthodoxy has been less inclined to ignore the role of political power in organizational life. Politics is recognized as a principal fact of decision making in organizations. Organizations have been increasingly recognized as 'political systems' (Handy, 1976), defined by competing interests (Dawson, 1986), fuelled by 'the tactics of conflict' (Handy, 1976), powered by hierarchical position (Burns, 1969) and subject to a plethora of tactical decision-making strategies (Bacharach and Lawler, 1980). Each of these principal areas of debate will be examined here, with a view to introducing the pluralist account of politics, organizations and political behaviour.

Mainstream account of political activity in organizations

To illustrate the mainstream approach, this section provides an adapted case study of Burns and Stalker's (1966) account of politics and organization within the Scottish electronics industry during the 1950s. Entitled *The Management of Innovation*, Burns and Stalker's classic study is a highly insightful example of mainstream political analysis (see also Chapter 7). The research was originally motivated by a desire to study an industrial company as a 'community of people at work' (ibid., p. 1). The proposed aim was to research into organizational conduct and relationships using the same terms of reference as would be applied to urban neighbourhoods and small communities. Despite changes to this original remit a committed interest in 'the adaptation of relationships between individuals' continued to guide the focus of their research. Consequently, Burns and Stalker (1966) set about studying the organizational relations, which in the mid-1950s defined firms involved in the Scottish Council's innovative 'Electronics Scheme'.

The Scottish Council was, at that time, a voluntary body financially sustained by industrial firms, the local government and trade unions. The Electronics Scheme was a joint venture involving the Scottish Council, the Scottish Home Department and the Board of Trade. It operated as an incentive scheme, to actively encourage the growth, in Scotland, of industries willing to adopt new technologies. The declared agenda of the scheme was to provide firms with assistance necessary to build up technological expertise so as to attract suitable contracts from the defence ministries. Companies that entered the scheme would be assisted in setting up a laboratory team dedicated to advancing the company's technological expertise. To this end the scheme was intent on instigating a rapid change in the rate of electronic development in the Scottish electronics market. It was this condition of rapid change and development that attracted Burns and Stalker's (1966) research interest. For their part, they hoped to observe 'how management systems changed in accordance with changes in the technical and commercial tasks of the firm' (ibid., p. 4).

Burns and Stalker's (1966) initial findings produced curious anomalies. They analysed the major incentives that encouraged firms to enter the scheme. Most firms entering the scheme were prompted by a fear of market competition. But only a few firms were prompted by a desire to expand their technological know-how and enter into new markets. The reticence of firms to embrace an 'expansionist urge' was reflected in the role and status firms ascribed to the laboratory teams, which they were required to form as part of their entry into the Scottish Council's scheme. Firms generally appeared

Box 8.2: Key concepts – classical tradition

1 Focus on the formal structure of the organization.

2 Concern to identify the right formal organization.

3 Belief in the existence of one best form of organization.

4 Seeking to describe organizational rules, often called principles.

5 Belief that organizational principles are applicable to all types of formal organization.

6 Keenness to identify the best way of dividing up the task to be done.

7 Stress on the need for clarity in role specification and performance.

8 Placing emphasis on hierarchical control and similarities between members.

9 Insufficient attention paid to the diversity of problems experienced in different types of organizations.

less inclined to exploit the team as a technical resource, often sidelining their efforts or confining them to specific activities. Burns and Stalker (1966, p. 4) describe how 'in half the cases laboratory groups were disbanded or disrupted by the resignation of their leaders'. In other instances laboratory groups were 'converted into test departments, "trouble-shooting" teams or production departments' (ibid.). Three features were common to all these predicaments. First, the dire fate of the laboratory group was often sealed from the outset. Established organizational members were, in many cases, determined to exclude the laboratory group from the rest of the organization. Burns and Stalker (1966, p. 139) provide verbatim evidence of this intention to exclude the laboratory group:

> These 'cultural' differences were openly accepted by the senior managers with whom we were first in touch. 'Physicists', we were seriously told by one managing director, 'are very difficult people to work with'. But the same differences showed up in remarks to the effect that a good production engineer was a person who would tackle any problem given to him and solve it unaided, while a good design engineer in a laboratory was a person who could say 'I don't know'; again they appeared in references to 'long-haired types' and to 'the production clots'.

Burns and Stalker's observation here, illustrates the conflicts of power that constituted, for them, a second noticeable response by existing organizational members to the introduction of the laboratory group. A third noticeable response was evident in the tendency for senior managers to convert what were clearly management problems into difficulties defined as caused by the 'ignorance and obstructiveness' of opposing interests. Burns and Stalker (1966, p. 140) defined this latter course of action as 'The price of adapting the working organization – and the refusal to pay it'. They had observed that for some managers adapting to the rate of commercial and technical change carried with it too many demands on their existing relationships and 'heavier mental and emotional commitments' (ibid., p. 7). For these managers a method of coping was either to control their personal situation or claim exemption from a problem so as to protect the special conditions attached to their status. But such manoeuvres were problematic as they compounded the company's 'inability to adapt the management system to the form appropriate to conditions of more rapid technical and commercial change' (ibid., p. 5).

The difficulties encountered by these firms in adjusting to rapidly changing technology and commercial situations led the researchers to identify the **political structure** of a company as a vital determinant of effective organizational management. They defined the concept of political structure as follows: 'The political structure of a [company] is the balance of competing pressure from each group recognizing a common interest for a larger share of all or some benefits or resources than they have now or think they may have in the future' (ibid., p. 145).

What Burns and Stalker (1966) sought to establish was, first, that political systems and status systems exist within firms, and, secondly, that they do not exist as isolated entities, for 'political and status considerations constantly influence the working organization, and influence it so as to reduce its effectiveness' (ibid., p. 146). It needs to be recognized that Burns and Stalker's (1966) position here is firmly committed to a mainstream account of politics and organizations. They fall short of claiming the existence of endemic irreconcilable power struggles within organizations in contrast with, for example, a Marxist perspective of political analysis. Instead they suggest that the political structure of specific types of organization have detrimental consequences. To this end Burns and Stalker (1966) set about elucidating two divergent forms of organizational structure operating within the sample of Scottish firms studied. The first of the two ideal types is the **mechanistic organization**. They describe this system as appearing 'appropriate to an enterprise operating under relatively stable conditions' (ibid., p. 5). The mechanistic organization is very similar to Weber's model of rational-legal bureaucracy (see Chapter 13). It includes a specialized **division of labour** within which each individual carries out an assigned and precisely defined task. This takes place within a clear hierarchy of control where senior persons take responsibility for major decisions, the direction of operations, and the coordination of specialized tasks. Communication is mainly vertical (i.e. between superiors and subordinates): instructions are directed downward through the chain of command. Information flows upwards and is processed at specialist levels before reaching the top. As they describe it:

> This command hierarchy is maintained by the implicit assumption that all knowledge about the situation of the firm and its tasks is, or should be, available only to the head of the firm. Management, often visualized as the complex hierarchy familiar in organization charts, operates a simple control system, with information flowing through a succession of filters and decisions and instructions flowing downwards through a succession of amplifiers. (*Burns and Stalker, 1966, p. 5*)

Burns and Stalker (1966) contrast this bureaucratic structure with the organic organization. They describe how this system 'appeared to be required for conditions of change' (ibid., p. 5). A rigid hierarchical structure was far less evident in the organic organization and the authors claim that this makes it better able to respond quickly to changing and unpredictable conditions. For this reason, organic organizations 'are adapted to unstable conditions, when problems and requirements for action arise which cannot be broken down distributed among specialist roles' (ibid., p.p. 5–6). In rapidly changing, unstable conditions it is difficult to operate mechanistically and break down new emerging difficulties into precisely allocated tasks. When a problem arises within an organic organization all those who have relevant knowledge and expertise contribute to its resolution. An emphasis is placed on knowledge as a contributive resource rather than restricted to a specific job specification. Consequently there exists a continual adjustment of tasks as they become shaped by the nature of the problem rather than predefined. Although a hierarchy exists, interaction and communication may occur at any level as required by the process and conditions at hand. Indeed organizational charts detailing the requirements of specific jobs are less prevalent or relevant in the organic organization, as they are seen to hamper the flexibility necessary for an efficient flow of communication and cooperative participation.

Burns and Stalker's (1966) two ideal-types of organization provide a particularly relevant framework through which to understand the politics of conflict within organizations. They were particularly interested in establishing why some of the Scottish firms did not change their system from 'mechanistic' to 'organic'. Despite being faced with unstable conditions, only some of the firms in their study attempted to adopt an organic system. Burns and Stalker (1966) chart the experiences of those firms that hung tenaciously to mechanistic systems, which were obviously failing to meet the demands of the rapidly changing environment. They pose the question why? And state that:

> The answer which suggested itself was that every single person in a firm not only is (a) a member of a working organization, but also (b) a member of a group with sectional interests in conflict with those of other groups, and (c) one individual among many to whom the rank they occupy and the prestige attaching to them are matters of deep concern. (*Burns and Stalker, 1966, p. 6*)

This leads them to suggest the existence of political systems and status structures within organizations. These informal structures exist in conjunction with the formal structures of the working organization. The authors describe how in those companies studied the political and status structure of the organization was directly threatened by the introduction of the new laboratory group. Organizational members were particularly wary of the technical information available to the newcomers as this was perceived as a source of 'political control' (ibid., p. 6). Consequently the 'laboratory engineers claimed or were regarded as claiming elite status within the organization' (ibid.).

Individuals within mechanistic organizations were observed as not only committed to the organization as a whole but also political players with affiliations to their departments, stable career structures and sectional interests. As Burns and Stalker (1966, p. 6) describe it:

> Neither political or status preoccupations operated overtly, or even consciously; they gave rise to intricate manoeuvres and counter-moves, all of them expressed through decisions, or discussions about decisions, concerning the internal structure and the politics of the firm. Since political and status conflicts only came into the open in terms of the working organization, that organization became adjusted to serving the ends of the political and status system of the [company] rather than its own.

Such practices are political in their endeavour to meet career pursuits and sectional interests to the detriment and or displacement of organizational goals. Burns and Stalker (1966) identify how established interest groups are preoccupied with retaining status and power, thus preventing the required transformation of the mechanistic systems into an organic form.

Three of the 'pathological' systems, which developed as part of the determination of established groups to sustain their status position and power, are particularly informative. They are autocracy; elites in the mechanistic jungle; and committee systems.

- *Autocracy*. This refers to the development of an 'autocratic system' constituted by the official hierarchy and non-official pairings between chief executives and senior managers. As the mechanistic organization tenaciously tries to cope with rapidly changing conditions, an accumulation of information flowing upwards (i.e. as subordinates encounter new conditions) begins to consume the activities of executive management. Burns and Stalker (1966, p. 6) describe how 'the individual manager became absorbed in conflicts over power and status because they presented him with interests and problems more immediately important to him and more easily comprehended than those raised by the new organizational milieu and its unlimited liabilities'. Many of the managers found it difficult to maintain control of the stream of new information pouring into their occupational lives. Autocratic rule provided a means of managing the information overload and seemingly preserving the status attached to their managerial role. But these practices persistently involved manoeuvres that mitigated against the development of an organic system in response to the changing external environment.

● *Elites in the mechanistic jungle.* A second pathological system generated by the mechanistic organization's attempts to operate in unstable conditions is the emergence of an **elite**. Many of the electronic firms in Burns and Stalker's (1966) study had employed technologically adept scientists and technicians to respond to the new information required by the market. These newly recruited employees were sometimes seen as a threat to the established order of rank, power and privilege. Existing personnel feared seeming inept as the currency of knowledge within the organization shifted away from their traditional areas of expertise. Concerns were raised about a loss of status and power in decision making. In an attempt to hold on to power some managers tried to distance the new department operationally and administratively from the rest of the organization. Elsewhere, whole new departments were created to respond to the changing conditions. But this also proved conflictual as these departments clearly depended for their existence on the perpetuation of the existing difficult conditions. Success in resolving the conflicts would be like turkeys voting for Christmas.

● *Committee systems.* A third pathological response, as discussed by Burns and Stalker (1966), is the proliferation of **committee systems**. The establishment of committees is the traditional method for dealing with new conditions while not upsetting the balance of power of existing structures. But the formation of committees is only effective as a temporary measure. When used as a permanent device the committee begins to compete with the loyalty demanded, and career structure offered, by the established departmental structure.

Image 8.1 Politics of exclusion in autocratic systems

In terms of a political analysis, several other important issues arise from Burns and Stalker's study. First and foremost their research draws attention to the form and function of the organization as subject to the internal politics of the organization. Thus the failure of the Scottish companies to adapt to an organic system was seen as the consequence of the strength of political status structures. Burns and Stalker's (1966) study also emphasizes the importance of conceiving organizations as operating at three levels or social systems. The first refers to the formal authority structure, which is defined by the organization's goals, technology and **organizational chart**. This is a clear systematic representation of the organization and a clear basis for the analysis of decision-making processes. Political analysis also reveals organizations to be constituted by covert 'cooperative systems' based on negotiation and bargaining. The tendency for organisations to be simultaneously systems of cooperation and competition means that decisions taken in the formal structure inevitably have differential effects on members' interests. As sites of both conflict and cooperation, a third level or system of organizational relationships is its 'political system'.

Key issues raised by the discussion of Burns and Stalker (1996)

1 Discuss how Burns and Stalker's (1966) case study draws our attention to the form and function of the organization as largely defined by internal politics.

2 Discuss how Burns and Stalker's (1966) case study draws our attention to the many interactions that take place between different parts of an organization.

Political analysis reveals all organizations to be at one and the same time formal structures and political systems. Decisions in the formal structure, therefore, impact on cooperative relations and set the scene for political activity. But it would be naive to assume a downward flow of forces that serve to instigate political activity. As Morgan (1986, p. 166) states: 'the politics of organizational decision making often involves preventing crucial decisions from being made, as well as fostering those that one actually desires'. Morgan (ibid.) suggests that a political analysis of decision making requires a distinction to be made between three interrelated elements 'decision premises, decision process and decision objectives'.

Central problems in the mainstream agenda

The analysis of organization as a process of government provides unique opportunities to understand the day-to-day political dynamics of organizations. Mainstream political analysis focuses on explaining:

- typologies of political rule
- how rules are maintained
- how conflict is contained and
- how legitimacy is sustained.

Constructing typologies Implicit parallels between the nature of organizations and political systems have enabled writers to construct useful political rule typologies and the processes through which rules are maintained. Organizations, like governments trade upon rule systems as a means of sustaining order among members. Political rule involves goals, interpersonal influence, skills and tactics of negotiation. In other words it is action-based, dependent on the practices of organizational members and limited by the norms, values and foresight of informed actors (Kakabadse et al., 1988). Furthermore, organizational decision making is a political activity undertaken by purposeful actors (Fincham and Rhodes, 1996). Individuals retain their pursuit of self-interests and sectional loyalties throughout the processes of organizational decision making.

Identifying rule systems in everyday situations Organizations, like governments, operate according to 'rule systems' as a means of sustaining order among members. These rule systems relate to the existence of formal and informal procedures/structures for managing decision making. The following are organizational events that you might be familiar with. Discuss each event and identify the formal rules that generally characterize these decision-making instances.

1 *Student union elections.* The election of a student representative depends on the adherence by delegates and voters to predefined norms, values and rules. Can you identify several of these rules?

2 *Implementation of no-smoking policy at work.* Many organizations have implemented no-smoking policies at work. Can you identify the formal rules that a senior manager would have to recognize if she/he wished to reverse this no-smoking policy?

Image 8.2 The organization of a politically negotiated order

How rules are maintained Political analysis reveals organizations as constituted by a plethora of interests, each with the potential for conflict, agitation and manipulation. Interest groups have the capacity to exploit both the legitimate authority bestowed on them by virtue of their formal position and the power drawn from controlling resources, forming alliances and managing boundaries. This mainstream image of politics and organization relates directly to what is generally recognized as the 'pluralist' frame of reference. The pluralist vision of organizational politics emphasizes the free interplay of interest groups, as operating to check and balance the potentially authoritarian tendencies of governing bodies. This approach is evident in the following quotation drawn from Bacharach and Lawler's (1980) account of decision making as a 'politically negotiated order'. In adopting this view they describe how:

> we can observe organizational actors in their daily transactions, perpetually bargaining, repeatedly forming and reforming coalitions, and constantly availing themselves of influence and tactics . . . politics in organizations involve the tactical use of power to retain or obtain control of real or symbolic resources. In describing the processes of organizations as political acts, we are not making a moral judgement: we are simply making an observation about a process. (*Bacharach and Lawler, 1980, pp. 1–2*)

Exercise 8.3

Conflict management Recollect a time when you or someone you know has been involved in some conflict with mates or in a more formal situation and think how events unfolded.

1 Did the conflict end in outright aggression?
2 If so, how did it end? Did someone seek to arbitrate? Alternatively did it end through a stand-off in which the parties refused to acknowledge each other?
3 If not, were there some compromises made through negotiation?
4 Can you think of other ways in which the conflict might have evolved?
5 How do these processes compare with politics as you know it?

Discuss and analyse your various answers with other students in your group.

How conflict is contained To recap, pluralist perspectives perceive organizational relations as defined by bargaining, competition and the use of politics to achieve a 'negotiated order that creates unity out of diversity' (Morgan, 1986, p. 185). The strength of the pluralist perspective is that it places emphasis on diversity, conflict and power. Indeed it regards power as a crucial medium through which conflicts and divergent interests are managed and resolved. In this sense the pluralist model differs considerably from a classical perspective, which assumed the organizations to be a unitary whole. Conflict in a classical perspective is seen as a source of trouble, a dangerous deflection away from the quest to sustain an apparent synergy between the interests of individuals and the goals of the organization. The management of conflict in classical theory tends not to emphasize the balancing and coordination of divergent interests. Rather, conflict is perceived as an unwanted intrusion, which must be eliminated at every possible opportunity.

How legitimacy is sustained The classical approach to organizational analysis is a powerful ideology, which trades upon a notion of compliance between organizational members as a basis for achieving

Table 8.1 Comparison of political analysis in classical and pluralist traditions

Classical tradition	Pluralist tradition
Emphasis on formal structure	Emphasis on informal structure
Achievement of common interests	Organization as loose coalition of diverse interests
Principles of decision making	Decision as outcomes of political bargaining
Eradication of conflict	Conflict as inherent and ineradicable
Power as formal authority	Power drawn from myriad of sources and groups
Hierarchical structure as disciplinary	Free interplay of interests as a check to power
Rationality in decision making	Rationality through communicative discussion
Unity through adherence to rules	Politically negotiated unity

individual interests. When translated into management practice, the notion that 'unity' and 'working together' is important provides a powerful mechanism through which to adapt organizational relations to meet management goals. Morgan (1986) discusses how the concept of a 'team' conspires to eliminate any acknowledgement of difference. Instead, individuals subordinate themselves to the service of the team. Elsewhere, the classical approach is identified as overly concerned with the formally sanctioned aspects of behaviour in organizations (Fincham and Rhodes, 1996). Table 8.1 provides a brief summary of these comparative features.

Decision making is perceived in classical theory as a rational process in which managers act jointly and consensually to resolve problems. Where conflict does arise, the formal organizational structure is attributed the responsibility of producing consensus and preserving unity. The classical approach, therefore, has little scope from which to theoretically embrace the prospect of chaotic political systems operating in many directions. In approaching the concept of power, classical approaches fall short of regarding power as plural, and organizations as constituted by a plurality of power holders drawing upon a diversity of often-conflicting power resources. Conversely, pluralist approaches recognize that management is about balancing and coordinating difference. Rather than disrupting organizational goals, conflict and its political resolution can function as both a positive and negative force. The pluralist manager thus assumes a curious role in pluralist theory. He/she is positioned as the arbiter of conflict management and is assigned the duty of facilitating positive conflict. The pluralist manager is, therefore, reasoned in his/her management of conflict. The political arena is a context in which positive conflict is to be facilitated and negative conflict to be managed.

Exercise 8.4

Contrasting Burns and Stalker from classical tradition Read through the following extract from Burns and Stalker's (1966) case study:

> Members of an [organisation] are recruited to be used, by agreement, as resources to achieve its ends. The activities which are directed in this way, and the management system in operation, together form the working organisation . . . But the men and women it employs bring in with them other, private purposes of their own. To an extent which varies a great deal from person to person, these purposes may be achieved partly by the return they get from the contract with the employing [organisation] to allow themselves, their physical and mental capacities, to be used as resources. But men and women do not ordinarily yield themselves wholly to use as resources by others; indeed, to do so infringes the human purpose of controlling the situation confronting the individual. In every organised community, therefore, . . . individuals seek to realize other purposes than those they recognize as the organization's.
> *Source*: Burns, T. and Stalker, G. (1966) *The Management of Innovation*, second edition, London: Tavistock, p.p. 97–102.

Having read the above extract, answer the following questions:

1 Identify differences between Burns and Stalker's account of organizational goals and those of the classical tradition.

2 Are there any similarities between Burns and Stalker's account of organizational goals and those of the classical tradition?

Mainstream concepts

Decision making is indeed a political process in which power is exercised and a range of tactics deployed by people or groups seeking to gain particular advantage. Political analysis highlights seven key concepts relevant to the study of interpersonal relations in organisational analysis, and these are examined in the following sub-sections.

Micro-politics (freedom) Pluralist perspectives highlight the relevance of micro-politics to organizational relations. The concept of micro-politics refers to those strategies and activities that groups (and individuals) within an organizational context are free to seek to secure their preferred outcomes in a situation in which there exists dissension.

Decision process (knowledge) Pluralist perspectives situate knowledge as a valuable resource in decision making. Knowledge limitation and restriction provide for crucial conditions for the manipulation of power in organizations. Pluralist discourse attempts to demonstrate the relevance of knowledge in their account of the decision process. They distinguish three interrelated elements that distinguish a decision-making process. Each element has relevance as a point of entry for micro-politics and control. The first element is the 'decision premises'. Morgan (1986, p. 166) observes how 'one of the most effective ways of getting a decision is to allow it to be made by default'. He describes how, as a consequence, much of the activity in organizations involves controlling the structures and processes that constitute the apparatuses of decision making. These are defined as the decision premises. An example of a decision premise is the agenda to meetings. Control of this agenda enables one to manipulate how a decision is approached. The second of the three elements of decision making in pluralist theory concerns 'decision processes'. This refers to the formal systems through which a decision travels and the authorized controls on this passage. For example, the decision within an academic institution to elect a new student representative has to progress through a formal system dictated by rules of procedure. The final of the three elements of decision making is 'decision issues' and 'objectives'. These features refer to an established account of the intended outcome of a decision. All three elements provide avenues for the mobilization of bias.

Negotiated order (identity) Pluralist perspectives describe organizations as arenas of political struggle. Formal structures remain of significance, but are of marginal consideration when compared to the significance ascribed to informal relations. Consequently, the concept of negotiated order is one that both reflects and reproduces individual and group concern to establish and secure specific identities (such as class, gender, roles, status and authority) as immanent – continuously moulded and remoulded by flows of interaction, shared meaning and negotiating processes.

Plurality of power (power) Pluralists perceive organizational relations to be defined by bargaining, competition and the use of power to resolve conflicts and represent conflicts of interest. Power is pluralistically dispersed throughout the organization and operates to prevent any one group or individual monopolizing influence. But the problem with mainstream concepts of power is that they are based on the ideas of power as a property of persons or groups rather ideas one of relations.

Contingency (insecurity) Pluralist accounts of organizational processes are predicated on a belief that uncertainty, for an organization, stems from technological developments and the extrinsic conditions derived from its external environment. Reducing uncertainty is a vital precondition of effective management and those groups deemed capable of controlling uncertainty gain power and status. The concept of contingency appears in the case study provided by Burns and Stalker (1966). In this sense, insecurity is an unacknowledged resource in the mainstream analysis since controlling uncertainty is, to a significant extent, about managing insecurity for self and organization.

Mobilization of bias (knowledge) This refers to the process whereby groups (and individuals) manipulate core beliefs in such a way so that potentially threatening ideas and alternative positions are marginalized, 'filtered out' or re-represented in a more acceptable form. The mainstream neglects to discuss how knowledge is drawn upon and yet produced in the exercise of power.

Conflict (inequality) Classical perspectives in decision making are predicated on the existence of harmony of interests. This is reproduced in classical decision-making models that emphasize rationality and unity as achieved through the adherence, by employees, to formal rules. The existence of conflict is either neglected in classical theory or marginalized by the reification of rational harmony. Indeed, classical theorists define disagreement in ideas to be the product of rational systems and not endemic disharmony. For example, the introduction of a new computer system would be anticipated to generate temporary disagreement. But this disagreement will be resolved rationally, as individuals become familiar with the new operating system. Pluralist perspectives challenge the tendency of classical theory to reify organizational relations into a model of harmonic coordination and shared goals. Instead pluralists emphasize the significance of implicit and explicit conflict, which arises as a consequence of the technical specialization and functional differentiation within organizations. Members are enticed into cooperative relations to maximize their abilities to mobilize interests in their favour. It follows from this that organizations are political coalitions, in the sense that allegiances are formed to enhance the bargaining power and influence of individual members.

Political rule systems   Pluralist analysis depicts organizations as constituted by definable modes of power mobilized into a rule system. Examples of political rule systems include the following:

- **Autocracy** is a term used to describe a political regime or person that rules by coercion rather than consent, as is expected in democratic regimes (discussed later). The coercion is possible largely because the regime or person is able to punish deviants or withdraw rewards from those who fail to comply with its rule. It signifies absolute modes of governing where power operates dictatorially through the intentions of an individual or small group. Power is wielded to confer on supporters valued rewards. Coercive power refers to the reverse side of this coin and a situation in which compliance is achieved through the threat of withholding valued rewards.

- **Bureaucratic** power equates with rational-legal authority. It refers to the legitimate use of authority based on an acceptance of hierarchy and rules that are believed to result in rationally organized or efficient activities and thereby a willingness of people to consent to them or at least be compliant with them (see Chapter 13).

- **Technocratic** rule is exercised through expertise, technical aptitude, knowledge and experience. Power and accountability are directly linked to the perceived relevance and marketability of an individual's technical knowledge and expertise. French and Raven (1959) describe this form of influence as '**expert power**' and draw attention to the proximal nature of its potency. For unlike previously mentioned forms of influence, expert power is usually highly specific and limited to the particular area in which the individual has expert knowledge (see Chapter 11).

- **Co-determination** refers to a form of influence predicated on the cooperation of parties with possibly opposing or competing interests in the pursuit of a mutual or common outcome. Clear parallels exist here between the coalitions that define the world of politics, and the politicking that may be an essential aspect of achieving a collective organizational goal.

- **Representative democracy** also draws closely upon political reality to describe a form of democratic influence predicated on legitimate forms of electoral selection, accountability and representation.

- **Direct democracy** refers to a system of collective decision making in which everyone participates and has equal rights in influence. Morgan (1986) describes how 'self-organization' and 'active citizenship' are key modes of organizing direct democracy.

All six styles are inextricably political in their emphasis. Differences as and between these forms of political rule relate mostly to the different principles of legitimacy that they draw upon. Yet the mainstream still see power and politics as disruptive and thus seeks to eradicate it wherever possible, rather than see it as an inescapable aspect of social and organizational life.

Exercise 8.5

Role playing political rule systems   Refer to the Burns and Stalker (1966) case study discussed earlier. The authors identify several 'pathological systems' that developed as part of the established group's determination to sustain status position and power. Drawing upon the key concepts in the mainstream approach (outlined here) match a mode of political rule system to each of Burns and Stalker's 'pathological systems'.

Key ideas and contributions to mainstream thinking

Decision making as a rational political process The process of making choices from among two or more alternatives is defined as decision making. Mainstream theorists have long since been concerned to identify the most effective thoughts and actions associated with a sequence of choices. These processes comprise the content of an influential and relatively new field called decision theory. Decision theorists emphasize the importance of constructing systematic procedures for approaching and solving problems. The study of decision-making processes is believed to provide managers with a valuable repertoire of problem-solving techniques to be applied in similar contexts. Mainstream models of decision making rely on a strong degree of rationality. That is, alternatives are evaluated 'objectively' in terms of their meeting specified criteria for contributing to delivering a set of objectives. The choices made involve becoming aware of a problem and selecting from among an array of value-maximizing options, within specified constraints. The decision is rational in the sense it is objective, logical and designed to achieve coherently defined goals with maximum efficiency (Williams *et al.*, 1985, p. 126).

Managers would like to think that all their decision making emulates the rational model depicted in Box 8.3. In fact it is only really applicable to a limited amount of routine consensual decisions. If there is less than full knowledge and there exist divergences in agreement – as is invariably the case within organisations – then creative thinking and political activity will be crucial facets of the decision-making process (Dawson, 1986).

Pluralist model of power and decision making Although hierarchical position is a significant source of organizational influence, a pluralist perspective in decision-making analysis encourages us to consider the unofficial resources that people can mobilize in the decision-making process. Political analysis here has focused on the twin concepts of uncertainty and dependency (see Box 8.4 and Chapter 6 for discussion of resource dependency theory where uncertainty is a key factor).

Box 8.3: Steps in rational decision making!

1 **Define problem**. A problem is thought to exist when there is an objectively definable discrepancy between an existing and preferred state.

   Case study example. Suppose that your leisure centre or gym has to comply with the Disability Discrimination Act (1995). Identify what would be the problem.

2 **Identify the decision criteria**. Relevant information is selected by participants in the decision-making process.

   Case study example. The managers of the leisure centre consult official documents detailing the design and architectural features encompassed in the Disability Discrimination Act (1995).

3 **Allocate weights to the criteria**. Once information is selected it tends to occupy a notional space in which it can be ranked according to levels of relevance.

   Case study example. The managers of the leisure centre consult the design features stipulated as compulsory by the Disability Discrimination Act (1995). Having identified these design features (such as lifts or slopes supplemental to stairs; special toilets that can be used by customers in a wheelchair; special weight training equipment, etc.),

the managers of the leisure centre attempt to prioritize those renovations that require immediate commission and those that can be deferred into the next financial year.

4 **Develop the alternatives**. Identification of possible alternative courses of actions as solutions.

   Case study example. The managers of the leisure centre consider alternative sources of financing for those renovations that have been deferred into the next financial year.

5 **Evaluate the alternatives**. Evaluate alternatives through a process of rating each alternative on each criterion. Having computed the alternatives, an optimal decision is achieved by determining the alternative with the highest score.

   Case study example The managers of the leisure centre compare the alternative sources of financing and decide which of these sources are viable alternatives.

6 **Implementation of chosen course of action**

7 **Monitoring**. The chosen course of action is then continuously observed in light of the achievement of objectives.

Source: Adapted from Robbins, S. (1998) *Organizational Behaviour*, Englewood Cliffs, NJ: Prentice Hall, p. 104.

Uncertainty as a source of power Research on the interdependent nature of organizational relations has revealed how organizational departments (or 'sub-units') are rarely equally powerful (see Box 8.5). Perrow (1970) identifies how the strategic position of a department, with respect to the environmental context, significantly determines the degree of its influence. In 11 of the industrial firms studied by Perrow (1970), managers invariable described the strategic position of the sales department as sustaining its leverage. Elsewhere attention has been drawn more specifically to uncertainty and its significance to the strategic power of organizational sub-units. Thompson (1967) identifies how leadership and influence within organizations tends to be achieved by those perceived as dealing with the sources of greatest uncertainty (see Chapter 6).

Strategic contingency theory These ideas concerning uncertainty have been developed further by Hickson *et al.* (1971) in their strategic contingencies theory of power (see Box 8.6). This theory suggests that uncertainty for an organization stems from its systems of operation, which include technology and work operations, and from its environment. As it is imperative for management that the conditions of uncertainty be reduced, any group or individual that can 'cope with uncertainty' gains powerful influence.

Box 8.4: Definition of dependency

Political analysis reveals how any organizational member engaged in a form of exchange is party to some form of dependency. Dawson (1986, p. 158) identifies how 'the degree and direction of dependency of each individual on others will be based on the availability of satisfactory alternatives for each party . . . and the importance or centrality of the desired resources or commodities to the fulfilment of their needs, goals and objectives'. Consider once again the process of campaigning to become a representative of the students' union. Each delegate is engaged in a relationship of dependency with his/her supporters and sponsors. The higher the stakes the greater the degree of dependency between individuals. Thus the stakes for selecting the head of the students' union are higher as against a delegate to the NUS annual conference. Consequently, the selection of the head of the students' union will produce a greater degree of dependency between individuals.

Box 8.5: Definition of uncertainty

The politics within an organization tend to revolve around the conflicts that surround complex and uncertain relations between individuals, departments, divisions and between those outside the organization (e.g. suppliers, customers, competitors). A common strand of argument is that the plurality of group activities and interests within an organization creates complexities that cause uncertainties. But uncertainties also can create diverse interest groups, cabals and political conflict. Effective management requires the development of communication channels to alleviate potential conflict and appropriately channel the outcome of communicative exchange.

Box 8.6: Definition of strategic contingencies

If one part of an organization (e.g. department work unit) is indispensable (i.e. cannot be easily substituted) and deals with uncertainties either in the environment or externally, it will exert significant influence in decision making. Dawson (1986, p. 114) succinctly defines the theory of contingency as follows: 'A central theme of this analysis is that the more uncertain and complex the context, the more organic the structure needs to be, and the more need there is for information to flow vertically in both directions between levels, and horizontally between functions.' In these circumstances, a sub-unit of an organization can mobilize its power by ebbing the information flow, so as to maximize its indispensability to deal with strategic uncertainties.

The more strategic the form of uncertainty for the organization, the more powerful an individual or group deemed irreplaceable and capable of dealing with uncertainties will become. Organizations, therefore, become heavily dependent on groups that appear to cope with uncertainties, especially where these threaten the survival of the enterprise.

Exercise 8.6

On uncertainty and power Think of an example from your own experience where a parallel situation to that in Box 8.7 exists. Discuss this in groups then summarize your conclusions in reporting back to the whole class.

Box 8.7: Uncertainty and decision-making influence – a brief case study

Crozier (1964) has shown how the location of individual agents within the operational structure of a company influences their relative autonomy and access to career rewards. His study demonstrated how skilled production workers were able to lucratively exploit a source of uncertainty within an otherwise routine system. Routine breakdowns had plagued the production system for some time. These machine breakdowns constituted the only major source of contingency and were a constant threat to operations, a consequence of which was that the organization became increasingly dependent on the maintenance crew who dealt with the machine malfunctions and, in turn, enhanced their status and access to rewards.

Another important political analysis of uncertainty is Pettigrew's (1973a) *The Politics of Organizational Decision-Making*. The study was based on a longitudinal analysis of an expanding computer system within a retailing organization. The installation of the computer system coincided with a rapid expansion of business. Computer installation skills were (especially at that time) of high order and in significant demand. All of these factors contributed to conditions of uncertainty, and the organization became heavily dependent on the new systems analysts responsible for computer installations. But the new breed of systems analyst did not fit into the organization. The culture of the existing programmers was very bureaucratic and a far cry from the young, dynamic, technological literate culture of the new systems analysts. An intense antipathy developed between these two groups, fuelled partially by an imbalance of expert power. Pettigrew traces the political struggles that ensued as management tried systematically to undermine the system analysts control of technical information.

Pettigrew's (1973a) study is important in its illustration of how the mobilization of expert power over others can change or maintain structures as well as incite conflicts between groups. The very powerful antipathy between the new computer programmers and established personnel challenged formal authority structures. Managers resented their reliance on the technological expertise of the new programmers. Attempts were made to break up the programming function through the reallocation of selected activities to other members of staff. The new system programmers responded defensively to the erosion of their power base. In an attempt to re-evaluate their expertise, the new systems programmers mystified their skills, withholding crucial information. In seeking to defend the company's reliance upon their technological expertise, the new systems programmers challenged the authority structure of the organization. This reveals how the attempts to weaken an irreplaceable skill will be met with resistance. By withholding information, the new computer programmers threatened to disrupt operations, thus creating uncertainty.

Exercise 8.7

Limitation of rational decision-making model In groups of four, discuss the following case study as a critical example of mainstream decision-making theory. A retail department store is keen to increase the quality of its customer services in all its national outlets. The management decide to commission a research agency to conduct a marketing survey. The agency is informed that a time limit has been placed on the research and development of the company's intended turnaround in customer services. The research agency is renowned for generating vast amounts of statistical data. The agency conducts a huge marketing survey consisting of a sample of approximately 5000 customers over a period of six months. The data yielded is immense. During a meeting with the retail department's marketing directors the research agency provides 10 volumes of findings. A rational approach to decision making would insist that each volume of findings was read through and implemented. In your groups, reflect upon the scenario presented to the marketing directors and answer the following questions:

1. To what extent would it be justified for the marketing directors to abandon the task of reading all 10 volumes of findings?

2. How might the marketing directors have avoided the information overload scenario?

3. Given the wealth of information provided to the marketing directors and the short time span available for implementation, how might compromise and bargaining dictate the decision-making process?

Major controversies

Political activity as a rational process?   Although rational procedure is the preferable emphasis in mainstream theory, the actuality of decision making in everyday circumstances involves significant elements of irrationality. Table 8.2 contains a list of conditions that contribute to irrational decisions.

Managerial decisions are never totally rational; they are better characterized by what March and Simon (1958) termed **bounded rationality**. Limitations in the human capacity to process information are defined as restricting individuals *to simplified models that extract the essential features from problems* without capturing all their complexity as is evident in the retail study in the exercise in Exercise 8.8.

Exercise 8.8

Bounded rationality   Think back to when you were considering which university to attend. Recall the wealth of choices available to you. The concept of 'bounded rationality' recognizes that with so many options available an individual might not consider every viable alternative. Rather, when faced with a complex problem – such as selecting a university – most people reduce the problem to a level at which it can be easily comprehended and managed. These constraints on rational decision making are effectively summarized in Table 8.2. In small groups, identify the potential contributions to irrational decision making that influenced your choice of university.

Key mainstream studies

Groups – particularly specialist groups – coalitions, networks and sponsors all provide a source of power from which to control the process of decision making. One common power strategy, based on

Table 8.2 Potential contributors to irrational decisions

Ideal rational decision-making model	Potential contributors to irrationality
Problems identification	Conflicting goals
Problem definition	Changing goals
Data collection	Limited information
Seeking alternatives	Misinformation
Analysis	Errors in logic
Authorization	Personal ambition
Deliberation	Jealousies
Compromising	Personality domination
Evaluation	Power struggles
Sub-decision	Rationalization
Decision/action	Time pressure

Source: Adapted from Willams, J., DuBrin, A. and Sisk, H. (1985) *Management and Organisation*, fifth edition, South Western Publishing Co., p. 127. Reprinted with permission.

group formation, is the sponsor–protégé relationship. These are informal relationships between senior and junior personnel and motivated by mutual advantage. The junior organizational member might provide the senior with direct access to sensitive information or alert him/her to relevant events. In return the senior will guide the career development of the protégé. Burns (1963) provides some indication of this phenomenon in his account of organizations as interlocking cliques and coalitions. The skilled organizational politician actively cultivates informal allegiances with powerful interest groups operating in his/her field. A 'coalition' refers to a special type of power resource. As Fincham and Rhodes (1996, p. 445) express it, a coalition is 'an informal relation between two or more interest groups for the purpose of increasing their joint power in relation to some other group or groups'.

Differentiating cliques and coalitions To recap, a clique or coalition is 'an informal relation between two or more interest groups for the purpose of increasing their joint power in relation to some other group or groups' (Fincham and Rhodes, 1996, p. 445). This definition takes for granted coalitions as premised on an alliance between employees with shared interests. But coalitions and other forms of alliance are not necessarily based on shared identities. That is to say, members of a coalition may not identify with each other except for the opportunistic activity that has brought them together. Rather, their recruitment maybe be motivated by disparate aims and objectives, tenuously converged around a similar interest. Organizations reflect this definition of coalition when they comprise formal and informal groupings united by an interest or stake but whose ultimate intentions and preferences might differ (Morgan, 1986, p. 154). Political analysis often makes contrasts between cliques 'that become aware of common goals' and coalitions who 'unite to pursue a joint interest, often working against a rival network' (ibid.). Given the potential power of coalitions to advance specific interests and pursue particular objectives, it is important to reflect upon their formation (see also Chapters 6 and 11).

Factors motivating group formation Fincham and Rhodes (1996) identify three distinct factors relevant to the formation of coalitions. The first objective condition, which might encourage a coalition group forming, is the relative power of the interest groups. If a single interest group is deemed sufficiently powerful to gain advantage in the decision-making process, they might well decide that a coalition is not worth forming. A second feature, which plays a part in coalition formation, is managerial differentiation. If interests within the organization are extremely diverse, any coalition will be unstable and subject to factious tensions. In these circumstances, the interdependent cooperation required for the successful operation of the coalition will be so difficult that the very existence of the coalition will be jeopardized. A third feature relevant to the formation of a coalition is the issue itself. If an objective is suitably realizable through the one-time pooling together of interests, this might

---

Box 8.8: Power, interest groups and goal achievement – brief case study

As part of a large-scale study of the Imperial Chemical Industries (ICI), Pettigrew (1985) examined the relationship between political process and corporate culture. He identified how in the period up to 1980 the 'segmentalist' corporate culture of ICI meant that real power resided with the organization's divisions and divisional managing directors. This 'segmentalist' corporate culture was radically challenged in the period 1980–1982, when a change in financial profits had paved the way for radical changes at the higher echelons of ICI. Innovations challenged the organization's previous commitment to short-termism and financial targets. These operational features were now seen as a fetter to strategic action. In their place was instigated systems and practices geared towards the development of a strategic culture.

Pettigrew (1985) charts how the vision of a more strategic culture had significant historical trajectories. At least a decade prior to the organizational changes that occurred between 1980 and 1982, a powerful interest group of managers had begun to articulate problems and inadequacies in ICI's corporate culture. Pettigrew (1985) provides a useful account of the communication channels utilized by the powerful interest group of senior managers. Networks of contacts and loyalties provided communication channels through which the group promoted its preference for ICI to adopt a more strategic culture. Pettigrew (1985) concluded that organizational change is enabled when powerful interest groups align with the intended alterations.

tempt unlikely groups into a temporary coalition. In summary, conditions relevant to coalition formation are as follows:

1. Coalition attracted by relative power of the respective interest groups.
2. Limited amounts of managerial differentiation.
3. Likelihood of coalition formation as issue-based.

The coalitions and alliances built through these conditions may remain highly informal and to a degree virtually invisible. And yet their operation in the control of decision-making processes is a force to be recognized. Pettigrew (1973b) provides an important case study detailing the use of power by interest groups as illustrated above (see Box 8.8). The case study is particularly significant in its demonstration of the potential for interest groups to operate successfully in securing power, so as to achieve specific organizational ends.

Power, group formation and decision making In his paper entitled 'Occupational Specialisation as an Emergent Process', Pettigrew (1973b) distinguishes between strategies for power acquisition and strategies for power maintenance. As you may recall, his research charted the response of a group of computer programmers to the arrival in the organization of a new breed of systems analysts. The programmers were said to have used four protective strategies to defend their power status against the threats presented by the new systems analysts. The first of these strategies was the development of norms, which denied the outsider's competence. Pettigrew (1973b, p. 271) provides the following excerpt drawn from a conversation with a chief programmer to illustrate this particular protective strategy:

> We knew it would not work, people trying to tell programmers what to do – they knew nothing about computers. We objected to suggestions from people who didn't even know what they were talking about. This was particularly so with the Systems Manager who tried to dictate what we did.

CONTROL BUILT ON BELIEF SYSTEMS This quote exemplifies how much of the unobtrusive control within organizations is built upon belief systems, norms and values. The derisive response of the programmers to the competencies of the new systems analysts was intended to normalize the antipathy that had emerged between these two groups. It served to conceal what was in fact a protective strategy adopted by the established programmers in a rapidly changing organizational context. The second protective strategy utilized by the established programmers was the construction of 'protective myths' drawn upon to bolster the group's image. One of these myths is revealed by a deputy to the chief programmer saying that: 'The chief programmer has always argued we cannot work under time constraints. This isn't true, it's just his way of giving himself plenty of room for manoeuvre' (Pettigrew, 1973b, p. 272). Our attention is drawn here to how organizational members may gain power from their role in, and commitment to, an informal alliance. Narratives exaggerating the productive capacities of the group operated in this case study as a means of amplifying existing forms of organizational influence and status.

The third protective strategy employed by the established programmers was the deliberate control of information through secrecy. Pettigrew (1973b) describes how a routine transfer of information between the two conflicting groups was hampered by the creation of informational channels, designed to by-pass formal procedures. One of the analysts described its operation as follows:

> . . . we found there was no record of what had been happening. We found we were becoming terribly reliant on the persons who did the programming . . . in its worst light it seemed that the programmers were trying openly to manipulate the situation. It looked like their attitude was 'I know what's going on, therefore I'm indispensable'. (*Pettigrew, 1973b, p. 273*)

Evident in this particularly excerpt is the significance of *knowledge* as a resource through which persons are able to influence the decision-making process (see Chapter 5). By controlling the flow of information, the established programmers were able to create *patterns of dependency*, which in turn amplified their existing status and power. A final strategy utilized by the programmers was the protection of their knowledge base through the control of recruitment and training policies.

Boundary management Any discussion of power and group behaviour within decision making must include a reference to **boundary management**. The concept of boundary management refers to strategies and actions intent on controlling the interface between different elements (or departments) within an organization (Morgan, 1986). Pettigrew's case study details how the monitoring and controlling of boundary transactions can help to isolate a unit so it can function in an autonomous way. The established programmers were keen to retain control over recruitment, as this helped preserve their distinction and impede moves towards the routinization of their core expertise. Elsewhere, Morgan (1986, p. 170) describes how 'Groups and departments often attempt to incorporate key skills and resources within their boundaries and to control admissions through selective recruitment'.

One outstanding feature of boundary management is that it is characterized by competing strategies for control and counter-control (Morgan 1986, p. 170). Organizational members generally try to preserve the control over their life space, which entails responding to similar attempts made by others to gain a degree of autonomy and control.

In summary, decisions are inherently political. Managers often have to settle for less then ideal decisions to placate powerful interest groups and other political affiliations. As indicated earlier, the art of effective organizational decision making entails cultivating influential allies, controlling the flow of vital information and influencing through power of personality.

Contributions and limitations of mainstream approaches

Political analysis clearly encourages us to recognize that organizational decisions are often made by coalitions of individuals and groups. Organizations are constituted by a diversity of individual and group interests, each with the potential of influencing decision making. Limited organizational resources precipitate ceaseless competition between individuals and groups. Although many mainstream thinkers prescribe strategies for preventing such competition bursting into uncontrollable conflict, sometimes it heralds the conflict as stimulating innovative change. The intended imagery is one of vibrant political behaviour and ongoing processes of change and development (see Box 8.9).

Decision making in the pluralist model is conceptualized as operating through the continual resolution of conflict. Political analysis often converges towards a model of decision making predicated on negotiation and bargaining between divergent interests. Conflict takes centre stage in this bargaining model, because it is conflicting interests that motivate actors to draw upon tactics and skills in advancing their position (Fincham and Rhodes, 1996). Figure 8.1 provides a diagram that simplifies the conditions in which conflict tends to arise. The diagram is particularly pertinent as it highlights the possibilities as opposed to dysfunctions of conflict.

But this pluralist account of decision making has been subject to considerable critique by those adopting a **structuralist approach** in organizational theory.

Challenge to the concept of plural power A significant challenge to the pluralist position is presented by structuralist accounts of organizational decision making. Structuralist decision making theories, as

---

Box 8.9: Decision making in organizations – summary of mainstream contributions

1 Decision making encompasses both 'rational' activities in respect of perceived opportunities and constraints and 'irrationality', insight and chance occurrences.

2 Decisions vary in the extent to which they are programmable and amenable to standardization.

3 Decision processes revolve around perceptions of issues, objectives and means.

4 Information is purposively selected for inclusion in decision making.

5 Complete agreement between different parties on objectives and means is rare.

6 Complete knowledge and information on objectives and means is rare.

7 Different patterns of agreement and knowledge about ends and means in decision making provide a typology of decision processes.

8 This typology has implications for the political strategies that are likely to be followed, such as:

   (a) negotiation between groups

   (b) control of information

   (c) alleviating conflict

   (d) compromises and bargaining.

Source: Adapted from Dawson, S. (1986) *Analysing Organisations*, London: Macmillan, p. 179.

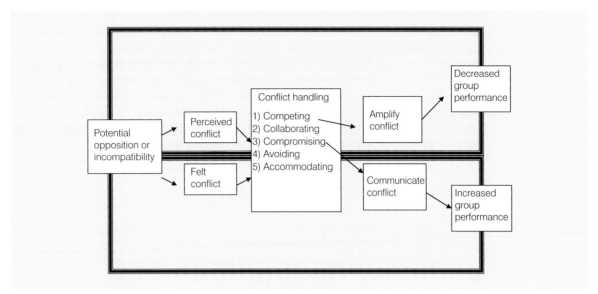

Figure 8.1 The conflict process in mainstream pluralist theory

with pluralist approaches, primarily assume the organization to be a complex social unit in which a multiplicity of social groups interact. Pluralists see differences of interests as potentially productive of innovation and change as well as allowing greater levels of participation in decision making among a wider array of individuals. Interest groups make it possible to alter specific features of organizational programmes while also retaining those which the majority supports. Furthermore, the political wrangling of conflicting interests functions as a check on power and prevents any one party being constantly successful in realizing its goal. Conversely, the structuralist contribution pays less attention to the individual decision maker than to the complexity of organizational alternatives. In short, the organization conditions are seen to determine the decisions that can be made.

Structuralist challenge to the concept of decision process March and Simon (1958) were one of the earliest exponents of a structuralist perspective that focuses on the substance and complexity of decision making without reducing organizational theory to propositions about individual behaviour. At the centre of their contribution is a premise concerning the limits to rationality. In pluralist models of decision making the rational individual is thought to make 'optimal choices in a highly specified and clearly defined environment' (ibid., p. 137). Conversely, March and Simon (1958) argue that decision makers are only 'intendedly rational'. They attempt to be rational but 'the limits of human intellective capacities in comparison with the complexities of the problems that individuals and organisations face' prevents anything near complete rationality (March and Simon, 1981, p. 148). Their account of the 'complexities' that obstruct effective rational decision making is summarized in Box 8.10.

According to March and Simon (1958) the complexities of the problems faced by organizational decision makers means that simplified models have to be constructed to 'capture the *main features* of a problem without capturing all its complexities' (ibid., our emphasis). Limits on rationality are

---

Box 8.10: Restrictions on rational decision making

1 Impossibility of obtaining complete knowledge of the consequences of action.

2 The inability to control for both anticipated and unanticipated outcomes.

3 Lack of complete knowledge regarding alternative courses of action.

4 Even when there exists knowledge of several alternatives, it is difficult to rank these according to the most desirable and least desirable outcomes.

Source: Perrow (1973).

mainly linked to the inability of the system as a whole to provide complete information for decision making and the inability of the decision maker to comprehend the multitude of options and alternatives available. It is clear that the more far-reaching the consequences of a decision, the greater the number of factors that require consideration by the decision maker. The ability to comprehend the multitudinous expanse of relevant information is often an impossible expectation placed on decision makers. The result is that decision makers often construct simplified models of the real situation. Otherwise they would be impotent to make decisions for fear of committing the organization to inappropriate actions or appearing not to be fully rational. In effect, a commitment to total rationality would render decision makers incapable of making decisions.

Exercise 8.9

Think about some purchase you have made recently and examine whether you can consider it to have been perfectly rational or influenced by other factors.

Even though your decision might not have been perfectly rational on the grounds of discovering the best possible quality and price, could the decision still be seen as rational?

What would an irrational decision look like and would we ever be prepared to admit to such outside of the influence of a drug such as alcohol or other substance?

Discuss your deliberations with other students.

Structuralist account of the concept of contingency The simplification has a number of characteristic features. First, the pluralist emphasis on optimizing information available for the production of rational decisions is replaced by a focus on satisficing (see Box 8.11). Satisficing refers to the 'requirement that satisfactory levels of the criterion variables be attained' (March and Simon, 1981, p. 148).

Secondly, repertoires of action programmes are developed by organizational members – over time – and form the basis for alternate choices in recurrent situations. Definitions of a situation are therefore built out of past and present experience. Decision makers draw upon solutions used in similar situations. Organizations are said to construct repertoires of available action programmes, which decision makers draw upon as sources of information.

In summary, March and Simon's (1958) model of limited rationality suggests that, in 'reality', decision makers conduct a limited search for alternatives along familiar and well-worn paths, eventually selecting the most immediately accessible solution (Perrow, 1973). The outcome of these 'limiting factors' is that the decision maker 'satisfices' instead of 'optimizes'. Decision makers select the most immediate solution available rather than search for the optimum.

Box 8.11: Satisficing rather than optimizing

Re-read the discussion of rational decision making in Box 8.3. Recall how the procedure for rational decision making emphasized the need to evaluate and prioritize alternatives. This feature of locating and selecting the best possible course of action is defined as optimizing information.

Exercise 8.10

Satisficing versus optimizing March and Simon (1958) draw our attention to a specific limitation in pluralist analysis of decision making. While pluralist theory focuses on the use of rationality to effect the optimum solution, March and Simon (1958) identify how limitations in managing vast amounts of information require that the decision maker selects the most immediate solution available.

Consider the brief case study provided in Box 8.7. To what extent is this case study an illustration of 'satisficing' rather than 'optimizing' in the decision-making process?

Structuralist challenge to the concept of micro-politics The central significance of this structuralist contribution to decision-making theory is that it ascribes organizational variables with the predominant control over behaviour. The control presented by existing structures, norms and procedures within organizations is considered to be so pervasive that we need not account for individual behaviour in all its multiplicity and variability. This model of decision making 'calls for simplifying models of individual behaviour in order to capture the complexities of organisational behaviour' (Perrow, 1973, p. 285). Decision making is considered as an outcome of 'organization structure', which is defined as consisting of 'those aspects of the pattern of behaviour in the organization that are relatively stable and that change only slowly' (March and Simon, 1981, p. 149).

Exercise 8.11

Enduring structures The concept of enduring features within organizations can be illustrated by their use of technical vocabulary. Specialist organizations, such as academic institutions, develop concepts that form a technical vocabulary. Examples of this technical vocabulary are evident in the administration of examinations. This formal process contains distinguishing events, which are given technical titles. Here are some examples of the formal titles attached to the administration of examinations:

- course code
- candidate number
- invigilation
- examination paper.

Can you think of any additions to this list?

The fundamental premise here is that, in order for an organization to adapt to changing circumstance, it needs some stable regulations and procedures. Examples of these stable regulations include organizational goals (see Box 8.12). In March and Simon's (1958) model we learn that goals are devised by senior managers and broken down into sub-goals at each level of the organization. Sub-goals are constructed in order to facilitate the accomplishment of higher-order goals. Organizational members are not assumed to accept goals because they necessarily identify with them, but rather because cooperation will assist in realizing personal goals.

Box 8.12: Goal adoption and the endurance of structure

The training of organizational members provides for an opportunity to introduce personnel to the organization's goals, ethos and ideals. The successful completion of a trainee induction programme will invariably involve him/her demonstrating knowledge, understanding and commitment to the organization's value systems. In so doing the trainee demonstrates de facto compliance and agreement.

Structuralist challenge to the concept of a negotiated order Simon (1957) suggests that in commercial, governmental and voluntary organizations, the higher echelons of management tend to directly identify with the objectives of the organization, while junior personnel need not. Despite not necessarily identifying with the organization's goals, however, junior personnel contribute to the reproduction and dissemination of these goals. This occurs through the translation of wider organizational goals into categories of evaluation, forms of classification and operating procedures.

Once established, organizational goals are stabilized through such features as the capital invested in their design and implementation. Perrow (1973, p. 286) discusses the high cost of innovative activity in terms of time, resourcing and money. Large capital outlays to formulate and establish programmes, procedures and structures results in them not easily being changed. He goes on to state that 'regardless of wants, motives and desires or the dynamics of decision making of individuals, these non-personal aspects stabilise objectives and activities' (ibid.).

Structuralist challenge to the concept of democratic political rule systems The concept of organization structures highlights numerous other sources of stability, which also function to limit the potential of interest groups to determine the outcomes of decision making. The 'routinization' of activity through the establishment of standardized operating procedures has a significant effect in limiting the possibility of change through political action. Perrow (1973) describes how the existence of routinized activity restricts the introduction of change to those instances where objectives are not being met. But even when objectives are not met, the search for alternative programmes follows familiar paths 'minimising the disruption; the satisficing solution is to select the least disruptive alternatives' (ibid.). The imagery here is that of the organization's decision making as firmly embedded in the enduring structure and goals as defined by senior management. The adaptation of decisions and indeed the limits of what can be discussed are largely defined by the organizational structure. Even more constraining is the existence of established procedures, which the organization uses for developing, elaborating, implementing and revising decisions.

The organizational structure is defined by structuralist perspectives as a limiting factor in decision making. It provides for a formidable boundary to rationality insofar as 'there are elements of the situation that must be or are in fact taken as givens, and that do not enter into rational calculations as potential strategic factors' (March and Simon, 1958, p. 149).

The model of authority, which is implied here, is clearly not one in which subordinates grant authority to the superior or emphasize participation. Rather, superiors have the power to structure the context of decision making in accordance with the operation of existing structures. Communication

---

Box 8.13: Summary of contributions and limitations of the mainstream pluralist and structuralist approaches

Contributions

- A primary focus on examining the micro-politics of everyday organizational life to reveal the plurality of political processes through which decision making is performed. In contrast to the classical theorists' image of stable formal structures, pluralist analyses depict organizations as 'organized anarchies'. Coherence and order in organizational life emerges out of the accommodations, compromises and negotiations that reflect and reproduce political activity.

- An understanding of organizations as negotiated orders. Order and stability within an organization is the negotiated outcome of relations between the interest groups and coalitions, which contain and manage overt conflicts.

- The adoption of a contingency approach, which rests on the view that an organization is constituted by informal sub-systems and boundaries, which delineate it from its wider environment. The contingency approach seeks to identify the sub-systems that define the organization and the conditions that foreground their interrelationships.

- A rejection of a universal and unitary model of organizations. Rather, the form an organisation adopts is framed by how it copes with specific contingency factors, group dynamics and political negotiations.

- A pluralist concept of power that acknowledges how diverse interests, competition and conflict characterize decision making in organizations.

Mainstream approaches in the form of pluralist and structuralist theories contrast with the classical approach in recognizing the importance of power, competition, conflict and limits to rationality rather than simply consensus around organizational goals and their achievement. The limitations of the mainstream revolve around the failure to interrogate the conception of power. This reflects and reinforces the belief in an established order within which political contests, competition and conflict take place.

Limitations

- Politics and negotiations are restricted to minor issues and conflicts within accepted or agreed rules of the game, so that the prevailing structure of inequality, freedom and identity cannot be challenged.

- Managers are presumed not to have their own interests above and beyond a concern to reconcile diverse and conflicting interests.

- Power is still seen to be located in persons or groups rather than in the relations between them.

- While rationality is seen as bounded or limited, it is not itself recognized as political such that power defines what can be accepted as rational.

- Because satisfactory rather than optimal outcomes are seen as the new form of rationality, big issues of conflict, say over world poverty, the environment, consumerism, etc., are marginalized.

strategies centre around the confirmation of favoured procedures that 'screen out some parts of reality and magnify other parts' (Perrow 1973, p. 288).

In summary, the pluralist framework fails to take account of how prevailing structures of inequality are a limitation on any shared decision making (see Box 8.13). In short, different interest groups may influence decisions but only so far as this does not challenge the structure of power and inequality. Although recognizing how organizations are adaptive, even structuralist theorists are extremely reticent about the potential for group activities to dramatically change enduring procedures and normative values. The enduring nature of organization structure means 'only a few elements of the system are adaptive at any one time; the remainder are, at least in the short run, "givens" ' (March and Simon, 1981, p. 148).

Critical approach

Broad overview of the critical approach

Mainstream accounts of politics and organization focus on explaining: (1) typologies of political rule; (2) how rules are maintained; (3) how conflict is contained; and (4) how legitimacy is sustained. A perspectival link to each of these concerns is the acceptance that coordination and cooperation between members constitutes a vital condition for organizational survival. No one would deny that cooperation is a legitimate topic of organizational analysis. But mainstream analysis focuses almost exclusively on the dynamics and strategies that sustain the political status quo or organizational stability. Moreover, the rules and regulations that sustain existing political relations are seen as politically and morally neutral devices. An image is developed of a complex network of political actors jostling for power and, somehow, largely unaffected by the deep-rooted structural features of class, gender, sexuality and race. A degree of myopia is clearly evident here, in that a concentration at the micro-level of interaction underestimates the extent to which the practices of dominant power groupings may have the effect of reproducing wider inequalities of power, status and wealth. Critical perspectives have been keen to locate decision making within the political and economic context in which organizations operate. Critical theorists refuse to focus only on the micro relations internal to organizations, but also demand to reflect on broader configurations of power and inequality in society, which simultaneously constrain and enable the political activities of organizational members. A clear example of this perspective is embodied in Marxist political analysis (see also Chapters 6 and 7).

Marxist political analysis emphasizes the necessity to be historical and contextual when studying organizational relations. Work organizations are uniquely linked to the capitalist productive economy and thus require an analysis that appreciates the dynamics of capitalist accumulation and the labour process (Thompson and McHugh, 1991, p. 40). In this sense the structures and everyday processes of organization can only be comprehended in terms of control initiated by class-based interests (Reed, 1992, p. 95). Organizations are social arenas in which wider social and political inequalities of power are played out. While groups display differences of interests and thereby behave in distinctive ways, these differences present limited challenges to the enduring structures of capitalist production. Organization relations, structures and processes do indeed have political significance. But political analysis, according to the Marxist perspective, needs to extend beyond the confines of the physical organization and embrace the wider 'political economy' (Thompson and McHugh, 1991). Organizations are perceived as mechanisms through which dominant groups secure conditions necessary for the reproduction of their economic, political and cultural advantage. As Salaman expresses it: 'organizational structure – the design of work and control – can only be seen in terms of a general process of organizational control initiated by, and in the interests of, those who run or dominate the organization' (quoted in Reed, 1992, p. 95).

Major controversies relating to limitations of the mainstream

Functionalism or systems approaches have dominated the mainstream study of politics, even when accounts of decision making have regarded power as plural and dispersed throughout the organization. Power is a crucial medium through which conflicts of interest are brought into the political arena and resolved. Conflict resolution through communication is a central principle of mainstream thinking. Organizations are made up of individuals who, when aggregated into coalitions, constitute formidable sources of power. The imagery here is of loosely connected coalitions with just a passing interest in the formal goals of the organization. An often-acknowledged adversary to the pluralist account of political behaviour in organizations is the critical structuralist approach. A critical structuralist approach is in part a synthesis of the classical and human relations school, drawing also on Marxist and Weberian approaches to organization theory. Critical structuralism is particularly sceptical of the emphasis ascribed to 'harmony' or consensus as a condition for effective decision making within pluralist approaches. In summary, mainstream pluralist theories premise their accounts of decision making on the existence of negotiable interests as and between organizational members. Conversely, the critical structuralist perspective describes relations between organizational members as mediated by systemic conflict and antagonisms concerning the distribution of scarce and valued material (income, capital) and symbolic (status, prestige, esteem, social significance) resources. Before examining these critical approaches, we turn to some studies that help to illuminate the limitations of the mainstream.

Selection of studies within the critical approach

In our Burns and Stalker (1966) case study example earlier in this chapter we saw how some researchers within the mainstream were beginning to recognize and take account of internal politics within organizations. Burns and Stalker understood that individuals within organizations are competitors for scarce material (remuneration) and symbolic (hierarchical position, status) rewards as well as collaborators, cooperating to accomplish organizational outputs (see also Chapter 9). However, these developments tended either to be selectively absorbed into mainstream thinking or eclipsed by a more dominant concern to show how organizations adapted to their environments or were conditioned by the nature of the technology, albeit sometimes mediated through human or social arrangements surrounding it.

A focus on process only emerged with more detailed, 'ethnographic' studies of organization that directly engaged and challenged the apolitical character of most mainstream thinking. Pettigrew's (1973) *The Politics of Organizational Decision-Making* was path-breaking in this regard. Single causal or determinist analyses had been prevalent in the post-classical period of management, perhaps partly to claim some scientific respectability after the long period of anecdotal management theory, but Pettigrew sought to avoid such simplistic approaches.

Pettigrew showed how politics was a central internal as well as external feature of organizations. There was a refusal to accept that management practice was politically neutral, although until the development of a sub-specialism called organizational politics, little attention was given to the political character of management theory itself. In addition to the UK studies, there were also two important North American theorists. An industrial sociologist, Melville Dalton (1959) carried out a non-participant observation study of a group of managers and found that they were continually fighting and manipulating one another in pursuit of specific political advantage (see Chapter 14). The management theorist Henry Mintzberg (1973) can also rightly claim to have broken convention by arguing that management is deeply political, in the sense that it seeks to acquire, but also is involved in the allocation of, scarce resources and rewards. The acknowledgement of a political dimension in management could be seen as a major breakthrough except that **processual** theorists persist in treating politics largely in terms of conflict and as essentially pathological – something to be understood only for purposes of bringing about its eradication. In this sense, as Knights and McCabe (1998, p. 771) have observed, 'despite appearing to challenge traditional management theory, an element of functionalism can be detected':

> politics has functional roles to play in organizations too (as well as no shortage of dysfunctional ones), sometimes over the resistance of planning . . . Politics in an organization can promote necessary strategy change blocked by the more legitimate systems of influence. *(Mintzberg, 1994, p. 200)*

Mintzberg's focus is exclusively on how politics might be *functional* for management's goals. He believes the it might be possible for a more sensitive management to manage politics precisely for the benefit of the organization rather than just for those playing political games. Otherwise politics has to be seen as an illegitimate aberration. And, indeed, the importance of managing politics so as to remove its destabilizing or disruptive effects has been a central emphasis of influential authors such as Child (1969) and Pfeffer (1981) who, like Mintzberg, have argued that dysfunctions are removed less by the application of seemingly infallible techniques (e.g. total quality management or business process re-engineering, both considered in Chapter 7) than by the politically sensitive and astute mobilization of insights into process and forms of persuasion through the formation of alliances, etc.

The problem with the 'functional' view of power and politics is that it:

- Takes for granted the existing structure of power relations and thereby justifies and helps to reproduce prevailing inequalities of power, status and wealth.
- Presumes 'organizational politics' is only about conflict, which is an aberration to eradicate.
- Is individualistic in its approach.
- Perceives power as something to be possessed usually by individuals or groups.
- Explains organizational politics in terms of its presumed negative/disruptive consequences.
- Fails to consider organizational politics as a mode of resistance to legitimate concerns such as incompetent management, diversity discrimination, environmental pollution, corporate ethics, etc.

If the formal organizational goals are treated as sacrosanct then any action designed to change them will be defined as organizational politics and be condemned as subversive. Yet, interestingly, there is another literature in the mainstream called 'change management' that celebrates change as the oil that lubricates the wheels of organizational life. Examples discussed in Chapter 7 include business re-engineering and total quality management, but any new theory or set of principles (e.g. scientific management, human relations, teamworking, etc.) could be seen as vehicles of change management when first developed and introduced to organizations. Management innovation is another label given to the same processes.

Thinkpoint 8.1

Can you think of any reasons why change management or innovation is not described as organizational politics?

'Organizational politics' tends to be associated with conflict largely because, instead of recognizing it as an inescapable feature of any organizational activity, the presumption of or desire for consensus leads functionalists (i.e. those who subscribe to a functional view of power) to seek to eradicate conflict. While 'organizational politics' often reflects or generates conflict, it need not since there is no automatic relationship between differences of interest and their polarization into two extreme camps of mutual antagonism. Sometimes differences and conflicts point to important failings that a majority feel should be corrected or alternatively they focus people's minds on alternatives that can be the basis for acceptable compromises. Organizational politics or even conflict therefore need not be seen as inevitably negative since it can be highly productive in the sense of being the stimulus for important changes that eventually even the 'hardest' opponents might come to recognize as beneficial. However, these changes are not necessarily consistent with preserving existing structures of power and inequality. They might, for example, be equivalent to the suffragette protests that achieved the vote for women earlier in the last century, or the civil rights movements that resulted in the outlawing of racial discrimination, both of which were subsequently welcomed by some of those antagonistic to them.

The functional view of power tends to see organizations as simply an aggregation of individuals rather than as collective communities. Yet, this individualistic view is itself highly political since it facilitates the identification of individuals engaged in organizational politics who can then be isolated and 'picked off' by those who see it as a threat to their power and privilege. Once organizational politics is attributed to awkward or ambitious individuals, it is effectively destroyed through divide and rule techniques. Such an individualistic view will generally perceive power as the property of persons that is perfectly legitimate when exercised by formal leaders. However, if individuals lower down the hierarchy exercise power, it is then described as politics and an aberration, except for those occasions where it prevents conservative or complacent resistance to necessary changes that support the goals of the organization.

Critical thinking subscribes to a conception of power not as an individual possession but as a relationship such that its exercise is always dependent on the compliance or consent of those over whom it is exercised. Of course, in order to secure that compliance or consent, power will almost always be exercised in ways that claim to be following and promoting what are believed to be the agreed collective aims of the organization. Politics is just a term to describe the activity of individuals, groups, organizations or institutions in mobilizing resources and enrolling people to support a policy, plan or project (see Chapter 11 for an elaboration of this actor-network perspective). In other words, politics is the practice of securing compliance or consent, so cannot really be described as aberrant. Where there are conflicting views about either the goals or the means to achieve them in an organization, politics might be the practice of resistance to the established power relations. This may take the form of subordinates resisting management through, for example, trade union militancy or bargaining. On the other hand, it is just as likely to be a question of power struggles between different groups of managers.

Exercise 8.12

Power and resistance at M&S In June 2004 the well-known UK retailer Marks & Spencer was caught up in a major power struggle when Philip Green threatened to make a formal bid for the company. Philip Green had a reputation for transforming loss-making major high street retailers into highly profitable enterprises. Through the media, he offered shareholders a price of £4 per share when, prior to the offer, the shares had languished below £2.70p. The board of directors of Marks & Spencer sought to resist the takeover but had to take some drastic actions in order to win the support of shareholders, particularly the big financial institutions. Ordinarily it is thought that the latter are more interested in short-term profits rather than the long haul, and £4 a share in the hand might have been thought worth more than promises of more in the proverbial bush. M&S brought in a new Chief Executive, Stuart Rose, who ironically had worked previously for Philip Green. Amid massive media hyperbole, he had to develop a strategic plan to sell to the City if he was to ward off the predator Philip Green. The defence package was successful, not least because it offered shareholders a £1 per share payback to be paid for largely by selling off M&S's highly successful financial services arm to the global bank HSBC.

Divide up into small teams and, by consulting newspaper commentaries of the time, company reports and other literature, and write a report answering the following questions:

1 Why in your view did the bid fail?
2 Why do you think the board was so keen to avoid the takeover?
3 Does the discussion of power above but also the other five concepts (i.e. freedom, knowledge, identity, inequality and insecurity) around which this book is organized assist in developing your analysis.

In the mainstream approach to organization behaviour, we have already seen that the focus is often on how organizations adapt to their environments such that *adaptation* overrides any other issue. This is clearly a product of the systems or functional perspective, where attention concentrates on maintaining order, stability and consensus and this means adapting to an environment that otherwise might disrupt the organization. A critical 'organizational politics' perspective, however, does not presume order and consensus, and insofar as there are claims within organizations about adapting to their environments, it identifies these very claims as inherently political. The environment is merely a linguistic description whose content has to be articulated and perhaps mobilized as a way of enrolling others to a particular definition of reality for the purposes of pursuing specific political objectives. This political activity concerns individuals or groups securing power to advance not just their material interests in terms of career, income and security but also their symbolic interests in relation to identity, social recognition and status. From this perspective, management and leadership are seen to be inescapably political, as may be seen in Case study 8.1 (Knights and Murray, 1994) of a medium-sized UK mutual life insurance company, where organizational politics is seen to have determined the direction followed by the company.

By contrast to processual theorists, this research identified organizational politics not as 'aberration or pathological condition' but 'as the motor of organizational life' (ibid, p. 245). Clearly the participants are struggling not merely to have their ideas or knowledge accepted by significant others in the organization, although that does enhance the sense of their own identity, but they are also competing for career progress (power, wealth, freedom and status) and seeking to achieve greater levels of security. While not entirely obvious from this brief synopsis of the research, it also challenges the over-rational view of organizational processes that is common both among theorists of organizational behaviour and practitioners themselves. It is this belief in rationality that precludes an admission that organizational outcomes are often the relative arbitrary result of political processes of competing career and identity-securing strategies that are anything but rational. From this perspective, management activity is a political process constructing a reality that denies its own political character – to paraphrase Oscar Wilde, 'a politics that dare not speak its name'. Were it to be recognized, let alone admitted publicly, that management is arbitrary and accidental rather than rational and planned, this would be to threaten the very basis of its power and privilege. If organizational outcomes cannot be perceived as a result of managerial competence, then why are managers rewarded so much more than their staff? By avoiding blowing the cover, as it were, the mainstream contributes to reproducing the myth of management rationality and the maintenance of existing power relations. In this sense, it reflects and reinforces the identity of managers as indispensable to organizations and thereby helps to sustain their security.

Rationality in our society is a highly valued concept. It is at the heart of science, administration and business and it is reinforced in all three by dominant masculine discourses that privilege 'cold', 'hard' and calculating rationalities against 'warm', 'soft' and intuitive emotional relations. Consequently, there is a conspiracy of silence regarding the existence of bodies and emotions, in addition to cognition and calculation, in management and leadership. Theory and practice present management in a 'disembodied' fashion. In *Beyond Management*, Ian Lennie (1999) carried out his research while acting as a full-time manager in public welfare. He was aware that management was a messy, fully embodied process; and yet all the literature seemed strangely disembodied, speaking only cognitively and at a distance from the everyday experience of managing. He writes of this as the difference between management and managing, and admitted that managers seeking a professional status and through their training were increasingly made to feel that management was technical, abstract and completely separate from what it means to be bodily as well as mentally involved in work on an everyday basis. He is convinced that a disembodied manager cannot manage well since managing is largely about social relations and we only know whether we have managed well through the quality of those relations: 'The results of managing well are not control and accumulation, but civilization' (Lennie, 1999, p. 141).

Exercise 8.13

Managers, leaders or teachers Think of some examples where you have experienced being managed, led or taught in a way that impressed you. What were the typical characteristics of the manager, leader or teacher? Alternatively, think of examples of management, leadership or teaching that have failed to inspire you and examine why you think that was the case. Discuss your deliberations with other students before drawing up some conclusions.

CASE STUDY 8.1 Pensco

At the time of the research in the mid-1990s, a fundamental political struggle was occurring between managers in marketing and those in other divisions but, in particular, Information Systems (IS). Ostensibly it was over how the environment was to be understood, but the effect of having one definition of the environment accepted as opposed to another had major political consequences. The IT division interpreted the environment as one in which competition had made the provision of good customer service vital and this was dependent on adequate administrative procedures, which in turn required a complete overhaul of IT systems. The marketing division, however, interpreted the environment somewhat differently. In response to a new government initiative to persuade consumers to contract out of the state earnings-related pension scheme (SERPS) and make private arrangements, the marketing division was convinced that competition would be focused more on providing the most attractive products – one being a group pension product. While there were many complex shifts of position of the various parties that would take up too much space to record here, the outcome was that marketing forced the issues through more resilient arguments but eventually by enrolling the CEO on their side. In order to deliver a new suite of pensions products, IS was forced to 'botch up' a number of systems rather than completely overhaul them, which was its preference. Customer service was sidelined in this struggle and just had to hope that the administration of policies would not be too severely affected by the deflection of IS resources to new products.

A 'disembodied' way of managing is often attributed to the growing scientific, professional or technical content of management practice, but it may also be seen as reflective of dominant masculine discourses within organizations (Collinson and Hearn, 1996; also Chapter 2) and society more generally.

As was seen in Chapter 7, despite legislation designed to promote and enforce equal opportunities, organizations reflect and reproduce the inequalities and discriminations that exist in wider society. According to the ONS (2005) the median gross annual earnings for males was £24 137, compared to £18 500 for women.

Racial and ethnic minorities suffer enormous discrimination at work both in terms of where they are likely to secure jobs but also in relation to climbing the hierarchy. It is interesting that given the prevalence of diversity, inequalities and discriminations, leading organizational behaviour texts virtually ignore it. Huczynski and Buchanan (2001), for example, devote less than three out of 837 pages to this topic, and even then use it as a vehicle to discuss the attribution theory of Fritz Heider and how sexual attractiveness may be seen as a causal attribute of success at work. In effect, then, they simply ignore the much more significant evidence about sexual, racial or lesser mobility discrimination in favour of an analysis of the more trivial, albeit still unacceptable, ways that physical appearance affects work life chances. Of course, physical appearance in relation to discrimination is extremely significant in relation to skin colour but this is not mentioned in their account.

Racial and ethnic discrimination is often accounted for in terms of British imperialism and the historical legacies of a colonial age where when they were not actual slaves, blacks were treated as inferior and sometimes like animals. Civilization, the law and the **liberal enlightenment** seem only marginally to have eroded this at the level of consciousness, or should we say the unconscious of the white population in Western societies, even if it has curtailed explicit discriminatory practices. If we examine membership of the National Front and other racist political groupings it will be found that they are dominated by comparatively socially and economically deprived white men. Inequality and identity but also power and insecurity would seem to provide some analytical ways of understanding this form of racism since, in a society that emphasizes material and symbolic success, the less successful may seek to find a scapegoat that passes the blame for their situation away from themselves – 'xyz are taking our jobs and our homes' referring to some minority group is the mantra for these people, and stopping immigration is seen as the political solution. Middle class political correctness rightly condemns the racism but often fails to understand the concerns. While exaggerated for political rhetoric, the increasing popularity of this politics in deprived areas of Western cultures suggests that, whether the case or not, many believe it to be so and will always be able to find one or two examples to strengthen their case. The liberal middle class majority set the rules but are not directly affected by them whereas deprived people feel that they are the victims of the middle classes salving their conscience. There are perhaps other explanations, some of which link to aspects of masculine identity. Being a man within modern *masculine discourses* means being in control and demonstrating high levels of achievement.

Modern organizations have been described as cultivating forms of political rivalry between human interest groups. This assumption is based on the premise that modern organizations are designed as systems of simultaneous competition and collaboration (Kakabadse, 1983). In this sense, organizations consist of a dual reality. On the one hand there is the formal structure of operating systems designed to generate rational decision making. But this formal structure exists in conjunction with a parallel system based on struggle, conflict and power. The day-to-day politics of everyday organizational life is reflected in Burns's (1969, p. 232) definition of organisations as 'plural social systems':

> Business enterprises are cooperative instrumental systems assembled out of the unstable attributes of people. They are also places in which people compete for advancement. Thus, members of a business concern are at one and the same time cooperatives in a common enterprise and rivals for the material and tangible rewards of successful competition with each other. The hierarchical order of rank and power, realized in the organization chart, which prevails in all organizations is both a control system and a career ladder.

Contradictions in the pluralist model of competition Competition is accredited in pluralist perspectives of political decision making as having the capacity to 'stimulate and channel energies'.

It provides groups with a common purpose 'which helps to channel their energies in a common direction' (Handy (1976, p. 218). Competition is assumed to motivate organizational members to extend their abilities by 'testing oneself, of discovering new sources of talent and energy' (ibid.). Competition is believed to have the capacity to 'sort out' those organizational members who are underperforming and to communicate collective standards. Above all, productive political rivalry can be used to stimulate creative discussions and liaisons between members (ibid., p. 219).

Rethinking power and control in decision making Morgan (1986) provides an extensive account of the range of strategies organizational members can use to prevent an issue entering into decision-making contexts. Such actions are defined as intentioned attempts to control 'decision premises'. The concept of control of decision premises relates to Stephen Luke's (1974) 'second face of power', namely the ability of individuals to control the conditions that enable an issue to be debated. Tactical power can enable the control of organizational agendas so as to influence how an issue is to be approached, perhaps in ways that prevent selected issues from ever surfacing. Morgan (1986) describes how the tactic of preventing certain issues from entering the bargaining arena often proves popular to those groups and individuals who have a vested interest in maintaining the prevailing distribution of material and symbolic privileges.

The manipulation of decision-making premises relates quite significantly to the forms of control built into belief systems, structures of communication and negotiation. Political analysis draws our attention to decisions as not simply determined or taken, but as emerging from interaction. Systems of communication have the effect of defining the ways we come to recognize an issue as warranting a decision and the course of action available. The subtlety of this 'second face of power' contrasts with the overt strategies used when controlling the process of decision making. Determining how the decision should be made is a powerful strategic resource in the control of decision making. By determining how the decision is to enter the bargaining arena a manager has available to him/her a powerful resource for affecting particular outcomes. Direct parallels exist here with the political strategies employed in the wider world of parliamentary democracy. In brief, the passage of bills through the parliamentary systems involves a transition through various committees. These committees contain representatives from the major political parties. Opposition between the political parties are often played out within the committee stages, whereby a party in opposition might use their presence in the committee to hinder the government's bill. Consequently, the government in power often attempts to steer sensitive bills away from specific parliamentary committees. Similarly a manager, when arranging a meeting, might include on the agenda only those issues he/she wishes to be discussed. In so doing, he/she has determined how a decision has entered the decision-making arena.

Controlling decision-making processes It is the conflictual nature of specialist interests that encourages people to use political strategies to promote outcomes favourable to them. Political analysis thus draws our attention to the use of personal power resources as the tactical basis of decision making. Probably the most basic of power resources utilized in tactical control of the decision-making process is the control of information. In classical readings of organizational dynamics, information flows upwards to high-ranking organizational members as part of their decision-making responsibilities. Information gives power in that it reinforces the formal power and status of the senior personnel who have access to strategic information. The withholding of information is also a powerful mechanism of controlling the decision-making process. The manager who withholds crucial information from subordinates, the specialist department which obstructs the distribution of vital information to committees, and the censorship of sensitive documents are mechanisms by which information is controlled in order to affect decision-making processes. But this classical reading tends not to recognize the possibility of lower-ranking members of the organization mobilizing information to their advantage. The manager confronted with a completed report detailing technicalities and procedures to which he/she is not a specialist can easily be persuaded into accepting its content. He/she is deprived of any real influence over the content of the decision, instead having to rely on the competence of subordinates. Box 8.14 provides a summary of these general issues relating to informational control in decision making (see also Chapter 5).

Contribution and limitations to thinking about the field

Rethinking the pluralist account of decision-making dynamics   Critiques of the pluralist tradition in political analysis draw attention to a shortfall in the theoretical analysis of deep-rooted social cleavages. This radical view, influenced by Marxist theory, introduces a political focus on the social and cultural reproduction of endemic inequalities. Pluralist accounts of political activity regard conflict as an inherent characteristic of organizational life. Conflict stems from a multiplicity of sources drawing upon an innumerable plurality of power resources. The negotiations, coalitions and alliances, which characterize the organization as a political system, are with difficulty contained by reference to a single focal point of power. Critiques of the pluralist tradition emphasize the inherent oppositional and irreconcilable conflicts that define the nature of power in capitalist society. Conflict theory identifies how incompatible class-based interest mediates organizational politics.

While the mainstream has made often-exaggerated claims about the participation and involvement of lower hierarchy staff in decision making, 'critical structuralist' approaches see employee participation schemes as largely attempts to secure the consent of staff. Important decisions still remain with senior management, leaving only minor operational decisions as the prerogative of employees. Structuralist approaches define unresolved conflict as a conspicuous feature of organizational decision making. Organizations are constituted here as arenas of power struggle between incompatible interests. The pluralist model of loosely aligned, shifting coalitions is assumed to deny the existence of incompatibilities between the interests of capital and those of labour, between men and women or different ethnic groups. These endemic differences of interest translate into deep-seated oppositions between the interests of management and workers.

Following the analyses of Marx and Weber, structuralist approaches argue that decision-making practices and outcomes are, at least partly, controlled by factors external to the organizations themselves. According to Marxist analysis, economic conflict between management and labour demonstrates how decision-making processes are 'instruments of capital' (Braverman, 1974; Clegg and Dunkerley, 1980). Decision making is defined in these Marxist terms as enabling the owners of the means of production to further exploit workers through paying them much less than the value of their labour. In contrast to this Marxian analysis, Weberian approaches (see Chapter 13) identify how organizational roles might conflict with systems of authority, formal and informal operating procedures, and patterns of expertise (Fligstein, 1992; Perrow, 1973; March and Simon, 1958). Weberian approaches shift the structuralist emphasis from the experience of being oppressed by broader economic factors to a focus on oppression in terms of a worker's internalized obligation to comply with company directives. Decision making is thus defined in Weberian structuralist theory as compelling workers to submit to authority through rules and regulations that have secured some legitimacy. This legitimacy, however, has been achieved largely through the ability of those exercising power to define the situation for others.

Considering limitations of the critical alternative   Having set an agenda for the study of structure and institutional conflict within organizations, we do not want to fall into the theoretical trap of dismissing all that went before. Indeed the critical structuralist approach has significant limitations – namely

---

Box 8.14: Key issues and processes in the control of information flows within organizations

1 *Formal and informal communication networks.* Information is a scarce and valued resource within organizations. Access to information can increase the power and influence of group members. Consequently, hierarchies often emerge according to who has access to important sources of information.

2 *Gatekeepers.* Informational flow is invariably controlled through restrictions on access and interpretation.

3 *Partiality.* Information held and transmitted by people is often partial and reflects their interests and resources.

4 *Suppression.* Some information may be consciously or subconsciously excluded from consideration if it questions or counters the dominant view.

Source: Adapted from Dawson, S. (1986) *Analysing Organisations*, London: Macmillan.

Exercise 8.14

Try to list the number of situations in your own life that have been defined for you by others – parents, teachers, police, the government, peers, etc. Often, especially when you completely agree with what is defined, it may seem like it is your own definition of the situation so you may have to think deeply to trace the source. Compare this list with another list where you have most definitely defined a situation for yourself. How do the two sets of situations differ in terms of your commitment and feelings about them?

its neglect of the individual. In pluralist political analysis conflicts result from a plurality of divergent interests among individuals as well as groups. This micro-politics of organizational decision provides at least some opportunity to focus on the individual or group interest. Conversely, structuralist analysis describes how conflict in organizations rests on ideological foundations and fundamental questions of structural relations and power. Both positions insufficiently acknowledge how organizational members are engaged in the pursuit of their own personal interests and their own commitments related to beliefs and values. Purely structural forms of analysis tend to obviate the experiences, views and interpretations of the individual actors that make up any organisation (Ball, 1987).

Synopsis and conclusion

Classical models of decision making place less emphasis on individual action, focusing instead on the operation of collective norms, values and social structures. They describe decision making as a response to organizational structures rather than directed by political activities and interest groups. Many writers within this tradition base their theories of decision making on the premise that members of organizations share common interests. Successful decision making is defined by its ability to achieve organizational goals, so that all its members can be more highly rewarded.

Conversely, pluralist approaches recognize political behaviour as a crucial feature of decision making. Political behaviour involves cultivating influential allies, controlling the flow of information and influencing decisions through the informal use of one's power base. The imagery invoked in pluralist analysis is that of loosely connected coalitions vying for limited resources, in an organizational context characterized by contested cultures and shifting alliances. The pluralist model is indeed a vibrant, optimistic account of power and its distribution throughout the organization.

However, structuralist analyses raise considerable doubts about the pluralist conception of power. There are assumed to exist significant limits on the degree to which incompatible interests can be articulated and reconciled within decision-making processes. Questions are raised concerning the extent to which informal groups cut across formal divisions (Etzioni, 1964; Dubin, 1954). Questions are also raised concerning the scope of informal groups (Etzioni, 1964). Whether mainstream or critical, structuralists have a propensity to neglect individual behaviour, thus transforming the complexities of interpersonal influence into nothing more than the outcome of structural processes.

Possibilities, however, exist in the synthesis of structuralist and pluralist approaches within those critical perspectives that emphasize individual identity and insecurity as the medium and outcome of the exercise of power conditioned by structures of inequality generated by global and national capitalist, gender and race relations.

Exercise 8.15

1　Critically review the classical model of decision making.

2　Provide fictional examples of the pluralist model of organizational decision making.

3　Provide fictional examples that illustrate the limitations of the pluralist model.

4　Discuss the limitations of the mainstream structuralist model of decision making.

5　Discuss the limitations of the critical structuralist approach to organizational politics.

9 Culture

Joanna Brewis

Key concepts and learning objectives

By the end of this chapter you should be able to:

- Outline the origins of the interest in organizational culture.

- Understand the 'culture is something that an organization has' perspective.

- Critique the central link this mainstream perspective makes between the 'right' culture and high levels of organizational performance.

- Understand the 'culture is something that an organization is' perspective, and the important ways in which it challenges the orthodoxy.

Aims of the chapter

This chapter will:

- Identify the origins of organizational behaviour's interest in culture.

- Outline the mainstream perspective on culture.

- Identify the extent to which the key claim of this perspective stands up to empirical and conceptual scrutiny.

- Outline the critical perspective on culture, and the ways in which it departs from its mainstream counterpart.

Overview and key points

Organizational behaviour (OB) as a discipline, as should be fairly obvious by now, seeks to understand why people behave as they do in organizations. The literature on **culture** is no exception. Borrowing from anthropological studies of societal cultures, the study of organizational culture focuses on the values, beliefs and norms about what is important and how things should be done in a particular organizational setting. Culture is seen to represent some kind of shared commitment to particular ways of relating to the organization, to superiors, to colleagues and to role.

For example, you (hopefully!) share a certain kind of organizational culture with your fellow students. You might share, to some degree, a belief that higher education is important, that your university will deliver the best kind of education for the future you have planned, that your tutors are qualified to deliver such education, that your task is to participate in lectures and seminars, study independently outside of these sessions, abide by course work deadlines and so on. And you will undoubtedly be expected to comply with such beliefs even if you are not committed to them. The key argument here is that values like these influence behaviour in organizations and so are worthy of study in their own right.

This interest in organizational culture emerged in the late 1970s as a result of a series of challenges facing Western management practitioners and theorists at the time. These have been said to include the following:

- *A general decline in religious belief.* This can be linked to the longstanding claim that modern society is alienating – as discussed in preceding chapters. Westerners, it seemed, therefore began to look to work as a source of 'identity'. Organizational culture became seen as a way for them to find answers to questions like 'Who am I?' as well as 'What is my job for?', 'What is my organization for?' and so on (see also Chapter 2).

- *The expansion of highly technical work and the growth of service industries.* These developments meant that workers required more skills and expertise (and therefore could not be managed using the traditional authoritarian approach) but also needed to behave in 'customer-pleasing' ways. The emerging New Right politics also emphasized individualism (e.g. Thatcherism in the United Kingdom and Reaganomics in the United States), and workers were becoming more educated and demanding more autonomy as a result. Again, culture here can be understood as a way to give employees more day-to-day discretion or freedom – the idea being that there is no need for strict rules and/or management surveillance if workers already have the 'correct' values, such as 'the customer is always right'.

- *The limitations of a mechanical, 'Theory X' approach to managing people.* The 'management science' approach, which dominated theory and practice during the 1960s and 1970s, had become discredited because employees could not in fact be managed purely through 'objective' and mathematical analysis of organizational operations. This led to a renewed focus on the 'soft', 'human' elements of organizations. The culture literature represents part of this backlash in its emphasis on what Peters and Waterman (1982, p. 11), as we shall see later, call 'the intractable, irrational, intuitive, informal organization'.

- *Innovative production methods.* Techniques like 'just-in-time' were making organizational operations more efficient (see Chapter 4). But this required increased flexibility and therefore greater commitment from workers. Given that culture supposedly provides a reservoir of meaning for the individual worker and also enhances a sense of collectivity among workers, a strong set of shared cultural values should – it was argued – enhance their commitment.

- *The 'Japanese miracle'.* The emergence of Japan following the Second World War as a world economic power was seen to have something to do with the cultural values informing Japanese management techniques. Globalization – the breaking down of economic, political, cultural and technological barriers between countries (see Chapter 12) – meant that the West was paying more attention to other countries. And if Japan could create such dramatic success through underpinning its economic activities with a strong value system, why couldn't this also work elsewhere?

In this chapter we will discuss both mainstream and critical approaches to organizational culture. First we review the mainstream perspective, which sees culture as something that an organization *has*, as something that managers can shape and modify. It also dominates the literature. This 'has' perspective urges managers to make every effort to ensure that employees have the 'right' values, beliefs and norms. Creating culture 'at the top' in this way is said to engender harmony and stability in the organization, as well as ensuring that employees behave in the 'appropriate' ways. 'Has' theory therefore draws a strong link between the management of culture and organizational success, but there is controversy as to whether there is 'one best culture' for all organizations or whether culture is in fact a matter of contingency. In this part of the chapter we also review some of the (many) mechanisms that the mainstream approach suggests can be used to manage culture, and end with a more critical look at the empirical and conceptual support for its key claim – for instance, whether a strong culture always leads to excellent organizational results.

In the second part of this chapter we discuss the critical alternative, which argues that culture is something that an organization *is*: in other words, everything in the organization, from the market segment it targets to the number of people it employs, speaks in some way of underlying values, beliefs and norms in that environment. Culture here is also seen to emerge organically as workers learn together to cope with what their jobs require of them. Plus, because workers differ both in terms of what they face within the organization and their experiences outside work, 'is' theory argues that any one workplace is likely to house a number of potentially antagonistic *sub*cultures. For these reasons, this perspective is much more sceptical about the management of culture and argues that such initiatives will either be resisted by employees anyway, or that they come close to an attempt at brainwashing – an unethical use of management power.

Introduction

> [A]nyone who has spent time with any variety of organizations, or worked in more than two or three, will have been struck by the differing atmospheres, the differing ways of doing things, the differing levels of energy, of individual freedom, of kinds of personality. For organizations are as different and varied as the nations and societies of the world. They have differing cultures – sets of values and norms and beliefs – reflected in different structures and systems. *(Handy, 1993, p. 180)*

Despite OB's relatively recent interest in culture, it has nonetheless become a major, perhaps *the*, focus of attention in the area. We already know broadly speaking what culture is – shared organizational values, beliefs and norms – but it is worth breaking the concept down a little before we embark on the chapter proper. Aspects of organizational culture might include some or all of the following:

- Mission and goals: what is the organization aiming towards? – e.g. to be the UK market leader in a particular product, or to expand into markets in other parts of the world.

- The **psychological contract**: what employees can expect of the organization beyond the formal employment contract (e.g. job security, exciting work) and what the organization can expect in return (e.g. long hours, customer responsiveness).

- Authority and power relations: these are not the same thing. Someone can have formal authority but no real power to influence what others do, and vice versa (see Chapter 8). This is nicely illustrated in Ackroyd and Crowdy's (1990) study of abattoir workers, where the authors suggest that teams in this environment were formally led by chargehands, but in reality the chargehands were often fairly low down in the informal hierarchy that had developed.

- The qualities or characteristics that members should have (or not have): some organizations for example stress innovation, initiative and risk-taking, others emphasize caution, conservatism and attention to detail. (Dembrow, Markow and Thompson Inc. is probably an example of the latter.)

- Communication and interaction patterns: do staff address managers by their first names? Do they see colleagues as competitors or collaborators? Do they see co-workers in the evenings or at weekends?

- Rewards and punishments: how is 'good' behaviour rewarded – praise or something more tangible like a bonus or a promotion? What kind of sanctions are available for 'bad' behaviour? Is it OK to be late three days in a row? How far does an employee have to go to get the sack?

- Ways of dealing with the outside world: how committed is the organization to protecting environmental resources? Are recycling schemes, electricity saving policies or car sharing arrangements in place, and how seriously are they taken? Moreover, is information shared with competitors or are all organizational processes shrouded in a veil of secrecy?

Image 9.1

Organized activity demands that people work together in coordinated ways, whether they are in a university, a shop, a factory, a call-centre, a publishing house or wherever. So it would be impossible if the individuals concerned did not agree to some extent on issues like those identified above. Culture therefore provides a source of organizational 'common sense' upon which members draw when deciding where, when and how to act. And if organizational structures, strategies, regulations and policies frame the possibilities for behaviour formally and explicitly, culture could be argued to bring the organization to life. In other words, much of what is outlined above will already be spelt out in written documents like strategic plans, job descriptions and disciplinary procedures. But if cultural values, beliefs and norms in any way contradict these documents then members will probably subvert or ignore the formal rules in their real-life workplace activities – as we have already seen in the abattoir example.

How do some of the questions on p. 346 relate to your university? For example, what do lecturers guarantee to students – prompt feedback on assessed work, perhaps, or maybe they have an open door policy so you can see them whenever you want to? What do they expect in return – essays always being handed in on time or thorough preparation for seminars maybe? Do you ever socialize with your lecturers? To what extent are you encouraged to work with other students on assessed essays or presentations? How would your department deal with plagiarism? And what might the answers to these questions say about the values, beliefs and norms that exist at this institution?

Can you think of instances in your university where what happens in practice goes against institutional rules? For example, perhaps extensions are sometimes granted over the phone when the rules state that forms must be filled out in order for students to make such a request, or attendance registers are not always kept for seminars.

Moreover, because organizational culture consists of values, beliefs and norms that exist in people's heads, we can only actually identify it at the level of what Schein (1992) refers to as cultural artefacts. These are tangible phenomena that embody organizational culture, such as types of people employed (personalities, levels of education, etc.), traditions and rituals, technology, architecture, logos, heroes, stories, myths and so on. Schein argues though that there are in fact three levels of culture, and that, as Figure 9.1 suggests, artefacts represent the tip of an iceberg in the sense that the other two levels are hidden from view.

Values incorporate answers to questions like 'What are we doing?' and 'Why are we doing it?': they involve ethical statements of 'rightness'. So an organization's values might include a commitment to equality of opportunity, to solving human problems through the application of technology or to profit maximization for shareholders – but these can be brought to light only through careful and directed questioning.

Basic assumptions on the other hand are almost impossible to surface. These are unconscious and taken for granted ways of seeing the world and are *the source of values and artefacts*. They concern questions about:

- Our relationship to our environment (should we seek to master nature or to live in harmony with it?) and to each other (should our prime orientation be to ourselves as individuals, or is it more important to be a member of and offer loyalty to a group?).

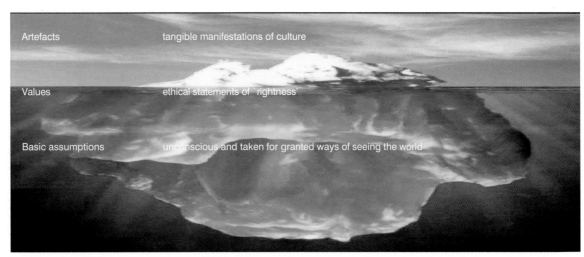

SOURCE: © SCHEIN, COPYRIGHT © (2006) JOHN WILEY & SONS INC.

Figure 9.1 Schein's iceberg model of culture

- Reality and truth (is there such a thing as a universal, timeless human truth or reality or do we live in dynamic worlds that are largely of our own making?).
- Human nature (are we essentially good, bad or a mixture? Is it appropriate to place our trust in others or do we need to take steps to avoid being exploited by them?).
- Human activity (should we focus on measurable achievement and see our activities as a means to an end, or is it more appropriate to live for the moment and enjoy the actual process of our activities?).

With the context for the chapter now established, we turn to the mainstream perspective.

Mainstream perspective on organizational culture

Introduction to the mainstream perspective, AKA culture is something that an organization 'has'

Most of the relevant literature views organizational culture as, in Smircich's (1983) words, something that an organization *has*. From this perspective culture is understood to be:

- *A variable.* Like capital or other assets such as information technology, culture – how employees think and feel – is something that can be manipulated by managers.
- *Integrating and stabilizing.* Because culture is shared between organizational members, it is seen to provide a ' "natural" force for social integration' (Meek, 1988, p. 455). Culture brings people together: it ensures that they all think, feel and act in relatively similar ways, that they all develop similar workplace identities. Thus it creates consistency and reduces conflict. The 'has' theorists suggest that culture simplifies people's choices about how things work, what is important and how to behave in organizations.
- *Created at the top.* Culture is set by senior management and disseminated downwards throughout the organization. This can be referred to as **cultural engineering** (Jackson and Carter, 2000, p.p. 27–28) – creating the 'right' kind of organizational culture such that management-imposed values rule out particular courses of action or narrow the range of options for a decision.

Culture here then is understood overall as a management 'lever', a means of ensuring that employees direct their efforts towards organizational goals. Peters and Waterman (1982, p. 11) sum the 'has' perspective up neatly in their suggestion to managers that:

All that stuff you have been dismissing for so long as the intractable, irrational, intuitive, informal organization *can* be managed. Clearly, it has as much or more to do with the way things work (or don't) around your companies as the formal structures and strategies do . . . you [are] foolish to ignore it.

So what might cultural engineering look like in practice? Case study 9.1 describes one of the best known examples of an apparently successful cultural change, which took place at British Airways between 1982 and 1996.

Key issues and controversies

In the BA case, we see fairly striking evidence to suggest that the 'has' theory account of organizational culture is plausible in terms of the link it forges between the management of culture and organizational effectiveness. Indeed, this claim – that 'a culture has a positive impact on an organization when it points behavior in the right direction . . . [a]lternatively, a culture has [a] negative impact when it points behavior in the wrong direction' (Kilmann *et al.*, cited in Alvesson, 2002, p. 43) – is probably the most important one that it makes.

As already suggested, 'has' theory sees the 'appropriate' culture as leading to organizational effectiveness in two ways: first, by providing meaning for employees so that their work makes some kind of sense to them, which can be seen as motivating; and, secondly, establishing particular ways

CASE STUDY 9.1 Cultural engineering at British Airways, 1982–1996

BRITISH AIRWAYS

Image 9.2

British Airways was produced by a 1974 merger between British Overseas Airways Corporation (who offered long-haul flights) and British European Airways (specializing in flights to continental Europe). In its early years, BA was very bureaucratic and rules-oriented (see Chapter 13). It is described as having an introspective, inflexible culture where over-staffing was routine, hierarchy was all-important and little attention was paid to customer service, employee opinion or profitability.

There were also substantial cultural differences post-merger. BOAC staff tended to look down on their BEA counterparts, believing they provided flights for 'tradesmen' whereas their own services were for 'gentlemen'. BEA employees on the other hand regarded the BOAC staff as snobs who had no real sense of the cut-throat world of commercial competition. The result was disastrous in terms of performance – indeed in 1980 BA was voted the airline to avoid at all costs and, at the time, was also the most unpunctual European carrier flying out of the United Kingdom.

When John King was appointed by Prime Minister Margaret Thatcher as BA Chairman in 1981, he saw a need for drastic action because of the huge losses the company was making. His 'survival plan' created nearly 20 000 staff redundancies, closed routes and disposed of BA's cargo-only service. By the time Colin Marshall took over as CEO in 1982 an operating surplus had been created for the first time since the merger. Marshall's objective was to build on this by encouraging all BA staff to take responsibility for customer satisfaction, and also to develop a more holistic outlook on the company, bridging functional and cultural divides. An extended training initiative was therefore developed. Marshall was quoted at the time as talking about 'designing' BA staff to deliver good service, just as BA already designed the seats on its planes, its inflight entertainment and its airport lounges to do the same.

The first of these training events was launched in 1983. Two days long, it was called 'Putting People First', and was eventually attended by 40 000 staff. The course focused on encouraging effective personal relationships, the idea being that if staff felt good about themselves they would also feel good about interacting with customers. A senior director was present for question and answer sessions at each of these events and Marshall himself frequently attended. Other

programmes followed, including 'Managing People First' for BA's 1400 managerial and supervisory staff, launched in 1985. Its objectives were to foster a more caring and trusting relationship between managers and their teams, and to improve communication and staff motivation. Another – 'Day in the Life' – was introduced in the same year to improve cooperation and break down barriers between BA's various functions.

At the same time other more tangible changes were afoot, including privatization in 1987 and a takeover of British Caledonian Airways in 1988. Both marked how much progress BA had made towards becoming a market-oriented, customer-facing organization. The organization's structure was also changing – Marshall revamped BA into 11 profit centres, streamlining its bureaucracy and allowing for greater cross-functional communication and cohesion. Executives who he felt weren't up to the changes were removed and performance-related pay, linked to the new BA values, was introduced.

But the developments didn't end there: in 1987, 'Awards for Excellence' were brought in to recognize high levels of-performance among staff, and the suggestion scheme 'Brainwaves' was introduced. In 1988 BA began to offer an in-house MBA in conjunction with Lancaster University; and the initiative 'Winning for Customers', consisting of a training event to signal that every staff member makes a difference to the customer experience, and an associated course for supervisory and managerial staff, was launched in 1992.

All in all, this lengthy and expensive programme seems to have transformed a loss-making public organization colloquially known as 'Bloody Awful' into a profitable private company, which won the *Business Traveller* 'World's Best Airline' award for seven years up to and including 1995. Indeed, former CEO Bob Ayling (who took over from Colin Marshall in 1996, when Marshall became Chairman) suggested in a BA magazine that the organization 'has been one of the great turnaround stories of the late twentieth century. The image this airline has built for itself in the past 14 years has stood it in great stead' (*Business Life*, 1997, p. 45). The BA example therefore suggests that culture can indeed be engineered, and that a substantial hike in performance can be achieved by managers embarking on this kind of initiative.

"It's just a familiarity we like to go through with new employees."

Image 9.3

SOURCE: © NAF/CARTOONSTOCK.COM

to think, feel and act, which are linked to the achievement of organizational goals. The 'has' theorists believe that the strength of an organization's culture – the extent to which employees buy into management-directed values, beliefs and norms – has a direct impact on its performance, however that is measured. The basic 'guarantee' of this literature is that, properly managed, culture can help to build employee commitment, convey management philosophy and legitimate their policies, motivate staff and facilitate socialization of new employees.

The 'swearing in' cartoon pokes gentle fun at the socialization of new staff into a particular company's culture, suggesting that this amounts to asking them to swear an oath of allegiance to hard work, turning up on time and putting in extra hours as and when required. But the 'has' literature takes these possibilities more seriously. As established in the chapter overview, it believes that, once employees have taken on board the 'right' values, these will guide their behaviour without the need for costly and demotivating direct supervision. Indeed Deal and Kennedy (1988, p. 15) go as far as to claim that it is possible to increase every worker's productivity by one or two hours a day if culture is managed effectively.

'Has' theorists, then, are functionalist and technical in their outlook. Their **functionalism** can be seen in the claim that culture performs a function in its maintenance of organizational equilibrium and consensus. The 'has' perspective is also **technical** because it seeks to develop knowledge about organizations which enables managers to manipulate specific variables (workers' values, beliefs and norms) in order to achieve a specified outcome (organizational effectiveness). And of course the suggestion that culture might be the solution to the age-old problem of getting employees to work hard because they enjoy it and feel fulfilled has a broad populist appeal among organization theorists and managers alike – perhaps this is why there are so many contributions to the 'has' camp.

Exercise 9.1

Going back to your university, try to identify the ways in which academic staff endeavour to

- Encourage you to commit to your studies (e.g. by emphasizing the reputation of the university and its good graduate employment record).
- Convey their philosophy (e.g. my institution believes in encouraging students to critique everything they are exposed to and bases all teaching on offering several sides of the same theoretical or empirical story).
- Justify practices like a plagiarism policy or the rules that govern how your degree grade is calculated (e.g. by suggesting that plagiarism policies protect students against others who cheat and thus gain higher grades by unfair means).
- Teach freshers or direct entry students 'the rules of the game' (e.g. by holding social events at the beginning of each year or operating a student mentor system).

How successful are they in these endeavours, in your opinion?

But its suggestion that getting the culture 'right' results in high levels of performance aside, there are two areas on which there is disagreement in the 'has' literature. The first of these is the question as to whether there is one culture, which, if implemented in any organization, will result in high performance (the 'one best culture'/'one size fits all' argument) or whether the right kind of culture is actually a question of the variables affecting the organization (the contingencies/'horses for courses' argument). So that you can get to grips with this debate, this section begins by reviewing the two sides, identifying the best known contributions to each and suggesting that the second is probably more plausible in common-sense terms.

The second 'has' theory controversy surrounds the mechanisms that should be used by managers to change, consolidate or establish organizational culture. Again, the central points of this discussion are rehearsed here, to draw your attention to the many cultural tactics that managers might have at their disposal, and to focus on some of the key decisions that 'has' literature suggests they need to make in this regard. We end the section by acknowledging that, although 'has' theorists are not universally optimistic about the end result of cultural management strategies, this has not had any noticeable impact on wider public demand for its prescriptions and advice – perhaps because of the aforementioned attractiveness of the primary link it makes between culture and organizational performance.

In terms of the 'one best culture' argument, Peters and Waterman (1982) – whose work is discussed in more detail in the 'Important empirical studies' section later in this chapter – and Ouchi (1981) are probably the most notable proponents. Their position suggests a kind of magic formula for organizational success. Peters and Waterman identify eight cultural values that they say exist in America's best performing companies, and which should be introduced into all organizations to ensure 'excellence'. Indeed the subtitle of their best-selling text *In Search of Excellence* is *Lessons from America's Best-Run Companies*.

Similarly, Ouchi analyses what he sees to be a distinctive form of culture in Japanese organizations – in fact his work is an example of OB's 'Japanese turn' as described in the chapter overview. Ouchi calls this approach Theory Z, after Maslow's claim that type Z is the highest form of self-actualization (see Chapter 2). It is based on the assumption that, instead of the competitive ethos of the 'market' organization or the rules-driven bureaucracy, workers in a Theory Z organization behave in appropriate ways because they share a commitment to the same value system. This also helps them to counter the apparently alienating characteristics of the modern world – something we have already touched upon. Ouchi recommends that US managers should try to socialize their employees into just such a culture – and the subtitle of his book (*How American Business Can Meet the Japanese Challenge*) once again makes his message very clear.

More common in 'has' theory, however, is the contingencies/horses for courses argument. These theorists pick and mix a range of different internal and external variables to which, they argue, managers should attend when deciding what kind of culture best fits their particular organization. The best known of these writers are Deal and Kennedy (1988) and Handy (1993), who borrows extensively from earlier work by Harrison (1972). Deal and Kennedy (whose ideas are also developed in the 'Important empirical studies' section) identify a four-fold 'typology' of organizational culture, where the suitability of each cultural type depends on the level of risk involved in an organization's activities and how quickly it receives feedback on those activities. Handy, similarly, identifies four key categories of culture to fit a range of organizational situations, as follows:

1 *The power culture (represented by a web)*

- Depends on a central power source, usually the founder or owner.
- Trust between centre and 'outlying' staff is key to effectiveness, as is personal interaction.
- The central figure needs to select staff who have similar ways of thinking so they can be left to get on with their work: thus members have a lot of freedom.
- Few rules and routines; decisions depend on balance of power rather than procedure.
- A strong, cohesive and flexible culture where politically minded risk-takers thrive.
- Centre's influence declines as organization grows bigger (and the web weaker), which may prompt break-up into smaller divisions or a shift towards role culture (see below).
- Tough and competitive, possibly causing low morale and high labour turnover.
- Replacement of the centre at the end of their career is a key challenge because 'a web without a spider has no strength' (Handy, 1993, p. 184).
- Likely to be found in small entrepreneurial organizations such as trading, finance or property companies, new businesses and/or family firms.

SOURCE: © ISTOCKPHOTO.COM/JESSE YARDLEY

Image 9.4

2 *The role culture (represented by a Greek temple)*

- Reason and logic are key values here.
- A bureaucratic and highly structured organization; temple's pillars are specialist departments like marketing or production, and roof is senior management team.
- Organizational operations controlled by job descriptions, reporting procedures, communications policies, etc.
- Staff are selected on basis of capability/expertise and are not required to do anything more than their roles require.
- Power comes from hierarchical position, not personal charisma.

SOURCE: © ISTOCKPHOTO.COM/BART PARREN

Image 9.5

- Works well where the market is predictable or a monopoly/oligopoly exists.
- Provides security and predictability for workers, who are able to climb the 'career ladder'.
- 'But Greek temples are *insecure* when the ground shakes' (Handy, 1993, p. 186 – emphasis added): they do not respond quickly to changing circumstances, and can be frustrating for those who seek freedom.
- The civil service, car manufacturers, oil companies, life insurance companies and high street banks are all likely to be role cultures.

3 *The task culture (represented by a net or a matrix)*

- Centres on getting the job done, bringing the right people and resources together at the right time to work on a project; staff may be simultaneously involved in several different projects.
- Key values are expertise and teamwork.
- Overall control maintained by central allocation of resources and people to projects.
- Suited to competitive and volatile markets with short product cycles, where responsiveness, cooperation and creativity are vital.
- Project teams can be formed and abandoned rapidly and decision making is often faster, being devolved to team level.

SOURCE: © ISTOCKPHOTO.COM/JIM JURICA

Image 9.6

- But no real attention to economies of scale and staff may have little opportunity to develop expertise when working across a range of projects (can also generate confusion and insecurity).
- May be found in venture capital firms, management consultancies and advertising agencies.

4 *The person/cluster culture (represented by a galaxy of stars)*

- Key value here is individuality or freedom.
- Organization exists only for its members' benefit; it comes into existence when people find that sharing office space, desks, an IT network, etc. helps them, but there are no collective goals as such.
- Overall control is only possible by mutual consent, and power is shared.
- Tends not to last: 'Too soon the organization achieves its own *identity* and begins to impose on its individuals.

SOURCE: © ISTOCKPHOTO.COM/JUSTIN HORROCKS

Image 9.7

It becomes, at best, a task culture, but often a power or role culture' (Handy, 1993, p. 191 – emphasis added).

● Unusual but may be found in barristers' chambers or architects' partnerships, or in small organizational enclaves like consultants in an NHS hospital.

Handy, as we can see, stresses size, market and individual worker preference as the key variables in identifying the best culture for a particular organization. Other contingencies that have been identified as important include:

● National culture – see, for example, Hofstede's (2001) discussion of differences between IBM subsidiaries in various parts of the world.

● Political environment – such as Tayeb's (1988) comparison of industrial relations legislation and government attitudes to market regulation in the United Kingdom and India.

● Founder/leader – like Henry Ford, whose approach to management is discussed by Corbett (1994, p.p. 123–132), and Konosuke Matsushita of the Matsushita Corporation, analysed by Pascale and Athos (1981).

● Technology – Anthony's (1994) discussion of production processes in coal-mining, for instance.

Our intuition should tell us that the contingency stance is a more sensible position to adopt when organizations vary so widely in terms of size, sector, ownership, location, staff and so on, especially given the advent of the so-called 'global village'. As Handy (1993, p. 183) points out: 'It must be emphasized that [any culture] can be a good and effective culture; but people are often culturally blinkered, thinking that ways that worked well in one place are bound to be successful everywhere. This is not the case.'

Exercise 9.2

If you are a student who is studying abroad, think about how educational practices in universities at home differ from those in the country where you are doing your degree (you might have to e-mail a friend at home for information). If you are a 'home' student, ask a friend who comes from elsewhere. Some examples might be:

● How essays are marked (some higher educational cultures typically award much higher marks in general than others).

● How degrees are graded (some use grade point averages, others prefer 'bands' like the British class first upper second/lower second/third system).

● How students treat academic staff and vice versa.

● The extent to which you are expected to write in your own words or submit course work as part of your assessment, and so on.

The contingency literature also acknowledges that organizations may house subcultures because of the particular circumstances facing different departments or functions. This cultural differentiation requires that managers work to integrate these various groups of employees, to encourage them to understand each other despite their differing values, beliefs and norms. Typologies – such as the four cultures identified by Handy – might therefore be best understood as ideal-types for benchmarking real organizations, indicating the dimensions that could be important in understanding why particular values exist and whether these values come together to 'form a coherent [organizational] . . . whole' (Brown, 1998, p. 72).

Thinkpoint 9.3

Think about the different departments or functions in a 'typical' manufacturing organization – marketing, R&D, production, finance, human resources and so on. Using Handy's typology, identify the kind of culture you would expect each department to have and suggest why this might be.

The second controversy in the 'has' literature centres on the most appropriate ways to manage organizational culture. These discussions tend to focus on changing an existing culture – as in the BA case study. But it is worth remembering that cultural initiatives may also involve managers trying to preserve the status quo, which can be particularly challenging in the face of large numbers of staff leaving or joining the organization. Alternatively, they could be trying to build a specific type of culture in a new organization. Daymon (2000), for example, discusses efforts to encourage commercial values around high profit and low costs as opposed to 'traditional' broadcasting values of creativity, artistic merit and production excellence among incoming staff at Countrywide Television.

However, it is also true to say that the cultural transmission mechanisms (CTMs)[1] used are broadly speaking the same whether managers are trying to change, maintain or build a culture. Also, change is probably more difficult than the other types of cultural engineering, '[b]ecause it entails introducing something new and substantially different from what prevails in existing cultures' (Trice and Beyer, 1993, p. 393). For present purposes, therefore, we will concentrate on cultural change.

As implied above, although there are many different explanations available, there is no real agreement in the 'has' literature as to the best way to change a culture. It has been argued in fact that the approach management chooses to shift employees' values, beliefs and norms ought to be based on criteria such as how many people need to change and how much of their behaviour needs to change; how different the new culture is from what exists at the moment; and whether people either inside or outside the organization already espouse the new values, so that they can be used as role models.

Exercise 9.3

Evaluate the BA case study in terms of what it suggests about how many people and how much of their behaviour needed to change in this organization; how different the new culture was from the old; and whether there were any external or internal role models for the new ideas and behaviours. How might it have felt to be an employee experiencing this series of interventions?

There are also many empirical examples of the CTMs managers have deployed to change (or maintain or build) a culture. These have been claimed to fall into two main categories:

- Devices that are the responsibility of the human resources department and focus on employee resourcing (getting the 'right' people into the organization and ensuring that they perform in a particular way once there, as well as 'disposing' of the 'wrong' people), employee development (training staff in 'appropriate' ways) and employee relations (encouraging 'suitable' forms of communication between management and staff).
- 'Symbolic leadership' devices – the ways in which senior members of the organization go about managing the rank-and-file employees and how these tactics embody various values, beliefs and norms to those employees.

These measures are also said to be more effective when used in a kind of cultural package, as on their own they are unlikely to have much impact. Moreover, a 'consistent cues' approach is said to be necessary such that 'all aspects of every . . . programme must unequivocally promote the desired state culture' (Brown, 1998, p. 166).

We have already seen a very good example of the use of human resource devices to change a culture in the British Airways case study – where employee resourcing, employee relations and employee development tactics were all used to shift the prevailing values towards an emphasis on customer service and internal staff cooperation.

Thinkpoint 9.4

Can you classify the various CTMs used at BA into the categories of resourcing, relations and development? Some may fall into more than one.

In terms of symbolic leadership devices, on the other hand, **management by example** (MBE) is probably the epitome of such techniques. It involves, quite literally, 'walking the talk', acting out the organization's cultural vision because, in the old adage, actions speak louder than words. Indeed, according to the 'has' theorists, managers should 'be seen as spending a lot of time on matters visibly related to the values they preach' (Deal and Kennedy, 1988, p. 169). After all, management talk begins to sound like so much hot air after a while if it is not backed up by behaviour.

There are some very evocative examples of such 'embodiment leadership' in cultural change projects, including Lee Iacocca's refusal to draw more than US$1 a year salary until he got General Motors on its feet again and Colin Marshall of British Airways (them again!) assisting check-in staff on the first day of the company's Super Shuttle service when they were overrun with customers. We have also seen other BA instances of MBE in senior directors always being present for Q&A sessions at the 'Putting People First' events and Marshall himself frequently turning up into the bargain.

Thinkpoint 9.5

Which values do you think Iacocca, Marshall and the latter's senior BA colleagues are trying to embody to staff in the MBE examples discussed above?

In sum, then, 'has' theory disagrees on (a) whether one culture fits all organizations, and (b) how managers ought to go about changing, maintaining or constructing cultures – in other words, no clear message emerges here about the appropriate combination of cultural transmission mechanisms.

But to conclude this section we should also note the cautionary tales that appear periodically in the 'has' literature with regard to the realities of managers embarking on a cultural intervention. For example, it has been suggested that many initiatives of this kind fail because any initial enthusiasm on the part of staff fades and training is not used to properly support the changes. Another recommendation is that sufficient time and space is given to employees to voice their resentment about the changes and 'grieve' for what has been lost (rituals, heroes and so on).

Managers contemplating changes of this kind are also counselled to attend to organizational **multiculturalism** – i.e. not to assume that the organization has one culture through and through. They should allow for the fact that different groups of workers may have different sets of values (as we saw above in the discussion of cultural differentiation) and thus could respond to a cultural change programme in varying ways. The UK National Health Service is a particularly interesting example here. In the wake of the Griffiths Report and the importation of managers with no medical expertise, there was an attempt by the new incumbents to impose a culture of efficient use of resources. This led to clashes with clinicians, who argued that patients simply needed the best care regardless of cost. Such debates persist to this day, but here the *managers* were the *minority subculture* trying to impose their values on a *dominant* culture – as may often be the case when a new management team arrives in an organization.

Overall, then, it would be unfair to say that the 'has' literature necessarily sees cultural change as a 'quick fix' or a panacea for all managerial problems. As Deal and Kennedy (1988, p. 163) have it, 'let us summarize the dismal economics of effecting real and lasting cultural change: it costs a fortune and takes forever'. They suggest that achieving even half the change in values, beliefs and norms that management propose in any one initiative necessitates spending between 5–10 per cent of the salaries of the staff being targeted, and so strongly recommend that managers ask themselves whether embarking on cultural change is either necessary or worth it.

However, the above warnings (which certainly emphasize the possibility of cultural change but also alert managers to the potential pitfalls along the way) seemingly do little to sap the enthusiasm of the corporate market in particular for 'how to' texts on organizational culture. Indeed, one of the best selling books in this area – Deal and Kennedy's (1988) *Corporate Cultures* – also issues, as we have seen, a clear warning about the economic and temporal costs of trying to change culture. It is to two such texts – the key empirical contributions to the 'has' literature – that we now turn.

Important empirical studies

In this section we will briefly review two of the central empirical texts in the 'culture is something that an organization has' school in order to draw out their central lessons. These are Peters and Waterman's (1982) *In Search of Excellence: Lessons from America's Best-Run Companies* and Deal and Kennedy's (1988) *Corporate Cultures: The Rites and Rituals of Corporate Life*. They have been chosen because there exists 'something of a consensus that [they] were central to stimulating the growth of popular managerial interest in organizational culture', along with Ouchi's (1981) *Theory Z* (Parker, 2000, p. 10). As we know already, Peters and Waterman fall into the 'one best culture' camp, whereas Deal and Kennedy prefer to argue for cultural horses for organizational courses.

Peters and Waterman gathered their data by interviewing managers in 43 top performing US companies, all Fortune 500 listed. They began with a list of 62 of McKinsey's[2] 'star' clients and subtracted 19 – including General Electric – on the basis of specific performance measures. The organizations left included Hewlett Packard, McDonald's, Procter and Gamble, and Disney. Peters and Waterman's conclusion, as we have seen, was that these 'best-run' companies operated on the basis of eight cultural tenets that were at the heart of their performance. These constitute the authors' recipe for success: they argue that every organization needs to live by the same tenets in order to create excellence. The eight tenets outlined in the book are as follows:

- *A bias for action*. Instead of discussing and planning everything in minute and pernickety detail, go out and make things happen – use the trial and error approach.
- *Close to the customer*. Listen to what the customer wants and tailor business activities accordingly.
- *Autonomy and entrepreneurship*. Empower employees and encourage innovation, creativity and risk-taking.
- *Productivity through people*. Regard employees as the organization's most important resource and the source of quality goods and services.
- *Hands-on, value-driven*. Managers must get involved in the work that their staff do as well as demonstrate their own commitment to the central corporate values (referred to above as management by example).
- *Stick to the knitting*. Stick to producing whatever it is that the organization is good at; don't be tempted by diversification.
- *Simple form, lean staff*. The organization's structure should be as flat and flexible as possible; top-heavy bureaucracies are inimical to excellence.
- *Simultaneous loose–tight properties*. Employees should have a great deal of discretion all the way down to the shop floor (loose properties), as management exercises control through a strong set of centralized values (tight properties).

Of course this list sounds almost commonplace now – we would expect that the majority of businesses would seek to operate on the basis of such values. But *In Search of Excellence* is probably also the most prominent management book of recent times, having sold millions of copies worldwide and been translated into many different languages. It would be surprising, then, if it had not had some effect on managerial thinking. And in the early 1980s it was certainly heady stuff, given the aforementioned backdrop of management-by-numbers (Parker, 2000, p.p. 10, 12, 16).

Recap	Peters and Waterman's key message is 'My way or the highway' – i.e. there is 'one best way' to business excellence via cultural management.

Deal and Kennedy, in a text originally published around the same time as *In Search of Excellence*, similarly stress that 'people make business work' (1988, p. 5). Their research encompassed 80 US companies, 18 of which had strong cultural values and were all high performers. The latter group included DuPont, the chemical, energy and materials giant, and vehicle component manufacturer

Dana Corporation. But unlike Peters and Waterman, Deal and Kennedy argue that the type of culture that is most likely to breed business success depends on particular features of that business's environment – specifically the level of risk that the business faces and the speed of feedback it receives. On this basis they develop a four-part typology, similar in form to Handy's, which unfolds as follows:

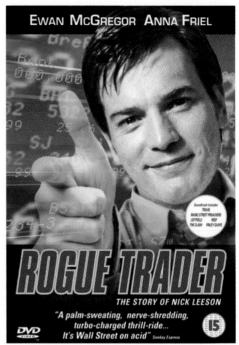

SOURCE: © GRANADA

Image 9.8

1 *Tough-guy culture*
- Key values are speed (making decisions quickly) and emotional resilience (living with the consequences).
- A high-pressure, individualistic, all-or-nothing culture, nicely illustrated by 'rogue trader' Nick Leeson's claim that he needed 'balls of steel' to survive the Baring's Bank trading floor; it respects risk-takers and mavericks.
- Suits organizations, particularly new ones, where operations are risky (e.g. millions of dollars invested in a film) and feedback rapid (e.g. when using dynamite to explode the last stretch of a tunnel under construction).
- But has a short-termist outlook, plus there is little cooperation between members and no real incentive to learn from mistakes.
- Constant pressure also makes employee burnout likely.
- Those who thrive are tough and competitive, want to do well on their own merits and prefer to work alone.
- The police force, construction companies, management consultancies, advertising agencies, television, film and publishing companies and sports teams might all be tough-guy cultures.

2 *Work hard/play hard culture*
- Values customers, trying to meet their needs and solve their problems.
- Also emphasizes action, or what Deal and Kennedy (1988, p. 114) call the 'try it; fix it; do it' ideology, and teamwork.
- Performance measured by results, such as sales generated.
- As its name suggests, a friendly culture where having fun (e.g. staff parties) is as important as hard graft.
- Suited to organizations where the risks are small (e.g. no one sale makes or breaks a retail organization like Tesco, Marks and Spencer or Next, a car salesroom or an estate agency) but feedback is quick (e.g. you either close the sale or you don't).
- Manufacturing companies may also fall into this cultural category: workers here know when mistakes are made but checks along the production line mean no single error is a disaster.
- Good for extraverts.
- But emphasis on volume can override attention to quality, not always adaptive to change and has a tendency to prefer quick fix solutions.

3 *Bet-your-company culture*
- Attention to detail and precision are key values here.
- Has a long-term orientation and believes in giving a good idea the chance to work.
- A relentless 'drip drip' pressure culture where technical expertise is emphasized because errors are costly.

- Knowledge is shared and staff interdependence seen as important.
- Suitable for high-risk, slow-feedback environments where running a business 'means investing millions – sometimes billions – in a project that takes years to develop, refine, and test, before you find out whether it will go or not' (Deal and Kennedy, 1988, p. 116), and a quick fix ideology could be disastrous.
- Produces high-quality inventions and breakthroughs.
- But vulnerable to short-term fluctuations: always waiting for the 'pay-off'.
- Survivors have character, confidence and the stamina to 'wait it out'.
- Oil companies, the nuclear arms industry, mining corporations, investment banks and the forces (who spend considerable time and money preparing for wars they may never have to fight) could all exhibit this culture.

The 43rd **Civil Service Year Book**

SOURCE © CROWN COPYRIGHT 2005 REPRINTED WITH PERMISSION

Image 9.9

4 *Process culture*

- Very bureaucratic; the emphasis is on caution and getting processes right.
- Status-oriented and formal; hierarchy is visible in artefacts like size of desks, office space, etc.
- Suited to low-risk, slow-feedback environments: 'This lack of feedback forces employees to focus on *how* they do something, not what they do' (Deal and Kennedy, 1988, p. 119).
- Organizes and routinizes work when required, and may allow other sorts of organizations to survive.
- Survivors are orderly, attend to detail and work by the book.
- But an inflexible and potentially stifling culture.
- May be found in insurance companies, government departments, public utilities and highly regulated industries like pharmaceuticals.

Exercise 9.4

Compare Deal and Kennedy's cultural types to Handy's. Where are the similarities and the differences?

Recap

Deal and Kennedy's key message is 'It depends' – i.e. there are several different routes to excellent performance via cultural management, according to the circumstances that organizations face. The challenge is to match the culture to the circumstances.

Despite their differences, these key contributions to the 'has' perspective both make fairly unequivocal and empirically grounded claims about the connection between culture and organizational performance. Rather than just accepting these claims, however, we should subject them to scrutiny. Before we do so, we will briefly revisit the British Airways case, because developments following Colin Marshall's apparently successful re-engineering of culture in this organization foreshadow both this and later critical discussion of the 'has' perspective.

CASE STUDY 9.2 Cultural engineering at British Airways: What happened next?

Although BA had apparently been 'turned around' in the 1980s and early 1990s, there were during this period also several warning signs that all was not entirely well. In 1993, for example, Richard Branson of Virgin Atlantic won a libel case against John King and Colin Marshall. This arose from Marshall's claim that Branson had lied in alleging that BA was engaging in 'dirty tricks' (i.e. forms of unfair/illegal competitive activity). Branson's accusations included the suggestion that, after Virgin relocated from Heathrow to Gatwick in July 1991 and thus began to compete directly with BA, BA sought to steal Virgin customers by encouraging their staff to pose as Virgin employees. He also said that BA had gained access to confidential Virgin files, and that the BA public relations guru Brian Basham had been deliberately spreading detrimental stories about both him and Virgin in the City and the British media. Branson was eventually awarded £500 000 in damages, Virgin won £110 000 and BA were also held liable for some £3 million in legal costs as well as being forced to publicly apologize.

In addition, there was conflicting evidence regarding just how far the customer service ethos had been taken on board. Heather Höpfl's anecdote about a BA flight attendant who offered passengers six leftover cartons of milk after a flight could be seen to suggest that this employee was going out of her way to 'delight' customers, even though her actions were in fact against company rules. On the other hand, Bob Ayling claimed in the aforementioned *Business Life* (1997, p. 47) interview that:

I believe we already have a caring team working for us . . . who make every effort to make our passengers feel as comfortable and as at home as possible. But somehow we haven't been able to communicate that properly and I don't know why . . . Perhaps because, up to now, we've concentrated on projecting the more macho side of the company, how strong we are, how powerful and business-like.

These are fascinating claims from the Chief Executive of a company that had spent the previous 15 years or so (and enormous sums of money) trying to promote customer care in all

aspects of its operations! But, then again, perhaps Ayling's comments can be read as reflecting back on the dirty tricks episode?

Ayling himself was to create his own controversies during a stormy four years at the BA helm. After a very healthy first 18 months, the June 1997 announcement of a new corporate identity caused a not-so-positive stir. The changes included a brand new livery for BA, dubbed World Images and to appear on plane tailfins, cabin crew scarves, business cards and ticket jackets. World Images featured 50 new designs commissioned from artists all over the world to replace the traditional red and blue BA logo. The key intention was to revamp BA (yet again) into something more cosmopolitan, diverse and friendly, to reflect its growing numbers of both overseas staff and customers and play down the potentially offputting associations of the organization's 'Britishness'. But shareholders called the rebranding unpatriotic and extravagant and Margaret Thatcher demonstrated her own feelings when she draped a hanky over a model BA plane tailfin featuring a World Images design at a Tory party conference.

Moreover, the announcement of this initiative coincided with two ballots on strike action by BA staff. One, concerning the sale of the inflight catering division, was resolved without industrial action being taken. The other related to an aspect of Ayling's cost-cutting Business Efficiency Programme (BEP) which meant that cabin crew stood to lose out financially. This ballot – for a 72-hour strike – was successful by a majority of 3 to 1. In the event, and arguably due to what was widely regarded at the time as intimidation by BA management,[3] only 300 staff went on strike but a further 1500 called in sick. The action ended up costing the airline £125 million. In the aftermath of the strike, Ayling did however began to put restorative measures in place, such as an internal task force focusing on staff motivation and patching up relations with customers.

1998 also proved to be somewhat of a curate's egg for Ayling and BA. It featured, among other things, the decline of the 'Asian Tiger' economies, rising levels of customer dissatisfaction and more legal action by Branson, this time alleging that BA had no business using their 'World's Favourite Airline' slogan. Although the Advertising Standards Authority found in BA's favour in the end, a Consumers' Association survey published at the same time suggested that they had lost considerable ground in terms of being an airline that people recommended to each other. By late 1998 Ayling had had to declare BA's first ever third quarter loss.

In 1999 an internal opinion survey entitled 'It's Your Shout!' proved rather damning – staff apparently did not believe BA directors could cut costs and still maintain quality, were cynical about their commitment to honest and straightforward communication with employees and also did not believe that the board cared about them. 'Putting People First' was

Image 9.10

SOURCE: © SAM SMITH/CARTOONSTOCK.COM

therefore rejuvenated as 'Putting People First Again', involving all 64 000 staff. BA's financial performance began to improve after the announcement of a six-year low in annual profits in May, but was not helped by the decision in June 1999 to cease using the World Images designs on planes – Ayling's claims that the movement away from the traditional BA logo had been welcomed notwithstanding.

In August 1999, Ayling was forced to announce 1000 job losses. However, things started to look up again later in the year as new service innovations (such as flat beds in business class) and an e-commerce initiative to increase online sales were publicized. Customer satisfaction measures began to improve and BA's low-cost airline Go was also doing well – somewhat ironically when its parent company was moving strategically away from the economy end of the market and focusing its attentions on 'front cabin' passengers.

Nonetheless, a further 6000 job losses were made public in February 2000 and the BA share price then nosedived as part of wider market trends. By March Ayling had been forced to resign. The charismatic and charming CEO had apparently failed to persuade BA customers or staff of the viability of his vision. Even his planned alliance with American Airlines, which would have given the two airlines joint control of over 60 per cent of transatlantic flights, was eventually diluted into a marketing agreement after regulator objections – and one that did not permit the partners to work together to set prices.

On top of the difficult task of continuing to cut costs whilst simultaneously improving staff morale, Ayling's Australian replacement Rod Eddington also had his fair share of additional turbulence to negotiate. This included the grounding of all Concordes in August 2000 following the Paris air crash in which 113 people lost their lives,[4] the UK foot and mouth crisis of March 2001, which had a substantial impact on British tourism, and of course the horrific events of 9/11. A total of 7000 redundancies were made as a result during 2001, followed swiftly by the announcement of 5800 additional job losses in the following February. BA also declared its worst annual losses since privatization later in the spring. However, things were improving by September, with the airline netting seven awards from *Business Traveller*, including Best Business Class and Most Innovative Airline.

But a further round of industrial action – this time unofficial – caused more havoc in July 2003. Some 500 flights were cancelled as BA check-in staff protested about the introduction of electronic swipe cards for clocking on and off, because of their concerns about possible changes to staff rosters as a result. Despite a fairly speedy resolution, these events again had a very negative impact on service and were also disastrous in PR terms – indeed BA issued both televised and newspaper apologies to its customers as a result.

Then there was the announcement that, from August 2004, all UK staff would be subject to drug and alcohol testing under certain circumstances. This policy was developed, say management, for safety reasons and it came in the wake of several controversies involving the use of alcohol by BA staff. Although unions agreed the move, it was publicized just as major research findings suggested such testing is likely only to have a small effect on numbers of accidents, productivity, etc. This research also argued that it could also be very expensive, not to say divisive, if introduced across the board in an organization. While the researchers accepted that testing may be worthwhile in occupations where safety or public trust are of paramount concern (as of course is the case with many jobs at BA), the jury may still be out as to whether it is justified for *all* BA employees.

At the time of writing, the latest development in the BA saga, at the height of the August 2004 holiday season, was chaos at Heathrow created by a shortage of check-in staff. Many flights were either cancelled or delayed as a result, meaning hundreds of travellers having to camp overnight at the airport and losses running to millions of pounds for the company. The cause was a combination of factors including delays in taking on replacement staff and sick leave. Ironically, only days earlier, BA had narrowly avoided strike action over pay planned for the English bank holiday weekend by hammering out a last-minute deal with unions.

| Recap | Before we move on to examine some of the limitations of the 'has' perspective on organizational culture, remember contributors to this body of thought agree that culture: |

- Is an organizational variable that managers can manipulate.
- Integrates and stabilizes organizations because it ensures that everyone thinks, feels and acts in the same way.
- Is created at the top and disseminated down through the organization.
- If properly managed, generates excellent organizational performance.

They disagree, however, on:

- Whether there is 'one best culture' for all organizations.
- The best way to change, maintain or build a culture.

Limitations and contributions

One area of contention over whether the claims made by the 'has' perspective stand up to scrutiny is the issue of whether *strong* cultures are always *good* cultures. Here we could note, for example, the argument that while strong cultures enable stability, coordination and rapid decision making they may also encourage complacency, lack of creativity, inflexibility and groupthink (see Chapter 4). So a strong culture might actually harm performance. Indeed, work by Kotter and Heskett (1992) suggests organizations with strong cultures are no more likely to perform well than organizations whose value systems are relatively weak. 'Strong culture' organizations which performed poorly during the US economic boom years of 1977–1988 include Sears, General Motors and Goodyear, whereas some of their 'weak culture' counterparts – such as GlaxoSmithKline and McGraw-Hill – did well. Likewise, Miller (cited in Trice and Beyer, 1993, p. 380) suggests that overly strong cultures create 'paths of deadly momentum . . . [so] productive attention to detail . . . turns into an obsession with minutia; rewarding innovation turns into gratuitous invention; and measured growth becomes unbridled expansion'.

Thinkpoint 9.6

Thinking back to Bob Ayling's comments about BA showing a rather 'macho' face to its public, and the 'dirty tricks' campaign waged by BA against Virgin, how might these episodes suggest that BA's new culture had by the early 1990s begun to demonstrate some of the problems relating to strong cultures discussed above?

Then there is the question of whether there is any real evidence that cultural change programmes guarantee *long-term* organizational success. Some commentators suggest that all we have available are 'brief, anecdotal stories of the dramatic impact of founders, leaders, heroes, in establishing or rescuing their enterprises' (Anthony, 1994, p. 15) – and we could also reflect on 'what happened next' at BA in the light of this argument.

Moreover, the validity and reliability of the texts establishing the culture–excellence link have been heavily criticized. Peters and Waterman, for example, have been accused of failing to focus on key US economic sectors like car manufacturing and financial services, as well as carrying out most of their interviews with senior managers who would be expected to sing the praises of their organizations. The companies they researched were also all high growth and employed large numbers of professional staff – both conditions that could be argued to make management-by-values more feasible, at least in terms of the required investment of resources and the likely reaction of the workforce.

Perhaps most damningly, by 1985 nearly a quarter of the firms surveyed by Peters and Waterman were having real economic difficulties; a point which is taken up by Chapman (2003) in the wryly titled *In Search of Stupidity*. The platform for Chapman's discussion is that it was the high-tech firms in particular in the Peters and Waterman sample that subsequently began to struggle. Chapman claims that these firms (perhaps *because* of their cultures – bearing in mind the argument above about strong cultures and complacency) often fail to learn from past mistakes and therefore continue to repeat avoidable errors. One example is Lotus' misguided 18-month long project to enable Lotus 123 to run on 640kb computers, by the end of which such machines were virtually obsolete.

Relatedly, it has been suggested that the 'has' theorists over-privilege culture as *the* factor that leads to business success. For example, consider this claim, taken from a biography of IBM founder Tom Watson. Here a former colleague is responding cynically to Watson's claim that IBM's success was founded on its corporate philosophy and not its capital investments, its R&D and so on:

> Well, what the hell could he say? He couldn't very well [say] that IBM had the money, recruited the scientists, or was ready to spend half a billion dollars . . . to take over the computer market by making everything in it, including IBM's own machines, obsolete. He couldn't very well say that it didn't make any difference what the company, or the employees, believed if they got eighty percent of the market. *(cited in Parker, 2000, p. 25)*

As we can see, then, it is possible to level several empirical and conceptual critiques at 'has' camp claims about the connection between culture and business excellence. Nonetheless, as Parker (2000, p.p. 12, 20 – emphasis added) suggests, 'these gurus *were* attempting an interesting reformulation of organizations and organizing' in their reinterpretation of the manager as committed champion of the organizational cause, not boring, numbers-obsessed cipher. This is also worth remembering with regard to the BA case study, the airline's more recent problems aside. That is to say, the cultural change effected by Colin Marshall did to some extent at least transform a moribund organization with a very formal and 'people-unfriendly' style of management into an outfit where staff apparently felt more valued, and translated this into better customer service.

Because of its emphasis on the ways in which organizational life can be constructed and reconstructed, moreover, the 'has' narrative reminds us of the fact that it is *people* who make organizational processes happen, not machines or money or information technology. In other words, it is only through human creativity, vision, efforts and interactions that goods are produced, services delivered, profits made, government targets met, budgets adhered to, shareholders satisfied, and so on.

But there are other issues we need to consider when analysing the contribution of the organizational culture orthodoxy. These relate specifically to what we might call its ontology – the assumptions about workplace reality on which its key assertions are based, and the various anthropological, sociological, political and ethical implications of those assertions. It is to these issues that we now turn in considering an alternative reading of organizational culture. Instead of suggesting that 'has' theory perhaps exaggerates the claims that it makes – as we did earlier in this sub-section – this perspective takes critical issue with *the ideas that lie behind* these claims.

The critical perspective

Introduction to the critical perspective, AKA culture is something that an organization 'is'

The broad alternative to understanding culture as something that an organization 'has', again in Smircich's (1983) formulation, is the claim that culture is something that an organization 'is'. This perspective is closer to the original anthropological conceptualization of culture than its mainstream counterpart. Indeed some 'is' theorists argue that 'has' theories have gone too far in their analysis of culture, because 'Most anthropologists would find the idea that leaders create culture preposterous: leaders [according to anthropology] do not create culture, it emerges from the collective social interaction of groups and communities' (Meek, 1988, p. 459).

On a related point, and emphasizing how 'is' theory shies away from the functionalist, technical, managerialism of 'has' theory, Alvesson (2002, p. 25) suggests that 'Advocates of the [is] . . . view of culture are inclined to play down the pragmatic results that can help management increase effectiveness in favour of more general understanding and reflection as the major emphasis of cultural studies.' That is to say, 'is' thinkers are interested in interpreting organizations rather than generating a series of management 'how to's' regarding improvement of the bottom line, as 'has' theorists are inclined to do. The focus of the 'is' perspective, then, is primarily a practical-hermeneutic one. In particular, it directs our attention to how coordinated action (without which, as we saw in the introduction to the chapter, organizations would not exist) becomes possible among disparate aggregates of individuals with varying aspirations, views, experiences and so on.

'Is' theorists begin from the claim that culture is *not* a variable – i.e. it is not just one organizational element. Instead they see it as a metaphor for the organization. If culture is something that an organization is, then everything in the organization is in some way cultural, evoking prevailing values, beliefs and norms:

> Seemingly 'objective' things, such as numbers of employees, turnover, physical products, customers, etc. become of interest (almost) only in terms of their cultural meanings. The size of a company may be seen as 'small is beautiful' . . . [or l]imited size may . . . signal exclusiveness and elitism.
> *(Alvesson, 2002, p. 25)*

Alvesson here clarifies how numbers of employees, for example, may be interpreted by 'is' theorists as signifying particular values. In the same way, turnover figures, product range, target market segment/s and so on would all be seen to express something about the relevant organization's culture. 'Is' theorists, then, focus on the symbolic significance of organizational phenomena as a way of understanding them.

The 'is' perspective also sees organizational culture as a *jointly produced* system of intersubjectivity. In other words, it develops the aforementioned notion of organizational common sense to examine how shared assumptions emerge and are passed on in day-to-day organizational activity. Here culture is an ongoing product of 'learning the truce' (Mills and Murgatroyd, 1991, p. 62). The principal values in any one workplace come about as the result of a collective accommodation between organizational requirements and individual members' aspirations. Here we see a particular understanding of freedom and identity: the common sense of culture allows workers to come to terms with what is asked of them at work, to arrive at a compromise between their own personal desires and the demands of their employment.

Ashforth and Kreiner (1999), for example, discuss what are usually referred to in the OB literature as **dirty jobs** in an attempt to understand the occupational cultures that grow up around this type of employment. They categorize these jobs as 'physically' dirty – where individuals deal with literal dirt, do dangerous tasks or work in areas that bring them into contact with death (e.g. refuse collectors, deep sea divers or mortuary attendants); 'socially' dirty – necessitating association with stigmatized groups or having to be servile in the job itself (e.g. prison warders and personal maids); and 'morally' dirty – the job is regarded as morally problematic or requires some form of 'cheating' (e.g. prostitution or professional gambling). Those involved in occupations like these, argue Ashforth and Kreiner, therefore work to reconcile their sense of themselves as upright and functional human beings with what they do for a living.

Thinkpoint 9.7

Think of examples where you have engaged in the process of reconciliation – maybe during your studies at university – or have observed others striving to do the same.

One example of this process of reconciliation, to which we have already referred, is Ackroyd and Crowdy's (1990) abattoir workers. Their work is both physically and morally dirty – it involves contact with blood, organs and excreta and centres on killing 'innocent animals' (p. 4). In the face of these exigencies, these men celebrate their own toughness and resilience – stressing, for example, that 'Only one in a thousand has the stomach for this job' (p. 8) – and attributing highest status to those who actually kill the animals. Their pride in what they do is also visible in the fact that they bring their sons to the plant for visits. Moreover, the men rarely shower before leaving the abattoir – indeed some deliberately splash themselves with blood before departing – and only change their overalls and hats when they are absolutely filthy. This culture therefore turns external social values upside down and prizes exactly what it is about the work that others view as negative. As Ackroyd and Crowdy (1990, p. 5) put it, 'the occupational culture of the slaughtermen grows out of the barrel of polluted products they are seen to handle' – it therefore insulates those who participate from wider society's moral condemnation and disgust.

For 'is' theorists, then, *everyone* participates – although, as we shall see, not necessarily as equals – in the ongoing construction of an organization's culture. It is not a matter of values being transmitted by managers and passively accepted by the lower ranks. This is a much more organic, 'socially emergent' view of culture as a product of the ways in which groups of people come to accept the limitations on their freedom or the challenges to their identity that working for a living entails. In short, culture here is understood to be a *coping mechanism* rather than a handy management tool. It involves the collective negotiation of a particular form of organizational reality, which allows workers to accommodate what they do for a living, however demanding or restrictive it might be.

Exercise 9.5

Another example of learning the truce can be seen in the 'dirty job' of prostitution. For example, sex workers rarely allow their punters to kiss them, and will almost always insist on the use of condoms at work when they may not bother in their personal relationships (see, for example, Brewis and Linstead, 2000, Chapter 8). How might selling sex for a living threaten a woman's identity, and how might these coping mechanisms allow her to deal with this threat?

'Is' theory therefore focuses on:

> explor[ing] the phenomenon of organization as subjective experience and . . . investigat[ing] the patterns that make organized action possible . . . When culture is [seen as] a root metaphor, attention shifts from concerns about what do organizations accomplish and how may they accomplish it more efficiently, to how organization is accomplished and what does it mean to be organized?
> *(Smircich, 1983, p.p. 348, 353)*

As already stated, of course, at least a measure of cultural agreement is necessary in order for organizations not simply to descend into anarchy.

Here we see further evidence that this is a very different approach to the one adopted by the 'has' camp, where a case is made for managers' ability to change, build or maintain culture in order to enhance competitive advantage, improve quality, increase productivity and so on. The 'is' camp, in contrast, understands culture as a means of adjusting to organizational demands, which develops jointly and gradually. Culture here turns on the daily accomplishment of an organizational reality within which members can feel psychologically 'safe' – where their identities are protected and they have come to terms with restrictions on their freedom. Perhaps, then, we should use different terms when referring to 'has' and 'is' readings of culture; 'corporate culture' when we are discussing interpretations based on the possibility of management-led cultural engineering initiatives, and 'organizational culture' for the 'is' claim that culture develops more organically (Linstead and Grafton-Small, 1992).

We now discuss the implications of 'is' theory's claims in more detail, as well as exploring a key debate around power and inequality within this area of the cultural literature.

Key issues and controversies

Because it sees culture as a day-on-day social product, enacted by all the members of the organization, the 'is' concept of 'culture-from-everywhere' emphasizes both the fragility of organizational life and its dynamics. 'Is' theorists attend closely to the ways in which *rank-and-file* members of organizations produce and reproduce systems of values, beliefs and norms – and therefore also amend and adapt them.

In addition, they emphasize 'cultural traffic' – the ways in which cultures shift 'with the flow of meanings and values in and around organizations'. For example, as new recruits join a firm, they may bring different ways of seeing with them, especially given the increased probability in our globalized world that these newcomers originate in another country. So culture here is understood as fluctuating in accordance with changing organizational circumstances (Alvesson, 2002, p.p. 191–192).

Exercise 9.6

BA apparently attempted to accommodate 'cultural traffic' – its growing numbers of non-British staff and customers – through its World Images rebranding exercise. But the initiative lasted only two years. Bearing in mind 'is' theory's suggestion that culture is an organic, collective product, can you suggest why it was so short-lived?

Because of these central precepts, 'is' theory is also much more emphatic than 'has' theory on the multicultural nature of organizations. In other words, it suggests that:

> ideas within a social group are not homogenous but plural and often contested . . . An organization's culture could thus be viewed as a struggle for *hegemony* with competing factors attempting to define the primary purpose of the organization in a way that meets their perceived definitions.
> *(Parker, 2000, p. 75 – emphasis added)*

'Has' theory does, as we have seen, accept that different cultures may exist in different organizational departments or functions because of the different challenges that they face. However, it tends to confine its analysis to the argument that managers need to devise ways of overcoming the resultant differentiation, whereas for 'is' theory this does not go far enough. For 'is' commentators, the organization represents a site in which there is an ongoing contest between various groups to make their voices heard, to control or have power over the overall direction that is taken, to shape activities in ways that meet their particular desires and aspirations. We will now develop this idea in a little more depth.

First, because of the idea that culture comes from 'everywhere' in an organization, 'is' theory makes the related claim that different sets of values, beliefs and norms (i.e. subcultures) *inevitably* develop at different loci within the organization in response to different situations. In other words, it sees cultural heterogeneity as 'situation normal' – especially given power structures within organizations and the fact that ordinary employees' experience of work may therefore be rather different from managers'. This heterogeneity and the consequent 'struggle for hegemony' often become very visible when workers feel their interests are being ignored or marginalized by management. The two episodes of industrial action at BA in 1997 and 2003, the UK firefighters' strike during the winter of 2002–03, the Association of University Teachers' strike in early 2004 and 24-hour stoppages by London Underground drivers are all good examples. 'Has' theory only rather grudgingly accepts that such heterogeneity *may* exist *despite* managers' best efforts. As Willmott (1993, p. 525) argues, it is 'responsive to the presence of value conflicts within modern (capitalist) organizations' but sees them 'as a sign of cultural weakness that can be corrected'. 'Is' theory, by way of contrast, suggests that organizations are *always* highly internally differentiated in terms of values – that they are almost mosaic-like in this respect.

Secondly, 'is' theory asserts that cultural differences are not just a product of varying experiences *inside* the organization: it adds to these considerations the issue of 'extra-organizational' identity. In other words, for 'is' theory, subcultures do not just spring up among those who participate in specific activities within the organization, but also among those who share things 'outside the factory gates'. These might include membership of a profession (like medicine, accountancy or academia), being male or female, belonging to a particular racial, ethnic or religious group, socio-economic or educational similarities and so on. Such affiliations will further cut across, dilute or undermine any connection employees have with the values, beliefs and norms that management attempt to hegemonically impose.

Thinkpoint 9.8

Think about the students in your year at university. To what extent would you say that they tend to 'split off' into subcultural cliques based on gender, racial, ethnic, religious, class or educational differences? If such 'divisions' are noticeable, how do they manifest themselves?

Moreover, these shared 'external' experiences may well be *reinforced* by internal organizational processes, perhaps creating subcultures that span organizational boundaries. A good example of this are the professional women's networks that bring together women from various organizations to discuss and advise each other on the challenges they face within traditionally masculine workplace hierarchies.[5]

This analysis also suggests further complications in that one person may simultaneously be a member of several organizational subcultures, the values, beliefs and norms of which potentially contradict each other. For example, I am female, a UMIST graduate, a Reader in Management, a lecturer in OB and research methodology, someone who researches the intersections between the body, identity and processes of organizing, the course leader for a specific Master's degree and Caucasian as well as Geordie[6] – all at the same time. This complexity could, moreover, mean that individual employees 'switch' between or emphasize specific cultural allegiances at different times in their working lives – for instance, when they receive a promotion or decide to blow the whistle (see Chapter 14 on the latter issue). It certainly makes the lines of 'Them' and 'Us' much more difficult to draw. In this understanding of organizational multiculturalism, then, 'Individuals are nodes on the [workplace] web, temporarily connected by shared concerns to some but not all the surrounding nodes' (Meyerson and Martin, 1994, p. 124).

So the 'is' version of multiculturalism means that organizational values, beliefs and norms are just as much the source of organizational *dis*agreement as they are of harmony and consensus. As Figure 9.2 indicates, for instance, some groups may buy into the culture that management wishes to impose, fervently and without reservation ('enhancing' subcultures that bolster the management message), others ('orthogonal' subcultures) accept the basic corporate culture but have an independent set of values of their own and still others ('counter' cultures) may be resistant to what management is attempting to instil.

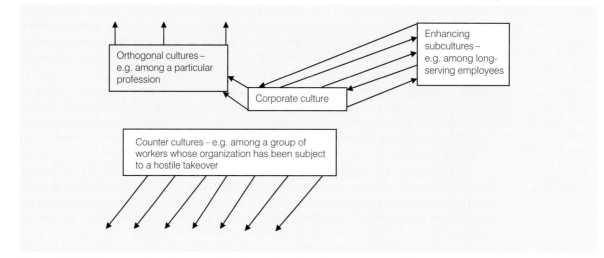

SOURCE: BASED ON MARTIN AND SIEHL (1983); MEYERSON AND MARTIN (1994).

Figure 9.2 Different subcultures and their relationship to corporate culture

---

Thinkpoint 9.9

Thinking back to the early days of the BA cultural change initiative, how would you classify the former BOAC employees and the former BEA employees using the above framework – are these groups enhancing, orthogonal or counter cultures? Or are the lines not that easy to draw?

The argument here is that, instead of being passive recipients of management hegemony, employees will 'accept, deny, react, reshape, rethink, acquiesce, rebel, conform, and define and refine the[se] demands and their responses' (Kunda, 1992, p. 21) in various ways. This then raises the question of the extent to which it is actually possible for managers to change, maintain or build organizational culture – a capacity, which, as we know, is a central tenet of 'has' theory. 'Is' theory, however, is much more sceptical. Golden (cited in Brown 1998, p. 93) argues, for example, that there are at least four possible reactions to corporate culture as 'sold' by senior management:

- *Unequivocal adherence.* Unquestioning acceptance of management values, likely, as Brown asserts, 'to be the exception rather than the rule', and humorously depicted in the cartoon below.

- *Strained adherence.* Employees have concerns about the ethics or effectiveness of these values, but for the most part 'buy in'.

- *Secret non-adherence.* Workers outwardly comply with management values, usually because management have more power than they do and thus they fear for their jobs. But underneath this workplace 'act' they do not accept these values and will demonstrate this non-acceptance when it is safe to do so. Höpfl's (1993) BA research, for example, highlighted the potential flipside of the friendly greeting we receive when we board an aeroplane. One flight attendant told her that, while the staff are verbally wishing us 'Good morning', in their heads they are saying 'fuck you'. The 'fuck you' preserves some measure of personal identity and individual freedom in the face of corporate demands.

SOURCE: © JIM SIZEMORE/CARTOONSTOCK.COM

"This is wonderful—pathological loyalty is *exactly* what we're looking for!"

Image 9.11

Thinkpoint 9.10

Drawing on your experience of situations (at university or elsewhere) in which you were expected to behave according to particular values – e.g. respect for your seniors or neatness and tidiness – can you think of times when you have demonstrated secret non-adherence? An instance might be to have private, derogatory nicknames for disliked tutors to whom you show deference in public. You could also reflect on the following question: if workers display adherence to corporate values in public, does it matter whether they have actually taken them on board as part of their 'identities' or not?

- *Open non-adherence*. Out-and-out resistance to management values, such as the profound resentment displayed by certain brewery workers in Aktouf's (1996) research. Their dislike of colleagues who conformed to the corporate culture was manifest in insults including 'traitor', 'brownnose', etc. These epithets seem to demonstrate that these workers felt so strongly about their individuality, identity and freedom that they were not prepared to put on a workplace front even for the sake of a quiet life. Here Parker's struggle for hegemony again becomes very visible, as it did in the various forms of industrial action discussed above.

In short, 'has' theory is seen by 'is' theory to take a rather naive view of the extent to which culture can be managed. 'Is' theory sees meanings as contested within organizational settings. It emphasizes the multicultural character of organizations and suggests that different groups within a workplace constantly work to make their voices heard, to persuade others of the legitimacy of their interpretations of the organization. Here culture is the ongoing, dynamic product of contests of power, in which the advantage rests with managers because of their position within the organizational structure and the inequalities which this creates, but whose hegemonic attempts to persuade workers to take particular values on board are likely to be resisted in various ways.

For example, Kunda's (1992) fascinating study of High Technologies Corporation (Tech) suggests that management in this organization remorselessly reinforce their corporate message via manifold CTMs. Tech employees are thereby encouraged to invest in the company in terms of time, effort and identity, indeed to cease to think of themselves and their employer as separate entities. And these very overt forms of cultural control do seem to be successful: most Tech workers put in long hours and enjoy what they do for a living. But they also routinely distance themselves from the organizational ideology, describing it as 'the bullshit that comes from above', for instance (p. 158).

Nonetheless, while this may seem to undermine the Tech ethos, it actually serves as a safety valve through which employees can express frustration with management attempts at manipulation, thus forestalling any more damaging forms of dissent (such as industrial action). Workers also know that to *really* get on at Tech they must 'buy in' – mere behavioural compliance is not enough for managers who want to possess their hearts and souls, not just their time. Resistance to management 'bullshit' is therefore routinely tempered by the greater power that managers possess to shape and control staff's working lives.

In developing the idea of inequality in particular, moreover, some 'is' theorists pose a rather different set of questions. Rather than critiquing 'has' theory's naiveté for ignoring or downplaying organizational multiculturalism, contested meanings and worker dissent, they focus on what they see as its problematic aspirations. Willmott (1993), for example, claims that cultural management is similar in its objectives to the activities of the totalitarian[7] Oceania government in George Orwell's famous novel *1984*, because they both operate on the basis of what Orwell calls 'doublethink'. Cultural management initiatives, Willmott suggests, effectively promise autonomy for the individual employee if they submit to the company ideology. Such interventions therefore celebrate an idea (autonomy) while simultaneously rejecting it (through requiring submission). In other words, says Willmott, the 'has' gurus are recommending doublethink as a management tool, advocating that managers create a situation in which employees *believe* that they determine their corporate existence yet have no real freedom to make choices for themselves. So the basic 'has' theory message to managers is reinterpreted by this strand of 'is' thinking as follows:

A stupid despot may constrain his slaves with iron chains; but a true politician [/ manager] binds them even more strongly by the chain of their own ideas; it is at the stable point of reason that he secures the end of the chain; this link is all the stronger in that we do not know of what it is made and we believe it to be our own work. *(Servan, cited in Foucault, 1977, p. 35)*

What this quote means is that overt forms of management control or open displays of management power – use of rules, reward and punishment, direct supervision and so on – are much more obtrusive and likely to be resisted than the subtle manipulation of employee values, especially where workers really do buy into what is being 'sold' to them. Authors like Willmott see this as the central tenet of 'has' theory. In this version of 'is' thinking, then, the emphasis is less on organizations as pluralist arenas in which a cacophony of different cultural voices can be heard, and more on the ways in which managers attempt to exercise their superior power to silence these voices, and impose their own hegemony. Our attention is thus drawn to the ways in which management values – such as the idea that 'the customer is always right' – might conceivably assume an organizational normality that is difficult to question. Instead, they may simply become what the organization and its members 'are all about'; just 'the culture'. 'Is' theory here becomes more explicitly political, more 'emancipatory', more to do with identifying the organizational forces that 'prevent [workers] from acting in accordance with their free choices' (Alvesson, 2002, p. 8).

Exercise 9.7

'A bad manager says
I'm sorry. You'll have to work all the hours that God sends.

A good manager says
I'm proud. This is a 24/7 organisation.'
(Beaton, 2001, p. 17)

"You do as you're told, we pay as we please. You work like a slave, we punish at random. That, in a nutshell, is our corporate culture."

Image 9.12

Why might this extract from Beaton (2001) be considered an 'emancipatory' 'is' theory joke about organizational culture? Is the manager in the cartoon a 'good' manager or a 'bad' manager in this respect?

We can reconsider the apparent 'success' stories told by 'has' theory in this light – like the one about the Honda worker who adjusts all the windscreen wipers on the Hondas he passes on his way home because he wants them to look perfect, or the Procter and Gamble employee who bought an entire range of P&G products in his local supermarket because the labels were wrongly positioned.[8] Colin Marshall's comments about the need to 'design' BA staff so that they give good customer service just as the organization designs seats, lounges and inflight entertainment are also relevant here. Perhaps these examples now begin to seem just a little sinister, a touch more like organizational cloning. Perhaps Honda, P&G and BA are examples of what Coser (1974) calls the **greedy institution**, demanding unswerving loyalty and enormous amounts of employee effort, such that its members have little time or energy for anything outside work, given the strength of the bond with their employer. Perhaps strong cultures such as these are apt to produce Whyte's (1957) **organization man** (/woman); employees who put what the corporation demands before their own needs, maybe without realizing that this is what they are doing. And then there is Kanter's (1983, p. 203) claim that strong corporate cultures offer workers 'a high' akin to that derived from alcohol or drugs – perhaps they are just as addictive as these substances, with equally problematic results? Here in fact the management of culture begins to look very much like a perpetuation of organizational inequalities and an abuse of management power.

Relatedly, we can also consider what 'is' theory would tend to identify as a gulf between the values senior management claim to promote in their public relations literature, annual reports, recruitment brochures and so on, and what it is actually like to work in that organization – what kind of values really shape organizational behaviour. A real-life example is the fact that most large organizations – and many smaller ones – now claim to be equal opportunities employers. They say they recruit, reward and promote all employees on the basis of merit and not ascribed characteristics like gender or race. But there are still marked inequalities between, for example, men and women in terms of their organizational experiences. These include the fact that full-time women workers in Britain are paid only 81 per cent of what their male counterparts earn (Equal Opportunities Commission, 2003, p. 11), and findings of this kind are only really explicable if we accept that sexism is still at large in the vast majority of workplaces.

Exercise 9.8

Following the launch of BA's 'Putting People First Again' initiative in 1999, one commentator wrote: 'Admirable though this may be, it does rather beg the question of where BA has been putting people recently' (*The Times*, 1999, p. 23). We know that the impetus behind this training intervention and its 1980s predecessor was to make staff feel good about themselves so they would also feel good about their dealings with customers. But then there are the various cost-cutting and redundancy exercises that have been characteristic of BA management practice since 1981, and which *The Times* journalist is presumably alluding to above. What might all of this suggest about what BA management claim regarding the organization's culture versus what it is actually like to work there?

In sum, then, the 'is' perspective is not functionalist or technical, but rather critical in the sense of refusing to accept things at their face value and appreciating the role of power and inequality in establishing organizational cultures. These writers emphasize that organizational values, beliefs and norms are both multiple and contested, that workplaces represent environments where there is an ongoing struggle for hegemony. However, an equally strong motif within the 'is' camp is that the management of culture can represent a problematic attempt by the senior members of the organization to clamp down on this multiplicity, to impose ways of thinking and feeling – to, in effect, brainwash employees into accepting the official organizational 'line'. So, while 'is' analysts generally seek to adopt a practical-hermeneutic stance on organizational culture because their key interest is to create meaningful knowledge about our working lives, as opposed to generating prescriptions about how to enhance the corporate bottom line, some as we have seen are also avowedly emancipatory. This later emphasis is even more at odds with the managerialist focus of 'has' theory because it views management activities as potentially oppressive.

In order to illustrate some of the issues discussed above in more depth, the chapter now considers two key empirical studies within 'is' theory. In contrast to those quoted for the 'has' camp, and perhaps reflecting different intellectual traditions in the two countries, these are both by British authors. They are Collinson's (1988) 'Engineering humour' and Ackroyd and Crowdy's (1990) 'Can culture be managed?'. These studies have been chosen because of their impact on the field of OB, and in particular their alternative take on some of the claims made by 'has' theory. Both studies, then, stress the idea of culture emerging as a coping mechanism, as well as suggesting that the specific cultures discussed are effectively counter cultures, resistant as they are to management ideology and precepts. Interestingly, however, Collinson and Ackroyd and Crowdy also go on to suggest that, despite their counter cultural form, neither generated unproblematically emancipatory consequences.

Important empirical studies

Collinson's (1988) study was set in the components division of a lorry-making factory in north-west England, where 250 men were employed. It examined humour in this context, and suggests that the various ways in which the men joked with each other 'reflected and reinforced the central values and practices of these male manual workers and contained elements of resistance and control, creativity and destructiveness' (p. 184). Examples included:

- Nicknames like 'Electric Lips', who couldn't keep a secret.
- Initiation rites – e.g. being sent to another colleague for 'a long stand'. The initiate would then be asked, after standing waiting for some time, 'Is that long enough?' (p. 189).
- Jokes at each other's or the management's expense, such as one colleague sending a rate-fixer (who set the payment rates for the men's work) to examine another rate-fixer's job, the implication being that he was not working hard enough.

The men's humour was generally unforgiving, macho, highly sexual and peppered with curses. Collinson suggests that it was a product of what we referred to earlier as 'learning the truce'. These men did repetitive, mundane work and also worked the longest hours in the company, in insecure jobs with very poor terms and conditions. This employment situation sent a clear message that they were both disposable and of little value. In the face of this challenge to their masculine pride, they established a culture that preserved their identities. The men's humour emphasized that, while they could laugh at themselves, they were also different from the managers and the white-collar workers, the 'twats and nancy boys' who didn't have the freedom to joke around (p. 186).

'Having a laugh' also helped them to get through the dull working day, plus it was a means of achieving group acceptance. Being able to withstand humiliation by one's colleagues as well as meting it out (i.e. being a 'real man') was a passport to becoming 'one of the gang'. But jokes were also directed at those who were seen as skiving (e.g. the rate-fixer gag above), because part of the men's wages was calculated using a collective bonus system. As Collinson points out, then, working in what appeared to be a creative culture of resistant shop floor humour was actually an edgy, competitive experience, which allowed no real basis for a sense of belonging. This is illustrated by a vote in 1983 where workers accepted a lump-sum redundancy payout with no resistance following the announcement of the closure of the components plant.

Recap	Collinson's key argument is that culture in this environment had evolved to allow the male shop floor employees to deal with the demands of their working lives, but that the humour involved did not really produce a cohesive or supportive community of co-workers or any basis for collective resistance to an oppressive regime in which these workers effectively colluded.

Like Collinson, and as we already know, Ackroyd and Crowdy (1990) discuss the culture in an English abattoir as a product of the particular demands of the occupation of slaughterman. The work here, like that in the lorry-making factory, is monotonous and partly remunerated using team-based bonuses. It is also dirty in moral and physical terms. Equally, the prevailing values are similar in some ways to those in the components division. The men emphasized hard and fast work, often not taking scheduled breaks, and taking pride in completing tasks in the shortest time possible.

Moreover, the slaughtermen's culture was macho and aggressive: every man had to measure up in terms of output as well as being able to withstand and/or participate in certain production line rituals. These included:

- 'Harassments' and 'degradations', where the men might speed up their own efforts such that work piled up at the stations of slower colleagues, or throw entrails at 'inadequate' workers.

- 'Demonstrations', where individual workers expressed boredom in acts such as spraying excreta from an animal's intestine and yelling 'It's raining' – identified here as a manifestation of that worker's individual toughness (p. 7).
- 'Set pieces', which were 'targeted', but 'also statements of [personal] effectiveness' (p. 7). These necessitated groups of workers cooperating to, for example, fill the boots of another with blood, having judged its temperature so that the unfortunate victim would not notice until it was too late.

Ackroyd and Crowdy's study, like Collinson's, is very evocative of the uncompromising atmosphere in the slaughterhouse, of the desire to show others up which lies beneath what might look like jolly workplace japes. They also emphasize though that there was little resistance from the lower status workers (usually the targets) to such 'japes'. But perhaps their central point is to question 'the extent to which a culture is something a management can create or control' (p. 4). Indeed they argue that the slaughtermen's culture, despite its contravention of health and safety regulations and formal abattoir hierarchies, actually suits management very well because the work gets done and there is no need for direct supervision.

Recap	Ackroyd and Crowdy's key argument is that this organizational culture developed organically to allow the abattoir workers to accommodate the exigencies of their employment, and that what resulted was highly competitive and highly macho. However, they also suggest that management had no need to intervene because the prevailing values among these men also guaranteed that they worked extremely hard.

Recap	Contributors to the 'is' perspective agree that culture:

- Is a metaphor for the organization – every organizational phenomenon says something about the prevailing values, beliefs and norms in that workplace.
- Is jointly produced by everyone in the organization, representing a means of coping with the demands of members' working lives.
- Is multiple and fragmented in complex and conflicting ways – different subcultures inevitably emerge in different organizational loci because of varying external and internal influences.
- Can therefore be very difficult to manage.

They disagree, however, on the extent to which managers are able to impose a culture on their employees – some see cultural management as tantamount to brainwashing, others suggest that groups of employees will often resist management attempts to manipulate them.

Conclusion

In drawing the chapter to a close, it seems plausible to conclude that some organizational values will be shaped by management, and taken on board in different ways by different member sub-groups, and others will be a product of collective or subcultural accommodation to the slings and arrows of organizational life. Moreover, although managers tend to act as what Hines (1988, p. 255) calls 'Official Communicators of [Cultural] Reality' ('has' theory), this does not mean that other groups within the organization do not try to influence the ways in which the organization operates ('is' theory).

We should take on board what 'has' theory says because it offers us another explanation of organizational success and failure, which we can add to more obvious factors such as technological innovation, high-quality products and market dominance. However, 'is' theory asks us to acknowledge that workers are not simply embedded in a culture where they passively accept what management feeds them. Even senior managers do not have this much power, and those further down the organization have even less in terms of their overall visibility, control over resources, numbers of people they interact with and so on – however much it may appeal to their vanity to believe the contrary.

Indeed, the more reflective analysis offered by the 'is' perspective, which seeks to understand how it is that people in organizations actually come together to work in more or less coordinated ways, is probably a precondition of any effective cultural initiative by management, as would be recommended by 'has' theorists. That said, the difficulty for many managers is that 'is' views are more complex, less accessible and do not assume the legitimacy of managerial values. 'Is' thinking is thus more likely to threaten managerial identity than to enhance and inflate it.

Finally, Smircich's (1983, p. 355) claim that thinking about organizational culture may encourage us 'not to celebrate organization as a value, but to question the ends it serves' also reminds us that organizations and management as we know them today are in themselves cultural (and relatively recent) phenomena. In other words, they are not natural, historical human activities. With this in mind, we can also think about the outcomes of organizations and management – which include space travel, university education (hurrah!) and the cure for smallpox, but also nuclear arms, developing world sweatshops and environmental destruction – and consider possible alternatives. As Alvesson (2002, p. 2) suggests, then:

> Insights and reflections [into/on organizational culture] may be useful in [relation] . . . to getting people to do the 'right' things in terms of effectiveness, but also for promoting more autonomous standpoints in relationship to dominant ideologies, myths, fashions, etc. To encourage and facilitate the thinking through of various aspects of values, beliefs and assumptions in industry, occupations and organizations seem to me to be a worthwhile task.

Discussion questions

1 What does it mean to say that culture brings an organization 'to life'?

2 Can you identify the four key differences between the 'has' perspective and the 'is' perspective on organizational culture?

3 What are some of the contingencies that might help managers to identify the 'right' culture for their organization?

4 Is a strong organizational culture always a good thing in terms of achieving business excellence? What other problems might such a culture create?

5 To what extent do you think it is possible to manage organizational culture?

Further reading

Important empirical studies

Ackroyd, S. and Crowdy, P. (1990) 'Can culture be managed? Working with raw material: The case of the English slaughtermen', *Personnel Review* 19(5):3–13.

Collinson, D. L. (1988) ' "Engineering humour": Masculinity, joking and conflict in shopfloor relations', *Organization Studies* 9(2):181–199.

Deal, T. E. and Kennedy, A. A. (1988) *Corporate Cultures: The Rites and Rituals of Corporate Life*, Harmondsworth: Penguin.

Peters, T. J. and Waterman, R. H., Jr. (1982) *In Search of Excellence: Lessons From America's Best-Run Companies*, New York: Harper and Row.

Reading highlights

All the texts below represent good overviews of the organizational culture literature. You may find some more challenging than others.

Alvesson, M. (2002) *Understanding Organizational Culture*, London: Sage.

Anthony, P. D. (1994) *Managing Culture*, Milton Keynes: Open University Press.

Brown, A. D. (1998) *Organizational Culture*, second edition, London: Financial Times Pitman Publishing.

Linstead, S. (2004) 'Managing culture', in S. Linstead, L. Fulop and S. Lilley (eds.) *Management and Organization: A Critical Text*, Basingstoke and New York: Macmillan, p.p. 93–122.

Parker, M. (2000) *Organizational Culture and Identity: Unity and Division at Work*, London: Sage.

Smircich, L. (1983) 'Concepts of culture and organizational analysis', *Administrative Science Quarterly* 28(3):339–358.

References

Ackroyd, S. and Crowdy, P. (1990) 'Can culture be managed? Working with raw material: The case of the English slaughtermen', *Personnel Review* 19(5):3–13.

Aktouf, O. (1996) 'Competence, symbolic activity and promotability', in S. Linstead, R. Grafton-Small and P. Jeffcutt (eds.) *Understanding Management*, London: Sage.

Alvesson, M. (2002) *Understanding Organizational Culture*, London: Sage.

Anthony, P. D. (1994) *Managing Culture*, Milton Keynes: Open University Press.

Ashforth, B. E. and Kreiner, G. E. (1999) ' "How can you do it?": Dirty work and the challenge of constructing a positive identity', *Academy of Management Review* 24(3):413–434.

Barsoux, J-L. and Manzoni, J-F. (2002) 'Flying into a storm: British Airways (1996–2000)', INSEAD, Fontainebleau, France (case number 02/2002–4906).

BBC News Online (1999a) 'Business: The company file – Turbulent times at British Airways', 9 February. Online. Available at http://news.bbc.co.uk (accessed 5 July 2004).

BBC News Online (1999b) 'Business: The company file – Airline passengers Go against BA', 9 March. Online. Available at http://news.bbc.co.uk (accessed 5 July 2004).

BBC News Online (1999c) 'Business: The company file – British Airways hits more turbulence', 25 May. Online. Available at http://news.bbc.co.uk (accessed 5 July 2004).

BBC News Online (1999d) 'Business: BA to fly the flag again', 6 June. Online. Available at http://news.bbc.co.uk (accessed 5 July 2004).

Beaton, A. (2001) *The Little Book of Management Bollocks*, London: Pocket Books/Simon and Schuster.

Bjerke, B. (1999) *Business Leadership and Culture: National Management Styles in the Global Economy*, Cheltenham: Edward Elgar.

Brewis, J. and Linstead, S. (2000) *Sex, Work and Sex Work: Eroticizing Organization*, London: Routledge.

Brown, A. D. (1998) *Organizational Culture*, second edition, London: Financial Times Pitman Publishing.

Business Life (1997) 'The way ahead', July/August, p.p. 44–47.

Chapman, M. R. (2003) *In Search of Stupidity: Over 20 Years of High-Tech Marketing Disasters*, Berkeley, CA: Apress.

Clark, A. (2004) 'Heathrow turned into makeshift camp site as troubled BA hits fresh turbulence', *The Guardian*, 25 August. Online. Available at: http://www.guardian.co.uk (accessed 15 November 2004).

Collinson, D. L. (1988) ' "Engineering humour" ': Masculinity, joking and conflict in shopfloor relations', *Organization Studies* 9(2):181–199.

Corbett, J. M. (1994) *Critical Cases in Organizational Behaviour*, London: Macmillan.

Coser, L. A. (1974) *Greedy Institutions: Patterns of Undivided Commitment*, New York: Free Press.

Dalton, A. (2003) 'Peace deal in BA row over swipe cards', *The Scotsman*, 31 July. Online. Available at: http://news.scotsman.com (accessed 5 July 2004).

Daymon, C. (2000) 'Leadership and emerging cultural patterns in a new television station', *Studies in Cultures, Organizations and Societies* 6(2):169–195.

Deal, T. E. and Kennedy, A. A. (1988) *Corporate Cultures: The Rites and Rituals of Corporate Life*, Harmondsworth: Penguin.

Equal Opportunities Commission (2003) *Facts about Women and Men in Great Britain 2003*, January. Online. Available at: http://www.eoc.org.uk/cseng/research/factsgreatbritain2003.pdf (accessed 18 December 2003).

Foucault, M. (1977) *Discipline and Punish: The Birth of the Prison*, A. Sheridan (trans.), London: Allen Lane.

Handy, C. (1993) *Understanding Organizations: Managing Differentiation and Integration*, New York: Oxford University Press.

Harrison, R. (1972) 'Understanding your organization's character', *Harvard Business Review*, 50 (May–June):119–128.

Haurant, S. (2004) 'Drug testing at work "to increase" ', *The Guardian*, 28 June. Online. Available at: http://www.guardian.co.uk (accessed 5 July 2004).

Hines, R. (1988) 'Financial accounting: In communicating reality, we construct reality', *Accounting, Organizations and Society* 13(3):251–261.

Hofstede, G. (2001) *Culture's Consequences: Comparing Values, Behaviors, Institutions, and Organizations Across Nations*, Thousand Oaks, CA: Sage.

Höpfl, H. J. (1993) 'British carriers', in D. Gowler, K. Legge and C. Clegg (eds.) *Cases in Organizational Behaviour*, London: Paul Chapman, p.p. 117–125.

Innes, J. (2004) 'BA to test all staff for drug and drink use on duty', *The Scotsman*, 25 June. Online. Available at: http://news.scotsman.com (accessed 5 July 2004).

Jackson, N. and Carter, P. (2000) *Rethinking Organisational Behaviour*, Harlow, Essex: Financial Times Prentice Hall.

Kanter, R. M. (1983) *The Change Masters*, New York: Simon and Schuster.

Kotter, J. P. and Heskett, J. L. (1992) *Corporate Culture and Performance*, New York: Free Press.

Kunda, G. (1992) *Engineering Culture: Control and Commitment in a High-Tech Corporation*, Philadelphia: Temple University Press.

Legge, K. (1994) 'Managing culture: Fact or fiction?', in K. Sisson (ed.) *Personnel Management*, Oxford: Blackwell, p.p. 397–433.

Linstead, S. (2004) 'Managing culture', in S. Linstead, L. Fulop and S. Lilley (eds.) *Management and Organization: A Critical Text*, Basingstoke and New York: Macmillan, p.p. 93–122.

Linstead, S. A. and Grafton-Small, R. (1992) 'On reading organizational culture', *Organization Studies* 13(3):331–355.

Martin, J. and Siehl, C. (1983) 'Organizational culture and counterculture: An uneasy symbiosis', *Organizational Dynamics* Autumn:52–63.

Meek, V. L. (1988) 'Organizational culture: Origins and weaknesses', *Organization Studies* 9(4):453–473.

Meyerson, D. and Martin, J. (1994) 'Cultural change: An integration of three different views', in H. Tsoukas (ed.) *New Thinking in Organizational Behaviour: From Social Engineering to Reflective Action*, Oxford: Butterworth-Heinemann, p.p. 108–132.

Mills, A. and Murgatroyd, S. (1991) *Organizational Rules: A Framework for Understanding Organizational Interaction*, Milton Keynes: Open University Press.

Morgan, G. (1997) *Images of Organization*, second edition, Thousand Oaks, CA: Sage.

Morgan, O. (2003) 'Besieged BA left with strike baggage', *The Observer*, 27 July. Online. Available at: http://guardian.co.uk/Observer (accessed 5 July 2004).

Ouchi, W. G. (1981) *Theory Z: How American Business Can Meet the Japanese Challenge*, Reading, MA: Addison Wesley.

Parker, M. (2000) *Organizational Culture and Identity: Unity and Division at Work*, London: Sage.

Pascale, R. T. and Athos, A. G. (1981) *The Art of Japanese Management: Applications for American Executives*, New York: Warner Books.

Peters, T. J. and Waterman, R. H., Jr. (1982) *In Search of Excellence: Lessons From America's Best-Run Companies*, New York: Harper and Row.

Schein, E. (1992) *Organizational Culture and Leadership*, second edition, San Francisco: Jossey Bass.

Smircich, L. (1983) 'Concepts of culture and organizational analysis', *Administrative Science Quarterly* 28(3):339–358.

Tayeb, M. H. (1988) *Organizations and National Culture: A Comparative Analysis*, London: Sage.

The Times (1999) 'Not such a bad air day for Ayling', 10 February, p. 23.

Thompson, P. and McHugh, D. (2002) *Work Organisations: A Critical Introduction*, third edition, Basingstoke: Macmillan.

Trice, H. M. and Beyer, J. M. (1993) *The Cultures of Work Organizations*, Upper Saddle River, NJ: Prentice Hall.

Vedpuriswar, A. V. with Kamachandran, U. (2003) 'British Airways: Leadership and change', ICFAI Knowledge Center, Hyderabad, India (European Case Clearing House Collection, case number 403-044-1).

Whyte, W. H. (1957) *The Organization Man*, London: Jonathan Cape.

Willmott, H. (1993) 'Strength is ignorance, slavery is freedom: Managing culture in modern organizations', *Journal of Management Studies* 30(2):515–552.

Wilson, F. M. (2004) *Organizational Behaviour and Work: A Critical Introduction*, second edition, Oxford: Oxford University Press.

Wray, R. (2004) 'BA begins chaos inquiry', *The Guardian*, 30 August. Online. Available at: http://www.guardian.co.uk (accessed 15 November 2004).

Notes

1. Exercise 9.1, when you identified ways in which the staff at your university attempt to convey their 'philosophy', teach newcomers the 'rules of the game' and so on, would have identified some of the CTMs in use in this organization.

2. The management consultancy that Peters and Waterman – and indeed Deal and Kennedy – worked for at one time.

3. Management apparently threatened anyone planning to strike with removal of their staff perks, a block on promotion, dismissal or even being sued for damages.

4. These planes were subsequently phased out completely.

5. See for example the Business and Professional Woman UK website at http://www.bpwuk.org.uk/.

6. In other words I hail from the north-east of England.

7. Controlling all aspects of its citizens' lives and quickly and mercilessly suppressing any resistance.

8. He was, the story runs, reimbursed at a later date.

10 Change and Innovation: New Organizational Forms

Frank Worthington

Key concepts and learning objectives

By the end of this chapter you should understand:

- The terms 'Fordism' and 'post-Fordism' as key concepts for describing the rise and development of contemporary forms of production and work organization.

- How and why post-Fordist forms of production and organization have come to replace conventional Fordist forms.

- How new, post-Fordist organizational forms are conceived to release the creative and competitive potential of employees in organization.

- How new organizational forms are seen by critical organization and management theorists as subtle forms of power, control and surveillance.

Aims of the chapter

This chapter will:

- Examine the nature of organization innovation and change.

- Explain how mainstream thinking accounts for the rise and development of new organizational forms.

- Analyse how and why new forms of production and organization have come to replace previous forms.

- Demonstrate how new forms of production release the productive potential of employees in organizations in novel ways.

- Explain how new organizational forms are viewed from a critical perspective.

Overview and key points

During the last quarter of the 20th century the nature and organization of work in advanced industrial society is said to have undergone a radical transformation, resulting from the emergence of forms of organizational innovation that are both quantitatively and qualitatively different than those that existed at the beginning of the Century (Delbridge, 1998). These innovations are said to have brought about major changes not only in the way in which goods and services are produced, but also major changes in business practices, management control methods and management–labour relations.

Over the past two decades or so, this change has been widely celebrated in mainstream management literature in that both business organizations and their employees are said to have benefited considerably from these changes. The changes are said to provide businesses with the means to operate more flexibly to improve productivity, product quality and reliability, and therefore customer satisfaction, and to respond more rapidly to shifting economic and market conditions (Child, 2005). Employees benefit because change offers them an opportunity to be much more involved in the day-to-day planning and organization of production in ways that make their work much more interesting and rewarding.

According to the leading advocates of these new organizational forms, employees in organizations today no longer face a life at work governed by regimented working practices, simplified and repetitive work tasks, narrowly defined roles and responsibilities and 'low-trust' management control methods associated with **bureaucracy** and **mass production** (see Chapters 6 and 13). Instead, it is claimed, in both the public and private sector, employees at all levels can now enjoy a very different and much improved lived-experience of work that is based on 'high-trust' 'employee involvement' practices rather than **direct management control**.

Critical organization and management theorists, on the other hand, have a rather different view of these developments. They acknowledge that the contemporary workplace has changed considerably in recent decades in terms of job design, the nature and organization and control of production, business practices and the management and control of employees. But, from their perspective, fundamentals have not changed. Today's ostensibly progressive organizational forms are no less exploitative (the gap between a wealthy elite and the mass of people is not narrowing) or necessarily less alienating than those that existed before (Sewell, 1998). In the workplace, as many commentators, especially labour process theorists, have shown, innovative forms of organization, production methodologies and working practices comprise subtle forms of self-disciplinary managerial power, control and surveillance that lead to **work intensification**.

In this chapter you will become familiar with these two perspectives as we examine how mainstream and critical organizational and management theorists offer very different assessments of innovation in the contemporary workplace. Before we consider these two perspectives, let us first take a look at a case study as a way of gaining an insight into the nature and lived-experience of the various new forms of organization that this chapter examines (see Case study 10.1).

CASE STUDY 10.1 Northern Plant: 'The factory that time forgot'

Coming here has been an absolute nightmare and a career disaster. Everyone talks about Northern Plant as being militant. But militancy is normally associated with formal trade union activity. Well it doesn't mean that here. This is one of the most militant shops I've ever seen but none of it is union led.

This statement was made by Mike, a senior manager from Northern Plant's North American Corporate Headquarters, who had been drafted in as a member of a human resource management 'change' team charged with facilitating the full introduction of an innovative approach to work production, called 'lean production' (see Box 10.1), at Northern Plant. Lean production was viewed by Northern Plant's parent company as the most competitive form of manufacturing within the high-tech sector of the automotive industry in which the company operated. Prior to Mike's arrival, Northern Plant had experimented for over a decade with a number of 'new wave' flexible manufacturing and production methodologies, including just-in-time, lean production, teamworking and total quality control, but with little success.

Workers at the plant resisted lean production because in their view it was designed not simply to improve productivity but to enable their managers to gain greater control over working practices, which they believed would lead to work intensification. The actual nature of their resistance, however, was not something that managers at the plant found easy to understand or to explain. As a long-standing senior human resource specialist, who had joined the plant some years earlier, explained to Mike's change team, 'When you join this plant you quickly come to realize that it's not managed properly, that there are no basic rules and professional human resource standards in place that managers should be working to, which has resulted in workers becoming ill disciplined'. Senior managers at the plant attributed this problem to the poor man-management skills of first-line managers, which over time had led workers to become accustomed to 'getting away with "murder" ' in terms of their approach to their work and their attitude to authority. What frustrated managers at Northern Plant most, however, was that workers never actually *openly* challenged their authority. As long as managers left them to their own devices, they were in fact highly cooperative. It was only when managers interfered in the 'informal' organization of production and working

Box 10.1: Lean production

Lean production/manufacturing describes a system of production first used in Japan that is designed to maintain the smooth flow of production by using minimum resources to reduce cost, work in progress and other overheads. Lean production commends the reorganization of production into dedicated multi-skilled and multi-functional teams of workers who, wherever possible, operate high-tech multi-purpose machines and automated assembly operations that require less physical effort, less manufacturing and factory space, less machine hours, fewer tools and less inventory.

practices (see Chapter 6) that they refused to cooperate with them.

What these managers didn't fully explain to Mike's change team was that prior to the plant's interest in lean production, workers had in fact been encouraged to 'manage' themselves, as a way of enticing them to meet production quotas in the fastest way possible. Workers valued this arrangement because it gave them a considerable measure of autonomy from direct management control. Basically, as long their output was of a sufficient quantity and quality, and as long as each day's production of finished products were 'right first time' and dispatched to customers *on*-time, workers were allowed to take as many unofficial rest times as they liked during the working day itself, and also to build up considerable 'free time' at the end of each working shift, time which they were allowed to spend in various leisure activities. These activities included reading books or newspapers, chatting to friends, playing table tennis, cards, darts or chess, studying the day's race card and placing bets with the plant's bookie, sleeping during the night shift, taking leisurely strolls around the plant or the surrounding area, and even making the occasional visit to a local pub during working hours.

Although they pretended that they did not to know what was going on behind the scenes, first-line mangers went along with this arrangement because of the constant high market demand for the plant's products and the tight delivery schedules they were required to meet. Some first-line managers did in fact join in many of the workers' leisure activities. Without giving workers 'responsible autonomy' from direct management control in this way, and without encouraging them to complete production quotas in the fastest time possible, and rewarding their efforts with 'time off' during working hours, targets would not have been achieved as easily. This kind of give-and-take arrangement between managers and workers is not so unusual. But at Northern Plant it went far beyond what most managers in manufacturing would normally be willing to accommodate, or likely to subscribe to. What was the outcome apart from meeting the deadlines? Ironically, it actually cultivated 'high-trust' flexible teamworking practices. It is ironic because such practices are normally associated with the kind of lean production that managers at Northern Plant were now seeking to introduce. These practices were operational in Northern Plant long before they were championed within the industry. Managers therefore assumed that Northern Plant would be ideally suited to lean production. How wrong could they be?

Thinkpoint 10.1

How would you account for managers' failure to understand the differences between what worker' at Northern Plant had been used to, and what 'lean production' involved?

When attempts were made to introduce new working practices associated with lean production, workers refused to cooperate with managers by distancing themselves from any involvement in its planning and organization (see Collinson, 1992, 1994). They did this by claiming that although they did not object to its introduction, as far as they were concerned it stood to reason that *responsibility* for its success ultimately lay with management, not workers. We will explore the reasons why workers employed this particular form of resistance when we revisit this case study later in the chapter.

For now, to give you an indication of what it is like to face this kind of resistance, imagine for a moment you are a member of Mike's human resource 'change team'. Like Mike, you arrive at Northern Plant to help re-engineer the plant into a lean production facility. You are informed how management at the plant has been attempting to fully introduce lean production for some years, but without much success. You have been briefed about the 'worker resistance' problem. You see the problem as a challenge, as a difficult barrier to change that obviously needs to be overcome, but this does not faze you. From your experience as a 'change agent' elsewhere, you already have a good idea what the likely problem is: *a lack of leadership and poor communication*. You know this from studying for your 2.1 BA Human Resource Management Degree at a reputable university. As your favourite 'change management' lecturer pointed out many times, 'scratch

below the surface of any "change management" problems in organizations and what you will undoubtedly find in almost every case is poor leadership and poor communication'. You also recall how she explained to you that you may of course come across the odd militant worker, or a few 'bad apples', who seem to have a chip-on-their-shoulder, who have a propensity to resist management's prerogative to manage, but how this resistance is almost always due to a 'fear of change' to which everyone is susceptible when facing the unknown.

You make these points at Mike's first team meeting, and as you are seen to have a clear view of the problem and how to solve it, you are given the task of tackling these problems. Pleased with having been given this responsibility, you arrange for a series of meetings and workshops to be held with the plant's workforce. In these meetings you give an excellent presentation, drawing upon your lecture notes on the topics of lean production and change management, about the aims and objectives and benefits of lean production, both in terms of its competitive advantage for the company and also, in particular, in terms of the benefits for workers themselves.

You feel confident from these presentations that workers at the plant will at least appreciate that lean production is essentially about working *smarter* not *harder*, how they will be empowered to make decisions and the opportunity to take greater responsibility for the planning and organization of production, 'quality control' and customer satisfaction. You feel quite confident that this will undoubtedly put their apparent 'fear of change' to rest.

Their response to your account of the benefits of lean production, however, is not quite what you expect. Not only are the workers apparently unconvinced that lean production will give them a greater say in decision making, they totally refuse to accept that it will make their work more interesting. In any case, they say, they are quite happy with the way things are at present and don't particularly want to work differently. You try to convince them that their views are misguided by recounting how lean production offers them job enrichment and skill enhancement. This doesn't seem to get you very far. They just become more hostile, not only to your ideas but also to you personally by claiming that your attempt to convince them to accept new working practices is motivated purely by your own personal ambitions. As they put it, getting them to 'buy into' lean production will probably get you a 'bonus' of some sort, and help you to move up the corporate ladder as a reward for your efforts, while they will be left to work much harder than they did before within a system of production that does not offers then the same rewards and opportunities. They also claim that you know full well that the proposed changes are designed not to empower them but to subjugate them to greater management control, for no other reason than to increase productivity.

You refute these claims emphatically. You admit that yes, as a management graduate you certainly do want to one day hopefully progress to the top of your profession – who wouldn't. You also concede that ultimately lean production is obviously designed first and foremost to increase productivity, but you insist it is not designed to do this simply by 'sweating labour'. A chorus of laughter erupts from around the training room. As the laughter dies down you're told to 'come clean', to be honest with workers and with yourself. You are told that if you want to be taken seriously as a manager you need to stop insulting their intelligence by treating them 'as if they were born only yesterday'.

You begin to realize that you are being baited into a situation in which these workers are using what they claim are your own selfish, personal, professional goals and interests to question your integrity as a ploy to expose what they claim to be the *real* motives behind your attempts to induce them to accept new working practices. Your attempts to counter these accusations serve only to produce further gales of laughter. They then finish their attack on you by claiming that everyone – including you – knows that first and foremost management's job is to 'screw' workers as much as they can to get as much productivity out of them as possible! At this point you lose your composure, you blush and become lost for words, not quite sure what's going on, but you have a sinking feeling that you're getting nowhere.

Summary of the issues raised by this case-study so far

This is just a brief insight into a number of subversive forms of misbehaviour (see Ackroyd and Thompson, 1999) that workers at Northern Plant employed to resist lean production. Having read Box 10.1, you will appreciate how workers did not openly challenge management's right to re-engineer the plant's manufacturing arrangement. Instead, they questioned managers' integrity as a method of 'spoiling' their professional and personal identity as a method of undermining the legitimacy of their power and authority within the workplace. Conventional organizational behaviour and management textbooks rarely examine such misbehaviour in any detail. And yet, as Ackroyd and Thompson (1999) and Collinson (1992, 1994) show, misbehaviour of this kind is just as much a feature of life in organizations, yet it is generally ignored or downplayed in most case studies that fill the textbooks used on so many management courses.

Exercise 10.1

- Make a list of the challenges that you think Mike's change team faced at the lean production briefing meetings described in the case study.
- Make a separate list of what you think are the likely reasons for worker resistance to lean production at Northern Plant.
- Sketch out a strategy that Mike's change team might adopt to counter worker resistance at the plant.
- Assess the strategy of resistance that involves questioning managers' integrity and 'spoiling their identity'.

We will return to these issues again when we revisit the case study later in the chapter. What we need to do first is to look in more detail at how 'new organizational forms' have come to replace conventional ways of producing goods and services in advanced industrial society during the late 20th century.

Mainstream approach

Introduction to the mainstream approach

The new organizational forms that emerged during the latter part of the 20th century have acquired a wide variety of labels. In the sphere of production, the following are widely used:

- 'just-in-time' (Schonberger, 1986)
- 'lean production' (Womack, Jones and Roos, 1990)
- 'Innovation-mediated production' (Kenney and Florida, 1993)
- 'cellular manufacturing' (Alford, 1994)
- 'product-focused manufacturing' (Alford, 1994)
- 'the integrated factory' (Bonazzi, 1994).

Along with these various terms and concepts, new theories have also been developed that are used to describe their nature and characteristics. The most common include:

- 'flexible specialization' (Piore and Sabel, 1984)
- 'post-Fordism' (McKinlay and Starkey, 1992; Wood, 1989)
- 'Toyotaism' (Imai, 1989)
- 'Japanization' (Bratton, 1992; Oliver and Wilkinson, 1992)
- 'neo-Fordism' (Agglietta, 1979).

What all of these terms and concepts have in common is the notion that in advanced industrial societies in recent decades a radical change has been occurring (or must occur if 'the West' is to remain competitive) in the way that work is organized and experienced.

Here we will concentrate primarily upon 'lean production', an innovation that is intended to revolutionize the organization and productivity of shop floor work. As Womack *et al.* (1990), leading champions of lean production, explain, in contrast to traditional Fordist mass production arrangements, post-Fordist organizational forms, such as lean production, comprise of small dedicated multi-skilled and multi-functional teams of workers who operate high-tech multi-purpose machines and automated assembly operations that require less physical effort, less manufacturing and factory space, less machine hours, fewer tools and less inventory. Within this new, high-tech manufacturing environment workers are *empowered* to take greater responsibility for decision making, problem solving, product quality control and production maintenance. According to Womack *et al.* (1990), directly involving

SOURCE: © ISTOCKPHOTO.COM/PAUL LARAGY

Image 10.1 Lean production

workers in the day-to-day running of production and the planning and organizing work not only makes work more interesting for workers themselves, organization also become more competitive.

One of the most popular forms of flexibility in use in many organizations today is just-in-time (JIT), which forms an integral part of most lean production systems. JIT is essentially a system of production that is designed to improve productivity and competitiveness by reducing waste. According to JIT enthusiasts, forms of waste include idle machine time, waiting time, lost production due to machine breakdowns, defective parts, poor-quality finished products, high levels of work-in-progress, late deliveries, the need for overtime to meet output quotas not achieved within normal working hours and so on. JIT is designed to eliminate these various forms of waste by controlling stock levels and the level and flow of work-in-progress at each stage of production. The key aims of JIT are to:

- Reduce stock and work-in-progress to the minimum possible level.
- Prevent large quantities of work-in-progress from building up within the production system.
- Reduce the level of finished goods held by the organization, by dispatching them to the consumer as soon as they are produced.

All of this rests on organizations being able to buy in small batches of materials from suppliers, delivering them to the point of production *just in time* for when they are needed, and to arrange for finished goods to be dispatched to, or collected by, customers immediately they reach the end of the production process. This requires close buyer–supplier cooperation, simple workflows, fast machine set-up and changeover times, rigorous in-process quality control methods designed to guarantee that things are made 'right first time', and, most importantly, a workforce that is both aware of, and committed to, the principles of JIT (see Schonberger, 1986). Workers are the most important resource in this system because JIT ultimately relies on them to keep the flow of production going at all times by addressing problems quickly, as and when they occur, so as to minimize stoppage time and avoid faults or breakdowns within the system. The underlying rationale behind this is to 'build in' quality at each stage of production rather than 'inspecting out' defective or sub-standard parts or products only at the end of the production process. Figure 10.1 illustrates how the JIT process works in practice.

There are various accounts of the origins of JIT. One of the most popular states that it was first introduced at Toyota in the 1950s after one of the firm's senior executives visited an American supermarket where he observed workers restocking shelves immediately after customers had purchased goods rather than when shelves became empty. According to Schonberger (1986), following its introduction at Toyota, JIT was widely adopted in other post-war Japanese manufacturing industries, especially shipbuilding, and later in other high-tech industries. Its introduction and subsequent widespread popularity in North American and Western European industries, however, as you will see below, only came about as a result of spiralling production costs triggered by a series of economic crises in the 1970s, which left Western industries unable to compete with their Japanese counterparts.

Many industrial sociologists, especially those working within the labour process tradition for example, contest the claim that new organizational forms, such as those promoted by JIT and lean

Thinkpoint 10.2

On what basis would you assess the claims made by the advocates of lean production, bearing in mind the case study of Northern Plant? How would you defend this basis?

production, make work more interesting and rewarding. Oliver and Wilkinson (1992) demonstrate how under lean manufacturing arrangements workers are often simply required to do several boring and monotonous jobs instead of just one. Similarly, Diane Sharpe (1998), who worked for a full year on the shop floor in a Japanese manufacturing company in the United Kingdom, shows how 'so-called' **multi-skilling** often involves little more than **multi-tasking** in that more often than not workers merely acquire *company-specific* skills as opposed to genuine *transferable skills* that are applicable to other organizational settings.

Others working within the labour process tradition have also shown how so-called multi-skilling, along with teamworking and total quality control methods, do not just fail to live up to their promise to make work more interesting and rewarding but in reality lead to work intensification. Delbridge *et al.* (1992, 1998), Garrahan and Stewart (1992) and Sewell and Wilkinson (1992) show

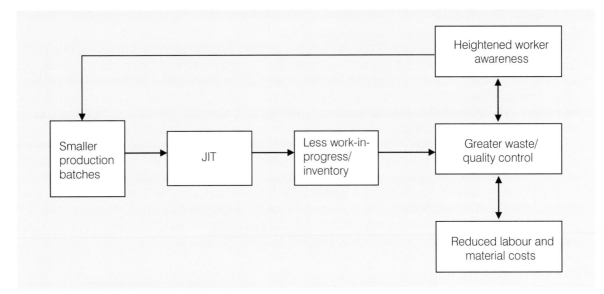

SOURCE: ADAPTED BY AUTHOR FROM: R. SCHONEBERGER: JAPANESE MANUFACTURING TECHNIQUES NINE HIDDEN LESSONS IN SIN/A

Figure 10.1 The JIT production process.

how under lean production, which they refer to as 'mean' production, rather than being empowered workers are in fact subject to subtle forms of managerial surveillance that extend rather than reduce management control over the labour process. As they show from their research, flexibility, team-working and total quality management, which mainstream management theorists claim are intended simply to reduce 'waste' and 'slack' time within the system – which workers have traditionally used to gain a respite from the boredom and monotony and fatigue of the production line – are designed first and foremost to increase output, through 'cost-cutting'. The advocates of lean production claim that these criticisms of it are unjustified.

Table 10.1 summarizes in most textbooks what critical theorists see as the rhetoric and stark reality of the nature of work practices within new organizational forms based ostensibly on flexibility and high commitment.

In this opening section, we have looked at how new organizational forms are viewed from two perspectives. On the one hand, mainstream theorists have celebrated the advent of post-Fordism as not only a radical departure from the past, from traditional Fordist organizational structures based upon rigid hierarchical and bureaucratic command and control regimes, but also as the beginning of the end of the problem of workplace alienation and degradation. On the other hand, we have seen how critical commentators challenge this rosy view by arguing that post-Fordist production methods and working practices do not deliver what they promise. We will return to examine these claims later in this chapter in the 'Critical approach' section.

Key controversies surrounding the mainstream approach

So far, we have talked mainly about the advent of new forms of organization in manufacturing. However, it is not only manufacturing industries that have been subject to change in recent decades. Similar major changes in organization structures, working practices, job design and management control methods have also taken place in both private and public sector organizations. As in manufacturing, changes have been driven, or at least justified, by reference to the emergence of highly complex and competitive economic and market conditions, which some would say have been brought about by the forces of globalization. To cope with these conditions, managers across diverse sectors and across the world have all turned to 'new wave' management ideas and novel organizational forms.

In the name of competitiveness and commercial success – which could equally be interpreted in terms of a response to a crisis in profitability, or a determination to reassert control over value-producing activities – they have sought to re-engineer their business processes and human resource practices. In many cases, this involves the formation of alliances and complex inter-organizational relationships as firms cooperate with one another to minimize their individual limitations and vulnerabilities or to capitalize upon synergies. As Child (2005) has recently pointed out, many firms no longer compete solely on a national basis. They operate globally, distributing products and providing services across

Box 10.2: The benefits of lean production

Womack *et al.* (1990) argue that first and foremost lean production is simply a system that combines the advantages of mass production with the benefits of craft-production, and claim that whether this actually leads to genuine skill-enhancement is not important. In their view, the more important issue, which they claim their critics fail to appreciate, is that lean production is undoubtedly a far 'better way of making things', which organizations have no choice but to adopt given today's highly competitive global markets (ibid., p. 225). Even if this is accepted, we can see from the 'mean' production perspective that we need to be very careful about automatically viewing new post-Fordist organizational forms as a radical departure from the demands placed upon workers by Fordism. As Womack *et al.*'s response to their critics indicates, even leading advocates of such new organizational forms are willing to concede that flexible production arrangements and working practices do not necessarily lead to skill enhancement and job enrichment. It is difficult to resist the conclusion that their advocacy of lean production is based upon its cost-effectiveness and ultimately upon its inevitability in the face of global competition, and not on its enrichment of the experience of work, even when it does fortuitously bring such benefits.

Table 10.1 The rhetoric and reality of new production methods

Rhetoric	Reality
Customer first	Market forces rule supreme
Total quality management	Doing more with less workers
Lean production	Mean production
Flexibility	Management 'can do' whatever it wants
Core and peripheral workers	Reducing the organization's commitment to its employees
Devolution/de-layering	Reducing the number of middle and first-line managers
Downsizing/rightsizing	Expanding part-time insecure
New working patterns	jobs, reducing full-time jobs and increasing redundancy
Empowerment	Making workers take risks and responsibilities with rewarding them with status, pay or promotion
Training and development Employability	Manipulation. No employment security
Recognizing the contribution of the individual	Undermining trade unions and collective bargaining
Teamworking	Reducing and controlling individual discretion

Source: Sissons (1994).

national and cultural boundaries in ways previously unimagined. For example, firms that previously operated independently of each other now operate in 'clusters' within retail or technology parks (Wilson, 2004), or within Japanese style spatially concentrated, preferred buyer-supplier production sites (Oliver and Wilkinson, 1992).

Note how at the same time, new information and communication technology has also played a part in forging new forms of organization and business relationships. Zuboff (1988), for example, shows how advances in information and communication technologies and knowledge transfer capabilities have enabled, if not compelled, business organizations in general to transform the way they operate, both in terms of their business and customer relationships and their use of material and human resources.

Re-engineering in the public sector   Public sector and voluntary service organizations have similarly sought ways to achieve ambitious improvements in performance (McNulty and Ferlie, 2005) by re-engineering their organizational structure and human resource capabilities (Legge, 2005). Attempts include the introduction of leaner, flatter, flexible organization practices (Beattie and McDougall, 1998), business process re-engineering (BPR) (Hammer and Champy, 1993), quality audit systems (Morley, 2003), 'new public management' (Corby and White, 1999) and cultural change initiatives (Hope-Hailey, 1998) (see also Chapter 6). In the United Kingdom, as in other advanced industrial societies, these investments are designed to erode the rigidities and inefficiencies associated with traditional post-war welfare state hierarchical and bureaucratic organizational structures, which are seen as having made public sector services 'wasteful and bloated' (Ferlie *et al.*, 1996), and to provide taxpayers with more value-for-money public services that better serve their needs and expectations (Howkins and Thornton, 2002).

Here again, critical management and labour process theorists draw out important differences between the rhetoric and reality of the outcomes of new organizational forms in the public sector (e.g. Dent, 1998; Ferlie *et al.*, 1996; McNulty and Ferlie, 2005; Wilson, 2004; Worthington, 2004). These studies show how, BPR and TQM (see Chapter 6), for example, have resulted in widespread dissatisfaction, discontent and alienation. To take the example of healthcare, it has been found that clinicians, nurses, medics, auxiliary and catering and cleaning staff alike have tended to experience the new working practices resulting from these investments as '*dis*-empowering' rather than 'empowering', leading to work-intensification rather than work enrichment.

In further and higher education a similar picture emerges. The application of quality methodologies to job role analysis, output requirements and performance targets, teaching and learning methods, student support and methods of assessment has also resulted in widespread employee discontent, stress and alienation. So much so that university vice-chancellors, teachers' trade unions and academics themselves have all expressed concerns about the purpose of quality assessment in higher education, both in terms of its financial cost and also its drain on time and resources (see Howie, 2002; Harley, 2001; Morley, 2003; Strathern, 2000). But what most concerns them is how the notion of quality in higher education has led to the marketization of education (Willmott, 1996), and with this the subordination of academic work to managerial priorities resulting in work intensification.

Benefits of new organizational forms

It should be apparent from what we have covered thus far that lean production and flexible working practices are attractive to organizations because they promise to improve productivity. But do these organizational forms benefit workers? As we have noted, lean production enables organizations to use their manufacturing, financial and human resources in more cost-efficient ways. John Atkinson's (1984) flexible firm model (sometimes referred to as 'flexible specialization') is widely used to illustrate the benefits of flexibility not only to firms but also to their employees.

The flexible firm Atkinson's flexible firm model has three distinct but interrelated characteristics: (i) *functional* flexibility; (ii) *numerical* flexibility; and (iii) *financial* flexibility.

- Functional flexibility refers to how firms assign (multi-skilled) employees to different roles, activities and work tasks to meet changes in market demand and customer requirements.
- Numerical flexibility refers to how firms adjust the size of their workforce in relation to fluctuations in output requirements and market demand by using employment agencies, such

---

Box 10.3: Supply chains and the clustering of firms

Spatially concentrated business clusters, as they are referred to, comprise small to medium-sized firms located in close proximity to each other, or to larger (often) multinational manufacturing and business organizations for whom they are contracted to supply outsourced small sub-assembly and sub-component parts and accessories that can be delivered on a just-in-time basis to the buyer organization. The underpinning rationale of preferred buyer–supplier relations is to allow (large and small) firms to collaborate to 'continuously improve on cost savings by reducing transport and distribution costs, smoothing the flow of production, reducing lead times, eliminating waste, sharing the costs of investment in new technology, research and development and maintaining quality control (see Oliver and Wilkinson, 1992).

as Manpower, or 'non-standard' employment practices such as part-time, short-term and fixed-term employment contracts.

● Financial flexibility refers to how firms adjust their wage costs to make savings by moving away from uniform and standardized pay structures, or by introducing performance-related pay in keeping with the objectives of functional and numerical flexibility.

Within this model, workers fall into one of two distinct groups: *core* or *peripheral* employees. Core employees, who normally perform what Atkinson refers to as 'functionally flexible' roles. Workers who fall into this category are usually highly skilled (e.g. craft workers, and research and design engineers), experts in a particular field (e.g. computer technicians and technical sales staff), or essential to the firm's core operations. Given their importance to the firm, this group normally enjoys relatively secure terms and conditions of employment, higher salaries than other workers, good company benefits such as bonus payments, generous holiday pay, sick-pay and company pension rights. Peripheral employees on the other hand (e.g. part-time, contract and agency workers, and public subsidy trainees), perform what Atkinson calls 'numerically flexible' roles. Workers who fall within this category, who are easily replaceable, tend to have rather less secure employment conditions and more often than not receive less pay and less access to the company benefits enjoyed by functionally flexible workers.

For many mainstream theorists the 'flexible firm' model captures some of the key benefits of new forms of organization. However, they tend only to flag up how 'flexibility' reduces costs and improves organizational performance. They rarely look beyond these priorities at the potential implications of the flexible firm for core and peripheral employees, in terms of job security, skill development and career opportunities. One way of exploring this issue is to imagine for a moment what it might be like to be a core or peripheral employee. Chris Smith and Anna Pollert, who critique Atkinson's flexible firm model from a labour process perspective, provide a good starting point (see Box 10.4).

The important point to draw from this is that the mainstream literature gives an impression that training, education and skill enhancement are a priority in all organizations, irrespective of the employees' position and role within the firm. The reality of employment conditions in the flexible firm, however, shows clearly that this is not the case at all. Only *certain* workers, those who are valuable or cannot be easily replaced or disposed of, are likely to receive good pay and conditions, and have access to training and education. Whereas others, who are not as valuable to the firm, for the reasons outlined above, are more often denied these opportunities. Changes in the technical and social organization of production, and the flexible utilization of labour, in other words, do potentially create opportunities for multi-skilling and job-enrichment, but not necessarily for all employees. By focusing mainly on the technical superiority and competitive advantages of new organizational forms over older forms of production, mainstream theorists fail to recognize this, how the trend towards

---

Box 10.4: A critique fo the 'flexible firm'

According to Pollert (1988) and Smith (1991), it stands to reason that flexible firms will try hard to attract, and keep, their *core* workers by offering them good terms and conditions of employment: good pay, attractive company benefits, and opportunities for education and training, etc. *Peripheral* workers, however, as Pollert and Smith note, normally perform mainly routine tasks that require only generic skills. This makes them easily replaceable, and therefore less important to the firm. Not only does this disadvantage them in the workplace itself – in terms of the limited opportunities for genuine skill development, training and education and career development – their contract and conditions of employment have a detrimental effect on their economic well-being.

When it comes to taking out a mortgage or a loan, for example, which many of us take for granted, we need to demonstrate we are creditworthy by being in regular (relatively) secure employment that is not likely to disappear overnight. Peripheral workers do often work for one firm for long periods of time, but this does not mean they are in secure employment. On the contrary, the nature of the roles they perform and their position within the firm, especially when they are recruited through employment agencies, means that they can easily find themselves out of work at very short notice. Another issue that is also ignored in mainstream literature is that women and ethnic minorities are over-represented in many peripheral employment groups (see Warhurst, Grugulis and Keep, 2004).

flexibility in organizations has different outcomes for different employee groups, and how this can just as easily lead to 'skill-polarization' as 'skill expansion' (Warhurst, Grugulis and Keep, 2004). The problem is that investments in new flexible organizational and working practices, that clearly do provide firms with genuine opportunities for skill expansion, are driven first and foremost by managerial priorities concerned with cost reduction, profit maximization and market share.

- Make a list of the advantages of *functional*, *numerical* and *financial* flexibility for organizations.
- Make a list of the advantages and disadvantages of being a *core* worker.
- Make a list of the advantages and disadvantages of being a *peripheral* worker.
- Are firms likely to be concerned about skill polarization, and to what extent are they likely to seek ways to address this 'problem'? Is it a problem for employers?
- Make a list of how the 'problem' of skill polarization would be addressed from: (i) a management perspective; and (ii) an employee perspective.

The skill polarization versus skill expansion issue discussed in this section, along with the issues you may have considered in carrying out Exercise 10.2, will more than likely have raised at least some doubts about the claim that new flexible post-Fordist organizational forms represent a radical break from the past, and the notion that they (can) significantly improve the lived-experience of work. As we have seen, flexibility certainly brings some benefits for 'core' elements of the workforce, but such improvements are largely a coincidental outcome of the drive to gain competitive advantage. So how different are Fordist and post-Fordist working practices? The following section deals with this question by assessing the reasons for, and outcomes of, the apparent shift from the former to the latter.

The shift from Fordism to post-Fordism in context

The term 'Fordism' refers to a form of manufacture and work organization that was developed at the beginning of the 20th century by Henry Ford at the Ford Motor Company in the United States.

Fordism can be loosely defined as a system of mass production for mass consumption. Its principal feature is a moving production line, along which a highly detailed division of labour is governed by rigid hierarchical command and control structures, and 'low-trust' inflexible management control methods based upon the principles of 'scientific management' (see Chapters 2 and 6). An underlying premise of this system is the view that workers 'should be paid to work not to think', and that it should be management alone that determines how work is organized and how jobs and work tasks are performed.

The politics of scientific management We are told in the mainstream literature that 'scientific management' came into being due to the rapid expansion of mass markets in North America at the turn of the 20th century (Huczynski and Buchanan, 2003; Burnes, 2002; Mullins, 2001; Watson, 2002). According to Huczynski and Buchanan, scientific management provided a practical solution to two basic problems. Many workers employed in large-scale manufacturing organizations at that time were from agricultural regions in the United States, or were immigrant workers who had little knowledge of the English language, few job skills and little or no experience of

SOURCE: © ROYALTY-FREE/CORBIS

Image 10.2

factory work. By simplifying manufacturing processes, scientific management, which could be easily applied to different factory settings, overcame these problems by making it easier for managers to train workers to perform simplified repetitive jobs and monitor their performance. This implies that Ford and Taylor were simply concerned with productivity and efficiency. This is not the case. Their aim was to exercise direct control not only over work tasks but also workers, and to instil in them a more ordered and disciplined attitude to work (Anthony, 1977).

Labour discipline was a particular concern for Ford and Taylor. Having passed up the opportunity to go to Harvard in order to work on the shop floor, Taylor had been appalled by what he saw as the lack of management knowledge and control of working practices, and more so with what he referred to as 'soldiering'. This term refers to what Taylor saw as the natural human tendency to try to 'take it easy' by working no harder than was absolutely necessary. What most concerned Taylor, however, was what he referred to as '*systematic* soldiering', the tendency of both individuals and work groups to seek to control the pace and duration of work and effort needed to perform tasks to make the working day as comfortable as possible. What alarmed Taylor was management's apparent inability to address this problem.

Soldiering was a by-product of 19th century craft production arrangements, which Taylor, whose middle class background impeded any knowledge of such traditions, attributed to laziness. As Littler (1982) explains, before the 1880s, factory, mill and mine owners employed workers indirectly through subcontractors who took responsibility for the selection, recruitment and disciplining of workers. In this period it was 'master craftsmen' and 'gang masters', rather than management, who determined how work was organized, how jobs were performed and the speed at which work was done (see Littler, 1982). There was no real incentive to seek to improve productivity for its own sake. On the contrary, it was believed that excessive increases in output would reduce the market demand for labour and therefore result in redundancies and unemployment. Taylor's view was that soldiering would be overcome by directly employing workers, by bringing order and discipline to the shop floor, and by preventing workers, especially craft workers, from keeping their knowledge to themselves.

What Taylor failed to appreciate is that restrictive practices, such as soldiering, and other forms of misbehaviour and resistance to management control, are not simply due to laziness but to the prevailing subcultural norms and values that may, for example, regard certain forms of labour as degrading and/or undignified, and therefore associate their avoidance not with laziness but with good sense.

UNDERSTANDING RESISTANCE   Change in organizations, including the introduction of new working practices, is always susceptible to some resistance. Not only from lower level staff but also middle and senior managers and other occupational and professional groups will also resist change. Not because they 'fear' change but because of its effect on established working practices and occupational and professional interests and values.

Child (2005) notes how senior managers see downsizing as reducing their positional power and influence (Thompson and McHugh, 1998) in the workplace, their control over budgets and other resources as well as opportunities for promotion. Similarly, middle and first-line managers see the introduction of flatter organizational structures, self-managing teamworking arrangements and the concept of empowerment as a threat to their role and job security (see Oliver and Wilkinson, 1992). Trade unions resist change for the same reason. For them, change represents a serious threat to traditional management–trade union relations and their right to represent worker interests (see Pollert, 1996). It is likely that workers will resist change, as our case study shows, when change leads to work intensification.

Many mainstream theorists, Child (2005) included, interpret and dismiss these responses by invoking the argument that resistance is ultimately irrational due to 'fear' of change, a misconception of its aims or a failure to recognize the need for, and benefits of, new organizational arrangements and working practices. At the same time, Child claims that managers can overcome resistance; that is, although some resistance to change is inevitable, as long as management recognize this they will be in a position to deal with it. What he claims is that when faced with resistance, managers simply need to explain to workers the underlying rationale for change, strive to involve workers in the change process, then move forward as quickly as possible to minimize any further potential 'disturbances'. By following this simple formula, managers are able to turn 'resistance into commitment to the change so people contribute their knowledge and experience to working out its details and ensuring its successful implementation' (Child, 2005, p. 299).

Thinkpoint 10.3

What does Child's recommended formula for dealing with resistance ignore? Is adequate attention given to how the outcome and potential consequences of change can result in individuals experiencing intense feelings of powerlessness, angst and insecurity?

Is this response because employees do not understand the goals and underlying rationale for change? Or is it because of the sudden realization that 'downsizing' can reduce not only their status and power and position within an organization, and with this opportunities for career advancement, and may even lead to their unemployment? It is worth pondering that:

- Both 'victims' *and* 'survivors' of downsizing often feel betrayed by organization.
- Both are also prone to feelings of angst and guilt.
- For victims, this is because they can find themselves unable to account for, or come to terms with, why they and not others were made redundant.
- For survivors, this is because they feel guilty about the fact that others have lost their jobs when they themselves have kept theirs.

Critical management and labour process theorists view the mainstream lines of reasoning as rather naive. That is because mainstream thinking tends to assume that fear of change is irrational, and that all that managers need to do to get employees 'on board' and committed to new working practices is to explain to them the need for change. As we saw in our case study of Northern Plant, however, employees often have a very different view of the rationale for change and what it may actually mean in practice.

What mainstream management theorists also omit is that it is not just the threat of work intensification and closer management control that provokes resistance. As Ackroyd and Thompson show, workers often resist both change, and management's right to manage, as a more or less rational or planned way of 'getting back' at management – either as compensation for the psychological and emotional depravation of boring and monotonous work and/or for 'fun' in order to gain some respite from the monotony of day-to-day working life.

Non-Fordist organizational forms   Not all organizations and management practices in the 20th century were Fordist, nor did all Fordist-type organizations fully embrace scientific management. Systems and contingency theorists show how certain business environments limit the scope and reach of *direct* management control methods (see Chapter 6).

In a study of 20 firms operating within different business environments, ranging from the relatively stable to the least predictable, Burns and Stalker (1961), for example, show how business environments and the nature of production rather than management alone play a key role in determining the structure of organizations and the nature of management control. For Burns and Stalker, organizations can be understood as being either *mechanistic* or *organic*, depending on the environment in which they operate. Mechanistic organizations are those that operate in stable and relatively predictable business environments. They have a clearly defined, specialized job, task and role demarcation within and between the different functions and departments. These tend to exemplify, or be amenable to direct control and Taylorist job design methods. Organic organizations, on the other hand, that operate in more turbulent and complex business environments, rely upon interdependent organizational and departmental networks and relationships to function effectively. Organic organizations tend to exemplify, or are amenable to, forms of control that rely upon employees acting in responsibly autonomous ways (see Box 10.5).

Thinkpoint 10.4

Do you see managers who employ a system of responsible autonomy as being more enlightened, more humanistic perhaps, than those who prefer direct control? What would be your counter argument to their views?

Post-Fordism   It is said that management control in Post-Fordist organizational forms goes beyond DC and RA, by taking responsible autonomy to the level of self-management. It is claimed that increases in productivity, product quality and market responsiveness through lean production can only be achieved by fully involving worker production. As Kenney and Florida (1993) and Delbridge, Kenney and Lowe (1998) point out, under post-Fordism the separation of task design from task execution is reversed as workers become empowered to take ownership of production planning and product quality. Similarly, as noted earlier, just-in-time is heavily reliant upon not only accurate and effective production scheduling, and efficient and reliable equipment. For JIT to function effectively, decision making and problem solving must be devolved to personnel at all levels, right down to the point of production.

Kenney and Florida (1993) use the term 'innovation-mediated' production to capture what they see as the differences between the rigidities of conventional Fordist mass production methods and post-Fordist methods. 'Innovation-mediated', they contend, brings together research and development, product design, manufacturing operations and supply chain management in a much more 'functionally integrated' and 'strategically focused' way. Kenney and Florida claim this produces what they refer to as a 'laboratory-type' 'learning by doing' (see Chapters 4 and 5) environment in which collective rather than individual effort is harnessed through knowledge sharing and problem solving within and between functionally integrated cross-functional teams of managers, product design and production engineers, and front-line managers and workers.

Work transformation in the public sector

Mainstream accounts of transformational change in the public sector make similar claims. As Howkins and Thornton (2002) and McNulty and Ferlie (2005) explain, management's role in today's public services is to exploit the benefits of new organizational forms to create a climate 'in which everyone acknowledges that changes in [working practices and relationships] must occur and then become committed to the change' (Howkins and Thornton, 2002, p.7). As in other public and private sector industries, the overall goal is to create more efficient and cost-effective public services, and to gain workers' commitment to the achievement of this goal by empowering them. As Cochrane (2001) points out, the goal of transformational change in the public sector is to release the essential creativity, ingenuity and enterprising spirit of people in organizations that is stifled by traditional public sector bureaucratic practices, and occupational and professional boundaries.

Box 10.5: Direct control versus responsible autonomy

The term 'responsible autonomy' (RA) is used to differentiate organic forms of organization from mechanistic forms that rely upon 'direct control' (DC). These two terms were coined by Andrew Friedman (1977, 1990), who argues that all management control strategies fall somewhere along a continuum between DC and RA. Freidman has been criticized for overly simplifying management strategy. Nevertheless, the DC/RA typology is very useful for understanding the contingent nature of management control in organization.

These two 'ideal types' of control, Friedman argues, are determined essentially by the level of skill needed to perform tasks in any given industry or work situation. DC, which is associated with 'low trust' Taylorist management thinking and found normally in low-skilled work, whereas RA is found in highly skilled workplaces. RA is used to give workers leeway and encourage them to be proactive in decision making and problem solving to assist managers to achieve organizational goals. Its aim in releasing workers from DC is to harness their creative powers and adaptability to achieve organizational goals.

What is particularly noteworthy about this typology, as Friedman points out, is that management can find it extremely difficult to shift from RA to DC, and vice versa, once either one has become embedded in organizational practices. Both DC and RA, in other words, create their own habits and rules and related inflexibilities. As Friedman shows, employees subject to RA are usually reluctant to automatically surrender the relative freedom and self-determination they enjoy under this system of control. By the same token, those subject to DC are often disinclined to embrace a shift to RA, and are often suspicious about management's motivation for change, believing that the introduction of (ostensibly) autonomous work practices is likely to lead to work intensification, job losses and the erosion of their collective power.

"Just measuring your job performance..."

Image 10.3

SOURCE: © DAVE CARPENTER/CARTOONSTOCK.COM

Within the NHS for example, work organization has traditionally been 'centralized, hierarchical, authoritarian, closed [to change], formal, tightly controlled, top down and reactive' (Howkins and Thornton, 2002, p. 8). Today's public services, Howkins and Thornton suggest, can ill-afford this form of organization. Moreover, public sector workers, they claim, are no longer prepared to tolerate such a mechanistic organizational environment in which 'they are [simply] given orders, work only for monetary reward and remain in the same job for life' (Howkins and Thornton, 2002, p. 8).

The modernist faith in formal, objective and technical-rational decision making is evident in the way in which modernist organizations are governed by management thinking that is shaped by traditional hierarchical command-and-control mentalities and bureaucratic and administrative organizational structures. Under these arrangements, individual and group identities, careers, roles, responsibilities and opportunities are essentially fixed within boundaries determined by the power and position and status of the skills, expertise, knowledge and qualifications possessed by various professional and occupational groups.

Box 10.6 From modern to modern organizational forms?

For Howkins and Thornton, the concept of post-modernism usefully captures the reasons for the shift to new organizational forms in public services. Prior to the 1970s, public sector organizations were essentially modernist. Modernism is the traditional belief system of industrialization that stems from the Western scientific 'enlightenment' in the late 18th century (Hassard and Parker, 1992). Its basic premise is that the advancement of human knowledge and the unfolding of social progress over the past 200 years of industrialization has rested upon the logic and rationality of a valid set of 'value free' universal scientific laws, social assumptions and organizational arrangements, that bind human beings and organizations together (Hancock and Tyler, 2000). In short, modernist management thinking is a belief in the idea that there is, and can be, a 'one best way' of managing people in organizations in that a unified set of professional values and principles (e.g. systems and contingency theory, see Chapter 6) for guiding human judgement and social conduct can be discovered and harnessed for the greater benefit of a society (Hancock and Tyler, 2000). Post-modernism rejects

this idea that human knowledge and social organization are coherent, stable and unified (Hatch, 2002). It sees this as the 'myth' of modernist thinking, which is no more that a 'convenient fiction' that lays claim to an all-encompassing truth about organizations (Hancock and Tyler, 2000). As Hatch points out, the post-modern view is that knowledge in organizations is fundamentally fragmented, something that is 'produced in so many different bits and pieces [in so many different ways and contexts] that there can be no reasonable expectation that it will ever add up to an integrated and singular view' of reality that is shared by all members of an organization or a society (Hatch, 2002, p. 44). Post-modernism challenges the idea that organizations comprise of a coherent logically ordered and stable structure that remains fixed over time. As Burnes puts it, for post-modern theorists, organizations are 'inconsistent, ambiguous, multi-plitious and in a constant state of flux' (Burnes, 2002, p. 155). Burnes usefully illustrates the differences between modernist and postmodernist organizational forms in the following table (see also Clegg, 1990, p. 203).

Table 10.2 Modernist and post-modernist organizations

	Modernist organizations	Post-modernist organizations
Structure	Rigid bureaucracies	Flexible networks
Consumption	Mass markets	Niche markets
Technology	Technological determinism	Technological choice
Jobs	Differentiated, demarcated and de-skilled	Highly de-differentiated, de-demarcated and multi-skilled
Employment relations	Centralized and standardized	Complex and fragmentary

Source: Managing Change, Burnes, p155, reproduced with permission from Pearson Education Ltd.

performance, productivity and competitive advantage in organizations was precipitated by a series of distinct but related social, political and economic events that took place during the last quarter of the 20th century:

- The flagging performance of North American and Western European industries in the wake of global economic crises triggered by the 1973 and 1979 OPEC 'oil shocks'.
- The rise of new strong South-east Asian economies, mainly the Japanese economy, that in the 1970s and 1980s were suddenly outperforming Western organizations in world markets.
- The rise of highly competitive global capitalist market conditions, and increasingly diverse socio-cultural and consumer trends, within and between newly emerging supranational political-economic trading blocs.
- The emergence of new organizational forms, comprising novel complex 'customer/consumer-driven' flexible production regimes and business practices, pioneered by Japanese organizations, designed to meet these challenges (Oliver and Wilkinson, 1992; Storey, 1994).

Turning Japanese

For many theorists it is the Japanese economy and Japanese management and business practices that, directly or indirectly, have had the most influence on the emergence of new organizational forms, especially in manufacturing. During the 1970s Japan's phenomenal post-war economic growth was considered an 'economic miracle' (Whitehill, 1990). Its continued growth and competitiveness in the wake of a severe global economic downturn in the 1970s earned it unprecedented Western management attention (McKinlay and Starkey, 1992). One need only consult any current textbook on organizational behaviour (e.g. Huczynski and Buchanan, 2003; Mullins, 2001), human resource management (e.g. Legge, 1995; Redman and Wilkinson, 2002; Storey, 1994), change management (Burnes, 2002) and employee relations (Hollinshead, Nicholls and Tailby, 2002) to see the extent to which Japanese management and organizational practices were seen in the 1970s and early 1980s as a new way of improving productivity and competitiveness. As the 'excellence theorists' claim, Japanese managers were seemingly doing something 'right' in the face of these severe economic conditions that Western organizations failed to recognize and incorporate, or were not accustomed to. Japan's dominance within the emerging global economy was attributed (Whitehill, 1990) to a number of factors that were identified as peculiar to the Japanese post-war economy:

- Closely integrated and highly efficient family-owned and controlled cooperative business cartels.
- Japanese state supported capital investment in key strategic domestic and export industries.
- Novel manufacturing and market-responsive production regimes and a customer-driven business strategy.
- Japanese organizational culture and flexible teamworking practices and total quality control methods.

For the excellence theorists, the most important of these factors is Japanese organizational culture (Ouchi, 1982; Morgan, 1986; Whitehill, 1990). In the early 1980s, belief in the link between Japanese organizational culture and Japanese economic competitiveness gained widespread Western attention (McKinlay and Starkey, 1992). Japanese organizations were said to comprise highly motivated and committed employees, who shared a common sense of purpose, encouraged by clearly articulated corporate values and organizational goals communicated by strong 'visionary' management leadership. In contrast Western organizations were seen as overly bureaucratic, rule bound and governed by low-trust, inflexible, top-down, typically Fordist command-and-control management styles (McKinlay and Starkey, 1992) that tended to create conflict rather than cooperation between management and workers.

Thinkpoint 10.5

If Japanese organizational culture is strongly rooted in Japanese national culture, the social values of which are distinctly different from those of Western cultures, what implications does this have for learning from Japan?

As Dore (1976), Morgan (1986) and Whitehill (1990) show, Western cultures hold dear the belief that self-worth and social recognition is gained essentially by individual enterprise, hard work and personal achievement through competition with others. Japanese culture, on the other hand, rests on a belief that self-respect and social recognition at work and in society at large are achieved through collective and cooperative involvement with others, personal sacrifice, and a strong sense of commitment to the system as a whole, however much particular aspects of the system can be oppressive (see Kamata, 1979; Kondo, 1990). These values are in many ways anathema to the ideology of individualism that pervades traditional Western cultural beliefs and values (Morgan, 1986). That said, following an extended period of economic stagnation and scandals, there is less confidence in Japan about the long-term effectiveness of their form of economic organization. Reforms have been slowly and unevenly introduced and there is a clear break with tradition by new generations of urban Japanese who have not acquired the commitments (e.g. work ethic) and collective orientations that were so taken for granted by their parents. Likewise, in the West, techniques that were once applauded simply because they were applied in Japan are now assessed on the basis of notions of 'best practice' – notions that are no longer equated with what goes on in Japanese companies.

But why let the facts get in the way of a good story? The discovery of the apparent 'secret' of Japan's success led to a wholesale shift in (Western) management thinking during the 1980s. This cultural turn, as it has been referred to, coincided with a significant loss of faith in traditional Western modes of production and management (Burnes, 2002). Japanese-style organizational forms and organizational cultural practices, it seemed, suddenly held the key both to greater organizational effectiveness and human resource efficiency.

Critical management theorists challenge this. They show how cultural management is much more problematic than 'excellence theorists' assume (see Chapter 9), how it downplays the complexities of organizational culture and ignores, in particular, the politics of organizational culture change. As Edwards (1979) argues, management–employee relations is a 'contested terrain'. Conflict over culture change and work transformation arises not simply because of employees' fear of change, ignorance, weak management, inadequate leadership or poor (visionary) management communication, etc., as mainstream management theorists and practitioners are prone to argue. Conflict occurs, as noted already, because it threatens certain employee interests. It is a manifestation of more deep-seated tensions – what some would call contradictions – that are built in to capitalist work organizations. Conflict occurs also because of its real or perceived threat to the norms, values and identity concerns of the various professional and occupational groups within organizations upon whom managers rely in order to secure productive work and output. Moreover, these norms, values and identity concerns are developed within an institutional context (see Chapter 1). As they are endemic to this context, it is necessary to transform the entire context – including the established relations of inequality and power – in order to bring about a deep and sustained change in the 'culture'.

Occupational identity

Resistance to change in organizations occurs, in its various forms, for a whole host of reasons. As noted earlier, these include the real or perceived threat of unemployment, disempowerment, de-skilling, work intensification, loss of autonomy, and the erosion of traditional professional boundaries and demarcation lines that so often accompany organizational restructuring (see Scarborough and Burrell, 1996). Change, however, is also resisted in order to defend the symbolic realms of the organization, and to maintain prized working practices and occupational values (Ezzamel *et al.*, 2001). This is because work in modern society is not just a means of producing goods and providing services. It is also an important site of social identity.

For Deal and Kennedy (1982), along with most 'excellence theorists', a strong organizational culture can provide employees with a valued sense of purpose and self-identity. This assumption ignores the presence and role of *occupational* and organizational *sub*cultures in shaping employees' interests and identity concerns. Occupational as opposed to organizational culture, in other words, is more often than not the bedrock shaping identity (Trice, 1993). As Trice illustrates, occupational cultures mediate how members of an organization relate to each other, and also to how they make sense of their role and status in relation to others, especially to 'outsiders'.

Identities (occupational, professional or otherwise) are socially constructed through the processes of occupational and professional socialization. Through these processes, new members of a group learn to adopt the norms, values and beliefs and subscribe to the behaviour patterns of a (sub)culture, and how to act in accordance with its social codes, behavioural expectations and day-to-day rules and habits. Giddens (1991) explains how culture provides individuals with a sense of personal and group identity; a way of being something that is greater than the self, that is forged and maintained through distinctive codes of practice, rituals, ceremonies, discourses and sanctions against deviant behaviour. Although these codes, etc. are sometimes ambiguous, inconsistent and often contradictory, they still serve to produce and preserve a sense of group identity and feelings of solidarity that are highly resistant to change.

We can see from this that becoming a member of an occupation or profession involves not only acquiring formal training and education and entry qualifications through examination, professional licensing and accreditation or other formal 'rites of passage'. New entrants are also taught to act in ways deemed appropriate to a profession, to recognize and internalize its values, by observing its rituals, ceremonies and codes of practice and to protect the profession from interlopers. New entrants to a profession not only learn professional knowledge, skills and expertise from established members; at the same time they also learn how to conduct themselves towards client groups and others within organizations (including management and other non-management employees) not of their group or profession. As Trice (1993) points out, new entrants to a profession are not only required to learn that which gives them entry to their chosen career, they are also taught to observe and to internalize the values and ideology of their profession and to defend its ethos, interests and integrity from being undermined, transgressed or eroded by 'rogue' in-group members or 'outsiders'. It is all 'part of the package' of becoming a competent, credible member within a particular institutional context.

Becoming and being a doctor   The medical profession is a case in point. Like accountants, lawyers, engineers and architects, doctors are a distinct, self-conscious occupational group whose professional identity and ideology is forged over a long period of time through extensive professional training and education (Freidson, 1988). The most distinctive and highly prized characteristic of the occupational identity of the medical profession is its traditional autonomy from state control, management regulation, or lay interference in matters concerning medical work (Dent, 1995, 1998). This autonomy is not absolute. It is conditional and bestowed upon the medical profession by the state (and society) in return for their guarantee to ensure proper ethical, professional conduct and self-regulation that puts patient care and public interest before individual or professional self-interest (Dent, 1995).

Thinkpoint 10.6

In what sense is the autonomy so jealously guarded by doctors a product of their positioning within healthcare systems?

The high level of autonomy enjoyed by doctors within healthcare is entirely their preserve. Others, such as nurses, ambulance staff and various healthcare and community care workers supplementary to medical work do not enjoy the same special professional privilege, status and autonomy as doctors (Allsop and Saks, 2002). This gives doctors considerable professional power. The acknowledgement of the legitimacy of this power by both the state and society at large, bestowed upon them by the nature of their work, in turn gives doctors a strong sense of elite professional status and self-identity along with considerable social status and prestige (Freidson, 1988). Notwithstanding recent scandals concerning medical ethics in the NHS, following the Alderhey Hospital, Bristol Infirmary and Shipman Inquiries, the medical profession is still highly resistant to outside interference and government scrutiny of medical practices.

However, for the NHS the problem today is that the traditional 'positional power' of doctors and privileged status of the occupational boundaries are seen as dysfunctional – something a 'modern' NHS can ill afford. As Allsop and Saks (2002) point out, government intentions to introduce multi-professional education, more flexible career structures and the licensing of new professional groups in healthcare places considerable pressure on the traditional mainstream professions such as medicine and dentistry to reform themselves to accommodate these developments.

Doctors are not unreceptive to the claims that the NHS is under pressure to modernize through organizational transformation. What doctors object to is the basis of the reasoning behind attempts to alter the regulation of medicine; that is, to transform healthcare from being a citizen's right into a customer service, governed by quasi-market values and associated modes of accountability that render the medical profession open to what they themselves see as increasingly hostile government, management, media and public scrutiny (Dent, 1998).

Change and conflict at work in the NHS

Government and NHS managers are clearly aware that re-engineering the NHS has had a considerable negative effect upon motivation and morale within the medical profession (Department of Health, 2003). What doctors themselves object to is the way change has led to demands for them to adopt a managerial attitude to healthcare, to take on new roles and responsibilities and to meet government performance targets when, as they see it, they are already overworked and underpaid. However, by far their overriding concern behind the strength of their stance against organizational re-engineering is the question of their professional autonomy.

As a way of overcoming this problem, the NHS has sought to harness what they refer to as the 'creative tension' that they believe exists between doctors and managers in innovative ways. That is, rather than seek to erode tension they have sought to exploit it to release 'its creative potential', which they see as a means of reaching a genuine consensus for change, one in which both doctors and managers openly acknowledge and respect professional values and priorities. This is contingent upon creating a climate of 'responsible autonomy', whereby doctors maintain prime responsibility for clinical decision making, unhindered by management control, in exchange for acting *responsibly* towards the roles and responsibilities of management (Dent, 1998). What is remarkable here is the level of faith the NHS has in the ideology and principles of human resource management. It is remarkable because this is also the actual *source* of doctors' distrust of the NHS modernization agenda.

The problem for doctors is that the rhetoric of HRM – its call to enhance performance through 'more staff working differently' (Department of Health, 2003) to achieve higher standards of healthcare that privilege the sovereignty of individual consumer/customer expectations – bears little resemblance to their lived-experience of change. As this DoH report shows, doctors perceive change in the NHS to have led only to increasing stress and feelings of alienation and degradation due to a loss of social recognition, compounded by ever-increasing workloads, and constant pressure to meet government performance targets. Thus, far from winning doctors' 'hearts and minds' for change (Thompson and Warhurst, 1998), cultural management in the NHS has instead led to widespread disaffection. From the point of view of doctors, cultural management has severely ruptured the psychological contract between doctors and society, for example, by distorting traditional clinical priorities and by disregarding the sense of responsibility that clinicians have to the needs of individual patients, rather than financial budgets.

From professional to responsible autonomy? The NHS uses the term 'responsible autonomy' to capture the kind of working practices they are trying to instil in doctors and other healthcare workers. We have discussed this concept earlier (see Box 10.4). In this context, however, the NHS are not attempting to create a shift from direct control to responsible autonomy – rather they are attempting create a shift from *professional autonomy* to *responsible autonomy*. Friedman's concept of responsible autonomy does not include consideration of 'professional autonomy' (PA), although there are certain parallels between the two.

That said, there are also crucial differences. Both forms of autonomy give certain groups in an organization special status that differentiate them from others, and also certain 'situational power' in relation to management. Friedman's notion of RA originates from his analysis of private sector management expediency towards the problems of labour control in relation to the competitive pressures of capitalist political-economic market conditions and the possibility of worker resistance. PA, in contrast, is the outcome of competition and conflict between professional and managerial groups and, in the public sector, their relationship to the state, rather than in relation to a struggle between 'capital' and 'labour', as in Friedman's original analysis (Dent, 1995).

Of relevance in this context is Friedman's point that management usually finds it extremely difficult to shift from RA to DC, and vice versa, once either strategy is embedded in organizational practices. Friedman shows how employees subject to RA are usually reluctant to surrender the relative freedom and self-determination they enjoy under this system of control. By the same token, those subject to DC rarely take at face value the introduction of autonomous work practices, designed (ostensibly) to harness their commitment to the pursuit of new organizational norms, goals and values. Both systems of control, in other words, create their own *cultural* inflexibilities. That being the case, it follows that professional groups, in this case the medical profession, as Friedman's typology indicates, would be no less reluctant to surrender their PA to closer managerial scrutiny and state control.

Dent argues that RA is not a new concept within manager–doctor relations in the NHS. In his view RA has 'long been the preferred control strategy of the British State towards the medical profession' (Dent, 1995, p. 87), but one which it has been unable to establish because of persistent counter measures by the medical profession to prevent themselves from 'being incorporated into the state apparatus of healthcare' (ibid, p. 88). As he points out, the current attempts to renegotiate the medical profession's relationship to the state is just the latest in a long line of similar attempts stretching back as far as the advent of the UK post-war welfare state (Dent, 1995). What has prevented the state from realizing this goal has been the medical profession's determination to maintain the privileged status of their professional right to 'clinical autonomy' as *the* principal mechanism for governing the 'frontier of control' (Friedman, 1977) between doctors and the state, doctors and managers and other occupational and professional groups supplementary to medicine within healthcare.

New organizational forms

It was noted in the 'Mainstream approach' section of this chapter that non-mainstream organization and management theorists claim that working practices under new organizational forms are not what they are cracked up to be. They lead to greater not lesser management power and control (Garrahan and Stewart, 1992). On the face of things, workers are seemingly empowered to take 'responsibility' for the organization of production, but in reality their performance is closely controlled and constantly monitored through management surveillance (Sewell and Wilkinson, 1992) and information technology (Zuboff, 1988). As a result, the brave new post-modern workplace fails to live up to its promise of providing a more interesting and satisfying experience of work, and seldom if at all results in any meaningful empowerment.

Critical organization and management theorists acknowledge that employees in many organizations today do work in ways that differ significantly from traditional Fordist work practices. However, they also point out that hierarchy, rigid bureaucracy, command-and-control management practices, low-skilled detailed divisions of labour, strict demarcation and unequal rewards, recognition and remuneration determined by class, gender, race and social inequalities have far from disappeared in the new workplace (Thompson and Warhurst, 1998). There is a wealth of empirical evidence suggesting that there is a considerable difference between the espoused values of

"Remember the good old days when it was a suggestion box?"

Image 10.4

post-Fordist organizations and the extent to which post-modern values and beliefs are actually embraced, let alone internalized, by their members (Casey, 1996; Kunda, 1990). Many commentators also question the claim that cultural management alone can raise employee performance and productivity, change values and reshape beliefs and attitudes.

As Burnes (2002) points out, there is an assumption in culture change literature that 'attitude change' leads to voluntary 'behavioural change', and that individuals will willingly (want to) put aside their individual self-interest for the greater good of their organization. This mainstream literature assumes that good management communication and effective leadership will always overcome internal conflict and struggles between individuals or occupational or professional groups over the outcomes of change. Hope-Hailey (1998) shows how such assumptions ignore the influence of organizational structures – in the form of hierarchy, specialist organizational, departmental and occupational boundaries, etc. – on organizational culture change. The cultivation of new roles, responsibilities and relationships in organizations is often driven as much, if not more, by structural change rather than cultural change. These writers also show how new organizational forms are heavily reliant on new forms of accountability and surveillance techniques that are concerned

HORRORSCOPE®

New office equipment will greatly increase your productivity. This won't go unnoticed by higher-ups!

Image 10.5

with more than simply attempting to win employees' hearts and minds (see Thompson and Warhurst, 1998).

The assumption that culture change leads to behaviour change ignores the spatial and temporal domains of organizations and cultures. There is evidence that improvements in productivity and employee performance through cultural management programmes, in so-called 'excellence' organizations, have rarely been sustained over time (Burnes, 2002). Power, politics and conflict are widely ignored or trivialized. This is because a fundamental assumption in 'excellence' cultural management theory is that organizational cultures are essentially unitary and apolitical (Anthony, 1995; Hatch, 2002; Martin, 2000; Thompson and Warhurst, 1998; Willmott, 1993). As labour process theorists in particular demonstrate, workplace cultures comprise a complex web of competing occupational and organizational cultural and subcultural work groups, whose norms, values, beliefs and behaviour patterns are conditioned by particular occupational and professional values and interest rather than those of the organizations that employ them (Thompson and McHugh, 1998; Thompson and Warhurst, 1998; Knights and Willmott, 1990). In this context, the idea that organizations are open to change through top-down strategic human resource intervention is highly questionable.

Here we return to 'lean' production and to the argument made by Delbridge (1995, p. 803), for example, that it is a subtle system of managerial power, control, surveillance and accountability that could hardly be more distant from its humanistic image of empowering employees (Delbridge and Turnbull, 1992). Empowerment within and between teams in the new workplace takes place only in accordance with narrowly defined boundaries that closely monitor and control, rather than expand the scope for workers to exercise discretion (Delbridge, 1995; Delbridge and Turnbull, 1992; Sewell, 1998; Sewell and Wilkinson, 1992). Even where scope for increased levels of worker involvement and decision making does exist, ideas put forward that go beyond those that offer up productivity gains or cut costs are largely ignored or marginalized (see Buchanan and Preston, 1992; Kamata, 1979). In short, their conclusion is that 'total quality control', 'teamworking' and 'flexible' working practices do not really empower workers to play a more active and autonomous role in production. And, for this reasons, it should come as no surprise to us when workers fail to respond positively to efforts to introduce it.

Resistance in the new workplace

There are many studies within the literature that have examined how and to what extent new forms of work organization, whether on the factory floor, in the office or in the public sector domain of healthcare, can be resisted. Leaving aside the view that resistance is minimal or even impossible because the power of management, supported by the state's employment laws, is ultimately overwhelming, resistance of one form or another is always possible. It has been shown by McKinlay and Taylor (1998), in their research in the UK microelectronics industry, that even under conditions that could hardly be more favourable for close management control methods to flourish uncontested, resistance occurred. A considerable number of critical case studies support McKinlay and Taylor's findings (e.g. Graham, 1994; Pollert, 1996; Rinehart, Robertson, Huxley and Wareham, 1996; Stephenson, 1996). Even those studies that proclaim the 'end of worker resistance' show evidence of resistance. For example, Zuboff (1988) argues, through the use of information technology the contemporary workplace is now a site of consolidated managerial disciplinary power, control and surveillance from which there is no escape. But at the same time, as Sakolosky (1992, p. 241) points out, Zuboff herself shows evidence of resistance. The workers she studied were able to avoid the disciplinary 'power effect' of computer surveillance by cheating on certain working practices and operational procedures. Managers also manipulated output and productivity records in a way that could not be detected. Sewell and Wilkinson (1992, p. 293) talk about the inescapability of 'panoptic' power, control and surveillance under lean production, but at the same time also note evidence of workers falsifying output and productivity figures. Misbehaviour of this kind is not uncommon (Ackroyd and Thompson, 1999), for no other reason than that new organizational forms promise much but often deliver very little in terms of improving the lived-experience of work. It is also worth noting that resistance is often not so much an attempt to *escape from work* as an attempt to *escape into work* (Sturdy, 1997). This term, escape into work, refers to how workers deal with boring and monotonous work by establishing routines and rituals that enable them to 'turn off' and perform tasks without actively thinking about the work being performed and what is taking place around them.

CASE STUDY 10.2 Resistance at Northern Plant

At the beginning of this chapter is was shown how workers at Northern Plant refused to accept management's claim that lean production provides more interesting and satisfying work, and how they resisted new working practices through misbehaviour rather than through industrial action. The reason for their resistance was that although lean production would in fact lead to significant changes to the organization of the plant's manufacturing resources, as workers saw it, the actual nature of work itself would change little.

When Northern Plant first invested in lean production in the early 1980s, it comprised of five main manufacturing sections. Over the ten years prior to Mike's (the new HR manager) arrival these sections were re-engineered a number of times, and given different labels each time: lean manufacturing cells, product-focused cells, customer-focused cells, autonomous business units, strategic business units and then finally profit centres. Workers themselves were also organized into teams: manufacturing teams to begin with, then autonomous production teams, self-managing teams, and finally 'high-commitment teams'. Yet,

from their point of view, the work they performed remained what it had always been, a dull and tedious process of operating drilling, boring, grinding, turning, de-burring and spot-welding machines that turned out various parts and sub-components that were assembled into finished products along traditional Fordist assembly lines that required little if any real skills.

When lean production was introduced managers were, however, at a loss to understand why workers resisted it and saw it as work intensification. What these managers failed to appreciate was that it was not simply the opportunity to work independently of direct management control that motivated workers to work 'smarter' to 'make the numbers'. What they valued most was the opportunity to earn 'free time' during working hours. They resisted lean production, therefore, not just because it was perceived as work intensification but because they saw it as an attack on the 'free time' and leisure activities they had become accustomed to, which they believed they earned and were rightfully entitled to in exchange for their efforts to meet production targets ahead of schedule.

Thinkpoint 10.7

If you were Mike, how would you go about addressing this problem?

In the introduction to the case study at the beginning of this chapter, you were asked to imagine that you were a member of Mike's change team who had been given responsibility for calming workers' fears and concerns about lean production. Imagine now that you are a first-line manager who had worked at the plant prior to Mike's arrival, and who had subscribed to the informal system of production described above.

For years, not only had you condoned the unspoken agreement that once output quotas had been reached shop floor workers could spend their time as they saw fit, but from time to time you and some of your first-line management colleagues had also taken part in various leisure activities yourself, including sleeping on nightshift and occasionally spending time in the local pub during working hours. Then suddenly, overnight, following the launch of lean production at the plant, along with

other first-line managers you find yourself charged with the responsibility for introducing new teamworking practices and quality control methods. You can no longer continue to accommodate previous informal agreements whereby you trade time for output and then turn a blind eye to how workers spend their time once they have reached the agreed output quotas.

At team briefings you and your colleagues explain the need for change, the need for workers to accept new working practices and the benefits these can offer them in terms of skill enhancement. You are required to 'sell' these new ideas to workers, and convince them that the 'old way of doing things' can no longer continue. In response, both the shop stewards and workers remind you that any proposed changes in working practices are ultimately subject to trade union agreement, which can only be reached through formal negotiations with senior management, and, therefore, although they are willing to listen to what you have to say you should not assume that this means that they are willing to accept new ways of working. At the end of your briefing both the shop stewards and shop floor workers claim that you have done a very poor job in selling lean production to them because you have made it more than apparent that it will undoubtedly lead to work intensification and possibly redundancies. You don't accept this.

Fearful of what senior managers will make of these claims, you respond by trying again to explain that 'working smarter rather than harder' and 'doing more with less' does not necessarily mean doing more with less shop floor personnel. You remind them again that the old ways of doing things cannot continue, and that whether they like it or not, corporate management are determined to introduce new systems and work practices.

You suddenly find yourself being denounced as a hypocrite. Along with the other first-line managers, you are reminded of your own 'misbehaviour' under the old system: your poor time-keeping and attendance, the extended lunch breaks and rest allowances you were happy to take, and how, like workers themselves, you also enjoyed participating in card schools, sleeping during nightshifts and how you (with other first-line managers) occasionally accompanied workers to the pub during working hours. In the light of this, you are asked how you have found the nerve to now condemn these activities, and how you are going to explain to Mike's change team why you have lost your credibility as a manager.

You witness other similar instances of workers using such tactics designed to discredit other first-line managers. What you find particularly frustrating and humiliating is the enjoyment workers get from ridiculing you and your colleagues, by threatening to expose how you previously failed to manage workers properly and allowed them to 'skive off' so much during working hours, and how you yourselves also regularly 'skived off'.

You witness a cell manager, who as a shop floor worker had regularly slept in a comfortable cardboard construction he made for himself while working the nightshift, being told during a briefing session, at which he announced that productivity needed to improve, that 'people who live in cardboard houses shouldn't throw stones'! Similarly, a first-line manager who had acquired the nickname 'Disco Dave', as a consequence of making regular visits to a local night club during his nightshift, is told by workers that they do appreciate that things may well need to change, but that there is still no need to make a 'song and dance' about it!

Above and beyond this kind of banter, workers also presented 'reasonable' arguments against the proposed new working practices, which they know you cannot accept. Certain workers, for example, who claimed that they do of course recognize the benefits of teamworking, argue that in practice teamwork would be unworkable due to the age of certain workers and because of personality clashes. To support this claim they point out that, as they see it, under lean production the stamina of younger workers would put undue stress upon older workers, which was unfair. Some argue that workers who are fundamentally 'lazy' would end up being 'carried' by other team members. Carrying lazy workers, they explain, would not only impede team performance but also possibly lead to 'hard working' team members being perceived as 'lazy'. Others claim they are 'loners', who are unsuited to teamwork, and state that they would therefore rather work independently from others and have their own individual output targets. Some simply question the need for change, and argue that if is true that lean production empowers them to have a 'say in things', they would prefer things stayed as they are! Others exercise their 'say in things', by identifying fellow workers who they feel they could perhaps work well with within a team environment, those who they believe they would find it difficult to work with, and those who they are not prepared to work with at all. Some others announce that they intend to refuse to work in teams with certain workers because they simply don't like each other. To further ridicule the situation, others announce to you that they do in fact 'like each other', but that they had better not be allowed to work together because their mutual interests would distract them from 'getting on with the job'.

All these comments and arguments are used to point out to you that it stands to reason that if management were to put certain workers in teams together this would undoubtedly undermine the discipline of the team and impede its performance, and therefore it was only right that any responsibility for subsequent poor performance should ultimately lie with those – that is management – who decide to put them together in the first place.

When you attempt to counter these arguments you are told that although you obviously have considerable management experience you still don't really understand the shop floor, nor appreciate the problems teamworking can cause. In the end, like Mike's change team, you are challenged to come clean and admit that all you *really* want is to regain control of the shop floor – something that has been lost over the years because of management's own 'shenanigans' and poor 'man management' skills. In the process you are also asked how you are going to explain to senior and corporate managers why flexibility, teamworking and total quality control methodologies had *seemingly* been introduced but are not working because you have gone through the motions of being committed to introducing change but, in practice, you have allowed, things to continue as before.

Exercise 10.3

- How would you counter the claim that you are a hypocrite?
- How would you explain to Mike why you subscribed to, and why you sometimes took part in the plant's leisure activities?
- Do you think the way you ran the shop floor and managed production before Mike's arrival makes you a 'bad' manager?

Summary of the issues raised in this case study

These episodes of resistance at Northern Plant show how workers in organization use humour and misbehaviour to expose what they see as the inconsistencies and contradictions in the effort to engineer change, such as the change to lean production, including 'teamworking' and 'continuous improvement'.

It might be argued that this account of resistance at Northern Plant shows how discrediting teamworking and new organizational practices and working arrangements in this way, and with them the credibility and authority of those presenting them, is simply a tactic used by workers to entertain themselves and to inflate their own sense of self-importance. But we should be aware that such misbehaviour is also a 'consciousness-raising' exercise. It may be a method used by shop stewards and 'politically astute' workers to alert others to what is at stake in 'change management' programmes. By using humour, it is possible to demonstrate, in an accessible and enjoyable way, how these programmes are ostensibly human-centred, yet on closer examination are perhaps more to do with management's concern to gain control of production and working practices. Greater control is needed in order to improve productivity, rather than to empower workers to have a greater say in the organization and management of production. Empowerment is simply a means to the end of productivity because, in a leaner more flexible manufacturing system, it is necessary to obtain the ('responsible') involvement and cooperation of workers in order to make the system function effectively.

It is worth mentioning that this is not a fictitious account of resistance through misbehaviour. Northern Plant does, or rather *did* exist. The plant was closed down by MotorCo, its multinational parent company, in 2004 and relocated to an eastern European country where labour costs are much lower than in the United Kingdom (see Chapter 12). Plans to shift production to this new location were drawn up by corporate management even when they were claiming that the introduction of lean production, which would improve the plant's productivity and competitiveness, would serve to guarantee its future within the industry and, with this, security of employment for its workforce.

We can draw several conclusions from this, including the capacity of managers who seek the respect and trust of employees to engage in forms of deception and disingenuousness that subvert this quest. But what is perhaps most noteworthy is that it is profit maximization above all else that ultimately governs (corporate) management thinking and decision making, at least at MotorCo. For all the talk about employee-centric work organizations, empowerment, enlightened management thinking and the rhetoric of workers being stakeholders in the organizations they work for, labour nevertheless is regarded and remains primarily a resource to be exploited and then disposed of when more promising opportunities to reduce costs and/or to increase returns on investments for *shareholders* are calculated to exist elsewhere. Likewise, in the case of the NHS, doctors found themselves being treated more like workers (or wage labourers) who were required to place the achievement of targets set by politicians and managers above their control of the quality of healthcare. They, too, were the recipients of lectures from management, which enjoined them to reorganize and 'modernize' their working practices, but which paid little or no regard to their own well-being or the logic of their organization of work. Instead, their way of working tended to be viewed as, at best, irrational and, at worst, entirely self-serving.

Strengths and limitations of the critical approach

The critical view of the shift from 'low-trust' Fordist organizational forms and work practices, to flexible 'high-trust' employee conditions questions the mainstream claim that under these conditions managers seek to utilize not only the physical but also the subjective and intellectual capacities of the human subject. As we have seen in this section, under so-called 'high-trust' innovative production regimes workers are still exploited. The principal contribution of a critical approach, then, is to challenge the credibility and expose the limits of mainstream thinking. It also anticipates the possibility of organizing work differently but without providing any blueprints for such change. Indeed, to do so would be rather contradictory as it would assume or promote the existence of an intellectual elite, equivalent to a managerial elite, that would tell everyone else what to do. Not only would this simply reinvent the division between managers and workers but it would also likely produce the same kinds of difficulties, tensions and frustrations.

The critical approach raises questions about the contradictions and oppressive outcomes of new organizational forms, but it does not show how there may be overcome. In other words, it does not demonstrate how more democratic and emancipatory conditions of employment could be realized so as to replace dominant market-driven management priorities and concerns about the all-importance of growth and corporate profit. This is not to say that understanding organizations in a critical context is a fruitless exercise. It leaves open important questions about how organization might (one-day) shift to more genuine human-centred organizational conditions and practices. As our case study shows, people in organization are capable of 'messing with power', to protect valued working practices but remain limited in the challenges they pose to managerial power and control (Alvesson and

Willmott, 1996). As we can see, worker resistance at Northern Plant, which is the case in most organizations, had no clear or explicit political or emancipatory aim or purpose. It was, above all, a 'game', an end in itself, that enabled workers to retain a degree of self-respect at management's expense. But it was in a context of resignation to the overwhelming capacity of big business to move its manufacturing capability elsewhere. In principle, critical analysis can challenge and counter such resignation and defeatism by suggesting how, for example, struggles in different workplaces and across different domains of society (e.g. gender relations, environmentalist movements) can be linked together through an appreciation of their relatedness as aspects of subordination within a wider totality of modern capitalist economies.

Conclusions

In this chapter we have considered the rise and development of various new organizational forms in both public and private sector organizations. In the 'mainstream approach' section we looked at how mainstream theorists see them as a positive development that has created new opportunities and possibilities for both organizations and their employees, which (in theory at least) represent the beginning of the end of alienating work. As the mainstream theorists see it, efficiency, competitiveness and profitability continue to be of key importance to organizations, but what has become more important is continuous innovation and adaptability to ever-changing global market conditions and business environments. This, managers increasingly believe, can only be achieved through people who are highly motivated and committed; and that this approach to work necessitates them being allowed to exercise greater discretion. Workers must be allowed to operate more freely from direct management control, to use their ingenuity and creativity to achieve organizational goals.

In the 'Critical approach' section, we looked at the rather different interpretation of change and innovation offered by critical organizations and management theorists. Without denying that employees in many organizations today do evidently work in ways that differ significantly from those of traditional modernist organizations, critical students of organization suggest that new organizational forms and work practices are not necessarily as they are described in mainstream accounts. Hierarchy, rigid bureaucracy, command-and-control management practices, low-skilled detailed divisions of labour, strict demarcation and unequal rewards, recognition and remuneration are hardly swept away in contemporary organizations. At the very least, there is reason to believe that a considerable difference exists between the *espoused* 'excellent' management ideas, values, beliefs and control methods in (so-called) post-modern organizations and how these ideas and values are worked out in practice.

Mainstream theorists seem to think that employees are passive yet enthusiastic recipients of 'excellence' management jargon, and are likely to 'buy into' new working practices without looking critically at what empowerment and teamworking will mean in practice in terms of workloads, their career prospects and job security. But, equally, we should not assume that employees will always, automatically resist change. It means only that employees are unlikely to take what managers say at face value and that they may be somewhat reluctant to put aside individual personal advancement and individual self-interest for the greater good of their organization. As Flemming and Spicer (2003) show, at the level of the self, employees in organizations who are mistrustful of management promises often adopt a cynical distance from the normative control and behavioural expectations of the rhetoric of empowerment, teamworking and notions of self-management. They may, for example, conform outwardly while doing the absolute minimum to implement or facilitate the desired change. Cynicism and other 'distancing' strategies of resistance (Collinson, 1994), it is worth emphasizing, do not prevent employees in organizations from performing their roles. Cynicism can allow workers (and managers in some cases) to deal with the contradictions and superficiality of 'new wave' management philosophies and values.

So where do we go from here? Change and innovation, in the form of lean manufacturing, 'new public management' and many other 'advances' in work organization have given rise to a whole host of new structures, networks, business and management practices and new ways of working, and people in organization have adapted to them – to the new roles, relationship and responsibilities they have brought with them. What mainstream theorists ignore is how the cultivation of new roles,

Knights, D. and Willmott, H. (1990) *Labour Process Theory*, Aldershot: Gower.

Kondo, D. (1990) *Crafting Selves: Power, Gender and Discourses of Identity of a Japanese Peripheral Worker*, Chicago: Chicago University Press.

Kunda, G. (1990) *Manufacturing Culture*, Philadelphia PA: Temple University Press.

Legge, K. (1995) *Human Resource Management: Rhetorics and Reality*, London: Macmillan Press Ltd.

Legge, K. (2005) *Human Resource Management*, London: Macmillan.

Littler, C. (1982) *The Development of the Labour Process in Capitalist Societies*, London: Heinemann.

Martin, J. (2000) *Organization Culture: Mapping the Terrain*, London and New York: Sage.

McKinlay, A. and Starkey, K. (1992) *Strategy and the Human Resource*, Oxford: Blackwell Business.

McKinlay, A. and Taylor, P. (1998) 'Through the looking glass: Foucault and the politics of production', in A. McKinlay and K. Starkey (eds.) *Foucault, Management and Organization*, London: Sage.

McNulty, T. and Ferlie, E. (2005) *Reengineering the NHS: The Complexities of Organizational Transformation*, Oxford: Oxford University Press.

Morgan, G. (1986) *Images of Organizations*, London: Sage Publications.

Morley, L. (2003) *Quality and Power in Higher Education*, Milton Keynes: Open University Press.

Mullins, L. (2001) *Management and Organizational Behaviour*, London: Pitman/Financial Times.

Oliver, N. and Wilkinson, B. (1992) *The Japanization of British Industry*, Oxford: Blackwell.

Ouchi, W. (1982) *Theory Z*, Reading, MA: Addison-Wesley.

Pascale, R. T. and Athos, A. G. (1982) *The Art of Japanese Management*, Harmondsworth: Penguin.

Peters, T. and Waterman, R. (1982) *In Search of Excellence: Lessons from America's Best-Run Companies*, London: Harper & Row.

Piore, M. and Sabel, C. (1984) *The Second Industrial Divide*, New York: Basic Books.

Pollert, A. (1988) 'Dismantling flexibility', *Capital and Class* (34):445–567

Pollert, A. (1996) 'Team work on the assembly line: Contradiction and the dynamics of union resilience', In P. Ackers, C. Smith and P. Smith (eds.) *The New Workplace and Trade Unionism*, London: Routledge.

Redman, T. and Wilkinson, A. (2002) *Contemporary Human Resource Management*, London: Financial Times/Prentice Hall.

Rinehart, J., Robertson, D., Huxley, C. and Wareham, J. (1996) 'Reunifying conception and execution of work under Japanese production management? A Canadian case study', in P. Ackers, C. Smith and P. Smith (eds.) *The New Workplace and Trade Unionism: Critical Perspectives on Work and Organization*, London: Routledge.

Sakolsky, R. (1992) 'Discipline, power and the labour process', in A. Sturdy, D. Knights and H. Willmott (eds.) *Skill and Consent: Contemporary Studies in the Labour Process*, London: Routledge.

Scarborough, H. and Burrell, G. (1996) 'The axeman cometh: The changing role and knowledge of middle managers', in S. Clegg and G. Palmer (eds.) *The Politics of Management Knowledge*, London: Sage Publications.

Schonberger, R. (1982) *Japanese Manufacturing Techniques: Nine Hidden Lessons in Simplicity*, New York: The Free Press.

Schonberger, R. (1986) *World Class Manufacturing*, New York: The Free Press.

Sewell, G. (1998) 'The discipline of teams: The control of team-based industrial work through electronic and peer surveillance', *Administrative Science Quarterly* 43(2):397–428.

Sewell, G. and Wilkinson, B. (1992) ' "Someone to watch over me": Surveillance, discipline and the just-in-time process', *Sociology* 26(2):271–289.

Sharpe, D. (1998) 'Changing Managerial Control Strategies and Subcultural Processes: *An Ethnographic Study of the Hano Assembly Line*'. Paper Presented at the 14th Annual Labour Process Conference, Aston.

Sissons, K. (1994) *Personnel Management*, Oxford: Blackwell.

Smith, C. (1991) Automation to Flexible Specialisation: a déjà vu of Technology Panaceas, in Pollert, A. (eds) *Farewell to Flexibility*. Oxford: Blackwell.

Stephenson, C. (1996) 'The different experiences of trade unions in two Japanese plant's', in P. Ackers, C. Smith and P. Smith (eds.) *The New Workplace and Trade Unionism: Critical Perspectives on Work Organisation*, London: Routledge.

Strathern, M. (2000) *Audit Cultures: Anthropological Studies in Accountability, Ethics and the Academy* London: Routledge.

Storey, J. (ed.) (1994) *New Wave Manufacturing Strategies: Organizational and Human Resource Management Dimensions*, London: Paul Chapman Publishing.

Sturdy, A. (1997) 'The consultancy process: An insecure business?', *Journal of Management Studies* 34(3):389–413.

Thompson, P. and McHugh, D. (1998) *Work Organization: A Critical Introduction*, London: Macmillan.

Thompson, P. and Warhurst, C. (1998) *Workplaces of the Future*, London: Macmillan Press.

Trice, A. (1993) *Occupational Culture*, Chicago: Chicago University Press.

Warhurst, C. Grugulis. I. and Keep, P. (2004) *Skills That Matter*. Macmillan Press

Watson, T. (2002) *Organising and Managing Work*. 2nd edition. Prentice Hall. Finance Hall.

Whitehill, A. (1990) *Japanese Management: Tradition and Transition*, London: Routledge.

Willmott, H. (1993) 'Strength is ignorance, slavery is freedom: Managing culture in modern organizations', *Journal of Management Studies* 30(4):681–720.

Willmott, H. (1996) 'Managing the academics: Commodification and control in the development of university education in the UK', *Human Relations* 4(9):993–1027.

Wilson, F. (2004) *Organization at Work: A Critical Introduction*, Oxford: Oxford University Press.

Womack, J., Jones, D. and Roos, D. (1990) *The Machine That Changed the World: The Triumph of Lean Production*, New York: Rawson Macmillan.

Wood, S. (eds.) (1989) *The Transformation of Work*, London: Unwin Hyman.

Worthington, F. (2004) 'Management Change and Culture in the NHS: Rhetoric and reality', *Clinicians in Management* 12(2):55–68.

'Why British Doctors Are So Unhappy?' The National Health Confederation (2003).

Zuboff, S. (1988) *The Age of the Smart Machine*, Oxford: Heinemann.

11 | Technology

Theodore Vurdubakis

Key concepts and learning objectives

By the end of this chapter you should understand:

- Why the role of technology in organizations has received so much attention.

- The main different approaches that have been used to analyse the complex interrelationship between technology and organizational behaviour.

- A number of major studies that illustrate the strengths and limitations of these approaches.

- The main disputes and debates about the value of the different approaches in explaining the patterns of potential relationships between human behaviour and technology.

- How the concepts of power, knowledge, freedom, identity, inequality and insecurity can be used in the analysis of these relationships.

Aims of the chapter

This chapter will:

- Introduce the different strands in mainstream and critical thinking on the issue of the interrelationship between technology and organization.

- Present, explain and illustrate the key concepts that are relevant to mainstream and critical analysis, such as technological determinism and the social shaping of technology.

- Present a number of major studies that show mainstream and critical thinking on this topic 'in action'.

- Evaluate the assumptions and values underpinning mainstream and critical perspectives associated with technology, management and organizations.

Overview and key points

Technology plays a key role in the ways we organize ourselves and in the ways we work and live our lives. This chapter will review and evaluate the main approaches that can be used to understand the complex interrelationship between technology and organizational behaviour. Technological determinism, while somewhat out of favour in certain academic circles, is still prevalent in mainstream accounts of technology and organization. At the core of technological determinist thinking is the assumption that the technical properties of particular technological devices are the cause of corresponding developments in organizations or even society. Therefore, a crucial question for much of the mainstream literature is how organizations can best adapt to the demands placed upon them by new technologies. More critical approaches, however, condemn this perspective as rather too simplistic and one-sided. To counter the dominance of technological determinism a number of alternative forms of explanation have been proposed, among them the social shaping of technology, the social construction of technology and actor-network theory. What most of these approaches have in common, apart from their rejection of technological determinism, is the desire to redress the balance by bringing to the fore the role that organizational, social and cultural factors play in the shaping of technology itself.

The 'just so story' in Box 11.1 narrates a typical encounter between new technology and organization. For as you know from personal experience a university lecture is a remarkable feat of organization. The one or two hours it takes to attend this particular lecture represent but the tip of a (bureaucratic) iceberg. Months ago, syllabuses and curricula were compiled, scrutinized and approved by the relevant academic decision-making bodies. University timetables were compiled, time-slots and rooms allocated, lecture notes were prepared and presentational aids assembled. Registration and option forms were filled in and submitted to specified deadlines. Even the room itself could be understood as but the material expression of a set of 'social technologies' in Fox's (1974) sense. A lecture room embodies a particular set of organizational relationships, for instance, between the lecturer and her audience or between those who have the right, and often the obligation, to be there and those who do not. (Remember how tough it was to gain admittance to university?) Many people have to carry out particular tasks in prescribed ways (including students and lecturers but also secretaries, cleaners, security staff, etc.) in order for this particular lecture to take place.

The mobile phone's merry ringtone could be a sign that this picture is about to be dramatically transformed. To paraphrase Philip Agre (2000) (from whose work this little vignette has been adapted), anyone in the world can now reach into the controlled space of the lecture theatre and make a technological device vibrate or emit a little tune. Suddenly the whole of the 'outside' world of activities and relationships can no longer be kept out of the lecture room. A sign of the times?

Thinkpoint 11.2

Let's note at this point that Jon's or Raj's activities during the lecture may be hidden from the lecturer but are of course visible to the mobile phone network which 'knows' where they are and what they are doing. Indeed our everyday activities and interactions are increasingly technologically mediated and generate as a matter of course a multitude of electronic traces – a version of the phenomenon Zubuoff (1989) descrebes as the 'information panopticon' (see Chapter 9; Garfinkel, 2001). Can you identify the electronic traces you generated today? Mobile phone calls? ATM usage?

Go to http://aclu.org/pizza/images/screen.swf and watch the clip. Make sure you pay attention to the cursor movements. Is this the future? Are we witnessing as some suggest the 'death of privacy? Is that a bad things? What, if anything, can be done and by whom?

In the days before mobile communication every social activity and relationship had its place. You would interact with your friends at the Dog and Duck, with your bank at your local branch and with your boss at work. You could conceivably run into someone from your bank in the Dog and Duck but you would not attempt to do your banking there. Your Significant Other could always ring you on the telephone, but telephones were located in specific places. Insofar as communication devices have now become truly mobile, the close correspondence between activities, relationships and places is starting to break down. The many relationships (family, partners, friends, work) that traditionally made up a person's life can no longer be kept as separate as they used to be. They now, so to speak, follow you around in a form of electronically mediated continual presence. Many see here a symptom of the imminent 'death of distance' (Cairncross, 1998). Be that as it may, we certainly appear to be witnessing 'a tremendous shift in human relationships: from episodic to always-on' (Agre, 2000, p. 10). Boundaries between inside and outside previously marked by the lecture theatre walls are now permeable. Furthermore, the boundaries between home and work, work time and leisure time, are also blurred.

For those of a technologically optimistic disposition, these are all positive developments bringing with them individual empowerment and a new freedom of association. For others, these are negative developments heralding the erosion of leisure time, intensified control and increasingly shallow social relationships. Organizations as we know them (universities, theatres, churches) tend to be dependent upon, and a reflection of, the (until now) episodic and place-specific character of social life. The way that the mobile phone disrupted the organization of the lecture could be seen as an example of that. Note also, however, that mobile communications also enable new practices of micro-coordination – recall for instance Y's organizing of his little excursion. As discussed in Chapters 7, 10 and 13, for many management and organization researchers we are witnessing the dawn of a remarkable technologically induced-transformation of prevailing structures of organization and enterprise, such as the emergence of the 'post-bureaucratic' organization. What would an electronic-age, post-bureaucratic university look like?

Thinkpoint 11.3

The UK e-University (UKeU) was launched with much pomp and publicity in 2000. Its aim was to allow (mainly) overseas students to earn a British university degree by studying online. Its failure was acknowledged in 2004 when the scheme was terminated. In four years of operation, the project had cost £62 million in public funding and had only managed to enrol 900 students (a cost of around £56 000 per student). In your view, and based on your experience of university learning, what are the reasons for this debacle? Does it mean that distance is not quite dead?

You can find more information at the website of *Computing* magazine (e.g. http://www.computing.co.uk/specials/1156350). You can also go to Langdon Winner's website at http://www.rpi.edu/~winner/apm1.html and check out the 'Automatic Professor Machine' (or APM for short). What are the concepts of knowledge and technology being satirized here?

Mainstream perspectives: Technological determinism

You will have read (or heard people express) views along the lines: 'Technological developments X and Y are all but inevitable. The best people can do is try to adapt to them'. Such views are typically espoused by both those who are exceptionally optimistic and those particularly pessimistic about current technological advances. It is the theoretical outlook of choice for both those who dream that technology will ultimately deliver a society of freedom and plenty *and* for those who fear that out of control nano-robots will someday munch the world into grey goo. For large sections of the mass media it is something of a commonplace that the existence of a technology will inevitably lead to its use, whether for good or ill. Technology, we are told, will transform our jobs, 'educate our children, revolutionize our families, erode our privacy and modify our genes' (Winner, 1997, p. 1). Such views are also quite common in the literature on management and organizations and the theoretical perspective behind them is technological determinism. As discussed in Chapter 13, determinism is the view that there is an inevitable direction in which events move determined by some cause. For technological determinists, that cause is technology. In other words, certain key technologies are the primary movers in developments in organizations, the economy or even society itself:

> In technological determinism, research and development have been assumed as self-generating. The new technologies are invented as it were in an independent sphere, and then create new societies or new human conditions. *(Williams, 1979, p. 13)*

It follows that from the viewpoint of technological determinism that the key problem for OB is to understand a technology's – positive or negative (depending on one's point of view) – impacts upon individuals and groups, organizations and society. Countless studies have thus focused upon the impact of computers on employment patterns, the distribution of skills, spans of control, firm strategies, competitive advantage, managerial decision making and worker alienation.

For technological determinism (TD), social and organizational changes are caused (or at least shaped) by technological developments. But what are the causes of these technological developments themselves? For TD, technological developments are determined by technological superiority in a manner resembling a Darwinian 'survival of the fittest'. Sociologist William Ogburn for example, suggested that if collectively people select the same technology, it must be because it is that technology that best satisfies their needs. In the words of Ralph Waldo Emerson, the American writer, if you invent a better mousetrap, the whole world will beat a path to your door. How does the invention of a better

Technology → Society

Figure 11.1 Technological determinism

mousetrap come about according to the proponents of TD? Ogburn claimed that since technologies follow an inherent internal logic of their own, once all the necessary elements are present, an invention will become inevitable: 'given the boat and the steam engine is not the steamboat inevitable?' (Ogburn quoted in MacKenzie and Wajcman, 1999, p. 9). The fact that the same invention may be made almost concurrently in geographically dispersed locations adds weight to this argument. In sum, new technologies emerge out of older technologies by means of (techno-scientific) 'breakthroughs' which *subsequently* have social and organizational consequences – whether intended or unintended. For TD technology is the engine of organizational and social change. It is what takes us from the 'Stone Age', to the 'Bronze Age', to the 'Iron Age', to the 'Age of Steam', to the present 'Information Age' and forever onward. The transition from say the Bronze Age to the Iron Age came about because of the technological superiority of iron tools and weapons over bronze ones, and all other aspects of this changeover are consequences of this technological superiority rather than causes of the change in their own right. In summary, the key ideas in the deterministic outlook are summarized in Box 11.2.

Box 11.2: Key ideas in Technological Determinism (TD)

- Technology is seen as extraneous to the rest of society, an autonomous force that causes social and organizational changes.
- TD concentrates on the impacts of technology on human organization and action.

- Key mainstream problem: How can organizations best adapt to new technologies?

Key issues and controversies

In other chapters various determinisms (biological, economic, etc.) come in for a fair amount of criticism. It should then be clear by now that determinism is on the whole considered an intellectual gaffe. Thus, in social scientific debates, 'technological determinism' is more often than not an accusation, employed to show that one's intellectual adversary has an irredeemably naive perspective on technological and organizational change. That is not to say that social scientists are unlikely to harbour deterministic views (quite the opposite), but rather that writers very rarely explicitly identify their own arguments with that school. Technological determinism is, so to speak, the theory that dare not speak its name.

SOURCE: © COPYRIGHT © ROY EXPORT COMPANY ESTABLISHMENT

Image 11.1 The alienation of the workforce reduced to 'repetitive servitude' by the machinery of the (Fordist) assembly lines was memorably, albeit satirically, portrayed in Charlie Chaplin's (1936) Film *Modern Times*

Among the more explicitly determinist arguments we should include Joan Woodward's (1965) view, also discussed in Chapters 6 and 13, to the effect that organizational structures will reflect the type of technology being employed. As Woodward argued, 'there are prescribed and functional relationships between [organizational] structure and technical demands' (ibid., p. 51). There is, in other words, 'a particular form of organization [that is] most appropriate to each technical situation' (ibid., p. 72). Similar arguments were (and are) made concerning what we might call the more informal aspects of work organization. In their classic study, Walker and Guest argued in 1952 that the impact of technology upon assembly line work meant among other things that social interaction among workers decreased and that work groups were now difficult to form. Therefore, the social needs of employees were not met under the 'Fordist' (see Chapter 10) organization of work. In the same vein, Blauner (1964) claimed that the particular production technologies employed in car assembly and chemical processing resulted in alienated workforces. Blauner described this experience of alienation in terms of feelings of powerlessness, meaninglessness, isolation and self-estrangement. Nevertheless, Blauner believed that the gradual introduction of new, more advanced technologies would eventually rid the workplaces of the future from the malady of alienation. Jaques Ellul (1967, p.138) on the other hand, did not share the (techo-) optimism of Blauner. For him 'there can be no human autonomy in the face of technical autonomy'. Technological autonomy, he claimed, means that the human individual is reduced to 'a slug inserted in a slot machine' (ibid., p. 135).

As described in Chapters 7 and 13, more recent TD inspired contributions to management literature and practice have argued that bureaucratic forms of organization reflect the technological imperatives of a previous (Industrial) Age and are therefore totally unsuited to the requirements of the present Information Age (e.g. Kelly, 1999; Evans and Wurster, 2000).[1] New computer technologies are indeed widely regarded as the impetus for fundamental changes in the scope and range of organizational activities. The call to urgently adapt our behaviours and associated forms of organizing and enterprise in line with the new technological imperatives has, for instance, been a common refrain in the literature and practice of business process re-engineering (BPR). As you will recall, BPR proposes that information technology should be a catalyst for revolutionary organizational changes leading to 'dramatic improvements in critical contemporary measures of performance, such as cost, quality service and speed' (Hammer and Champy, 1993, p. 32; cf. Grint, 1994). Indeed, much theoretical and empirical work in a wide range of management disciplines has routinely claimed that contemporary societies are in the throes of a new and fundamentally different phase of development (Toffler, 1980). The ongoing ICT revolution, many argue, signals a fundamental shift in the underlying dynamics of societal and organizational change, pushing inexorably in the direction of flatter more decentralized and dispersed forms of organizing (e.g. Negroponte, 1995; Peters, 1997).'Network' forms of organization are said to be in the process of replacing bureaucratic ones as the dominant structure in the Information Age (Davidow and Malone, 1992; Van Aken *et al.*, 1997; Friedman, 2005; see also Chapters 10 and 13). As we have seen, Frances Cairncross has argued along similar lines that the rapid advancements in ICTs are bringing about the electronically facilitated 'death of distance'. This 'death of distance' is in turn having a number of important consequences for work, organizations and society. These range from increased amounts of telework, to looser organizational structures, to near frictionless markets, to reduced immigration and emigration, to strengthened national secession movements everywhere (e.g. Cairncross, 1998, p. xi–xvi).

Most of the works mentioned in this section are significantly more complex than the more 'straightforward TD' one finds in many media accounts of new technologies, while at the same time still in debt to particular deterministic assumptions.[2] TD themes typically permeate arguments concerning organizational change without being named as such. As an even cursory examination of the many works currently crowding bookshop shelves that claim to guide management through the actions necessary in order to ride the latest wave of technological change will show, technologically deterministic assumptions tend to underpin much of mainstream management thought and practice. In many ways, technological determinism has achieved the status of a common-sense perspective on matters technological. As Rosalind Williams (2000, p. 652) of the Massachusetts Institute of Technology (MIT) has put it:

> Most historians condemn technological determinism as a dangerous fallacy, but my MIT colleagues are convinced it is simply true . . . Over and again people talk about the inevitability of change . . . understood as a series of [technologically originated] shocks, an endless catch-up game.

Nevertheless, and as various chapters in this book have argued, when critically investigated, 'common-sense' views often turn out to be neither common nor to make much sense. This turns out to also be the case with TD. At the same time, we must resist the temptation many textbooks succumb

CASE STUDY 11.1 The stirrup

By way of illustration of how technological deterministic explanations 'work' analytically, we can point to Lynn White's (1962) influential analysis of the relationship between medieval technology and social change, a key case in the development of the TD perspective. Briefly, White claimed that the diffusion westwards of an Asian invention, the stirrup, brought about a new form of military and social organization in western Europe: feudalism. Up until that time fighting on horseback had been severely constrained by the ever-present danger of falling off. The stirrup gave the medieval rider a far more secure grip on the horse, welding them together into a single fighting unit capable of an entirely new level of violence in combat.

White illustrates the argument about the social and organizational effects of this technological device, by recounting the story of Charles Martel (c.689–741 AD). In the early 8th century Charles Martel created a new type of cavalry force in order to repel Moorish incursions into France. A mounted warrior (knight) similar to those Charles Martel deployed to such good effect against the Moors is shown in the picture. Note the stirrup and also how the mounted warrior in the foreground of the picture is holding his lance: the long lance is held under the arm in the 'couched position'. Now compare this hold with that of a mounted warrior of an earlier age as shown in the lower left corner of the second picture. The difference between the two ways of holding the lance could be ascribed to the fact that the medieval knight enjoys the benefit conferred by the stirrup, an advantage that the ancient mounted warrior lacks. The former can strike home with the combined momentum of horse and rider, the latter with little more that the force of his arm.

Charles Martel's battlefield s successes, marked, or so the TD argument runs, the emergence of the mounted knight as the specialized practitioner of a new kind of 'mounted shock combat' – made possible by the stirrup. A strike force of knights thus conferred a competitive advantage that no European ruler or potentate could do without. The armoured knight would therefore dominate European battlefields for centuries to come. At the same time the maintenance of such a force posed some acute economic problems: armour was expensive, horses were costly to acquire and maintain, while the acquisition of horsemanship skills takes a long time. In order to ensure the ready availability of such a strike force in their domains, western European rulers granted knights fiefs of land in return for military service. A new mounted warrior nobility was thus created, endowed with land, castles, retainers and all the other accoutrements we now associate with chivalry, and upon whom European monarchs grew increasingly dependent. According to TD then, a new form of military, social and economic organization comes about not because of the whims of kings and queens, nor out of the operation of 'social forces', but as the direct result of the introduction of 'a simple mechanical device' (Darby, 2001). As White put it:

Few inventions have been so simple as the stirrup, but few had so catalytic an influence in history. The requirements of the new mode of warfare which it made possible found expression in a new form of Western European Society, dominated by an aristocracy of warriors endowed with land so that they might fight in a new and highly specialized way.

Image 11.2 After the stirrup: Carolingian mounted warriors as represented in the St. Gall Psalter (9th century AD)

Image 11.3 Before the stirrup: A detail from the so-called 'Issus' mosaic discovered in the Roman city of Pompeii. It shows the charge of Alexander the Great and his Companion cavalry in the course of the battle of Issus, which took place in 333 BC

The story of the knight ends the way it began, with yet another technological device – gunpowder – revolutionizing European warfare: increasingly accurate firearms were the knight's undoing. Firearms can penetrate armour at a distance, so the infantry gains the upper hand in the battlefield over the mounted warriors. As Cervantes' Don Quixote lamented, the gun was 'an invention which allows a base and cowardly hand to take the life of a brave knight'. A new technologically induced transformation of both military organization and of society was afoot. Useless against cannon, the knightly castles dotting the European continent were either demolished or transformed into what we now call 'stately homes' devoid of any military function. The title 'knight' became an essentially honorific one. It no longer described a mounted warrior but a courtier. 'Feudalism' was no more and the 'Early Modern Age' was upon us (Cameron, 1999).

to of treating TD as nothing more than an intellectual error, thus leaving the causes of its popularity an incomprehensible mystery. Rather, in order to gain a clearer view of its strengths and limitations, we need a better understanding of how it 'works' as a mode of explanation.

All this was so long ago that the relevance of White's analysis to the world of modern technology and contemporary organizations may appear obscure. And yet, from a TD point of view, what matters is *the way* it all happened. In modern management-speak, the introduction of a new technology, the stirrup, radically altered the cost/benefit equation of medieval armies by introducing remarkable efficiency gains (Darby, 2001). It was a cheap, easy to implement technology, which offered the irresistible competitive advantage of economy of effort, combined with increased productivity. The stirrup brought within the grasp of the average rider levels of control of his mount hitherto only achievable by the most talented and highly skilled riders. A process not dissimilar you might say to the way graphical user interfaces (GUI) brought computing power within reach of the least technically adept (thus launching the so-called PC revolution), or the way in which search engines and the world wide web have made the resources of the internet (until relatively recently accessible only by the highly computer literate) available to the many millions (thus initiating the so-called internet revolution). In TD accounts then, the *dramatis personae* may change but the plot remains much the same.

How much space do technological determinist accounts allow for human choice? White himself was careful to state that 'a new device merely opens a door, it does not compel one to enter' (1962, p. 28). The acceptance or rejection of a technological invention therefore appears to remain a matter for society to decide. Nevertheless, one could claim with some justification that what TD explanations give with the one hand, they take with the other. Since as you will recall, for technological determinists technological change has as its cause the technological superiority of one device or technique over another, individuals, organizations and societies that choose *not* to adopt a new and more effective technology will not survive long against competitors who *did* choose to adopt the technology in question. One example that can be used to illustrate this point concerns the knight's Japanese counterpart, the samurai warrior. Competition for power among the nobility in Japan had by the beginning of the 16th century turned into all out civil war in which cannon and firearms often played a decisive role (Turnbull, 1996).[3] During the civil wars Japan built itself a substantial firearms industry to keep the combatants supplied. By the 17th century, however, the civil wars having been concluded, the seemingly inexorable spread of the gun was put into reverse. The population was disarmed and weapons collected to be melted down (it was said) for the construction of a giant statue of the Buddha. After the experience of the civil wars, guns came to be seen as a recipe for social disorder and as forever tainted by their association with European Christianity. They were considered as incompatible with samurai martial virtues and with the culture of Japan. By the end of the 17th century the use of guns had effectively been eliminated in Japan (Perrin, 1979). From then on, the samurai warrior class would only carry swords. This then could be seen as an example of – in White's terms – a society's refusal to enter the door opened by the technological innovations of gunpowder and the gun. We could therefore say that the Japanese made the choice *not* to undergo the changes in military and social organization necessary for effective exploitation of the destructive power of guns. This choice, however, appears to have been open only for as long as Japan remained isolated from the Western world. In 1853, ships of the US navy entered Tokyo Bay and forced the Japanese government to open up trade with Western nations thus ending centuries of Japanese isolation. The door was, so to speak, reopened and entry forced at gunpoint. Western technologies, including firearms, were introduced as part and parcel of Japanese modernization. The modernization of Japan meant that the samurai were now essentially redundant and their social privileges withdrawn. This led to sporadic uprisings

CASE STUDY 11.4 The bicycle

Consider the picture of the penny-farthing – a popular bicycle type of the Victorian era. To us the reasons for this popularity concepts which may be something of a mystery. In our eyes the high front wheeled penny farthing may appear as a hilarious example of a design so bad that it made it difficult and dangerous to ride. What could these Victorians have been thinking off? A tempting answer would be to see the penny farthing as little more than an inept predecessor to the modern bicycle we all know and love. However, Pinch and Bijker (1984) in their influential account of the social construction of the bicycle, seek the answer in the study of the '*relevant social groups*' that were involved in 'negotiating' and 'stabilizing' the meaning of the bicycle. From the point of view of one such group – adventurous young men – the penny farthing was essentially a sporting machine. The fact that it was difficult and hazardous to ride was for them part of its attraction:

Young and often upper-class men could display their athletic skills and daring by showing off in the London parks. To impress the rider's lady friends, the risky nature of the [penny farthing] was essential. Thus the meaning attributed to the machine by . . . [its] users made it the macho bicycle.
(Bijker, 1995, p. 75)

In other words we cannot understand the technical design of the penny farthing unless we also understand its cultural connections with particular late-Victorian ideas about male (often upper-class) 'youth culture' and identity. It follows, that for those social groups who did not share that culture or identity, the penny farthing would have been a highly dysfunctional device. Its design functioned to exclude particular groups, including women (impossible to ride in a skirt) and the elderly. For Pinch and Bijker (1984) these people constitute another relevant social group – the 'non-users'. In the eyes of this group, the very same characteristics that made the penny farthing attractive to the young 'macho' riders were reasons to avoid it. The machine 'was difficult to mount, risky to ride and not easy to dismount. It was in short the unsafe bicycle' (Bijker, 1995, p. 74). The 'macho bicycle' and the 'unsafe bicycle' are thus descriptions of the same machine. What were advantages from the viewpoint of one social group were disadvantages from that of the other:

The macho bicycle was . . . radically different from the unsafe bicycle – it was designed to meet different criteria; it was sold, bought and used for different purposes; it was evaluated to different standards; it was considered a machine that worked whereas the unsafe bicycle was a nonworking machine.
(Bijker, 1995, p. 75)

The moral of the story then, is that the questions of whether a machine works or not or whether one technological device is superior to another are not straightforward technical matters as TD might lead us to expect, but are socially determined. Pinch and Bijker (1984) use the example of the penny farthing to illustrate a key SCOT concept – that of the '*interpretative flexibility*' of technological devices. What it means in practice is that there tend to be as many different machines (macho bicycle, unsafe bicycle) as there are relevant social groups. That is why an engineering understanding can never be by itself sufficient, and what makes a social scientific investigation of how over time we might come to share a common interpretation of the artefact essential.

Here enters another set of key SCOT concepts: '*closure*' and '*stabilization*'. Bijker (1995, p. 270) describes them in terms of 'the process by which interpretative flexibility decreases, leaving the meaning attributed to the artefacts less and less ambiguous'. In the case the penny farthing (also known at the time as the 'ordinary bicycle'), social agreement (closure) was achieved and it was the non-working/'unsafe' and not the working/'macho' interpretation that stuck. As a result, the penny farthing has now become a museum exhibit. The 'ordinary bicycle' is now considered to be extraordinary, a technological curiosity. 'Stabilization' is represented by another machine, called at that time the 'rear-driven safety bicycle'. This had not been conceived as a sports machine but as a means of transportation. It is now known simply as the bicycle.

Image 11.7 The Penny Farthing – a difficult design to understand

SOURCE: © BETTMANN/CORBIS

SOURCE: © HULTON-DEUTSCH COLLECTION/CORBIS

Thinkpoint 11.9

Is the skateboard a kind of penny-farthing for the present age? Identify and make a list of the relevant social groups of the skateboard.

SCOT argues that a new technology may mean different things to different social groups. More specifically, a device may be seen as a response to different problems, represent a variety of solutions and be associated with a range of social impacts. Hence the concept of 'interpretative flexibility'. This may be defined as the different meanings various relevant social groups give to a particular technology. For example, the views held by young clubbers on the properties of 'recreational' drugs may be very different from those held by the medical profession or law enforcement authorities. When a technology is relatively new, there is a higher degree of flexibility in how people may think of it or interpret its artefacts and in how those artefacts are designed. It is not therefore surprising that if we go back far enough in the history of any technological process or device, we are likely to find interpretations of 'what this technology is for', and what it can and cannot do that may appear bizarre to us now.

For example, in his study of the history of radioactive waste,[16] Bruhèze (1992) describes how that the Atomic Energy Commission's (ATC's) Division of Military Application considered radioactive waste, not as waste but rather as a useful by-product of the nuclear industry that could be used as raw material in weapons construction or in the irradiation of food. In the ATC's Division of Reactor Development, radioactive waste was perceived as an essentially economic problem (waste was expensive to store). The ATC's Division of Biology and Medicine saw it in terms of risks to human health while the ATC's headquarters considered radioactive waste to be a relatively normal problem, to be solved in due course through technological advances and therefore not requiring immediate attention. Even within the same organization then, different relevant social groups held radically differing interpretations of the 'same' thing.

This interpretative flexibility associated with a technological innovation can be curtailed by various means including, force, agreement and compromise on a particular design, standard, or specification. 'Closure' may be reached in many different ways – including rhetorical closure where the relevant social groups perceive (or are persuaded) the problem as being solved; the obscuration of alternatives; the redefinition of the problem, and so on. Misa (1992, p. 109), for instance, defines 'closure' as 'the process by which facts or artefacts in a provisional state characterized by controversy are moulded into a stable state characterized by consensus (. . .) it is how artefacts gain their hardness and solidity'.

The decrease in interpretative flexibility typically leads to one variant of the technology becoming dominant (e.g. the 'rear-driven safety bicycle' becomes 'the bicycle'). The dominant artefact will then develop an increasing degree of stabilization within the various RSGs. Processes of closure are almost irreversible – but not quite. Clearly not all rival interpretations will necessarily vanish; instead we may see the development of distinct devices that meet different groups' needs. 'Closure' tends to be a two-sided process. It tends to involve the stabilization of both technological device *and* relevant social groups. As Bijker (1995, p. 273) argues, 'all stable [socio-technical] ensembles are bound as much by the technical as by the social'. Organizations and other social arrangements and institutions are stabilized by the technical means as much as technologies are stabilized by them.

Exercise 11.2

Below you will find a brief description of a new (at the time of writing!) technology called AWOL™, which, its makers claim, can change the way alcohol is consumed. On the basis of this information, you are invited to consider whether you would recommend the installation of such a device in any of the following establishments:

- a 'hip' urban bar
- a traditional family pub
- an 'ethnic' restaurant
- the Dog and Duck.

AWOL™ (Alcohol With Out Liquid™) is a machine that mixes spirits with oxygen. A cloudy alcohol vapour is created that can be inhaled or snorted. As the makers of the device put it:

> Up the nose or breathe in the mouth, straight to the brain. Finally, a solution to the two greatest problems today's drinkers have: hangovers and calories. This is the dieter's dream, this is the Atkins diet alcohol and diabetes alcohol, low carbohydrates, low calorie and low sugar alcohol. The AWOL machine includes the hand-held diffuser into which the booze of choice is poured; this, in turn, is connected to an oxygen generator the size of a school backpack. The drink is then snorted up the nose like a nasal decongestant, or breathed through the mouth – instead of swallowed down the throat with a sweet mix like Cola or ginger ale.

Once inhaled, the alcoholic vapour enters the 'bloodstream to give an instant buzz'. Its promoters claim that the device offers among other things (source: www.awolmachine.com)

- 'A very mild way to enjoy the aromas and flavors of fruit-infused spirits.'
- 'The Ultimate Face Lift! Oxygen facials are the natural alternative to Botox and Surgery, instantly reducing lines and wrinkles.'
- 'The Ultimate Workout! Oxygen workouts will make your routine easier, improve your endurance, speed recovery and reduce post-workout stiffness.'
- 'The Ultimate Urban Cure! Beat pollution and stress with extra oxygen. Nature's antidote for re-vitalizing, rejuvenating and re-energizing your mind and body.'

A number of medical experts and alcohol concern groups have condemned AWOL™, fearing it is an unsafe machine that could lead to brain damage and have called for an investigation by (UK) Trading Standards officers (*The Daily Telegraph*, 19 February 2004; see also the BBC http://news.bbc.co.uk/go/pr/fr/-/1/h/england/bristol/349348.stm and https://securethepublican.com/cgi-bin/item.cgi?id=128348d=328h=248=238dateformat=%25o-%25B-%25Y

'The technical is socially constructed and the social is technically constructed (. . .) social classes, occupational groups, firms, profession, machines – all are held in place by intimate social and technical links' (ibid., p. 273).[17]

Whether you remember the earlier discussion of SCOT or not, it is still likely that in attempting to answer the question you began by reflecting upon the meaning of this particular technology. Chances are that using the sparse cues provided in the above description, you set out to identify the relevant social groups – that are relevant to the various establishments – including publicans and different categories of drinkers and non-drinkers (e.g. students, families) and the ways they may relate to the various 'technical' claims (and counter-claims) made about this machine. You may have considered how these groups of people do things and what the things they do mean to them. Are they potential as user or non-user groups? A quiet family outing 'means' different things to the participants than a pub-crawl or a stag party. You may have reflected for instance upon current drinking rituals and their place in what is understood as 'student behaviour' and (if you have read the rest of this book), upon how they ultimately figure in the construction of what we might call 'student identity'. Or more accurately the construction of a *particular* student identity – given that many students may not share it or wish to share it (more non-users?). However unsystematic, such musings are inescapably tied up to the interpretative flexibility that still characterizes this particular machine. We may speculate that were the machine to become successful, this interpretative flexibility would diminish. Perhaps one day it might appear as self-evident a piece of pub equipment as the beer pump looks now ('closure' and 'stabilization'). If it is unsuccessful, for instance through lack of interest or if 'closure' is achieved around the 'unsafe machine' interpretation instead, the machine may appear one day at least as bizarre in our eyes as the high-wheeled penny-farthing now does.

Social construction of technology: Review and implications Social constructivists could be described as the 'radical wing' of SST (Pinch, 1998). SCOT is concerned to demonstrate how various social processes influence the technical characteristics of a technology. SCOT's key claim is that the meanings of a technology, including the facts about how or whether it works, are socially produced. Hence, there is no such thing as a 'pure technology' developing under its own immanent logic independent of its creators' world views, cultural assumptions, prejudices or biases. Rather, technological processes and devices are outcomes of social conflicts negotiations and compromises. Clearly the meanings of a technology are not simply free-floating and random, but more often than not, are channelled through power relations. This channelling is especially evident in relation to organizations where there is contention as to which world views or interpretive frameworks 'will be employed to guide the definition and choice of technologies' (Thomas, 1994, p. 212). SCOT thus provides a useful perspective on socio-technical change that allows us to highlight how culture, social arrangements and institutions – and the patterns of power, inequality and identity that comprise them – are important influences upon, or even constitutive of, technology. At the same time SCOT is subject to a number of different criticisms from both mainstream and critical perspectives:

- From a mainstream perspective, it is often argued that SCOT accounts over-stress social choice and human factors at the expense of technological ones. SCOT is thus accused of having *replaced technological with a social determinism.*

- For TD critics, SCOT is in fact pernicious, as it sets out to obscure the (to them) self-evident fact that the study of society may indeed be about differences in interests, values, world views and the like, but the study of technology is about indisputable facts and observable relationships (Thomas,1994, p. 246). Furthermore, technologies are not infinitely plastic – technological design is constrained in fundamental ways by the physical, chemical, or in the case of software, logical properties of its material: 'We are not dealing with ectoplasm here nor the stuff that dreams are made off' (Miles, 1988, p. 1).

- From a critical viewpoint, SCOT is often seen as inattentive to the broader social context and the role of inequalities of power between social groups. For instance how do particular groups become relevant? What of those social groups that do not have a voice?

- SCOT is also said to be inattentive to the social *consequences* of technological choices, including an apparent lack of concern for the ways in which we might judge whether particular technologies make the world better or worse.

From a number of critical points of view then, including that of many feminist Marxist and post-colonial authors, SCOT appears politically disengaged, debilitating and insipid and of little use to those seeking to transform society and organizations. Some of these criticisms are more justified than others. The debate appears destined to run and run (for criticisms and responses see, for instance, Pinch, 1998; Grint and Woolgar, 1999). Over the last few decades, a number of researchers originally associated with SST/SCOT (such as Bruno Latour and John Law) have developed yet another theoretical alternative that is critical of both TD and SST/SCOT. This is commonly known as actor-network theory or actor-network analysis, and we will consider this next.

Actor-network theory

The third alternative to technological determinism is actor-network theory (ANT for short), from the viewpoint of which the arguments between TD, SST and SCOT over the role of technology in society and organizations are in essence chicken and egg debates: various perspectives propose different answers to the question of what comes first, the social chicken or the technological egg (Bromley, 1994). For ANT the solution is to stop viewing technology and society as two separate but related domains and instead as different *phases* in the same action. We cannot, ANT claims, draw hard and fast distinctions between what is social and what is technological in order try to find out which one determines the other: the social and the technological already presuppose and contain one another. As MacKenzie and Wajcman (1999, p. 23) note, the various 'material resources – artefacts and technologies, such as walls, prisons, weapons, writing, agriculture – are part of what makes large scale society feasible. The technological, instead of being a sphere separate from society, is part of what makes society possible – in other words, it is constitutive of society'. We cannot, in other words have a society without technology any more than we can have a technology without society.

Researchers, ANT insists, *should not* switch registers and use different types of explanation when they move from the analysis of the technical to that of the social aspects of the problem studied (Callon, 1986a, p. 200). They should in other words *resist* the temptation of providing (purely) social explanations (say in terms of social group interests, social values or cultural world views) for social phenomena, while giving (purely) technical explanations (say in terms of physical or chemical) properties for technological ones. Instead, technological (and organizational) processes are both to be understood as processes of network building. Such networks are constructed through the enrolment of both human and non-human actors[18] by various means including negotiation and conscription.

The idea of an actor-network then refers to the bringing together of various actors – whether human individuals, groups, technical standards, money, or natural forces – whose *actions* are to be somehow aligned for a particular purpose. A car cannot function without roads, petrol stations, car mechanics, traffic codes or qualified drivers. Drivers need cars and cars require drivers. Petrol stations need roads and roads need petrol stations (Stalder, 2002). All these actors give one another specific identities and roles in the network. Each is influenced by, and in turn exerts influence upon, all other actors, playing an active part in the eventual outcome of every process of network building and maintenance. ANT is therefore the study of the creation, maintenance and demise of actor-networks. It makes the claim that the creation of both technology and organization (or for that matter society) involves the building of such heterogeneous networks (see Box 11.5).

If what this 'actor-networking' entails is not altogether clear, then the example in Box 11.6 might help. Even in a relatively simple situation like the one described there, the *act* of switching off the

---

Box 11.5: Key ideas in actor-network theory

- The creation of both technology *and* organization involves the creation and maintenance of *heterogeneous* actor-networks involving both human and technological actors.

- 'Actors' therefore may be either persons or things. It should not matter to researchers whether the various actors assembled in a network (say cars, drivers, roads) should be classified as 'social' or 'technological'. What matters is such entities' ability to *act* on one another.

- Every technological device is dependent on a heterogeneous network that supports the specific ways in which this device is being used.

- The different elements in a technology's actor-network are held together by chains of 'translations'. Translations build actor-networks out of otherwise unrelated entities.

- Key question: how can we best explain the processes whereby such relatively stable networks of aligned actors are created, maintained and dissolved?

Box 11.6: Mobile phone troubles (2)

Suppose you were asked to devise a strategy for preventing the use of mobile phones in lectures. How would you proceed? Take a moment or two to devise your strategy.

Clearly there are many strategies you could adopt. Let's for the sake of simplicity discard from the outset those that are too unreasonable or intrusive to implement (such as employing staff – 'human actors' in ANTspeak – to search everyone at the door and confiscate their mobiles). Let us look instead at some of the strategies actually used in such situations. A notice on the door and/or in the student handbook to the effect that 'all mobile phones must be switched off' is by far the most typical of these. We will call this Strategy 1. It should be largely successful in 'enrolling' most mobile users. Everyone, that is, except the forgetful (such as Z in our story), and those intent on contravening this regulation (such as X and Y) who might put their phones on 'silent' and continue using them. Together, these two groups constitute what we might call 'anti-network 1' (see Figure 11.4).

What can be done about them? The addition of a verbal reminder from the lecturer at the start of the session might take care of all but the most brazen and the extremely absent-minded (Strategy 2). This is the typical strategy used in, for instance, examinations in order to prevent cheating or

disruption. This means that using your mobile is now not merely a distraction, likely to attract censorious looks, but an offence. The university disciplinary code can now be enrolled to discipline offenders. You will also find this strategy in use in air travel.

We have perhaps now reached the limit in terms of the number of mobile users we can enrol without employing more drastic measures and recruiting more powerful allies. Facing us is the real hard core of mobile users, perhaps including the type of person who will attempt to use a mobile during a flight. We could, of course, recruit further (non-human) allies to our cause. We could, for example, seek to insulate the room with material that would prevent the transmission of the signal – to cut off, so to speak, phone from phone network (Strategy 3). There is, for instance, special wallpaper containing a metallic mesh that will screen out mobile phone signals (e.g. Howell, 2004). When we employ this strategy, the task of 'switching off mobiles' is no longer performed by the users (the human actors) but is delegated instead to the insulating material (a non-human actor). This is a strategy that might prove useful in theatres, the opera or in other sites where it is considered worth making the investment in order to ensure that performers can perform their roles without distractions. (It is also a possibility in aircraft where, as we know, mobile usage might interfere with flight instruments.) There are reports, for instance, that a number of chinese provinces have ordered the installation of 'mobile telephone blocking devices around University entrance examination halls to prevent answers being sent in by text message (Spencer, 2006).

Similarly, the French Ministry of Trade has authorized the installation of equipment in theatres and cinemas able to jam mobile phone calls in the premises while permitting emergency calls (Randall, 2004, p. 12). The three strategies described here and the actor-networks and anti-networks (enrolled versus resistant actors) are illustrated in Figure 11.4 (based on Akrich and Latour, 1992).

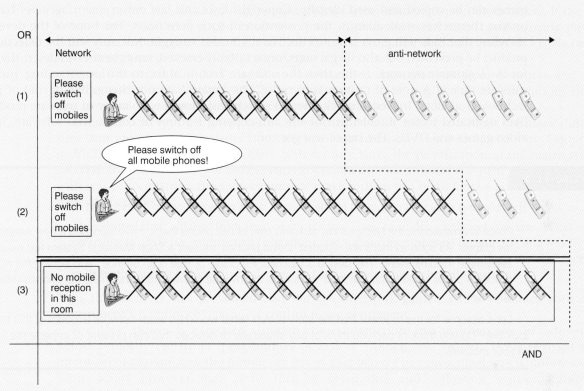

Figure 11.4 Actor-networks and anti-networks

mobile phones of the audience is carried out (or resisted) by a number of different configurations of human and non-human actors (including lecturers, air-stewards, mobile users, texts, building materials, etc.). As we have seen, the various networks involve various acts of delegation between the human and non-human entities that comprise them. The delivery of an instruction for instance ('switch off your mobile'), can be delegated to a human actor, a written notice and so on. Similarly, the physical act of 'switching off' can be performed by a human actor or, alternatively, delegated to particular insulation materials. In fact delegations to non-human actors are frequently initiated in order to overcome perceived deficiencies in human actors.

From an ANT perspective, a working technological device is dependent on the operations of the heterogeneous network that supports the ways in which that particular device functions (Callon, 1993). A working mobile phone, for example, presupposes functioning handsets, competent users, a telephone network plus a network of masts (in tall buildings or concealed behind billboards and petrol station signs) to supply coverage. It requires the signing of legal contracts and the establishment of business relationships between the user and the various organizations and institutions that provide coverage, sell upgrades, or are otherwise involved in the development, distribution and maintenance of the technology. Changes in actor-network, are also changes in what a device does and how it is being used. The stabilization of a technological device is therefore at the same time the stabilization of its actor-network. All this may sound rather esoteric but is well understood by those involved in the design, production or marketing of a device.

be able to construct this kind of package it is necessary to define in advance and standardize (script) elaborate procedures to be followed in the performance and documentation of organizational tasks (Kallinikos, 2004). Deviation from the correct 'script' can easily disrupt the operation of the system. An organization therefore does not merely buy, but also buys into an ERP system. Although such 'scripting' is said to represent the industry best practice for each particular process designed into the system, it can also cause problems, particular in areas of the world with business practices that are different to the United States and Europe where most systems originate. For example, in a study of ERP use in a Middle Eastern manufacturing company, El-Sayed and Westrup (2003) found that haggling over prices was commonplace and valued customers expected prices *not* to be fixed until after the receipt of goods. This was not a notion of business supported by the company's ERP system so staff only entered sales order data *after* payment was received so that they could then create an invoice that satisfied the ERP system. Company accountants had in other words found a way to evade the ERP script in order to preserve established practices.

Actor-network theory: Review and implications Actor-network theory helps us understand the course of technological *and* organizational innovations (these are but different *phases* in the same action). Actor-network theory proposes that technologies and organizations are both enacted through networks of actors (where the actors can be both human and non-human). ANT allows us to investigate issues such as 'How did it come to turn out this way?' (through the changing alliances of [heterogeneous] actors), 'Who is influencing it?' (who has been doing what scripting?) or 'Why are some actors acting this way?' (what scripts are they carrying?). These are not questions with deterministic answers but allow a rich interpretation of the situation' (Underwood, 1999). On the other, ANT has had its fair share of criticism, with the following being among the most common:

- ANT has been criticised for generating jargon-ridden accounts that describe but do not explain. ANT analyses it is said to offer a 'homogenous model, where everything is part of everything else and mutual influence is effective everywhere at once, [which] may be less misleading, but at the cost of offering little guidance: how do you proceed and where do you look first?' (Bromley, 1994, p. 14).
- One symptom of ANT determination to make no analytical distinctions between human actions and the behaviour of objects is, as we have seen, the symmetrical treatment of human and non-human 'actors'. Critics find this intellectually and morally problematic, as reducing people to the status of objects (e.g. Collins and Yearley, 1992a,b). While this flattening of human/non-human differences might make analytical sense it is not without political implications.
- ANT, critics have argued, seems to view and describe 'networks' from the standpoint of the manager, the innovator, the victor, the entrepreneur. From a critical viewpoint then, ANT has been criticized as 'apolitical' or even insensitive to those social structures and institutional sources of power and inequality and oppression – such as gender inequalities (see Chapter 6) – which severely limit the spectrum of social actors' choices and behaviours.

At the same time we need to acknowledge that ANT is a not stable body of knowledge that can be used in unproblematic way, but still very much a work in progress, subject to regular revision (and even criticism) by its developers.[22] Unavoidably then, many of the above criticisms have different applicability for different ANT authors.

Thinkpoint 11.9

You can find additional information about ANT (and also about SST and SCOT) – including frequently asked questions and further readings – at John Law's website at http://www.lancs.ac.uk/fss/sociology/css/jlsts.htm and at http://www.lancs.ac.uk/fss/sociology/css/antres/antres.htm.

Conclusion

The role technologies play in the ways we organize our affairs is a topic that can provoke heated discussions. The aim of this chapter has been to selectively present the main interpretative frameworks that provide the 'toolkit' for both mainstream and critical investigations of this topic. In the mainstream literature, the influence of technological determinism has long been dominant. As a result, much of what has been written about technology and organizational behaviour has often tended to focus on the power of technology to determine what happens in organizations and society. Social shaping, social constructivism and actor-network theory have also had their share of influence on critical approaches concerned with the ways technology can become a vehicle for relations of domination in the workplace and elsewhere.

It should by now be apparent that these 'toolkits' can be used to construct a variety of stories about technology. What stories we choose to tell about this topic *is* important because stories about technology are never just that. They are also stories about human behaviour and have implications for the ways we act in the world. What do these stories tell us? Do they tell us that technology determines the ways we organize and coordinate our activities or even the ways we live our lives? Or do they tell us that we have the freedom to do things differently, to do technology differently? To what extent and in what way does our identity, our vision of who 'we' are, influence what technologies we end up with? What do these different stories hide, obscure or leave unsaid?

Perhaps there are no single answers to such questions. All the frameworks reviewed in this chapter have their strengths and weaknesses and we have devoted some space to discussing those. It may well be that our understanding of the topic would be unduly limited if our knowledge was restricted by the viewpoint afforded by a single theory. Perhaps we need to consider such issues from *multiple* perspectives. Perhaps again, this is a piece of advice that is easy to dispense but less easy to follow.

Discussion questions

1 Go back to the list you were asked to compile in the opening section of this chapter (p. 407) of those future technological developments that you thought will most affect your life. Review the answers you gave to the questions about who/what have control over or bear responsibility for those technologies. Did the reading of this chapter cause you to revise your answers and in what way?

2 What do you understand by the term 'technological determinism'? What are the main strengths and limitations of that approach to understanding the role technologies play in the ways we organize our activities?

3 What does it mean to say that a technology is 'socially shaped'? Illustrate your answer with examples.

4 What does it mean to say that a technology has been 'socially constructed'? In what way – if at all – does 'social construction' differ from 'social shaping'?

5 What do you understand by the term 'actor-network' and how can a 'theory' based on this concept help us better understand technology? Illustrate your answer with examples.

6 What, in your view, is the best theoretical approach to understanding the role that *management* plays in deciding what technologies we get and how they are implemented? Illustrate your answer with examples.

7 In your judgement, which of the theoretical approaches outlined in this chapter best helps us understand the role of technology in relations of power and inequality?

8 Take a technology with which you are familiar (say music downloading). Then pick *two* of the frameworks presented above and try to sketch out what an analysis of this technology conductive from these two different perspectives might look like. For instance, which aspects of this technology each approach focuses on.

Further reading

Mainstream approaches

More recent examples of work heavily influenced by TD include Frances Cairncross' (1998) *The Death of Distance: How the Communications Revolution Will Change Our Lives* (London: Orion Business Books). The book is an analysis of how recent developments in information and communication technologies have caused the rapid decline in the importance of factors such as physical location and geographical distance in processes of organizing. Also influenced by technological determinism is P. Evans and T. Wurster's (2000) *Blown to Bits* (Boston: Harvard Business School Press), a very readable account of how technology is transforming contemporary organizations. A potted version of their argument can be found in the same authors' 1997 article 'Strategy and the new economics of information', *Harvard Business Review*, September–October, 71–84. See also Kevin Kelly (1999) *New Rules for the New Economy* (Harmondsworth: Penguin). (A less optimistic take on some of the same developments can be found in J. Rifkin and R. Heilbroner (1996) *The End of Work: The Decline of the Global Labor Force and the Dawn of the Post-Market Era*, New York: J. P. Tarcher). Among the most influential mainstream texts in recent times has been M. Hammer and J. Champy's (1993) *Reengineering the Corporation: A Manifesto for a Business Revolution* (London: Nicholas Brealey). The gist of their argument can be found in Mike Hammer's (1990) 'Reengineering work: Don't automate, obliterate', *Harvard Business Review*, July–August, 104–112.

Alternative approaches

An alternative treatment to that of Hammer and Champy can be found in Soshana Zuboff's (1989) *In the Age of the Smart Machine*. Zuboff's argument is closer to 'social shaping' approaches to the role of technology in that she puts emphasis on the role that managerial choices play in determining the role of technology in organizations. Among the classic studies of the shaping role of managerial choices and (through them power and inequality) in determining the characteristics of a technology is David Noble's classic, article 'Social choice in machine design: The case of automatically controlled machine tools' in D. MacKenzie, and J. Wajcman (eds.) (1999) *The Social Shaping of Technology* (Milton Keynes: Open University Press). Harry Collins' and Trevor Pinch's (1998) *The Golem at Large* (Cambridge: Cambridge University Press) contains a number of very readable empirical studies from a SCOT perspective. For those in search of a more demanding read, check out Lucas Introna and Louise Whittaker (2005) 'Power, cash and convenience: The political space of the ATM', available at http://www.lums.lancs.ac.uk/publications/viewpdf/002697/, and Wiebe Bijker's and John Law's (eds.) *Shaping Technology/Building Society* (Cambridge, MA: MIT Press), which contains a range of empirical explorations of SCOT and related matters.

For an introduction to the actor-network approach, see Bruno Latour (1988) 'Mixing humans and non-humans together: The sociology of a door-closer', *Social Problems*, 35:298–310. For demonstrations of how this approach might be used in empirical work, see Barbara Czarniawska and Tor Hernes (eds.) *Actor-Network Theory and Organizing* (Copenhagen: Copenhagen Business School Press). For those in search of something shorter and less demanding, Felix Stalder's (2002) 'Failures and successes: Notes on the development of electronic cash', *The Information Society* 18(3):209–219, is another good illustration of ANT-influenced empirical work.

For a good overview of the different approaches to technology see the different contributions to William Dutton (ed.) (1996) *Information and Communication Technologies: Visions and Realities* (Oxford: Oxford University Press). See also

the introduction to Donald MacKenzie and Judy Wajcman (eds.) (1999) *The Social Shaping of Technology* (various editions, Buckingham and Philadelphia: Open University Press). Keith Grint and Steve Woolgar's (1999) *The Machine at Work* (Cambridge, Polity) is another interesting, albeit more demanding overview – this time with a constructivist flavour. For ANT, see Bruno Latour's (2005) *Reassembling the Social: An Introduction to Actor-Network-Theory*, Oxford: Oxford University Press.

Websites

http://www.wired.com/

Wired magazine is a good source of technologically deterministic reflections on 'cutting edge' technological developments.

http://www.lancs.ac.uk/fss/sociology/css/jlsts.htm

http://www.lancs.ac.uk/fss/sociology/css/antres/antres.htm

John Law's site has a lot more on ANT (but also on social shaping and social construction) – including frequently asked questions and further readings.

http://www.ensmp.fr/~latour/

For more on actor-network theory and its recent evolution, Bruno Latour's website has a number of accessible articles and opinion pieces on the topic.

Important empirical studies

Technological determinism

Woodward, J. (1980) *Industrial Organization: Theory and Practice*, Oxford: Oxford University Press.
Blauner, R. (1964) *Alienation and Freedom; The Factory Worker and His Industry*, Chicago: Chicago University Press.

Social shaping of technology

MacKenzie, D. and Wajcman, J. (eds.) (1999) *The Social Shaping of Technology*, Milton Keynes: Open University Press.
Zuboff, S. (1989) *In the Age of the Smart Machine: The Future of Work and Power*, New York: Basic Books.

Social construction of technology

Bijker, W. (1995) *Of Bicycles, Bakelites, and Bulbs: Towards a Theory of Sociotechnical Change*, Cambridge, MA: MIT Press.
Collins, H. and Pinch, T. (1998) *The Golem at Large*, Cambridge: Cambridge University Press.

Actor-network theory

Law, J. (1994) *Organizing Modernity*, Oxford: Blackwell.
Latour, B. (1996) *Aramis, or The Love of Technology*, Boston: Harvard University Press.

References

Aaronson, B. and Osmond, H. (eds.) (1971) *Psychedelics: The Uses and Implications of Hallucinogenic Drugs*, Boston: Schenkman Publishing.

Agre, P. (2000) 'Welcome to the Always-On World', *IEEE Spectrum Online* (www.spectrum.ieee.org).

Akrich, M. (1992) 'The de-sciption of technical objects', in W. Bijker and J. Law (eds.) *Shaping Technology/Building Society*, Cambridge, MA: MIT Press, p.p. 205–222.

Akrich, M. and Latour, B. (1992) 'A summary of a convenient vocabulary for the semiotics of human and nonhuman assemblies', in W. Bijker and J. Law (eds.) *Shaping Technology/Building Society*, Cambridge, MA: MIT Press.

Arnold, M. (2003) 'On the phenomenology of technology: The 'Janus-faces' of mobile phones', *Information and Organization* 13:231–256.

Bacharch, B. (1970) 'Charles Martel, mounted shock combat, the stirrup and feudalism', *Studies in Medieval and Renaissance History* 7:46–75.

Barham, N. (2004) *Disconnected: Why Our Kids are Turning Their Backs on Everything We Thought We Knew*, London: Ebury Press.

Barnes, B. (1985) *About Science*, London: Basil Blackwell.

Barnes, B., Bloor, D. and Henry, J. (1996) *Scientific Knowledge: A Sociological Analysis*, London: Athlone Press.

BBC News (2004) 'Child-proof packs baffle adults', 25 April, available at http://news.bbc.co.uk/1/hi/health/3652607.stm.

Bennett, W. (2004) 'Expert who told Bond to hang up his "lady's gun"', *The Daily Telegraph*, 6 September, 6.

Bijker, W. (1992) 'The social construction of fluorescent lighting or how an artifact was invented in its diffusion stage', in W. Bijker and J. Law (eds.) *Shaping Technology/Building Society*, Cambridge, MA: MIT Press.

Bijker W. (1995) *Of Bicycles, Bakelites, and Bulbs: Towards a Theory of Sociotechnical Change*, Cambridge, MA: MIT Press.

Bijker, W. and Law, J. (1992) 'Postscript: Technology, stability and social theory', in W. Bijker and J. Law (eds.) *Shaping Technology/Building Society*, Cambridge, MA: MIT Press.

Blauner, R. (1964) *Alienation and Freedom; The Factory Worker and His Industry*, Chicago: Chicago University Press.

Bloomfield, B. P. and Vurdubakis, T. (1994) 'Boundary disputes: Negotiating the boundary between the social and the technical in IT systems development', *Information Technology and People* 7(1):9–25.

Bromley, H. (1994) 'The social chicken and the technological egg', paper presented at the American Research Association Annual Meeting, April.

Bruhèze, A. de la (1992) 'Closing the ranks: Definition and stabilization of radioactive waste in the US Atomic Energy Commission, 1945–1960', in W. Bijker and J. Law (eds.) '*Shaping Technology/Building Society*, Cambridge, MA: MIT Press, p.p. 140–174.

Cairncross, F. (1998) *The Death of Distance: How the Communications Revolution Will Change Our Lives*, London: Orion Business Books.

Call Centre Europe (1999) 'Call centre locations', Issue No. 21, 31–40.

Callon, M. (1986a) 'Some elements of a sociology of translation: Domestication of the scallops and the fishermen of St Brieuc Bay', in J. Law (ed.) *Power, Action and Belief*, London: Routledge and Kegan Paul.

Callon, M. (1986b) 'The sociology of an actor network', in M. Callon and J. Law (eds.) *Mapping the Dynamics of Science and Technology*, London: Macmillan.

Callon, M. (1993) 'Variety and irreversibility in networks of technique conception and adoption', in D. Foray and C. Freemann (eds.) *Technology and the Wealth of Nations*, London: Pinter.

Cameron, E. (ed.) (1999) *Early Modern Europe*, Oxford: Oxford University Press.

Cockburn, C. (1983) *Brothers: Male Dominance and Technological Change*, London: Pluto Press.

Collins, H. and Yearley, S. (1992a) 'Epistemological chicken', in A. Pickering (ed.) *Science as Practice and Culture*, Chicago: Chicago University Press, p.p. 301–326.

Collins, H. and Yearley, S. (1992b) 'Journey into space', in A. Pickering (ed.) *Science as Practice and Culture*, Chicago: Chicago University Press, p.p. 369–389.

Computing (2004) 'The failure of UkeU', Special Report, Monday, 19 July. Available at: http://www.computing.co.uk/specials/1156350.

Connect (2004) 'When cars become human', No. 65, 5 January.

Cranz, G. (1996) *The Social Purpose of Chairs: Maintaining Hierarchy in Ancient Societies and Contemporary Institutions*, paper presented at the AASA Conference, New York, August.

Daniel, W. W. and Hogarth T. (1990) 'Worker support for technical change', *New Technology, Work and Employment* 5:85–93.

Dant, T. (1999) *Material Culture in the Social World*, Milton Keynes: Open University Press.

Darby, D. (2001) *How the Stirrup Changed Our World*, unpublished manuscript, Darby Consulting Group LLC.

Davidow, W. and Malone, M. (1992) *The Virtual Corporation*, New York: HarperCollins.

Ellul, Jacques (1967) *The Technological Society* (trans. John Wilkinson), New York: Vintage.

El-Sayed, H. and Westrup, C. (2003) 'Egypt and ICTs: How ICTs bring national initiatives, global actors, and local companies together', *Information Technology and People* 16(1):76–92.

Evans, P. and Wurster, T. (2000) *Blown to Bits*, Boston: Harvard Business School Press.

Finnegan, R. (1975) 'Communication and technology' in *Making Sense of Society*, Milton Keynes: Open University Press.

Fox, A. (1974) *Man Mismanagement*, London: Hutchinson.

Fox, B. (2003) '"Subversive" code could kill off software piracy', *New Scientist*, 10 October. Available at: http://www.newscientist.com/news/print.jsp?id = ns99994248.

Friedman, T. (2005) *The World Is Flat: A Brief History of the Globalized World in the 21st Century*, Harmondsworth: Penguin.

Garfinkel, S. (2001) *Database Nation: The Death of Privacy in the 21st Century*, Sebastopol, CA: O'Reilly.

Grint, K. (1994) 'Reengineering history', *Organization*, 1(1):179–202.

Grint, K. and Woolgar, S. (1999) *The Machine at Work*, Cambridge: Polity.

Hammer, M. and Champy, J. (1993) *Reengineering the Corporation: A Manifesto for Business Revolution*', London: Nicholas Brealey.

Head, Simon (2003) The New Ruthless Economy: Work and Power in the Digital Age, Oxford: Oxford University Press.

Howell, J. (2004) 'Why wallpaper does a cracking good job', *The Sunday Telegraph (House and Home)*, 8 August:6.

Hughes, T. P. (1983) *Networks of Power: Electrification in Western Society, 1880–1930*, Baltimore: Johns Hopkins University Press.

Hughes, T. P. (1987) 'Edison and electric light', in D. MacKenzie and J. Wajcman (eds.) *The Social Shaping of Technology*, Milton Keynes: Open University Press.

Introna, L. and Whittaker, L. (2005) *Power, cash and convenience: The political space of the ATM*, paper presented at the 2005 Critical Management Studies Conference, University of Cambridge.

Kallinikos, J. (2004) 'Deconstructing Information Packages: Organizational and Behavioural Implications of ERP Systems', *Information Technology and People*, 17(1):8–30.

Kelly, K. (1999) *New Rules for the New Economy*, Harmondsworth: Penguin.

Knights, D., Noble, F., Vurdubakis, T. and Willmott, H. (2002) 'Allegories of creative destruction: Technology and organization in narratives of the e-economy', in S. Woolgar (ed.) *Virtual Society? Technology, Cyberbole, Reality*, Oxford: Oxford University Press, p.p. 99–114.

Knox, H., O'Doherty, D., Vurdubakis, T. and Westrup, C. (in press) 'Zeno's shadow: flux and stability in computer mediated organization'.

Kuhn, T. (1970) *The Structure of Scientific Revolutions*, Chicago: University of Chicago Press.

Kumar, K. and van Hillegersberg, J. (2000) 'ERP experiences and revolution', *Communications of the ACM* 43(4):23–26.

Latour, B. (1987) *Science in Action*, Milton Keynes: Open University Press.

Latour, B. (1988a) 'Mixing humans and non-humans together: The sociology of a door-closer', *Social Problems* 35:298–310.

Latour, B. (1988b) 'The prince for machines as well as for machinations', in B. Elliott (ed.) *Technology and Social Process*, Edinburgh: Edinburgh University Press.

Latour, B. (1992) 'Where are the missing masses? A sociology of a few mundane artifacts', in W. E. Bijker and J. Law (eds.) *Shaping Technology/Building Society*, Cambridge MA: MIT Press.

Latour, B. (1993) *We Have Never Been Modern*, London: Harvester Wheatsheaf.

Latour, B. (2004) *A Prologue in Form of a Dialog Between a Student and His (Somewhat) Socratic Professor*, available at: http://www.ensmp.fr/~latour/articles/article/090.html.

Law, J. (ed.) (1986a) *Power, Action and Belief*, London: RKP.

Law, J. (1986b) 'On power and its tactics: A view from the sociology of science', *Sociological Review* 34(1):1–38.

MacKenzie, D. and Wajcman, J. (eds.) (1999) *The Social Shaping of Technology*, Buckingham and Philadelphia: Open University Press.

Marx, L. and Smith, M. R. (eds.) (1994) *Does Technology Drive History? The Dilemma of Technological Determinism*, Cambridge, MA: MIT Press.

May, Thornton A. (2002) 'Technohits, technomisses', *Fast Company*, March 2002: 64.

Metro (2003) 'This game will self destruct in . . .' Thursday 9 October: 11.

Miles, I. (1988) *On Technology*, paper presented at PICT Network Conference, Edinburgh, 19–21 September.

Miles, I. (1989) 'Review of S. Hill, the Tragedy of Technology', *Sociology* 23(3):489–490.

Misa, T. (1992) 'Controversy and closure in technological change: Constructing "Steel" ' in W. Bijker and J. Law (eds.) *Shaping Technology/Building Society*, Cambridge MA: MIT Press.

Morgan, G. (1986) *Images of Organization*, London: Sage.

Negroponte, N. (1995) *Being Digital*, London: Hodder and Stoughton.

Noble, D. (1999) 'Social choice in machine design: The case of automatically controlled machine tools', in D. MacKenzie and J. Wajcman (eds.) *The Social Shaping of Technology*, Milton Keynes: Open University Press.

Ogburn, W. F. (1950) 'Social evolution reconsidered', in W. F. Ogburn (ed.) *Social Change*, New York, Viking, p.p. 369–393.

OU (1996) *Information Technology and Society*, Block 1 of course text for THD204, Milton Keynes: Open University.

Perrin, N. (1979) *Giving Up the Gun: Japan's Reversion to the Sword 1543–1879*, New York: David Godine.

Peters, T. (1997) *The Circle of Innovation*, London: Hodder & Stoughton.

Pinch, T. (1998) 'The social construction of technology: A review', in R. Fox (ed.) *Technological Change*, Amsterdam: Hartwood.

Pinch, T. and Bijker, W. E. (1984) 'The social construction of facts and artefacts: Or how the sociology of science and the sociology of technology might benefit each other', *Social Studies of Science* 14:399–441.

Pippin, R. (1994) 'On the notion of technology as ideology', in Y. Ezrahi, E. Mendelsohn and H. Segal (eds.) *Technology, Pessimism, and Postmodernism*, Boston: University of Massachusetts Press.

Randall, C. (2004) 'France silences cinema mobiles', *The Daily Telegraph*, 12 October:10.

Rapoport, A. (1969) *House, Home and Culture*, Englewood Cliffs, NJ: Prentice Hall.

Rheingold, H. (2000) *The Virtual Community: Homesteading on the Electronic Frontier*, Cambridge MA: MIT Press.

Rifkin, J. and Heilbroner, R. L. (1996) *The End of Work: The Decline of the Global Labor Force and the Dawn of the Post-Market Era*, New York: J. P. Tarcher.

Schaefer, S. (2003) *Tech Bubble: Who Benefited? An Interview with Michael Hudson*. Available at: http://www.michael-hudson.com/interviews/030830_counterpunch.html.

Schwartz, E. I. (1999) *Digital Darwinism: 7 Breakthrough Business Strategies for Surviving the Cutthroat Web Economy*, New York: Broadway Books.

Schwartz Cowan, R. (1985) 'How the Refrigerator Got its Hum', in D. MacKenzie and J. Wajcman (eds.) (1985) '*The Social Shaping of Technology*', Milton Keynes: Open University Press.

Selby, A. (2004) 'Against the grain: The Amish are old-fashioned farmers but their approach is remarkably successful', *Financial Times*, 22/23 May: W7.

Sheffield University Packaging Research Group (n.d.) *User Capabilities and Problems*. Available at: http://www.shef.ac.uk/packaging/paper3.htm.

Spencer, R. (2006) 'Mobiles blocked in exam crackdown', *Daily Telegraph*, June 8: 18.

Stalder, F. (2002) Failures and successes: Notes on the development of electronic cash, *The Information Society* 18(3):209–219.

Thomas, R. (1994) *What Machines Can't Do*, Berkley: University of California Press.

Toffler, A. (1971) *Future Shock*, London: Pan.

Toffler, A. (1980) *The Third Wave*, London: Collins.

Tsoukas, H. (1994) *New Thinking in Organizational Behaviour*, Oxford: Butterworth-Heinemann.

Turnbull, S. (1996) *Samurai Warfare*, London: Cassell & Co.

Turnbull, S. (1998) *The Samurai Sourcebook*, London: Cassell & Co.

Underwood, J. (1999) 'Not another methodology: What ANT tells us about systems development', in T. Wood-Harper, N. Jayaratna and J. Wood (eds.) *Methodologies for Developing and Managing Emerging Technology Based Information Systems*, London: Springer.

UNPD (2001) *Making New Technologies Work for Human Development*, Oxford: Oxford University Press.

van Aken, J., Hop, L. and Post, G. (1997) *The Virtual Company: A Special Mode of Strong Inter-company Co-operation*', paper presented at the XVII Annual International Conference of the Strategic Management Society, Barcelona, 5 October: 8.

van Dulken, S. (2004) *Inventing the American Dream: A History of Curious, Extraordinary and Just Plain Useful Patents*, London: British Library.

Walker, C. R. and Guest, R. (1952) *The Man on the Assembly Line*, Cambridge MA: Harvard University Press.

Warschauer, M. (2003) 'Demystifying the digital divide', *Scientific American*, August.

Weinberg, A. M. (1966) 'Can Technology Replace Social Engineering?' *University of Chicago Magazine*, 59, October:6–10.

Weizenbaum, J. (1984) *Computer Power and Human Reason*, Harmondsworth: Penguin.

Wernwick, A. (1994) 'Vehicles for myth: The shifting image of the modern car', in S. Maasik and J. Solomon (eds.), *Signs of Life in the U.S.A.*, Boston: Bedford Books, p.p. 78–94.

White, L. T. (1962) *Medieval Technology and Social Change*, Oxford: Oxford University Press.

Williams, R. (1979) *Television: Technology and Cultural Form*, Glasgow: Fontana.

Williams, R. (2000) ' "All that is solid melts into air": Historians of technology and the information revolution', *Technology and Culture*, 41, October:641–668.

Winder, B., Ridgway, K., Nelson, A. and Baldwin, J. (2002) 'Food and drink packaging: Who is complaining and who should be complaining' *Applied Ergonomics* 33(5):433–438.

Winner, L. (1977) *Autonomous Technology*, Cambridge, MA: MIT Press.

Winner, L. (1997) *How Technomania is Overtaking the Millennium*. Available at: http://www.rpi.edu/~winner/How%20Technomania.html.

Woodward, J. (1965) *Industrial Organization: Theory and Practice*, Oxford: Oxford University Press.

Woolgar, S. (1988) *Science: The Very Idea*, London: Routledge.

Zuboff, S. (1989) *In the Age of the Smart Machine: The Future of Work and Power*, New York: Basic Books.

Notes

1 As Thornton A. May ('Chief Psychographer' for the US consulting firm Toffler Associates Inc., puts it (2002, p. 64) 'basically we have *Star Wars* technology, factory-level deployment, and sit-around-the-campfire [i.e. Neolithic] human behavior'.

2 Even Karl Marx is sometimes described (e.g. Ellul, 1967) as a technological determinist because of his remark to the effect that the hand-mill gave us feudal society and the steam-mill bourgeois society.

3 In the battle of Nagashino (1575), for instance, warlord Oda Nobunaga used 3000 men armed with firearms to unceremoniously mow down the mounted samurai of his opponents (the Takeda clan). The Portuguese had introduced firearms to Japan in 1542.

4 This particular historical episode has recently received the Hollywood treatment in *The Last Samurai* (Edward Zwick, 2003).

5 The Luddites are named after a certain Ned Ludd or Ludlam from Leicestershire, said to be the first to smash his machine in 1779.

6 While many concede that technologies may well be put to political uses, they often argue that it is the *purposes* to which a society puts its technologies that are political, not their technical content. Technology, the United Nations' Programme for Development (2001, p. 27) report argues, 'is not inherently good or bad – the outcome depends on how it is used.'

7 For example, the nomads of central Asia may have invented the stirrup but did not adopt the knights' heavy armour nor – needless to say – feudalism.

8 Indeed technological determinist perspectives are sometimes described as 'science push' theories.

9 A the old joke has it, 'on the internet nobody knows you are a dog'.

10 From a TD perspective, the explanation of 'technology itself' should be left to technical experts: For TD the technical 'content' is beyond social scientific understanding – what engineers call a 'black box' (MacKenzie and Wajcman, 1999).

11 For instance, it is customary to see the factory system as the product of a technological revolution. However, the first factories 'contained the same machinery as had been used previously in the cottage production system'. It was only *after* such factories were set up, 'that there existed the demand for new technologies' (OU: 1996, p. 62).

12 Yes, buildings – machines for living as Le Corbusier would have it – do qualify as technologies according to the definition provided earlier.

13 For instance, the choice between building an apartment block or a number of semi-detached houses for private accomodation has a lot to do with fashion (tower blocks were very popular in the United Kingdom in the 1960s), socio-economic class (it was the poor that often ended up in the tower blocks) and our ideas about identity or the good life (say urban versus suburban living).

14 The safe disposal of the ozone layer damaging CFCs found in electric fridges is now a major concern throughout the world. Thus recently the EU has demanded that decommissioned fridges should be treated as hazardous waste and disposed of accordingly, a complex and resource-intensive process.

15 For similar reasons, British novelist Ian Fleming was told to change the weapon of his secret agent hero James Bond from a Beretta – considered a 'lady's gun' – to a (presumably more 'masculine') Walther PKK (Bennett, 2004: 6).

16 Although some might argue that radioactive waste is not a technology as such, the perception of nuclear waste clearly influenced the development of both nuclear and waste disposal technologies.

17 SCOT analysts often employ the concept of 'technological frames' (TF) to describe the diversity of interactions among social actors in RSGs. If existing interactions tend to move members of an emerging RSG in the same direction, a technological frame will build up. If not, there will be no shared technological frame, the RSG will fall apart and interaction will decline. A TF includes elements such as goals, technological and scientific theories, testing procedures and design methods and criteria, which members of RSGs use to make sense of a technology.

A technological frame is therefore a social space, a kind of arena, within which the meaning attributed to an artefact by the members of the social group is negotiated. It is where the problems of the technology are identified, and solutions proposed using the problem-solving strategies characteristic of that frame (recall for instance the Atomic Energy Commission's various deliberations over the problem of radioactive waste mentioned above). In other words, describing the TF of a relevant social group helps one explain a particular course of events (Bijker, 1995, p. 124).

18 One casualty of ANT determination not to indulge in the separation of what are social (i.e. human) factors from what are technological/material (i.e. non-human) factors appears to be all taken for granted distinctions between 'human actors' (people) and 'non-human actors' (such as technological devices, institutions, forces of nature). To underline this point, ANT writers often prefer to speak of 'actants' rather than actors. To keep things simple, this neologism has been avoided here. However, ANT is not intended as an exercise in anthropomorphism. ('Anthropomorphism' is the attribution of human qualities to non-humans.) This is not what is intended here.) Rather it is a recognition that the boundary between what people do and what machines etc. do, is in constant flux across the whole spectrum of human life. Flying a plane, for instance, requires inputs from pilots and the onboard computers. As accident investigations have shown it is very difficult to separate their activities. See Latour (2004).

19 ANT's concept of 'translation' is a deliberate departure from the more common concept of interaction. As Stalder (2002) puts it, whereas interaction presupposes 'two (or more) stable entities that are linked together in a stimulus response relation . . . translation instead focuses on the mutual (inter)definition of actors as they become linked together'. ANT is often called the 'Sociology of Translation'.

20 In practice these 'steps' may occur in a different order.

21 One could say that you explored various such scripts when attempting to decide upon an appropriate environment and clientele for AWOL™.

22 The central concerns and conceptual tools of ANT have remained relatively unchanged, thus allowing us to present a rather simplified version here.

Part III
Emergent Issues

Part III provides a review of wider, emergent issues that are of contemporary significance. The global economy is examined within the context of the strategic plans of corporate managers who increasingly have to take some, if rather a limited, responsibility for the consequences of their activities for sustained ecological and environmental stability. The characteristics of new forms of organization, the nature of regulation and the relevance of ethics are examined from mainstream and critical perspectives.

12 Globalization and Organizations

Glenn Morgan

Key concepts and learning objectives

By the end of this chapter you should understand:

- The concept of globalization.

- The economic factors that generate increasing internationalization of firms.

- The mainstream models of how multinationals should be structured.

- The potential barriers to an efficient multinational structure that come from national cultural differences.

- The limitations of the mainstream approach with regard particularly to the neglect of issues of power, control and inequality.

- The importance of understanding multinationals as concentrations of economic and political power.

- The impact that multinationals can make on governments and society more generally.

- The multinational as a transnational social space in which groups from different local contexts bargain and negotiate.

- The necessity for a critical approach to the study of globalization and multinationals.

Aims of chapter

This chapter will:

- Explain the meaning of the term 'globalization'.

- Examine how globalization impacts on organizational behaviour and management.

- Identify the factors that lead to the development of multinational firms, their strategy and structure.

- Analyse how multinational firms respond to national cultural differences.

- Demonstrate the contribution that a critical approach to globalization and multinationals can make.

Overview and key points

The 21st century will be the century of globalization. Organizations increasingly plan their production, their innovation and their marketing on a scale that goes beyond the national. There are profound economic drivers for this process that come from accessing resources, skills, labour and technology in the most efficient way. That means crossing national borders in order to create economies of scale and scope that will enable goods and services to be produced as cheaply and flexibly as possible in order to respond to customer demands. Multinationals become hugely powerful actors in this process, influencing governments and international regulators as well as profoundly reshaping national societies and the natural environment as they seek to create the conditions that enable them to achieve these economies of scale and scope.

From an internal organizational point of view, however, the problem of coordinating all these activities across national boundaries is immense. For much of the 19th and 20th centuries, social life in the industrial societies of the West was constructed in a predominantly 'national' way. The state constructed school and education systems that taught individuals the rudiments of disciplines such as time-keeping and obeying authority that were essential to running large collective efforts such as the civil service, factories, offices and armies. In different countries, however, these processes occurred in distinctive ways. In the 19th century, states were constructed around strong national identities – being English, being French, being German, etc. – and this was reflected in the systems of work and industry that were established. In particular, the way in which work was organized (how much did it occur in big factories, how standardized was it, how skilled were the employees) and the way in which relations between employees and employers was structured (were employees allowed to join independent trade unions, what rights did these unions have in terms of negotiating wages or conditions of work, what links did trade unions have with political parties and the state) was different across the major industrial societies. This led to profound differences in how businesses were organized across these societies (Bendix 1956 was an early classic study trying to conceptualize those differences in relation to the United Kingdom, the United States and Russia). There was no standard model of work and industry but rather a series of models of what have now become known as 'divergent capitalisms' (Whitley, 1999). These differences remain significant even in an era of globalization.

Thinkpoint 12.1

Motivation and the Japanese employee It is not unusual for office workers in Japan to work until nearly 11.00pm in the evening. However, their overtime is almost always unpaid. Moreover, unlike workaholics in the United States and the United Kingdom, they will not receive a personal individualized bonus. There is in effect no material incentive for them to work such long hours. We cannot understand this on the basis of a single universal explanation of how people are motivated at work. We must understand how different societies place different values on work, family, participation, control, etc. In Japan, the employment relationship in the large firm sector is profoundly different to that in the United Kingdom. It is long term; there are expectations of commitment on both sides; the fates of the firm and the individual are intertwined. Employees are expected to demonstrate a life-long loyalty to the employer and to the people with whom they work. This loyalty overrides the individual's loyalty to the family and even to him/herself. Japanese employees take few holiday days, preferring instead to reserve them for moments of sickness or ill-health. Some Japanese firms have been so concerned about this that they present prizes to employees willing to take holidays. This sense of loyalty is not a 'natural' characteristic of Japanese people; rather it is drummed into them from a very early age by schools, families, the media, employers and the state that they must conform to authority. Even in the 21st century when Japanese young people love to display themselves in outrageous dress and show their openness to Western influence, this seems still a temporary rebellion before the onset of the pressures of work and conformity.

This reflects the way in which Japanese society industrialized, with strong links between the state and firms in order to maintain social stability by making employees highly dependent on the firm and limiting the role of independent trade unions. In Japan, there is a phrase which reflects this process: 'the nail which stands out is hammered down'. This reflects the broader problem for Japanese businesses and Japanese society that this sort of conformity leads to 'groupthink' – i.e. a collective inability to disagree or be innovative – which in turn has implications for businesses more generally. In the United Kingdom, on the other hand, employees expect to have to move from one company to another over the course of their working lives. They expect to be treated as individuals rather than a part of a collective. Work is only one part of their wider life. People do not expect the firm to look after them forever and are used to the prospect of having to move between firms either because they are searching for better wages and conditions or the firm has made them redundant. Management in the United Kingdom faces much bigger problems than Japanese management in terms of getting employees to do as they are told!

These differences across national contexts create a deep problem for multinational firms. What do they do about these different expectations? How can a Japanese firm manage UK or US employees? Do they accept the differences and construct an organization that is highly varied and diverse? Or do they seek to homogenize and standardize values and practices across the firm?

In this chapter, you will be introduced to these debates and arguments. First, we will look at what we mean by globalization and place this in a broad historical context. In the following section we will look at how mainstream theories have developed these arguments. In particular, we look at why globalization is an economic necessity for large firms, what frameworks have been produced to show how multinationals can be coordinated, and finally what concepts can help us understand national cultural differences and how multinationals relate to these. Secondly we will consider the critical approach to globalization. In this section, we look at how globalization potentially centralizes power into the hands of those people who control multinationals and the effect of this on societies and the natural environment. This raises the issue of resistance. Here we can identify two distinct dynamics. One relates to the external context of organizations and in particular the rise of anti-globalization movements. The other relates to the differences between different national contexts and how employees and others build on their local resources to resist attempts to standardize processes and controls on a global scale.

On most measures, the extent of globalization is increasing. This presents organizations with massive challenges. By the end of this chapter, you will understand what these challenges are and how they will shape the agenda for organizational behaviour and management in future years.

Introduction

The term 'globalization' is now commonly used and familiar to everybody and yet even as recently as the early 1990s 'globalization' was not included in the list of keywords in the social sciences compiled by the cultural theorist, Raymond Williams (1992). Globalization has, in effect, become one of the key ways in which we define our sense of ourselves in the current era. On a simple, everyday level it is easy to understand why. We only have to check the labels in our clothes to see that in some basic way our lives are connected to those of others across the world. The shirt I am wearing as I type this was made in China, the jeans in Mexico, the shoes in India. The food that I ate last night included vegetables bought from Kenya and Guatemala. The computer I am using was probably assembled in the Far East from parts made in China, Taiwan, Malaysia and the United States. The car I drive was made in Japan. The drinks in the average British pub come originally from all over the world; Carlsberg from Denmark, Heineken from the Netherlands, Fosters from Australia, Tequila from Mexico, Tiger Beer from India, vodka from Russia, Jack Daniels from the United States, wine from Australia, South Africa and Chile.

Globalization is not just a matter of trade and economic interdependence. It also relates to our whole way of life. Who or what do we think we are? What do we aspire to be? In sport, we see this very clearly. Although 'our teams' compete on the basis of their local and or national affiliations (Manchester United, Chelsea, Arsenal; England, France, Germany, etc.) what draws the biggest crowds and the highest media interest are events like the Olympic Games or the World Cup. What makes us more aware of being 'One World' than watching great performances in events like these? Even so-called local or national teams are in reality often multinational and global. Take the example of football teams in the English Premier League. The takeover of Chelsea football club by the Russian billionaire, Roman Abramovich, and the purchase of footballers from all over the world to make the team, is part of the growing globalization of sport as a business and as a way of life for its many fans. In recent years, other clubs like Manchester United, Real Madrid, Barcelona and Liverpool have seen not just their team internationalize but also their fans becoming increasingly international. Real Madrid were keen to buy David Beckham for his footballing skills but they also knew that he had become highly recognizable in Southeast Asia and would therefore help them build up their fan base there. International fan bases are now a crucial revenue generating opportunity for football clubs, allowing them to sell merchandise and more importantly TV rights to their games in new and expanding markets.

The growth of cheap air travel together with the growing popularity of 'gap years' for students between school and university have both contributed to high levels of travel in and experience of different countries. The flow of overseas students into UK and US universities impacts not just there but in the countries from which they come as graduates return with new ideas and approaches. Styles of life cross national borders easily. The influence of TV programmes such as *Friends* and *Sex in the City* is to construct mythical views of what life can be like, which in turn become aspirational targets for young people in many parts of the world.

Of course, we can raise questions about such a picture both at the descriptive and the evaluative level. At the descriptive level, the great age of mass migration was the 18th and 19th centuries when European populations spread into the Americas, Australasia and parts of Africa and when many Africans were forced into slavery and transported to the Americas. Our time is characterized both by a partial reversal in the process, particularly as far as Europe is concerned (i.e. populations wishing to enter Europe rather than leave it), but also by high levels of border controls and rigid quotas on migrants. Looking back, it is also possible to see that this flow of styles of life and accompanying material goods, such as clothes and ceramics, has often occurred. The Brighton Pavilion was built in the late 18th century under the influence of architectural styles from India and interior decoration patterns from China.

Everyday staples of the British diet for centuries originated from trade with other countries – potatoes, coffee, tomatoes, chocolate from the Americas, tea from China, spices from the islands that eventually became Indonesia. We have to be careful, therefore, not to exaggerate the uniqueness of the current era.

Nevertheless, many authors argue that the current era is unique and therefore globalization is something new. In one of the most important and detailed analyses of globalization, Held and his colleagues state that 'Globalization may be thought of initially as the widening, deepening and speeding up of worldwide interconnectedness in all aspects of contemporary life' (Held *et al.*, 1999, p. 2). This is a useful definition in that it allows us to see that globalization is a process. In this respect, we can identify different degrees of globalization across different spheres of social life. We can also identify different authors in terms of the degree to which they believe this process has proceeded. Held *et al.* (1999, chapter 1), for example, differentiate three categories of interpretation:

- *Hyperglobalizers* who tend to emphasize the decline of the nation state under the pressure of economic processes and the development of cross-border trade and multinationals (e.g. Ohmae).

- *Sceptics* who argue that the extent of these processes has been much exaggerated. Nation states remain crucial actors and even multinationals are dependent on their home state in many ways (e.g. Hirst and Thompson).

- *Transformationalists* who argue that there are profound changes occurring but the direction of these processes is uncertain, uneven and contradictory. Held *et al.* place themselves in the transformationalist camp and it is from a similar position that the current author writes in this chapter and elsewhere (Morgan, 2001a, 2001b).

Image 12.1 The Royal Pavilion in Brighton was transformed into Indian style for the Prince Regent, later William IV, in the period 1815–22, by the famous architect, John Nash, whose 1826 painting this is. The interior was decorated in a Chinese style with imported silks, fabrics and porcelain

In evaluative terms, globalization sets us many moral conundrums and this reflects the uncertain, uneven and contradictory processes involved. The reason why production of many standard commodities (such as clothes, toys, electrical components, etc.) has spread to areas like China, Vietnam and India is because the people in those countries can be paid very much less than their counterparts in the United Kingdom or Germany or France. Similarly, these countries do not have the same standards of health and safety in their factories, the same level of taxes on companies to fund employment relief or healthcare, the same legislation restricting hours of work for children, etc. The result has been a profound improvement in the standard of living of the Western countries with prices of standard manufactured goods (from televisions to computers and toys) continuously falling relative to wages over the last two decades. In this respect, we have become dependent on globalization and in the process we have become dependent on the low wages paid to workers in other parts of the world.

Thinkpoint 12.2

Look at the labels on your clothes and shoes. What proportion of them were made in the United Kingdom? Do you see a difference in origins between your more expensive clothes items and your cheaper ones? Why do you think this is? Should you care about where your clothes are made?

Similarly globalization pressures draw societies into the world economy in ways that both threaten traditional ways of life at the local level and more broadly the global ecology. The deforestation of large areas of the world such as in Brazil, India and Indonesia drives local people off the land and often leaves them marginalized and demoralized in shanty towns or reservations that become human sink-holes. The same process also robs the world of the unknown resources that come from the high levels of biodiversity that characterize rainforest environments. Deforestation and other environmental changes seem also to have impacts on global weather systems that are hard to predict, while locally it makes areas more susceptible to flooding and other natural disasters (such as happened in Haiti in the floods that Tropical Storm Jeanne brought to the island in September 2004, and in New Orleans in September 2005 with Hurricane Katrina). In the short run the benefits of deforestation flow to the global corporations that organize and manage the process, the local landowners who sell the rights to timber, and to the companies and consumers of the affluent societies who purchase the goods made out of these trees. In his analysis of globalization, Giddens (1999, chapter 2) has associated this with the idea of risk. Events in one part of the world are interdependent with those in another part, and thus risks become magnified. Global warming does not respect national boundaries, and although President George W. Bush might reject the Kyoto Protocol on reducing the harmful emission of gases (because it would impose a burden on US industry), Hurricane Jeanne does not stop and divert its destructive path away from the coastline of Florida.

Organizations are central participants in this process. Multinationals in particular scour the globe looking for new opportunities – to find new markets, to find new resources, to find a cheaper labour force, to find new ideas. Their restless search takes them anywhere that money can be made, subject only to the constraints of geo-political dynamics and public opinion as the headlong rush of US companies into Iraq after President Bush declared 'Victory' illustrated. Authors such as Giddens (1999) emphasize the contribution made to this process by new information and communication technologies. It is now simple enough for European and North American managers to be in instantaneous contact with factories in China and Brazil, call centres in India and Scotland, suppliers in Taiwan and Mexico, distributors in Australia and South Africa. Systems of transportation and logistics mean that products and people can move around the world quickly, efficiently and (mostly) predictably in planes, trains, lorries and massive container ships. Giddens argues that our notions of time and space have been changed as a result of these developments. He refers to this as time-space distanciation, by which he means that we expect instant communication with others (and can achieve this thanks to mobile phones and e-mail technology) and we expect geography to be a limited barrier to this communication thanks again to technology (see Table 12.1).

When you are in another country, how do you communicate with friends and family? How do you think you would have communicated if you had been travelling abroad in the 1970s? Most young people now have mobile phones. Do you know anybody who has not?! Access to the internet is increasing and soon VoIP (Voice over Internet Protocol) is expected to become a significant competitor in the telephone market. What are the limits to Giddens' idea of time-space distanciation in your experience?

Table 12.1 Top ten countries with the highest internet penetration rate

Rank	Country or region	Penetration (% population)	Internet users latest data	Population (2006 est.)	Source and date of latest data
1	Malta	78.1	301 000	385 308	ITU – Sept/05
2	New Zealand	76.3	3 200 000	4 195 729	ITU – Sept/05
3	Iceland	75.9	225 600	297 072	ITU – Sept/05
4	Sweden	74.9	6 800 000	9 076 757	ITU – Oct/05
5	Denmark	69.4	3 762 500	5 425 373	ITU – Sept/05
6	Hong Kong	69.2	4 878 713	7 054 867	Nielsen//NR Feb/05
7	Australia	68.4	14 189 544	20 750 052	Nielsen//NR Dec/05
8	United States	68.1	203 824 428	299 093 237	Nielsen//NR Dec/05
9	Canada	67.9	21 900 000	32 251 238	eTForecasts Dec/05
10	Norway	67.8	3 140 000	4 632 911	C.I.Almanac Mar/05
World total users		15.7	1 018 057 389	6 499 697 060	IWS – Dec/05

Managers need no longer worry about their actual physical distance from a factory in China because they can get close to it through monitoring various output and performance indicators. Nor need they worry about how long it might take to deliver goods from one side of the world to the other. This can be planned and speeded up by modern technology. Time and distance are being conquered in the interests of the (Western) consumer and the market system.

For those of us who study organizations, however, this story is too simple. Of course, organizations can do amazing things. By bringing individuals together and coordinating their actions with inputs of capital, technology and other resources, organizations have contributed to a vast expansion in our material well-being. But as you are well aware from the previous chapters in this book, this process is highly conflictual, generates and reinforces inequalities of power, income and wealth, and has unanticipated effects on individuals, groups, localities and the planet more generally. In this chapter, therefore, we want to look at these two sides to globalization and organizations.

- On the one side, there is the mainstream approach in which the expansion of the global market contributes directly to this improvement in living standards as firms become more efficient. From this perspective, the considerable problems of organization that arise from internationalization can be solved if we apply sufficient rational decision making to the issues faced, such as that of national differences.

- On the other side is the critical approach, which uncovers the costs of this process in terms of the concentration of economic and social power and the fact that it is in the hands of a few who are unaccountable to the populations affected by their actions. The critical approach also dissects the rational model of the multinational, revealing how groups are struggling inside the organization to make a difference to how they live and how their localities are affected by these processes of globalization.

(Shell, BP, Esso), sugar (Tate and Lyle) and minerals (RioTinto Zinc, Anglo-American Mining). Alongside this, three other trends emerged. First, there was increased export of capital from Europe; often this went into the development of infrastructure such as railways and later the supply of gas, electricity and water. Secondly, there was increased export of manufactured goods from Europe into other parts of the world, often in payment for the raw materials extracted from these countries. Thirdly, there was the gradual establishment of overseas subsidiaries.

Approaches to internationalization

From an organizational point of view, the key issues were those of control, predictability and profitability. Investing overseas brought with it risks as well as opportunities. We can identify four broad approaches that organizations have taken when they have sought to internationalize their activities – selling, licensing and franchising, subcontracting and, finally, setting up production outside the home base.

Selling: Export strategy   The least risky strategy for a firm which wishes to benefit from overseas demand for its products is to simply export from the home base. This requires very little investment in other countries. Sales might be handled by an international office in the home country with independent agents operating as intermediaries overseas. Traditionally most small and medium-sized enterprises tend to be come 'international' by exporting their products. Even large companies have been reluctant to move beyond this. Until the late 1980s, for example, German manufacturing companies, including some of their large car companies, tended to become international through exports rather than any more direct involvement in overseas contexts. The main disadvantages of such a strategy are

1 The firm incurs high transport costs in shipping products overseas.

2 The products are made additionally expensive because of customs duties levied on entry to the foreign market.

3 It tends to limit the market overseas. This is for two reasons:

   ● The firm is unlikely to be able to adapt its product to the specific consumer needs of the overseas market (at least partly because, without actually being in the country, it finds it hard to know what those specific needs are).

   ● Because it relies on agents, it does not have direct access to knowledge about the scale of the market or how to develop it further (at least partly because agents may find it in their interests to keep the company ignorant of these specific details).

Licensing and franchising   In this system, the agent (i.e. the licensee or franchisee) pays a fee to the company in order to use its system/design/invention in its own country. The fee can be negotiated in various ways but often is set so that there is an incentive to build the market because each new sale directly brings in a reward to the franchise holder. The company that has the idea or product does not have to risk its own capital and managerial time in setting up overseas in this system. Instead it relies on the local knowledge and the capital of local investors to bear most of the risk. There are many variations on this model. McDonald's, for example, has grown through a franchising system. It sells the rights to become a McDonald's to investors in different countries. Part of the franchise is the commitment of the owners to follow the McDonald's model in terms of décor, menu, methods of cooking and customer service. This process enables McDonald's to be present in all parts of the world without having to find the capital or managerial expertise itself to make this work in a diversity of cultural and social contexts.

Exercise 12.2

Find five other global franchises besides McDonald's. Choose one of them and find information on how its franchising system works and how truly international it is. As an initial starting point for your research, you can look at the website of the British Franchising Association (http://www.british-franchise.org/index.asp).

Franchising has a number of disadvantages:

1 Loss of control over the brand raising the risk that it may be undermined by the poor performance of franchisees.

2 Loss of control over the knowledge and processes that are transferred overseas, enabling franchisees to transfer that knowledge to other operations that may eventually change the competitive environment for the renewal of licences – what is referred to as 'opportunism', i.e. that people will act in ways that benefit themselves to the detriment of others in a contract if they think they can get away with it.

3 Loss of knowledge about market changes in different contexts and how this might be relevant to either the adaptation of the original product or the development of new products.

4 Loss of direct control over the production process; the franchisor is thus unable to squeeze maximum revenue out of employees through increasing the level of effort demanded of the employees. These decisions are left to the local franchisee.

These disadvantages can of course all be overcome by increased monitoring of the licensee, but this then begins to undermine the economic logic of the bargain. Increased monitoring and surveillance of the franchisee costs the franchisor in terms of money and managerial time. Clearly there will inevitably be a point where the costs of monitoring exceed the benefits of franchising and therefore the franchisor or licence holder may withdraw the franchise and move to set up its own subsidiary operations in the country.

Subcontracting   In this system, the firm contracts with an independent manufacturer to produce goods and services according to the terms of a carefully specified contract. Again the firm reduces its risk as it does not have to commit its own capital or its own managerial time to direct control and coordination of the labour process. Subcontracting of this sort is also popular because it increases flexibility for the firm and reduces its costs. This is the model that Nike follows. In general, this set of relationships is known as the supply chain. Researchers who have been particularly concerned with the construction of international, cross-border supply chains have labelled these relationships 'global commodity chains' (Gereffi, 1996, 2001) or 'global production networks' (Dicken, 2003). Global commodity chains are common in the retail industry. Supermarkets such as Tesco and Sainsbury enter into contracts with farmers in many parts of the world to ensure year-round supply of products like strawberries, asparagus, apples, etc., which have short harvests in the United Kingdom itself. Clothes stores such as Gap, H&M and TopShop contract with independent firms in India, China, Malaysia, etc. to produce according to designs supplied by UK designers aiming to keep up or develop fashion trends for the various seasonal collections of clothes and accessories. Any manufactured product is likely to contain within it components from many different subcontractors, often in different countries and even continents.

Exercise 12.3

Check out the computer you normally use. It may be branded as IBM or Dell or HP, but where was it actually assembled and by whom? You may find that this was done by another company. This subcontractor is known as an OEM (own equipment manufacturer) – i.e. it is an independent company producing under contract for a buyer such as IBM, which will brand the end-product. When firms sell their own products, we call this the development of own-brand manufacturing (OBM) capability. Acer in Taiwan have both OEM and OBM capability – i.e. they produce for IBM and under their own brand name (at a cheaper price).

Look at commercial websites for the retail sale of computer components (e.g. Maplins) and you will see the range of producers who specialize in various parts that the OEM and OBM assembler puts together, such as memory chips, microprocessors, flash memory devices, logic chips and screens. Follow through to manufacturer websites (such as Intel, AMD, Motorola, Fujitsu) and look at where their production facilities are located and how they themselves are embedded in global commodity chains.

Where products are simple and designs can be standardized, it is relatively easy to establish contracting relationships as there will be high amounts of competition between contractors.

However, as products become more complex and more knowledge has to be transferred to the contractor involving more specific investments in order to meet the contracting firms' requirements, so the relationship becomes difficult. Both sides become open to potential opportunism (i.e. they may be tempted to cheat each other). Thus the main firm may respond to this problem in the same way as in the previous case – i.e. by cutting the contract and setting up its own subsidiary.

Overseas production   Levels of what are known as foreign direct investment (FDI) – i.e. directly investing in buying or establishing production facilities overseas – have grown massively in the last decade after a slower and more steady period of growth in the period since the 1950s. These figures reflect two things. First, they reflect multinational companies investing in the building and creation of new manufacturing or office facilities overseas. Secondly they reflect cross-border mergers and acquisitions. In the latter case, no new productive facilities have been added to those already existing. It is simply a case of ownership being transferred so that, for example, a firm based in the United States is now owned by a firm based in the United Kingdom. In 2000, the most recent peak for cross-border merger and acquisition deals, the total amount spent on these deals was US$1143 billion. Economists measure these statistics in terms of annual outflows and inflows. In 2000, US$1393 billion dollars of FDI flowed into countries, so 82 per cent of this flow was in terms of cross-border mergers and acquisitions and only 18 per cent went directly to develop new productive facilities. FDI growth began to outstrip growth rates for exports in the late 1980s and whereas export growth in the period 1996–99 averaged only 1.9 per cent per annum, FDI outflows (in other words the amount of new money being sent overseas each year for investment) grew by 37 per cent per annum. Why has this happened? Why are firms increasingly confident that both the political and economic uncertainties of the past can now be handled sufficiently to encourage them to make these investments?

In political terms, the dominance of capitalism is more or less complete since the collapse of the Soviet system at the start of the 1990s. The United States is the dominant superpower. What was known as the Cold War between the United States and the Soviet Union and their allies in the period from 1945 through to the early 1990s was a different sort of international order. The two sides struggled for influence in all parts of the world, giving military and financial aid to countries or parties that supported them. This led to high levels of political uncertainty in Africa, Asia, Latin America and the Middle East, reflected in occasional outbreaks of hostilities – e.g. in Korea in the 1950s and in Vietnam in the following decade, as well as promoting coups and civil wars in many other parts of the world. Although the 1990s and 2000s has seen new wars in places like the former Yugoslavia (Serbia, Croatia, Bosnia), Iraq and Afghanistan, together with continued civil wars and massacres in Africa (such as Rwanda), this is less a reflection of hostilities between 'superpowers' (inevitably as there is only one now – the United States) and more a consequence of internal struggles for power and influence in the new post-Cold War setting.

In this period, the dominant economic orthodoxy has been that poor countries with low savings and low internally generated capital cannot develop on the back of their own resources. The only way of building infrastructure (such as roads, railways, airports, education systems, health and safety systems, etc.) and manufacturing capability is to encourage the investment of foreign capital. Loans from developed countries and institutions such as the World Bank and the International Monetary Fund may serve to start this process, but a central element is to persuade large multinationals to locate new production facilities in their country. For many countries, this is a losing battle. Africa, for example, is not an attractive site for foreign investors in manufacturing due to political instability, a small internal market (due to large numbers of people in poverty), a relatively unskilled workforce (low levels of literacy and numeracy), and poorly developed infrastructure (in terms of both the physical setting – rail, roads and airports – and the broader social context of health services and the problems stemming from the AIDS crisis). The only possible exception at the moment is South Africa in post-Mandela times, but even here it is still extremely difficult to get large foreign investors. Of course, Africa has huge natural resources – diamonds, gold, copper, tin, oil (known as the extractive industries) as well as agricultural products – and these are often owned and operated by overseas companies. However, the impact on the broader economy is often limited as most technology in the extractive industries is imported from overseas, managers tend to be expatriates from overseas and employees develop few skills that are more widely transferable. Moreover the huge riches from these industries (particularly diamonds and gold) circulates into the political system in ways that has often led to corruption and civil war as groups struggle for control of the wealth, as in Angola in the last two decades.

Countries that have been particularly successful in encouraging inward FDI tend to have political and economic stability and a skilled (or if not skilled, cheap and disciplined) labour force. These factors are reinforced by locational factors (close to major markets) and language factors (English-speaking). As Table 12.2 illustrates, some countries have become highly dependent on inward FDI for their overall economic well-being. In the early 1990s, this was the route by which the so-called Asian tigers (Hong Kong, Singapore, South Korea, Malaysia) developed (see Table 12.3 for the contrasting outward FDI). The late 1990s saw the label of 'Celtic tiger' being applied to Ireland as it became a huge importer of capital, particularly from the United States.

Other countries have also begun to swallow up large amounts of FDI, although, because of the size of their overall economy, their dependency is lower than the small countries in Table 12.2. In the period 1999–2001, for example, China held 5.87 per cent of all inward FDI stock (stock is a measure of the total amount of foreign investment in a society, whereas flow refers to the amount coming in or going out in any one particular year); if Hong Kong (at 7.14 per cent) is added, it would make a total of 13.1 per cent. No other developing country comes close to this; India, for example, is only 0.32 per cent. Only the United States is ahead of China plus Hong Kong at 19.48 per cent, reflecting the fact that, in absolute terms, the great bulk of FDI flows are across developed countries, not into the developing world. In 2002, US$460 billion flowed into the developed economies, compared to US$162 billion into the developing economies, of which Africa received barely US$10 billion (less than the total inflow to a single mid-sized European economy such as Sweden and significantly less than the sum that China alone received, US$52 billion).[1]

Table 12.2 Inward FDI as a percentage of gross domestic product, 1990 and 1999

	1990	1999
Singapore	76.3	97.5
Malaysia	24.1	65.3
Chile	33.2	55.2
Ireland	12.2	50.7
Netherlands	23.6	50.1
Developed countries overall	8.4	14.5
Developing countries overall	13.4	28.0

Source: Reprinted by permission of Sage Publications Ltd, from Dicken, Global Shift 4th edition,.1993.

Table 12.3 Percentage of world total of outward FDI, 1960, 1990 and 2000

	1960	1990	2000
USA	47.1	25.1	20.8
UK	18.3	13.4	15.1
Japan	0.7	11.7	4.7
Germany	1.2	8.6	7.4
France	6.1	7.0	8.3
Netherlands	10.3	6.0	5.5
Share of top ten countries in total outward FDI stock	93.0	86.8	74.0

Source: Reprinted by permission of Sage Publications Ltd, from Dicken, Global Shift 4th edition,.1993.

The big multinationals

Multinational companies (MNCs) are key mechanisms in the flow of inward and outward FDI. They establish overseas production facilities through the transfer of capital (and also technology and people). One of the most important measures of multinationals is one developed by the United Nations Conference on Trade and Development. UNCTAD has produced what it terms 'transnationality' index for MNCs. This aims to show in very broad terms which are the most multinational firms in the world. The transnationality index measures MNCs by three criteria. These criteria are the ratio of home to foreign in the following categories – assets, sales and employment. So by each measure it is possible to measure the percentage of 'foreign' as opposed to home activity in each category – e.g. what percentage of total employment is outside the home country, etc.? Weighting each of these dimensions equally, it is then possible to construct a table of the most transnational firms in the world. Table 12.4 ranks the top 10 MNCs in foreign assets in 2001, and from the point of view of the overall transnationality index.

Table 12.4 Top 10 MNCs by foreign assets, 2001

Foreign asset ranking	Transnationality index ranking	Name of company	Home economy	Industry
1	13	Vodaphone	United Kingdom	Telecoms
2	83	General Electric	United States	Electrical and electronic equipment
3	15	BP	United Kingdom	Petroleum
4	36	Vivendi Universal	France	Diversified
5	82	Deutsche Telekom	Germany	Telecoms
6	39	ExxonMobil	United States	Petroleum
7	85	Ford	United States	Motor vehicles
8	87	General Motors	United States	Motor vehicles
9	48	Royal Dutch/Shell	United Kingdom/ Netherlands	Petroleum
10	21	TotalFinaElf	France	Petroleum

Source: UNCTAD.

Exercise 12.4

Go to the UNCTAD website and find the latest *World Investment Report*. Look for the data on the world's top 100 non-financial transnational companies.

1 Which companies are highest on the transnationality index and why?

2 Which industries are most highly represented on the transnationality index and why?

3 Which industries are most likely to be high on the ratio of foreign employees to home-based employees and why?

4 Why do small countries like Switzerland, the Netherlands and Sweden have companies that are so high on the transnationality index?

5 How transnational is Japanese industry and in which sectors?

6 What weaknesses do you see in this way of measuring the transnationality of firms?

Recently, a strong argument has been made that the internationalization of firms is not so much global but more regional. In his book *The End of Globalization*, Alan Rugman (2000) argues that firms' activities are closely concentrated in their particular part of the world triad – i.e. the world conceived of as being divided into three powerful trading blocs, the EU, NAFTA (the North American Free Trade Agreement covering the United States, Canada and Mexico, and increasingly incorporating in various ways most of Central and Latin America) and Asia Pacific. For example, he presents Table 12.5 on the distribution of the assets of global car firms in 1998.

Rugman follows a rigid methodological approach which conceals some important issues, such as the degree of distribution across different countries within the same trading areas. His methods also cannot show the degree to which components are sourced from outside the home trading area, so it may be that a car assembled in North America is significantly composed of components made in China. Nevertheless these arguments are suggestive about the need to think carefully on what is meant by the term 'multinational'.

The economic logic for the multinational firm

Why do firms decide to establish overseas production and incur the economic risks associated with this instead of making do with exporting, licensing and subcontracting? There are three broad answers to this question: (a) extending the product life cycle; (b) internalization advantages; and (c) the eclectic theory.

Extending the product life cycle One early analyst of multinationals, Vernon (1966), argued that the internationalization of production was a way of extending the life cycle of particular products. In this logic, firms in one country invest in producing a particular commodity which soon becomes outmoded. The investment is then effectively lost and written off. However, there may be other countries where the market is not so advanced that would be willing to buy the product. The company can therefore extend the life cycle of its products and investments by shifting production overseas to where new markets exist. Thus its home base is characterized by a continual process of product upgrading and innovation while its overseas facility receives 'last year's model'.

Vernon's ideas may seem a little dated now when globalization suggests the idea of simultaneous global launches of new products, yet it remains important. Take, for example, the Japanese car industry and its subsidiaries in the United Kingdom. The UK subsidiaries have been built to produce a small handful of standard designs that have been established in Japan for some years. More innovative cars, such as variants of four wheel drives, electric cars, sports cars, etc. are designed, developed and manufactured in Japan for export to the United Kingdom. Innovations such as satellite navigation or the placing of TVs and videos in cars have been developed first in Japan, not in their UK subsidiaries. In general, most firms still seem to do their key development work in their home base and their overseas subsidiaries concentrate on standard products.

Internalization advantages The argument (developed by authors such as Buckley and Casson, 1976, 1985) is that a firm invests at home in developing assets such as production systems, routines of coordination and control, methods of innovation and research and design, systems of management and management development. If the firm licenses its products to overseas manufacturers or sets up subcontracting relationships, it runs the risk that its agents will act opportunistically. In other words, agents will try to conceal the benefits that they receive from the licence or contract and maximize the costs that they incur. Similarly, agents need to be carefully monitored to ensure that they keep to the standards the licence demands of them in order to prevent damaging the broader reputation of

Table 12.5 Asset distribution of global car firms, 1998

	North American assets as % of total	Japanese assets as % of total	European assets as % of total
US MNCs	64.3	11.6	24.3
Japanese MNCs	26.5	66.3	7.2
European MNCs	2.8	4.7	92.5

Source: From 'The End of Globalization' by Alan Rughman, published by random House Business Books. Reprinted by permission of the random House Group, Ltd.

SOURCE: © REPRODUCED COURTESY OF SONY

Visit the websites of two well-known Japanese companies such as Sony and Toyota. Can you see any radically new products that they are developing? Are they developing them mainly in Japan or overseas? Are they launching them in Japan before they launch them elsewhere? Does the product life cycle argument still seem valid in these cases? Do you think this is just a peculiarity of the Japanese MNCs? Check out Sony's QRIO robot as a possible example.

Image 12.3 Sony's QRIO

the brand. Thus the threat of opportunism and cheating on the part of agents will encourage firms to move to tighter control of other contexts, e.g. by setting up subsidiaries or buying ownership of existing independent contractors. If the firm has its own overseas production facility it can reduce the risk of opportunism (through the use of its monitoring and control system).

The eclectic theory   One of the most well-known commentators on the dynamics of multinationals, John Dunning, has put these arguments together with others to construct what he terms the 'eclectic' theory of multinationals. Dunning's theory is also referred to as the OLI theory of multinationals (for summaries see Dunning, 1998, 2001). 'O' stands for ownership advantages, 'L' for locational advantages and 'I' for internalization advantages. In Dunning's view, firms decide whether to set up overseas by calculating whether the costs and uncertainties of such an endeavour are larger or smaller than the advantages that can be gained from these three sets of advantages. Ownership advantages refer to the advantages derived from the firm's build-up of its own assets, expertise and knowledge. Building on Vernon's argument, this relates to the ability of the firm to reuse the same assets in other contexts and thus to increase the productivity of those assets. Locational advantages refer to being near to various sorts of markets – e.g. to product markets, to markets for raw materials, to labour markets (with low wage employees) and to markets of expertise. Internalization advantages refer to the ability to avoid the opportunism of agents and maximize internal economies of scale and scope.

In summary, we can see that internationalizing is a complex task for firms, requiring from the mainstream perspective highly rationalistic decision-making processes in order both to identify measures of advantage and disadvantage and to reach a final decision about the economic viability of the process (see Table 12.6).

The last two decades have seen a simultaneous intensification of each of these processes creating stronger webs of interconnections across national and organizational boundaries. These theories have provided a formidable set of tools for analysing the development of multinationals. What they have told us less about is the organizational and management implications of this. Clearly, the internationalization of an organization, whatever form it takes, adds new layers of complexity to issues of management. What can we learn from the mainstream about how this complexity is controlled and managed? For this we need to turn to another group of authors for whom issues of organization and management have been central in their analysis of multinationals.

Strategy and structure in multinationals

Once a firm has decided to pursue a particular type of internationalization strategy, how does it ensure that it controls and coordinates these activities effectively? This concerns the relationship between the headquarters of the company, the overseas subsidiary and the market context of the activity. Two counteracting factors are influential here. On the one hand, there is the impetus arising from the achievement of economies of scale. The more a firm can standardize its products and manufacture them in large plants with continuous working, the lower the price at which it will be able to sell, thus the higher its market share. This argues for a 'global' decision-making process whereby the firm decides the best location for its production, and exports from this base to all its main markets. On the other hand, national markets are often subject to different consumer tastes and different

Table 12.6 Modes of international activities

Types of international expansion	Advantages	Disadvantages	Organizational implications
Export strategy	Low on coordination costs	Low on learning possibilities; high dependency on agents	Minimal: establishment of 'international' division
Franchise and licensing	Improves income stream and spreads costs further	Dependence on local franchise owners – potential loss of and control of brand which may impact negatively; danger of opportunism and poor management	Requirement for established procedures for offering franchises monitoring performance
Subcontracting	Improves flexibility of supply while keeping costs low	Problem of coordinating across different firms and managing problems of opportunism and poor performance	Central importance of supply chain management and logistics linked to improved methods of coordination
Overseas production (FDI)	Production closer to markets enables stronger learning; also economies of scale and scope can be maximized	Problems of integrating overseas plants into broader system; issues of standardization, benchmarking and restructuring	Increasingly complex management system associated with problems of integration, coordination and differentiation

Thinkpoint 12.4

SOURCE: © AFP/GETTY IMAGES

Image 12.4 Advertising the global brand McDonald's in India (where the majority Hindu population do not eat beef)

Global integration and local responsiveness: The case of McDonald's We may assume that McDonald's is highly globally integrated. Its core products are the burger bun. Its 'golden arches' are ubiquitous across the world. Its business model of fast, reliable food with limited but clean and hygenic eat-in facilities is reproduced in all its branches. But McDonald's has been trying to change in response to national differences. Some changes have gone from a local adaptation to a common product across the world, such as the introduction of salads. Other experiments in the same direction eventually failed to become global products – e.g. the McDonald's pizza. Still others remain just local adaptations, like the lamb burger in India and the teriyaki burger in Japan.

For more details on McDonald's and how it has adapted in East Asian countries like Hong Kong, China, Korea and Japan see the fascinating collection of papers in Watson (1997), *Golden Arches East*.

regulations, thus making global standardization difficult. Furthermore, states may set import taxes at levels that equalize the price of products from outside its boundaries and in this way support and sustain employment internally. These two tendencies were analysed by Prahalad and Doz (1987) in terms of the dynamic between integration (the global imperative) and responsiveness (adaptation to local markets). A product like Coca-Cola is highly standardized and can be produced in bulk, while many other products are affected by national preferences – e.g. in terms of taste (the sphere of consumer preferences) or in terms of what is socially acceptable (the sphere of governmental regulation).

Bartlett and Ghoshal's model What are the implications of this for how the firm is organized? Bartlett and Ghoshal (1989) identified four models of organization: multinational; global; international; and transnational firms.

MULTINATIONAL FIRMS In these firms the emphasis is on a strong local presence through being highly responsive to national differences. Each subsidiary is run relatively independently as the different national markets require different variations in the products. For example, until very recently there were strong differences between European countries in terms of how they did laundry. Bartlett and Ghoshal (1989, p. 20) state that:

> As late as 1980, washing machine penetration ranged from less than 30% of households in the United Kingdom to over 85% in Germany. In northern European countries 'boil washing' had long been standard, whereas hand-washing in cold water represented an important demand segment in Mediterranean countries. Differences in water hardness, perfume preferences, fabric mix and phosphate legislation made product differentiation from country to country a strategic necessity.

GLOBAL FIRMS This describes firms where efficiency of production, and economies of scale are high because products can be standardized across different countries. Consumer electronics tend to have these characteristics, particularly at the component level (e.g. semiconductor chips that are increasingly produced in massive highly efficient plants according to standardized designs) and also at the consumer product level (e.g. standardized designs for TVs, videos, DVD players, etc.). There are no strong market pressures towards national differentiation and, on the contrary, high pressures towards global standardization, economies of scale and strong price competition.

INTERNATIONAL FIRMS This category refers to the ability of firms to transfer knowledge and competencies across national boundaries. Thus subsidiaries are neither totally based on local capabilities nor totally driven by global economies of scale. Subsidiaries utilize the knowledge generated in the head office to create distinctive products in varied national markets where local knowledge is important.

TRANSNATIONAL FIRMS For Bartlett and Ghoshal, this was the most interesting category of firm and also represented the direction in which firms were heading. The transnational firm is characterized by a wide variety of different subsidiaries that perform their own specialized role in the organization as a whole but are also interdependent and interacting. This enables the firm to learn from different contexts and to spread this information around different subsidiaries. Thus, in theory, best practice can be identified in one setting and transferred to another. All subsidiaries can be subjected to a form of benchmarking – e.g. how many mistakes or rejects and how long to do a certain process. By benchmarking subsidiaries against each other, high performers and low performers can be identified and there can be transfers of learning, knowledge and people across the boundaries, which will enable the low performers to catch up. Early innovations can be communicated to other parts of the firm more widely and this can contribute to further improvement and development. Thus the transnational firm is locally responsive, globally efficient and internationally innovative.

The management and organization challenges arising in these different models are distinctive (see Table 12.7).

- In the global firm, production becomes concentrated in large integrated sites. Managers tend to be international, moving around the organization with an expertise in production technology. The central task is coordinating and controlling the supply chain in order to achieve company goals. Broadly, one might expect a Taylorist work system, highly controlled and monitored in order to achieve standardized outputs.

Table 12.7 Bartlett and Ghoshal's model adapted

	Low global integration	High global integration
Low local responsiveness	*International* Skills and knowledge in headquarters transferred to subsidiaries in local markets	*Global* Highly efficient: production organized on a global scale to maximize economies of scale in standardized products
High local responsiveness	*Multinational* Main focus on the national markets; little integration of production, management skills or knowledge across national contexts	*Transnational* Production planned to maximize economies of scale but local contexts remain central, so that products are adapted to local contexts and learning is transferred across subsidiaries

- Multinationals (in the Bartlett and Ghoshal terminology) are quasi-federations of firms with national identities. The head office will monitor performance primarily on a financial basis. There will be few transfers of managers or technologies or practices either across subsidiaries or to or between head office and subsidiaries. Work systems will differ depending on the history of the subsidiary and the normal pattern of control in its particular national context.

- The international firm will have intensive contacts with local subsidiaries but this is primarily in an advisory capacity and will be reflected in the transfer of technology. This will involve some international assignments for both managers and engineers but there will be relatively little lateral communication or movement between subsidiaries.

- The transnational firm involves dense communication and movement across subsidiaries and the head office. This will be reflected in frequent overseas assignments for managers and the use of international project teams to ensure the transfer of ideas and processes across the firm.

Exercise 12.6

Select a well-known firm and, using the information from its website, analyse where it fits in terms of Bartlett and Ghoshal's model. The key things to look out for are:

1 Is its strategy to produce for global markets, national markets or regional markets?

2 Where are (a) its major production sites and (b) its main research and development sites located and are they serving global, national or regional markets?

Try, for example, brewing. How do firms like Carlsberg, Heineken and Fosters fit into this model?

Bartlett and Ghoshal's model has been highly influential. It moves from the broad question of why do firms internationalize as posed in Dunning, etc. to the question of how do they organize themselves when they internationalize, with the answer arising from the market contexts in which firms are located. It is based, however, on a highly rational view of how managers and firms behave, in which it is economic incentives that are the dominant influence, and more social and political considerations are ignored (see Chapters 2, 6 and 7).

Harzing's control focus Harzing (2000) has elaborated on these processes by focusing particularly on the ways in which headquarters seek to maintain control over their subsidiaries.

PERSONAL CENTRALIZED CONTROL In this mechanism of control, all key decisions are taken by the head office and are then monitored by frequent personal visits to the subsidiary. This has obvious disadvantages in that as the number of subsidiaries grows and the number of decisions that need to be taken increases, it becomes impossible to sustain personal control. Such a system is therefore only likely to occur when the degree of internationalization is low and the complexity of decision making limited.

BUREAUCRATIC FORMALIZED CONTROL These controls are impersonal and consist of sets of rules and procedures that must be followed in subsidiaries. The problem with this system is that it tries to impose a single set of rules across diverse environments and can therefore run up against the problem of national differences. Also, bureaucratic systems more generally are inflexible and make it difficult for managers to respond to new contingencies (see Chapter 13). Given the diversity of contexts within multinationals, this can be highly problematic.

OUTPUT CONTROL This refers to setting targets for the subsidiary management to achieve. Frequently these are financial targets but they may also relate to sales, productivity, market share, etc. Many multinationals use this as a primary means of control as it relieves the headquarters of detailed involvement in work processes (allowing local managers to respond flexibly to local conditions) and provides an easy way to compare performance across subsidiaries as well as in relation to the performance against targets set. The difficulties of such systems relate first to the diversity of output measures and the problem of choosing, which is the most important one (though in US and UK multinationals financial targets are usually given top priority) and secondly to the problem of information asymmetry. Information asymmetry refers to individuals having different amounts of information about the same thing and the problems that can follow in terms of economic relations. Economists frequently cite the example of the buying and selling of used cars. Almost inevitably the seller has more information about the quality of the car than he/she is willing to provide to the buyer. In organizational terms, this leads to the possibility of key actors in the firm distorting the figures in order to serve their own interests.

CONTROL BY CULTURE AND NETWORKS This technique of control is more complex and difficult to create (see Chapter 9). It relates to bonding different levels of management together and creating a strong shared culture among managers of subsidiaries and managers in headquarters. International management training programmes supported by an integrated international programme of management career development are ways in which such a shared culture can be established across managers from different national backgrounds. In these contexts, expatriate assignments and international project teams between different parts of the organization can be systematically constructed in order to both strengthen and develop formal and informal networks within the multinational. Thus, while subsidiaries necessarily remain geographically distinct, the managers within them have access to wider networks in order to monitor and control the tension between the local and the headquarters.

Harzing's model of control mechanisms (see Table 12.8) does not map directly onto Bartlett and Ghoshal's model of different types of MNCs but it is highly suggestive:

- Global firms are likely to be characterized by 'bureaucratic formalized control' to ensure efficiency.
- Multinationals are likely to be held together by a strong personal centralized control as the constituent parts of the firm share little else in common.

Table 12.8 Harzing's classification of control mechanisms

	Personal/cultural (founded on social interaction)	Impersonal/bureaucratic/technocratic (founded on instrumental artefacts)
Direct/explicit	Personal centralized control	Bureaucratic formalized control
Indirect/implicit	Control by culture and networks	Output control

Source: From Harzing 'An Empirical Test and Extension Test and Extension of the Barlett and Ghoshal Typology', in Journal of International Business Studies, 31(1) 2000. Reproduced with permission from Palgrave Macmillan.

- International firms are concerned to ensure that national subsidiaries improve their performance with the help of the head office, which will be reflected in strong output control.
- Transnational firms, with their dynamic internal processes and structures, are likely to require a strong, shared culture and the frequent use of networks to ensure that common goals, standards and processes are continually renegotiated in line with developments in individual subsidiaries.

These arguments are basically a variant of the contingency model of organizations. In other words, if we know the market that the firm is aiming at we are able to assess the balance between efficiency considerations (price, in particular: generally lower prices will come from larger and more concentrated sites of production where economies of scale and scope can be realized) and responsiveness considerations (adapting to local tastes and local regulations). From this we can decide the type of firm that we have and we can then deduce the implications for management and organization. A solution to our problem of organization structure and strategy follows quite naturally from this. Is life so simple?

National cultures and universalist solutions: The problems for MNCs

The most important challenge within the mainstream to this idea comes from the cultural differentiation thesis. In broad terms, this argument states that the values and beliefs that people hold about themselves, their society, their work and their position in the world are deeply embedded in particular social contexts, the most significant of which in the modern world is defined by the nation state. Of course, it is relatively simple to reduce this to the level of stereotypes – the English 'stiff upper lip', the French '*joie de vivre*' and the German '*schadenfreude*' (enjoyment of others' misfortunes) are just a few examples. It is also very easy to exaggerate the degree to which this model has spread to other contexts – e.g. the states of Africa may seem similar on the surface but they are often creations of the period of European imperialism and have found it difficult to establish a single national identity over strong religious, ethnic and regional differences.

Nevertheless, if we accept that there is something in some contexts that constitutes a national culture, this is a considerable challenge to any universal theorizing about management and organizations. You cannot motivate a Japanese person the same way in which you would somebody from the United States. Japanese groups work differently from those in France. Leadership means something different in Sweden than it does in the United Kingdom. This instantly raises a problem for multinationals. How is it possible to create coherence and stability when people in different subsidiaries see the world differently depending on their cultural backgrounds.

But can we prove national cultures exist? The predominant framework within the study of organizations that has been established to answer this question derives from the work of the Dutch researcher and management consultant, Geert Hofstede. Hofstede initially developed his ideas through accessing a large database of questionnaires about job satisfaction, which had been collected from among its employees by IBM in the late 1960s (Hofstede, 2002). Altogether Hofstede had around 116 000 questionnaires to deal with, collected from a variety of levels of employees within IBM's 46 national subsidiaries. IBM was a classic global company in Bartlett and Ghoshal's terms. It manufactured mainframe computers from a number of research and innovation intensive centres in the industrialized world. These products, subject to some local adaptation, were sold all over the world by IBM's salesforce which was renowned for its uniformity, not just in terms of the way in which mainframe computers were sold but also in terms of its style of dress (navy blue suit and white shirt) and their general approach to business. IBM was seen as a company with a strong central culture, enforced by the presence of US expatriates in subsidiary offices and by common training systems.

However, Hofstede argued that the research showed that there were significant national differences in relation to key attitudes towards work and that therefore multinationals had to decide how to adapt to these differences. At first, Hofstede identified and labelled four key attitudinal complexes; he later added a fifth following further research, and this is included in the discussion that follows.

- *Power distance*. Hofstede identified that there were significant differences in terms of how national cultures viewed power. In some societies, those at the bottom of the organization felt very separate from those at the top, those in power (e.g. France). Surprisingly high power distance was often accepted by those at the bottom; they thought that it was legitimate. Other countries rejected the idea that there should be a big distance between bosses and others and felt there should be more equality and less hierarchy (e.g. Sweden). In high power distance contexts, there tended to be more levels in the hierarchy; authority centralized at the top and

Thinkpoint 12.5

Some views on 'national character' 'The Englishman likes to imagine himself at sea, the German in a forest. It is impossible to express the difference of their national feeling more succinctly'. (E. Canetti: *Crowds and Power*)

'German managers visiting France are appalled at finding that their French colleagues will spend much of their time deciding where to eat lunch. The German does not speak the French language of time, which requires evoking the whole gustatory apparatus and setting the proper inter-personal relationship before business can be taken up. If the German insists on adhering to a rigid schedule, the French will label the visitor as uncouth, someone with little appreciation for life and no feeling for people.' (Adapted from Hickson and Pugh, *Management Worldwide*)

'Wittgenstein had to abandon his plan to produce a book of philosophy written entirely from jokes, realizing he had no sense of humour. German wit, famously, is no laughing matter.' (J. Paxman: *The English*)

'There are three things that concern the loyal servant. The Master's Will, his own vitality and the condition of his death.' (17th century Japanese Samurai manual, *Hagakure*)

'The Japanese are to the highest degree, both aggressive and unaggressive, both militaristic and aesthetic, both insolent and polite, rigid and adaptable, submissive and resentful of being pushed around, loyal and treacherous, brave and timid, conservative and hospitable to new ways.' (R. Benedict: *The Chrysantheum and the Sword*, 1946)

For an amusing view of what constitutes the 'real England', have a look at the novel *England, England* by Julian Barnes. The book is based on the idea of creating a theme park along the lines of Disneyland, which encompasses the 'essence of Englishness'. Before that, the intrepid entrepreneur has to decide what that essence is. On the basis of market research across the world, the following top ten emerge as 'quintessences of England':

1 The Royal Family
2 Big Ben/Houses of Parliament
3 Manchester United Football Club
4 Class system
5 Pubs
6 A robin in the snow
7 Robin Hood and his Merrie Men
8 Cricket
9 White Cliffs of Dover
10 Imperialism

---

low involvement of employees. In low power distance settings, managers and employees were expected to work more cooperatively together; there were fewer levels in the hierarchy and decision making was more devolved.

- *Uncertainty avoidance.* The extent to which 'the members of a culture feel threatened by uncertain or unknown situations'. In societies characterized by high uncertainty avoidances there is a highly formalized conception of management. The power of superiors depends on the control of uncertainties and managers are more involved in details. Overall there is strong loyalty to the employer and long average duration of employment as a means of managing uncertainty (e.g. Greece, Japan). In low uncertainty avoidance contexts, there is tolerance for ambiguity in structures and procedures, the power of superiors depends on position and relationships (rather than the direct control that they exercise). Managers are more involved in strategy and relationship-oriented with weak loyalty to the employer and short average duration of employment (United States and United Kingdom).

● *Individualism/collectivism*. Are the ties between individuals loose, with everyone expected to look after him or herself and his/her immediate family only (high individualism) (e.g. the United States)? Are people from birth onwards integrated into strong, cohesive in-groups, which throughout people's lifetime continue to protect them in exchange for unquestioning loyalty (high collectivism) (e.g. Pakistan)? In individualistic settings the employer–employee relationship is a business deal in a 'labour market'. Employees perform best as individuals. Direct appraisal of performance improves productivity. Treating friends better than others is nepotism and unethical. In collectivist settings, the employer–employee relationship is basically moral, like a family link. Employees are seen to perform best in in-groups. Treating friends better than others is normal and ethical. Direct appraisal of individual performance is a threat to harmony and the employee has to be seen in a broader family and social context.

● *The masculinity/femininity dimension*. This describes attitudes to work centrality. The work ethos in masculine cultures tends toward 'live in order to work' whereas the work ethos in feminine cultures tends to 'work in order to live'. This reflects the degree to which gender roles are segregated or overlap: where men and women share child care responsibilities, there has to be a work–life balance (e.g. Sweden, the Netherlands): where men work and women stay at home, men tend to become very work-centred (e.g. Japan). Thus societies where there are high levels of female participation in the labour force tend to be characterized by what Hofstede calls a 'feminine' culture – i.e. one where people are expected and encouraged to take time out from work to look after family and more generally to balance their work commitments against their home life. In masculine countries, managers hold ambitious career aspirations and are expected to be decisive, firm, assertive and competitive. In feminine countries, managers hold modest career aspirations and are expected to use intuition, deal with feelings and seek consensus.

● *Long-term orientation*. Hofstede developed this dimension later in his researches following more work on cultural values in Asian contexts. Long-term orientation was identified in terms of 'fostering of virtues oriented towards future rewards, in particular perseverance and thrift', while a short-term orientation reflected the need to preserve 'face' (i.e. the respect of others) and fulfil social obligations in the present. The long-term orientation is linked to what Hofstede terms 'Confucian dynamism'. Confucianism is a significant cultural influence in Asian contexts. It is associated with the wisdom of age and the importance of the long-term development and prosperity of the family. Hofstede identifies this with a willingness to work extremely hard in the present in order to build for the future (a future that may be conceived in terms of generations of the same family, not just a single individual or a single generation).

Hofstede argues that countries can be placed on each of these dimensions, and by understanding where a particular country lies in the rankings, we can understand better how to develop organizations in those countries. Thus the Scandinavian countries tend to be low on power distance, low on

Table 12.9 Selected examples of Hofstede's rankings (out of 53 where 1 equals highest and 53 equals lowest on the dimension identified)

	Power distance	Uncertainty avoidance	Masculinity index	Individualism index
United States	38	43	15	1
United Kingdom	42/44	47/48	9/10	3
Japan	33	7	1	22/23
Germany	42/44	29	9/10	15
France	15/16	10/15	35/36	10/11
Top-ranked country	Malaysia	Greece	Japan	United States
Bottom-ranked country	Austria	Singapore	Sweden	Guatemala

Source: Adapted from Hofstede (2002).

uncertainty avoidance and predominantly feminine in their orientation to work. A US multinational setting up in a place like Sweden or Denmark would find that certain of its normal ways of doing things would be accepted and others would not. So the US firm could expect to find conflict if it pursued its normal strategy of expecting high commitment, long hours, and short holidays (its highly 'masculine' culture in Hofstede's words) in countries that held a very different view of the life–work balance. French managers with their expectations of high power distance would find that this would clash with Scandinavian expectations of low power distance, etc.

Figures 12.1 and 12.2 show Hofstede's profiles comparing Japan and the United States and a comparison of Singapore and the United Kingdom. What do you deduce from this data? There is a website where it is possible to access profiles of any particular country on the four (or occasionally five) dimensions and also to compare the profiles of two countries from his sample. If you have any foreign friends or family find out what their country profile is (http://www.geert-hofstede.com/geert_hofstede_resources.shtml) and discuss with your friends whether this is accurate or not, stereotypical or fair in its portrayal.

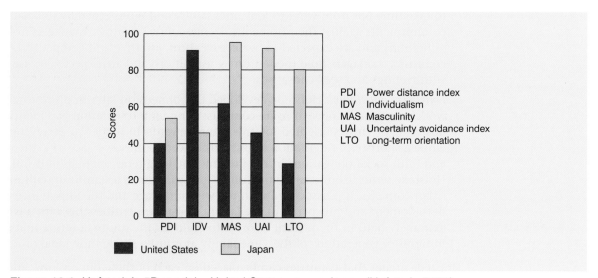

Figure 12.1 Hofstede's 5D model – United States versus Japan (Hofstede 2002)

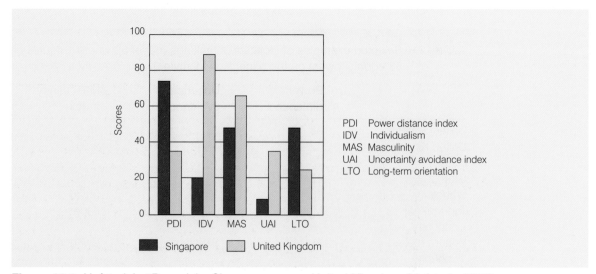

Figure 12.2 Hofstede's 5D model – Singapore versus United Kingdom (Hofstede 2002)

From this culturalist point of view, it is natural to expect conflict within multinationals as national cultural differences come into contact with each other. How local managers respond to output control mechanisms in Bartlett and Ghoshal's model of the international firm will vary depending on how they think of their status and position, what they consider their skills to be and how they relate to other parts of the organization. From this culturalist position, it is impossible to assume that all members of the firm will see these control mechanisms in the same way.

How does this culturalist approach supplement the more structural accounts of multinationals presented by authors like Bartlett and Ghoshal? Headquarters of multinationals may respond in a number of ways.

Leave alone   One way is to leave national subsidiaries as relatively independent entities and not seek to impose common practices and standards onto them. However, this is only feasible in what Bartlett and Ghoshal label as 'multinational firms' – i.e. where subsidiaries operate in highly distinctive markets and cannot make gains from a wider more global integration.

Train managers in cultural awareness   Where firms are global, international or transnational, there may well be high levels of investment in teaching managers from different contexts about different cultural values and expectations, particularly those going on expatriate management tasks. Cultural sensitivity training, using Hofstede's categories, is now a highly extensive and profitable business, but its problem is mainly its superficiality – it may take an awful long time for an American to understand why and how the Japanese rank people and alter their behaviour according to their perceptions of these rankings (which often derive from notions of age and the wisdom of age and experience).

Thinkpoint 12.6

Women in Japanese workplaces and the impact of multinationals   There are few women managers in Japanese organizations. Graduate women can aspire to the position of 'office lady' though they will be expected to leave when they have a child. As well as traditional office tasks such as typing, copying, filing, etc., office ladies are usually responsible for serving tea to their male colleagues. In Japan, this is a highly ritualized ceremony and being asked to serve tea involves the office lady in both intense mental and physical activity which in turn emphasized her subordinate role in the Japanese system. They may be asked to go out on errands to buy birthday presents for their male boss's family. They used to be called 'office flowers' to reflect their decorative function in the office, or alternatively 'office wives' to reflect the role they played in serving their male boss.

These expectations have a long history in Japan and are part of the taken-for-granted reality of Japanese society even in an era when Japanese women are learning to rebel and reject these roles. However, senior Japanese managers are reluctant to deal with even foreign women as equal. How does this impact on Japanese firms when they set up offices in societies where the genders are more equal? How does it impact on US and UK multinationals when they set up offices in Japan? Women have come particularly to the fore in US multinationals in recent years. How therefore should US MNCs respond when deciding on expatriate assignments to Japan?

You can read more about the office lady in Japan in: Y. Ogasawara (1998) *Office Ladies and Salaried Men: Power, Gender and Work in Japanese Companies* (University of California Press).

Create an international management cadre   This is where MNCs try to create a common culture through intensive training of a tier of international managers. This raises many questions and issues. Most managers are educated within one country in educational systems that reflect the history and inheritance of that country. When they join a multinational, they take that education in with them and may find it difficult to understand the meaning of the skills and education of managers from different countries. In order to create a common culture within the firm, there needs to be a massive investment in management training and development. Is this going to be worth it, especially given that there are high levels of mobility in many managerial tasks and any investment made can walk out the door' quite easily? Bartlett and Ghoshal try to anticipate these problems by their focus on diversity as a strength in the transnational firm so long as there can be communication across different people, different cultures and different units, but this simply assumes the problem away. Given the differences, how do we know that they can be productively as opposed to destructively harnessed?

Hofstede's results and his prescriptions have brought many plaudits, but equally many criticisms. Baskerville (2003, p.1) summarizes her criticisms as follows:

(i) the assumption of equating nations with culture (ii) the difficulties of, and limitations on, a quantification of culture represented by cultural dimensions and matrices; and (iii) the status of the observer outside the culture . . . A further problem is a general lack of confidence in the assumption of stability of cultural differences.

(see also, McSweeney 2002a and 2002b; and the replies by Hofstede to both authors; Hofstede 2003a and 2003b.)

The idea that national cultural differences can help us understand the tensions within multinationals is therefore highly contested though, as we will see, the broader point that there are differences of perspective inside the MNC and this creates substantial problems for management can be developed much further and does not have to rely on an amorphous concept of national culture.

Contribution and limitations of the mainstream approach

These mainstream approaches have created a fertile field of study. Broadly speaking we can summarize the research issues as follows:

- How and why do firms internationalize? (Dunning, Buckley and Casson, etc.)
- How do firms organize the coordination between headquarters and subsidiaries? (Bartlett and Ghoshal, Nohria and Ghoshal, Doz and Prahalad, Harzing)
- What impact do national cultural differences have on issues of managing multinationals? (Hofstede)

In turn, we can make an initial identification of the weaknesses of these approaches. They are all basically variants of the contingency model of organizations assuming that managers act rationally in the light of the information and knowledge that they have about how to ensure efficiency and market responsiveness. The contingency model relies on a number of presuppositions that are questionable and to which we will return:

- It assumes that it is possible to 'know' the market. However, as human beings our ability to process information is limited even when we supplement our decision making with technology.
- It assumes that managers have the power to implement a particular model of organization. Yet it is clear from many of the chapters in this book that managers have limited knowledge and limited power.
- An economistic and rational view of internationalization with little concern for the unevenness of benefits in this process is presented (inequality).
- There is little recognition of MNCs as constituted through social interactions of different groups and the power conflicts that arise (power).
- The view of 'identity' and 'culture' that is used is highly static and over-deterministic (identity).

In the following section, we present a critical alternative that builds on these themes.

The critical approach

Introduction

How do we understand globalization and multinationals from a critical perspective? Broadly speaking, the following themes are crucial:

- Multinationals cannot be conceptualized separately from the impact they have on social relationships, political systems (at the national and the international level) and the global ecology.
- Multinationals cannot be conceived as single unitary rational actors. They are transnational social spaces in which ideas, people, knowledge, technologies, procedures, practices and capital flow across borders undermining simple unitary models of multinationals and national cultures.

CASE STUDY 12.2 Nike: A critical approach

From a critical perspective, Nike reveals the way in which multi-national firms contribute to global inequality and how this relates to the emerging dominance of US style consumerism. It also reveals how both these processes promote resistance and conflict as actors in different social settings seek to reassert control over their own lives in countering the forces of global capitalism.

As has already been described, Nike's strategy depends upon keeping the design, brand management and marketing in the United States and transferring manufacturing processes overseas. The rewards of this strategy are distributed highly unequally, with the bulk of them returning to US employees and US shareholders even though the actual material object is not produced in the United States. If Nike wanted to produce shoes in the United States, it would have to cut its profit margins substantially because US employees are (in world terms) paid quite high wages. They also have certain rights in terms of employment and union membership. The company would also be liable for contributions to pension schemes and health insurance. Producing the shoes in China or other countries in South-east Asia reduces the costs significantly. Traditionally, regulations on hours of work, safety standards on machinery, and other aspects of labour discipline have been low. Nike's products are therefore manufactured overseas and well away from the high cost and high regulations of Western societies.

As described previously, this context enables Nike to squeeze its suppliers in terms of their costs. There are many potential suppliers to Nike in Asia, from India to China. Nike's representatives can bargain in this market-place in order to get the lowest price possible for the manufacture of their shoes. In these circumstances, how do contractors keep their costs down and still make a profit? The answer is of course that they pay very low wages, make employees work

long hours and keep other costs – e.g. health and safety, healthcare, sickness and pension rights – to a minimum. Exploring this further, who constitute the workforce of contractors for firms like Nike? The answer is that it is predominantly made up of young, single women. Carty states that in the early 1990s over 80 per cent of the women employed in factories in South-east Asia making Nike products were under the age of 25. In the Indonesian factories, the average wage was US$2.20 per day (Carty, 1997, p. 193). It is easier for male supervisors to subject young women to mental and physical bullying than it is for them to do this to other men or older women. Carty reports frequent complaints about this in Nike-related factories. In these countries, demographic and land pressures often result in young women being forced to look for work in such factories where frequently they are housed in company barracks and subjected to further high levels of discipline.

As also discussed earlier, Nike moved from owning their factories towards subcontracting. At first sight this had another advantage (besides the economic one) for Nike. The actual conditions of work in its factories were set by contractors and not Nike itself. Thus if Western observers saw child labour in Nike plants or watched young women working extremely long hours and suffering from poor working conditions and abusive employees Nike itself could claim that it was not their fault. Such a defence was, of course, very superficial and over the last decade Nike has found itself having to defend its reputation more systematically. This is for the obvious reason that in its contracts with manufacturers it has the power to specify certain conditions in terms of labour such as health and safety, wage levels, health and holiday entitlements, etc. The sorts of people that buy Nike products do not want to think that they are exploiting people in other parts of the world. Nike's website reveals their attempts to manage this part of their image and has many materials relating to how they ensure employees in their contract manufacturers work in acceptable conditions (http://www.nikebiz.com). However, this is an ongoing debate and many commentators remain sceptical about the degree to which these goals are actually achieved and how systematically Nike inspects its contractors to ensure that they are put into place. Nike's argument is that it is bringing work and wages to people who would otherwise have a lot less. It is also encouraging the development of manufacturing facilities that can then be used to compete for other contracts and thus create a multiplier effect of gradually extending the range of employment opportunities in less-developed economies. Ideally this creates a virtuous circle of more FDI or contract work leading to a population with more wages to spend, thus encouraging further the development of the internal market of the country.

Image 12.5 Asian women factory workers working on an assembly line

From a critical perspective, however, this argument can be countered with the view that whatever the limited local benefits (and these in turn can be contested), Nike reflects and reproduces inequalities within and across countries (see Box 12.1). Most obviously, there is the difference between the wages paid to the makers of its shoes and the salaries and other rewards received by its US management. For example, in 2003 Philip Knight, founder, chairman and chief executive of Nike, was paid US$2.5 million in salary and bonuses plus other benefits. The shareholders of Nike are predominantly institutional investors, mostly controlled in the United States and the United Kingdom. These institutional investors control the pension funds and savings of millions of individuals in the United States, Europe and Japan, who in turn are beneficiaries of Nike's success. In 2003, return on equity in Nike was 18.9 per cent. Although the price of Nike shares has fallen over the last few years from a peak of US$76.375 in 1997 to its lowest point of US$26.563 for a brief moment in 2000, it averaged around US$50 between 2000 and 2003, and in 2004 went back over US$70. The gains of Nike's success are highly unevenly distributed, with the bulk of them flowing to their senior employees and shareholders in the United States and the advanced capitalist countries and not to the people who actually make the shoes.

A further critical question pertains to the social constructions of identity that are central to the development of the Nike brand on a global scale. There are a number of aspects to such a discussion. One is to consider the messages that underlie the Nike adverts. The slogan 'Just Do It' relates to American traditions of individualism and individual ambition. Carty states that 'Nike clearly recognizes and plays upon American values which encourage and legitimate consumption;

an ideology of personal hedonism whereby commodities display the symbols of individual achievement. Hedonism, authenticity, irreverence, narcissism and the pursuit of pleasure through hard work and performance are the backbone of Nike advertising' (Carty, 1997, p. 195; see also Goldman and Papson, 1998, for a more detailed analysis of Nike's adverts).

The power of Nike was also revealed in the US$200 million sponsorship deal which it set up with the Brazilian national football team in 1996. This required the Brazilian team not only to wear the swoosh logo and appear in Nike adverts (most famous of which was the football game conducted in Rio de Janeiro airport) but also for them to play five friendly matches a year featuring eight regular first team members. Following the defeat of Brazil by France in the World Cup final of 1998, it was rumoured that Nike had insisted that Brazil's star player Ronaldo play in the match in spite of the fact that he suffered a convulsive fit just before it was due to begin. Playing Ronaldo at less than his full fitness was seen by many commentators as a significant contributory factor to Brazil's defeat. A similarly huge deal worth over £300 million has been made with Manchester United. The football team handed control of its global replica kit and merchandising business to Nike for the period 2002 to 2015. Manager Alex Ferguson is believed to have been offered an 'ambassadorial' role with the company when he retires.

In her best-selling book *No Logo*, Naomi Klein devotes a significant part of a chapter to an analysis of the resistance to Nike (Klein, 2000, chapter 16). One of the most contentious areas has been in the relationship between Nike and the sportswear of famous US colleges and universities. College campaigns against firms accused of employing sweatshop labour have been recorded and stimulated by Klein's book.

Exercise 12.8

Where does your student union or university buy its logo t-shirts, sweatshirts, caps and jackets from? Is it 'fair trade' or just the cheapest that it can find in the market-place?

Box 12.1 Websites critiquing Nike

- David Boje's website at http://cbae.nmsu.edu/~dboje/nike/nikemain.html.
- The adbusters website at http://www.adbusters.org/home/.
- Behind the label website at http://www.behindthelabel.org/.
- Campus campaigns against sweatshops at http://www.studentsagainstsweatshops.org/.

- Global exchange campaign at http://www.globalexchange.org/campaigns/sweatshops/nike/.
- Oxfam's community action abroad campaign maintains a Nikewatch at http://www.caa.org.au/campaigns/nike/.

Nike's own site also provides a lot of detail about their side of the story: http://www.nike.com/nikebiz/nikebiz.jhtml?page=0.

The anger that many people feel about Nike reflects both the issue of sweatshop labour in its subcontractors and its role in shaping culture and claiming a right of ownership and control over popular institutions, particularly in the area of sports. Not surprisingly, therefore, Nike has been the object of attack in many ways. For example, there have been spoof adverts for Nike products (such as that reproduced here) appearing on the internet reflecting what is called culture-jamming and ad-busting – 'the practice of parodying advertisements and hijacking billboards in order to drastically alter their messages' (Klein, 2000, p. 280).

Multinationals and power

In order to develop a critical approach, we proceed in two sections. First we consider the silences and absences in the mainstream approach. This relates primarily to a failure to reflect on the political, social and ecological significance of multinationals. Secondly, we consider the conceptual inadequacies of the mainstream model and present an alternative view of the multinational and global strategy.

Silences and absences in the mainstream

The mainstream approach generally limits its analysis within a framework of markets and the economic rationality of organizational forms. This ignores some key areas that have already been hinted at in the discussion of Nike. We can consider these under two main headings: economic power and political power. We then consider how resistance to this power is manifested.

The economic power of the multinational A recent report calculated that of the 100 largest economies in the world, 51 are corporations and only 49 are countries. Using a comparison of gross domestic product (for measuring country size) and annual sales (for measuring company size), General Motors (the largest company) is ranked at 23 above countries such as Denmark (24), Poland (29), Finland (34) and Singapore (54) (Anderson and Cavanagh 2000). In broad terms, the decisions made within these massive concentrations of economic power are reflected in patterns of FDI, labour adjustment and taxation payment, and in their global market management.

PATTERNS OF FOREIGN DIRECT INVESTMENT FDI is crucial to all sorts of economic benefits, not just in terms of direct employment but also in terms of the indirect employment effects generated – e.g. in supplying firms with products and services, in the increased expenditure of the employees leading to increased consumption locally and knock-on effects on local business. States, regions and urban areas compete against each other to attract FDI offering various deals on taxation and subsidies as well as on improving infrastructure. In this respect, multinationals' ability to shift investment around the globe places them in a very powerful position relative to most national governments. At the extreme, they can take all the subsidies and other benefits offered and then shift production again after the subsidies run out.

PATTERNS OF LABOUR ADJUSTMENT The ability of the multinational to move around also enables it to take advantage of different wage rates and employment conditions. This does not only work in terms of locating in cheap wage areas but also in terms of using such a threat to squeeze concessions out of unions and employees keen to keep jobs in their existing locations. This idea of the use of 'coercive comparisons' has become increasingly important in countries such as Germany where traditionally high levels of union organization and employee power have led to relatively high wages, short working hours and a welfare system that compensates employees at high rates for periods of unemployment or ill health. Trade unions, faced with the prospect of manufacturing moving out of Germany to eastern Europe or Asia have been willing to moderate wage demands as a way of keeping employment in its traditional base.

Thinkpoint 12.7

In the past few years German employers and managers have become increasingly demanding on their work-forces. Now that it is relatively easy and safe to move production into eastern and central Europe, German employers are increasingly threatening to do this unless trade unions and employees agree to certain conditions. Both Siemens and VW, two of the largest and most important multinationals, have reached agreements with their employees to extend working hours from 35 to 39 per week with no additional money. The increasingly realistic threat that they will remove production from Germany has led the unions and employees to capitulate to these demands.

PATTERNS OF TAXATION PAYMENT The multinational firm is highly complex in terms of its internal accounting system and the ways in which it calculates profitability and liability for tax. Such firms tend to have high levels of intra-firm trade; in intra-firm trades prices are set not by the market but by administrative decisions. Thus prices can be set so that profits appear higher in low-tax areas than in high-tax ones. Anderson and Cavanagh's (2000) report, for example, notes that of the 82 US corporations on the top 200 list, 44 did not pay the full standard 35 per cent federal corporate tax rate during the period 1996–98. Seven of the firms actually paid less than zero in federal income taxes in 1998 (because of rebates) including Texaco, Chevron, PepsiCo, Enron and General Motors.

MANAGING GLOBAL MARKETS Multinationals are able to use their power to manage global production networks in ways so that primary producers or subcontractors receive a very small part of the final retail price of whatever they produce.

Thinkpoint 12.8

Commodity chain analysis: Primary products

Coffee Coffee is a simple commodity crop, mainly grown in less-developed countries of Africa, Central and Latin America and South-east Asia. It appears in the cafes, shops and restaurants of the developed world as the product of global multinationals. The four largest roasters of coffee are Kraft, Nestlé, Procter and Gamble and Sara Lee. Their brands include Maxwell House, Nescafé, Folgers and Douwe Egberts.

The chain of relationships whereby the coffee goes from being grown to being consumed has been analysed in a recent report entitled *Mugged: Poverty in Your Coffee Cup*, published by the Make Trade Fair campaign organization (and located on their website at http://www.maketradefair.com). Taking the example of coffee grown in Uganda and sold in the year ended November 2002, the report shows the following stages and prices (in dollars):

- Stage 1: Farmer sells to middleman 1 kg of green coffee beans at a price of US$0.14.
- Stage 2: Middleman transports beans to local mill (US$0.05), bags and transports to capital city (US$0.02) and takes a margin of US$0.05, making the cost of 1 kg now US$0.26.
- Stage 3: Coffee is prepared for export and the exporter takes a margin (US$0.09); bagged and transported to port (US$0.10), giving a price of US$0.45 for the actual exported coffee.
- Stage 4: The price (which includes the cost of freight and insurance – US$0.07 – and the importers' cost and margin as well as delivery to the roaster – US$0.11) at which the importer sells the coffee to the roaster is US$1.64.
- Stage 5: The coffee is then roasted, prepared, packaged and delivered to the retailer who sells the coffee at US$26.40.

Apples A recent report published by Oxfam entitled *Trading Away Our Rights* (http://www.oxfam.org.uk/what_we_do/issues/trade/trading_rights.htm) looked at the export of apples from South Africa to the United Kingdom; of the price at which the apple was sold, the following shares were taken by the various elements in the chain:

- farm labour 5 per cent
- farm income 4 per cent

- farm inputs and packaging 17 per cent

- shipping 12 per cent

- UK handling 7 per cent

- importer's commission and duty 7 per cent

- supermarkets 42 per cent.

The political power of the multinational   Concentrations of economic power on the scale that have just been described are inevitably political in their impact. We can distinguish here between (a) visible and invisible power in relation to political decisions and (b) power exercised over national contexts and national governments versus power exercised over the development of international systems of economic regulation (see Table 12.10).

THE USE OF VISIBLE POWER IN NATIONAL CONTEXTS   Multinationals have huge resources available for employing lobbyists who work on the doorsteps of governments and legislatures in order to protect the interests of their clients. The US political system is notorious for the extent to which 'special interest' groups lobby Congress to protect themselves. Lobbying in the US context means trying to persuade politicians to support the point of view of the interest group. This persuasion can stretch from providing figures and data that support the argument through to providing money to fund political campaigns. Other lobbying methods include buying advertising space, organizing demonstrations and supplying researchers and personnel to politicians. K Street in Washington DC, an area a few blocks north of the White House, contains many of the firms employed by multinationals to act on their behalf.

An example of an area where this influence has been very significant is contained in a 2003 report published by the campaigning organization Public Citizen on drug companies and their lobbyists in the US.[2] This report shows that 'the drug industry hired 675 different lobbyists from 138 firms in 2002 – nearly seven lobbyists for each US Senator . . . The industry spent a record $91.4 billion on lobbying activities in 2002, an 11.6 percent increase from 2001.' The particular issue exercising the companies was the proposed extension of the Medicare programme to prescription drugs. If this had happened, the drug companies would have faced a single large buyer of many drugs, which would have driven down their prices. Instead, they lobbied and succeeded in ensuring the situation was not changed from its existing position (where drug coverage is provided through multiple private insurers). The drugs industry is hugely affected by government in two ways. First, governments oversee the rules and regulations concerning safety in the industry and its products. Particularly as genetic research and more sophisticated forms of biotechnology engineering have emerged, this has become increasingly important. Secondly, governments are invariably involved (though to different degrees) in supporting health systems in which one of the biggest expenses is the drug bill. For both these reasons, therefore, multinational drug companies see it as essential to their business that they should be closely connected to government. The Public Citizen report states that since 1997 'the drug industry has spent nearly $478 million lobbying the federal government. In that same period, the top 25 pharmaceutical companies and trade groups gave $48.6 million to federal campaigns. Well over $100 million more went to paying for issue ads, hiring academics, funding nonprofits and other

Table 12.10 Types of exercise of political power

	Visible	Invisible
National level	Governmental lobbying, e.g. in Washington DC	Covert involvement in political coups, e.g. in Chile 1973
International level	Lobbying at the European Union or in the negotiations in the World Trade Organization	Formation of private interest agreement associations, e.g. international arbitration

activities to promote the industry's agenda in Washington'. Also, 342 of the lobbyists had what is termed 'revolving door' connections; this means that they had worked inside the US government system previously to their lobbying employment. This figure includes 26 who were actually former members of Congress. Not all systems are as open or visible about lobbying as that in the United States. Nevertheless, the important point is that such firms have many more resources to influence governments and legislatures than, for example, citizens' groups.

THE USE OF VISIBLE POWER IN INTERNATIONAL CONTEXTS When it comes to international tiers of governance, the gap between democratic lobbying and paid lobbying by multinationals becomes even greater. In 2001, for example, the *Guardian* (3 September) reported that:

> Development campaigners have reacted with outrage to the news that American and European corporate lobby groups will outnumber organisations from third-world countries at the World Trade Organisation's next summit at Qatar in November. Among the 200 accredited western industry groups are a long list of US corporate lobbyists, including the Motion Picture Association, the American Sugar Alliance and the United Egg Producers Association. Twenty six of the groups are industry committees advising the US government on trade. Development campaigners, already furious that the WTO has told all observer groups to send a single representative, said corporate lobbyists outnumbered developing country groups by six to one.

In Europe, there are 4803 people who have accredited lobbyist status to the European Parliament.[3] In 2003, a draft report of the European Parliament called for greater transparency and visibility of the activities of the lobbyists.[4]

THE USE OF INVISIBLE POWER IN A NATIONAL CONTEXT US multinationals have frequently been accused of behind the scenes activities in order to elicit support from the US government and, in particular, the CIA to overthrow governments that have threatened their interests. In 1954, for example, the legally elected government of Guatemala was overthrown by an invasion force of mercenaries trained by the CIA. The President who was overthrown was Jacobo Arbenz, a left-of-centre socialist; four of the 56 seats in the Congress were held by communists. What was most unsettling to American business interests was that Arbenz had expropriated 234 000 acres of land owned by the US multinational United Fruit, offering compensation that United Fruit called 'unacceptable'. The new government gave the land back to United Fruit, abolished the tax on interest and dividends to foreign investors, eliminated the secret ballot and jailed thousands of political critics. A long list of other names could be added to this, of governments and leaders who were threatening the interests of US multinationals and therefore prompted intervention by the CIA to support anti-government forces. For example, in March 1964, Brazil's elected president, Joao Goulart, ordered the nationalization of all private oil refineries. By 1 April, a military junta brought down his government ushering in an era of an exceedingly brutal tyranny which introduced the use of death squads. The CIA was involved in a major way in bringing about the coup d'état in Brazil. Similar fates were met by Prime Minister Mossedeq of Iran (because he had nationalized the oil industry) and Salvador Allende of Chile (who also threatened nationalization of the property of US multinationals). Similarly, the US government, lobbied by US multinationals, has supported undemocratic regimes that have protected their property rights – e.g. right-wing death squad leaders in El Salvador, contras in Nicaragua, Suharto in Indonesias and apartheid South Africa.

Exercise 12.9

The war in Iraq and its subsequent aftermath has led to a host of accusations that the US government was primarily interested in making sure that it had access to Iraqi oil. It was also accused of awarding contracts for the reconstruction of Iraq to certain favoured US multinationals, most particularly Haliburton, a company which used to be run by President Bush's vice-president, Dick Cheney.

Use the internet to track down these allegations. Do you think there is any truth in them? Is this yet another example of US multinationals and the US government working hand-in-hand to create a government favourable to US interests rather than responsible to its own citizens?

THE USE OF INVISIBLE POWER IN AN INTERNATIONAL CONTEXT In an era when international economic transactions increasingly cross borders, an important area of development that is almost totally invisible to public scrutiny concerns the establishment of private international law. In an interesting analysis of this phenomenon, Dezelay and Garth (1996) have revealed how companies that find themselves in dispute with each other are increasingly unwilling to reveal this in the public arena. As a result, a whole new area of law has begun to develop that is separate from normal, national jurisdictional contexts. The court has been set up by the International Chamber of Commerce to deal with contract disputes between large companies or between countries and companies. In order to resolve these disputes by agreement, the parties are brought together in front of a neutral party to whom the facts of the case are presented. This neutral party then makes the decision in what is known as an 'arbitration'. This sounds like a normal legal procedure. The difference is that the parties to the contract decide which laws will apply and who will be the judge so they are not bound by the laws of the country in which the dispute takes place. With this flexibility, it is generally possible to structure a neutral procedure offering no undue advantage to any party. The website for the court states (amongst other things):[5]

- Judicial systems do not allow the parties to a dispute to choose their own judges. In contrast, arbitration offers the parties the unique opportunity to designate persons of their choice as arbitrators, provided they are independent. This enables the parties to have their disputes resolved by people who have specialized competence in the relevant field.

- Arbitration is faster and less expensive than litigation in the courts. Although a complex international dispute may sometimes take a great deal of time and money to resolve, even by arbitration, the limited scope for challenge against arbitral awards, as compared with court judgements, offers a clear advantage. Above all, it helps to ensure that the parties will not subsequently be entangled in a prolonged and costly series of appeals.

- Arbitration hearings are not public, and only the parties themselves receive copies of the awards.

Dezelay and Garth reveal how the arbitrators themselves are chosen from among establishment figures across a range of societies. These figures are generally highly esteemed members of the legal elites sharing similar class backgrounds and connections. In these settings, multinational firms can ensure that their 'dirty linen' is not washed in public but kept discreetly behind closed doors. The rules that bind the sides in the arbitration can be chosen from many different jurisdictions; they do not have to reflect where the case is actually conducted or the national jurisdiction in which the case arose. Thus this sphere of international law emerges without any democratic accountability. In 2003, 580 requests for arbitration were filed with the ICC Court, concerning 1584 parties from 123 different countries and independent territories; the place of arbitration was located in 47 different countries throughout the world; arbitrators of 69 different nationalities were appointed or confirmed under the ICC rules.

This has been just a small selection of the silences and absences of the mainstream. The key point is that this mainstream neglects issues of economic and political power. However, before we leave this topic it is necessary to reiterate that this power is continually opposed and contested. Any quick internet search will reveal a massive list of websites devoted to anti-globalization.[6] It has been argued both by the opponents of globalization and its adherents that the communication possibilities among protestors have been improved by the internet enabling rapid and unexpected mobilization of protestors. Events such as the Seattle anti-globalization protests in 1999 have revealed both the strength of feeling and the role of the internet in mobilizing such forces.

Moreover, there have been many efforts within existing international institutions to control multinationals. The International Labour Organization, which was originally founded under the Treaty of Versailles ending the First World War, and then became part of the United Nations, has been campaigning since 1919 for the promotion of fair labour standards across the world. The ILO has been active in developing conventions and regulations about the treatment of labour, many of which have been accepted by national governments, though much obviously remains to be done.

More recently, the UN itself set up a Global Compact bringing together multinationals, government and labour organizations to discuss and agree forms of regulation and control.[7] Resistance to globalization ranges from radical attempts to criticize and undermine the system (see e.g. Hardt and Negri, 2000) through to organizations that seek to reform multinationals and the process of globalization by creating public accountability systems (see Chapter 14).

Image 12.6 Protests against globalization at a meeting of the World Trade Organization

Retheorizing the multinational

Another approach to developing a critical analysis of multinationals, however, is to theorize in a different way the nature of multinationals. Here the emphasis is on attacking the vision of the multinational as an economically rational form, not just by emphasizing its political character but also by showing that the multinational in fact consists of multiple groups of actors involved in ongoing conflict and negotiation. One way to discuss this is in terms of the concepts of 'transnational social space' and 'transnational communities'. This terminology is initially drawn from the interface of ethnic studies, labour migration, economic globalization and cultural identities (see Morgan, 2001a, 2001b for a more extended discussion; also the contributions in Morgan *et al.*, 2001). Underlying it is the sense that forms of social action and identity are increasingly coordinated across national boundaries and it is therefore important to understand the modes of social organization, mobility and communication that enable these processes to hang together. This in turn is related to the idea of dialogues of communication that can emerge and be sustained across national boundaries, out of which new definitions of identity and interest can emerge. While these new definitions in themselves remain contested, they embody a dual movement. On the one hand, the importance of the local (in its cultural and social manifestations) is affirmed, but, on the other hand, the contrast between different 'locals' becomes the means whereby more general definitions of the collective become defined.

Such an approach turns the normal model of the MNC upside down as it means that the focus is on multiple local sites rather than a coherent hierarchical structure in which decisions are taken and implemented on the basis of an abstract, economically rational mode of acting. In this view, the multinational is not a 'thing' or an actor; rather it consists of multiple local sites that each have their own conditions of existence and their own type of embeddedness in local social relations. By 'embeddedness' is meant work and authority relations reflecting the distinctive national and local history of the particular site (see the earlier discussion on 'varieties of capitalism'). From the point of view of senior managers and the capital markets, the multinational as an organization is a means of coordinating these local sites into a single legal and financial entity that can produce 'shareholder value'. The management headquarters of multinationals, within the constraints set for them by financial governance mechanisms operated through capital markets, develop specific sets of practices to bring order and coordination to these local sites. They seek to impose the terms of the debate in which 'general' and 'collective' interests are represented – e.g. profitability, shareholder value and efficiency. However, the degree to which these are imposed and accepted by local sites is clearly variable (see for instance the excellent studies by Belanger *et al.*, 1999 and Kristensen and Zeitlin, 2005). Also, the actors within the local sites may themselves seek to develop linkages across sites or with actors that are outside the multinational – e.g. the local state, local and international suppliers and customers, local, national and international social movements such as trade unions or other collective bodies. Other dialogues across national, organizational and institutional boundaries can potentially emerge in these contexts. These in turn may give rise to alternative definitions of the collective interest that may not be encapsulated in concepts of 'shareholder value' but may revolve around discourses of 'employee rights', 'sustainable development', 'respect for local communities', etc.

One aspect of such an institution is the European Works Council. Any company with subsidiaries in two or more members of the European Union is supposed to establish a European Works Council (EWC). The EWC has the right to receive and be consulted about the company's strategy in so far as it affects employment and conditions of work. Employee representatives are nominated at national level and then meet in the EWC with other employees as well as managers. The EWC is a top-down institution emerging out of the EU rather than being the result of employees agitating for such a body. Nevertheless, it is one example of a formal institution that allows employees to make connections with each other and discuss common issues. It seems clear that when BMW management was discussing how to get rid of its loss-making Rover operation in the United Kingdom, employee representatives from both the United Kingdom and Germany strenuously opposed the closure of Rover in Birmingham.

Exercise 12.10

The growing significance of European Works Councils The following is an extract from an Opinion adopted on 24 September 2003 – the European Economic and Social Committee on the practical application of the EWCs Directive and on any aspects of the Directive that might need to be revised:

> Out of a total of 1,865 companies or groups of companies employing 17 million people which come under the scope of the EWC Directive, 639 of them, with 11 million employees, had an EWC at the end of 2002. More than 10,000 workers' representatives are now directly involved in the work of EWCs and in implementing intercultural exchanges and practices. This is one of the most striking and significant features of social Europe.

Using an internet search engine, find two examples of European Works Councils based in MNCs from different countries in Europe. Can you find out what they have discussed? Do they have any power? What problems do you think emerge on the employee side coordinating their approach to these discussions?

In a critical approach to multinationals, local sites and subsidiaries can be seen as having their own social dynamics. They are not reducible to the outcome of the control measures undertaken by the headquarters. Two dimensions are relevant here. The first concerns the degree of autonomy and independence that the local site can exercise vis-à-vis headquarters control. The second concerns the nature of social relationships within the local subsidiary. With regard to the former, local sites will be more powerful if the following conditions apply:

● They have technical expertise that is unavailable elsewhere in the company and yet perceived as important.

● Their production system is perceived to be among the best in the company and therefore not easily replaceable.

● Their products and services are important for other sites and other products (i.e. rather than being only destined for local consumer markets).

This independence can be reinforced by conditions outside the firm itself. For example, where a local area constitutes what is called an 'industrial district' or an 'innovation cluster' in which there are multiple social relationships crossing firm boundaries and supported by local government, local training and innovation centres and local financial institutions, the subsidiary may be deeply embedded in these relationships (Solvell and Zander, 1998; Kristensen and Zeitlin, 2001). Moreover, the multinational may have set up or purchased the subsidiary precisely so that it can tap into these local resources. It cannot therefore act in a way that interferes with the operation of these local networks or else it destroys what it set out to gain.

Exercise 12.11

Look in recent editions of the *Financial Times*. What examples can you find of multinationals doing the following?

- Closure of an existing subsidiary plant.
- Sale or divestment of a subsidiary plant.
- Acquisition of a subsidiary.
- New investment in an existing subsidiary plant.
- Setting up a new plant.

You will find it a lot easier to find examples of closures or the threat of closures.

What reasons has the MNC given for its decisions? What have local political actors had to say about these decisions? What impact will these have on the local community and/or the broader region/nation?

Whether and how a local site might exercise its power against the headquarters, however, depends on the nature of the social relationships within the local site. The most important issue in this context is the form of social cohesion in the local context. The literature on 'varieties of capitalism' has revealed that authority relationships within the firm can vary immensely depending on the nature of the national context. Simplifying this literature, one can distinguish on the one side local sites that are embedded in a social democratic or collectivist ethos of economic activity; on the other side are those systems based more on individual rights and responsibilities and/or in which collective organizations are weak.

Thinkpoint 12.9

The varieties of capitalism approach In recent years there has been strong interest in how different forms of capitalism are structured. For example, in countries like Germany, Sweden and Japan, decisions about how firms should behave in relation to investments, how they treat employees and how they treat suppliers tend to be decisions that are taken not just inside the firm but through coordinated action with others, such as their bankers, the state, their employees and their trade unions, and other employers in the same industry. Hall and Soskice refer to such systems as 'coordinated market economies'. Where these same decisions are taken primarily by the management of the firm on the basis of their perceptions of the market (for labour, for components, for capital, for products), this is referred to as 'liberal market economies' (the United States and the United Kingdom). These two models have profound implications for power and inequality as well as for how firms are managed and organized. Broadly speaking, coordinated market economies tend to be more consultative and participative both inside and outside the firm; they are often dominated by broadly social democratic politics. Liberal market economies tend to have firms that are led by managers who are keen to exercise power without restraint from other stakeholders. Liberal market economies are characterized by more flexible employment arrangements and higher disparities of reward than coordinated market economies. They tend to be dominated by more individualistic and market-dominated forms of politics.

The two systems tend to work better in different industry environments. Thus traditionally coordinated market economies have developed very strong capabilities in engineering, automotives and electronic products areas while liberal market economies have tended to be more successful in rapidly evolving market areas where flexibility is important – e.g. software industries, professional services, entertainment and broadcasting.

In the 1980s, the coordinated market model was favoured by some commentators as it seemed to offer a protection against the sort of 'deindustrialization' that the United Kingdom and the United States under Thatcher and Reagan suffered. In the 1990s as new industries sprang up in computers, internet technology and biotechnology, the United States and United Kingdom seemed very much more successful than countries like Germany and Japan. However in the early part of this decade, the dot-com crash and the subsequent fall of Enron, Arthur Andersen, WorldCom and a number of other companies seen as exemplars of the strength of US capitalism in the 1990s made people question US dominance.

As well as Hall and Soskice (2001) and Whitley (1999), there are more accessible introductions to this debate in Coates (2000) and Crouch and Streeck (1997). Journalistic accounts are available in Turner (2001) and Hutton (1995).

In local sites within societies where social democratic movements have been strong and the outcomes of their activities have been put into the legal framework, a form of social cohesion exists that emphasizes the collective fate of the local economic activity and the rights of those concerned to be, at the least, consulted. Such systems would, for example, include Germany and the Scandinavian countries where trade unions and works councils have generally had access to high levels of information. These systems in turn are generally based upon a form of class compromise between labour and capital; in return for certain rights to consultation, stability of employment and high wages, workers accept managers' rights to continually upgrade technology and production processes. This class compromise is also reflected in wider social relations. In social democratic systems, welfare rights (e.g. unemployment benefit, sickness pay, pensions), tend to be the outcome of collective processes organized through the state or the trade unions.

Workers also accept the responsibility to learn and develop their own skills in the light of changing technological and competitive conditions (for the broader debate on skills and learning see Chapter 5). In its most worked out form, there exists a strong set of institutional links between the innovative capacity of local production sites, local government systems, forms of training inside and outside the firm and the legislative framework for labour and capital. These sites are locally embedded in a variety of ways, not least that employment in the locality is long term and has been built up on the basis of sustained collective investment in local training and research facilities. This is reinforced by strong linkages between local banks, local political institutions and the livelihoods of communities. It is also strengthened by the collective institutions at the national level in which the employee representatives of the local sites can access management information and form their own perspective on the 'collective good'.

In more individualist systems, on the other hand, collective institutions are weak and individuals have to develop their own responses to labour market conditions with little help from trade unions or the government. They are much more reliant on their own earning power to fund both gaps in employment or efforts at further training and their old age and retirement. Increasingly, the savings necessary for this tend to be invested in private sector investment management companies. All this reinforces the dependence of the individual and the family on movements in the stock market and reduces dependence on state provision of welfare. The power of capital in liberal market economies is relatively unconstrained by legal blocks or trade union power. Decisions about production and location are taken by managerial elites in response to 'market pressures'. Local objections to closures or rationalizations of production sites are treated as ill-informed and short-sighted about the conditions necessary for economic welfare. There are few strong institutional linkages between firms, local political institutions and the development of a social and training infrastructure for the workforce. The conditions for reproducing the locality as a community with a strong collective identity have been dismantled. The collective purpose is defined by unconstrained free markets, which will, in the end, supposedly, benefit all.

In collectivist systems, the local subsidiaries of multinationals are usually controlled at middle and lower management level (and sometimes higher) by managers who have long been associated with the local system. This is likely to lead to a stronger sense of solidarity and collectivism binding managers and employees in a common 'community of fate' than where the managers have been put in by headquarters and see themselves as part of a global management cadre with their first loyalty to the company rather than the local site (Kristensen and Zeitlin, 2001). Therefore, local sites can exercise power and, within certain limited contexts, can create and sustain alternatives to the dominant managerial logic.

In any multinational, therefore, the degree to which the headquarters can enforce its power over the local sites will vary according to the degree to which a local site has some independence and also the degree to which there is a form of social solidarity/coherence among local managers and employees that enables that local power to be exercised (see e.g. the differences between sites in the study of a division of ABB by Belanger *et al.*, 1999; see also contributions in Morgan *et al.*, 2001; Geppert *et al.*, 2002).

Managing the multinational across national and institutional divides

Managers at various levels of the firms (the divisional, the geographical business unit, the head office functions as well as those actually working within the local sites) attempt to bring order into the diversity of the localities. There are various ways in which control can be exercised. Among the most obvious are the quantitative controls that are placed on local sites. These may be financial measures, quality measures, productivity measures, manpower measures and other efficiency measures. Where such systems are in operation, the next tier of management is most concerned with the quantitative outcomes and less interested in how they are achieved.

This can have two obvious effects, though how this works out in practice will relate to issues of independence and solidarity as discussed in the previous section. The first effect is that the quantitative indicators themselves become sites of social construction and negotiation. What appear to be 'hard', quantitative indicators usually dissolve on further inspection into figures that have to be constructed and interpreted. What are taken as objective 'facts' are the outcome of processes in which actors negotiate over what is to count and what is to be 'dis-counted'. This is not to understate the importance of such quantitative targets and their use as a way both of coordinating across sites and providing the basis for management action. However, it is important to question within multinationals decisions, for example, about plant closures where the argument is made on the basis of so-called 'hard evidence' about lack of profitability, efficiency and so on.

This relates to the second effect of the use of quantitative indicators, which is the role of negotiation and meaning construction that occurs between local sites and various tiers of management at divisional and headquarters level. If multinationals hold to multiple quantitative targets, negotiation and power to define which are the most important measures becomes crucial. Senior management measures of productivity and efficiency may be challenged in themselves or even placed against other locally developed measures, such as 'serving the local community', 'innovating' and providing useful employment.

Control and coordination can also be exercised, as previously discussed, by positioning expatriate managers in the most important roles within subsidiaries. Expatriate managers can be expected to have been socialized within the headquarters and be committed strongly to achieving according to head office criteria. This will normally be their route to career advancement within the company. Even if their career expectations lie beyond the company, they will be more likely to rely on an assessment of their achievements by the head office for future advancement than the local site. Expatriate managers act as 'the eyes and ears' of the head office. They exercise control and coordination by implementing practices defined by the head office as essential to its global functioning. However, there may be other sorts of managers who have developed their careers in the locality and are committed to this site. They are less likely to accept the logic espoused by the headquarters and can in fact be in a good position to debunk and challenge this approach on the basis of their knowledge of local conditions.

Instead of perceiving a multinational as a 'thing-like' object with goals that are determined by the necessities of market survival, the approach here has been to see the multinational firm as a transnational social space that binds together in various ways a variety of social contexts. The nature of these local sites, how they become bound together through processes of control and coordination and how all of this fits into a broader process of capitalism becomes the focus of analysis. The approach is concerned with process, with 'becoming' rather than 'being'. From this point of view, the analysis of the multinational could be much more usefully concerned with analysing these sites, in terms of how they relate to their local context, to other local sites, to social and political movements beyond their local boundaries and to the headquarters.

This has a crucial effect on issues of policy and strategy for those seeking to resist multinationals because it emphasizes that local struggles can be successful. The multinational is not all powerful; it cannot simply close down a plant or reduce numbers employed. In order to do that, it has to be involved in some sort of negotiation and this negotiation is structured by the social relationships in the local site, the local community and the broader political context.

Thinkpoint 12.10

When BMW saw that they would be continuing to lose money on Rover for some time, their senior management looked for ways to sever their ties. BMW saw that simple closure of the site was not an option because the impact on the local area was too large in terms of jobs. Politicians, trade unionists and local community leaders would inevitably resist this. BMW therefore sought to pass on responsibility by selling Rover to a venture capitalist company, Alchemy partners. As it became know what Alchemy was planning, there was huge disquiet. Alchemy proposed to massively thin down production at Rover's main Longbridge plant. Trade union officials saw the implications of this and quickly moved to block this by threatening to take Alchemy and BMW to court for potential breaches of EU law in relation to the supply of information to employees, among other things. The coalition of local, national and international forces that had defeated BMW's initial moves to closure stayed together to defeat Alchemy. Instead, a new bid was put together by previous Rover managers under John Towers (who had left soon after BMW took over). They took over the Longbridge plant and other assets for a nominal sum and BMW made a less than graceful exit.

In April 2005 Rover Cars went into liquidation. The company had failed to generate sufficient revenue from its existing fleet of cars and needed substantial backing from another partner if it was to succeed. To that end, it had sought an alliance with a major Chinese car company, Shanghai Automotive Industry Corporation. These efforts were unsuccessful and Rover closed. There was a great deal of controversy because, while many thousands of employees in Rover and in the local area lost jobs, the owners of the company had managed to secure themselves large pensions that were not lost. For a comprehensive account of this see the report by the National Audit Office see http://www.nao.org.uk/pn/05-06/0506961.htm.

In comparison, other car plants have been effectively closed without this degree of opposition. Ford's earliest and biggest plant in the United Kingdom at Dagenham, Essex has been downgraded from assembly to engine work with significant loss of jobs with very little resistance. In September 2004, Ford announced its intention to close one of its Jaguar plants in Coventry, and in 2006 Peugeot decided to close its plant in Ryton, near Coventry.

Why are there such different reactions to factory closures? Is it simply a matter of scale or are some closures politicized in ways that others are not. Does it matter how strong a local community there is associated with the factory?

These arguments point to the role critical management theorist can play in developing resistance and not just standing on the sidelines; it opens space for engagement. In fact, by virtue of its very structure, the multinational creates the space for new forms of dialogues across nations, across the developed and the less-developed regions of the world, and across different institutional contexts. Developing and using these spaces to create an emancipatory agenda is a fundamental challenge to critical theorists.

In conclusion, critical management studies can open up the sphere of international business and multinationals to much wider scrutiny than has previously been the case. It can shift the agenda away from technical and economistic analyses of these processes and link more closely with the critical social science literature that has emerged over the last few years in this area. It can do this best by building on its own strengths in terms of examining the conflicts and contradictions that emerge within multinationals as managers seek to control and coordinate different interests as well as different sites of production.

Discussion questions

1 Why do multinational firms exist?

2 How do the dynamics of different markets affect (a) how firms internationalize and (b) how international firms organize?

3 Should multinationals aim to create a single common culture among all their managers?

4 Do multinationals exert too much power? If so, who should control them and how?

5 Can and should local communities exercise influence over the decisions of multinationals to invest in or disinvest from an area?

6 Do you want to work in a multinational? If so, why, and how do you expect this would be different from working in a firm located in just one country?

Further reading

Bartlett, C. A. and Ghoshal, S. (2002) *Managing Across Borders: The Transnational Solution*, second edition, Boston MA: Harvard Business School Press.

This book is the classic account of different models of multinationals' strategies and structures. It uses some simple and clear illustrations of MNCs from different countries to show how organizational structures can vary depending on the strategy of the firm.

Crouch, C. and Streeck, W. (1997) *Political Economy of Modern Capitalism*, London: Sage.

This is a clear introduction to some of the main differences between countries in terms of their economic system and how this affects the development of firms, industrial relations systems, skill systems, etc.

13 Bureaucracy and Post-bureaucracy

Christopher Grey

Key concepts and learning objectives

By the end of this chapter you should understand:

- The two models of organizations – bureaucracy and post-bureaucracy – and what is claimed about the reasons for their existence and the benefits and limitations of each.

- The disputes about their value from the point of view of efficiency, but you should also understand that efficiency itself is a disputed concept.

- The different concepts of **rationality** in organizations and how these relate to the two models.

- The political and ethical issues that inform debates about the two models.

Aims of the chapter

This chapter will:

- Explain bureaucracy and post-bureaucracy as models of organization.

- Explain the deficiencies of each model from mainstream perspectives.

- Examine some major mainstream studies.

- Identify critical approaches to each model.

- Examine some major critical studies.

- Explain the strengths and weaknesses of the critical approaches.

Overview and key points

Bureaucracy is a model of organization based upon rules, hierarchy, impersonality and a division of labour and has been the dominant form of organization for over a century. However, it suffers from problems such as poor employee motivation, producer-focus and inertia. In view of this, post-bureaucracy has been proposed as a new organizational model more suited to today's business environment. Post-bureaucracy is based on trust, empowerment, personal treatment and shared responsibility. But this brings its own problems in terms of loss of control, risk and unfairness.

These models and problems derive from mainstream thinking. Such thinking is concerned with narrow views of efficiency and is guided by a search for control and performance. Critical approaches provide a more radical analysis of bureaucracy and post-bureaucracy. From a critical perspective bureaucracy is seen as dehumanizing and post-bureaucracy is interpreted as an extension of control. Moreover, both are criticized for seeking efficiency from the point of view of those with power, to the neglect of other people and of the ethical purposes and consequences of organization. However, among other limitations, critical approaches can be seen as utopian.

Mainstream approach

Introduction

Imagine that you have been asked to manage student admissions to your course, and imagine that for some reason you have to do the job from scratch. What kinds of things would you do? The chances are you would set up some kind of system. As a minimum, you might set up a system that established a closing date for applications; which sent out a standard letter acknowledging receipt of applications; which set a rule that once the closing date has passed you will accept the 100 best-qualified applicants; and which sent a standard letter of acceptance or rejection to each applicant, asking those you had accepted to confirm by a set date that they will take up your offer. You might well also employ other people to do some aspects of the job. For example, you might employ a secretary to send out the letters, but make the decisions about the wording of the letters and about whom to accept yourself. And on what basis would you have the right to make those decisions? Obviously, the fact that you are the Admissions Manager.

What other kinds of procedures might you put in place?

No doubt there would be quite a lot of other aspects of the system you devised. What is sure is that you would devise a system, and that if you did not then you would be unlikely to do a very good job. Think for a minute about what would happen if you did not adopt a system similar to that just outlined. You might accept or reject applicants when later on you got better or worse qualified applicants; you would write a different letter each time you dealt with an application; you would accept applicants on the basis of something other than qualification (at random? first come, first served? the sound of their name? where they were born?), and you would have no way of knowing who had accepted their places because you had not asked them to confirm acceptance of your offer.

In order to perform this relatively straightforward task efficiently, you would have designed a system characterized by:

- rules (e.g. closing date)
- standardized procedures (e.g. letters)
- rationality (e.g. accepting applicants for a logical reason)
- division of labour (e.g. between you and your secretary)
- hierarchy (e.g. you are in charge of your secretary)
- authority (e.g. you have the right to make decisions).

Take any other task of any size and you will find that these kinds of systems will enable you to do the job better than any alternative. What does 'better' mean here? It means more efficiently (with less waste of time and resources) and more effectively (in terms of getting the result you require).

Exercise 13.1

Imagine another task you might be asked to organize. What system would you put in place and how does it illustrate the characteristics discussed? Can you design a system that would be effective that does *not* have these characteristics?

This example illustrates themes that have been at the heart of the theory and practice or organization for at least 100 years. One of the founding figures of organizational behaviour was Max Weber (1864–1920), a German social scientist who was interested in a wide range of social and political questions in his time. One of these was the question of what held societies together, and this, he thought, was to do with authority.

Authority comes in different forms in different societies at different times. It may be based on 'charisma' (the personal authority of particular individuals) or on 'tradition' (the established authority of institutions, such as the monarchy). But according to Weber, modern societies were increasingly based on rational-legal authority – that is, systems of rules (e.g. legal rules) devised for rational reasons. Hence the term rational-legal. People in society accepted that they had to follow the dictates of these systems. Hence they were a form of authority.

Rational-legal authority was the basis not just of the legal system, but the state, the civil service, industry and most other kinds of organization. We can already see how it relates to the example of setting up an admissions system, where terms such as 'rule', 'reason' and 'authority' appeared. Applied to organizations, rational-legal authority means bureaucracy. Nowadays we often use this word to imply something inefficient – 'red tape' (and we will come back to that later). But in its pure form (which Weber called an 'ideal-type') it refers to a highly efficient form of organization. Indeed, this was the reason why, according to Weber, it was becoming more and more dominant from the late 19th century onwards. Bureaucracy, he said, was the most technically efficient and rational form of organization. It simply got the job done better than any other system, and this was why it was adopted.

Let's take a closer look at what these bureaucracies consist of:

- *Functional specialization*. There is a formal division of labour so that some people are paid to do one kind of function as their official duty and they do not do anything other than their official duty. They are employed full-time within the context of a lifetime career structure and are appointed and promoted on the basis of qualifications and experience.

- *Hierarchy of authority*. There is a structure such that those holding a superior position have the authority, solely by virtue of holding that position, to give orders to those in subordinate positions. Subordinates, in turn, report upwards to their superiors.

- *System of rules*. Everything that goes on in the organization is based upon following a formal, written set of rules about procedures and practices that must be adhered to.

- *Impersonality*. Rules are followed and authority is held with regard for emotions, personality or personal preferences. Employees and customers are treated in accordance with these rules.

Some of these ingredients look pretty obvious to us. Does it really need to be said that people get paid in money? But Weber was trying to pin down all the features that separated bureaucracy from

Image 13.1 Cogs in the machine?

all other kinds of organization. Other features are familiar from the admissions system example – which isn't surprising because Weber's 'model' was based on his observation of what efficiently organized systems actually did. Some features look a little dated – full-time, permanent jobs for life, for example, are not necessarily a feature of modern bureaucracies. But overall, the reason why the list seems obvious is that Weber was right to think that these kinds of organizations were becoming dominant. Now, they seem so familiar that we hardly recognize them as anything other than 'the way things are'.

However, a bureaucratic way of organizing is one bound up with tasks of a particular kind. Specifically, it is effective in situations where very large numbers of identical, standard operations are needed – processing social security claims or mass producing cars, for example. It also suits situations where a rigid chain of command is favoured, where little training or initiative is required, since all that people need to do is to follow rules and orders.

Many commentators believe that these kinds of conditions no longer obtain or, at any rate, are increasingly rare. Since at least the 1970s, but with a growing insistence, it has been claimed that such 'industrial' conditions are giving way to a 'post-industrial' era. This argument takes many forms, but in essence it says that the economy has moved from the mass production of standard products towards short product runs for niche markets. At the same time, it is suggested that people in organizations need – and perhaps want – to be more flexible and innovative, rather than simply following orders.

Thinkpoint 13.2

What do you regard as the benefits and costs of a working in a bureaucracy from the point of view of the employee?

Against that background, there has arguably been the development of a range of new organizational forms. These are given many different names, but as an umbrella term we can call them 'post-bureaucracies'. Charles Heckscher (1994), one of the leading writers on post-bureaucracy, has devised a list of characteristics he calls the post-bureaucratic ideal-type, in contrast to Weber's ideal-type of bureaucracy:

- Rules are replaced with consensus and dialogue based upon personal influence rather than status. People are trusted to act on the basis of shared values rather than rules.

- Responsibilities are assigned on the basis of competence for tasks rather than hierarchy, and are treated as individuals rather than impersonally.

- The organization has an open boundary, so that rather than full-time permanent employment, people come into and out of the organization in a flexible way, including part-time, temporary and consultancy arrangements. Work is no longer done in fixed hours or at a designated place.

CASE STUDY 13.1 Universal

Robertson and Swan (1998) explain the development since 1986 of a consultancy firm that specializes in advising high-tech companies and start-ups on innovation and the exploitation of intellectual property rights. The firm – which they call 'Universal' – is also involved in incubating (providing resource and assistance for new ventures) and taking equity shares in some client companies. The Universal case is an interesting one for illustrating aspects of the basic models of bureaucracy and post-bureaucracy and also some of the complexities of these models, which we will come to later in this chapter.

To give a very brief summary, Universal grew from a charismatic founder and handful of consultants in 1986 until it employed around 120 consultants plus almost the same number again as associates in other countries. In the early years, Universal was explicitly egalitarian, non-hierarchical and non-bureaucratic. Many of the early members were recruited from more traditional consultancies and were attracted by the freer atmosphere. Project teams were self-organizing and trusted to do their work well and efficiently. Projects were initiated on the basis of their scientific value. People joined projects that interested them and rewards were fairly equally shared. Knowledge about projects was shared on a word of mouth basis. In short, bureaucracy was not much in evidence. From the early 1990s onwards, the combination of growth and also tougher market conditions led to the creation of divisions and divisional managers. Under a new performance management system, each division and each individual was given a revenue target, and this was linked to financial rewards. Projects were undertaken on the basis of their financial viability. Although there was still relatively little formal hierarchy, there was an informal pecking order among staff. There was an internal labour market for project staff, which used e-mail systems to advertise opportunities.

Exercise 13.2

Imagine that you had joined Universal in 1986. How might you feel about the changes now?

Case commentary

How we read this case depends on where we look from. Entering Universal now, we might see it as a good example of a post-bureaucratic organization. It is relatively flatly structured and project based, and it makes heavy use of 'virtual' organization. Looked at by someone who had worked at Universal since 1986 we might see it as a good example of an organization which has become more bureaucratically structured in order to compete in tougher market conditions by increasing efficiency. Although we will return to the case as we go through the chapter, the point to note for now is that bureaucracy and post-bureaucracy are to some extent relative terms. In other words, reality is usually less clear-cut than the models or 'ideal-types'. Robertson and Swan (1998, p. 561) make almost exactly this point when they show how cultural and systemic forms of control are interlinked at Universal.

Key problems

Bureaucracy Although bureaucracy has been adopted in probably every large organization in every country in the world, organization theorists and analysts have always recognized that it poses problems. Some of these problems are to do with the social impact of bureaucracy, and these will be picked up in the 'Critical approach' section later in this chapter. But there are also problems from the more narrow perspective of organizational design and efficiency. Many of these are the kinds of problems that give rise to the everyday sense that bureaucracy equals 'red tape' – needless waste and pedantic obsession with rules. Later, we will cover some of the technical reasons for these problems, but for now we will just give a brief outline of them.

Bureaucracy can be thought of as a form of organization which is like a 'machine'. In principle, each part is perfectly designed to perform its task, and the whole thing operates 'like clockwork' in an entirely predictable, standard way. It is this that makes a bureaucracy efficient. But it also means that the people within the organization have to function as if they were mere 'cogs' within the machine. This leads to at least three key problems for bureaucracy.

One is the problem of motivation (see Chapter 2). Because people in bureaucracies have to follow rules, and have no choice or discretion about doing so, they may well have little personal commitment to the organization, and gain little interest or stimulation from their work. Theorists of motivation have long recognized that very often motivation is linked to factors such as job satisfaction and to a sense of achievement and responsibility at work. Bureaucracies rarely deliver this and, *if* high motivation leads to better work performance then it follows that employees will perform sub-optimally in bureaucracies. In this sense, they may not be so efficient as they seem at first sight.

Linked to this is the problem that bureaucracies, as rule-based systems, may not be very good at customer service. If the workforce are poorly motivated they are unlikely to care much about customer service but simply follow rules grudgingly or blindly. These rules are there for the good of the organization rather than customers, and will not be changed to suit the particular demands an individual customer may have. For this reason, bureaucracies are sometimes described as producer-focused. There is an expression – 'a jobsworth' – which describes the typical mindset of an employee of a bureaucracy. When asked by a customer to bend the rules in some particular case, such an employee replies 'that would be more than my job's worth'. They know that failing to follow rules will lead to their being punished, or even sacked. This can also lead to a situation where no decision is taken until it is passed up to the competent 'authority'. This 'buck-passing' leads to people 'hiding behind the rules' and is sometimes called bureaupathy.

This kind of inflexibility is a microcosm of a third key problem for bureaucracy: it seems to be resistant to innovation and to change (see Chapter 10). Rules, once made, are enshrined for all time and will only change very slowly. This may not matter in contexts of, say, producing large quantities of standard products the specifications of which do not vary for long periods of time, perhaps several years. However, in more volatile and uncertain conditions bureaucratic inertia will mean that these organizations fail to adapt and therefore will either disappear when faced with competition; or survive only because of being protected by government from competition, but deliver goods and services in an inefficient way.

Thinkpoint 13.3

How does the system for student admissions, described at the beginning of this chapter, illustrate the problems of bureaucracy?

Post-bureaucracy   Post-bureaucracy is very much a response to the kinds of problems believed to characterize bureaucracies and it proceeds, as we have seen, from the analysis that many or most sectors are in fact unstable and rapidly changing. This means that bureaucratic inertia will indeed be a problem. However, as an alternative model of organizations, post-bureaucracy generates its own set of problems, many of them, of course, being precisely those which bureaucracy seems to solve.

If bureaucracy is like a machine, then post-bureaucracy is more like an organism – a living, growing, changing entity with a mind of its own. But this means that it is far less predictable than a machine, and prey to illnesses and malfunctions. Again, we can see at least three linked problems.

The first of them is that of control. Bureaucracies use detailed rules to control what goes on in organizations. Without such rules, how can control be exercised, especially in large organizations that may spread over many countries? In essence, post-bureaucracy proposes a different, normative, form of control based upon some version of culture management (see Chapter 9) and trust. But that is a rather fragile form of control, resting as it does on self-control rather than external monitoring. Trust may be difficult to sustain, especially over long distances where relationships are mediated 'virtually' rather than face-to-face, and trust, of course, may be betrayed. Since post-bureaucracies are also characterized by a 'porous' organizational boundary, this means that employees will be coming in and out of the organization on short-term and consulting contracts. These seem like particularly unpromising conditions to build shared values and trust. In short, there is a danger that post-bureaucracies will descend into anarchy.

Related to this problem of control, there is the problem of risk. It is all very well to give people more freedom to innovate and to do away with rules, but what happens if this freedom leads to decisions that go wrong? The consequence will be failures of service delivery and lost money. Fixed

Image 13.2

rules may deter good ideas and improvements to products and services, but they also prevent bad ideas and damage. We can see that, in the case of Universal, these issues informed the development of more bureaucratic systems. Whereas, in the early days, projects were developed with little concern for their financial consequences, the later systems tried to ensure that these consequences were considered.

The third main problem is also linked to the issue of control. As well as the business risks of innovation there are also questions of fairness. Bureaucratic systems are impersonal; they do not discriminate between people except on the basis of experience and qualifications. Post-bureaucracy stresses individual treatment – again, a move away from rigid rules. But this opens up the possibility of all kinds of irrationalities and prejudices. For example, while you might want to be treated 'as an individual', would you want your promotion prospects to depend upon whim? Suppose a male project leader only chooses attractive young women to work on prestigious contracts. Wouldn't those of us who are not attractive young women (and, indeed, those who are) prefer to be chosen on the basis of a rational system? And the issues here are not only moral but also pragmatic, since businesses that allow discrimination may face legal penalties and also suffer sub-optimal decisions about staffing. This also applies to the flexible treatment of customers. We might be delighted if an organization, say, rushed our order through and so responded flexibly to our needs. But what about the other customer whose order is therefore pushed down the queue? Would that customer be so pleased?

Thinkpoint 13.4

How does the development of Universal illustrate an attempt to deal with the problems of post-bureaucracy?

Key ideas and contributions to thinking

Because bureaucracy has had such a long history, there is a very wide range of studies that have tried to understand and refine it. Post-bureaucracy has a shorter history, but this has coincided with an upsurge in writing and thinking about organizations, so there is plenty of material to cover there as well. However, it would not be unfair to say that the earlier generation (say, 1945–1970) of organizational theorists, who were concerned with bureaucracy and its problems, contributed more to the key ideas in this area. This is partly because ideas about post-bureaucracy have actually been around for a long time (as we will see later) and so the earlier theorists had already developed several ideas about them. And it is partly because the later generation (say 1970 to the present) seem less to generate new ideas as to reformulate what has become something like an orthodoxy about the deficiencies of bureaucracy.

Does size matter? In much of the earlier material, and explicitly in the case study of Universal, it has been implied that there is something significant in the impact of organizational size upon bureaucracy. And this is surely true. If we go back to the opening example of an admissions system for a university course, then it is fairly obvious that if, for the sake of argument, there were only three applications for the course, it would hardly be necessary to devise the systems described. There would be no need for standardization of letters, no need for a division of labour and no need for an authority structure. There might still need to be a rule on whom to accept (if, for example, there was only one place available) but this would hardly call for a bureaucratic system.

There can be no doubt that part of the reason Weber observed a growth in rational-legal, or bureaucratic, organization was because he also lived at a time that was witnessing a phenomenal growth in organizational size – whether that meant the army, the state or factories. Later studies confirmed this. Some of the classic work was done by Peter Blau (1955, 1970). In studies in the United States of over 50 government employment agencies involving over 1200 branches and 350 head offices, Blau found a consistent relationship between bureaucratization (which he measured in some technical ways that do not matter here) and organizational size, measured in numbers of employees. As employee numbers increased, so to did bureaucratization. An organization with, say, 10 000 employees was much more bureaucratized than one of 10, or even 100.

But, more than that, although bureaucratization increased with size, it did so at a declining rate. In other words, adding employee numbers to small organizations had a bigger impact on bureaucratization than adding the same numbers to large organizations. It is not difficult to see why. Imagine a firm employing 10 people, which then expands to employ 510. That is likely to call for all kinds of new systems and rules. But imagine a firm of 20 000 people that expands to 20 500. That will have much less impact. So numbers of employees increase bureaucratization, but at a declining rate, and this observation gives rise to the 'Blau curve'.

That size was linked to bureaucracy was also supported by the Aston Studies, conducted at Aston University in the United Kingdom in the 1960s and 1970s (Pugh, Hickson and Hinings, 1968; Pugh and Hickson, 1976). These studies asserted a causal relationship between size and bureaucratic structure. However, their explanation was different, and more complicated, to that of Blau. The Aston researchers proposed that in larger organizations there was a greater statistical probability of recurrent and repetitive events. This being so, such organizations were more likely to develop standardized rules since they were faced with standardized situations. And standardized rules are, of course, at the heart of bureaucracy. One way of understanding the developments at Universal consultancy is to see a growth in size as leading to the development of more standardized systems.

Although there is an obvious common-sense appeal in the idea that size is what drives bureaucracy, it is important to realize that the situation is less straightforward than common sense might suggest. First, there have been studies which argue that if there is a relationship between size and bureaucracy, then its causality may run against that proposed by the Aston Studies. In other words, it may be that sometimes size is a consequence, not a cause, of bureaucracy. Aldrich (1972) reanalysed the Aston data and argued that this was so. Why? Imagine an organization setting up a new division (e.g. a personnel division or an overseas office). This is an increase in the division of labour, one of the measures of bureaucracy. This new division has to be staffed, so more people are employed. So an increase in bureaucratization has led to an increase in size, not vice versa.

Another classic study questions the size–bureaucracy link in a different way. Joan Woodward, who was not just one of the pioneers of organization studies but one of the few women among those pioneers, looked at the relationship between technology and bureaucracy. She studied around 100 manufacturing firms, of varying sizes, in the United Kingdom and argued that what affected the extent of their bureaucratization was not their size but the type of technology they employed (Woodward, 1965). Thus firms engaged in mass production of standard goods did indeed have bureaucratic structures, but those – even large firms – that were developing one-off products (e.g. hydroelectric turbines), or that had continuous high-tech production technologies (e.g. chemical refining), were far less bureaucratized.

How do these questions relate to post-bureaucracy? Is the implication that large organizations must be bureaucratic? This can be answered in two ways. First, the case for post-bureaucracy rests heavily on the proposition that new information and communication technologies have had a decisive impact upon ways of organizing. So the Woodward findings are relevant to this, because they suggest that there is not an iron law linking size and bureaucracy. Technology also comes in to the

SOURCE: © RONNIE KAUFMAN / CORBIS

Image 13.3 Pre-industrial or post-Fordist?

Image 13.4

equation. Secondly, at least since Peters and Waterman's influential thinking on organizational culture it has been claimed that organizations can 'be big' and 'act small' at the same time. They can use cultural norms, instead of bureaucratic rules, to combine personalized service and organizational control. Whether that is true remains, of course, an open question.

The dysfunctions of bureaucracy Whatever it is that leads to bureaucracy, what are its effects? Classic studies here have focused on whether bureaucracy is really as rational as it appears. We have prefigured this question when, in discussing the problems of bureaucracies, we considered how efficient they were. A group of writers, sometimes called the 'bureaucratic dysfunctionalists', posed these issues with considerable sharpness, by probing some of the realities of bureaucratic life.

The American sociologist Robert Merton (1940) addressed a core theoretical and practical issue with his concept of goal displacement. He argued that, over time, people in bureaucracies came to see 'following the rule' as the goal or purpose, rather than the effect that the rule was supposed to produce. This is the theoretical way of talking about the 'jobsworth' mentality referred to earlier. What matters in goal displacement is, so to speak, 'doing the thing right' rather than 'doing the right thing'. A slavish adherence to the rules as an end in itself is central to the 'red tape' associated with bureaucratic life.

To see how it might work, let's return to the hypothetical admissions system discussed at the start of this chapter. Imagine that having set up the system described you receive an application from a student who has not filled in the application forms, but has provided evidence of already having achieved six 'A' grade A-levels at the age of 16. She also has an impressive record of non-academic achievement and a clutch of references attesting to her academic and personal qualities. But, for some plausible reason, she needs a decision on whether she will be accepted to the course before the closing date for applications has passed.

A reasonable response might be to offer her a place. You know that she fills the criteria and is almost certainly better qualified than any other applicant you will get. Yet the rules say that application forms must be completed and that no decisions will be made before the closing date. So, quite legitimately, you refuse to give a decision and she goes elsewhere. This is goal displacement. Goal displacement does not just mean that you have been inflexible. The point (or 'goal') of the rule is to ensure that the organization maximizes the quality of its student intake. Yet the effect of applying the rule has been to sub-optimize the intake: the person who takes the place you might otherwise have offered the unorthodox applicant will not be as well qualified. You have acted as if the goal of the rule is to *follow* the rule.

Exercise 13.3

How would a post-bureaucratic organization deal with this applicant? What problems might this lead to?

A particular version of the goal-displacement thesis is found in the work of Philip Selznick (1949). His studies suggested that the divisionalized structures of a bureaucratic organization led inevitably to people identifying with the aims of their divisions, not the aims of the organization as a whole.

Thus they would pursue divisional interests at the expense of the organization. In this way, a bureaucracy not only could, but, because of the divisionalization most likely would, deliver organizationally sub-optimal outcomes. This line of thinking has opened up significant wider issues in organizational analysis, including the relationship between sub-cultures and organizational cultures (see Chapter 9) and the nature of organizational politics (see Chapter 8).

All this might seem to deal a fatal blow to the whole theory of bureaucracy. The key idea of this theory is that a system of rules enshrines the most efficient way of doing things. Yet goal displacement suggests that following the rules does not always lead to the best outcome. Someone might respond by offering this (sophisticated) defence of bureaucracy. The defence would be that bureaucracy offers not an optimum solution to each case it deals with but an optimum *average* solution. In other words, overall a bureaucratic system is more efficient even if, in particular cases, it is less than optimal.

Yet, against this, we would have to set the argument presented by Peter Blau. Apart from the Blau curve, this researcher also advanced a very elegant argument suggesting that bureaucracy *always* delivers sub-optimal solutions to problems. Blau observed the trade union tactic called 'work to rule'. A work to rule falls short of a strike and consists of workers refusing to do anything other than follow the formal, established rules of their workplace. Anything that they do which is not in their contracts and not in the organizational rulebook, they refuse to do. If the rules say that they stop at 5.00pm, they stop at 5.00pm on the dot, for example. Similarly, if the rules fail to specify how a particular job should be done then they repeatedly ask for assistance or guidance before doing it. Blau explains that the reason why a union adopts 'work to rule' is in order to disrupt the organization (typically, in pursuit of a pay claim). Yet, if bureaucratic rules enshrine the most efficient way of organizing, then how could it be that following those rules to the letter made the organization less efficient? Blau's answer is that, in fact, following the rules exactly is *not* the most efficient way of organizing, just as goal displacement tells us that following the rules, rather than trying to meet the underlying purpose of those rules, is inefficient. But this means that bureaucracy is not the most efficient kind of organization. Therefore, the whole model of bureaucracy must be wrong.

These insights are very much in line with the case for post-bureaucratic organizations. This case invites us to 'tear up' the rulebook and allow individual discretion. Yet, although this is plausible in the light of Blau's analysis, it has its own problems. Workers may, in following the set rules, be less efficient than if they had used their own discretion. But it does not follow that, left to themselves, they would have adopted the most efficient way of working. They might have adopted an even less efficient approach than that enshrined in the rules. If so, a post-bureaucratic way of working would not only be less efficient during times of industrial action, it would be less efficient at all times!

Thinkpoint 13.5

Do you think that Universal is more or less efficient because it has adopted a more bureaucratic system? Do you think that the admissions system would be more or less efficient if it adopted a post-bureaucratic system?

The studies of Merton, Selznick and Blau show us that the close following of bureaucratic rules may not lead to efficiency. But there is also a second stream of work within the bureaucratic dysfunctionalist literature that advances a diametrically opposed set of problems. Here the issue is not one of an over-attachment to the rules but the observation that, very often, organizational rules are completely ignored. This was Crozier's (1964) finding – that employees in bureaucracies did, as a matter of fact, indulge all manner of prejudices whether or not the formal rules allowed it. These prejudices may be presumed to be sub-optimal from the point of view of organizational efficiency, but this is not necessarily so (as they might be cases of the Blau finding that ignoring organizational rules offers better outcomes than those delivered by the rules). But whether or not they are sub-optimal, they certainly deal a blow to the idea that bureaucracies are impersonal.

The work of Alvin Gouldner elaborates Crozier's insights by introducing the concept of mock bureaucracy. Gouldner (1954) found cases of organizations that have elaborate rulebooks but, in practice, the rules are ignored. Examples include safety regulations. In many dangerous industries, from mining (discussed by Gouldner) to building sites, it is commonplace for the formal rules to exist but not to be followed – as the phrase has it, 'more honoured in the breach than the observance' – because people see them as inconvenient or getting in the way of the job. Other examples might include equal opportunities regulations.

Mock bureaucracy and goal displacement are opposites – one is about following rules blindly, the other about ignoring rules – but both undermine the rational, machine-like picture of organizations found in the bureaucratic model. But their implications for post-bureaucracy are different. An over-attachment to rules vindicates the case for post-bureaucracy as a solution to this myopic inertia. But if bureaucracies ignore rules and find their own way of working then it might be argued that, in practice if not in theory, they end up being little different to organizations that dispense with rules, so why not stick with bureaucracy?

Key issues and controversies

Many key issues and controversies have already been indicated in the chapter, such as why do bureaucracies exist, whether they are efficient and what is the alternative? However, the major overriding controversy is whether bureaucracy is being, or should be, consigned to history to be supplanted by post-bureaucracy (see also Chapter 4).

The idea that bureaucracy is on the way out is one which has been touted for many decades – certainly since the mid-1960s when Warren Bennis (1966) proclaimed the imminent death of bureaucracy. His case for this was very similar to that heard today – namely that there was no longer the stable business environment within which bureaucracy made sense, and that more collaborative organizational relations rendered the rigid rules of bureaucracy obsolete. This analysis was disputed at the time, for example by Miewald (1970), and later by Perrow (1979), on the basis that bureaucracy, at least for large organizations, retained an efficiency advantage, and that the extent to which environmental turbulence had increased was exaggerated.

Despite this, there have been continual claims along the same lines as those of Bennis, although the vocabulary shifts over time. For example, Piore and Sabel (1984) advanced the idea that the world was moving from mass production and stable markets towards niche production in volatile markets. This in turn had the implication of a move from bureaucracy to 'flexible specialization'. More recent outings of the argument have probably been more widely, or at any rate more vocally, made than ever before. In particular, management gurus such as Tom Peters and Charles Handy have been highly influential in proclaiming versions of the same basic claim. This analysis has also been popularized by more public policy oriented writers such as Charles Leadbetter (1999) and in this way it has informed political debate in many countries, especially the United Kingdom and the United States. At the political level, the end of bureaucracy thesis links to attempts to reform public sector organizations and to devise education and training policies that are consistent with the emerging 'knowledge-economy' (see Chapters 5 and 12).

But it would be wrong to see all these arguments as deriving from the self-publicizing efforts of some influential popular writers. On the contrary, their claims are only accessible versions of some very sophisticated studies. For example, Manuel Castells has written several very detailed analyses (e.g. Castells, 1996) pointing to the rise of the network society and network organizations, which he links strongly to the information technology revolution of the last quarter of a century. More directly in the organization studies community, Heckscher and Donnellon (1994) have provided both a theoretical framework and several empirical illustrations of post-bureaucracy.

As with earlier predictions of the demise of bureaucracy, the more recent obituaries have also been met with a great deal of scepticism (see Chapter 4). Warhurst and Thompson (1998) have been particularly acute critics arguing that mass production and, for that matter, manufacturing are by no means in decline globally, and that new working practices based on trust and empowerment are more rhetorical than

SOURCE: © ISTOCKPHOTO.COM / SEAN LOCKE

Image 13.5 Brave new world?

Image 13.6

real. About the only attribute of the post-bureaucratic model that is unequivocally proven is an increase in the use of part-time and short-contract workers. But, even if increasing, this is not new, and it does not in and of itself demonstrate post-bureaucratization.

Later in this chapter we will return to some of these issues from a different perspective, but in terms of mainstream views, what is the answer to this controversy? In a sense, precisely because it is a controversy, there is no definite answer. It may be that it is just too early to tell. It may be that, as with Universal, there is no absolute answer because it depends on where, and when, you look at things. Thus it is possible to interpret Universal as being bureaucratic or as being post-bureaucratic. This perhaps reflects another important issue: both bureaucracy and post-bureaucracy as 'ideal-types' may not actually exist in practice. Instead, organizations may exhibit a range of characteristics, some of which are bureaucratic and others post-bureaucratic.

Finally, though, precisely because of the long history of this controversy, it is interesting to consider the now classic work of Burns and Stalker (1961). Their study suggested that organizations might be mechanical or organic (meaning roughly bureaucratic or post-bureaucratic) depending on 'contingencies' such as the nature of their business environment, the technologies they used and the skill levels of their workforces (a similar finding to the Woodward studies discussed earlier). This **contingency approach** might suggest to us that the idea that all organizations are, or will become, post-bureaucratic is simplistic. It is notable that most of the empirical examples given of such organizations are in high-tech business sectors such as computing and biotechnology, which are yet to 'mature'. In the end, then, the mainstream answer to the current version of its main controversy may be a restatement of contingency theory.

Important empirical studies

In the chapter so far, we have identified many of the main empirical studies in this area, all of which would repay closer attention. Because the theme of bureaucracy, in particular, has been present since the start of organization studies (indeed, in some ways, it is the bedrock of the subject) there are an almost literally endless number of studies we could examine. But the three discussed here are especially interesting.

The first study is Melville Dalton's (1959) classic *Men Who Manage*. This was in many ways a pathbreaking piece of research because it represents one of the first applications of **ethnographic** methods to the study of organizations. Although ethnography had been used from at least the 1920s to study social groups within Western societies, they had tended to focus on 'marginal' or relatively powerless groups, such as street gangs or prostitutes. Dalton's study was innovative because it was one of the first ethnographies of powerful elites.

Men Who Manage was a study of four bureaucratic organizations, codenamed Milo, Fruhling, Attica and Rambeau, but the centrepiece of the book was the study of Milo, which was the most extensive of the four cases. Strictly speaking, we should in fact say that, as its title implies, this was a study of bureaucratic managers rather than of entire organizations. Apart from being methodologically innovative, this study was highly revealing about the realities of managerial work and did much to debunk the rational image of such work and, indeed, bureaucracy itself. Among other things, it illustrates some of the issues that Crozier discussed concerning how individual prejudices (e.g. about religious beliefs) were not left outside the office but played a central part in decision making about, for example, who to employ and promote. The study also illustrates Selznick's point about how different divisions within bureaucracies pursue their own goals through political in-fighting, rather than there being a single, shared, organizational goal (see Chapter 8).

A second study in a recognizably similar tradition to Dalton's is Rosabeth Moss Kanter's (1993) book, *Men and Women of the Corporation*. The title itself seems to stand in some kind of relation to Dalton's work, published almost 20 years earlier. For not only had organizations become somewhat less male dominated in the intervening period but, more to the point, Kanter was one of the pioneers of applying feminist ideas to the study of organizations. Thus, while much of the detail of her study of the firm code named Indsco reveals some similar issues to that of Dalton, Kanter draws particular attention to how they relate to gender. For example, Kanter suggests that the relationship between (largely) male managers and (exclusively) female secretaries takes a form that is recognizably pre-bureaucratic and is quite resistant to the rational-legal ideal-type of bureaucracy. She suggests that the relationship is highly personalized and therefore unstandardized, and is in part bound up with displays of status on the part of both manager and secretary.

Good studies of this detailed type post-bureaucracy are, as yet, more difficult to find. The 'after-word' to the second edition of Kanter's book is worth reading in this regard as it updates some of the Indsco story into the 1990s. A less academic study of post-bureaucracy is Ricardo Semler's (1993) account of his company Semco, a Brazilian engineering firm. Semler regards himself as a 'counsellor' rather than a chief executive, and this illustrates the idea that post-bureaucracy discounts hierarchy. Overall, Semco is characterized by an approach that rejects formal rules, employees set their own working hours and pay rates, and is relaxed about unionization and strike activity.

It is important to recognize that this study is the work of someone describing and justifying his own experience and activities: it does not purport to be detached or analytical, and it would be interesting to hear the voices of others within the firm to see how far they endorse Semler's account. Nevertheless, there is no doubt that Semco represents a departure from traditional bureaucratic models of organizing and, moreover, that it has been able to perform profitably and successfully and that it is no small high-tech start-up. From that point of view it offers a documented example of the existence and viability of something like the organizations that Heckscher and others argue are the future of work.

Limitations of the mainstream approach

Like most of the mainstream approach to organizations and management, a major limitation of its treatment of bureaucracy and post-bureaucracy is its one-sided and restricted focus on efficiency. Weber's ideal-type of bureaucracy has – wrongly, as we will see – been treated as if it were a design template for how organizations should be. In the process, this has elevated one particular kind of rationality – **instrumental rationality** – at the expense of others.

Why is this a limitation? There are two related reasons. One is that by its focus on *means*, instrumental rationality is only concerned with the 'how' of organizing and not with the 'why'. In the next section we will explore why this is such an important omission. Secondly, by seeing efficiency in terms of minimum inputs and maximum outputs, the mainstream only considers efficiency from the partial viewpoint of someone who has an interest in this kind of efficiency. Normally this means the powerful – the people who own and run businesses being the obvious example. As soon as we shift position, efficiency can look quite different.

Think of the now common way that all kinds of organizations use automated telephone systems. When we phone up, we are told to press different keys for different options and eventually, probably after waiting in a queue, we are connected to an operator. This is efficient for the organization as it is a low-cost way of managing enquiries, partly because some of the work of transferring calls formerly done by a paid employee is now done, for nothing, by the caller. Sometimes, as with computer support lines, for example, the caller actually pays while they do this unpaid work for the organization. So from the caller's point of view it is not efficient because it involves a waste of time, sometimes a cost and, often, frustration. It also usually leads to a less personalized service (compare, for example, the traditional contact between a customer and a bank manager with that offered by national call-centres).

Thinkpoint 13.6

What other examples can you think of where things that are efficient for an organization are inefficient for you as a customer?

SOURCE: © JAGADEESH / REUTERS / CORBIS

Image 13.7 Back to the future?

This one-sided view of rationality and efficiency can be seen to run through almost all of the debates about bureaucracy and post-bureaucracy discussed so far. For example, concerns about 'motivation' in bureaucracy are animated by the idea that demotivation will lead to employees working less hard – it is not a concern about happiness or well-being (see Chapter 2). Much of the bureaucratic dysfunctionalist literature is concerned with the alignment (or otherwise) between the formal rules of the bureaucracy and what actually happens. Something similar could be said of Dalton's preoccupation with politics 'getting in the way' of rationality.

As for post-bureaucracy, the whole basis of the shift towards these new organizational forms – if, indeed, the shift is occurring – is the fear that failure to do so will lead to declining competitiveness and shrinking profitability. The more trust-based ways of working, like traditional concerns with motivation, are animated by a belief that these will render employees more productive, which again reveals the underlying view of efficiency in the mainstream approach. It is surely no coincidence that moves away from bureaucracy are typically associated with harder work and more stress. So, again, we must ask the question: efficient for whom?

Exercise 13.4

Thinking of the admissions system and the changes in the Universal case, for whom are they efficient and for whom are they inefficient?

In this sense, the limitations of the mainstream approach are, partly, to do with the partial picture it offers. But more fundamentally, it is to do with power. On the one hand, most mainstream approaches are concerned with deriving organizational methods – whether bureaucratic or post-bureaucratic – that best exert power and control over employees. On the other hand, by having this focus, mainstream approaches conform to and support the view that what 'matters' are the interests and perspectives of the privileged, the powerful and the elite.

Critical approach

Introduction

In many respects, the central dividing line between mainstream and critical approaches to bureaucracy and post-bureaucracy runs back to Max weber. Perhaps we could even say that it runs 'through' him.

For Weber on the one hand was persuaded that bureaucracy was becoming the dominant organizational form while, on the other hand, he bemoaned and even despaired of this fact. Weber did not use his term 'ideal-type' to mean that bureaucracy was a desirable ideal, or the ideal form of organization, but this is how mainstream approaches to organization studies have often interpreted it.

There is quite an interesting story that helps to explain why the mainstream did this (although there are many other reasons). Weber's work (which was written in German) was for a long time not widely read in the United States, where the bulk of organization studies has been conducted. It became popular through the translation of eminent Harvard sociologist Talcott Parsons. Parsons' translation and interpretation of Weber put a 'spin' on it that emphasized bureaucracy as an 'ideal'. This had an impact on the development of the organization studies field in a general way, but more particularly on Merton, who was a student of Parsons. Merton in turn supervised Blau, Gouldner and Selznick. As we have seen, these authors provided the bedrock of the literature on bureaucracy.

A different (and it is fair to say that most scholars would agree a more defensible) interpretation of Weber is to see his work as being concerned with two different kinds of rationality. One is the technical or instrumental rationality which, as we have seen, bureaucracy embodies. The second is value or **substantive rationality**.

It is worth dwelling a little on the rather complicated issue of why substantive rationality is sometimes called value rationality. This is because deciding whether an outcome is rational involves a value judgement – is something good or not? Some people believe that this is not just a matter of opinion but can be decided on rational principles. Others would say that what is good or bad is a matter of what we generally agree is good or bad. So, for example, most people would accept that child pornography is bad (and those who think that these judgements have a rational basis might say that it is also irrational because it treats children as objects rather than people with rights). From this point of view, no matter how efficient an organization was in producing child pornography (that is, no matter how instrumentally rational it was), that organization would not have value or substantive rationality. If this seems complicated, there is an easier version of the definitions. We could say that instrumental rationality means 'doing the thing right' and substantive rationality means 'doing the right thing'. Of course, someone might object that instrumental rationality *does* embody a value – the value that efficiency is the sole criterion in deciding what to do. This is true, but it is present as a hidden value and one which, when made explicit, would then provoke debates about its ethical adequacy which are suppressed when it is simply assumed that instrumental rationality is 'a good thing'.

Actually, even when the theory seems obscure and abstract, in practice we are all familiar with the kinds of issues that are at stake. Is it right (or rational) for organizations to produce guns, cigarettes or instruments of torture? And outcomes of organizational actions are not just to do with their products but with their by-products. So, for example, is it right (or rational) for organizations to pollute the environment? This latter case is especially interesting because it does help to explain why there might be a link between what is right and what is rational. If it is the case that organizations need to live in a sustainable environment (e.g. because they need clean water to operate), then is it rational (let alone right) if they despoil that environment (e.g. by polluting water supplies)?

Exercise 13.5

What other examples of substantive irrationality can you think of?

A concern with substantive rationality is central to critical approaches to bureaucracy and post-bureaucracy, and later on we will return to it in several different ways. In one respect, it is another version of the question: efficient for whom? Is the efficient producer of landmines efficient for the Angolan child whose limbs are blown off? Is the efficient producer of cigarettes efficient for a Chinese peasant (who may never have heard about the risks) dying from lung cancer?

Image 13.8 Getting the job done?

Thinkpoint 13.7

One of the big management problems facing the British National Health Service is 'bed blocking' – which normally happens when an elderly person is using a hospital bed because no suitable nursing home place is available. In 2004, Barbara Salisbury, a nurse, was convicted of attempting to murder such elderly patients. According to the prosecution, her motive was that she was trying to improve the efficiency of her ward. Was she a good bureaucratic manager?

Specific products aside, Weber's case for thinking that bureaucracy was substantively irrational was based upon his reading of the overall societal effects of its rise. These he described as creating an 'iron cage of rationality'. Here the idea is that, because bureaucracy is becoming dominant, so more and more of people's lives are lived within the constraints of a rationalized (i.e. instrumentally rationalized) system. Living in a world in which every experience was organized, literally from the hospital in which we are born to the undertakers who take us to the grave, is there a sense in which bureaucracy undermines our very humanity? In particular, the experience of work within bureaucracies is, from a critical perspective, not just demotivating but actually dehumanizing. That is, by treating people as parts of a machine, bureaucracy denies everything that makes people human rather than inanimate objects – perhaps this was what made possible the hospital murders referred to in Thinkpoint 13.7? Again it can be said that this is both wrong and also irrational. Fundamentally, the functional reason for having organizations is to meet needs that no one could satisfy as an individual. But if the effect of organization (in its bureaucratic form) is to negate our human needs then there is a logical contradiction. Dehumanization, then, is not just wrong, it is irrational, and it is a profound negation of identity and freedom.

We will return to these issues shortly, but the final introductory point to the critical approach is to consider post-bureaucracy. In many respects it might be thought that, as an alternative to bureaucracy, this addresses some of the points made by the critics. Overtly, there is a stress on organizational values and a much less dehumanizing approach to work. However, as has been discussed in other chapters (e.g. Chapters 4 and 9), critical approaches are by no means reassured by such developments. At the heart of the problem is again the issue of power and control. Critical commentators believe that there is not an either/or opposition between the control of employees under top-down formal rule systems like bureaucracy and the freedom of employees under top-down value-based systems. Rather, both are seen as forms of control, the former operating at the level of behaviour and bodily actions; the latter at the level of belief and the mind. Indeed, many critical theorists regard the latter as the more insidious, because it seeks to exert control over the 'whole person'.

Thinkpoint 13.8

In a corner of the Dog and Duck, John and Richard are comparing their bosses. John is saying that his manager is inspirational: 'She just has a way of making you feel as if you want to do a really good job, for her and for the company'. Richard is impressed. 'Wow, you should have my boss – she's a real slave driver', he complains.

Who do you think works the longer hours, John or Richard? Would you rather be coerced into doing something, knowing that it was coercion, or be manipulated into doing something, without knowing that you were being manipulated?

One way of thinking about these issues is in terms of employee skill levels. Bureaucratic organizations rely upon, and to some extent create, a situation where skill levels are low. They require that employees follow set rules and work in standardized ways. Skill is in many ways a form of power. If skill levels are low, then employees are easily replaceable and so reducing skill levels is an effective way of increasing organizational control. If the employees do not like the organization, well, there are plenty of people who can replace them. When skill levels are higher, then this gives more power to employees possessing these skills. In Joan Woodward's work, discussed earlier, it was assumed that the bureaucracy was linked contingently to the type of technology being employed. But perhaps a better way of rendering that link would be to say that technologies that required a skilled workforce gave more power to that workforce and, hence, they could not be managed bureaucratically.

By extension, post-bureaucratic organizations are obliged to create (or at least pay lip service to) employee responsibility because such organizations are predominantly in business sectors that need high levels of skill. These employees, who Reich (1993) calls 'symbolic analysts' and who have also been called (Kelley, 1990) 'gold-collar workers' (to distinguish them from blue-collar, or manual, workers and white-collar, or clerical, workers) have the power to command better treatment. Such employees are the consultants and professionals who possess a knowledge that resides in their heads. Craft workers had such knowledge, until it was broken down by Taylorism (see Chapter 6). And, wherever it can be achieved, symbolic analysts are similarly de-skilled, one example being attempts to replace accountants with IT-enabled audit factories. More generally, expert systems are used to replace professional employees. Even academics, traditionally a very difficult occupation to rationalize, are increasingly required to produce work in standard formats, such as this book, and perhaps eventually could be replaced with computer software.

So, on this reading, post-bureaucracy reflects an accommodation with those occupations whose skill level cannot be bureaucratized and it will only persist until such time as it can. In the meantime, post-bureaucracy uses the discipline of value-based or **normative control** to get the maximum amount of work out of its employees.

These kinds of ideas can sound, at first hearing, like pure nonsense. After all, control is about stopping people from doing what they want. So if people choose to do what they want to do then they are free,

SOURCE: © CARL FLINT/CARTOONSTOCK.COM

Image 13.9

SOURCE: © RONNIE KAUFMAN/CORBIS

Image 13.10 Girl power?

not controlled. But consider the haunting, and slightly scary, title of Nikolas Rose's (1999) influential book, *Governing the Soul*. Who we are, and what our choices signify, may not be as simple as we think.

John has now left the Dog and Duck and is in the supermarket. There is an endless array of things to choose from. He buys some toothpaste because it gives him double reward points (he hasn't noticed that it is twice the price of the value brand). Then he considers whether to buy some traditional English sausages or the own-brand version – he chooses the traditional option because the packet is cardboard with a picture of a farmyard. The own brand are wrapped in cellophane. They are cheap and, frankly, look it (he doesn't know that both sausages are identical and come from the same factory) and after all he has been economical with his choice of toothpaste. He chooses some beer and, because everyone knows that German lager is passé, he gets a Hungarian brand (he doesn't remember that he saw an advert for it last night – it's just what he fancies). At the checkout there is a display of hand-cooked potato crisps with a Malaysian curry flavour and he puts one in the trolley – he wouldn't have thought of buying them if the supermarket hadn't helpfully put them there. Then he sees a sign that says he can have a second bag free, so he chooses to take two (he doesn't know it yet, but next time he goes to the supermarket he will seek out these crisps, even though they won't be on special offer).

John has made several choices. Is he free? Are you any different to John?

Key issues and controversies

One of the most remarkable books ever written about organizations is almost never mentioned, much less discussed, within mainstream literature on bureaucracy. The book in question is Zygmunt Bauman's *Modernity and the Holocaust* (1989). Bauman explores how the Nazi Holocaust, which murdered at least six million Jewish people as well as those from many other groups, was related to a highly developed European civilization. He analyses this is many ways, but in particular he explains how the genocide instigated by the Nazis represents the extreme application of a bureaucratic logic. What makes the Holocaust peculiarly horrifying is the way in which the mass extermination was conducted industrially – with a system of rules, impersonally applied, which made it as technically efficient as a genocide could be. The capacity to register and monitor populations so that Jews, communists, gypsies, homosexuals and the other categories to which the Nazis objected was itself a considerable administrative achievement. The shipping of these people to the camps was another, and their systematic extermination a third.

Image 13.11 Where it all ends?

The British novelist, C. P. Snow, has one of his characters, a wartime civil servant in London, reflect that, just as he was handling the memoranda relating to the development of atomic weapons, so his counterpart in Berlin would be reviewing figures on the death rate of Jewish people under different dietary regimes in the labour camps (this was written before the extermination programme was known about). That bureaucratic practice, the impersonal, scientific, ethically neutral pursuit of means made the Holocaust instrumentally rational while, clearly, not being substantively rational. This is perhaps the clearest illustration of how these two definitions of rationality differ. Bauman says that we should not, therefore, see the Holocaust as an aberration or anomaly when compared with mainstream Western culture: rather, it was a manifestation of the habitual ways of organizing within that culture.

The Holocaust example is very important, and not for emotive reasons. Almost everyone can agree that the extermination of a race of people is irrational on any meaning that might be given to that term. Yet the fact that (instrumentally) rational methods could be applied to it, as easily as to the production of toy cars or, for that matter, the distribution of food aid, serves to underscore the moral blindness of bureaucracy. It is not that bureaucratic techniques are necessarily 'immoral' but that they simply do not consider morality. So, if we want to live in a civilized society, we cannot simply be concerned with efficiency as envisaged by bureaucracy: we have to think about the purposes to which bureaucracy is put. Bureaucracy does not consider values: people do.

Thinkpoint 13.10

You are (probably) on a management course. Would you be willing to devise the most efficient way to exterminate people? If not, how is your course helping you to make moral judgements about how to use your skills?

Although the moral deficiencies of bureaucracy are a key issue within the critical approach, are they a key controversy? The British sociologist Paul du Gay (2000) has offered a sophisticated and important defence of bureaucracy although not, of course, one that would condone its genocidal use. It is worth pausing to reflect upon the context within which du Gay has made his arguments. It is a context in which the public sector within the United Kingdom (and elsewhere) has been accused of being far too bureaucratic, not in the sense of being amoral but in the traditional sense of being mired in 'red tape'. It stands accused of being characterized by goal displacement, producer focus and all the other mainstream complaints about bureaucracy. These complaints have their counterpart in other critical analyses which see bureaucracy as dehumanizing and morally blind (see also Chapter 14). Fighting on both flanks, du Gay argues, in the title of his book, *In Praise of Bureaucracy*.

Bureaucracy, du Gay explains, is actually imbued with morality, not because of Weber's concerns about substantive rationality but because of the demands of instrumental rationality for maximum efficiency. To satisfy these demands, argues du Gay, requires an ethic of impersonality and fairness so that employees and customers or clients are treated without prejudice. So, for example, bureaucracy does not care about employee's gender or ethnic background – it only cares about qualification since this is what will be most efficient. Clients, too, are treated the same, whoever they may be. Bureaucracy is a safeguard against discrimination. In this way it embodies, rather than ignores, a morality of fairness and due process. Post-bureaucracy or, as du Gay says, enterprise, has no such formal code.

Exercise 13.6

How does the admissions system example illustrate du Gay's point that bureaucracy is fair? In the last few years there have been many criticisms of the elitism of university admissions procedures, especially at Oxford and Cambridge. What would be better; a system based on A level results, an interview system or, as some have suggested, a standardized aptitude test? In what ways might each approach relate to bureaucracy and post-bureaucracy? Would there be a conflict between efficiency and fairness in each of these approaches? Would it be greater in some rather than others? Assuming you are at a university, do you feel that your application was dealt with efficiently or fairly or both?

In one way, there is no doubt that du Gay is correct. And his work has been important in answering the charge that bureaucracy is morally blind. Yet in another way it assumes far too much. It assumes that bureaucracies do, in fact, conform to Weber's ideal-type. Yet studies from the mainstream show how, in practice, bureaucracies allow all kinds of prejudice and discrimination – Crozier, Dalton and Kanter are all examples. Du Gay is right to say that the formal model of bureaucracy embodies an ethic. But it would be wrong to conclude that bureaucracy does invariably, in practice, exhibit this ethic.

Exercise 13.7

Jackie decides to rent a house with five other students. When they move in they draw up a rota to share the cooking, cleaning, shopping and so on. This is a (simple) kind of rule-based system with a division of labour. One of its features is that it divides the work up fairly. In your experience, is this likely to work in practice? What difference might it make if all Jackie's house-mates are male?

Du Gay's arguments are important because they question whether bureaucracy is discredited. Although he flies against mainstream thinking, he has a strong case. For all of the arguments against the death of bureaucracy advanced in the 1960s continue to hold true, and the basic advantages of bureaucracy, as illustrated by the admissions system example, are undeniable – both in terms of efficiency and those of fairness. But whether fairness is enough to offset the moral deficiencies of bureaucracy that Bauman illustrates is less clear – and remains a controversial issue.

A selection of important studies

There are many ways in which bureaucracy and post-bureaucracy can be criticized. Studies have focused on the problems of the former, of the latter, or of the distinction between them. From the many possibilities, we have chosen some that represent a range of these positions and are the most articulate in advancing their analyses.

One of the more readable studies of bureaucracy is George Ritzer's widely praised book *The McDonaldization of Society* (2000). Ritzer's is in effect a re-working of Weber's concerns about the iron cage of rationality – the idea that there is no escape from the growing presence of bureaucracy. But Ritzer updates this analysis by focusing on McDonald's, the fast food chain, which he says is the template for contemporary forms of bureaucratization, with its standardized menus, architecture and, even, the words used by employees. At the heart of Ritzer's critique is the familiar complaint that bureaucracy dehumanizes both employees and customers. The impersonality that is central to the bureaucratic ethos may, as du Gay says, guarantee fairness, but it also means that the 'person' is irrelevant and subservient to the organizational machine. McDonaldization exemplifies the logic of standardization, which is what bureaucracy is all about, and Ritzer sees standardization as spreading into all kinds of areas of life: the national curriculum and modularization in education; package holidays and mass-build housing estates, for example.

Thinkpoint 13.11

When you eat at McDonald's, sit in a lecture theatre or go on a package holiday, do you feel dehumanized? And if you do not, does that mean that Ritzer is wrong or that you have become so tamed that you do not even notice the iron cage around you?

Ritzer, like Weber, is critical of the instrumental rationality of bureaucracy. Kathy Ferguson puts a particular spin on such a critique in elaborating *The Feminist Case Against Bureaucracy* (1984). Within the mainstream approaches we saw how Kanter's work indicated the male biases within bureaucratic organization, but Ferguson's arguments are much more radical. She sees the instrumental rationality of bureaucracy as being one that is in principle 'masculinist'. Whereas, for critics in the Weberian tradition, instrumentality is an expression of specifically modern and industrial ways of viewing the world and organizations, for Ferguson they embody something more – a masculine search for control and mastery. The structures of hierarchy are an expression of this both in the simple sense of being an example of such masculinism and, in a more complex way, by positioning employees and customers as passive and dependent in a way that Ferguson, borrowing the expression first coined by Simone de Beauvoir, sees as analogous to the traditional position of 'the second sex' or women.

In a wider ranging way, Ferguson sees the development of bureaucracy as being part and parcel of the way in which the modern world has been divided into a public and private sphere. The public sphere, where bureaucracy is located, is characterized by masculinity, competition, aggression and rationality, while the private sphere of families and households is characterized by femininity, cooperation, tolerance and emotionality. In this way, a range of archetypically feminine experiences and values are seen to have been excluded from the public sphere of bureaucracy and not just excluded but also disparaged and discounted.

Thinkpoint 13.12

Think about the ways you behave with your friends and family and compare them with how you behave at work or in classes. How are they different? Why? What would happen to you if you behaved in the same way in both settings?

The next study is one less concerned with theory and more focused on the lived-experience of, in particular, post-bureaucracy. Richard Sennett's *Work and the Corrosion of Character* (1998) looks at a series of lives affected by the changing nature of work. In many cases, Sennett returns to people and workplaces he had visited 25 years before as part of the research for an earlier book, giving a useful insight into these changes. For example, he revisits what was formerly a Greek bakery run along bureaucratic rules by a stable unionized workforce with intimate knowledge of baking techniques. It is now part of a huge multinational firm, and uses a shifting workforce of non-unionized migrant workers operating computer-controlled ovens. These latter allow production to shift flexibly from one type of bread to another, yet the operators know nothing at all of baking techniques: they simply click on icons on a computer screen.

This example is interesting because it shows how new post-bureaucratic working conditions of flexibility (in employment and production) do not imply an idyllic, empowered kind of organizational life. Rather, the new ways of working are as 'alienating' and dehumanizing as before, if not more so, because the bonds of community among the employees (and with customers) and the involvement of the workers with their work and product has been fractured. But it is also interesting because the loss of the traditional bureaucracy serves to point to the ways in which such organizations are not necessarily as dehumanizing as the work of someone like Ritzer claims, nor as devoid of emotionality as Ferguson's analysis might imply.

Finally, a more conventional kind of empirical study, but one of the very best of its kind is Rick Delbridge's *Life on the Line in Contemporary Manufacturing* (1998). Like Dalton's classic book on managers, this is an ethnography reporting on the author's time in two British factories. One is a Japanese-owned electronics plant (Nippon CTV), the other a European-owned producer of automotive components (ValleyCo). Although strictly speaking this is not a study of bureaucracy and post-bureaucracy, it does contrast the more traditional approach at ValleyCo with the 'Japanized' approach at Nippon CTV where there is a focus on lean production, just-in-time management, innovation, customer focus and HRM. This is, at least, an adjacent theme to that of the present chapter.

While Delbridge found a number of contrasts between the plants, it is fair to say that his overall conclusion is that there is a considerable similarity between 'traditional' and 'new' forms of working in terms of things like hierarchy, participation or trust. His findings are very much in line with those in the various contributions to Thompson and Warhurst (1998) in relation to scepticism about post-bureaucracy: 'There is little to suggest that contemporary manufacturing is best characterized as "postfordist" and that the shop-floor is a hotbed of worker autonomy and knowledge creation' (Delbridge, 1998, p. 192).

One feature of this study which makes it 'critical' rather than mainstream is that it captures the experience and perspective of the front-line – or shop floor – workers rather than being an idealized and self-interested account written from a managerial perspective. In this regard it represents an antidote to some of the more hyperbolic claims made about the 'new economy' such as those found in the mainstream literature on post-bureaucracy.

Contributions and limitations of the critical approach

Contributions   Perhaps the most important contribution of the critical approach is to move away from a narrow focus on efficiency and the techniques of bureaucracy and post-bureaucracy towards a recognition of the political and ethical values that come into play when organizations are designed (see also Chapter 14). The idea that managing and organizing are not 'neutral', technical issues is one that runs throughout critical approaches, as is clear from most other chapters in this book.

Post-bureaucracy, of course, is claimed by its advocates to be precisely an organizational form concerned with values. They argue that it liberates employees and consumers alike from the stifling 'red tape' and inflexibility of bureaucracy. Critical approaches are unpersuaded by such arguments. Crucially, as with culture management (see Chapter 9), the problem is that values are defined hierarchically and within an overall purpose of gaining control. Another way of saying this would be that post-bureaucracy, as much as bureaucracy, is defined by an instrumental – and, feminists would argue, masculinist – rationality. It may use a different set of techniques to get the job done, but it is still, essentially, an exercise of power, using people as instruments in pursuit of some other goal. The examples of Sennett's bakers or of customers' experience of automated phone systems both illustrate this.

In any case, the other main contribution of critical approaches is to point out that the lived experience of post-bureaucracy is by no means the utopia that its advocates suggest. Bureaucracy dehumanized its employees, but at least offered the security of set routines. Post-bureaucracy marks an increase in insecurity and anxiety because it promotes job insecurity, an intensification of time pressures (the '24/7' society) and places the accent on the responsibility of individuals to manage their careers and lives without the collective protection that bureaucracies can offer.

Thinkpoint 13.13

Thinking about the people you know, particularly older people like your parents and their friends, do you think that they are anxious and insecure about work? Or do you think that people your age face more of a problem?

Thus critical approaches question a **binary** logic: either bureaucracy is 'right' or it is 'wrong'. A simple version of the mainstream–critical divide would be based on binary logic. Bureaucracy is good, post-bureaucracy is bad. Or post-bureaucracy is good, bureaucracy is bad. We have seen that many of the protagonists in the debate follow just this logic. Almost all of today's management gurus, and most policy makers, say that bureaucracy is bad. Paul du Gay is one of the few examples of writers who say the opposite. However, in our discussions of the mainstream approach we found that evidence was split and we also found that the division between bureaucracy and post-bureaucracy was much less clear-cut. Critical approaches go further, though. It is not just a matter of trying to find evidence on one side of the argument or the other. Rather, it is to see that there are continuities, based on instrumental rationality, between both.

Limitations   Despite what was just said about a refusal of binary logic within critical approaches, it is also true that some individual studies within these approaches do have a tendency to oversimplify. Ritzer, in particular, seems to imply that because bureaucracy is 'bad' then anything that is not bureaucracy is 'good'. Thus some of the forms of resistance to McDonaldization that he proposes end up endorsing some of the niche marketing practices associated with post-bureaucracy. Defences of bureaucracy, too, can carry a danger of romanticizing such organizations as places of fairness and, even, communities. Studies like Delbridge's can be a useful antidote to this kind of danger.

A second difficulty with critical approaches, which seems to be present in Weber's discussion of the iron cage and, again, in Ritzer is the problem of **determinism**. Many mainstream positions show this problem – for example, most cases for the rise of post-bureaucracy rest on the determinism of computer technologies – but so too do some critical approaches. The idea that bureaucratization is a 'juggernaut' that will inevitably sweep aside other forms of organization because of its technical efficiency is a common one in critical theory. The limitation of this view is that it pays no attention to the choices that people and societies make about how to organize themselves. In this respect determinism is a double problem. First, because it ignores choices, it is analytically problematic. Secondly, because it promotes the view that whatever choices are made they will have no effect, it encourages fatalism and quietism and is therefore a political problem as well.

Exercise 13.8

Politicians often use phrases like 'there is no alternative' or 'the fact of the matter is . . . '. Parents often respond to small children's favourite question ('why?') by saying 'that's just the way it is' or 'because I say so'. Many economists tell us that 'you can't buck the market' and some biologists say that 'it's all in the genes'. All these are, in different ways, deterministic arguments. How valid are they? Can you think of other examples?

Somewhat related to this is a third difficulty for critical approaches, especially the argument that post-bureaucracy is no more than the spread of even more intense forms of power and control. This then makes it very difficult to know what kinds of reform can be envisaged that would be acceptable to critics. If dehumanization and humanization at work are both versions of control, then what proposal for change does that leave? The answers typically seem highly utopian: for example, the suspension of masculinist and instrumental rationality. Given that this seems unlikely in the immediate future, does this mean that there is nothing to be done but bemoan the existing state of affairs until a complete social transformation has occurred?

Conclusion

In this chapter we have seen how a complex series of issues are involved in thinking about bureaucracy and post-bureaucracy. It is undoubtedly true that bureaucratic organizations have been one of the defining features of modern life. Weber was right to observe that they were becoming so in his time and right to predict that they would become more so in the future. Yet almost no one who has studied them seriously, whether from a mainstream or a critical perspective, has concluded that they are without problems. Mainstream and critical writers differ in the radicalism with which they explain these problems, however. As a broad generalization, mainstream approaches stress the ways in which reality diverges from the rationality of the bureaucratic model, while critics draw attention to the defects of the very rationality that underpins that model. Mainstream writers may be more likely to see possible reforms to bureaucracy but are perhaps over-optimistic about the likely efficacy of such prescriptions. Critics are likely to highlight the oppressive and dehumanizing consequences of bureaucracy and therefore will tend to want to reject it root and branch.

But of course things are never quite so simple. In recent years, there have been very pronounced rejections of the bureaucratic model from within mainstream thinking on organizations and, also, some defences of bureaucracy from critics. The mainstream proponents of post-bureaucracy, who repeat many earlier claims in their case, are in some senses 'critics' of bureaucracy, but not in the way normally implied by the term 'critical approaches'. This is because they make their case from within mainstream assumptions about efficiency and organizational purpose. They are saying, in effect, bureaucracy was fine for its time, but times have changed and now they favour post-bureaucracy. They do not question the underlying idea that organizations exist to deliver efficient outcomes for their owners, nor the need to maintain control. They just want to do it in a new way.

For that reason, critical approaches are critical of both bureaucracy and post-bureaucracy. They question the narrowness of the mainstream understanding of efficiency and the acceptability of pursuing control over others in pursuit of that efficiency. Although to polarize mainstream and critical approaches too much would be to fall into the trap of binary logic, there are some real and substantive differences between them. These differences reflect very serious and profound divergences of thinking, not just about organizations but about society as a whole. Critical approaches tend to be explicit that it is these political issues that are at stake, whereas mainstream approaches typically prefer to leave them implicit, and to treat organizational design as if it were simply a matter of developing and applying the most efficient technique. However, as we have seen, embedded within the very notion of efficiency there are some political assumptions, principally about the question of for whom organizations are efficient.

The mainstream approach is, in this regard at least, untenable, and its more reflective practitioners know it. Within the myriad of debates about bureaucracy and post-bureaucracy, what is ultimately at stake is how people choose to organize their collective activities and this goes to the heart of what we think those collective activities should be, and how we go about them. These are inescapably moral and political questions.

Discussion questions

1 Why did bureaucratic organizations come into existence?

2 Does the literature on 'bureaucratic dysfunctionalism' prove that bureaucracy is inefficient?

3 What kinds of contingencies could explain whether an organization will tend to be bureaucratic or post-bureaucratic?

4 Charles Heckscher says that the world is becoming more post-bureaucratic. George Ritzer says it is becoming more bureaucratic. Who is right? Could they both be right?

5 Is it substantively rational to make a profit? If so, then aren't private sector bureaucracies necessarily rational in all meanings of the word?

6 What kind of organizations would satisfy the critics of bureaucracy and post-bureaucracy? Do any exist?

Further reading

du Gay, P. (2000) *In Praise of Bureaucracy: Weber, Organization and Ethics*, London: Sage.

This is not an easy read, but it must stand as one of the most important books written in this area for many years. It offers what some might think is an audacious case for the virtues of bureaucracy, and challenges much conventional thinking in this regard. At its heart is a claim that bureaucracy embodies a specific ethic of impartiality that is of enduring value.

Ferguson, K. (1984) *The Feminist Case Against Bureaucracy*, Philadelphia, PA: Temple University Press.

Again not an easy book, but it should feature in any list of readings because it provides a fundamental challenge not just to bureaucracy but to the logic that informs many claims about post-bureaucracy. For Ferguson, bureaucracy exhibits a masculinist logic of control and this opens up the very fundamental terrain of the values underpinning any form of organization.

Head, S. (2003) *The New Ruthless Economy: Work and Power in the Digital Age*, Oxford: Oxford University Press.

Written from the perspective of an economist, this book provides an accessible exposé of how working conditions in the 'knowledge economy' are subject to intensified pressure and control. The writing is lively and fluent, and although the analysis is not always deep it provides a compelling account of post-bureaucracy.

Ritzer, G. (2000) *The McDonaldization of Society: An Investigation Into the Changing Character of Contemporary Social Life*, second edition, Thousand Oaks, CA: Sage.

This is a provocative, well-written book that makes the case that modern society is becoming increasingly bureaucratized and standardized, with McDonald's as the defining example. It offers an interesting reworking of Weber's concerns about bureaucracy in a way that is much more accessible than the original writings.

Sennett, R. (1998) *Work and the Corrosion of Character: The Personal Consequences of Work in the New Capitalism*, London: WW Norton.

This book can be commended for its readability. It offers very personalized accounts of how shifts from traditional bureaucratic organizations to those of post-bureaucracy impact upon the lives of real people. Sceptics might say that Sennett offers us stories not analysis, but, carefully read, this book provides a convincing critique of contemporary life.

Whyte, W. H. (1956) *The Organization Man*, New York: Simon & Schuster.

This classic work, which is available in many editions, was an early and perceptive critique of life in bureaucracy. Although 50 years old, it still reads freshly, not least because many of the features described seem to apply to post-bureaucracy as well, which in itself should caution us against an overly polarized view of the two 'models'. Whyte's concern that individuals are subsumed within the organizational order has a disturbingly modern feel.

References

Aldrich, H. (1972) 'Technology and organization structure: A re-examination of the findings of the Aston group', *Administrative Science Quarterly* 15:26–43.

Bauman, Z. (1989) *Modernity and the Holocaust*, Cambridge: Polity.

Bennis, W. (1966) 'The coming death of bureaucracy', *Think*, November: 30–35.

Blau, P. (1955) *The Dynamics of Bureaucracy*, Chicago: Chicago University Press.

Blau, P. (1970) 'A formal theory of differentiation in organizations', *American Sociological Review* 35:210–218.

Burns, T. and Stalker, G. (1961) *The Management of Innovation*, Oxford: Oxford University Press.

Castells, M. (1996) *The Rise of the Network Society*, Oxford: Oxford University Press.

Crozier, M. (1964) *The Bureaucratic Phenomenon*, Chicago: University of Chicago Press.

Dalton, M. (1959) *Men Who Manage*, New York: John Wiley & Sons.

Delbridge, R. (1998) *Life On the Line in Contemporary Manufacturing*, Oxford: Oxford University Press.

du Gay, P. (2000) *In Praise of Bureaucracy: Weber, Organization and Ethics*, London: Sage.

Ferguson, K. (1984) *The Feminist Case Against Bureaucracy*, Philadelphia, PA: Temple University Press.

Gouldner, A. (1954) *Patterns of Industrial Bureaucracy*, New York: Free Press.

Heckscher, C. (1994) 'Defining the post-bureaucratic type', in C. Heckscher, and A. Donnellon (eds.) *The Post-bureaucratic Organization: New Perspectives on Organizational Change*, Thousand Oaks, CA: Sage, p.p. 14–62.

Heckscher, C. and Donnellon, A. (eds.) (1994) *The Post-bureaucratic Organization: New Perspectives on Organizational Change*, Thousand Oaks, CA: Sage.

Kanter, R. M. (1993) *Men and Women of the Corporation*, second edition, New York: Basic Books.

Kelley, R. (1990) *The Gold-collar Worker: Harnessing the Brainpower of the New Work Force*. Reading MA: Addison-Wesley.

Leadbetter, C. (1999) *Living On Thin Air: The New Economy*, London: Viking.

Merton, R. (1940) 'Bureaucratic structure and personality', *Social Forces*, May: 560–568.

Miewald, R. D. (1970) 'The greatly exaggerated death of bureaucracy', *California Management Review*, Winter: 65–69.

Perrow, C. (1979) *Complex Organizations*, Englewood Cliffs, NJ: Prentice Hall.

Piore, M. and Sabel, C. (1984) *The Second Industrial Divide*, New York: Basic Books.

Pugh, D. and Hickson, D. (1976) *Organisation Structure in its Context: The Aston Programme*, London: Saxon House.

Pugh, D., Hickson, D. and Hinings, C. R. (1968) 'Dimensions of organisation structure', *Administrative Science Quarterly* 13:65–103.

Reich, R. (1993) *The Work of Nations*, London: Simon & Schuster.

Ritzer, G. (2000) *The McDonaldization of Society: An Investigation Into the Changing Character of Contemporary Social Life*, second edition, Thousand Oaks, CA: Sage.

Robertson, M. and Swan, J. (1998) 'Modes of organizing in an expert consultancy: A case study of knowledge, power and egos', *Organization* 5(4):543–564.

Rose, N. (1999) *Governing the Soul*, London: Routledge.

Selznick, P. (1949) *TVA and the Grass Roots: A Study in the Sociology of Formal Organizations*, Berkeley CA: University of California Press.

Semler, R. (1993) *Maverick*, London: Century.

Sennett, R. (1998) *Work and the Corrosion of Character. The Personal Consequences of Work in the New Capitalism*, London: WW Norton.

Thompson, P. and Warhurst, C. (eds.) (1998) *Workplaces of the Future*, Basingstoke: Macmillan.

Warhurst, C. and Thompson, P. (1998) 'Hands, hearts and minds: Changing work and workers at the end of the century', in P. Thompson and C. Warhurst, (eds.) *Workplaces of the Future*, Basingstoke: Macmillan, p.p. 1–24.

Woodward, J. (1965) *Industrial Organization: Theory and Practice*, Oxford: Oxford University Press.

14 Ethics at Work

Edward Wray-Bliss

Key concepts and learning objectives

By the end of this chapter you should understand:

- The core assumptions of mainstream writers on business ethics, and be aware of how these assumptions limit the ethical questions that mainstream writers have been able to ask of business.

- The connections between mainstream academic writing on business ethics and contemporary organization's socially responsible image.

- That there is a wealth of other, more critical approaches to ethics that enable us to question the appropriateness of this socially responsible image.

- How some of these critical approaches enable us to undertake a deeper examination of the values underpinning modern organizations.

Aims of the chapter

This chapter will:

- Examine the relationship between ethical values and organizational behaviour.

- Explore some of the key ideas and developments that have introduced ethics into the heart of the modern organization.

- Examine some key mainstream studies of business ethics.

- Explore some of the key ideas that mark the critical challenge to mainstream views of business ethics.

- Examine some key critical studies of ethics in organizations.

- Explore the linkages between ethics and the core concept of freedom, in order to better understand the issue of ethical values at work.

Overview and key points

Behaviour perpetrated within and on behalf of organizations affects all of us, everyday. Thankfully, much of the time we experience positive effects. So for instance, we buy products made within organizations. We drink water and eat food processed by organizations. We are educated and employed in organizations. However, organizational behaviour is not always so benign. We are also ripped off by organizations. Our environment is polluted by organizations. Many people are exploited or abused, harmed or even killed as a result of organizational behaviour. Much of this 'bad' organizational behaviour is regulated by the law. However, the law is often a very blunt tool. It can be limited in its reach. It is not always effectively enforced. It may be circumvented by the unscrupulous and the clever. It can even be blind to some seriously damaging events. There is, in short, potentially a large gap between how we may want organizations to 'behave' and how the law ensures that they behave. As a result of this, society is increasingly asking management to make sure that their organizations not only refrain from breaking the law but also, and this is potentially much more radical and far reaching though also less clearly defined, to ensure that organizational members behave *ethically*.

This chapter will examine this important emerging way of thinking about organizational behaviour. In the first section we explore the work of theorists in the academic field of business ethics. We examine how such writers have attempted to integrate the apparently quite different arenas of 'ethics' and 'business'. We also explore how the managers of business organizations have come to appreciate how important it is for their organization to now be seen to behave ethically, or, in the new ethical language of business, to demonstrate corporate social responsibility.

In the second section we take a more critical look at these recent developments in both the study and practice of 'ethics' in business. We re-examine the core assumptions of the business ethics/corporate social responsibility fields and highlight how these are themselves ethically questionable. As part of this we scrutinize the mainstream assumptions that organizations are or can be 'responsible'; the desirability of employees' subordination to managerial control; and the reduction of 'ethics' to the greater goal of 'profits'. By exploring the theories of critical writers and a number of compelling critical case studies, we see how critical approaches to the subject can help to reclaim ethics as a language that enables us to examine the values underpinning contemporary organizational behaviour.

Mainstream approach to values at work: Corporate social responsibility and business ethics

Introduction

The modern engagement with 'ethics at work' is conventionally thought to have started in the United Kingdom and the United States in the 1980s. The 1980s were shaped by neo-conservative governments that pushed an aggressively pro-business, 'freemarket' agenda. The agenda centred upon deregulation of markets, reducing the legal obligations upon business, and an ideology of self-management and self-reliance for both individuals and corporations. Crucially, for our account of the emergence of the modern engagement with ethics at work, this decade strongly promoted the idea and practice that business leaders should voluntarily *self-regulate*. The idea was that business leaders should be left alone to control their businesses rather than be more tightly regulated by the state or federal/national government. This was an ideology that the business community warmly welcomed then, and still jealously guards today.

Public faith in the effectiveness of business self-regulation was shaken, however, by a series of very public business scandals, disasters and frauds. People began to question the negative effects of business practice. Some even began to question the effectiveness of business self-regulation more generally. Of course, such scandals had occurred in the past, but in the 1980s more people (as a result of such things as the growth in small-scale share ownership) were directly affected by them, and social movements critical of business were better supported and had gained a greater visibility.

To regain public trust and ward off calls for more state regulation of business, the business community needed to reassure the public and policy makers that it was capable of taking responsibility for the potentially negative effects of its practices. This reassurance took the form of 'ethics'. The business community began to publicly present itself as concerned with the ethics of its actions and its effects upon the wider society. By drawing upon a discourse of 'ethics', business leaders could seek to reassure that they would take responsibility for their own actions. Business would be its own conscience if you like, and did not therefore need further governmental regulation. This modern concern by business leaders with issues of 'ethics' is generally given the shorthand title corporate social responsibility (CSR).

CSR is the term that has come to stand for the practices and policies undertaken by the business community to promote the idea that they are concerned with more than just profit at any cost. CSR practices can include:

- Appointing managers or directors with responsibility for CSR.
- Developing and publicizing ethical statements, policies or codes of practice.
- Joining environmental or other public groups or forums.
- Publicizing a track record of good corporate governance.
- Making well-publicized donations of money, time or resources to charities and other 'good causes'.
- Linking the business brand, through sponsorship, marketing, etc., with 'good' images such as ending child poverty, protecting the environment or inner city regeneration.

So widespread has the CSR movement now become that it is rare to find a large company these days that does not promote itself as 'socially responsible' (see Table 14.1).

However, just because business leaders now promote their organizations as 'socially responsible' does not mean that such claims are legitimate. One way the corporate world finds legitimacy for its claim to be socially responsible is through an association with the rapidly growing academic field of study called business ethics.

Table 14.1 Examples of corporate social responsibility practices

Company	Practices
Shell	• Shell sustainable development 'We remain convinced that engaging with stakeholders and integrating social and environmental considerations better throughout the lifetime of our projects makes us a more responsive, competitive and profitable company, in the long and short term.' (www.shell.com)
Ford Motor Company	• Ford of Britain Charitable Trust • Environmental policies 'As the number of motor vehicles around the world increases, so do environmental concerns. However, we have always aimed to be a model for the industry in this area. So we're working to reduce the environmental impact of our products, while providing the utility, performance and affordability customers demand. We want it to be easy for people to say, "I'm an environmentalist and a car enthusiast." ' (www.ford.co.uk courtesy of Ford Motor Company)
Nike	• Charitable donations • Code of conduct for subcontracted labour 'Nike's Corporate Responsibility mission is to be an innovative and inspirational corporate citizen in a world where our company participates. We seek to protect and enhance the Nike brand through responsible business practices that contribute to profitable and sustainable growth.' (www.nike.com)

SOURCE: A) SHELL UK LOGO COURTESY OF SHELL BRANDS, INTERNATIONAL, B) FORD LOGO-COURTESY OF FORD

'Business ethics' may be understood as the academic study and promotion of corporate social responsibility. Business ethics explores the ethical legitimations for, and effects of, a wide range of business practices. These academic arguments are then widely disseminated to students and managers through, for example, business ethics modules on MBA and other university management courses, through the large market for business ethics textbooks, and through a sizeable and constantly growing volume of academic journals, conferences and symposia on business ethics and CSR.

The field of business ethics is, as a result, broad and diverse and can therefore seem difficult to get an overall sense of. Despite this variety and volume, however, it is possible to discern a common approach in most mainstream business ethics work, consisting of:

- *A pro-business agenda.* Business ethics critiques particular business practices, but does not question the ethics of business more generally.
- *A free market agenda.* Business ethics endorses voluntary self-regulation of businesses rather than for instance control from outside (e.g. state regulation) as the way to ensure ethical practices.
- *A belief in the compatibility of 'profits' and 'ethics'.* Business ethics sees 'good ethics' as synonymous with 'good business'.

Recap question
- Summarize what 'corporate social responsibility' and 'business ethics' are.

CASE STUDY 14.1 Telebank PLC: A famous ethical organization[1]

Telebank PLC is a successful medium-sized UK financial institution employing around 4000 staff. These facts hardly make Telebank interesting. What does make it interesting is that Telebank was publicly heralded throughout the 1990s as perhaps the best example of a successful 'ethical business', a business that seemed to clearly, demonstrate that 'good ethics' and 'good business' could be synonymous. This case study, adapted from Wray-Bliss (1998) and

(2001), charts Telebank's rise to this moral and economic high ground.

In the United Kingdom prior to the 1980s financial service organizations were prevented from engaging in cross-sector competition. The market for financial service products that the 'big four' banks (Barclays, Lloyds, National Westminster and Midland) along with smaller banks like Telebank were involved in was protected by law, with many other financial service providers such as building societies prevented from supplying the banks' core products. Enjoying the benefits of a stable, protected and growing market, the big four had entered into an unofficial agreement not to undercut each other's products and services, thereby keeping their profits inflated. As a result, relatively small institutions like Telebank could carve out a profitable niche by offering service innovations that the 'big four' were reluctant to follow, and other financial service institutions such as building societies were legally prevented from providing.

In the 1980s, however, the UK conservative government radically changed the financial services market. The government embarked upon a programme of deregulating markets and freeing-up business and capital from historical constraints. As part of this programme historical restrictions on both banks and other financial service providers were lifted (e.g. The Building Societies Act 1986). The 'big four' banks now faced stiffer competition as other financial institutions could enter into their markets and undercut their products. The big four responded by providing their own new products and services, thereby competing more keenly both against each other and against smaller companies like Telebank whose profitable 'innovative' niche was suddenly under threat. By 1990 Telebank was making a loss of around £15 million.

Telebank had to do something, and fast. Its strategy was two-fold. First, like many of the other banks, it cut costs. It rapidly shed over 1000 employees, closed branches, dramatically cut staff numbers in its branches (typically from 40 to eight), and rerouted most of its contact with customers from over-the-counter face-to-face to telephone banking via remote telephone **call-centres**. Secondly, the management of Telebank decided to reinvent the bank as an 'ethical' corporation. In particular they represented Telebank as the bank that gave its customers the choice to invest their money ethically. Telebank management researched its customers' opinions on ethical matters, and then formulated and widely publicized a 12-point ethical policy, detailing whom the bank will and will not do business with. The policy prohibited the bank from investing its customers' money in, or indeed having business customers who are involved in, for example, the tobacco trade, the testing of

cosmetics on animals or operating in countries with oppressive regimes. As the Telebank ethical policy booklet expressed it: 'Do you know, do you approve of how your money is being used when you are not using it? Do you think you have a right to know at least in principle? . . . Can you put up the Second World War defence – I didn't know?'

By so positioning itself as an 'ethical' bank, Telebank implicitly and explicitly distanced itself from the big four banks and also from the bad press that these banks had experienced through such practices as their involvement in apartheid South Africa and aggressive selling practices in the United Kingdom. For some business commentators and media analysts however, Telebank's reinvention as an 'ethical' company was contentious. The *Financial Times* newspaper remarked at the time that: 'Sceptics have been quick to suggest that Telebank is cashing in on ethics. A number also indignantly suggest that banks have no rights to preach to their customers or discriminate against potential recipients of loans.'

However, from this early scepticism, most detractors in the business world have now been converted to the good business sense of Telebank's ethical policy. They have come to understand it as an example of clever market positioning, with little risk to Telebank PLC, that served to attract the custom of more affluent, 'middle class', customers whose social conscience was matched with a solid bank balance. 'There's no denying this is a marketing initiative . . . why else do it? But we are not part of the long-haired sandal brigade, we are socially concerned bankers.' (managing director, Telebank). Indeed the bank's own economic turnaround speaks for itself. Telebank has increased its market share year-on-year since 1990. Deposits rose approximately 10 per cent in 1993, 16 per cent in 1994 and 20 per cent in 1995, with 44 per cent of new account openings being attributed to its ethical positioning. By 1996 the bank made a profit of almost £37 million, compared to its £15 million loss in 1990.

Questions

The case of Telebank PLC illustrates several elements that were also common to the emergence of CSR and business ethics more generally. Some questions:

- How does the case demonstrate connections between the free market economic context of the time and the emergence of the bank's ethical stance?

- How does the case illustrate the self-regulatory/voluntary nature of the bank's ethics?

- What relationship does the case suggest between the issues of 'ethics' and 'profitability'?

Key problems in this field

Case study 14.1 presents a celebrated example of one company's contribution to the problem of integrating 'ethics' and 'business'. In the section after this one, some important academic contributions to business ethics are discussed, but first we look at some of the key problems facing the field. A field that focuses upon practical business issues as diverse as A(lcohol policies at work) to

Z(imbabwe business bribery), and utilizes the framework of something as long-debated as ethical philosophy to do so, will clearly generate a great number of debates and controversies. To illustrate the complexities of ethical issues in organization, Box 14.1 raises just some of the questions that we might need to consider when thinking about the ethics of one organizational issue that effects every-one of us: pollution (see also Chapter 11).

From just this one issue, it should start to become clear that any attempt to consider the ethics of almost any organizational practice is problematic. So business ethics is full of 'problems' – but perhaps it should be. Business ethics is after all concerned with questions of ethics – with what is right and what is wrong, with how to live a 'good' life and not just a 'comfortable' or 'profitable' life – and these are far from easy issues.

Underpinning all the problems associated with specific organizational practices and issues (like pollution for instance), however, are a number of more general 'macro' problems that the field of business ethics needed to find a way to resolve if it was to justify its existence to sceptical managers of business organisations. We focus upon three such problems here: relevance; conscience; and translation.

The problem of relevance As an academic who works within the broad field of business ethics, the response that I invariably get when I tell people about my work is a look of bemusement followed shortly by the quip 'that's an easy job then . . . there aren't any'. The field of business ethics as a whole faces this same problem, that of connecting 'ethics' with 'business' in a context where many people see them as separate. Beaton's (2001) tongue-in-cheek advice to managers relies upon this commonly perceived disconnection between ethics and business for its humour: 'You cannot gain professional respect if your personal integrity is damaged. Prevent damage to your personal integrity by leaving it at home in the mornings.'

It is not just cynics like Beaton however that reproduce such ideas. The (in)famous US free market economist, Milton Friedman (1970), has argued that *the only* social responsibility of business is to increase its profits. Friedman has argued that the corporate executive or manager may *personally* feel responsibilities to particular charities, or good causes, but should only act on these responsibilities in the private sphere when at home or in the community. If as an employee s/he practises these or other expressions of 'social responsibility' in the corporation's time or with the corporation's money, then far from being 'ethical' s/he is being dangerously 'subversive', misspending the shareholders' money, and failing to act as s/he has been contracted to. For Friedman therefore: (quoted in White, 2000, p. 238).

> there is one and only one social responsibility of business – to use its resources and engage in activities designed to increase its profits . . . so long as it engages in open and free competition without deception or fraud.

Apart from pursuing profit as if it were a 'moral crusade', ethics has little or no place in the business world for Friedman. Instead ethics is seen as private and personal and should stay that way, and should stay out of business. It clouds and compromises the open pursuit of money-making.

Box 14.1: The complexities of ethics: The example of pollution

How should we understand the question of pollution by business? As immoral or as inevitable? Should it be stopped or only limited? Who has rights in this case: the business, the community, the natural environment, the shareholders, or the workers whose jobs may rely on the company producing, and thereby polluting? Do these rights conflict or coincide? How do we decide between them? Is pollution an evil that we must accept for the 'greater good'? Or does the community's right to clean air and good health outweigh all other moral appeals? And what health has a community without employment? Is it ethical to shift pollution-generating activites to other, poorer countries? Is it right to limit the goods that consumers can buy so that pollution is minimized? Who is to decide on each of these questions? On what ethical basis will such decisions be made?

Image 14.1

The problem of conscience Assuming that business ethicists somehow solve the above problem of making ethics seem relevant for business, who is to decide what ethics are relevant and how to enforce them? To encourage us to behave ethically, individuals have concepts such as conscience, or fear of God or gods, we have ideas such as damnation, karma, rebirth, salvation or enlightenment, we have the desire to please, or the desire to live according to our principles or precepts, and more, that encourage us to abide by what we understand to be ethical and good. But a business organization would seem to have none of these. Where is its god? Who is its conscience? Where is its desire to be principled? Who is to be its ethical authority, its guru, its lord, its cleric, its rabbi, its enlightened being? And, even supposing that such a figure or figures can be found, how are they to enforce the ethical conscience of the organization? And should this enforcement override the ethical values of dissenting others in the organization, or those with whom the organization interacts?

Thinkpoint 14.1

Power/knowledge and ethics

- Who do you think should be the 'ethical conscience' of an organization, and why?
- Reflecting further upon your answer, what assumptions have you made regarding who you think has knowledge about ethical issues in organizations and how this relates to the power you think these people should have to define an organization's ethics?

The problem of translation The third underlying problem facing business ethics is one of translation. Even if some body or bodies are identified as the 'ethical conscience' of the organization, are the languages of 'ethics' and 'business' commensurable? Ethics can seem to be all 'philosophical' and 'abstract', concerned with 'goodness' and 'virtue' and 'justice'. Whereas business is 'practical' and 'rational', concerned with 'efficiency', 'outputs', 'products', and 'costs'. Business relies upon measurement and calculability – everything must have a cost, a value, a purpose. Business has profit and loss accounts, stock control systems, payroll systems, delivery schedules, contracts, human resource planning and a wealth of other management systems to plan and measure each tangible aspect of organizational behaviour. Surely a business cannot hope to plan or measure something as intangible or spiritual as 'ethics'. And anyway, isn't ethics essentially individualistic, a matter of conscience, one's personal relationship with the divine (however this is understood)? Whereas organization is, by definition, concerned with collective purpose and collective effort. How can business ethicists possibly hope to translate 'ethics' into something intelligible to, and manageable for, business?

Taken together, these three problems of relevance, conscience and translation present a significant challenge for business ethics. In the next section we explore some of the key ideas and contributions in the field that have sought to address these issues.

Key ideas and contributions

Overcoming the problem of relevance   To address the widely held belief that 'business' and 'ethics' are, and possibly should be, disconnected realms, social and economic arguments to the contrary have been made.

The social argument attests that business, its employees and management should properly be understood as part of the social world, rather than abstracted from it. They should be subject to similar expectations of ethical conduct that we would expect from other members of our communities. Stakeholder theory has been used to argue that shareholders are only one of the many groups of people whom business interacts with, and is therefore responsible for.

While shareholders principally demand profit, stakeholder theory argues that other stakeholders have equally valid demands that it would be unethical for the business to breach. For example, employees have the right to demand payment for their work and a safe and suitable working environment; suppliers payment for their goods or services; the local community employment and a non-toxic environment; the nation state taxes; and consumers safe, trustworthy and reasonably priced goods. Such expectations can be seen to form an implied *ethical contract* between business and the community, such that it is only by abiding by this contract that society effectively gives business the right to consume resources and be rewarded with profit. Even in the early 1980s this hidden, ethical dimension of legal contracts was being emphasized in response to the spate of corporate scandals.

> What is shocking about some of the current corporate scandals – bribery, falsification of records, theft, and corporate espionage – is that these acts violate the conditions for making contracts and market exchanges, conditions which are at the very heart of the free enterprise system. Such violations cannot be excused by saying that they do not appear on the contract. Such excuses are almost as absurd as someone defending the murder of a creditor by saying: I only promised to pay him back; I didn't promise not to murder him. Hence we can conclude that a company has moral obligations in the contract it makes with society and it has obligations to those moral rules which make contracts possible. *(Bowie, 1983 in White, 2000, p. 245)*

Business leaders must therefore ensure that their business is seen to be ethical, lest too many breaches lead us to start to question the usefulness of organizing our society according to the private profit making, free market, business model. We can see here a self-interested argument for the business community to be ethical. This self-interested reason for being ethical is even more clearly seen in the second type of argument for connecting ethics and business, the economic argument.

The economic argument presents ethics, in one way or another, as a business opportunity waiting to be exploited. Thus the company that is seen to be 'ethical' can attract more loyal staff and customers, can benefit from good public relations, can use their ethics as a unique selling point, can use ethics to develop a strong 'brand', and can even charge a premium for its products because of its ethical image. To impress upon business, and students of business, further the link between 'ethics and the bottom line' (Edwards and Goodell, 1994; Johnson, 1994) business ethics textbooks are frequently peppered with stories of highly profitable companies that have successfully traded upon a strong ethical image (such as Telebank PLC, above). Overall, the implicit, and increasingly explicit, message of many business ethics texts is that good ethics 'translates into increased profits' (Axline, 1990, p. 87).

Thinkpoint 14.2

Power/knowledge and ethics II

- What commercial organizations can you think of that have linked an 'ethical' or 'socially responsible' image with a profitable business?
- Can you think of organizations that have suffered or struggled because of an unethical public image?
- Your answers to these questions might illustrate further the ways that power, knowledge and ethics are related. By constructing in the public consciousness an image (knowledge) of being ethical, certain corporations have managed to become more economically powerful.

Overcoming the problem of conscience From the discussion above we can see that business ethics makes a confident appeal to the business community's own commercial self-interest to justify the contemporary focus upon ethics. But who is to control the organization's new-found ethics? Who is to be, in effect, the conscience of the organization? Once we reflect upon the way that much of the field has now effectively rendered 'ethics' a business resource, something from which profit and good public relations can be gained, then the answer that the business ethics field has come to might be fairly obvious – management.

Thinkpoint 14.3

Power/knowledge versus ethics?

- Can you think of any others inside or outside the organization who might question management's right to control what is defined as a matter of ethics? (We will pick-up this point later in the chapter.)
- Your answer might illustrate further the ways that the right to define the knowledge of what is ethical/ unethical in organizations is itself contested. This is because there are 'power effects' that can arise as a consequence of such definitions. For instance, if working long hours is constructed as a marker of an employee fulfilling their ethical commitments to give their energy to their employing organization, then it will likely continue. However, if long working hours are constructed as an unethical demand by employers on employees' right for leisure and family time outside of normal working hours, then there is likely to be a challenge to these expectations.

In choosing management as the ethical conscience of the organization, business ethicists are reproducing the dominant managerialist thinking of mainstream Western industrial thought. As industrialized societies, since at least the time of F. W. Taylor, we are long used to understanding management to 'naturally' bear the responsibility for all 'higher' reasoning, all strategy and all 'important' thinking in the organization (see Chapters 3 and 6; see also Parker, 2002). Business ethics reproduces this managerialism by assuming that management should necessarily have the right to define the organization's ethics and ensure other organizational members' compliance to these ethics.

Overcoming the problem of translation If managers are to be the ethical agents or 'conscience' of organizations, this still leaves the question of how the language and concerns of 'ethics' can be translated into the rational or bureaucratic task of organizing?

Business ethics has managed this through simplifying ethics down to a process whereby management formulate and disseminate organization-wide ethical codes and/or policies. Through this mechanism the issue of ethics is thus reduced to a single, organizational-wide, unitarist series of rules. Ethics can now, in principle, be quite easily managed, with the manager merely having to decide whether the employee has broken the ethical rule or not.

Thinkpoint 14.4

Freedom power and ethics

- What ethical rules does your university or college have? (Does it have rules on cheating in exams, sexual harassment, bullying, discrimination?)

- What mechanisms are in place to enforce these rules, who enforces them, and how effective do you think these are in regulating your behaviour?

- Some universities, in response to worries about the safety of students, have started to introduce rules regulating who students may have sexual relationships with. As part of this, some universities have started requiring students to obtain formal written consent from a prospective sexual partner before they have sex. If your university or college introduced this policy, would you consider this an unjustified exercise of power and interference into your private sexual freedoms, or a responsible policy to ensure your freedom from possible sexual attack?

Key issues and controversies

So far, we have seen several problems with the attempt to integrate 'ethics' and 'business' and we have introduced the broad solutions to these problems presented by the business ethics field. These broad solutions are relatively uncontroversial within the field. There are disagreements in this field, however, and mostly these centre around the question of which philosophical ethical framework should be applied to evaluate and make sense of behaviour in organizations. The main frameworks that business ethics texts draw upon are utilitarianism, stakeholder theory, deontology, justice and virtue (see also Beauchamp and Bowie, 1997 and Snell, 2004 for useful summaries).

Originating in the work of British philosophers David Hume (1711–1776), Jeremy Bentham (1748–1832) and John Stuart Mill (1806–1873), utilitarianism understands the ethical value of an act to be based on its *consequences*. Acts that lead to the greatest good for the greatest number of people are judged to be moral. This apparently straightforward proposition, however, hides much complexity. What exactly constitutes a 'good' outcome, for instance, is very debatable. How are we to measure the sum total amount of good that each of a range of potential acts that we may undertake might lead to? How can a manager know, with any real certainty, the full consequences of her actions for others in a complex business situation?

One popular variation of utilitarian ethical approaches to business ethics is that of stakeholder theory. Stakeholder theory, as we have seen, argues that the management of an organization have responsibilities not just to consider the happiness or demands of shareholders, but to recognize that organizational behaviour affects a range of other 'stakeholders' both inside and outside the corporation. Stakeholder theory can be understood to modify utilitarianism, reminding us that when we are considering the ethical consequences of particular organizational actions, we must consider the potentially quite different interests of different constituencies. These can include employees, shareholders, the environment, the local community, even an unborn generation that may be harmed by a company's products or the pollution it generates.

Clearly, trying to take into account all the possible consequences for all stakeholders of every organizational act could lead to a paralysis of indecision. Utilitarian thinking, including stakeholder variants, in the contemporary business world has recognized this and tends to focus upon the development of ethical rules to guide behaviour. Rules such as 'do not break contracts' and 'do not falsely advertise products' may be argued to be those that the business should always observe because the *consequences* of not doing so would be a loss of faith in business in general. However, even this rule-based utilitarianism, popular in business ethics, is not without its problems. For any rule formulated for organizational members to follow, we can always ask such questions as: Who decided on the rule? How can we be sure that this rule doesn't just reflect their self-interest?

Why should we be certain that following this rule would indeed lead to the greatest sum of ethical outcomes?

Deontology, like rule-based utilitarianism above, is also based upon rules or laws. However, unlike utilitarianism, deontological ethics does not build its rules on the basis of anticipated consequences of actions. For deontology this would diminish ethics, reducing it to a means–ends calculation. To judge the ethics of an action on the basis of its contribution to, say, 'happiness' would be to elevate happiness *over* ethics – to, in effect, see ethics as a subset of happiness. According to deontology, ethics does not serve any such other ends, it is an end in itself. To act ethically an individual should not be attempting to second-guess the consequences of their actions, but rather should reason what universal *ethical duty* or law applies, and they should follow this without hesitation or regard to personal friendships, personal risks or any other contextual features. For deontology, these duties are worked out through pure reason on the basis of what German philosopher Immanuel Kant (1724–1804) argued was a 'categorical imperative' of 'universalizability'. Kant's categorical imperative can be understood as 'only act in ways that could be made a general law for all human behaviour'. On the basis of this universalizable imperative, all other ethical duties can be worked out through a process of logic and reason. Thus, for instance, murder cannot be moral because if murder was universalized as a moral duty logically not everyone could follow it (you can't follow a 'duty' to murder someone if you've been murdered yourself!). Therefore, refraining from murder is a logical universalizable moral duty.

This universalizable imperative translates into far more subtle moral duties as well. Perhaps most difficult to resolve in the context of today's organizations is the universal duty on all of us to respect the dignity and autonomy of others – a precondition if each person is to have the freedom to reason about what is ethical and act accordingly. This universal duty is often translated as the duty not to treat other people as only a *means* (i.e. as a resource to achieve what *you* want), but always to treat people as an *end* in and of themselves. Some business ethics writers (e.g. Arnold and Bowie, 2003) have suggested that this last duty presents a difficult challenge for contemporary businesses organizations in that they tend to use people instrumentally as disposable 'human resources'.

Another approach to ethics used in many business ethics articles is that of justice. Justice based approaches to ethics, formulated by among others British philosopher John Locke (1632–1704), focus upon rights and fairness (Snell, 2004). The *Universal Declaration of Human Rights 1948*, passed by the General Assembly of the United Nations, is perhaps the most famous attempt to formalize such a justice-based ethics and Amnesty International[1] the best known example of an organization attempting to turn these espoused rights into a reality. Justice-based approaches to ethics have some similarities with deontology (for instance the attempt to formulate universal rights, above); however, they can also be seen to depart in a crucial way. Whereas deontology focuses exclusively upon the observance of rational ethical duties, ethics of justice also focus upon the more emotional, and often emotive, issue of *fairness*. Thus under an ethics of justice, punishment of infringements and compensation for victims, for instance, might be justified if members of an organization have acted in ways that deny others' rights.

If the talk of ethical consequences, ethical duties and ethical justice so far seems a little impersonal, the next ethical theory used in business ethics texts turns our attention right back to the individual. Virtue-based approaches to ethics are often traced back – in Western thought at least – to the work of Greek philosopher Aristotle (384–322 BC). These approaches focus upon the *character* of the person who acts. After all, we could have all the information about the likely ethical consequences of our actions (as per utilitarianism) and we could know there to be clear duties that ethically we should not breach (as per deontology), but if we have failings in our character (if we lack 'virtue') we could still simply not choose to behave ethically. Within the business ethics field, this virtue-based approach to ethics can be seen in a range of material that focuses upon the moral education and character of managers (e.g. MacLagan 1998). Occasionally, when being least critical, virtue approaches can slip into a trap of individualism, where ethics depends upon heroic individuals possessing the special qualities required to resist temptations or engage in selfless 'good deeds'. This sometimes finds expression in business ethics texts celebrating charismatic senior managers as paragons of unimpeachable virtue, single-handedly spreading purity throughout their organizations.

Knowledge, identity and ethics

- Think about some examples at your university or college where you believe that you have acted ethically.

- Which of the approaches to ethics outlined above seems to best explain the reason why you acted this way. (For instance was it because you thought about the consequences of your actions (utilitarianism); because you were obeying an ethical rule that you would never consider breaching (deontology); because you were owed something that you took back (justice); because you are simply an ethical person (virtue); etc.).

- Could your evaluation of your behaviour as ethical be different if you applied one of the other understandings of ethics?

- The issue of ethics is central to our identity. We tend to justify our behaviour and selves using ethical arguments ('I did what I thought was right in the circumstances'; 'I followed the rules'; 'I followed my conscience'; 'I am a good person'; etc.). However, as the preceding section shows, there are different forms of knowledge about ethics. Not all of these would agree on what is the ethical course of action for any one situation. Given these disagreements, how secure is our valued 'ethical' identity?

A selection of important studies

Two studies are reviewed here – Denis Arnold and Norman Bowie's (2003) 'Sweatshops and Respect for Persons' and Bill Richardson and Peter Curwen's (1995) 'Do Free Market Governments Create Crisis-Ridden Societies?' – that, in their different ways, both reproduce several familiar aspects of the mainstream business ethics discourse and also push the business ethics debate forward.

Arnold and Bowie's (2003) article, published in *Business Ethics Quarterly*, uses a Kantian (deontological) ethical theory of respect for persons to critique the ethics of exploitative 'sweatshop' employment practices of **multinational corporations** (MNCs). For Arnold and Bowie (2003, p. 222): 'Persons ought to be respected because persons have dignity. For Kant, an object that has dignity is beyond price. Employees have a dignity that machines and capital do not. They have dignity because they are capable of moral activity.' The authors draw upon evidence from trade unionists, labour activists and non-governmental organizations to argue that **subcontractors** working for MNCs routinely breach such respect for persons in the conditions of labour that they impose upon their employees.

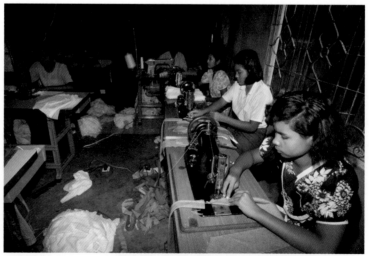

Image 14.2 An example of the overcrowded conditions common to sweatshops

Such conditions include widespread and well-documented breaches of labour law relating to wages and benefits, forced overtime, health and safety violations, sexual harassment, discrimination and environmental protection. Psychological and physical coercion to work also abounds. Such coercion can take the form of forced overtime through threat of job loss, and compulsion to work through verbal and physical assault. Working conditions are frequently appalling and include locking workers into the overcrowded and unventilated factories to prevent them leaving, resulting in fatalities when fires break out.

For instance, in 1993 200 employees were killed and 469 injured in the Kader Industrial Toy Company in Thailand because they were locked in. The Kader company produced toys for US MNCs such as Hasbro, Toys 'R' Us, J. C. Penney and Fisher Price (Arnold and Bowie, 2003, p. 231). In the 10 000-person Tae Kwang Vina factory in Vietnam, producing Nike products, employees were exposed to toxic chemicals at amounts up to 177 times those allowed under Vietnamese law (ibid.). Further, in addition to such unsafe, abusive and frequently illegal practices, these subcontractors producing goods for some of the worlds largest MNCs fail to provide workers with wages high enough even to meet basic needs for food, clothing and shelter, and this despite the fact that a living wage may only be as much as US$30.00 per week (see also Klein, 2001).

Drawing upon such evidence in conjunction with Kantian ethical philosophy and a variant of stakeholder theory, Arnold and Bowie (2003, p. 239) argue that MNCs are failing to meet their ethical responsibilities to these employees: 'We have argued that MNE managers who encourage or tolerate violations of the rule of law; use coercion; allow unsafe working conditions; and provide below subsistence wages, disavow their own dignity and that of their workers.'

Having criticised MNC treatment of their employees, the authors (ibid., p. 239) highlight MNCs as in a prime position to improve their ethics, thus reproducing the managerial focus of the mainstream business ethics field: 'MNE managers who recognize a duty to respect their employees, and those of their subcontractors, are well positioned to play a constructive role in ensuring that the dignity of humanity is respected.'

Thinkpoint 14.6

Inequality, power and ethics

- Critics of MNC's use of 'sweatshop labour' argue that these companies are unethical in exploiting stark inequalities in employment costs and conditions in developing countries compared to those in the West. Further, critics argue that MNCs are so large and powerful that they could, if they so wished, change these employment conditions and pay a sustainable wage.

- Imagine you are employed by one of the above companies and are given responsibility for improving your subcontractor's employment practices. What procedures would you recommend that the company undertakes?

- You may find it interesting to compare what Nike says about its own practices (www.nike.com/nikebiz/nikebiz.jhtml?page =25&cat=code) with what critics (such as those at www.corpwatch.org) say about the company's ethics.

Overall, Arnold and Bowie's argument is a powerful and important one. It blends traditional features of mainstream business ethics discourse with a powerful critique of the widespread exploitative practices from which the world's largest MNCs profit. It does, however, stop short of questioning the free market economic system that arguably encourages business to put profit before such ethical considerations. In the paper reviewed next we see an example of a mainstream business ethics article that does begin to question the prevailing freemarket economics.

Richardson and Curwen's (1995) article published in the *Journal of Business Ethics* is concerned with examining the causes of two fatal disasters, the *Herald of Free Enterprise* ferry disaster, and the Kings Cross underground fire, both of which occurred in the late 1980s. The 1987 *Herald of Free Enterprise* roll-on/roll-off passenger and freight ferry disaster occurred in good weather when the ferry capsized at sea after she sailed with both her inner and outer bow (loading) doors open. As a result, 150 passengers and 38 members of the crew lost their lives and many others were injured. The Kings Cross underground (below-ground passenger train) fire occurred in 1987, when grease and rubbish caught fire beneath the treads of the passenger escalators at the underground station level. The fire rapidly spread up the escalators and erupted into the ticket hall causing horrendous injuries and 31 deaths.

Analysing the causes of these disasters, Richardson and Curwen criticize management's inappropriate beliefs as contributing to, if not causing, the disasters by creating inappropriate organizational cultures, structures, systems and behaviour. They give an example (ibid., p. 556) of such inappropriate beliefs:

> Despite the existence of theoretical and real world warnings about the dangers inherent in organizations, a dominant premise of the free-market philosophy is one of organizations as economic (and only indirectly as social) wealth creators/bestowers. A society which concentrates excessively on the assumption that organizations are only – or even predominantly – beneficial wealth-creators, tends to be disaster prone.

The authors suggest that these fatal disasters are not 'one-off' examples of bad practice in an otherwise well-managed and safe economy. Rather, they highlight the free market economic system itself as strongly contributing to such inappropriate management beliefs: 'Free-market principles help sustain inappropriate beliefs about the nature of organizations and the kinds of cultures and systems which contribute to disasters' (ibid., p. 552).

So, we have in Richardson and Curwen what, for a mainstream business ethics article, is an unusually explicit criticism of top management's problematic influence upon the organization *and* of the freemarket philosophy that has so increased top manager's control. Though unusual in voicing these criticisms, however, the article also reproduces the managerialism and voluntarism of the business ethics field. Though critical of management for contributing to these fatalities, the authors see the solution merely as *management voluntarily changing the way they manage*. Managers, the authors conclude, must learn to 'think-upside-down' and develop a 'wider belief base for the creation of contexts by management strategies' (ibid., p. 558).

Ultimately, then, we have in Richardson and Curwen (1995) a compelling and persuasive critique of the most serious instances of organizational fatality and disaster. And while the authors reproduce the key assumptions of the business ethics field, they also push the field forward in examining more seriously the risks with management control and the free market economic system.

Although these studies are examples of some of the best work in the mainstream field of business ethics, critical approaches might suggest that they continue to display a number of serious limitations. We begin exploring these arguments by focusing upon the contribution and limitations of mainstream writing on business ethics in relation to the core concept of 'freedom'.

Limitations and contribution in relation to core concepts

Ethics is intimately connected to the idea of freedom. Ethics is concerned with choosing between different paths. At its simplest, ethics is choosing 'right' over 'wrong', 'good' over 'bad'. To choose, one must have the freedom to take different courses of actions, to make different choices. This core concept of freedom is illuminated in several different ways in the story of business ethics. First of all, the context of free market economics from which business ethics was born gave business more freedom from governmental control. Business self-regulation was to take the place of state regulation. With this freedom from state control came public examples of businesses abusing this freedom – leading to crisis, frauds, abuses, and disasters (much like those discussed above by Arnold and Bowie, 2003 and Richardson and Curwen, 1995).

Business ethics then emerged as a response to the problematic underside of this freedom, a response that promised to encourage business managers to think about the effects and ethics of their actions. Importantly, business ethics does not seek to limit the freedom that managers have under the free market/self-regulating economic system, it does not seek more state control, or stronger pressure groups, or unions, etc. Rather, business ethics endorses and reinforces the freedom and power of management to self-regulate, to be free from outside regulation, and to use this freedom to voluntarily behave more ethically.

The links between business ethics and freedom do not end here however. This is just the starting point of a whole series of questions regarding the nature of the 'freedom' that business ethics promotes. For instance, has the rise of business ethics and, 'corporate social responsibility' actually made the world freer from business exploitation, industrial accidents, environmental destruction, etc? Compelling evidence on this centrally important question is very elusive, but anecdotally it does not take much effort to find example after example of disastrous business behaviour in the local and national media – despite some of these companies having glossy ethical policies and codes. Indeed, if the industrial crises, abuses and disasters of the 1980s arose, as business ethics states, from a context of management having new found freedom to self-regulate, why does it make sense to see giving managers *more freedom*, freedom to define and police organizational ethics, as a likely solution to this problem?

Finally, under business ethics' managerial focus it is managers (and academics) only who have the freedom to define ethics – other employees and stakeholders seem to be cast in the subordinate position of merely submitting to these rules. Is their *unfreedom* the price that must be paid for more ethical organizations? Just how 'ethical' is it for a minority of organizational members (management) to impose their definition of ethics upon the majority?

Such questions and issues are among some of the concerns that critical approaches to the question of ethics at work address, which we turn to next.

Recap questions
- Why is 'ethics' considered important for today's organizations?
- Who in the organization is given responsibility for developing and enforcing ethical policy?
- Do you think organizations today are always ethical? If not, how would you like to see them improved?

Critical approaches to ethics at work

Introduction

One place to start an introduction to critical approaches to ethics at work would be to highlight the narrow range of ethical frameworks (utilitarian, deontological, justice and virtue) that mainstream business ethicists tends to draw upon. By so doing, business ethics tends to exclude a wealth of contemporary, and more critical, ethical systems including those of **feminism** (Brewis, 1998; though see Derry, 2002), **Marxism** (Wray-Bliss and Parker, 1998), and **post-modernism** (Phillips, 1991; Willmott, 1998).

Drawing upon such alternative ethical systems can provide us with fascinating and compelling different readings of ethics at work, readings that can make us radically question whether behaviour in today's organizations is indeed ethical. We start the introduction to critical approaches to ethics at work by questioning the ethics of organization; questioning the ethics of obedience; and questioning the corporate takeover of ethics.

Questioning the ethics of organization   As we have seen, business ethics seeks to make organizations socially responsible by giving the managers of these organizations more power to define and control other organizational members' ethics. On the surface this seems like an effective way to bring ethics into the organization. However, by drawing upon the work of post-modern sociologist Zygmunt Bauman (1989, 1993) this can be seen as potentially disastrous for ethics at work. It may provide the conditions to actually increase unethical organizational practices.

Organizations, like crowds, are comprised of a mass of people. Organizations differ from crowds however in that the behaviour of people in organizations is regulated and controlled so that it meets the collective purpose of the organization. By and large, employees do what they are expected to do and this harnessing of their collective effort is what makes organizations so powerful (Knights and Roberts, 1982). To achieve this, organizations must eradicate unpredictable behaviour. Thus we have rules, procedures, uniforms, targets, quotas and all manner of other bureaucratic and cultural mechanisms to control employees' behaviour in organizations (see Chapters 8 and 12). Bauman argues that one effect of these organizational pressures towards conformity and uniformity is that individual ethical responsibility is squeezed out of the organization. Ethics means doing what one feels to be right, not what may be profitable, what everyone else is doing, or what your boss or shareholders may want you to do. Organization and its leaders thus work, consciously or otherwise, to eradicate this unpredictable and disruptive ethics from the organization – to stop organizational members from feeling and acting upon individual moral judgements about their and others' organizational behaviour.

An example of such eradication of individual moral responsibility at work could be seen in the fact that we tend to apply different standards to behaviour at work versus behaviour outside of work. For instance, while none of us would probably consider attempting to take from a stranger on the street their wages, their car and their job, we might well, as managers, follow an instruction to make some employees redundant resulting in the same effects. And while taking these things from a stranger would be outlawed as immoral, taking them from an 'employee', as actually happens in an organizational context and in an organized way, is typically not viewed in the same way. So we see here precisely what Bauman is alluding to, the same act is removed from ethical accountability because it happens to take place in an organization. The ultimate message to be drawn from examples like this is, argues Bauman, 'that the organization as a whole is an instrument to obliterate responsibility' (Bauman, 1989, p. 163).

The implications of this argument for how we should understand business ethics are profound. By promoting the idea that management should take responsibility for deciding and enforcing 'ethics', business ethics can be argued to be further *removing* ethical responsibility from individual organizational members. This explanation of Bauman's might help explain how modern organizations, populated with thoughtful and educated people who may well act perfectly morally outside of work have, and continue to, perpetrate unethical behaviour at work.

From the above, rather than promoting the idea of 'obedient' organizational members following rules laid down by management, as mainstream business ethics does, perhaps we need to question such obedience and search for ethics instead in acts of *disobedience* and *dissent*. We turn to critical contributions on this issue next.

Thinkpoint 14.7

Power versus freedom and ethics?

- Explain Bauman's argument that making more rules for organizational members to follow can encourage less personally responsible behaviour.

- What is the relationship between power, freedom, and ethics suggested in Bauman's writing?

Questioning the ethics of obedience   A variety of ethical frameworks can be used to argue that one person's (e.g. an employee's) subordination to another (e.g. a manager) is unethical. For instance, it could be argued that employees' subordination is a breach of Kant's categorical imperative that states that a person cannot be used merely as a means by any other person. Alternatively, MacIntyre (1981) has argued that management can never be considered ethically virtuous because the concept and practice of management is manipulative. Management is about manipulating employees to do what they otherwise may not want to do (see Chapters 2 and 6; Roberts, 1984, also makes this argument very well). However, perhaps the most powerful critiques of the ethics of employees' subordination can be seen in Marxist critiques of capitalist working relations.

For Karl Marx what makes human beings unique is our potentiality and creativity. Through our collective effort (our labour) we transform ourselves, each other and the world around us. We fashion it according to our own designs and conscious intentions. However, under conditions of work in capitalist societies, many of us do not experience this human potentiality – even though our societies pride themselves on their 'freedom' and 'opportunity' and 'justice'. Our labour is bought by owners of corporations to service their need for profit. People are dehumanized, reduced to the status of things (e.g. 'human resources'), merely another factor of production to be used and exploited. Because of historical inequalities most people have to sell their labour for wages. Employees' labour then comes to seem like an alien thing to them, something owned by another. Work becomes resented – it turns into 'alienated labour' (Marx, 1844).

To help understand the concept of alienation, imagine some task either at home, work or at university that you really resented having to do – say a hated assignment for a course that you could not see the point of. Now imagine having to do such personally meaningless and hated tasks for the rest of your working life: this would start to give you an idea of Marx's concept of alienation at work.

As the group with a vested interest in ending their own alienation and exploitation, Marxism identifies employees as those most likely to act to challenge these dehumanizing workplaces. However, this group is routinely excluded from the decision-making processes in organizations, with such processes reserved for management. Therefore, Marxists focus upon employee resistance to management control as a potentially ethical and desirable act. Employee resistance is seen as employees' more or less conscious and strategic attempts to end their alienation and exploitation. This understanding of employee resistance as ethical is in direct contrast to the mainstream business ethics field that promotes increased managerial control as the only route to ethical renewal in organizations.

To illustrate the usefulness of this critical understanding of the ethical nature of workplace resistance, let's return to Richardson and Curwen's (1995) article 'Do Free Market Governments Create Crisis-Ridden Societies?' presented above. You will remember that this article was concerned with exploring the reasons behind two UK fatal disasters, the Kings Cross underground fire and the *Herald of Free Enterprise* ferry disaster. Throughout their paper the authors criticized top management as contributing to both disasters. Despite this the authors only identify *management* within the organization as providing any solution to such problems.

Drawing upon a critical understanding of the ethics of employee resistance, we can arrive at a less illogical solution. Taking the ferry disaster as an example, the investigation into this disaster discovered that it was caused because of the practice of ferries leaving port with bow doors open to save time on ferry turnaround and thereby maximize revenue. In this disaster 38 crew-members lost their lives, and many more were injured. All of these employees on board the ferry clearly had an acute vested interest in the safety and security of the ship their lives depended upon. An obvious conclusion from these facts would seem to be that if we are looking for a solution to improving workplace conditions and health and safety, we should be promoting employee resistance to such unethical and unsafe managerial demands. For example, by encouraging strong unions capable of voicing employee concerns, protecting them from victimization and generally exposing practices that put profit before people. This would seem to make more sense than, as the authors do, merely asking distant senior managers to develop a 'wider belief base', or indeed to write an ethical policy.

Thinkpoint 14.8

Inequality, power and ethics

- What is 'alienation' and why might employee resistance be seen as an ethical response to this?
- Your answer might illustrate the way that power even in a Marxist analysis does not just operate in one direction – i.e. *from* the powerful, *on* the powerless. Employee resistance demonstrates that employers are reliant upon employees behaving in productive ways. Once employees start resisting and not behaving in these expected ways, the workplace can be quickly transformed into a very difficult place to manage.

Questioning the corporate takeover of ethics From the above, we have an image of ethics as something that could and should be radical. We have an ethics that can be drawn upon to fundamentally question, for instance, the basis of management authority; the modern organizational form; and the basis of the capitalist economic system's promotion of local and global inequality. Understanding ethics as informing such wide-ranging critiques, how would critical approaches read the emergence of mainstream business ethics and corporate social responsibility? Perhaps the description that would fit best would be the 'corporate takeover of ethics'. Business ethics would be regarded as ethics made safe for business, where ethics is reduced to a corporate image exercise in support of the business drive for profits (see e.g. Parker, 2002).

By engaging in a few high-profile charity causes, producing some glossy ethical statements, or marketing themselves alongside images of smiling children, happy communities or green fields, business can apparently become wholesome and safe. For instance, giant fast food organizations according to their critics (e.g. Ritzer, 1993; www.mcspotlight.org) are complicit in reproducing health damaging obesity, environmental destruction and the rise in poorly paid, temporary 'McJobs'. However these organizations publicly project a very different image by linking themselves with children's charities and images of happy communities and families. We find, in short, ethics reduced to being just another resource that business can exploit to ward of criticism and/or attract the hapless consumer. This last point is illustrated well with a recent example from one of the world's largest defence (arms and weapons) contractors, Boeing (see Box 14.2).

Box 14.2: 'Boeing sacks finance chief in ethics row'

'Boeing, America's second largest defence contractor, yesterday dismissed Mike Sears, its chief financial officer, for unethical conduct in the hiring of a senior Pentagon official to run a $20bn (£11.8bn) refueling contract for the United States air force.

The aerospace group admitted that Mr Sears had violated company policy by communicating with Darleen Druyun about her future employment when she was still acting in her official government capacity on matters involving Boeing.

Ms Druyun – in effect head of air force procurement before joining Boeing as deputy head of its missile defence division – and Mr Sears covered this up, an internal investigation found. Ms Druyun was also dismissed . . . .

Mr Sears, who joined McDonnel Douglas in 1969, becoming head of its aerospace business in advance of Boeing's takeover in 1997, was widely tipped to succeed Phil Condit as chief executive when he steps down in 2006 . . . .

Mr Condit said "compelling evidence" of misconduct by Mr Sears and Ms Druyun had come to light "over the last two weeks", leading the board to order their dismissal . . . .

In July Boeing called in a former senator, Warren Rudman, from a prominent law firm to review its ethics programme and set up an office of internal governance. His work has now been extended to cover the hiring of government employees.

"Boeing must and will live by the highest standards of ethical conduct in every aspect of our business," Mr Condit said. "When we determine there have been violations of our standards we will act swiftly to address them."'

Source: David Gow, *The Guardian*, 25 November 25 2003, p. 17. © Guardian Newspaper Limited 1992.

In this example we might have expected a business that deals in the means to cause others' deaths to have some qualms about using a discourse of 'ethics' to describe its business. Not so. For critics of business ethics one possible reason why chief executive, Mr. Condit, finds the language of ethics so safe to use would be precisely because the field has functioned to bleach ethics of much of its critical potential. Instead of questioning business in general, business ethics has shied away from a serious analysis of the 'big picture', in favour of a blanket acceptance of capitalist society and the single-minded search for profit. The discourse of business ethics does not require Boeing to question the deadly business it is profiting from. Instead, ethics has been reduced to the much safer and much narrower question of whether its self-defined 'ethical' codes on recruitment have been followed. Instead of a serious, radical ethical critique of the nature of business in general, business ethics instead too often focuses upon local, specific and comparatively minor issues. This means, as Parker (2002, p. 98) argues, that: ' . . . business ethics is rarely utopian, or even moderately ambitious in its aims . . . if so little is expected, then perhaps little is likely to be achieved.'

This last point of Parker's is illustrated well by rereading Arnold and Bowie's (2003) business ethics paper critiquing the ethics of multinational corporations' use of sweatshop labour. This article (explored earlier) made a powerful ethical critique of the dangerous and exploitative conditions under which employees subcontracting for MNCs work. A radical critique of the ethics of such practices would likely lead one to question more generally the ethics of capitalism that promoted such disregard for the value of human life in the search for profits. However, Arnold and Bowie's paper, limited by its uncritical acceptance of the profit motive, does not argue for the above. Instead they merely ask that: 'MNEs and their contractors adhere to *local* labour laws, refrain from coercion, meet *minimum* safety standards, and provide a living wage for employees' (Arnold and Bowie, 2003, p. 222, emphasis added).

Critics of business ethics might suggest that we could be justified in feeling more than a little disappointed that an 'ethical' critique of such exploitative contemporary business practices ends by asking for so little. This last point is picked up in the following section, where we revisit the case study of the 'ethical' organization, Telebank PLC, showing what, for those critical of business ethics, would be the shallowness of the bank's ethical claims.

Key issues and controversies

Questioning Telebank PLC as an ethical organization The first of the critical approaches introduced above drew upon the work of Bauman. Bauman argued that organization exists by eradicating unproductive and unpredictable behaviour by its members, and especially such behaviour arising from employees' ethical sentiments. But how can we reconcile this argument with an organization such as Telebank PLC, which is celebrated for having explicit ethical commitments?

A critical reading of Telebank PLC might highlight how the bank's ethical policy functions as a controlling device. By taking the monopoly right to construct the bank's ethical policy, Telebank management can be understood to be taking this right *from* other organizational members. If others' concerns do not figure in what the bank's management has already defined as the ethical policy they are implicitly not a matter of ethics. The implications of these points can be seen in the history of Telebank's successful reinvention in the 1990s. Telebank PLC is celebrated for only *one* of its strategies in the 1990s: the publication of its ethical policy. However, if we return to Case study 14.1 we can see that its other major strategy at the time was a dramatic cost-cutting exercise:

> First, like many of the other banks, it cut costs. It rapidly shed over 1000 employees, closed branches, dramatically cut staff numbers in its branches (typically from 40 to eight), and rerouted most of its contact with customers from over-the-counter face-to-face to telephone banking via remote call-centres.

By taking control of what constitutes 'ethics', Telebank management effectively cast these redundancies as *not* an ethical issue. These redundancies, with their potentially devastating personal and social implications, are represented simply as a *financial* business decision. Returning to Bauman's arguments, we can see how this 'ethical organization' has effectively rendered redundancy outside of ethical discourse. As we will see below, this process of eradicating or removing issues from the status of ethics has occurred not only with the issue of redundancy at Telebank PLC. Other issues relating to conditions of employment are similarly absent from the organization's ethical policy.

Thinkpoint 14.9

Inequality, insecurity and ethics

- Do you think that redundancy should be regarded as an ethical, rather than a merely financial or legal issue? Why/Why not?

- Try to vividly imagine yourself in each of the following situations, and think whether your answer to the above question might have changed as a result:

  (a) Imagine that a member of your family was being made redundant.

  (b) Imagine that your job is to present before the board of directors the figures explaining the need for redundancies.

- Reflecting upon your answer to (a) and (b) above, can you see how our *closeness* to the effects of an action can change how we think about it ethically. It is very likely, for instance, that those who are made redundant and will experience the inequality of not having a job immediately and personally will understand redundancy as an acutely (un)ethical issue and not merely a financial decision. Whereas it is likely that those who get no closer to redundancy than providing some figures on corporate profitability may not experience the subsequent redundancies of people they may never meet as an ethical issue at all.

Questioning the ethics of obedience The second of the critical approaches to ethics and organization (introduced above) drew upon the writings of Marx. We saw how Marx's writings could be used to argue that one person's subordination to, and exploitation by, another is itself an ethical problem – it dehumanizes and alienates. Applying this critical ethical approach to the Telebank PLC case provides an unsettling and important reinterpretation.

The initial redundancies of 1000 employees can of course be critiqued as 'alienating' these employees from their productive human potential. Indeed there is perhaps little that can be regarded as more alienating in this respect than removing from people their ability to labour. However, oppressive and alienating relationships extend to those employees who remained in employment at the bank. We know from the case study that, in addition to the redundancies, many of the remaining employees were relocated in the bank's remote telephone banking call-centres. These types of organization have been criticized as oppressive places to work.

Call-centres are typically organized as large open-plan offices, where employees are permanently linked into a telephone and computer system that automatically distributes customers' calls to waiting staff. Staff have performance targets based upon number of calls answered per shift but little control over the automatic computerized allocation of their work. The work is high pressured and highly paced but routine, boring and repetitive. There is little chance for conversations and interaction among staff, so the social relationships that historically have been so important to quality of working life are damaged. There is little chance to interact with customers. The nature of the targets, the impersonal telephone service, and the lack of face-to-face interactions means that 'conversations' with individual customers typically last no more than a minute.

The chances for career progression are very limited, and salaries are not high. Timing on all of an employee's work (the number of calls they take, length of calls, actions between calls, time on breaks, time in the toilet, etc.) is recorded in the minutest detail by a central computer. Management can, at any time, examine each employee's statistics and make judgements about their performance, judgements that are linked to pay and/or discipline. Telebank staff have been seen to be crying at their desk after returning to work following holidays because of their intense dislike for the nature of the work. So notorious has the quality of working life at call-centres become that they have been described by some journalists and academics as the modern day equivalent of 'dark satanic mills' (Wylie, 1997).

For employees to experience their work so negatively, as so alien to their desires, and as so deadening of their potential, raises many ethical concerns about the nature of the work in Telebank's call-centres. For Telebank management, however, the working conditions were seen to be cost-effective – and matters of ethics just did not seem to figure. In fact, not one of the bank's celebrated 12 ethical commitments relates to the conditions their staff are required to work under. This indication of where management's priorities lie also lends weight to the suggestion of the critical writers that it is to employee resistance, rather than management largesse, that we should look if we wish to see such ethically questionable employment practices challenged. Indeed, an example of just this was when part-time Telebank employee, 'Sharon', refused to meet the target number of calls set by her manager, arguing that: 'If you pick up the phone 100 times a day and cut them off that's ok with the department manager. I'm at odds with him over targets, it's not good customer service. I've got a target of 40 calls but I don't care – I do the job as I think it should be done, we are here to help people' (Telebank employee 'Sharon', quoted in Wray-Bliss, 2001, p. 44).

Questioning the corporate takeover of ethics In Case study 14.1 I showed how Telebank PLC was rebranded as an ethical business. Through developing and publicizing a 12-point ethical policy and combining this with a profitable business, Telebank has become one of the hottest ethical business brands. The above critiques demonstrate how a business such as Telebank can gain this 'ethical' brand status despite serious questions that could be asked about shortcomings in its 'ethical' business practice. In particular, it has been argued here that it is often in the area of employment conditions that the contemporary business ethics discourse is most short-sighted. That so many redundancies and poor working conditions apparently do not affect a corporation's ability to brand itself as ethical can be seen to indicate just how successfully business has been able to take over the issue of ethics at work. What must be remembered from the Telebank case, and from similar celebrated ethical organizations, is that such organizations have not only deflected widespread public critical ethical scrutiny of such employment practices. More than this, they have been so successful in controlling what gets seen as an 'ethical' issue at work that they actually profit from the image of having the highest

Image 14.3 A call-centre

SOURCE: © SHERWIN CRASTO/REUTERS/CORBIS

ethical standards. For some critics, not only has business ethics removed its radical teeth, it is in danger of turning ethics into a lap dog of business (Neimark, 1995; Parker, 2002).

Important studies within the critical approach

In contrast to the often toothless nature of mainstream business ethics texts, the selection of articles in this section illustrate and emphasize the power and significance of critical approaches to ethics at work.

In her (1995) article 'The Selling of Ethics: The Ethics of Business Meets the Business of Ethics', Marilyn Neimark critiques mainstream business ethics, both in theory and in practice. Neimark draws upon the example of the multinational shoe-ware manufacturer 'Stride Rite' that sells its products under the registered trademark brands of Keds, Grasshoppers and Tommy Hilfiger Footwear. Like Telebank PLC, Stride Rite is celebrated for its ethical and socially responsible business practices, winning 14 social responsibility awards in the early 1990s. An example of the company's socially responsible policies published on its corporate website is paraphrased in Box 14.3.

However, also like Telebank PLC, Neimark argues that behind the public eye Stride Rite engages in practices that have a far less convincing 'ethical' justification. Alongside its ethical sentiments and numerous awards, Stride Rite has closed down production plants in deprived areas in the United States and shifted production to low-wage overseas plants, mostly in Asia. In addition to the financial exploitation of impoverished Asian employees, we already know from studies such as Arnold and Bowie (2003) and Klein (2001) how appalling the conditions of work in low-cost overseas production facilities can be. The result of this cost cutting is that Stride Rite has made very healthy profits indeed. As a result, Neimark argues, it can afford to channel a small percentage of this profit into high-profile 'socially responsible' deeds, thereby creating an 'ethical' brand image.

The conclusion that Neimark draws from such examples is very interesting. She does not just argue that companies like Stride Rite are cynically manipulating an otherwise 'good' business ethics discourse. Rather, she concludes that Stride Rite's behaviour is *acceptable* within the business ethics discourse because Business Ethics endorses the profit maximizing, pro-business, free market agenda:

> Within that discourse there are no penalties for corporations like Stride Rite which, on the one hand, benefit from the positive public relations associated with doing good deeds and, on the other hand, act in ways that contribute to the increasing degradation and deformation of life in the USA and the exploitation of workers abroad.

For Neimark, business ethics does not represent the emergence of new ethical organizations or increased ethical scrutiny of business. Rather, as examples such as Stride Rite demonstrate, Business Ethics actually *deflects* such ethical scrutiny. Ultimately, business ethics risks turning ethics into just another resource to be cynically exploited in the construction of the corporate brand.

Neimark's article can be summarized as highlighting the danger of buying into corporations' claims to be 'ethical' and thereby failing to question their less well publicised profit-seeking behaviour. The next study highlights the dangers with business ethics' promotion of organizational members' obedience to managerial authority.

The (in)famous psychological experiments conducted by Stanley Milgram in the 1960s illustrate the importance of questioning authority (Milgram, 1974). Milgram and his colleagues explored the ethical limits of obedience to authority in the following way. They put up posters in a university asking for volunteers to take part in a study of 'memory and learning', for which the volunteers would receive a small payment for their time. People that responded to the advert were each given a time to turn up at a laboratory in the university. Here they were met by a scientist and another 'volunteer'. The scientist gave both volunteers their payment, and then proceeded to give them a brief background to the study, explaining that it was concerned with the effects of punishment upon learning. Both volunteers then drew lots, to see who would be the 'teacher' and who the 'learner'. The learner is then taken into another room, strapped into a chair, and electrodes places on both wrists. The teacher sees all this, before being taken to a separate room, from which s/he can hear but not see the learner. S/he is seated in front of an electric shock generating machine with switches ranging from 15 volts to 450 volts in 15-volt increments.

The teacher is told to read a list of word pairs into a microphone to the learner. Having read through the list, the teacher then starts with the first word and reads four possible pairs. If the learner gets the correct pair the teacher moves on to the next pair. If the learner gets it wrong they receive a shock and are told the correct answer. With every wrong answer the shock level increases. The scientist remains in the room with the teacher throughout the experiment and encourages them to continue where necessary.

There is, however, a catch. The teacher is a genuine naive subject – a volunteer such as you or I might be. However, the learner is not actually a volunteer, but a trained actor. They are not actually being shocked. The volunteer teacher does not know this, however, and hears an escalating series of protests from the learner as the 'shock' level rises. These protests range from a grunt of pain at a fairly low shock level, through to a demand to be released, an agonized scream, complaints of heart problems, through to absolute silence (presumed death). The point of the experiment is not, actually, to test memory and learning at all, but rather, to see how far ordinary people will proceed to administer pain to a protesting victim.

Thinkpoint 14.10

Before reading on!

- Imagine yourself in the position of being the 'teacher' and that experiment was being conducted at your own university or college. At what level do you think that you would have stopped giving what you believed to be electric shocks to the 'learner'?

- Would you have stopped at the first exclamation of pain? Or the first demand from the learner to stop? Perhaps the first agonized scream would have been enough for you? Or do you think that you would have continued past the point that you thought the learner was seriously hurt?

- Remember your answer, and you can compare it to the results of the experiment, next.

The result of these experiments was extremely disturbing. For far from disobeying the command at a very early stage, as *all* psychiatrists Milgram surveyed prior to the experiment predicted (and you probably indicated as your likely behaviour) most people continued administering shocks to the victim right to the end of the scale. As Milgram recorded:

> Many subjects will obey the experimenter no matter how vehement the pleading of the person being shocked, no matter how painful the shocks seem to be, and no matter how much the victim pleads to be let out. This was seen time and again in our studies and has been observed in several universities where the experiment was repeated. (*Milgram, 1974, p. 5*)

In short, the adult subjects of this experiment continued to 'shock' the victim, even though they thought they were seriously hurting, even killing, another person who was pleading to be released. Why might this have been the case? A possible explanation might be that perhaps the subjects were, for some reason, unaware or uncaring of the suffering and harm that the other person was apparently feeling. The extract in Box 14.4 from the transcript of just one of these experiments (picked up at the 315-volt stage) shows this not to be the case.

As we can tell from the extract, Fred was neither unaware nor uncaring about the pain he believed he was inflicting. He clearly wanted to stop the experiment, indeed on numerous occasions he said that he would not continue the experiment any further. And yet he did continue right to the end of the scale. He continued even to the point that he thought he had killed the man next door, as did many others. Why? For Milgram, the explanation lies in Fred's and the other subjects' acceptance *of the decisions of those in authority*: 'it is the extreme willingness of adults to go to almost any lengths on the command of authority that constitutes the chief finding of the study and the fact most urgently demanding explanation' (ibid., 1974, p. 5).

The Milgram experiments are a dramatic experimental illustration of the consequences of giving up control to a perceived legitimate authority. In the experiments the authority was a 'scientist' but it might have so easily been a 'manager' demanding unethical behaviour from a subordinate. From these experiments, Milgram draws a very powerful conclusion. He argues that far from endorsing obedience to authority as an unquestionable good (as the *managerialist assumptions* of mainstream organizational behaviour and business ethics texts leads them to do) we should question any organizational members' subordination to another's authority. In such obedience there is always the potential for a loss or abdication of ethical responsibility, and ultimately, the possibility for inhumanity.

Power, identity and ethics

- To reflect further on the implications of the Milgram experiments, imagine that you are employed in a job that you really like and have worked hard to get. Now imagine that your manager insists that you carry out a task you believe to be morally wrong, and won't listen to your protestations that you don't want to do it. Imagine that your family, your house mortgage payments, your children, perhaps your health premiums, not to mention your relationship with your boss, all rely upon you following this direct order.

- Just how bad would the task have to be before you disobeyed and risked everything? Would you really throw your job away over the first, small immoral act? Or would you wait until the act you were told to do was very wrong? Just when would you draw the line?

- Thinking about these questions, we can perhaps begin to see how, when illegal and immoral acts are perpetrated in organizational contexts the perpetrators so often proclaim that 'I am not responsible, I was just following orders'. In such protestations, individuals are separating off their sense of self, their ethical identity, from their actions. They put responsibility for their actions onto those in positions of power. This is a dangerous process. Zygmunt Bauman (1989) pursues these points in Chapter 6 of *Modernity and The Holocaust* when he uses the results of the Milgram experiments to help explain the very worst example of organized immorality ever perpetrated.

Box 14.4: Fred Prozi, Unemployed (transcript excerpt from Experiment 5) – from Milgram (1974, p.p. 73–76)

The subject is about 50 years old, dressed in a jacket but no tie; he has a good natured, if slightly dissolute appearance. He employs working-class grammar and strikes one as a rather ordinary fellow. He begins the experiment calmly but becomes increasingly tense as the experiment proceeds . . .

SUBJECT: I think something's happened to that fellow in there. I don't get no answer. He was hollering at less voltage. Can't you check in and see if he's all right, please?

EXPERIMENTER (*with same detached calm*): Not once we've started. Please continue, Teacher.

SUBJECT (*sits down, sighs deeply*): 'Cool – day, shade, water, paint.' Answer, please. Are you all right in there? Are you all right?

EXPERIMENTER: Please continue, Teacher. Continue please. (*Subject pushes lever*)

SUBJECT: (*swivelling around in his chair*): Something's happened to that man in there. (*Swivelling back*) Next one. 'Low – dollar, necklace, moon, paint.' (*Turning around again*) Something's happened to that man in there. You better check in on him sir. He won't answer or nothing.

EXPERIMENTER: Continue. Go on, please.

SUBJECT: You accept all responsibility?

EXPERIMENTER: The responsibility is mine. Correct. Please go on. (*Subject returns to list, starts running through words as rapidly as he can read them, works through to 450 volts*)

SUBJECT: That's that.

EXPERIMENTER: Continue using the 450 volt switch for each wrong answer. Continue please.

SUBJECT: But I don't get no anything!

EXPERIMENTER: Please continue. The next word is 'white'.

SUBJECT: Don't you think you should look in on him, please?

EXPERIMENTER: Not once we've started the experiment.

SUBJECT: But what if something has happened to the man?

EXPERIMENTER: The experiment requires that you continue. Go on, please.

SUBJECT: Don't the man's health mean anything?

EXPERIMENTER: Whether the learner likes it or not . . .

SUBJECT: What if he's dead in there? (*Gestures towards the room with the electric chair*) I mean, he told me he can't stand the shock, sir. I don't mean to be rude, but I think you should look in on him. All you have to do is look in on him. All you have to do is look in the door. I don't get no answer, no noise. Something might have happened to the gentleman in there, sir.

EXPERIMENTER: We must continue, go on please.

SUBJECT: You mean keep giving him what? 450 volts, what he's got now?

EXPERIMENTER: That's correct. Continue. The next word is 'white'.

SUBJECT (*now at a furious pace*) 'White – cloud, horse, rock, house'. Answer please. The answer is 'horse'. 450 volts (*Administers shock*) Next word, 'Bag – paint, music, clown, girl'. The answer is 'paint'. 450 volts (*Administers shock*) Next word is 'Short – sentence, movie . . .'

EXPERIMENTER: excuse me, Teacher. We'll have to discontinue the experiment.

Contrary, therefore, to the business ethics field's practice of giving management sole moral authority to define ethical policies to which other organizational members should obey, we should look towards organizational members' *disobedience* as an ethical imperative. If only Fred Prozi, and all those others in the experiment like him, had simply *refused* to shock the protesting victim we could be far more confident that unethical acts are not being perpetrated as a result of organizational chains of command. The final critical article introduced here draws these points out strongly.

In their (1994) article, 'Whistle-blowing as Resistance in Modern Work Organizations', Joyce Rothschild and Terance Miethe demonstrate the importance of employee whistle-blowing in challenging unethical organizational practices. They define whistle-blowing as an organizational member's 'disclosure of illegal, unethical or harmful practices in the workplace to parties who might take action' (ibid., p. 254).

Whistle-blowers tend to be well-respected and conscientious employees. They tend to believe that once they have informed the appropriate managerial authority of these illegal or unethical acts the organization will take the appropriate measures to change its behaviour. In reality, what whistle-blowers often experience is that the organization's management do not see whistle-blowing as an act of good organizational citizenship. Instead, management tend to see the whistle-blower as a trouble-maker, as a potentially dangerous and unpredictable organizational maverick, or just plain crazy. The result too often is that rather than investigating the unethical practices brought to their attention, management investigates the whistle-blowing employee. The whistle-blower is disciplined, victimized or even dismissed. Undoubtedly, some who experience this unexpected victimization may be bullied or frightened into silence. However, for others, the experience of being victimized reinforces a belief that management is morally corrupt. Some of these individuals go on to pursue the issue they raised with a stronger sense of moral purpose.

Rothschild and Miethe (1994) illustrate their study of whistle-blowers with empirical examples, such as that of 'Anne'. Anne, 37 years old, was grateful to be hired in the late 1990s as a casting operator for a company making rubber belts. Within just a few days of starting the job, Anne began to experience some strange physical reactions. However, she continued to work hard and got a special commendation from her supervisor as well as an expansion of her role to include training other employees. Only a few weeks later, however, Anne was experiencing worse physical symptoms, including burning in the nose and mouth, headaches and bone pain. She told her boss and said that she planned to send for the papers that should be displayed on the chemical drums they were using, which would give details of the nature of the chemicals in the drums. Her supervisor told her this was a good idea, but the next day she was dismissed. Anne refused to accept this treatment. She contacted other employees of the organization and found out they too had suffered similar health problems. She then contacted a local university. With their help Anne discovered that the company was exposing its workers, with no protective equipment or warning, to over 100 times the legal exposure to certain toxic chemicals, and further that it was dumping toxic waste illegally. As a result of her own short exposure, Anne now had tumours growing in her mouth, liver damage, her skull began to soften and she had irreversible lung damage. Despite these serious health effects, she continued to campaign to end the organization's unethical and illegal practices. She prepared a civil law suit against the company, provided witness testimony at a national level, and was interviewed by the national hard-hitting TV journalism program *60 minutes*. Rothschild and Miethe quote Anne:

> I felt so completely victimized by the company. I had been such a trusting person. When they hired me, I thought they had picked me because they could see that I was an intelligent and responsible person. Now I know that when they picked me they were picking out a person to murder.
> (*ibid. p. 263*)

Rothschild and Miethe (1994) argue that for whistle-blowers such as Anne, a clear sense of ethics emerges that is in stark contrast to that of the managers of the organization. To quote the authors:

> To a person (whistle-blowers) come to see themselves as strong and moral. They have developed an understanding of how greed and self-aggrandizement can result in deceptive practices, harmful products and fraudulent services being built into the fabric of many organizations. They feel free of the abuse and above it. (*ibid., p. 268*)

Whistle-blowers' 'disobedient' personal ethical integrity does not always mean that they are successful in changing organizational practices. Often the power and resources of the organization are just too vast for an individual, no matter how committed, to change. The conclusion that Rothschild and Miethe arrive at reflects this, and they call for more widespread and collective organizational resistance to unethical organizational practices. Rothschild and Miethe's work is thus in stark contrast to the endorsement of stronger managerial authority in mainstream business ethics texts. Rothschild and Miethe's research argues that if we wish to have organizations that perpetrate less illegal and more ethical practices, we must look to and support those who *challenge* and *resist* managerial authority.

Thinkpoint 14.12

Ethics and power

- Have you or someone close to you ever refused to do something you were instructed to do because you thought it was morally wrong?
- How difficult was it to refuse, and how did the person who told you to do it react to your refusal?
- What does your experience tell you about the relationship between ethics and power?

Rothschild and Miethe's research, alongside that of Milgram's experiments and Neimark's case study, demonstrate the significance of critical approaches to ethics and organizations. Such studies show that, despite some business ethicists' attempts to make ethics palatable and profitable for business, 'ethics' can still be drawn upon to call organizations to account for their exploitative, dangerous or oppressive practices. Critically informed ethical studies of organizational behaviour present a troubling and potentially radical challenge to unethical organizational practices.

Box 14.5: UK whistle-blowing legislation – 'The Public Interest Disclosure Act (PIDA) 1998

Following a number of high-profile organizational disasters including instances of the abuse of vulnerable people in some care homes and children's homes, the collapse of the Bank of Credit and Commerce International and the Clapham rail disaster, legislation was introduced in the United Kingdom to protect whistle-blowers from being victimized by their organization in the kind of ways described by Rothschild and Miethe (1994).

The legislation (PIDA 1998) makes it illegal to victimize or dismiss whistle-blowers where they raise genuine concerns about misconduct and malpractice, as long as certain conditions and procedures are followed. If a whistle-blower is victimized or dismissed as a result of his/her whistle-blowing they can take their case to an employment tribunal to seek compensation.

While clearly welcome, the actual usefulness and extent of this legislative protection must still be looked at critically. For instance, Dr David Kelly, the weapons expert and senior government adviser who whistle-blew on his concerns about the UK government's 'sexing-up' or misrepresentation of evidence for engaging in the 2003 war in Iraq, seemed to

be very poorly protected by this legislation. Dr Kelly's name was given to journalists by government representatives, and a number of attempts were made by ministers to discredit him in the public perception by presenting him as paranoid and a fantasist. Dr Kelly committed suicide after these events, forcing a governmental inquiry. In addition to Dr Kelly's tragic case there have also been a number of other high-profile cases in the United Kingdom in recent years where senior professionals who have blown the whistle on practices ranging from child abuse, to medical malpractice (including the retention of dead children's organs without the parents' permission). Several of these people also seem to have been victimized and/or dismissed by their employing organizations despite the 'protection' of this legislation.

Such cases perhaps serve to illustrate again the argument that formal ethical 'rules' (including laws and/or company policies on whistle-blowing) do not take away the need for our continual ethical scrutiny of organizational behaviour.

For a comprehensive international review of whistle-blowing, see Drew (2003) at www.psiru.org.

Contribution and limitations of the critical approach to thinking about the field

Critical approaches to business ethics enable us to look again, and more deeply, at the ethics of business. Unlike mainstream business ethics, critical approaches are not tied to justifying their critiques in terms of what is profitable, comfortable or even necessarily sympathetic to business interests and managerial authority. Critical approaches enable us to understand that the consequences of and conditions of work are far from wholly positive or benign. They remind us that exploitation, oppression, abuse and rampant inequality abound in the contemporary business world. Critical approaches help us realize that management and other organizational participants can often have different, even contradictory, agendas and interests. They remind us that management practices are not necessarily those that lead to the most ethical outcome.

Critical approaches help us to reclaim 'ethics' as a language that can legitimize organizational members' right to radically question organizational behaviour. Overall, critical approaches help us to realize that ethical issues at work are far deeper, and more immediately pressing, than those contained within an organization's glossy 'mission statement' or 'code of ethics'. But, perhaps most importantly of all, critical approaches can help us reflect more deeply upon our *own* behaviour within, and assumptions about, organizations.

A limitation of some critical approaches is that, perhaps because they do not merely reproduce more widely accepted mainstream knowledge about organizations, they can sometimes seem abstract and distant from the lived-experience of working in organizations. Indeed, critical writers do not always help themselves in this regard, with academic critics of organization sometimes seeming to prefer the company of dusty old books and long-dead philosophers than the problems facing working people in today's organizations. As a result, you might find that some critical writing on organization needs to be persevered with – it may take some time to understand the densely packed arguments and concepts used. Persevere though, and your thinking about ethics and organization may be deepened, and changed, forever.

Thinkpoint 14.13

Power versus ethics?

- Why would critical writers see management control as ethically problematic?
- Why might 'corporate social responsibility' be viewed suspiciously from a critical perspective?

Conclusion

In this chapter we have explored the topic of ethics at work in a number of ways. In the first part of the chapter we examined the rise of business ethics as an academic subject area alongside the modern corporation's claim to be 'socially responsible'. We have unpicked these concepts and highlighted key assumptions upon which they have been built. These included assumptions that business and organization are generally ethical; that managerial authority is good; and that ethics and profits are compatible rather than contradictory.

In the second part of the chapter we saw how critical approaches to ethics at work enabled us to re-examine each of these assumptions. Through this critical lens we saw how, because it promotes and relies upon organizational members' conformity, organization is dangerous for ethics; how employee resistance can reintroduce alternative ethical values into organization; and how critical approaches are trying to wrestle 'ethics' back from the brink of becoming just another part of the corporate brand.

So this is what the chapter has done, but why do I think it has been important to do this? As an introductory chapter to ethics at work, indeed as an introductory book on organizational behaviour, this text is unusual in dedicating much of its space to critical approaches. These critical approaches

532 Part III Emergent Issues

have been introduced not just to give you more 'theories' to think about and learn (even though we have done so!). Nor are they included simply because academics love to argue with each other (although we do!). Nor even are they included principally because critical writers think that mainstream authors have been guilty of presenting a selective picture of organizations (although this would certainly be argued by many!).

Rather, as I understand it, critical approaches exist and have been presented to you principally because they signify an *ethical questioning* of, and unease with, the values and effects of organization. As I said at the start of this chapter organizational behaviour affects all of us, every day. Organizations are powerful, and this power can be beautiful and it can be terrible. For critical writers especially, organization must accordingly always be judged on ethical and not just on financial criteria such as profitability or share dividends. Critical approaches attend to the ethics of organizational behaviour, and do so whether the specific topic is motivation, bureaucracy, corporate culture, technology or any of the other chapters in this book. Critical approaches are always underpinned by ethical questions. Questions such as:

- Whether, and how, organizations contribute to happiness or suffering?
- How should we judge this?
- Who is harmed and who is helped by organizational behaviour?
- Whose lives and values have we neglected in the way we study and run our organizations?

Finally, and most importantly, such ethical questions and doubts should be regarded as never once-and-for-all resolved. Organizations do not stop being powerful, and the ethical questions about work and organization do not therefore come to an end either.

Discussion questions

1 Outline how mainstream business ethics overcomes the three problems of 'relevance', 'conscience', and 'translation' faced when trying to argue for a greater role for ethics in business.

2 Does the rise of interest in business ethics and corporate social responsibility mean that business is becoming more ethical? Answer this question first from a mainstream and then from a critical perspective.

3 From a mainstream perspective, can ethics be managed? And if so, how?

4 From a critical perspective, what is dangerous with the idea of trying to manage ethics?

Further reading

- Beauchamp, T. and Bowie, N. (eds.) (2001) *Ethical Theory and Business*, sixth edition, London: Prentice Hall. (Edited book. Includes a wealth of classic and contemporary writings on most mainstream aspects of business ethics.)
- Crane, A. and Matten, D. (2004) *Business Ethics: A European Perspective*, Oxford: Oxford University Press. (A thorough and sympathetic review of current thinking in business ethics.)
- Frederick, R. (ed.) (2002) *A Companion to Business Ethics*, Oxford: Blackwell. (Edited book of original articles. Mainly dealing with mainstream approaches, but with some critical work.)
- Jones, C., Parker, M. and Ten Bos, R. (2005) *For Business Ethics*, Oxford: Routledge. (An excellent critical discussion of business ethics.)
- Parker, M. (ed.) (1998) *Ethics and Organizations*, London: Sage. (Edited collection of critical writings on ethics and organizations. The first half reviews the main critical ethical approaches, while the second half critically explores a number of organizational practices. Not really written at an introductory level, but well worth persevering with.)
- Solomon, R. and Martin, C. (2004) *Above the Bottom Line*, third edition, London: Wadsworth Publishing. (Thoughtful textbook introduction to mainstream business ethics.)

Useful websites

- www.corpwatch.org (A website that pulls together critiques of contemporary business practice. A great resource for finding a wealth of unethical organizational behaviour.)
- www.McSpotlight.org (Similar to the above, with a strong focus on critiquing McDonald's restaurants in particular.)

References

Arnold, D. and Bowie, N. (2003) 'Sweatshops and respect for persons', *Business Ethics Quarterly* 13(2):221–242.

Axline, L. (1990) 'The bottom line on ethics', *Journal of Accounting* 170(6):87–91.

Bauman, Z. (1989) *Modernity and the Holocaust*, Oxford: Polity Press.

Bauman, Z. (1993) *Post-modern ethics*, Oxford: Blackwell.

Beaton, A. (2001) *The Little Book of Management Bollocks*, London: Pocket Books.

Beauchamp, T. and Bowie, N. (1997) 'Ethical theory and business practice', in T. Beauchamp and N. Bowie (eds.) *Ethical Theory and Business*, fifth edition, London: Prentice Hall.

Bowie, N. (1983) 'Changing the rules', in J. White (ed.) *Contemporary Moral Problems*, London: Wadsworth, p.p. 243–246.

Brewis, J. (1998) 'Who do you think you are? Feminism, work, ethics and Foucault', in M. Parker (ed.) *Ethics and Organizations*, London: Sage, p.p. 53–75.

Derry, R. (2002) 'Feminist theory and business ethics', in R. Frederick (ed.) *A Companion to Business Ethics*, Oxford: Blackwell.

Drew, K. (2003) *Whistle-blowing and Corruption: An Initial and Comparative Review*, Public Services International Research Unit (www.psiru.org).

Edwards, G. and Goodell, R. (1994) 'Business ethics', *Executive Excellence* 11(2):17–18.

Friedman, M. (1970) 'The social responsibility of business is to increase its profits', in J. White (ed.) (2000) *Contemporary Moral Problems*, London: Wadsworth, p.p. 233–238.

Gow, D. (2003) 'Boeing sacks finance chief in ethics row', *Guardian*, 25 November 2003:17.

Johnson, C. (1994) 'A free market view of business ethics', *Supervision*, 55(5):14–17.

Klein, N. (2001) *No Logo*, London: Flamingo.

Knights, D. and, Roberts, J. (1982) 'The power of organization or the organization of power?', *Organization Studies* 3(1):47–64.

MacIntyre, A. (1981) *After Virtue*, London: Duckworth.

MacLagan, P. (1998) *Management and Morality*, London: Sage.

Marx, K. (1844) *Alienated Labour* (ed. L. Simon, 1994) Cambridge: Hacket Publishing Company, Inc.

Milgram, S. (1974) *Obedience to Authority: An Experimental View*, London: Tavistock.

Neimark, M. (1995) 'The selling of ethics: The ethics of business meets the business of ethics', *Accounting, Auditing, and Accountability* 8(3):81–97.

Parker, M. (2002) *Against Management*, Cambridge: Polity.

Phillips, N. (1991) 'The sociology of knowledge: Towards an existential view of business ethics', *Journal of Business Ethics* 10:787–795.

Richardson, B. and Curwen, P. (1995) 'Do free-market governments create crisis-ridden societies?', *Journal of Business Ethics* 14:551–560.

Ritzer, G. (1993) *The McDonaldisation of Society*, Thousand Oaks, CA: Pine Forge.

Roberts, J. (1984) 'The moral character of management practice', *Journal of Management Studies* 21(3):287–302.

Rothschild, J. and Miethe, T. (1994) 'Whistle-blowing as resistance in modern work organizations', in M. Jermier, D. Knights and W. Nord (eds.) *Resistance and Power in Organizations*, London: Routledge, p.p. 252–273.

Snell, R. (2004) 'Managing ethically', in S. Linstead, L. Fulop and S. Lilley (eds.) *Management and Organisation: A Critical Text*, Basingstoke: Palgrave, p.p. 240–277.

White, J. (ed.) (2000) *Contemporary Moral Problems*, sixth edition, London: Wadsworth.

Willmott, H. (1998) 'Towards a new ethics? The contributions of poststructuralism and posthumanism', in M. Parker (ed.) *Ethics and Organizations*, London: Sage, p.p. 76–121.

Wray-Bliss, E. (1998) 'The politics and ethics of representing workers: An ethnography of telephone banking clerks' PhD Thesis, *Manchester School of Management*, UMIST, UK.

Wray-Bliss, E. (2001) 'Representing customer service: Telephones and texts', in A. Sturdy, I. Grugulis and H. Willmott (eds.) *Customer Service: Empowerment and Entrapment*, Basingstoke: Palgrave, p.p. 38–59.

Wray-Bliss, E. and Parker, M. (1998) 'Marxism, capitalism, and ethics', in M. Parker (ed.) *Ethics and Organizations*, London: Sage, p.p. 30–52.

Wylie, I. (1997) 'The human answering machine', *Guardian*, 26 July: 2–3.

Note

1 www.amnesty.org

Appendix: The Conceptual Framework

David Knights and Hugh Willmott

The theoretical framework for analysing management and organization in this book has been informed by six fundamental concepts: identity, knowledge, freedom, insecurity, power and inequality. In our view, these concepts offer a means of making sense of the complexity of social relations without involving excessive simplification, on the one hand, or student confusion and disorientation because of obscure jargon or difficult esoteric language, on the other.

As a concept, *identity* draws attention to the importance of who we are – a preoccupation that we believe is unique to the human species. Of course, we can never be entirely sure as to whether other animals (e.g. dolphins) share our '*freedom*' to attribute an identity to others and ourselves. However, we are the ones that put dolphins into (aquatic) circus roles rather than the other way around. So it seems that we exercise *power* over them rather than the reverse, although it can be argued that the way in which they capture our attention, and thereby receive some privileges relative to other, 'lesser' animals, means they do exercise some power over us. It only goes to show that power is a two-way relationship, but it is *we* who attribute 'captivating' qualities to dolphins and train them to repeat them on command rather than the dolphins developing a sales pitch in which they make us an offer we can't refuse. In the social world, power is largely about securing the consent or compliance of another person, group or even a collection of people, such as an organization or institution, to behave in a given way. Power is exercised only because those over whom it is exercised are free. If we could simply determine others to behave as we wish, there would not be a relationship of power but simply one of complete tyranny. The freedom that is a necessary condition of power relations, and which accounts for why everybody (even the lowest of subordinates) exercises some power, stems from our ability to reflect not only on what is outside of, but also on, ourselves – in short, our identities.

It is through our self-consciousness that we identify ourselves and are identified by others. Our actions are mediated by this *knowledge* of ourselves. Knowledge, as you are fully aware as students, is highly complex but it is grounded in the self-consciousness that makes us both free and concerned about our identities or how other people see us. The concern with how other people see us, however, is symptomatic of *insecurity* as we can rarely exercise sufficient power to make them see us how we would wish. Identity is always precarious. Think of some people who are generally considered or 'known' to be powerful – the President of the United States, for example. President Bush is repeatedly ridiculed for being a bit dumb; Clinton ended his Presidency in disgrace for his sexual antics, and President Reagan was viewed as a 'B'movie actor who had lost his marbles. We can never control how people see or 'know' us. So long as we are self-conscious and free, we will always suffer some insecurity about our identity. It can be argued that we often seek knowledge in order to address this insecurity. Not surprisingly, then, knowledge is widely considered to be of great value, but is perhaps most highly valued when it is perceived to have 'practical use' – which is generally understood to be useful for realizing our ambitions or allaying our fears.

Yet another source of our insecurity stems from the *inequality* between people, because, in addition to knowledge, material and symbolic wealth are highly valued. In earlier societies inequality was a function of birth since there was little social mobility. Today it is more a function of achievement (e.g. education or talent). This is not to say that the aristocratic past is completely dead – in the United Kingdom we still have a landed gentry epitomized by the Royal Family. In a capitalist society, those who have wealth can more easily make more wealth than those who have little. In the absence of government intervention to redistribute wealth, there is a polarization, which means some are extremely rich, and others extremely poor. Most of us end up in the middle and this is why there is not greater pressure to reduce inequality. Those not actually at the bottom of the hierarchy of wealth can feel a little less insecure, and even those at the bottom generally aspire to be a little higher up the ladder in order to occupy a more prestigious or dignified identity, rather than to tear it down.

Glossary

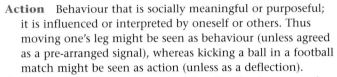

Action   Behaviour that is socially meaningful or purposeful; it is influenced or interpreted by oneself or others. Thus moving one's leg might be seen as behaviour (unless agreed as a pre-arranged signal), whereas kicking a ball in a football match might be seen as action (unless as a deflection).

Action-based   A concept used to describe the dynamics of organization. It assumes that political rule is dependent on the practices of organizational members and limited by the norms, values and foresight of informed actors.

Actor-network theory or analysis (ANT or ANA)   A theory that does not restrict action to that performed by humans but also involves non-human action as performed by material artefacts such as cars, phones or social institutions insofar as they and humans affect one another. Every technological device is dependent on a heterogeneous network, which supports the specific ways in which this device has been designed and used.

Agency   The sense of acting from an individual's own volition.

Alienation   Marx famously employed this concept to describe the experience of **labour** under capitalism; a condition in which individuals feel separated or estranged from some part of their existence (e.g. the product or process of their labour) because they are subjected to external controls.

Ambiguous figure system   The situation where the development of informal relations may clash with the formal hierarchy leading to considerable ambiguity as to who is responsible for what and/or to whom.

Anticipatory socialization   A process of learning to behave in ways appropriate to particular future roles, relationships or occupations. An example would be anticipating what is the expected behaviour of a student prior to leaving college.

Anxiety   Unlike fear, which has an identifiable source, anxiety has no specific object to which it responds. It is a *general* feeling of malaise or dis-ease for no particular reason, and indeed cannot be understood. In extreme form, it may be associated with **neurosis** or **psychosis**.

Apolitical   Absence of any acknowledgement of politics and power.

Appropriating   Taking possession of another's goods. Marx described it as legal theft since the law protected the capitalist when 'stealing' the surplus derived from labour, rather than returning it in the form of wages.

Ascribed   Behaviour that is imposed upon people by virtue of their position or role. In earlier societies roles were often ascribed at birth rather than achieved through demonstrating competence.

Asset specificity   Where an asset such as a skill, knowledge or machinery cannot easily be transferred to another organization and/or for which there are no ready substitutes.

Atomistic methodology   Approach to knowledge where complex 'reality' is broken down into simple 'components' that are then studied in abstraction from their natural habitat – in laboratories or other artificially constructed conditions. These components – or atoms – are then recombined to build ideal-typical models, which are then used to test, measure and intervene in the world.

Authority   Legitimate *right* to control, prohibit and judge the actions of others. It is when someone has the right to exercise power over you (e.g. tell you what to do) It is often distinguished from power, where there can be physical coercion or force, for that is based on 'might' not 'right'. Authority establishes rights recognized by subordinates as well as exercised by superiors.

Autocracy   A political regime or person that rules by tradition or coercion rather than consent, as might be expected in a democratic regime.

Barriers to entry   Corporate practices that develop or are deployed to deny or deter potential competitors entering the market.

Basic assumptions   A term used by Schein to refer to the origins of **values** and **cultural artefacts** in organizations. Basic assumptions are shared and deeply embedded presuppositions about issues such as whether human beings do or should live for the moment (immediate gratification) or see their activities as a means to a future end or goal (deferred gratification).

Binary   Division into two and only two opposites as in body/mind, female/male, black/white, positive/negative, true/false or the code of 0 and 1 in computing. Criticisms of this way of thinking, sometimes described as dualistic, argue that there are other alternatives that lie in between or beyond the two extremes.

Black box   Metaphorical term for describing something that need not be or never is investigated. It is as if to uncover what is inside the black box would destroy its benefits, much like discovering the sleight of hand of magicians undermines their mystique. The black box is often at the basis of **technological determinism**.

Boundary management   Strategies and actions intent on controlling the interface between different elements (or departments) within an organization.

Bounded rationality   Stipulates the existence of limitations in the human capacity to process information without resort to some arbitrary or non-rational selection. It suggests that these limitations restrict individuals to constructing simplified models that extract only the basic elements of a problem and thereby neglect its complexity.

Bourgeois   Critics of capitalism use this term to denote the privileged complacency of the relatively affluent middle classes.

Brainstorming   Involves people in a group exercising their creative skills to generate new ideas or innovations. The key aspect of it is that, in the early stages, all ideas put forward are considered valid and no criticism or selection is allowed until later on when ideas are evaluated.

Bureaucracy   Describes a form of business administration based on formal rational rules and procedures designed to govern work practices and organization activities through a hierarchical system of authority. Bureaucratic organization is often thought to be rigid, inflexible and overburdened by hierarchical rules sometimes pejoratively referred to as 'red tape'.

Business ethics   The academic study, and promotion, or the existence of, ethical practice in business.

Business process re-engineering (BPR)   An approach to organizational redesign that proposes that information technology should be the catalyst for revolutionary organizational change, leading to improved measures of performance in terms of costs, speed, quality and service.

Call-centres   Offices where staff are employed principally to process telephone calls with customers. Such centres involve heavily routinized and disciplined work processes where staff often work at very high levels of intensity and under conditions of technological surveillance and close monitoring.

Capital   In Marxist critical theory, capital is defined as assets (e.g. property, machines, money) used to finance the production of commodities for the private gain of the capitalist classes. Capitalists invest their capital in the production of commodities and accumlate profits by selling goods at a value exceeding the costs of their production.

Capitalist society   The dominant economic system around the world today. An economic system that concentrates the majority of wealth in private hands (capitalists) and requires the majority of people to sell their labour to secure a wage from this group.

Chain of command   Links within a hierarchy between the most senior and least senior of managers or supervisors.

Classical school   Writers who have focused on the formal organization of work. Classical theorists assume that an organization's structure formally unites organizational members into a well-integrated team dedicated to the pursuit of common goals.

Classify   Places ideas, phenomena, practices or events into categories that are then named. Most sciences begin by classifying the types of objects they study (e.g. types of plants in botany).

Cliques   Small exclusive group of friends and associates who constitute part of the **informal** structure of an organization.

Coalitions   **Informal** liaison between two or more interest groups intent on increasing their joint power and control with respect to another group or groups.

Co-determination   Form of influence predicated on the cooperation of parties with possibly opposing or competing interests in the pursuit of a mutual or common outcome.

Codified knowledge   A type of knowledge that has been written down or stored in a book or computer system, for example. It is therefore explicit, but might be better seen as information rather than knowledge.

Coercive power   Where compliance is achieved through the threat of withholding valued rewards.

Cognitive   Associated with thinking or mental processes such as perception; or traditional views of understanding such as those that are gained by reading or classroom learning.

Cognitivism   Psychological perspective on human behaviour that emphasizes the mental processes of thinking and perception rather than other influences such as the subconscious or social factors.

Colonized   Process where usually a larger, richer or more powerful unit (organization, country) takes control of a weaker one – as when, for example, in the 18th and 19th centuries, European states appropriated the wealth and labour of Africa, Far East Asia, the Indian subcontinent, Latin America and the New World.

Committee system   Where decisions are taken by committees rather than individuals – a situation that can lead to a proliferation of committees dominating the decision-making process of an organization.

Commodity   Something that can be exchanged for a price. While normally seen in terms of physical goods or services, the term is sometimes extended to human beings where they are treated, in a **dehumanized** manner, purely in terms of their economic value (price) as labour.

Common sense   What is assumed to be self-evident, obvious and fundamentally correct. It is often used to silence all alternative understandings on the basis that common sense is clearly and universally authoritative and dependable.

Communities of practice (COPs)   Refers to groups of people who interact (through meeting personally or electronically) and in so doing share knowledge and learn from each other through the interaction. Precise definitions vary, but emphasis is typically placed on the **informality** of such groups and interactions.

Competitive advantage   What is deemed to make an organization or nation more competitive or economically successful than another, such as access to important resources.

Conception   What characterizes human creativity is that it begins with a mental process of imagination or conception.

Consent   Wide-scale agreement relating to **authorities** and their decisions. For example, where production workers assent to, and approve of managerial strategies and mechanisms of work organization.

Content theories of motivation   These theories tried to identify the specific factors – individual needs, task factors, management styles – that shape individual motivation.

Contestability   Extent to which something can be disputed and debated.

Contextual embeddedness   Way in which any action on the part of, for example, managers or employees is ascribed different meaning and significance depending on the context in which it occurs. Highlights the historical and cultural conditioning (and relativity) of what may appear to be normal and natural.

Contingency approach   Way of analysing organizations so that rather than there being a single way of doing things, there are different ways depending (or 'contingent') upon different situations. For example, **technological determinists** believe that organizations have to adopt different structures depending upon the technology that they use.

Corporate social responsibility (CSR)   The practices and policies undertaken by organizations to promote the idea that they have concerns that extend beyond efficiency, performance, productivity and profit to embrace the public, customers, the environment and other stakeholders.

Critical structuralist Critical theory that identifies the political activity of organizations to be directly linked to the capitalist productive economy.

Cultural artefacts Phenomena accessible to the senses, including architecture, myths, rituals, logos, type of personnel employed and so on, which signify the **values** in an organization's culture.

Cultural barriers Are seen to prevent the transfer of ideas and practices because of differences in what is viewed as acceptable in different contexts.

Cultural differentiation Refers to differing sets of values, beliefs and norms, which co-exist in one organization. Also see **multiculturalism** and **subculture**.

Cultural engineering Attempt to change an organization's culture to accord with the interests or **values** of managers. It depends on a view that a 'culture is something that an organization has' rather than 'is'. If organizational relations are defined by culture, it is more difficult to impose a unified set of values, beliefs and norms that are designed to provide to impose a unified set of values, beliefs and norms that are designed to provide the basis for all organizational actions and decisions.

Cultural transmission mechanism (CTM) Techniques used by managers to build, maintain or change a particular organizational culture, to encourage employees to adopt specific values, beliefs and norms. Examples include **management by example (MBE)** and deliberately recruiting new staff who embody the desired culture.

Culture An anthropological term that refers to the shared values, beliefs and norms about key priorities and ways of undertaking particular tasks, or relating to colleagues among members of a particular organization.

Custom and practice Workplace behaviour that has been repeated over a lengthy period and is therefore routinely taken for granted.

Customer relationship management (CRM) A broad management approach that emphasizes the financial value of developing long-term relationships with and detailed knowledge of customers. For example, through the use of information systems databases, it is assumed that customers can be 'captured' so that customized goods and services may be targeted appropriately to them.

Death of distance View popularized by Cairncross, that, for the purposes of organizing, the importance of physical location and geographical distance is no longer a constraint because of the developments in information and communication technologies.

Decision objectives Aim/goal of a decision and the criteria through which outcomes can be evaluated.

Decision premises Structures and processes that constitute the apparatus of decision making. An example of a decision premise is the agenda for meetings. Control of this agenda can enable one to manipulate how a decision is approached.

Decision process Sequential processes and structures involved in the deliberation of a decision.

Decision theory School of thought that emphasizes the importance of constructing systematic procedures for approaching and solving problems.

Dehumanized A process by which human beings are treated like objects or things and thus their humanity is denied.

De-layering Reducing the number of levels in the hierarchy so as to have fewer managers.

Delegated The process of passing the responsibility to make management decisions down the **hierarchy** to those in less senior positions.

Dependency Indicates some degree of reliance upon others.

Deregulation of markets Process whereby greater competition is encouraged between commercial organizations through reducing regulations that previously restricted their behaviour or entry into certain markets.

Determinism View that there is an inevitable direction in which events move, as a result of some cause that is independent of the event. In organization studies and in everyday life, the idea that 'human nature' determines social arrangements is possibly the most common. See also **technological determinism**.

Dialectic of control Contested process whereby work and other activities are socially accomplished. Every activity is seen to involve an interdependence between diverse individuals and groups, such as managers and workers. While exercising differential power associated with their access to scarce and valued resources such as income, status and qualifications, none of these enjoy a monopoly of control. This is because each individual or group has a degree of dependence on the other.

Digital divide The term refers to the disparities between those who have access to the new information and communication technologies and those who do not – and who are therefore excluded from the 'brave' new digital economy. Research and debate on the subject typically focus on whether the social impact of computers reinforces or reduces existing social and economic inequalities.

Direct democracy System of collective decision making in which there is an opportunity for everyone to participate and influence how 'things' get done or are organized.

Direct management control Describes conditions where workers have little or no scope to decide how work is organized and conducted.

Dirty job A job that carries with it some form of social stigma and so may require its incumbents to reconcile this with their sense of themselves as 'decent' human beings. Examples include jobs that deal with literal dirt (e.g. refuse collection, lavatory cleaning) or involve what is regarded as morally problematic behaviour (e.g. prostitution, crime).

Discourse Often taken to mean the same as language or the spoken word and written text, but may also refer to a broad category of talk or text such as *managerial* discourse. Some approaches extend the meaning of the term to what is possible in a given context or era and to meaningful behaviour as well (discursive practices). Here, the term can be summarized as what can be said (and done).

Disembodied Analysis that relies purely on the cognitive aspects of human conduct, completely ignoring how bodily and emotional life is central to human existence.

Disintermediation Abandonment of intermediaries (e.g. wholesalers, retailers) that facilitate the distribution of goods and services so that producers trade directly with consumers. Mail order and internet trading represent common examples of disintermediation.

Dispositional factors   Internal personality aspects, traits and beliefs that are specific to each individual and may be seen to motivate a person to behave in a certain way. They are opposed to situational factors where the behaviour is due to factors or circumstances external to the individual.

Division of labour   The way that people divide up different tasks or jobs between one another to achieve greater levels of efficiency and productive output. Emile Durkheim (1947) argued that the division of labour was not only economically efficient but also socially effective in that it made clear how we are all dependent upon one another and this knowledge would help to generate social solidarity – a necessary condition of social survival.

Double-loop learning (DLL)   Involves highly reflective and creative actions that, through continuous feedback processes of self-learning, testing and exploration, facilitate organizational change. DLL is contrasted with single-loop learning (SLL), which is more incremental and mechanical and often likened to the role of a thermostat that regulates a domestic heating system in accordance with external temperatures.

Dysfunctions   Action, procedures and processes that impede or disrupt the ability of an entity to achieve its aims.

Economic deregulation   Part of the 'New Right' politics where there is an attempt to remove various restrictive practices on trade so as to open up companies to greater competition.

Elite   Selected group of presumably gifted or otherwise distinguished individuals.

Emancipatory   Political term associated with emancipation or freedom from control. An example is freedom from slavery, but freedom remains an important issue in other contexts, even where control may be less visible.

Empowerment   The distribution of power to people lower down the hierarchy so that they can feel a degree of autonomy and sense of personal identification in the decisions they make.

Entity   Something that exists as a solid or concrete thing. May refer to human institutions, such as organizations, as well as to objects.

Environment   What exists external to the organization, such as available technologies, markets and government.

Epistemology   Logic (*logos*) of knowledge (*episteme*). It is associated with the founding assumptions that make it possible to develop any kind of knowledge; and thereby it defines the methods and limits by which knowledge is constructed and advanced.

Equity theory   These ideas focus on the importance people attach to perceptions of fairness in how managers deal with them relative to others.

Esprit de corps   Positive morale – strong sense of belonging and purpose shared by a work group or organization.

Essence   That which is fundamental and unchanging in an 'object', situation or person and most commonly recognized in the phrase 'human nature' (see **determinism**). There is an assumption of some deep, inner essence that can be discovered and which defines the individual. Once an essence is attributed to an object, no further examination is seemingly required. That is why a phrase like human nature or commonsense gives the impression of providing the final and ultimate explanation of anything.

Ethnography   A form of study where the researcher lives and works as a member of the group being studied. It aims to provide an 'insider' account but, because it is conducted by a researcher, it has a degree of 'outsider' detachment. Ethnography developed from the techniques used by anthropologists to study what were often seen as exotic cultures or societies outside their own.

Experiential   Pertaining to direct experience rather than thought or imagination.

Exploitation   A process where people are used merely to further someone else's goals. In an economic context, 'exploitation' refers to using others for the purpose of creating a surplus that enables the exploiter to live without working or to supplement their income in this way.

Externalization   The process of creation through which what has been conceived in the mind comes to be embodied through work in an object.

Feminism   The theory and politics associated with critiques of society that make gender and the oppression of women as their central focus.

Flexibility   Systems of production and working arrangements that allow material and human resources to be utilized speedily to meet the fickle and fluctuating demands of the market and customer taste.

Flexible specialization   Approach to production and the organization of work that emphasizes the need for adaptation rather than repetition. Companies following this strategy simply transform their production regularly as there is a demand for more distinctive, customized products and services. **Flexibility** can come in the form of producing non-standard products for niche markets; varying the number of employees according to fluctuations in demand; and/or requiring employees to undertake multiple tasks.

Fordism   System of mass production based on hierarchical management control pioneered by Henry Ford during the early 20th century, adopted throughout most Western economies up until its decline in advanced capitalist economies in the 1970s when product differentiation and changing markets demanded more flexibility.

Functionalism   Theoretical model or framework that presumes organizational consensus and posits that activities continue to exist only because they perform the indispensable function of maintaining a coherent integration of the organization. Consensus is presumed to be the natural state of affairs and conflict pathological.

Globalization   Notion that countries are becoming economically, politically, technologically and culturally closer to each other. Examples of this process include the European Union, the internet and the worldwide popularity of branded products like Coca-Cola, Nike shoes and Mercedes cars.

Goal displacement   Occurs when the pursuit of a secondary or marginal objective assumes greater importance than the primary objective and/or when the means (e.g. complying with a procedure) becomes more important than the ends (e.g. attaining the objective).

Greedy institution   Coser's term for organizations that require unstinting effort and immense dedication from their employees.

Groupthink   Term used by Janis to refer to situations in which group make problematic decisions because individuals over-conform to the group ethos and fail to express personal doubts. There is comfort in groupthink in that the group as a whole feels protected given that the decision is collective, but silence is presumed to imply consent whereas it may signify a fear of resistance.

Headcount   Staff or employee numbers in an organization.

Hegemonic   Form of control that includes, if not focuses on, the control of people's values, their 'hearts and minds'. An example would be the instilling of a sense of respect for authority or for property rights or, more contemporaneously, a commitment to the organization. All these may help ensure that we do what we are supposed to do and want what we are supposed to want by those in authority such as employers and governments. This renders control through more overt reward or punishment (e.g. job loss) less necessary.

Hierarchy/Hierarchical levels   Positions in an organization associated with different levels of status, power and economic reward.

Hierarchy of needs   Maslow suggested that individual needs were organized in a hierarchy from physiological needs, to safety needs, to needs for love, affection and belonging, to esteem needs and finally at the top of the hierarchy the need for self-actualization.

Human capital   People or employees, as distinguished from other forms of (physical) capital, such as technology and buildings. It also suggests a particular, and restricted, view of people as economic assets.

Hybrid   Combination of two or more elements or characteristics that are normally separate.

Idealized picture   Description of a situation in a way that portrays only positive elements and it is cleansed of any negative aspects.

Idea-type   An ideal-type is the purest, most fully developed version of a particular thing (usually a concept). It does not mean that the thing itself is ideal. The ideal-type of a sadistic serial killer would be someone with all the characteristics of the cruelest mass murderer imaginable – but that does not mean that there is anything desirable about serial killers! It does not mean that the 'ideal' is good or bad. Instead it simply refers to an abstract, exaggerated image or a benchmark by which actual behaviour (e.g. the acts of an actual serial killer) can be assessed.

Ideology   A related set of ideas and beliefs held together by a set of values and sometimes used to justify particular political or sectional interests. A patriarchal ideology, for example, justifies male domination. However, definitions differ in the extent to which ideology is seen as reflecting or distorting the truth.

Idiographic approach to personality   An approach that is suspicious of the value of generalized 'scientific' categories of classification and thereby understands personality in the terms used by individuals to described themselves. It perceives individuals in terms of personal experience; their personality is learned through social and cultural interaction as opposed to biological or genetic determination.

Impersonal and disembodied   Relates to the way that our relations with one another can lack any sense of personal intimacy and be so instrumental and calculative or cerebral and cognitive (i.e. linked to powers of the intellect and logic) as to deny any bodily and emotional content.

Individualizing   The process through which people come to see themselves as separate from others and personally responsible for their actions and life chances rather than interdependent.

Informal or Informality   Behaviour that is not officially recognized or approved.

Inhibition   Inability to do or say something that one desires to say or do. There are numerous sources of inhibition from the fear of embarrassment of being wrong to the consequences of speaking your mind when in a position of subordination.

Innovation   The process of imaging something new in a given context (e.g. invention) combined with developing that idea into an applied form.

Institutional approach   A perspective that highlights the social shaping of activities at a broad level whereby institutions such as the state, education, professions and the church are seen to condition how things are done in a similar way within these contexts. Emphasis is placed on the importance of practices (such as managing employees) being seen as socially legitimate rather than necessarily technically efficient. When such practices and their legitimacy become taken for granted and established, they are said to be institutionalized.

Institutionalization   Process whereby people are fully integrated into an institution (repeated and routine practices) so as to rarely think to challenge them.

Instrumental rationality   Behaviour that is exclusively concerned with a self-interested end-result such that the end always justifies the means. It seeks the most efficient (i.e. high output/effort ratio) means to achieve a given end. The two terms often but need not go together to emphasize how the behaviour is single-minded in its 'technical' and non-emotional pursuit of specific goals.

Intangibles   Difficult or impossible to measure accurately yet remain important. For example, a new procedure or system might be seen to increase productivity or employee satisfaction, but the benefit is difficult to isolate and measure.

Integral   A necessary or inherent part of something.

Intellectual property rights (IPR)   A legal term referring to ownership of knowledge or ideas. For example, the copyright assigned to authors, editors or publishers means that others have to ask permission and, often, pay to reproduce material. Likewise, inventions might be patented.

Internalized   When an idea, norm or value is completely embedded in individual consciousness such that there is often an unawareness of its existence and influence on behaviour.

Interstices   That which exists in between two 'objects'.

Intersubjectivity   The existence of consensually shared ideas, values, beliefs and norms. Organizational **cultures** are a form of intersubjectivity.

Invoked   The drawing out, or encouraging, of some idea or action.

Isomorphic   A term associated with the **institutional approach** that means 'takes the same or a parallel form'. In particular, it refers to the ways in which organizations adopt the same practices as their peers in a given social context, because they are required to do so by **standard-setting bodies**, see it as 'best practice' or are uncertain of what to do and so copy others.

Japanization   Process of adopting practices associated with Japan. In particular, it refers to the adoption in the West of certain production practices such as team meetings based on quality improvements.

Job enrichment   Work arrangements that are designed to expand the number of tasks and roles workers perform to provide opportunities for them to gain greater satisfaction, reward, recognition and achievement.

Kaizen   This is the process of continuous improvement developed in the Japanese organization of work and then introduced as an important element in Western organizational designs, such as **total quality management**.

Knowledge diffusion   The spread of knowledge across contexts such as between organizational or national boundaries, as if knowledge acts like a gas. Recent challenges have been made to this traditional view such that knowledge does not exist independently, like a gas, but is produced and adapted or **translated** in context. See **contextual embeddedness**.

Knowledge-economy   One not based upon producing physical things but on using knowledge to deliver services. Consultancies like Universal, advertising agencies, software development houses, even universities are all examples of the knowledge economy. It is characterized by knowledge-intensive firms, knowledge-sectors and knowledge-workers.

Knowledge management   Process of capturing and codifying knowledge for management (e.g. profitable) purposes. It is often associated with information systems that store 'knowledge' in databases, but has become associated with the broader activity where management seek to **appropriate** the tacit as well as the explicit knowledge of their employees (see also **tacit skills**).

Labour   People or class people involved in the productive work, and can be distinguished from those who manage the processes of productive work.

Labourist   That which is seen to reflect, represent or celebrate the views of manual labour especially, but the working classes more generally.

Leakage   Used to refer to the **knowledge diffusion** where it was not intended, such as the loss of commercially sensitive information.

Lean production/manufacturing   System of production, first used in Japan, to maintain the smooth flow of production by using minimum resources to reduce cost, work in progress and other overheads. It is associated with just-in-time services and stock inventories where companies do not retain excess labour or stocks of goods but use information technology to ensure recruitment or reordering of stocks when actually needed.

Learning organization   Recent and managerially fashionable term to describe organizations that value collective and not just individual learning. May be reflected in more participative structures and a managerial emphasis on continuous learning (i.e. organizational improvement).

Learning styles   Variations in approaches to learning and the extent to which it is attributed to individual, cultural or other background differences, and subject to change.

Legacy systems   Old technology practices that have been superseded but still have to be serviced or managed since the cost and effort involved in merging all the data files and procedures to the new system is greater than the benefits of just allowing it to be 'run down' until extinct.

Legitimacy   Condition in which decisions or practices are widely acceptable to those whom they affect because there is broad level of consensus about the form or process of their adoption.

Liberal enlightenment   Belief in reason and rationality and generally supporting the freedom and autonomy of the individual.

Luddites   Name originally given to late 18th and early 19th century textile workers who, in defence of their livelihoods, set out to resist the mechanization of their trades. 'Luddite' is often employed as a term of abuse to describe those who attempt to stand in the way of 'progress'.

Management by example (MBE)   A symbolic leadership device, or **cultural transmission mechanism**, which involves managers embodying the values, beliefs and norms they wish employees to adopt in everything they say and do.

Management knowledge   Often associated with apparently discrete management ideas such as human resource management, but more generally linked to different types of knowledge used or possessed by management.

Managerialism or managerialist   Term applied by critical academics to describe the type of social science output that serves the objectives of managers, as these critics see them, rather than offering an independent or alternative perspective. Managerialism usually entails the idea that effective management is the solution to an array of socio-economic problems.

Marxism   Theory and politics associated with the writings of Karl Marx. The principal focus is a critique of the oppressive effects of social class in a capitalist economy.

Masculine discourses   Communication consciously or unconsciously reflects and reproduces a sense of being analytical and technical, and masterly and in control generated largely but not exclusively by men.

Mass production   The large-batch/mass assembly line/ conveyor belt systems of production, often referred to as Fordism because of its association with Henry Ford's production line.

Matrix   A form of organization where there are parallel lines of authority criss-crossing one another so that staff are accountable simultaneously to managers in a hierarchy and other specialists horizontally.

Mean production   Describes how critical theorists interpret lean production. They see it as having subtle controls and forms of surveillance over workers that result in work intensification.

Mechanistic organization   Similar to Weber's model of rational-legal bureaucracy. Includes a specialized division of labour within which each individual carries out an assigned and precisely defined task comparable to the discrete parts that comprise a machine. It is the opposite of **organic organization**.

Mentors   Those assigned the task of supporting others by providing advice and assistance to help in their personal and career development.

Mobilization of bias   Manipulation of decision-making premises, processes and objectives so as to ensure that a specific point of view or intention is supported.

Modernist   Label attached to a range of phenomena, including art and architecture. Here, it is a set of beliefs associated with the historical period of modernity. These beliefs value progress and include a faith in the rationality of science to discover truth and control nature. Things like ambiguity, chance, play, fun, unmanageability and multiple truths or rationalities (e.g. based on custom, religion, lifestyle) are denied or subjected to the scientific gaze in modernism. For example, emotion might be seen in terms of a quantitative measure of emotional intelligence. By contrast, such things are celebrated or brought to the foreground in what has come to be known as post-modernist views.

Monopoly   A market where only one supplier of a product or service exists. There is no competition and thus no other sources of the commodity, so the supplier is able to completely dominate the consumer. Also see **oligopolistic** and **oligopoly**.

Multiculturalism   In the organization studies context, another term for **cultural differentiation** or the existence of **subcultures** in an organization.

Multinational corporations   Very large corporations that have operations crossing multiple nations. Such corporations have been the focus of sustained criticism for the enormous economic and political power they wield.

Multi-skilling   Working arrangements in which workers acquire the full range of necessary skills required to perform a number of jobs, tasks and duties efficiently under minimum supervision.

Multi-tasking   Working arrangements where it is claimed that workers acquire the various skills needed to perform a number of jobs, tasks and duties.

Narcissism   Preoccupation with self-image, and with making the world enhance this image. In the ancient Greek myth, Narcissus became fixated with his mirror image as he saw it reflected in a pool of water.

Negotiated order   The idea that social reality is open to a degree of interpretation and mutual adjustment between actors (e.g. between members of a team or between a boss and a subordinate). This element of negotiability make possible a process of manoeuvring to influence other actors.

Neo-classical economics   A form of economics that emphasizes free markets and non-intervention by the state. It contrasts with the post-war consensus around Keynes's ideas of state intervention and public spending to maintain economic growth.

Neo-imperialism   Colonization other than by military force, typically associated with the spread of a particular dominant set of ideas such as religious beliefs or consumerism.

Network organization   Organizations which are not structured hierarchically but which make lateral connections, and connections across functions. Usually associated with claims of increased flexibility and often claimed to be modelled on 'Toyotaism' rather than Fordism.

Network society   A society composed of network organizations. More generally, a society in which there is a great deal of fluidity in social relations, multiple sources of information and multiple sources of authority, rather than fixed hierarchies and roles.

Neurosis   Unhealthy compulsion and attachment to routines or behaviour patterns that if taken away stimulate feelings of nervousness and anxiety.

Neutering   Rendering impotent or ineffective.

New Right   Political development or strategy popular in the final quarter of the 20th century where the 'free market' is advocated and state intervention stigmatized. New Right policies favoured the privatization of public sector corporations such as gas, electricity, the railways, etc.

Nomothetic approach (to personality)   Distinguished by the beliefs that there are underlying universals (e.g. of personality) against which everything and everyone can be measured and classified. Personality, for example, tends to be understood as an inherited phenomenon and one that is the product of biology, genetics and heredity. The nomothetic approach is based on large-scale quantitative and scientific study with the aim of discovering the mechanisms and 'laws' that explain human behaviour.

Non-participant observation   Method of research that observes the detailed activities of research subjects without participating directly in the experiences and tasks they perform.

Non-rigorous   Usually a pejorative term meaning the absence of in-depth analysis or systematic research procedures.

Normalize   A term to describe how discourses and practices are defined or perceived as proper and normal such that they become unquestioned; it serves to control or discipline individuals by transforming them into subjects that obey certain cultural or political norms or rules.

Normative   What is commonly accepted as normal and/or appropriate to an organization. Critical political analysis draws attention to the evaluation of behaviour using normative criteria, often the criteria favoured by supporters of the status quo (e.g. managers), as an exercise in classification and control. See **normative control**.

Normative control   Another term for the control of the 'hearts and minds' of employees. So when a manager or professional 'chooses', apparently from free will, to work through the night to complete a task because of values of being responsible, then s/he is being controlled, by being self-controlled.

Objectification   The end point of the creative process at which point what has been produced comes to have an independent existence in the world.

Objective   Free from bias, prejudice, judgement and emotion.

Oligopolistic   Market where a small number of very large suppliers of a product or service have removed the competition and are thereby able to dominate the consumer since there are few alternative sources of supply.

Oligopoly   The noun that describes the type of market discussed above.

One best way   Refers to anything that is regarded as the one solution for all organizational ills.

Ontology   Theories of reality; claims about the nature and contents of the natural and social worlds. It includes a concern with the nature of human existence or what it is to be human, so it is about our relationship to the world as a whole person, not just in terms of some aspect such as personality, motivation or attitudes.

Opportunism   Acting in one's own best interests regardless of others or any sense of wider social obligation or commitment.

Organic organization   An emphasis is placed on knowledge as a contributing resource rather than restricted to a specific job specification. There exists a continual adjustment to tasks as they become shaped by the nature of the problem rather than predefined. Opposite of **mechanistic organization**.

Organizational chart   Stylized but clear representation of the organization that may provide a basis for the analysis of decision-making processes.

Organizational politics   Label given to activities surrounding the competition between individuals, groups, units, departments or divisions for scarce rewards and resources within organizations. See also **negotiated order**.

Organization man   The term used to refer to a worker who is so committed to the organization that s/he automatically and perhaps even unconsciously prioritizes their job demands above what they themselves require or want.

Outsourcing   Business practice involving greater levels of intermediation (see **disintermediation**). Producers of goods and services establish contracts with other companies or specialists (e.g. payroll, web management, call-centres, or even distribution) to supply essential parts of their business. It has a long tradition stretching back to the early 19th century when producers bought their labour from contractors, but became less common in the 20th century, as companies directly employed their labour forces.

Panacea   This refers to a remedy that cures all complaints. Teamwork, for example, might be commended as a technology of work organization that solves all production problems from control, to productivity, to retention and commitment.

Paradox   Something that appears to be absurd, impossible or self-contradictory, but might be true.

Participant observation   Method of research originating in social anthropology where the researcher engages with the subjects of their study by attempting to live like them for some time.

Pathological   Derives from psychology or psychiatry to refer to mentally disturbed individuals. Emile Durkheim used the term 'social pathology' to describe a situation where individuals failed to see society as an objective reality, as discovered by the science of sociology, and thereby failed to see how their egoistic actions were destroying the very social fabric that is a necessary condition of civilized life. Managers tend to regard workers as pathological ('awkward', 'bloody-minded', 'uncooperative', etc.) when they fail to comply with the logic and reason of management.

Pathologized   See **pathological**.

Piece-work   Payment on the basis of what is produced rather than the time taken to produce it.

Pluralist   A recognition of diverse legitimate viewpoints, interests or approaches. A pluralist vision of organizational politics emphasizes the free interplay of interest groups as operating to check and balance the potentially authoritarian tendencies of governing bodies.

Political questions   These are characterized by an inquiry into how social relations are created, reproduced and charged.

Political structure   Balance of competing pressures from interest groups seeking to realize, or gain recognition of, their own particular concerns.

Political system   Boundaries, goals, values, administrative mechanisms and hierarchy of power, which constitutes a particular organization.

Politics of truth   Refers to the process of giving voice to ideas and voices that compete over what is taken to be accepted knowledge or **ideology**.

Positivism   Term used especially by critical analysts to identify a method of social science research in which the differences between the 'natural' phenomena of the physical sciences and human phenomena are downplayed. Positivists are those who presume, and or seek to emulate, the causal methods of the natural sciences. In doing so, they neglect the problems of meaning and interpretation, or how researchers are active agents (not merely passive recorders) in constructing the events and behaviour they may claim merely to report.

Post-Fordism   Describes flexible systems of production that are designed to produce differentiated goods and services for niche markets.

Post-modern   Has two broad meanings – an historical era following modernity and a philosophical/theoretical perspective. Both are seen to celebrate what modernism devalues and/or represses – surface appearances, emotion, play, chance and indeterminacy in life – the value of different rationalities (e.g. based on experience) rather than a single authoritative science or **truth**. See also **modernist**.

Post-modernism   The theory and politics principally associated with contemporary French thinkers. Post-modernism may be understood as a reaction to and critique of **modernism**.

Power   Often conceived as ability of A to influence B to do something that B would not ordinarily have done without A's influence. The attribution of power to individuals or groups as their 'possession' has been challenged by a view of power that is 'relational' – such as the disciplines and ideologies that operate to constrain as well as enable those to whom power is attributed by the 'possessive' view.

Power as plural   Pluralists perceive organizational relations as defined by bargaining, competition and the use of power to resolve conflicts and represent conflicts of interest. See **pluralism**.

Practical-hermeneutic   Describes theories that seek to understand and reflect on organizations as opposed to reporting them or issuing prescriptions as to how to manage them more effectively. Can be contrasted to **managerialist** theories and in some instances also to **emancipatory** theories.

Precepts   Refers to general instructions on a course of action and a set of principles that provide guidance. Taylorism, for example, has some explicit precepts such as a distinction between conception and execution, standardization, etc.

Privatization   Selling off public corporations, in part or in full, to individuals or corporations that anticipate increasing their wealth or value from this acquisition. See **New right**.

Procedural justice   Like equity theory, procedural justice is interested in the effects, either positive or negative, that arise from how fairly and transparently managers implement decisions affecting their staff.

Process theories of motivation   These theories look at motivation as the outcome of a dynamic interaction between the person and their experiences of an organization and its management. Such processes depend critically on the sense individuals make of their experiences at work.

Processual   Theoretical approach that focuses more attention on the political but also cultural and strategic process within organizations rather than the structure of the organization.

Procrustes   An ancient Greek mythological character who either stretched his guests to fit the bed or chopped off their legs, if they were too tall. Eventually, the same fate befell Procrustes himself!

Product differentiation   Refers to one way in which firms can maintain their competitive advantage; they differentiate their product, in ways that appeals to the customer, from all others on the market.

Product life cycle   Refers to how products move from being new to being mature to being obsolete. This impacts on the pricing and marketing of goods as well as the degree of competition.

Progressive   Favouring and believing in progress or moving forward by improving on the past.

Project teams   Group of people working together on a particular task with a discrete objective and time frame. Often such groups include different specialists, perhaps drawn from different departments, for the purpose of achieving the project task.

Psychodynamic approaches   Defined by a concern with internal processes and forces within the psyche that clash and conflict with varying degrees of intensity in each individual and in ways that take time to resolve. In this approach, individual behavioural routines, oddities or little peculiarities and idiosyncrasies are seen as surface acts of behaviour that are really 'symptoms' of more underlying, deep-seated and unconscious forces and desires. In the Freudian approach to analysis, psychodynamic forces are understood to reach eventual compromise or 'settlement' through the negotiation of a series of relatively well-defined stages – the anal, the oral and the oedipal, for example – the resolution of which help stabilize personality.

Psychological contract   The invisible or implicit set of expectations that employees have of their organizations (e.g. challenging, stimulating work that allows for career progression) and that their organizations have of them (e.g. loyalty and flexibility), but are not laid down in the formal contract of employment.

Psychosis   Breakdown of our normal ways of thinking and perceiving in which objects in the world lose definition and precision, merging and collapsing into one another in a surreal and agitated, highly charged riot of images. Objects in the world and even the sound of words can come to take on a seemingly malevolent force. In Freudian terms, psychosis is associated with the collapse of the distinction between the conscious and the unconscious so that our waking world takes on dream-like qualities.

Purposeful actors   Belief that individuals retain rational control (e.g. in their pursuit of self-interest and sectional loyalties) throughout the processes of organizational decision making.

Quality circles   These are meetings of group of workers committed to continuous improvement in the quality and productivity of a given line of production.

Quality of working life movements   Denotes programmes of organizational design and development dedicated to improving productivity and workers' retention and commitment by bettering the relationship between employers and employees and the work environment.

Quotas   Limits placed on something; in trade usually refers to limits placed on the number of goods, for example cars, which can be exported from one country to another.

Rationality   A commitment to reason, rather than faith, intuition or instinct. In the study of organizations, rationality is often claimed to consist of the adoption of optimally efficient means. However, critical approaches suggest that this is a one-sided view of rationality since it usually considers efficiency in terms of narrow goals such as profitability, without considering whether organizations are efficient for realizing the well-being of members of the organization, or for society more widely.

Rationalizing   Measures intended to increase the efficiency and/or improve the effectiveness of work practices. See **rationality**.

Rational process   Process that incorporates goals and a mechanism calculated to achieve agreed aims largely irrespective of its consequences for other dimensions of social existence (e.g. community well-being).

Receivership   Term used to describe a company that has gone bankrupt and has its assets taken over by an independent auditor who then allocates a distribution to the various creditors.

Red tape   A term of abuse applied to bureaucracies that enforce rules more elaborate and inflexible than is considered necessary. See **bureaucracy**.

Regression   Compulsion to repeat or return to earlier patterns of behaviour and interaction as a way of avoiding the challenges associated with more adult or demanding situations and relations. In everyday language we often hear people say 'stop being so childish!' This is often associated with behaviour that is deemed inappropriate for adults.

Reification   Describes the tendency to treat a human creation (say organization or technology) as if it had an independent existence of its own rather than being the product of human thought and work.

Relations of production   The basic set of social relations that allow production to take place. Typically they are the relations between those who own property and their agents (managers) and those who are dependent on them for their wage labour.

Relative power   Assumption that power exists in relation to the will and objectives of both superordinates and subordinates.

Representative democracy   A form of political reality in which democratic influence is predicated on legitimate forms of electoral selection, accountability and representation.

Rhetoric   Art of persuasion and may encompass a range of rhetorical techniques aimed at changing an audience's views or behaviour. It is also sometimes seen as meaning false or exaggerated, and is contrasted with reality or truth – 'that's just rhetoric or someone trying to convince you of their beliefs. For those who hold that knowledge is ambiguous, perhaps especially in management, and that what we say comes to shape what we do and think, the distinction is itself viewed as rhetorical, not least because it implies some direct or privileged access to reality.

Routinization of charisma   Charismatic leaders have been seen to inspire an organization by the force of their energy and passion but create a situation of over-dependence on one person. In order to remove the uncertainty and unpredictability associated with this dependence, an organization establishes routines, rules and procedures that institutionalize and thereby routinize the practices that have evolved.

Rule system   System of governance based on rules.

Sabotage   Conscious intention to disrupt 'normal service' or production. It is often considered a deviant activity. See **pathological**.

Satisficing   Describes (and sometimes prescribes) a situation where a satisfactory resolution to a problem is adopted, rather than an optimum resolution.

Scientism   A view where ideas and techniques that comply with [. . .] protocols are believed to be **objective** and politically neutral.

Self-esteem   A psychological term referring to how one thinks or feels about oneself in an evaluative (i.e. positive or negative) way.

Shareholder value   Associated with the idea that the first responsibility of firms is to deliver value to shareholders. Therefore, the interests of employees, consumers and communities are secondary. Most associated with US and UK firms.

Shop floor   Location in factories where industrial or manufacturing workers are employed.

Silos   Discrete functions, departments or divisions within an orgranization that through the routines of repetition have become ossified and self-absorbed.

Social capital   Economic value to organizations of the social contacts and networks people have, especially those where there is a sense of obligation (e.g. to return a favour). This concept has been given increasing attention in recent years as the learning value of networks has been recognized. For example, contacts, especially those outside of normal organizational relations, are useful as sources of new knowledge or innovation. Close relationships, by contrast, are seen as more suited for the transfer of elusive or tacit knowledge.

Social construction of technology (or SCOT)   A more radical variant of the approach known as the **social shaping of technology**. According to constructivists, in order to understand technological developments we need to study the social interpretations that have produced the definitions of what problems can or should be solved by a given technology. These interpretations, SCOT argues, guide the choices made by the designers, manufacturers and users. Technical choices in other words are not merely the application of an abstract techno-logic but are also vehicles for the expression of perspectives and ideologies of those social groups (including designers, opinion formers, users, non-users, etc.) that have a stake in the

development of a particular technology. Technologies are therefore the offspring of alternative constructions and compromise.

Social constructivists   or constructivists, those who adopt the **constructivist** approach.

Socialization   A term used in psychology and sociology that refers to the process by which an individual internalizes values, norms, beliefs and behaviours present within the socio-cultural environment in which s/he lives.

Social shaping of technology   A sociological approach that rejects the **technologically determinist** view of **technology** as being distinct from the rest of society. It focuses on social and economic interests as key influences on the eventual shape of the technology. For those who follow this approach, technology is just one aspect of the way we live socially (and is not inherently different to organizations, art or politics).

Social system   Refers to a specific pattern of relationship, maintained by a certain flow of interactions and a common goal.

Span of control   The number of people for whom a manager has responsibility.

Sponsor–protégé relationship   Informal relationships between senior and junior personnel, often motivated by mutual advantage.

Stakeholder theory   The idea that business owes responsibility to more groups than merely its shareholders. Stakeholders may include customers, the environment, suppliers, the local community, future generations. etc.

Standard-setting bodies   Regulatory organizations that set and monitor standards of practice for organization, such as those in health and safety or financial accounting.

Start-ups   New small businesses that have just begun to trade.

Static structural   A way of understanding that does not allow for processes of change over time and which presumes that the phenomenon can be divided into layers or structures. So, for example, knowledge can be classified as of different types that do not change over time.

Statistical probability   The chance of a given event happening across a population of events. For the probability to be robust, the population must be sufficiently large to be statistically significant.

Statistical process control   A statistical technique used by quality managers to ensure that product quality standards are maintained.

Stickiness   Sometimes used to denote how difficult it can be to **transfer knowledge** from one context to another – e.g. the **tacit skill** of a craft worker, developed over years of practice.

Strategic contingency   Theory suggesting that uncertainty for an organization stems from its systems of operation, which include technology and work operations from its environment.

Structuralist approach   Concentrates on the complexity of the design or structure of an organization independently of the human dimension. It tends to see organizational structures as determined by external conditions characterized as the environment.

Subcontractors   Those working to provide goods or services for one company but who are employed by another company. See also **outsourcing**.

Subculture   A set of values, beliefs and norms that is specific to one group in the organization, and may be at odds with the 'official' culture as promoted by senior management. See also **cultural differentiation** and **multiculturalism**.

Subjectivity   The sense of being-in-the-world that includes but is not reducible to the sense of identity and meaning that is associated with it.

Substantive rationality   Substantive rationality means whether the outcomes of an action are rational from the point of view of the actor regardless of the efficiency of the action itself. **Instrumental rationality** is concerned with means. Substantive rationality is concerned with ends.

Sub-system   One part (e.g. the heart) of numerous interdependent elements that comprise the wider system (e.g. the body).

Suggestion box   Box in which employees can write down their ideas for improvements.

Supply chain   Stages through which materials and other resources are passed in the process of their being combined, assembled and delivered to their ultimate customer.

Sustainable development   A term generally used to refer to a concern with balancing economic demands with a concern for future generations. For example, the use of timber is now controlled in many but by no means all of world, so that for every tree cut down another is planted in its place.

Sweatshop labour   This term generally describes any form of labour in factories or smaller workshops that is done in conditions where labour is poorly treated, lacks adequate rights, health and safely conditions are poor, and wages low.

Tacit skill   A form of knowledge that cannot be made fully explicit, such as in a training manual or through verbal instruction. Examples include riding a bike or changing gear in a manual car.

Teamworking   Working arrangements in which workers themselves are given responsibility for the planning and coordination of some aspects of their work and the roles and tasks they are required to perform.

Technical   In an organization studies context, this term refers to theories or ideas intended for application by managers so that they can improve the organizational 'bottom line'.

Technocratic   Form of governance, which is exercised through the technical knowledge of experts.

Technological determinism   Determinism is the view that there is an inevitable direction in which events move. For technological determinists, the cause is technology. According to technological determinists, certain key technologies are the primary movers in developments in organization, the economy or even society itself.

Technological determinists   Those who adopt the approach defined above.

Technology   At the most basic level the term 'technology' is used to refer to the 'entire set of devices' that facilitate the adaptation of human collectivities to their environments. A fuller definition of technology includes the human activities, knowledge and skills that are necessary in order to create, understand and operate such devices.

Theory X   McGregor used this term to characterize a set of negative assumptions by managers about the attitudes and capabilities of employees; people are passive and need to be persuaded, rewarded, punished and controlled if they are to align their efforts with the needs of the organization.

Theory Y   McGregor used this term to characterize a set of positive assumptions by managers about employees; that people are cooperative, able to take responsibility and set their own goals if managers provide the conditions under which they can do this.

Third way   Compromise political strategy that seeks to restrict state intervention to the minimum necessary to avoid the 'free market', having consequences that result in the less well off being excluded from certain aspects of society.

Tolerance of ambiguity   Used in Hofstede to differentiate between cultures that seek rules for everything and will not take action outside of a rule, and those cultures where rules are lacking and who use their own initiative and creativity.

Total quality management   A system of quality control that is designed to build in quality at every stage of production to minimize waste and defective parts that would otherwise be detected at the end of the production process.

Transaction cost economics   Theory that explains the existence of an organization in terms of its superiority, relative to markets, in controlling the cost of matching the supply of goods and services with their demand.

Transferability of knowledge   The capacity to move knowledge from one context or form to another. This may vary according to the people involved. For example, it might be easier to help another engineer learn a new theory of mechanics than it would be to teach an engineering novice (see also the **knowledge diffusion** and **cultural barriers**).

Transferable skills   Employee skills or knowledge that can be readily applied to a wide range of tasks.

Translated   Changed from one form to another. This might be in the sense of a complete transformation, as an idea is adapted to a particular context, or a more modest change such as a (good) linguistic translation (see also the **knowledge diffusion** and **cultural barriers**).

Transnational   This term emphasizes the importance of flows across the world but retaining contacts and lines across national boundaries. The term 'transnational corporation' is sometimes used to convey the same meaning as the term multinational.

Transnationality   Indicates that some or many of the assets, sales and employees of a firm are based outside its home base.

Truth   A common-sense term relating to that which is accepted as factual or verified beyond doubt, but also a philosophical issue, or claim, of some complexity. A core theme here would be the contrasting views on whether there can only be one truth or many truths.

Typologies   Form of classification that involves grouping together entities or subjects with like themes and ensuring that these groups are mutually inclusive and mutually exclusive from all other groups. For example, cars and aeroplanes might be different groups of entities within a typology of transportation.

Uncertainty   Branch of political analysis which argues that leadership and influence within organizations tends to be enjoyed by those perceived as dealing with the sources of greatest ambiguity.

Unitary Form of management in which the views of top management are assumed to be shared by everyone. Conflict is treated as is **pathological** rather than a reflection of different interpretations and interests.

Universalist Theories that claim applicability across all locations and all times.

Unobtrusive Intangible forms of control, which appear not to intervene overtly in a worker's daily activity and yet have the ability to influence their conditions of work (e.g. a racist canteen culture).

Utilitarian Useful, especially in a practical way, but also refers to utilitarianism, which is a doctrine that judges actions on their outcomes in terms of overall increases in 'good' or happiness, for example.

Value free That which is seen to be **objective** – i.e. detached from particular personal values. Critical theory questions its existence.

Value maximizing Pursuit of rational decision-making strategies that require the individual to select options based on their ability to best achieve the ultimate goal (e.g. if the goal is to seek promotion, value-maximizing would involve steering one's career away from activities that would undermine this objective). Often the 'value' is translated into material terms, such as salary improvements or value-for-money.

Values Has a variety of meanings in organization studies, but in the specific sense intended by Schein it encompasses his 'middle level' of organizational culture, located between **basic assumptions** and **cultural artefacts**. Values derive from basic assumptions and inform cultural artefacts. They involve shared organizational responses to questions such as 'What are we doing?' and 'Why are we doing it?', and might include a commitment to profit maximization or a focus on equal opportunities.

Vignettes Brief excerpts from a larger story that may help us to understand 'what happens' to people in everyday life.

Whistle-blowing When an organizational member tells the wider world of unethical or illegal practices being conducted inside their organization.

Work intensification Working conditions in which workers are subject to constant pressures to increase output and productivity levels.

Working to rule Way employees, when in dispute with employers, may revert to formally prescribed ways of working that disrupt efficiency and effectiveness by replacing informal practices with rigid and often time-consuming procedural requirements.

Work–life balance General term to refer to how far work dominates people's lives over and above any other considerations.

Index

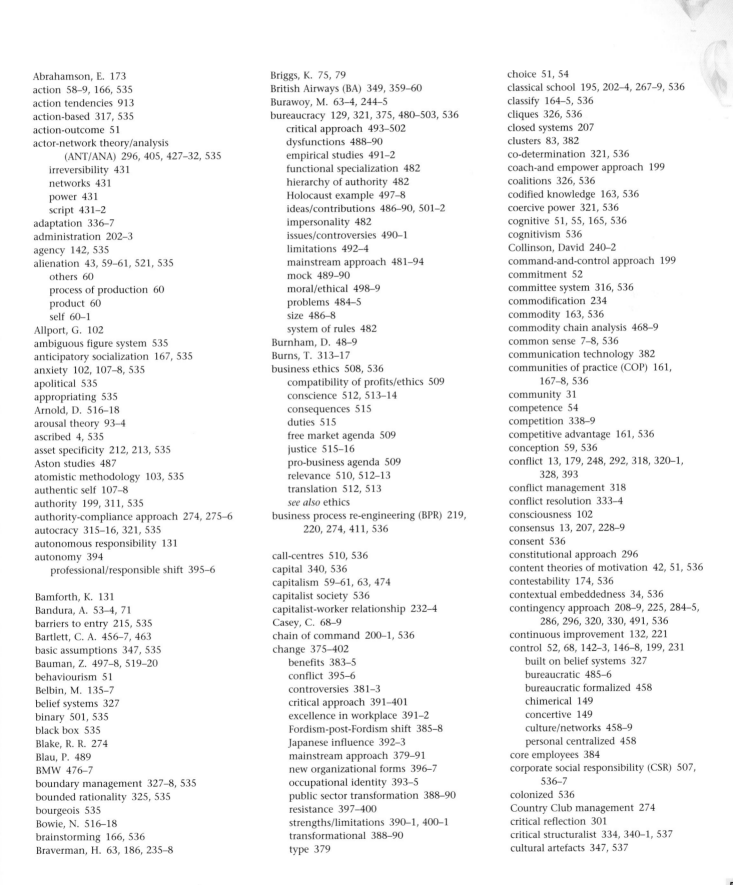